Real World Windows 8 Development

Samidip Basu

Apress®

Real World Windows 8 Development

ISBN-13 (pbk): 978-1-4302-5025-8

ISBN-13 (electronic): 978-1-4302-5026-5

President and Publisher: Paul Manning
Lead Editor: Jonathan Hassell
Developmental Editor: James Markham
Technical Reviewer: Matt Hidinger

Coordinating Editor: Katie Sullivan, Anamika Panchoo
Copy Editor: Kimberly Burton-Weismann
Compositor: SPi Global
Indexer: SPi Global
Artist: SPi Global
Cover Designer: Anna Ishchenko

Distributed to the book trade worldwide by Springer Science+Business Media New York, 233 Spring Street, 6th Floor, New York, NY 10013. Phone 1-800-SPRINGER, fax (201) 348-4505, e-mail `orders-ny@springer-sbm.com`, or visit `www.springeronline.com`. Apress Media, LLC is a California LLC and the sole member (owner) is Springer Science + Business Media Finance Inc (SSBM Finance Inc). SSBM Finance Inc is a Delaware corporation.

For information on translations, please e-mail `rights@apress.com`, or visit `www.apress.com`.

Apress and friends of ED books may be purchased in bulk for academic, corporate, or promotional use. eBook versions and licenses are also available for most titles. For more information, reference our Special Bulk Sales–eBook Licensing web page at `www.apress.com/bulk-sales`.

Any source code or other supplementary materials referenced by the author in this text is available to readers at `www.apress.com`. For detailed information about how to locate your book's source code, go to `www.apress.com/source-code/`.

Contents at a Glance

Contents

About the Author

Samidip Basu (`@samidip`) is a technologist, author, speaker, gadget-lover, and a senior software trainer for Telerik. With a strong developer background in the Microsoft technology stack, he now spends much of his time evangelizing Windows 8/Windows Phone platforms, as well as cloud-supported mobile solutions in general.

He passionately helps run The Windows Developer User Group (`http://thewindowsdeveloperusergroup.com`), labors in the M3 Conference (`http://m3conf.com`) organization, serves as the INETA Secretary (`www.ineta.org`), and can be found working on at least a couple of hobbyist projects at any time. His spare time calls for travel and culinary adventures with his wife. Find out more at `http://samidipbasu.com`.

About the Technical Reviewer

Matt Hidinger is a Microsoft MVP with years of experience developing top-tier consumer applications on XAML technologies. He has created a number of open-source projects, enjoys blogging at `http://matthidinger.com`, and has spoken at a number of community events and conferences.

Matt can be found on Twitter `@MattHidinger`.

Acknowledgments

This book would not have been possible without a lot of support from several sources.

Let me start with my gorgeous wife, Monali, who fills my life with love and brightness. Despite her long days as a college professor, she has patiently tolerated me when my entire evenings were devoted to book writing. With each passing day, I realize just how fortunate I am to have her in my life and can only hope that my boundless love for her offers some consolation for my almost constant technical preoccupations. I am also thankful to my parents, who have provided me constant verbal encouragement throughout the few months it took to get this book together.

Microsoft's support for making this book happen has been stellar. I am thankful to several Microsoft evangelist friends, like Jeff Blankenburg and Jennifer Marsman, for their encouragement, as well as their tracking down copyright permissions. Several images featured in the book are actually from Microsoft and shared with partner companies, and I am thankful to not have to reinvent the wheel. A lot of my developer friends in the community provided the buffer so I could crosscheck the technical accuracy of my content—notably, they were Doug Mair, Michael Collier, Hemant Purkar, David Fowler, Josh Twist, Tim Heuer, and Michael Crump. While I cannot mention everybody here, I am indebted to the countless developer blogs/articles that have helped shape some of the content in the book.

A big shout-out goes out to my buddy Matt Hidinger, the technical reviewer of the book. Despite being insanely busy, Matt found the time to meticulously review and provide feedback on the chapters and my sample code. Without him, a lot of technical inaccuracies would go unnoticed. Matt, thank you very much.

Lastly, sincere thanks go out to my brilliant editors at Apress—Kathleen Sullivan, Anamika Panchoo, Kimberly Burton-Weisman, and James Markham. It is not funny how much the focus on technical content makes way for bad spelling and grammar, and horrible organization in your writing. I have leaned heavily on the editors to shape things right. As tough as it was to stay focused on book writing on top of my normal workload, I am indebted to the Apress editors for keeping me disciplined and the schedule on track for a timely book release.

Introduction

I could say a thousand things here to introduce you to Windows 8 application development. But at the end of the day, everything boils down to your passion and excitement as a developer on the Microsoft technology stack. Windows 8 represents a significant opportunity for developers of both consumer-facing and enterprise apps. The whole Microsoft ecosystem is going through a huge change, based around mobile lifestyles, and our skills need to catch up if we developers want to stay on the cutting edge.

So, buckle down, roll up your sleeves, and get coding with me. This is an exciting new world and the potential for you to make a name for yourself is huge. Also, as you build your Windows Store apps, let's keep the conversation going. I am sure that you will have unique problems that you will have solved, or that you will find faster, better ways of accomplishing the same result. I want to know about these, since we developers make up one giant community and we support each other. So reach out to me with questions, concerns, or comments through Twitter; you can find me at `@samidip`. Let's talk—and happy coding!

PART 1

Knowing the Ecosystem

Windows 8 and the modern user experience represent a big change in Microsoft software and what it means for its future. Developers need to understand and truly enjoy the Microsoft ecosystem to be successful Windows 8 application developers.

Understanding the synergy between the PC, tablets, smartphones, the cloud, and Xbox gives us depth in knowledge that helps plan a Windows 8 application correctly.

We start this book by digging into the history, inspiration, and vision behind Windows 8 and the Microsoft ecosystem as a whole.

CHAPTER 1

Introduction to Windows 8

"Windows reimagined" has been a buzz phrase since Microsoft first announced Windows 8 late in 2011. Marketing aside, one needs to look no further than the software coming out of Redmond, WA, to realize the message between the words. Microsoft put together a monumental 2012—just about every product division saw major software updates rolled out for industry-leading products. What began as a user interface (UI) design overhaul for smaller form factors has been renamed "Modern UI," and it has spread its influence throughout the ecosystem of Microsoft products. At the pinnacle of this new wave of changes is Windows 8—the flagship Microsoft product and, arguably, the world's most popular operating system. The stakes are huge, the quality of work is premium, and the excitement is palpable. This is no longer just Windows reimagined—it is truly Microsoft reimagined!

Windows is an operating system (OS) used by computer users worldwide for work and at home. International Data Corporation (IDC) estimated in March 2012 that some 690 million PCs across the world used Windows 7. Add to that the PCs using Windows XP or earlier versions of Windows. It does not take a genius to figure out that Windows has a huge consumer base. And when there is an upcoming change to something so fundamental affecting many millions of people across the globe—it is a big deal.

Windows 8 does not feel like an incremental OS upgrade; it truly is Windows built from the ground up, as you shall see throughout this book. I'll peel back some of the layers of thought that went into Windows 8, discuss what Windows 8 means for consumers and enterprises, and most importantly to readers of this book - the developers, I'll talk about how things boil down for developers, and how we leverage several technologies/frameworks to create Windows 8 Store Apps. Rest assured, Microsoft's enormous consumer base and the significance of Windows 8 makes this one of the biggest opportunities application developers have had in a while.

The State of Computing

Before moving on, I'd like to provide a little perspective on the history of Windows 8. It reveals the bigger picture and context of where Windows 8 fits amidst the competition.

It's 2013 and computing as we know it is definitely going through a huge change. Human-computer interaction is evolving as our needs for on-the-go computing dictates tremendous innovation across computer form factors. There is no denying that Apple ushered in a whole new industry of smartphones with the 2007 launch of the iPhone. Since then, we are no longer content carrying cumbersome pagers or flip phones that just make phone calls. We want to have the Internet at our fingertips. Enter the modern smartphone: an all-in-one device that fits in our pockets and keeps us connected to work, family, and friends. Add to that real-time news, weather, maps, reviews, social media immersion, and other ways of staying connected—it's no wonder we no longer simply make phone calls with our smartphones.

The convenience of having a device that is always on, always connected, and ready to work purely with touch interaction, soon led to an App phenomenon: the need to control the various aspects of our lives and interactions through native applications built for smartphones. This brought on the explosion of the App Store model—a global but localized secure repository of Apps for our smartphones. These stores/marketplaces are mostly curated and maintained by the smartphone OS manufacturers. The submission and vetting process to get Apps from developers into the store is meant to give users confidence in the quality and safety of Apps downloaded from the store. This model has proven to be tremendously beneficial for developers of Apps, providing a global audience/customer base of users and monetization through paid Apps, Apps with advertisements, or in-App purchases leveraging existing e-commerce models.

November 2010: Microsoft launches Windows Phone 7. A completely new smartphone OS, written from the ground up and aimed at invigorating the Windows brand in the smartphone industry. With Apple and Google already out there for several years with their mobile OS offerings, the challenge was to do something fresh and exciting. What began with the Zune HD a couple of years back was a new kind of UI paradigm focused on content over chrome—and the user's lifestyle at the center of it all. With Windows Phone, this UI (first called the *Metro design language*) was now all grown up. It offered a breath of fresh air to the user experience.

Delightfully touch-oriented, Windows Phone OS excels at being fast and fluid, and offers complete personalization in putting the users' content and lifestyle at the center of the experience. No longer are we stuck with a grid of application icons. Apps come to life through what are called *live tiles* —visual, live representations of Apps (even when they are not running). Live tiles are updated locally or through push notifications from the cloud. They are a big selling point of the ecosystem, always inviting users back to the applications. Windows Phone also represents the best effort thus far toward bringing all of the Microsoft ecosystem service offerings (Xbox, Office, Live Services, etc.) together in one, shiny hardware device.

It might take Windows Phone a while to claw its way to the market share it deserves, but the innovation offered by the new platform is undeniable. Even better is the developer story. Because it's based on the Silverlight runtime, developing Apps for Windows Phone is a lot of fun for .NET developers, resulting in Windows Phone being the fastest-growing App marketplace/store among its peers in quickly reaching the 100K-App milestone and growing.

There is, however, a new kid on the block: the tablet form factor. As much as we love our smartphones, they are rather small devices for content consumption, multitasking, and business workflows. Users want an always-connected/always-on experience—but on a bigger form factor, which lends to expanded computing reach. Razor-thin, lightweight, and touch-friendly—tablets quickly grabbed consumer attention, and the computing transformation was well on its way. It didn't take the casual computer user, netizen, gamer, socialite, and movie buff long to realize that they didn't need a bigger computer—a touch-friendly tablet would likely meet most of their needs. Enterprises also began considering their line-of-business workflows for the mobile employee base; and the consumerization of IT became a reality. With the introduction of the iPad, Apple again pioneered the space; but it did not take the competition much time to see the iPad's shortcomings and come up with more compelling offerings.

Windows 8: The Overview

October 26, 2012, was the launch date for the general availability of Windows 8. Amid the waves of computing change, came an OS that promised to offer no compromises on a variety of form factors.

Windows 8 takes everything good about Windows 7 and tries to make it better. With full backward compatibility in Windows 8 Pro for applications running on Windows 7, the upgrade to Windows 8 promises to be painless. In addition to the desktop goodness, Windows 8 shines with its whole new UI, optimized for touch interaction. The ubiquitous Windows Start menu is no more! Instead, users get a full-screen Start touch menu—highly customizable, personal, and filled with live tiles that invites users back to their applications. The Start screen offers a brand-new Windows 8-specific user experience. It is the biggest change introduced in Windows since Windows 95. Figure 1-1 shows a sample of the Windows 8 Start screen experience.

Figure 1-1. *The Windows 8 Start screen*

The Windows 8 Start experience captures a lot of what Windows 8 craves to be: the one OS across all device form factors. Touch is not an afterthought; it is a first-class citizen. Equally supported are mouse and keyboard interactions. The Start screen is not a list or grid of application icons, but rather each App gets its own tile, which comes in two sizes: square or wide. The tile is not just an application shortcut; it is like a live representation of the App, conveying information to the user from the Start screen itself, without having to run the App. Live tiles, which update locally or from the cloud, started in Windows Phone and are all grown up in Windows 8. There are several combinations of text, pictures, and badges that make up a live tile, along with peek animations and the ability to cycle through content, leading to an energetic, inviting, and constantly alive Start screen experience.

Modern UI, which also began with Zune and Windows Phone, has center stage in the Windows 8 touch experience. The mantra is simple and minimalist, fast and fluid, content over chrome, rich use of bold flat colors, animations for liveliness, and putting the user first. The Windows 8 Start experience is full-screen and offers discoverability and personalization. The point is to make everyone's Start screen look different; users are free to move Apps around and arrange tiles based on what's important to their individual style and the given PC.

The Start screen content can pan left or right, but a feature called *Semantic Zoom* aids superbly in discoverability and navigation. To use it, you simply pinch the Start screen, or if you're on a traditional PC, you hold down the Ctrl key while scrolling the mouse scroll wheel. You are taken (with an easing animation) to a zoomed-out view of smaller App tiles that show the whole layout grouped in sections, as if from a height above. Pinch or scroll out, and you return to the regular Start screen tiles.

In addition to Semantic Zoom, another feature that aids in personal organization is *grouping*, which enables you to group the Start screen tiles easily into logical buckets, based on App types and position groups of tiles by preference. Grouping, combined with Semantic Zoom, is helpful with organization and way finding—simply zoom out, and then swoop back in on the App group of interest. Figure 1-2 shows my personal Start screen, with tile groupings under Semantic Zoom to give a feel for what's doable. The goal is to personalize to your heart's content. Windows is suddenly fun again—modern, fast, and colorful yet utilitarian!

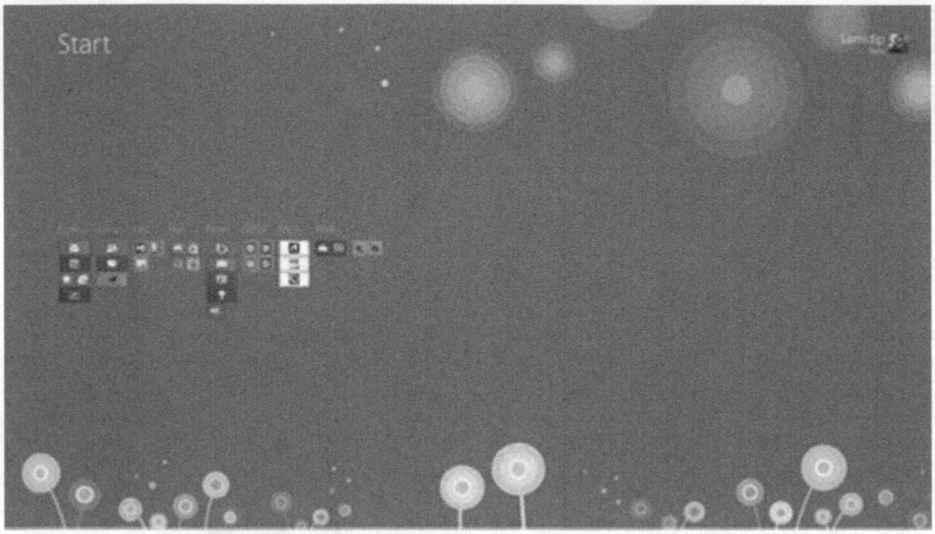

Figure 1-2. *The Windows 8 Start screen with grouped tiles under Semantic Zoom*

The Form Factors

It is no surprise that Apple's iPad dominates the tablet space, with Google Android–based tablets trying to wrestle away some of its market share. Tablets have captured the consumer imagination, and innovative computing scenarios are coming forward. For kids and younger generations, touch interaction comes naturally and computing is much more personal. Entire stacks of books or movie collections can be placed on a single tablet; and the thin and light form factors ensure ultimate mobility. There is one minor problem, however, that most would agree on: as handy as today's tablets are, they are mostly meant for consumption of content. While this works for the majority of folks, advanced users like developers might also want to do some actual work on tablets. Although there are competing products, Microsoft Office documents continue to be heavily used worldwide, but they are non-native citizens on today's tablets. Serious development work is possible only if the developer is remotely logged in to computers that are more powerful. Arguably, part of the problem is because both Apple and Google choose to use a mobile OS on their tablets. Although this approach is definitely working in terms of simplicity and market share, does it still leave something to be desired? Can work and play be combined?

Microsoft is definitely not new to tablets. There have been several experiments with the form factor, starting in the early days of Windows. The problem was that although Windows supported touch, the user experience was geared toward laptops and desktop PCs. This meant Original Equipment Manufacturers (OEMs) often tried putting their own touch-enabled skins on top of Windows, leading to somewhat clunky and inconsistent user experiences. Windows 8 throws away all of that clutter from the past and embraces touch first. The whole point is an uncompromising, single OS across all PC form factors, as shown in Figure 1-3. Windows 8 belongs in touch-based tablets and all-in-one PCs; but it is also perfectly comfortable with the mouse-keyboard setups of desktops and laptops. The point is that no matter your PC hardware, you get the same consistent user experience (UX) with Windows 8.

Figure 1-3. *Windows 8 across device form factors*

Although the Windows 8 Start screen experience and all Windows 8 Store Apps remain very touch-friendly, one tap of the desktop tile brings users back to the familiar desktop world—the same as in Windows 7 (sans the Start button), but with a ton of improvements.

Some applications are just too busy to be touch-centric, such as developer tooling or heavy image-editing software. Because advanced users appreciate the pixel density of complex applications, not all applications need to be designed for touch. Yet, Windows 8 shines for such workflows, letting PCs fully support desktop modes running applications with backward compatibility. Also, many advanced users may not need to interact much with the Windows 8 Start screen because they work primarily in the desktop world at work; a nice solution might be to use multiple monitors and keep the Start screen only on one display.

In fact, it is the dual and hybrid nature of the latest PCs that is a major allure for the Windows 8 ecosystem. No longer do we need to carry tablets that are mostly meant for consumption; we can be content producers on the same device. With Microsoft Office and all Windows 7-type desktop Apps (in Windows 8 Pro versions) running on the same devices, productivity is at your fingertips. Built from the ground up, Windows 8 supports a new chipset family—ARM processors, in addition to the Intel chips that Windows has always run on. ARM processors are the same chips that power many of today's smartphones and tablets; they specialize in low power-consumption and have long battery lives.

Opening Windows to ARM has major consequences on form factors running versions of Windows 8, which comes in two broad categories: Windows RT and Windows 8 Pro. The Windows RT version is meant for PCs running on ARM processors; whereas Intel-based devices normally run Windows 8 Pro. To the end user, Windows 8 should feel the same across chipsets, with the most juice coming from the more powerful processors. Both Windows RT and Pro run most Windows 8 Store Apps and support desktop mode, except RT versions only have compatibility with selected desktop applications, such as Office 2013.

With such wide support for devices, the Windows ecosystem is set to light up. Windows OEM partners are innovating in the various form factors, particularly the tablet, which now has enough processing power for advanced users, thus lending itself to the flexible workstyle concept. When you are at home or at the office, you can simply dock your tablet to a base to do serious development and other work. When you need to go mobile, simply pick up your tablet and walk away—all of your work stays on the same PC, and is now touch-optimized for access. There are also many hybrid PCs on the market, including tablets with snappable keyboards and bases, and laptops with flippable hinges on screens to fold them into tablets. Another interesting fallout from the Windows 8 shakeup is the emergence of high-quality *Ultrabooks*—extremely thin and light Intel-based PCs with full power and long battery lives for the mobile pro-user. The point is, no matter what your computing needs and lifestyle preferences are, there is a high-quality PC for you. The entire Windows ecosystem is changing for the good!

Platform Investments

Windows 8 is far more than a pretty UI skin—it is truly Windows reimagined from ground up. Strategic platform investments have been made so that Windows 8 can thrive and be flexible toward building an ecosystem around it. The following are the key platform investments:

- *Windows 8 user experience*: This is the Modern UI design-inspired UX that is superbly touch-friendly, uncluttered, and puts content over chrome.
- *Windows Runtime (WinRT)*: This is a whole new layer of APIs baked into Windows itself. The goal is to provide easy, consistent, and quick access to device internals, and Windows core services to Windows 8 Store Apps. Language projection is in use to make sure that the one set of APIs feels consistent and natural in any development language used to create Windows 8 Store Apps.
- *Windows 8 Apps and their execution model*: Windows 8 Store Apps take center stage in the user experience and introduce a new execution model as the applications live through their life cycle. The goal is to have delightfully immersive Windows 8 Apps that offer a natural continuation of the OS, and free the user from having to manage the App life cycle between launch/running/suspend/resume/termination; the entire experience is seamless.
- *Windows Store*: For the first time in the history of Windows, there is a Windows store, curated and hosted by Microsoft. It is the one-stop shop for users to discover and download Windows 8 Store-style Apps. It is available across all PCs, regardless of version or chipset. The Windows Store has tremendous reach and robustness in performance. It provides user confidence in certified Apps, it is optimized for App discoverability, and it supports various modes of monetization and e-commerce.
- *Consolidation*: Windows 8 also represents an effort to bring disparate Microsoft products/services together to form a cohesive ecosystem that is easy to develop on. The Modern UI design language, as seen in Windows 8, is shaping the UI of almost every Microsoft product, leading to unification of experiences. Windows Phone 8 will utilize (for the first time) the same core kernel as Windows 8 PCs, thus consolidating platforms into one uniform base to build around. The dream of "write once, run everywhere" isn't quite there yet—but we are getting closer.
- *Development investments*: As with any other Microsoft platform, Windows 8 has seen significant investments into developer tooling for authoring Windows 8 Store Apps and widespread community involvements.

I break down each of these investments and take a deep dive into each topic in upcoming chapters.

The One Ecosystem

As of the end of 2012, your Windows Phone smartphone, your laptop or ultrabook, your living room all-in-one PC, your Windows tablets, and your Xbox-connected TV all look very similar. This is a very conscious effort toward rebranding Microsoft in both enterprise and consumer markets. No more disparate devices or services. The goal is the one ecosystem called Windows, and Windows 8 is at the pinnacle of this strategy. Of course, there will be competition from other platforms/ecosystems, which are all trying to hook in the consumer. But competition is a good thing because it leads to relentless innovation. Windows has the most expansive reach of consumers through its worldwide market share of OS usage, and the three-screen unified ecosystem is just starting to kick in. Windows 8 undeniably presents one of the biggest developer opportunities as Microsoft reinvents itself around its flagship OS.

Are you ready?

CHAPTER 2

Modern UI Design

Modern smartphones and tablets have taught us one thing: user experience (UX) is of critical importance. No matter how complicated your operating system, no matter how well the apps are engineered, it comes down to this: is it fun to use? Design language guides the way content is presented and manipulated on smaller computing form factors, and as such, is arguably the biggest contributor to a pleasant UX. In this chapter, you take a close look at some history behind Microsoft's design approach in phones/tablets, as well as taking a deep-dive into Modern UI design language—the principles and guidelines for Windows 8 Store app developers. This is pivotal to understand and keep in mind as you develop your apps. It is the glue that holds it all together. Throughout the rest of the book, we'll get plenty technical; but for the best possible user experience, please keep coming back to this chapter to make sure that the design guidelines are being honored. Specifically, in subsequent chapters, as we talk about building Windows 8 Store apps through the use of right controls, content structuring, navigation, layout of content on canvas etc., you should see a very strong connection back to the basics we lay down about the Modern UI design language in this chapter. Onboard? Let us do design right.

The Backdrop

In a 1987 interview with *OMNI* magazine, Bill Gates predicted that tablets and other small form factors would dominate computing and the Internet, and along with ubiquitous services, they would put information at our fingertips. Fast-forward to 2013, and we begin to realize the vision of some of the best brains in the industry. Of course, much of this computing revolution started with another mastermind, Steve Jobs. With the iPhone and iPad, Apple quickly had two major hits and a substantial chunk of the mobile computing industry. Google came along next and reached the masses with Android smartphones and tablets. To restart the engines, Microsoft needed to think way outside the box.

Microsoft is no stranger to smaller computing form factors. Starting with the Pocket PC and Windows Mobile series (more history at `http://en.wikipedia.org/wiki/Pocket_PC`), we have always been able to run Windows on small devices. Operated through pen/stylus/touch, these smaller form factors often treaded the line between personal digital assistants (PDAs) and cellular phones. Although adored by geeks for customizability and adopted by enterprises for their unique workflows, it was clear that these mobile devices were not gaining mainstream traction. One of the key issues was the use of a desktop OS, retrofitted to run on a small form factor. Windows CE was an OS/kernel designed for lean, embedded systems that Microsoft licensed to OEMs (original equipment manufacturers); but it often felt like a toned-down version of the bigger Windows. And touch was often not a first-class citizen. As advancements in human-computer interaction has taught us, we humans are very adept at using our fingers on smaller form factors and touch leads to a better intimate a connected user experience. An overhaul was called for in Microsoft's mobile strategy and overall design language for presenting content on smaller devices.

September 2009. Microsoft launched the Zune HD portable media player. A direct competitor to Apple's iPod and iPhone series of mobile devices, the Zune HD came with an OLED touch screen, Wi-Fi capability, a browser, and the ability to run apps. Regardless of market penetration, Zune HD did something that was very well-received: offer a fresh design in content presentation. There was something about the simple UI that was rather enchanting: navigation through content and honoring typography.

October 2010. Windows Phone finally hits the market. The successor to Windows Mobile, Windows Phone 7 was nothing like its predecessor. Squarely aimed at consumers, Windows Phone was designed from the ground up with the smaller form factor in mind, and touch was a first-class citizen. Colorful, extremely personal, fast and fluid, and content over chrome were all adjectives used to describe the user interface (UI) offered by Windows Phone. See the similarities with Zune HD? What shone through was the new design language, which Microsoft called *Metro* for a while. This new design was the key toward making a product that brought all Microsoft's services under one roof in a small device—and it felt natural. Inspired from universal language-independent signage and global transit systems, the Metro design language oozed in speed of discoverability and simplicity in content presentation. Subtle animations and radiant but flat colors hold the user's attention. And if the content and the typography used to present it are strong, who needs extra adornment? Windows Phone users have been generally quite happy with the user experience that their devices provide, and this can be squarely attributed to the new school of design practices permeating the walls of Redmond.

The encouraging signs did not go unnoticed internally at Microsoft. The design language that first started in the Zune HD, and reached adolescence in Windows Phone, would be all grown up in Windows 8. The key difference from years past was the fact that Microsoft was not trying to retrofit the UX of desktop and laptops onto smaller form factors like smartphones and tablets. It is the brand-new imagination of what an OS can be if designed for specific devices and touch first; yet keeping it amenable to running on a variety of form factors, as we've seen with Windows 8. If the fundamentals are well-thought out, and if the principles are firm yet allow customization and branding, magical user experiences can be envisioned. The fundamentals of the Modern UI design principles came to change the face of almost every product and major business division in the Microsoft ecosystem. The importance of this new design language is culminated by the fact the Microsoft changed its corporate logo, for the first time in 25 years to symbolize the Modern UI that the company now stands for. More details about Microsoft's new corporate logo change and the inspiration behind it can be found at `http://www.youtube.com/watch?feature=player_embedded&v=OzkZWvAJUrO`.

Also, computing has taken on huge changes in recent past. User experience is no longer an afterthought; it is front and center in the way we start designing our applications. The once sturdy walls between developers and designers are evaporating. Developers need to understand design before their code makes a mark. It is important for all of us to understand this sea of change in UX so that we are building our applications right. So, let's spend a little time breaking down the tenets of this Modern UI design language from a developer's perspective.

Modern UI Design Principles

Let's examine the fundamentals of this new Modern UI design language before implementing them in our Windows 8 Store apps. The focus is on short to-do guidelines over descriptive text to understand each principle. The five broad Modern UI or Windows 8 style design principles, as recommended by Microsoft, are as follows:

- Show pride in craftsmanship
- Do more with less
- Be fast and fluid
- Be authentically digital
- Win as one

You'll look into each of these principles individually and try to follow them in a technical demo app that we will build in later chapters. The point is to make an honest attempt to understand these design principles. Be inspired!

Show Pride in Craftsmanship

Take a look at the screenshot of the Windows 8 weather app (see Figure 2-1), the one that comes preinstalled with Windows 8.

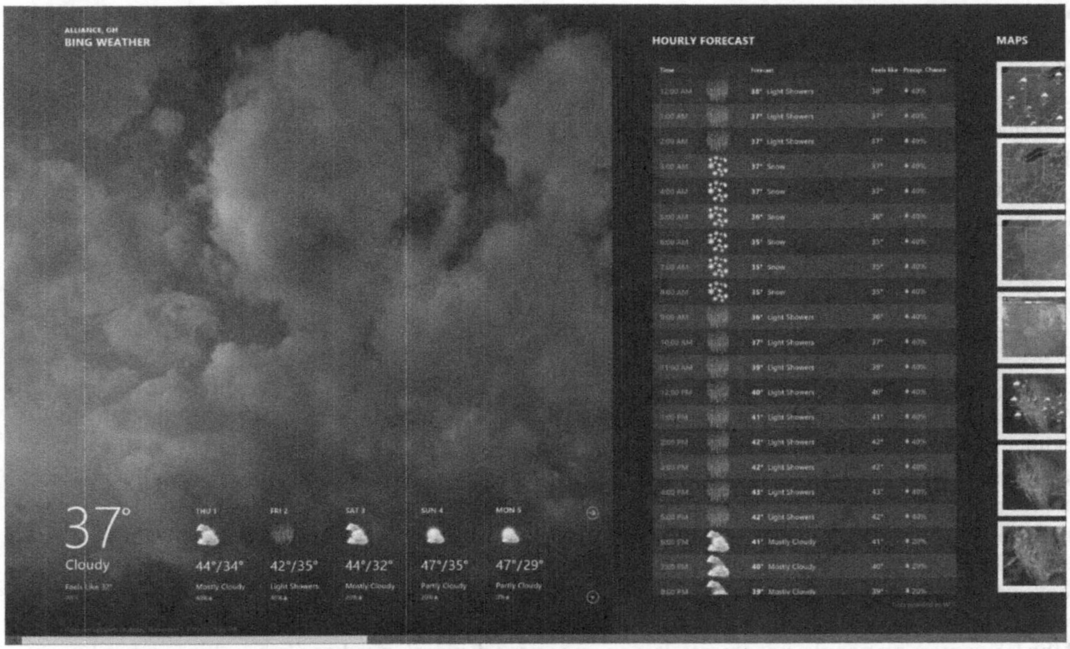

***Figure 2-1.** Screenshot of the default Windows 8 weather app*

This is awesome and a bit scary at the same time. As you can see, edge-to-edge, every pixel on the screen is occupied by the app. For the first time in the history of Windows, the OS completely steps out of the way and lets the apps shine. In fact, some might argue that Windows 8 is a bit of a misnomer because there are no "windows" anymore. This is content over chrome. But with power comes responsibility. The apps have all the pixels to shine or fail. This is where the pride in craftsmanship principle advocates sweating the details and making every pixel count. Software developers are craftsmen constantly trying to improve their craft. And software, in this case, the Windows 8 Store app, is the resulting art form. Caring for the end result shows, with every pixel aimed at delighting the user through a rich, connected UX. The Windows 8 apps we build will represent us—so let us do everything possible to be proud of our efforts and to stand by the fruits of our labor.

Do More with Less

Less is more. No, this is not defying physics but rather enforcing it. If applications are designed to be touch-friendly, one has to account for big human fingers so that touch targets are easily hittable. White space is our friend; busy screens and smaller content—not so much. This principle is also enforced by the content-over-chrome doctrine. Why have extra adornments, windows, borders, or navigation aids when none of it lends itself to easy touchability? If the content is presented in a seemingly simple and organized layout, it is easier on the user's eyes—and more importantly, their fingers. Give your content some breathing room.

Be Fast and Fluid

"Fast and fluid" is one of the most overused terms to describe the new Modern UI, but there is a really compelling story behind the hype. Pick up a tablet running any version of Window 8 and it immediately starts to make sense. Nothing is ever slowing down the UI; it is always fast and alive with motion. Yes, there may be heavy operations in the background, but the UI stays responsive. If a Windows 8 Store app is stuttering and not fluid on the lowest common hardware, the app has not been written per the design principles and it will probably never hit the Windows 8 Store. Interaction with app content is direct, and this leads to natural navigation through exploration.

Who doesn't like movies? Turns out, the new Microsoft design school takes several cues from cinematography. Motion captures attention and words can move. The Windows 8 UI has tiny deliberate animations all over to provide a nicely easing UX, especially on touch interactions. As seasoned designers would tell you, subtle motion is imperceptible to the user if done right, and it contributes to the overall UX. If anything is off, it sticks out like a sore thumb. It is thus important for third-party apps to embrace motion, because Windows 8 does it nicely all over and you want to feel like a part of a bigger whole.

Be Authentically Digital

The "authentically digital" design principle is often misunderstood, but has simplicity at its core. Imagine that you are making a Windows 8 app that shows the current time to the user. Would you rather make an elaborate wall clock replica with ticking hands showing the analog time, or just digitally show the time to the user? Therein lies the tenet of the "be authentically digital" design principle. Apps live a digital life in smartphones and tablets—so why bring in metaphors from the real world? This design principle is actually dramatically opposite to the skeuomorphism that we see in many Apple and Google devices, which explains the difference in the user experience provided by the Windows ecosystem. Neither one is right or wrong; just different. *Skeuomorphism* encourages imitation of original products or real-world objects in digital form, although it may be purely ornamental. The Modern UI design principles, on the other hand, break away from replicating physical metaphors and embrace a fresh, bold, digital representation. The reimagining of the UX centers on people, not objects. It is an important distinction to keep in mind as we developers design our Windows 8 Store apps.

Win As One

The one ecosystem. Right once, run everywhere within the ecosystem. These are dreams every major software vendor has. Microsoft's ecosystem is getting pretty darn close. As I have said before, our Windows Phones, Windows PCs, laptops, desktops, all-in-one PCs, tablets, and Xboxes all look very similar. And there is something in this similarity and familiarity that comforts end users. So, honor the ecosystem you're writing apps for so that the UX offered by your Windows 8 Store app does not feel jarring compared to the rest of the OS. Leverage the touch gestures and implement contracts to give your apps some Windows 8 character. The design principles are just what they say they are—principles, not strict guidelines. In fact, it is encouraged that you step outside the box to give your apps your own brand. However, it always helps to keep in mind the bigger ecosystem and the desired UX.

The Traits

Now that you have had a look at some of the guiding design principles, let's look at a few common traits that truly make a great Windows 8 Store app. I will skip over details because later chapters dig into every one of the features mentioned in the following sections. This section is meant to be an overview of all the things to keep in mind when creating your Windows 8 apps. Brevity and a quick checklist is the goal here. Once you are close to being feature-complete toward building your Windows 8 Store app, come back to this list to see how many you have gotten right.

Content Before Chrome

During the envisioning of Windows 8, Microsoft did numerous usability studies to figure out app usage patterns and chrome vs. content in today's Windows 7 applications. Figure 2-2 shows how an average user would draw a Windows 7 application if asked to describe one.

Figure 2-2. *User sketch of a Windows 7 application*

This is sad because what is drawn here is the chrome, not the actual application content. Border handles, application menus, and Close/Minimize buttons are great as chrome in desktop applications, but not so much for touch. The Windows 8 immersive UI removes the need to have Close/Minimize menus and "content as king" should drive navigation. Let the user explore.

Fierce Reductionism

"Fierce reductionism" comes straight out of the inspiration of the Modern UI design language from the *Bauhaus* school of design. Let's cut away all adornment and bring our Windows 8 Store apps down to the core essence of what's presented as content. The Windows 8 design style is also influenced by *Swiss Design,* which embraces cleanliness, readability, and beautiful graphic design. White space isn't a bad thing; it attracts attention to the content. Let's keep these principles in the back of our minds as developers.

Layout

Symmetry is the common definition of beauty across form, age, and species. Windows 8 Store apps are no exception. There is an invisible grid that we need to align all of our content to for aesthetics and symmetry. Actually, this grid is not so invisible in the Visual Studio/Expression Blend tooling. Small square units make up the drawing canvas for app content. We have a lot of flexibility in the way we layout our content; but everything aligns to this grid and adds to the symmetry. It is subtle to notice when done right; but it is immediately noticeable if something is off. Modern UI may look deceptively simple, but there is a lot of science behind the pixels and the exact measurements for alignment—all captured and made available to developers and designers through the Windows 8 app silhouette.

Let's take a closer look at this grid that forms a critical part of the Windows 8 silhouette. Figures 2-3 through 2-6 show the underlying grid for the Windows 8 app canvas, followed by various ways of placing content. Take note of how different content layout can be, yet everything adheres to the grid and highlights a sense of symmetry.

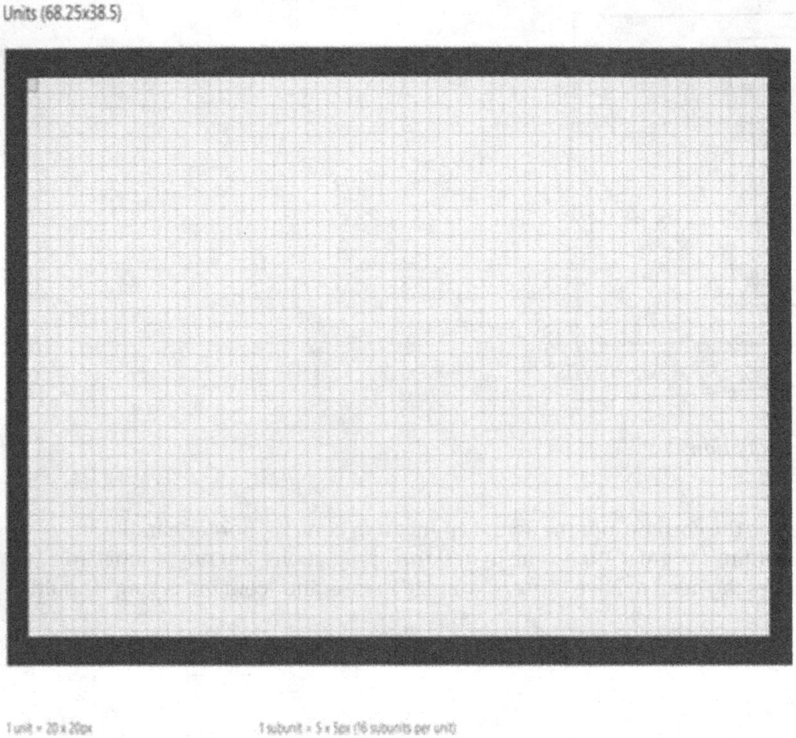

Figure 2-3. *The grid and content layout, option A*

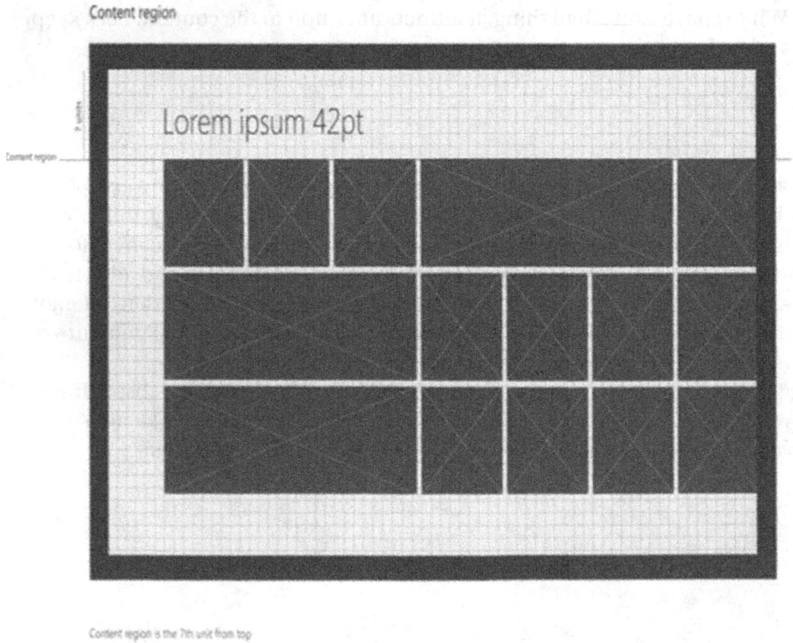

Figure 2-4. *The grid and content layout, option B*

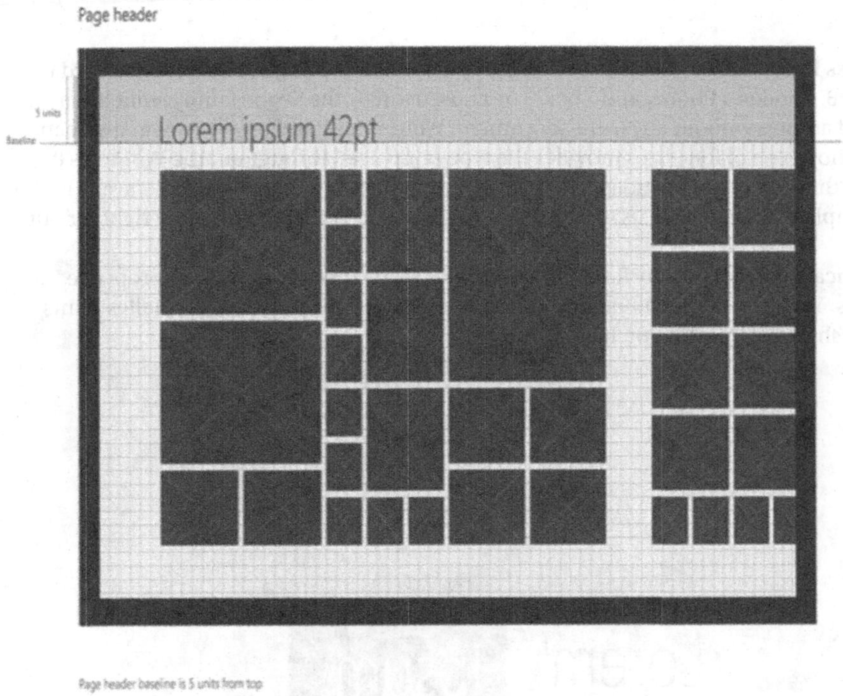

***Figure 2-5.** The grid and content layout, option C*

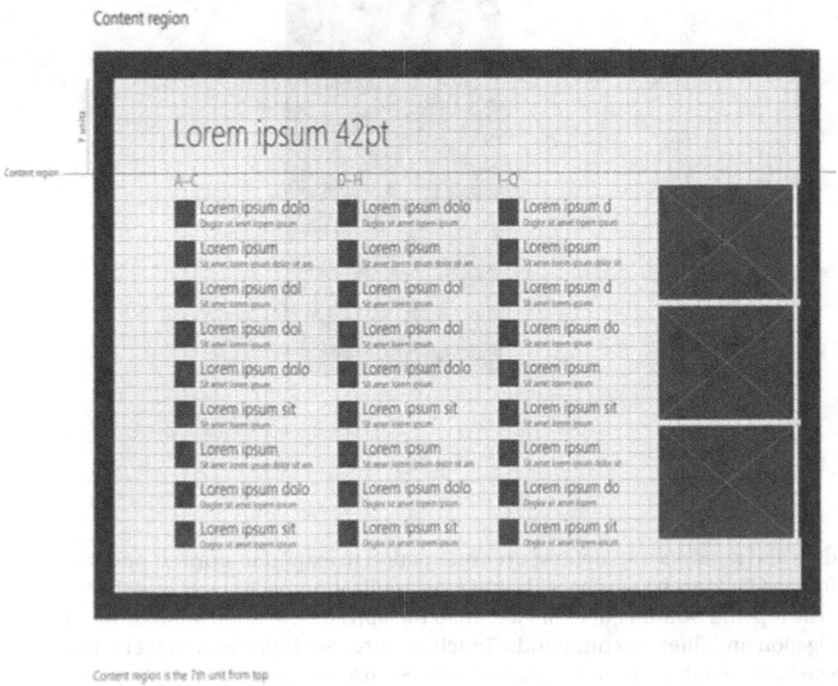

***Figure 2-6.** The grid and content layout, option D*

Typography

Another strong inspiration from Swiss Design comes in the use of typography, which is a huge contributor toward the user experience offered by Windows 8, Windows Phone, and Xbox. The chosen font is the Segoe family, which is a variant of Helvetica—both described as fonts without any extra adornment. Words can stand on their own, they can move, and they can be powerful. A chosen set of font sizes provides the type ramp used throughout the Windows 8 OS, and desirably carried forward in third-party applications. This provides structure and a consistent hierarchy in the content presented. Visual Studio templates already take us to a great starting point in getting typography right for our applications.

Figure 2-7 presents a typographical ramp commonly found in Windows 8 Store apps, along with appropriate usage guidelines for app UI elements. You'll notice the difference in font size between the largest and smallest fonts used. This difference is key to establishing the information hierarchy.

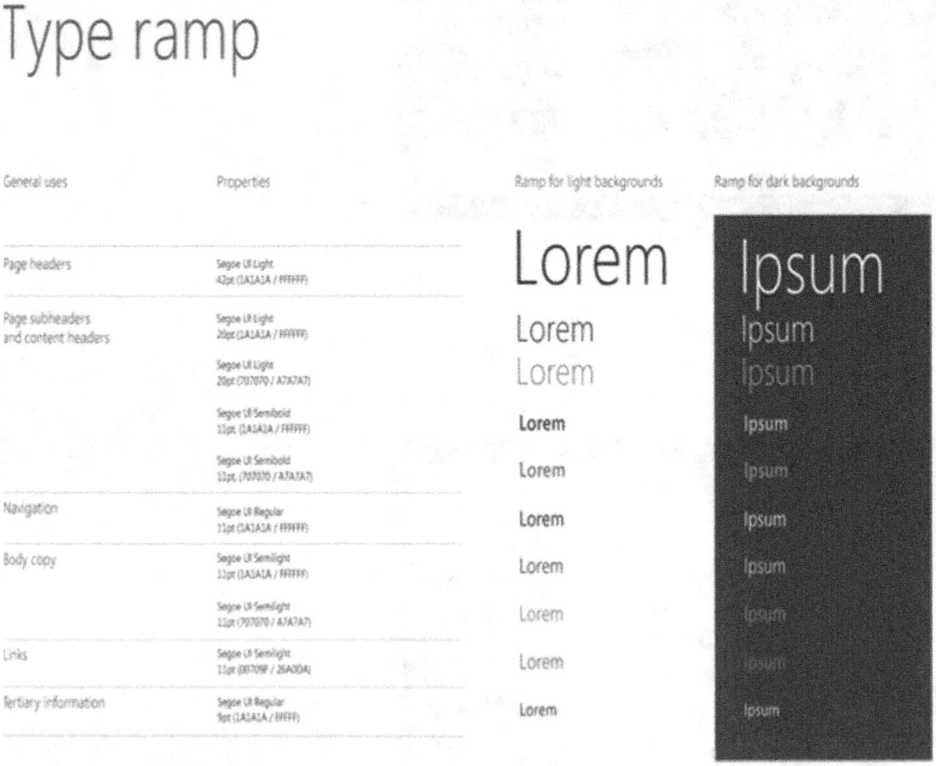

Figure 2-7. *The typographical ramp*

Leverage the Edge

Windows 8 is very sensitive around edges and it awaits the slightest user interaction to extend in-context options. The left and right edges are reserved for the OS: the left steps back through the application back stack, and the right brings up the ubiquitous charms bar. The top and bottom edges are left up to the apps for customization through the app Bars, which aid in placing navigation and filtering commands. Touch gestures are built-in to trigger edge commanding, and Windows 8 apps benefit from natural user muscle memory. So, use the edges to add natural functionality and branding, and to give your app some Windows 8 behaviors.

Figure 2-8 highlights the charms and application bars we see so commonly in Windows 8 OS and third-party applications. If you have access to a Windows 8 tablet, hold it with two hands to see where your thumbs can reach. The placement of the charms and app Bars will make complete sense to you.

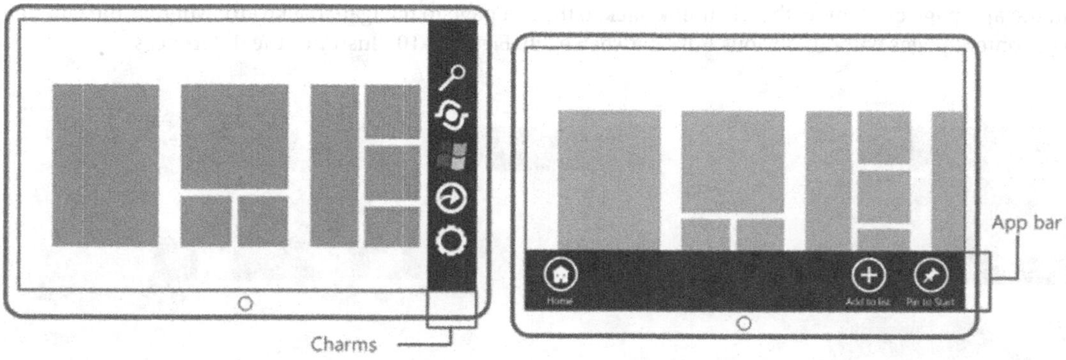

Figure 2-8. *The charms and a sample app bar*

Transiency

Fleeting information to draw optional attention or keep the user in context while showing or asking for extra information, are good traits for most user experience guidelines. Windows 8 apps can shine in transiency usage through the use of specialized controls called *flyouts*, which support light-dismiss by the user tapping outside the given flyout window. The notifications for Windows 8 also use transiency to briefly let the user know something important happened, before vanishing smoothly upon no interaction from the user.

Figure 2-9 provides a spattering example of the use of flyouts or other types of transient controls in Windows 8. The point is that the user is never taken out of context, but is shown a quick, context-sensitive pop-up window that goes away on light dismiss by tapping anywhere else.

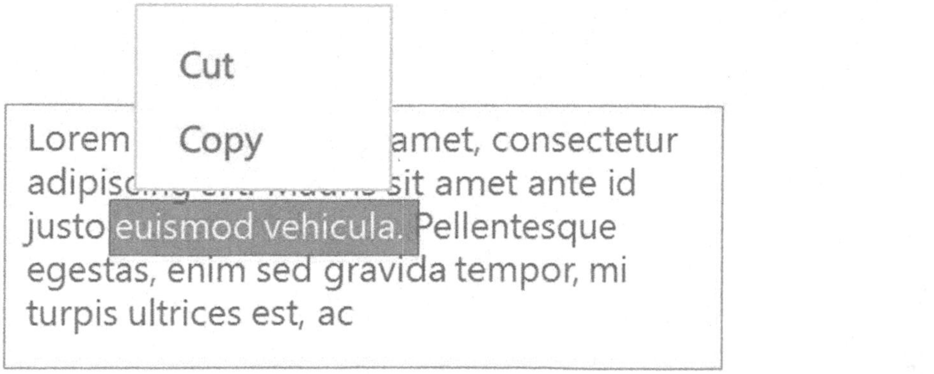

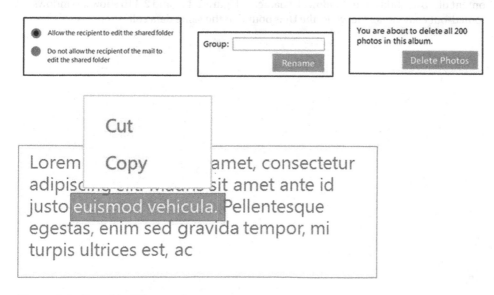

Figure 2-9. *Transient UI examples*

Navigation Models

Content is the navigation mechanism of choice. Invite users to touch the content they want to learn—and exploratory navigation will follow. There are two broad navigation patterns: *hierarchical,* as in the hub-and-spoke models seen in the actual Windows Store app, vs. *flat,* as seen in Internet Explorer 10 for Windows 8. The former takes the user down a nested path in the app page content, with a clear link back to the last page to navigate backward; whereas the latter is simply a chain of content pages without obvious links between each. Figure 2-10 illustrates the differences.

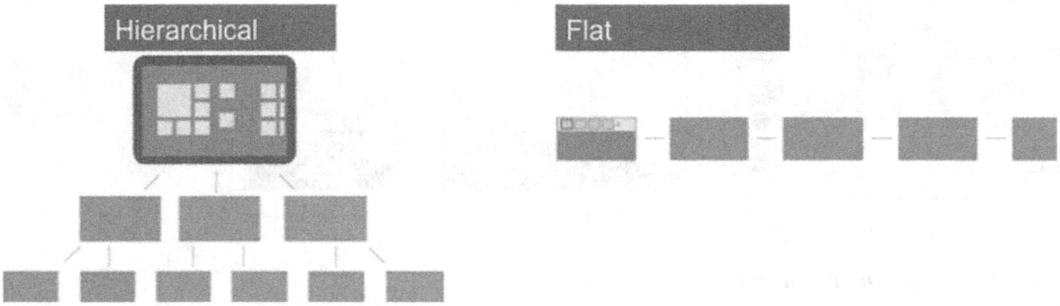

Figure 2-10. *The Windows 8 navigation patterns*

Semantic Zoom

Semantic Zoom is a new, wonderfully charming gesture experience in Windows 8. Are you browsing through a lot of content, leading to excessive panning around? With Semantic Zoom, you can simply pinch and zoom, or in mouse-keyboard systems, use Ctrl+Scroll—and voilà, the data is now grouped into buckets and you can jump into anything that interests you. This is called the *zoomed-out view* and it is supposed to show categorized summary information. The regular content is presented in a *zoomed-in view*. This is a must-do for Windows 8 app developers, because it immediately adds a lot to content discoverability and Windows 8 character. Figure 2-11a and 2-11b show a Windows 8 Store app with regular or zoomed-out content; all the while, the UI is bound to the same data collection.

Figure 2-11a. *The Windows 8 Store app—zoomed in*

Figure 2-11b. *The Windows 8 Store app—zoomed out*

Animations

Cinematography is inspiring. Motion keeps life interesting. These are heavy influences in the Windows 8 UX. Everything feels fast, fluid, and in motion. The key contributor behind the scenes is the design aspect of animations. Subtle and crisp, deliberate animations add zing to the Windows 8 user experience, without looking gaudy. Nothing in the OS is jarring. Content simply eases into position, just enough to raise the interest of users without being in their faces. Animations are not meant to decorate Windows 8, rather to smoothly nudge the UX around the continuity of content. Thankfully, developers have access to all the resources through built-in controls and animation libraries needed to re-create some of the animation magic that goes into Windows 8 in our own apps.

Snap and Scale

All Windows 8 apps can cycle through three visual states: full screen, fill view, and snapped. *Full screen* is when the app is edge-to-edge immersive on screen. A *fill view* is when the app is stacked to a side with most of the real estate. A *snapped view* is when an app is stacked to a side, with the smaller real estate (320 pixels wide, to be precise) with another app. Windows 8 users can always do this visual state change manually; so lack of a purposeful snapped state only leads to a bad user experience. The purpose of these visual states is to allow the user to multitask, with the less important app snapped to one side, as the main app is being used. Figure 2-12 shows the weather app snapped with Internet Explorer 10.

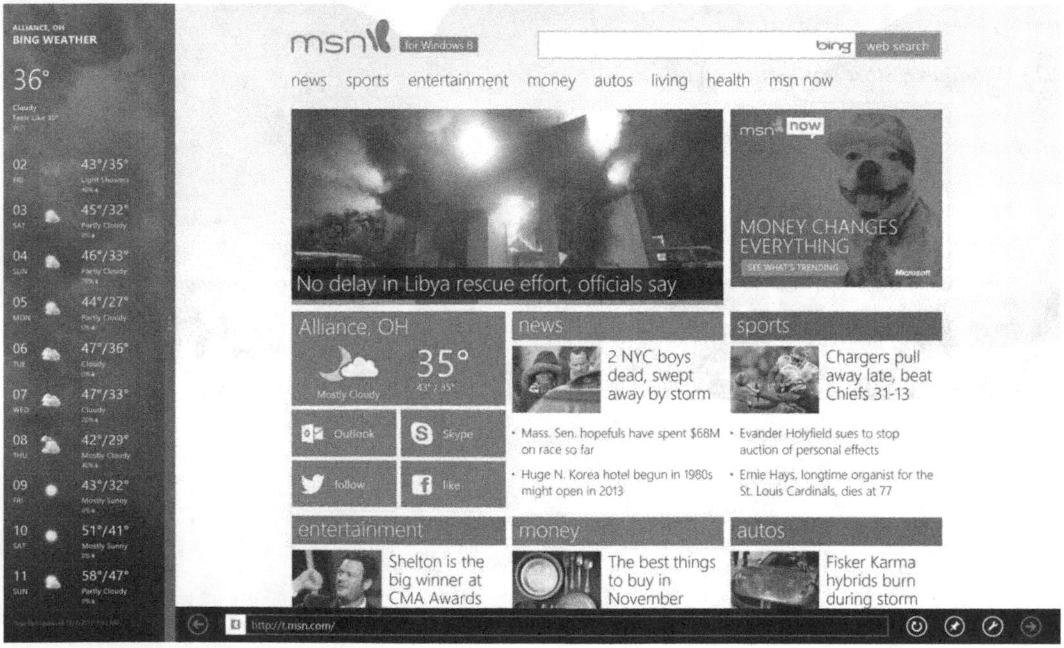

Figure 2-12. *Snapped Windows 8 apps*

Windows 8 also has great support for scaling. PCs come in various form factors with a variety of resolutions, and Windows 8 will scale content up or down given the pixel density available. Third-party apps can participate in automatic scaling and can offer native resolution support through the use of vector graphics or switchable assets based on resolution. Also, fluid layout of content, as compared to fixed layout, ensures that content flows naturally with varying screen real estate. There is help from the Visual Studio simulator to make sure developers can test their apps in a variety of screen resolutions. It is best to test apps for the best possible UX.

Contracts

Windows 8 Store apps run a silo for security reasons: so that there is no direct communication between apps. Through the use of *contracts,* however, the OS often acts as a broker to enable an app-to-app handshake. Features like Search, Share, Settings, File Pickers, and so forth, give the apps the unique Windows 8 flavor and deep integration with the host OS. It is highly suggested that Windows 8 apps try to implement at least some of the contracts to feel like a well-mannered citizen in the Windows 8 world and to leverage user muscle memory while providing a consistent UX.

Connected and Alive

The Windows 8 OS and hopefully all its apps feel connected and alive with information, always inviting the user back. This is major selling point for Windows 8 ecosystem as a whole. We have seen in recent history how much users cherish the always on and connected UX offered by today's computers and tablets. Windows 8 tries to extend that to the next level through the Start screen and beyond. Apps get to play a big role by providing the illusion of having fresh content, even though they are not technically running. Two features that go a long way toward this connected UX are live tiles and toast notifications.

Tiles are the squares and rectangles that represent apps on the Windows 8 Start screen experience. Tiles are the front door to the app and should exude branding. Along with the main content, a tile can show a little branding icon in its lower-left corner and a badge (number or glyph) that displays current information in the lower-right corner. For sustained energetic usage from the user, it is imperative that Windows 8 application developers and designers make the effort to create an inviting tile.

In addition to being the most common way to launch apps, the tiles serve another crucial role. They can be live tiles, fresh with information to invite the user back into the app. Live tiles are fed with tiny packets of fresh, personalized information, either from within the app on last run, from periodic or scheduled updates, or externally from the cloud through Windows push notifications. This preview of fresh information and peeking animations lights up the Windows 8 Start screen. A Windows 8 app may have a companion cloud service that can be polled for fresh content, or it may use Windows Push Notification Service (WNS) to send live tile updates to the app's tile, thus truly providing the connected and alive UX. The user gets fresh tile information in this case, without even having to run the app, which contributes to the glance-and-go design philosophy maximizing the amount of information a user gets just by looking at the Start screen. Live tiles can also flip through the last five pieces of content by using a unique peek animation, adding to the "alive" experience. Aside from the main app tiles, sections of the app can also be made pinnable on Start screen through the use of *secondary live tiles,* ready to provide contextual information about pinned content and to take the user directly back to the app content/section that was pinned.

Compared to tiles, *toast notifications* are meant to deliver transient messages outside the context of an app and only appear for a few seconds, generally in the top-right of the screen. To see a toast notification, the user does not need to come back to the Start screen; it will show up regardless of where the user is in Windows 8. Meant for real-time personal content push mechanisms, toast notifications can be acted upon when tapped, quickly taking the user to a contextually relevant part of the app. Because notifications show up at any time and place, user privacy must be taken into consideration to ask for permission. The user is also at liberty to turn off notifications if desired.

Figure 2-13a and 2-13b show a spattering of choices that developers have while designing content for their live tiles and toasts. There are system-defined API definitions for supporting live tiles and toasts, and they end up being tiny pieces of standard XML so that Windows 8 OS may process them. These templates are clearly defined in MSDN documentation, and developers and designers are encouraged to use the combination of text, images, and badges that best suits the needs of their apps. I'll discuss these at length later in Chapter 12.

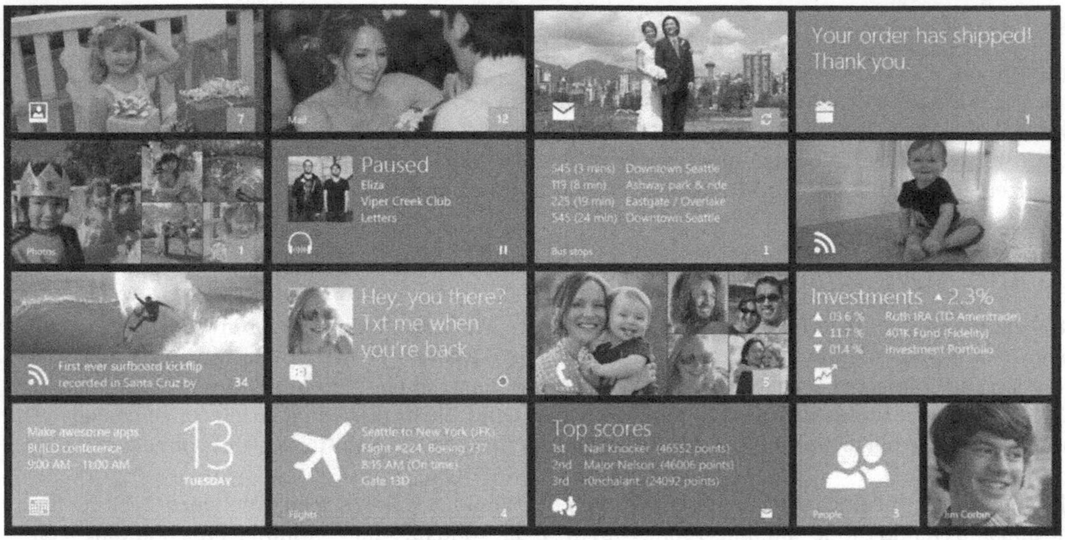

Figure 2-13a. Samples from Windows 8 Tile templates

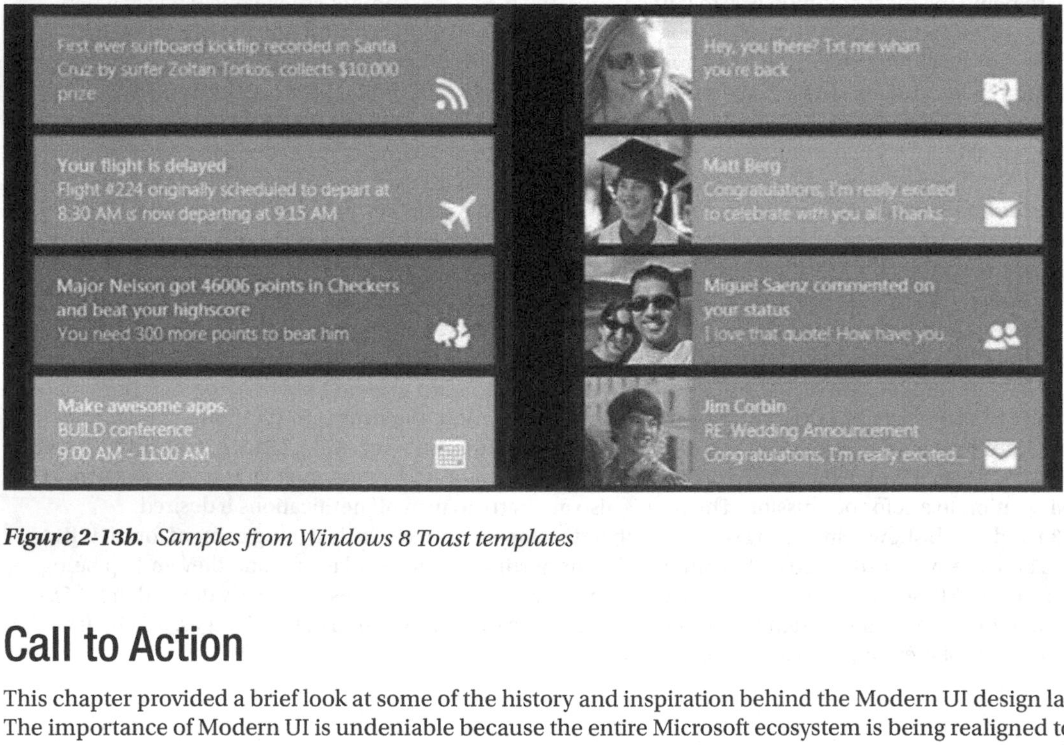

Figure 2-13b. Samples from Windows 8 Toast templates

Call to Action

This chapter provided a brief look at some of the history and inspiration behind the Modern UI design language. The importance of Modern UI is undeniable because the entire Microsoft ecosystem is being realigned toward this simple goal of a single, unified design language shaping the UX of major products. If you are a Windows 8 Store app developer or for that matter, any other types of applications in the Microsoft stack, it really does pay dividends to understand the design philosophy and customize your apps accordingly. Consistent UX leads to happy users, in turn leading to happier developers. So, what are you waiting on?

PART 2

Getting Started

Now that you've had a brief look at some of the history and inspiration behind Windows 8 and the new Microsoft software ecosystem, it's time to kick some dust as a developer. Let's get our hands dirty figuring out the magic behind the Windows 8 app user-experience and what it means for developers.

Chapters 3-6 are aimed at getting you quickly started in writing your first Windows 8 application. Less talk and more real-world code and scenarios. You'll learn about some of the tools and frameworks in the trade. You have the next big app idea and can't wait to get started? Time to discover what you need to keep in mind as the first few building blocks towards that dream Windows 8 app. All this and more are coming up.

In Microsoft CEO Steve Ballmer's words: "Developers, developers, developers . . . ".

CHAPTER 3

The App Platform and Developer Tools

Having covered some of the history and inspiration behind Windows 8 and the new Modern UI design language, let's unwrap what Windows 8 truly means for developers by looking under the hood of the platform. Built from the ground up, Windows 8 is Windows reimagined and presents one of biggest opportunities for developers. With the massive PC/Windows user base worldwide looking to upgrade to Windows 8 or purchase newer hardware, your Windows 8 Store Apps have a huge audience right out of the gate. The potential to make a name for yourself is definitely big, especially since the Windows 8 Store is starting from scratch. Every App has an equal opportunity to shine. But before you can embark on the journey to make your dream Windows 8 Store App, you should spend some time in this chapter to understand the moving pieces in the underlying platform, to learn how to make sane development choices, and to explore the tools and templates readily available to App developers. Let's get started.

Examining the Platform Architecture

First, let's agree on the starting point. Pick your favorite browser and please bookmark `http://dev.windows.com`. This is the Windows Developer portal home. This portal always has the latest and greatest documentation, code samples, and forum for discussions. It is an indispensible fallback resource while you are developing Windows 8 Store Apps.

Next, let's talk platform architecture. What is the system boxology behind the duality of Windows 8—the touch-first OS and the Windows Store Apps vs. the traditional desktop? Although available from Microsoft and various other sources, the following diagram (see Figure 3-1) by Doug Seven, executive vice president of Telerik, an end-to-end software development provider, stands out as the most accurate.

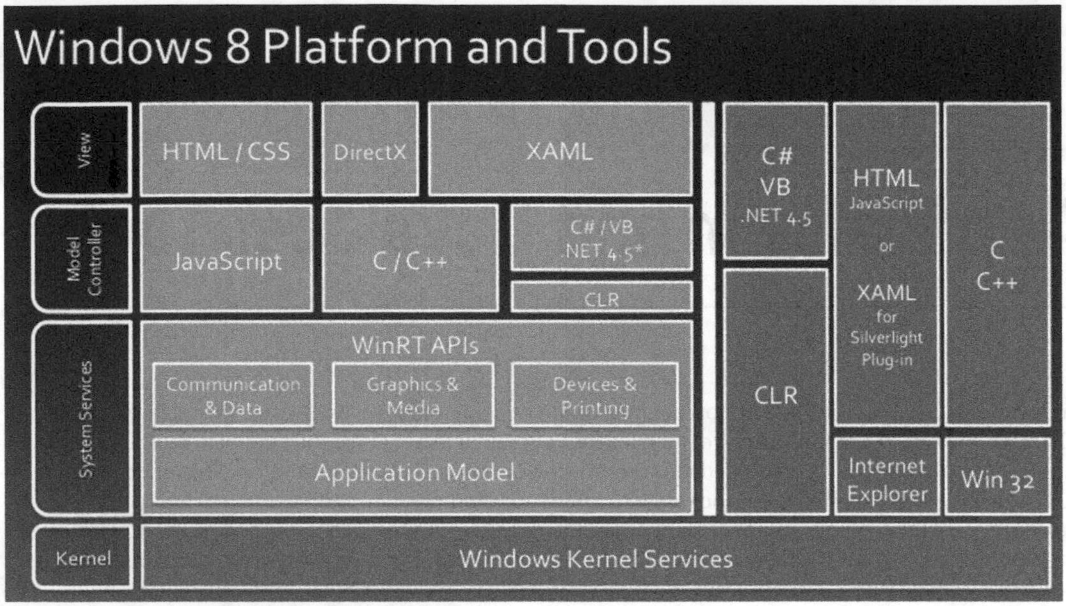

***Figure 3-1.** Windows 8 platform architecture*

Let's break this down a bit. Engineering teams will tell you that it is difficult to fit complex architectures in one slide deck because technical accuracy often lies between the lines. However, the diagram shown in Figure 3-1 offers, in one glimpse, what's changed in Windows 8. The monumental effort in making Windows 8 what it is for consumers and developers is apparent in the vastly different technologies present in this single diagram. The old and the new coexist happily. Here's how:

- The right area is similar to Windows 7 of the past, but with major improvements. It is the traditional Windows desktop and supports the millions of applications that have been written for Windows. Application technologies range from .NET, WPF, Silverlight within and outside browser, and games in various languages—C/C++, COM, Win32, and so forth. All of these applications can move into Windows 8 unchanged. Intel-based Windows 8 PCs run them all just fine, just as Windows 7 did.
- The left area represents the brave new world of touch-centric Windows 8 OS and the Store Apps. Application sandboxing is in place in this model to protect the end user.
- The right and left regions and applications within them, do not talk to each other; this is by design and it is meant for simplicity. At the lowest level, however, both types of Windows applications fall back on the Windows core kernel for OS-level interactions. The way one reaches this level is markedly different.

Windows has always allowed application developers access to core kernel features through Win32 APIs; it just hasn't been very easy to do. With Windows 8, Microsoft took the opportunity to ease access to the kernel features through a standardized API set called *Windows Runtime (WinRT)*. The projection of core features for easy consumption in native application development languages required extensive heavy lifting to make sure the Windows object model mapped to support for several development languages towards building Windows Store Apps. This was a big undertaking and the choice of several development languages remains the biggest investment in the Windows 8 App development ecosystem.

Development Choices

Windows 8 is out of the door, but the real slow-churning battle begins now. In order to have a thriving marketplace/store full of high-quality Apps, every software platform needs to woo developers. Not new to this game, Microsoft brings an arsenal of choices for developing Apps for Windows 8.

Choice in User Interface Technology

For building the user interface for a Windows 8 Store App, you have three choices when it comes to technologies used to render content on the screen:

- *XAML*: If you come from a .NET background, this will be the natural UI language of choice. The development ease of using XAML as the front end technology will be welcomed by developers, as well as, the managed stack of C#/VB.NET which is a first-class citizen in the Windows 8 App development stack. It also has a rich ecosystem of developer tooling and community support. In fact, this is the UI technology stack you'll focus on exclusively in this book. Interestingly, if you're a C++ geek, you can now use XAML natively as your UI language.

- *HTML/CSS*: News flash—if you have web development experience, you are already a long way ahead toward being a Windows 8 Store App developer. HTML5 and CSS3 act as UI for JavaScript-based Windows 8 Apps, with additional support from libraries like Microsoft-provided *WinJS* and other jQuery/custom frameworks.

- *DirectX*: If you need granular control over pixels and need to tighten the noose around performance without the managed stack overhead, DirectX with C++ may be the option for you. This will be true for a lot of game developers or Apps needing close-to-the-metal performance.

A Fair Bit of Choice in Development Language

Some portability magic is happening under the covers in Windows 8 to offer App developers their choice of programming language. Windows has always allowed access to its kernel features through InterOp or COM (Component Object Model) code; however, developers did not really enjoy writing COM components to interact with the OS. So Microsoft took up the task of writing a Windows Runtime component layer, called WinRT, that sits right on top of the kernel services. The goal was to ease developer access to OS features and make it native to whichever development language that was in use. The result was achieved through a system, depicted in Figure 3-2.

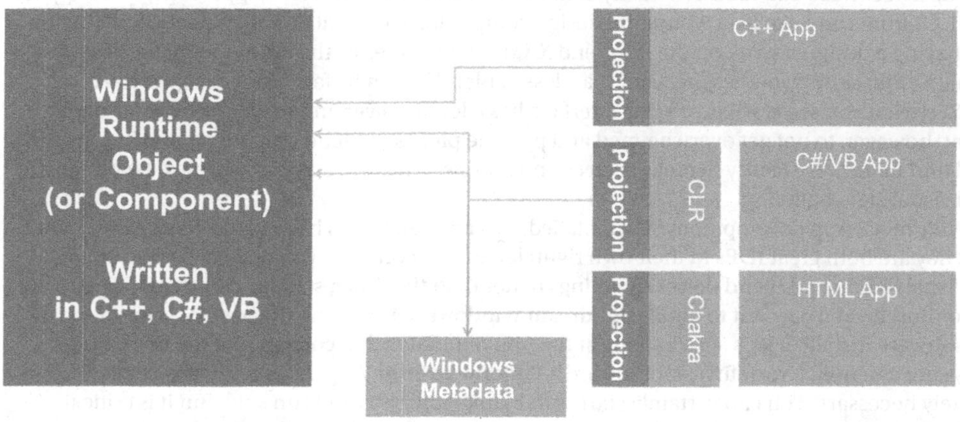

Figure 3-2. *Windows 8 language projections*

How do you support multiple development language all reaching into one API layer? The answer comes in the form of *language projections*, which are essentially a thin layer of abstraction that takes the object model type-system used in WinRT and maps them to types in the respective development languages (.NET, C++, or JavaScript). This mapping layer serves the brilliant purpose of masking the existence of WinRT from developers. Using Windows API through WinRT feels like an extension of the development language in use, which is easier than having developers learn a whole new language. This flexibility and natural extensibility to seamlessly access Windows features is a monumental shift in how Windows applications are going to be developed.

WinRT represents its entire API set in the form of *Windows Metadata*, which happens to be in ECMA 335 format. The language projections then read this metadata and do the mapping to its respective development language object model. The .NET CLR has a slightly easier job because the metadata is in the same format used internally in the WinMD metadata files; but at the end of the day, all languages have equal footing. Using WinRT APIs simply feels like natural code in C#/VB in managed stack, as well as C++ and JavaScript. You can, in fact, create your own Windows Runtime component to wrap additional Windows kernel features. The API details will be stored in a WinMD file and language-projected into all supported development languages for consumption. Essentially, this model lowers the learning curve for developers. Instead of learning WinRT as a language, the necessary bits are simply projected into the development language in use.

Tools: Required Software

Windows 8 Store Apps can only be developed if you are running the development tools from within Windows 8 OS. First, you need to download and run Windows 8. The OS can be installed on laptops, desktops, tablets, all-in-ones, or run in a virtual machine. The Windows 8 Enterprise 90-day free evaluation version is available for developers at `http://msdn.microsoft.com/en-US/evalcenter/jj554510.aspx`. Alternatively, you may use MSDN/Microsoft Partner Network subscriptions for access to Windows 8 final bits, or you can simply purchase Windows 8 from Microsoft.

The next order of business is to get Visual Studio 2012. Visual Studio is the one-stop integrated development environment (IDE) that you need to develop Windows 8 Store Apps. And thankfully, all that you need is free. The Visual Studio Express 2012 for Windows 8 includes Windows 8 SDK, Blend for Visual Studio, and App project templates. You may download the Express edition from `http://msdn.microsoft.com/en-US/windows/apps/br229516.aspx` or use MSDN subscriptions to gain access to fuller versions of Visual Studio 2012.

Visual Studio 2012 gives you everything needed to create code, debug, localize, package, and deploy a Windows 8 Store App. So everything you need to build successful Windows 8 Store Apps is contained in one tool. You do need to have a developer license to develop and test Windows Store apps before the Windows Store can certify them. Visual Studio provides one automatically as you begin to make your first Windows 8 App.

Blend for Visual Studio 2012, on the other hand, helps you design and build beautiful Windows 8 user interfaces by providing an accurate design surface and tools to visually create and edit Windows 8 Store Apps. Blend has support for both XAML and HTML UI fronts and can be a wonderful design companion to Visual Studio. In fact, Blend offers the unique advantage of having a designer work on the front-end XAML/HTML files as the developer of the Windows 8 App works on code. Visual Studio simply merges the work seamlessly. Blend began its fame as a designer tool. Accordingly, the WYSIWYG (what you see is what you get) interface has a lot of power and may look busy to some developers. It is important, however, to not get overwhelmed and pick the pieces of Blend that are helpful in a given scenario. Developers will find Blend very handy in areas such as animations, template editing, sample data binding, layout management, and visual state handling.

Once you have the Windows 8 App development SDK installed, you have access to both Visual Studio 2012 and Blend for Visual Studio. They are both great IDEs in their own right; let no one convince you one way or the other about their usage. Both Visual Studio and Blend do certain things better than the other, so your choice of IDE should be based on needs and comfort level. You want to build your dream Windows 8 App using the best tools for the job.

With the necessary software installed, let's start looking at the App templates that come out of the box with the developer tools. These are essentially your first steps toward a Windows 8 Store App. As you will see later, these templates are not absolutely necessary. You can certainly start with Blank templates and run solo. But it is critical to take a peek inside the built-in Windows 8 App templates to see how Microsoft envisions the plumbing inside a Windows 8 Store App.

Working with Templates

With Visual Studio 2012 Express or the full versions installed with the Windows 8 SDK, select File ➤New Project. Figure 3-3 shows the type of dialog box that you are greeted with.

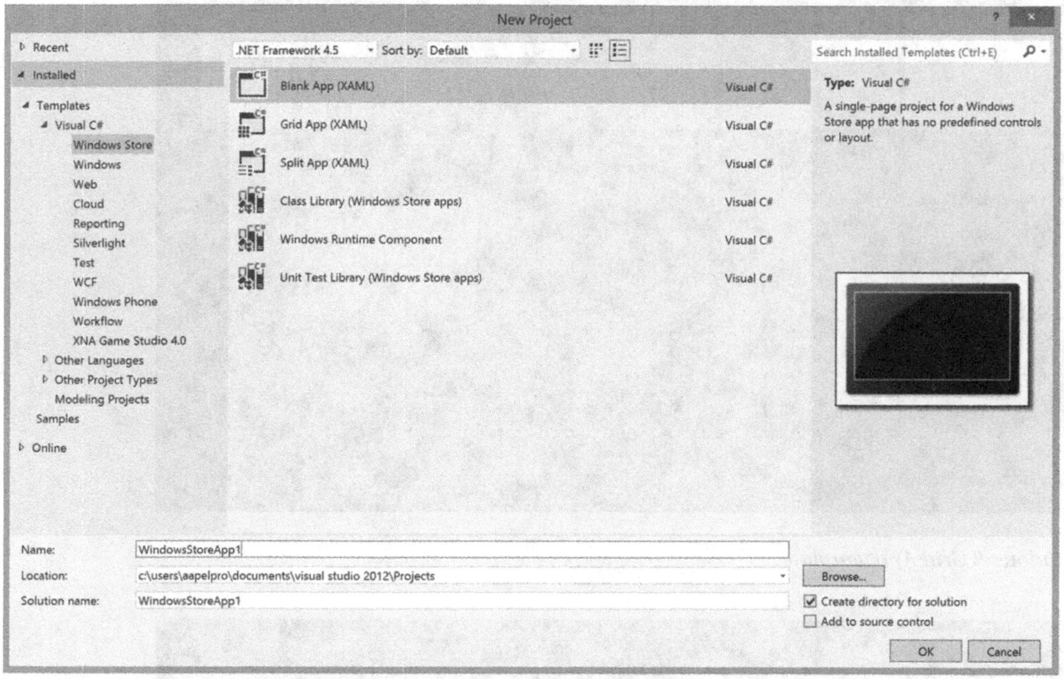

Figure 3-3. *Windows 8 Blank App template*

There are a couple of things to note here. Because you picked C#, the Windows Store options presents a list of XAML-based Windows 8 App templates supported by Visual Studio. Regardless of your development language choice between C#, VB, C++, or JavaScript, the same Windows 8 App project templates are available in Visual Studio. This indicates that every one of the languages offers a native first-class experience as you develop Windows 8 Store Apps. Once you select an App template, Visual Studio creates an application *solution*, with a project structure appropriately containing the necessary starting artifacts.

The project templates for Windows 8 Store Apps serve as a good starting point in getting a Visual Studio project ready with all the components that a Windows 8 Store App needs to be deployed to the Store and subsequently run on a PC. The other benefit of Visual Studio templates is that they give you a good head start toward correctly getting Modern UI in your App's user experience. As you saw in Chapter 2, there are guiding principles for design in Windows 8 Apps, but it may not always be easy for developers to get it right every time. The templates do a wonderful job in providing App pages that already conform to the design principles and the Windows 8 silhouette. All the design concerns about typography, spacing, and placement of content are already handled by built-in styles in the templates. All you have to do is start with the Windows 8 App templates and inject data along with building up your own App's brand.

The *Grid App* and *Split App* templates offer great visuals for designing your App and presenting content on-screen. You may also choose to start with a *Blank App* template and then progressively add items to your project; or you can start with the Grid/Split templates to have a visual for what your App may look like, and then trim out the unnecessary pieces.

With the Grid App and Split App templates selected, the Visual Studio project already has several files in place to help you start. Simply press F5 to run the Windows 8 App. You'll be greeted with Apps that look like the ones shown in Figures 3-4 and 3-5. Figure 3-4 shows a Grid App template and Figure 3-5 shows a Split App template.

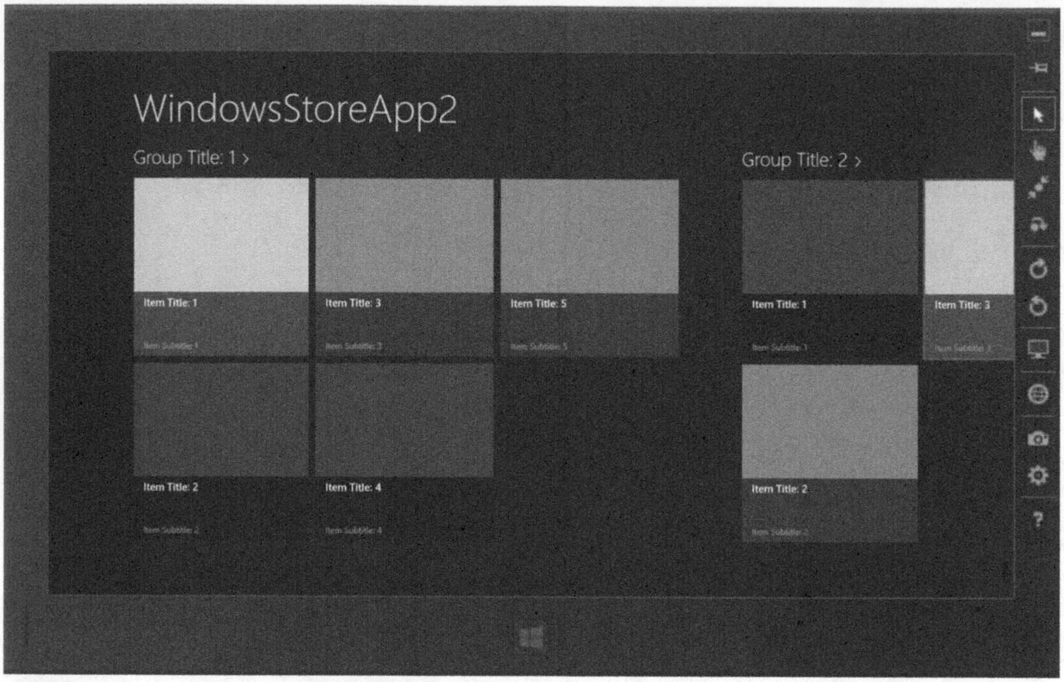

Figure 3-4. *Windows 8 Grid App template*

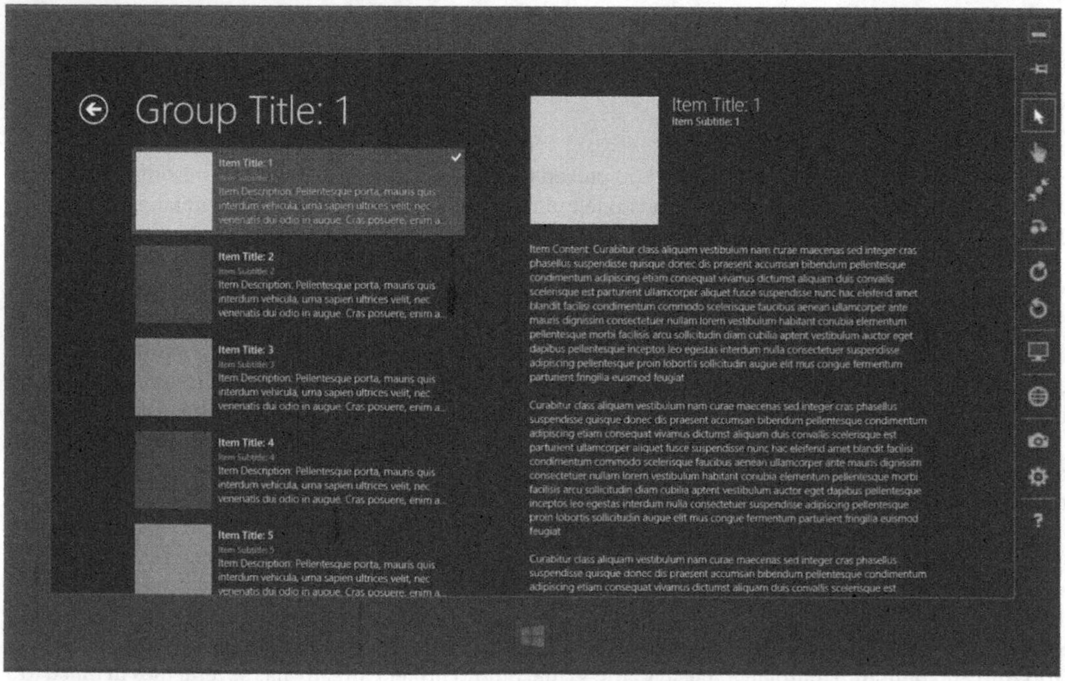

Figure 3-5. *Windows 8 Split App template*

The Grid App template drops files in your Visual Studio project to support a three-page hub-and-spoke layout, which includes a Summary landing page, a Grouped detail page, and an Item detail page. The Split App template simply provides a placeholder to have a page listing a collection of items on the left and their corresponding details on the right. Notice the common trend in these templates: the Apps that you can run by simply pressing F5 already emphasize the Windows 8 silhouette. Modern UI design is built-in the pages, controls, fonts, and spacing.

Though not strictly suggested, you could literally start with these templates, add custom data collections with appropriate imagery and branding, and data-bind to the existing UI—and voilà, you have a professional-looking Windows 8 Store App without designer help. That is one of primary goals of the Visual Studio templates—to show you a great starting point. What you do from here is your personal route to fame.

The other templates that you saw in Figure 3-3 do not necessarily contribute to the UI of your Windows 8 App, but they are important in getting you started toward that custom-class or WinRT component for reusability. Also, once you have a full-fledged Windows 8 Store App, your code base will be rather large and will grow as you enhance and provide App updates through the Store. It is in this context that the Visual Studio unit testing template is important. Start designing your App architecture where you can have separation of concerns between UI and business logic. Then, build up a battery of unit tests using the Unit Test Library template so that you have confidence that core App functionality is preserved across enhancements and updates.

Anatomy of a Visual Studio Project

No matter which Visual Studio template that you pick, few things remain the same, and it is important to understand the moving pieces and components that make up a Windows 8 Store App. So, let's dive into the anatomy of a typical Windows 8 App project in Visual Studio.

First, as with Windows Phone, Windows 8 Apps run in a sandboxed container. This means that every App operates in a silo with its own memory footprint and file/registry storage access. Every Windows 8 App is run by the OS in what's called an *application frame*—the container that houses all the pages within the App and allows for navigation between the pages. This model is true regardless of XAML or HTML pages, and lends to the easy design segregation of complex Apps into simple pages.

You will see references to this application frame in many places in your code. There are two essential backstacks in Windows 8: one within the App frame to keep track of the pages the user has visited within a given App, and the other maintained by the OS as an application backstack to allow the user to go back through Apps. On Windows 8 devices, this is the application backstack that you are seeing when you swipe from the left edge or use a mouse hover on the top-left corner. The page backstack within the application frame is more subtle, but it is a rather handy resource for developers to allow back navigation through the pages of their Apps. Refer back to Figure 3-5 for a moment. Do you see the little back-arrow icon in the top-left corner of the app? This is the visual cue to the user that the given App keeps a history of pages and allows back navigation. Later, you'll see more of this in the code.

Now that you've begun working on a Visual Studio project to create a Windows 8 Store App, the next obvious question is: where does the App run as you are developing it? Well, you have options here as well. By default (press F5 if you are following along), the App simply deploys/runs on the local machine running Windows 8; but that's not the only possibility, as the diagram in Figure 3-6 shows.

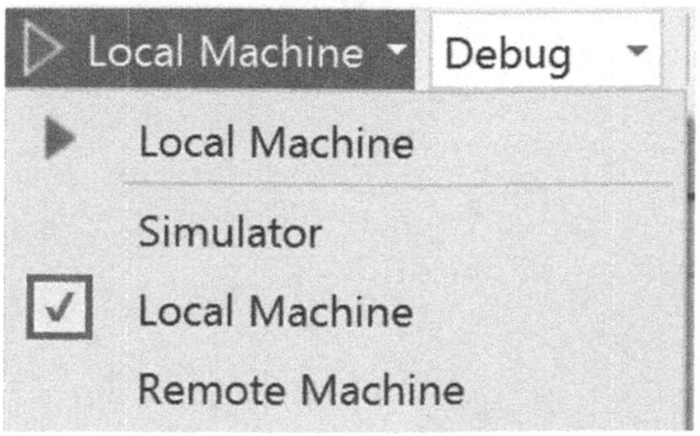

Figure 3-6. *Windows 8 debugging options*

The three options are described as follows:

- *Local Machine*: This is the default. The Windows 8 Store App being developed simply installs and runs on the same machine running Windows 8 with Visual Studio.
- *Simulator*: If installing in-development Apps locally isn't your cup of tea, there is a brilliant simulator to help you out, as shown in Figures 3-4 and 3-5. It essentially looks like Windows 8 running in a small tablet. It starts out with the same image as the host OS running Windows 8. The simulator can be kept open throughout development, with multiple Apps deployed to it. The huge benefit of using the simulator is the extras that you get. Windows 8 devices can respond to orientation changes, and the simulator helps you see how your App might adjust. Also, Windows 8 supports a variety of resolutions starting at 1024 × 768 all the way up to HD+ pixels. Wonder how your App scales up or down with this variety of resolutions? The simulator has a simple solution: grab the sidebar options on the right and simply change the resolution to see how your App looks! Want to see how your App responds to touch and two-finger pinch and zoom? The simulator has touch sensitivity built-in so that you may test your Windows 8 Apps without having access to a touch-screen device.
- *Remote Machine*: This is great new option for deploying Apps from Visual Studio. Many of you may already have Windows 8 Pro running on tablets or you have Windows ARM-based tablets like the shiny Microsoft Surface RT. Also, many consumers of your Apps may actually have ARM-based hardware. Wouldn't it be nice to deploy directly to these devices and know how your App looks on one? That is exactly what remote machine deployment does—run your App on a different PC straight from Visual Studio using a Home/Office domain network; you are even able to debug the application code while the App is running on remote device. Tim Heuer, from Microsoft, has a wonderful post on how to deploy Windows 8 Store Apps remotely to Surface or other ARM-based tablets. Read it at `http://timheuer.com/blog/archive/2012/10/26/remote-debugging-windows-store-apps-on-surface-arm-devices.aspx`. In an upcoming chapter, you'll also see a step-by-step mechanism on how to do this.

Now, let's go back to the Blank App template and see what makes up a Windows 8 App solution in Visual Studio. What you'll find in Visual Studio is a project structure like the one shown in Figure 3-7.

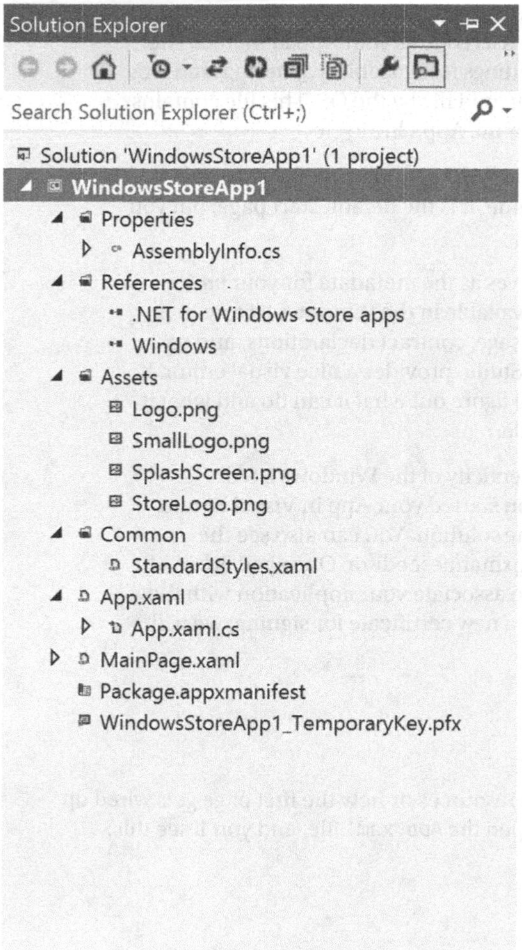

Figure 3-7. *Windows 8 Blank App solution*

Let's make sense of the individual pieces. This will be a nice foundation for building your Windows 8 App. The components of a Windows 8 App Visual Studio project are as follows:

- The *Properties* and *References* folders are no different from any other .NET solution. Assembly information and DLL (dynamic-link library)/service references show up here.
- All the images used in your Windows 8 Store App are conveniently housed in the *Assets* folder. The basic necessities support logos for your App's presence in the Windows 8 Store and get your App listed in various forms, such as the user's Start menu, Store search, Charms bar, App options, downloads list, Splash screen, and so forth. Pay attention to the exact pixel dimensions and replace with your own to inject your own brand.
- The *Common* folder may be used to house files that have potential use throughout the App. Prime candidates are global styles, base classes for pages, and anything you want to generalize for reuse within your App codebase.

- The *App.xaml* file and its corresponding code file are important starting points for your App. It is what the compiler parses first. The Windows 8 OS runs its code as your App launches. The `App.xaml` file contains all the App-level resources and settings for reusability. The `App.xaml.cs` file is where the first few lines of App code exist and is run initially by the OS. This file contains startup code and important milestone event-handlers for the App's life cycle.
- The *MainPage.xaml* and its corresponding code file is the first App page that the user sees. This is where your custom application code begins to shine. It is the default start page; but you are free to edit or replace it with a different starting page.
- *Package.appxmanifest* is an important file because it serves as the metadata for your entire App. It is a critical piece, especially if your App is to be available in the Windows 8 Store. It is the file that houses all the configuration, settings, logo usage, contract declarations, and so forth, for your App. The file is basically XML, but Visual Studio provides a nice visual editor. It is what Windows 8 OS and the Store read for your App to figure out what it can do and what it needs to run. It pays to be intimately familiar with this file.
- The *TemporaryKey.pfx* is the certificate signing the authenticity of the Windows 8 Store App. Every Windows 8 App needs to be signed. When you started your App in Visual Studio, it automatically creates a test certificate and adds it to the solution. You can also see the certificate in use in the Packaging tab of the Package.appxmanifest editor. Once you are ready to submit the App to the Windows Store, you will need to associate your application with the Microsoft Store and your developer account to generate a new certificate for signing; we will cover this later.

Some Boilerplate Code

You probably have a few questions about how an App uses its global resources or how the first page gets wired up for display behind the scenes. Let's buckle up and see some code. Open the `App.xaml` file, and you'll see this:

```
<Application.Resources>
        <ResourceDictionary>
            <ResourceDictionary.MergedDictionaries>
                <ResourceDictionary Source="Common/StandardStyles.xaml"/>
            </ResourceDictionary.MergedDictionaries>
        </ResourceDictionary>
</Application.Resources>
```

This is what tells the compiler to look for the global styles that you may have defined in the Common folder. Now, turn your attention to the `App.xaml.cs` file. Check out the default `OnLaunched()` method:

```
protected override void OnLaunched(LaunchActivatedEventArgs args)
        {
            Frame rootFrame = Window.Current.Content as Frame;

            if (rootFrame == null)
            {
                // Create a Frame to act as the navigation context and navigate to the first page.
                rootFrame = new Frame();
```

```
            if (args.PreviousExecutionState == ApplicationExecutionState.Terminated)
            {
                // TODO: Load state from previously suspended application.
            }

            // Place the frame in the current Window.
            Window.Current.Content = rootFrame;
        }

        if (rootFrame.Content == null)
        {
            if (!rootFrame.Navigate(typeof(MainPage), args.Arguments))
            {
                throw new Exception("Failed to create initial page");
            }
        }
        // Ensure the current window is active
        Window.Current.Activate();
    }
```

Did you notice how the application frame was initialized and how it was activated? Also, did you see the reference to `MainPage`? That is the cue to navigate to the first page of your App. So, make sure to update this line of code if you have changed your startup options. Also, check out the `OnSuspending()` and other events that you get to override. I will cover much of this in detail later, especially when I talk about application life cycle.

Summary

That's it! At this point, you should know about all the software that you need to install and have your development environment ready. With Visual Studio, you saw how to get started toward your first Windows 8 App and you inspected the anatomy of the moving pieces in the project. The most important takeaway from this chapter: play around with the built-in templates to realize how the component pieces work together and how the App templates portray the Modern UI design principles. Peek inside the built-in global styles or the base-class code in the Common folder. Create several dummy Apps and change the configurations around through the Package.appxmanifest editor to see the impact it has on the App's UI.

You are now ready for your developer fame towards writing the next big Windows 8 Store App!

CHAPTER 4

The Right Controls

Developing for mobile form factors is exciting. No matter what the platform, it is tremendously enticing as a developer to see your code running on a device that you can hold in your hands. It is as if all the code in the app just came alive in your hands to provide the perfect user experience. Add to that the breakneck competition in the quality and quantity of mobile apps from stores by Apple, Microsoft, and Google. And with a worldwide audience base to consume your app and its code, glory can be very near for many talented developers.

Although developer excitement to write mobile apps is commendable, there is commercial/business pressure to get the apps live and ready for download in app stores as quickly as possible. Peer developer pressure in using the latest and greatest development tools and techniques also adds to the urgency. The result: a lot of us on the Microsoft stack do a File ➤ New Project and proceed as quickly as we can with our dream app development.

Very soon, that pet app project may be riddled with the complexities of implementing patterns like MVVM (Model-View-ViewModel) and third-party vendor DLLs (dynamic-link libraries) to have access to the latest toolkits and controls. These are actually great add-ons and techniques to use as a Windows Store developer. In fact, you will spend time on these later in the book. The point is to show moderation, know the basics, and only do the things that are really needed. Slowing down to do the right things pays dividends. Content over chrome—one of the cornerstones of Modern UI design principles—prescribes that your UI should showcase content, minimize distractions, and provide the user with the right hints to explore the app further.

The controls that you put on your app canvas are very important for providing a consistent and compelling user experience (UX). They are the language that the end user uses to communicate with your app. The controls are pivotal, needless to say. You are going to spend time in this chapter learning a few details about the XAML stack and the native controls available for appropriate use in Windows 8 Store apps. Let's pick the right tools for the job and learn about the controls available out of the box for Windows Store app developers.

Framework and Namespace Basics

Before you start your journey toward the dream Windows 8 Store app, it is important to understand some of the moving pieces that make a Windows 8 app run the way it does. How do you choose the right framework when developing apps in XAML/C#? How do you get your page ready to start putting controls on it? Let's unpack.

Let's open Visual Studio, select C#/VB for Windows Store apps, and start a new project with a Blank template to follow along. You'll inspect a few internal workings to understand how a Windows Store app is really working. The first thing to note is that although you are writing your app in .NET, you do not have the luxury of the entire .NET framework; this is by design. MSDN documentation (`http://msdn.microsoft.com/en-us/library/windows/apps/br230302.aspx`) states: "The .NET Framework provides a subset of managed types that you can use to create Windows Store apps using C# or Visual Basic. This subset of managed types is called the .NET for Windows Store apps. It enables .NET Framework developers to create Windows Store apps within a familiar programming framework. Any types that are not related to developing Windows Store apps are not included in the subset."

You are leveraging a different .NET Framework profile as your Windows Store apps run inside Windows 8. Synchronous (or blocking) operations, types, and members that do not apply to Windows Store apps—types that wrap

OS functionality, performance counters, and so forth—are simply not included in the .NET Framework for Windows Store apps. However, to make sure that application developers can leverage the full power of the Windows 8 operating system as appropriate, we have access to the Windows RT (or WinRT) APIs. This is the unmanaged layer that exposes Windows' kernel features to consuming apps by projecting functionality natively into the app development language of choice.

Let's open the `MainPage.xaml.cs` code-behind file created through your Blank App template and inspect the *using* declarations. You should see two broad namespaces in use:

- *System.**.: This is the namespace that brings in functionality from .NET Framework for Windows Store apps.
- *Windows.**: This namespace brings in the WinRT features and API hooks.

Now, let's take a closer look at `MainPage.xaml`. This, as you know, is the UI view. It is written in eXtensible Application Markup Language (XAML, pronounced "zammel"). Generally, you'll define all your visual elements in XAML and take care of interaction/business logic in C#. However, just like HTML, XAML builds a visual tree while displaying content, and the tree can be manipulated in code. So, just about anything you do in XAML can also be done in the code-behind, albeit a little wordier.

My XAML file starts like so:

```
<Page
    x:Class="WindowsStoreApp1.MainPage" ....
```

This `x:class` attribute translates to a class called `MainPage` in the `WindowsStoreApp1` namespace and inherits from `Page` class. So, this is just like a class definition in C#. Now, if you go back to your `MainPage.xaml.cs` code-behind, you see the partial keyword in the class declaration. This continuation of the class declaration is the XAML component, thus directing the compiler to read both files. Parsing XAML is a two-step process—once during compilation to extract all the element names and generate intermediate C# files in `Obj` directory, and then again parsing at runtime to instantiate all XAML elements into the visual tree and obtain references to them for code edits.

Next, let's dive into what you actually put in your pages: the all-important controls.

The Placeholders

Let's talk a little bit about how content is placed in Windows Store apps. The top-level container in Windows Store apps is the *Frame*—the application frame that houses all other content in your app. To give you a little more clarity around the `Frame` class, here's the class inheritance hierarchy as you use the `Frame` in your app (see Figure 4-1).

Object
  DependencyObject
    UIElement
      FrameworkElement
        Control
          ContentControl
            Frame

Figure 4-1. *Frame hierarchy*

If you traverse up the object hierarchy before you use a Frame class, you can see all the element and framework properties that the Frame already inherits. The Frame in a Windows Store app is primarily responsible for housing pages and providing internal navigation between pages. As you have seen before, the App.xaml.cs sets up the initial application frame and it sets the content of the app's current window to the Frame. The result is that the app's window contains a Frame that contains the first page being navigated to. You will revisit Frames and look at navigation in more detail in the next chapter. There is no restriction preventing a Windows Store app from using multiple Frames; but most apps use only one for simplicity in maintaining the Page backstack memory during navigation.

Next up, let's look at the Page control. The class inheritance hierarchy is presented in Figure 4-2.

```
Object
  DependencyObject
    UIElement
      FrameworkElement
        Control
          UserControl
            Page
```

Figure 4-2. *Page hierarchy*

The Page class is designed to be a top-level placeholder for individual XAML views in a Windows Store app. It is housed inside a Frame. Remember the design principles around content layout? Let your content breathe—white space is your friend. As you envision the functionality of your Windows 8 Store app, look out for the risk of putting too much content in one view. Instead of making a view too busy, your users may be thankful if you split up the app into separate views, each doing one small task. What you are implicitly designing here are the app pages layout—the main placeholders of your content—and then figuring out the navigation between pages.

So the bottom line is that, most times, your app design is about one application frame and multiple application pages housed inside the Frame. This is often the most crucial part of envisioning an app. Take your time to get the design right. What is the right mix of breaking up content into discrete pages? How should the user navigate naturally between pages? Although you have lots of design tools at hand, pen and paper often work well in conceiving the Frame/Page hierarchy for your app.

Also, much of the modern XAML technologies that you use today have foundations in Windows Presentation Foundation (WPF) or the old Silverlight days. And the inheritance of Frame/Page controls show how important framework features trickle down to most of your controls. Although it's not essential to understand, almost all the controls I will talk about today work with dependency properties under the covers, inherited from DependencyObject. *Dependency properties* are an extension of .NET (common language runtime) CLR object properties, which allow establishing the value of a property, at run time, based on input from a number of sources (e.g., the current value of other properties, rapidly changing animation values, etc.). This often provides the crux of the property-change notification mechanism that you'll use extensively during XAML UI's data binding. If you are interested in learning more, Jesse Liberty nicely explains dependency properties on his blog at http://jesseliberty.com/2011/08/08/dependency-properties/.

The Container Controls

Layout is the process of sizing and positioning objects in your UI. *Container controls* can be your best friends because they are essentially what define the layout of content inside a *Page*—a container inside which all other controls are housed. You have three main options for Windows 8 Store apps:

- *Canvas*: This container control is for absolute positioning child elements using explicit X and Y screen coordinates. The `Canvas` control uses `Canvas.Left` and `Canvas.Top` to position child elements (as measured from the top-left corner) with absolute drag-and-drop support in Visual Studio. These types of properties on an XAML element are called *attached properties.* They are often treated as global properties, settable from any other object element. An overview of attached properties is on MSDN at `http://msdn.microsoft.com/en-us/library/cc265152(v=VS.95).aspx`. While absolute positioning pinpoints the UI look and feel, it does not consider screen size/resolution/orientation. Scaling could be an option to support a variety of screen sizes.
- *Grid*: This is the ubiquitous container control that supports dynamic layout by placing child controls in a maze of rows and columns. It is just like the HTML table, only less evil ☺. Child content is placed by defining `RowDefinition` and `ColumnDefinition` to fill up `Grid.Rows` and `Grid.Columns`. The flexible layout system is achieved by auto/*- sizing the height and width of controls so that content flows and wraps according to the space available to the parent container. You'll see examples of this in code.
- *StackPanel*: This is very similar to the `Grid` in supporting flexible layout, except that a `StackPanel` is one-dimensional. Child elements are "stacked" horizontally or vertically on top of each other based on the `Orientation` property of the parent `StackPanel`.

The Collection Controls

Turns out, most mobile applications (across platforms) commonly present data as a collection of items; for example—news items, photos, social feeds, and so forth. Windows 8 Store apps would have to present similar content in the form of collections. So, what ammunition do you have in terms of controls? To help keep your data presentation fashionable, Windows Store apps give you several choices through specialized controls to present a collection of items. The class hierarchy of the base class `ItemsControl` is presented in Figure 4-3.

Object
  DependencyObject
    UIElement
      FrameworkElement
        Control
          ItemsControl

Figure 4-3. *ItemsControl hierarchy*

The nice thing is that most of the following controls have a similar parent object hierarchy, which makes them behave similarly, but be cosmetically different. They all support data binding to a collection of items, but present the collection in different ways. Often, these collection controls, along with display templates to guide presentation, dominate the look and feel of Windows 8 Store apps.

Here's a rundown of the most commonly used collection controls:

- *GridView*: This is a ubiquitous control that presents a collection of items in rows and columns that pan horizontally. This will possibly be the most recognizable Windows Store app control, presenting data in appropriately sized rectangles with overlay description text. When bound to the right datasets and done right, the `GridView` is sure to provide an incredibly inviting touch UX and serve as the primary ingredient in defining the Windows 8 silhouette. Most importantly, the look and feel is completely customizable through `ItemTemplates` and `DataTemplates`. You shall look at a lot more code around `GridViews` in the next chapter.
- *ListView*: This control binds itself easily to a collection of items and is best suited for vertical/horizontal scrolling in one axis. Because it inherits from the same parent (`ItemControls` class) as the `GridView`, the display and touch interaction is completely customizable.
- *FlipView*: This is a unique Windows 8 Store app control that can be bound to a collection of items, but allows flipping through the items one at a time sequentially, thus resulting in visually stunning touch interactions. Flip buttons appear on either edge, which allows forward and backward navigation. Context indicator controls can be added to allow jumping to a control.
- *SemanticZoom*: The `SemanticZoom` control is the last in your collection of controls. It offers a wonderful and unique touch interaction in Windows 8, providing a zoomed-in and zoomed-out view of grouped data. It truly adds a lot of the Windows 8 flavor. You will devote a lot more time toward it later.

You can populate these collection controls inline in XAML, or more practically, by data binding them to a collection of items in code. When data bound, the controls can be populated either by adding items to its `Items` collection, or by setting its `ItemSource` property, but you can't use both at the same time. To change how an item is displayed within each collection control, you can apply a style to the item container by setting the `ItemContainerStyle` property to a custom style.

Collection Controls in Action

So, enough talk. Let's see some code, shall we? Now, let's say you were trying to build a Windows 8 Store app for Apress so that users can sift through the publisher's large collection of books. It would be nice to focus on one technology, like Windows Phone development, and flip through book titles one at a time. Hmm. That sounds like the `FlipView` control. Try using that and you'll get to learn a little more about the other container controls.

Start with a Blank App template and add a fresh XAML page to it called `FlipViewDemo.xaml`. For better organization, you may want to put all your XAML pages in one place, usually in a folder called Views. On the blank page that you just created, add the following code to the XAML, just under the page declaration:

```
<Grid Style="{StaticResource LayoutRootStyle}">
        <Grid.RowDefinitions>
            <RowDefinition Height="140"/>
            <RowDefinition Height="*"/>
        </Grid.RowDefinitions>
```

```
        <!-- Page title -->
        <Grid Grid.Row="0" Margin="40,30,0,0">
            <Grid.ColumnDefinitions>
                <ColumnDefinition Width="*"/>
            </Grid.ColumnDefinitions>
            <TextBlock x:Name="pageTitle" Grid.Column="1" Text="{StaticResource AppName}"
            Style="{StaticResource PageHeaderTextStyle}"/>
        </Grid>

        <FlipView Grid.Row="1">
            <Image Source="/Assets/MigratingToWP.png" Width="350" Height="480"/>
            <Image Source="/Assets/WPAppDev.png" Width="350" Height="480"/>
            <Image Source="/Assets/WPRecipes.png" Width="350" Height="480"/>
        </FlipView>
</Grid>
```

Having added some XAML in the form of a FlipView, update App.xaml.cs to make the new page the starting point of your app, as follows:

```
if (!rootFrame.Navigate(typeof(FlipViewDemo), "AllGroups"))
{
    throw new Exception("Failed to create initial page");
}
```

Your code is rock solid, right? Let's run it. Hopefully, you will see app views like the ones shown in Figures 4-4 and 4-5.

Figure 4-4. *Static FlipView demo showing an item at the start*

Figure 4-5. *Static FlipView demo showing an item at the middle*

There were several interesting things that happened. Let's break it down:

- First, you used a `Grid` control as your top-level container under the Page.
- Notice how the grid rows split up the screen real estate. The top 140 pixels are used for the Application title and the rest is used for content. The "*" in XAML essentially means "take up the rest of the space." This technique of dividing the screen real estate for various types of content is quite standard in XAML technologies for UI. You can do the same in Windows 8 Store apps.
- Did you see the use of `StaticResource`? This essentially is XAML styling declared globally so that you don't have all your eggs in one basket and can reuse the styles across multiple pages of the application. Remember what `App.xaml` did? Yep, wire up the solution to use global styles defined in the Common folder's `StandardStyles.xaml` file. This behemoth file is actually simple XML that defines reusable styles, like those used in your page and content. Don't settle on a default behavior—copy a style and change it to your heart's content. You'll look at some standard templates later.
- The Page title uses the `AppName` as defined in the `App.xaml`. This starts out the same as your solution name, but you can easily override.
- Aside from the Page header section, the goal of the XAML page is to use the `FlipView` control to highlight flipping through Apress publications. I simply added three static images to hold in the `FlipView`—the book shadow images have simply been added to the Assets folder prior to the first run. In fact, once you add images for use in your app, you can usually drag an image from Solution Explorer onto the app canvas (if added to a container control), so that you need not hand-type all hard-coded URLs.

- Did you notice that the FlipView is aware of its collection count? The left and right arrow marks only show up if the collection view can go back and front, respectively, compared to the item currently displayed. A flip view is also wonderfully touch-friendly—simply swipe/flick to the left or right, and a flip view obediently cycles through its collection.

As a developer, that must have felt dirty—you hard-coded the FlipView content with some images. Blasphemy! Let's fix it with somewhat more realistic content and learn about an important aspect of XAML in the process—data binding, which makes XAML-based UI development so much fun! Let's define a book class that acts as a placeholder for a generic Apress book—nothing fancy, just some appropriate properties to set/get:

```
namespace ApressDemo.Models
{
    public partial class ApressBook
    {
        #region "Properties"

        public string ApressBookISBN { get; set; }
        public string ApressBookName { get; set; }
        public string ApressBookAuthor { get; set; }
        public DateTime ApressBookPublishDate { get; set; }
        public string ApressBookDescription { get; set; }
        public string ApressBookUserLevel { get; set; }
        public string ApressBookImageURI { get; set; }

        #endregion
    }
}
```

The book class now defines a single book. In real life, your UI will more likely show a collection of books, like the FlipView control that flips through a book collection. Let's define another class to hold a collection of Apress book items:

```
namespace ApressDemo.ViewModels
{
    public partial class FlipViewDemoViewModel
    {
        #region "Members"

        public ObservableCollection<ApressBook> FeaturedWindowsPhoneApressBooks { get; set; }

        #endregion
    }
}
```

A couple of interesting things happened. Let's stop and take a closer look.

- Did you notice the namespaces in the classes that you defined? They all belong to the base ApressDemo, but then add their own subdomains of Models and ViewModels. This is somewhat of a convention. The Model-View-ViewModel (MVVM) is a software pattern that works really well for XAML-based technologies. The core idea is separation of concerns, minimal code in the code-behind, and easy-to-test business logic. Even if you are not doing true MVVM out of the gate, it helps to take some cues to be better organized. Create folders called Models, ViewModels, and Views to hold specific files—you'll be thankful later as your solution grows. The Models are purely data objects, like data transfer objects (DTOs), or inherited from some business service APIs. They are supposed to have their own validation and business logic around handling the objects. You may abstract out further by using a repository pattern, which has classes that know how to save and hydrate `Model/ViewModel` objects. The ViewModels are an aggregated collection of objects that together make up a certain view for the app and prevents you from having to manipulate business objects for UI binding. ViewModels usually handle the interactions the user has on screen to adjust the `ViewModel` properties, thus relieving the UI from having hard-coded event handlers. And the Views are supposed to be purely UI, in this case XAML, and lay out what the user sees on screen. Did some of that make sense? Don't worry too much if it didn't. You'll revisit it.

- The collection of Apress books is an `ObservableCollection<T>`. If this is your first time touching XAML technologies, you're in for a ride. Gone are the days of continuously having to bind data to UI for refreshes of underlying object collection. Shouldn't developers have some help in the plumbing so that the UI updates automatically when data-bound objects/collections change? The answer is ObservableCollections, which implements interfaces like `INotifyPropertyChanged` and `INotifyCollectionChanged`. The concept is simple: mark object properties that you need to listen to changes for and update your UI automatically through event bubbling. As the properties change value, events are thrown up to the UI, indicating the need to redraw after checking with the underlying object/collection. You can learn more about ObservableCollections at `http://msdn.microsoft.com/en-us/library/ms668604(v=VS.95).aspx`.

Data Binding with FlipView

Now that you have a couple of classes around Apress books, make your collection reusable. Open the `App.xaml.cs` and define a couple of global placeholders. It makes sense that a Windows Store app for Apress books could maintain a collection of books in memory for use throughout the app. The following shows you how to initialize and expose global properties for the `ViewModel` holding your book collection:

```
    #region "Global Members"

    private FlipViewDemoViewModel _flipViewDemoVM;

    #endregion

    #region "Properties"

    public FlipViewDemoViewModel FlipViewDemoVM
    {
        get { return _flipViewDemoVM; }
        set { _flipViewDemoVM = value; }
    }
#endregion
```

```
public App()
        {
            this.InitializeComponent();
            this.Suspending += OnSuspending;

            _flipViewDemoVM = new FlipViewDemoViewModel();
            LoadFlipViewDemoVM();
        }
```

The app constructor called a simple Load ViewModel method. This is a simple way to have some dummy books added to your collection. In the real world, your collection of custom objects may come from a database or some network service call; you simply want a collection of books to play with. So, here goes:

```
private void LoadFlipViewDemoVM()
        {
            _flipViewDemoVM.FeaturedWindowsPhoneApressBooks = new
            ObservableCollection<Models.ApressBook>();

            ApressBook WPMigration = new ApressBook();
            WPMigration.ApressBookISBN = "978-1-4302-3816-4";
            WPMigration.ApressBookName = "Migrating to Windows Phone";
            WPMigration.ApressBookAuthor = "Jesse Liberty, Jeff Blankenburg";
            WPMigration.ApressBookDescription = "This book offers everything you'll need to upgrade your
            existing programming knowledge and begin to develop applications for the Windows Phone.";
            WPMigration.ApressBookImageURI = "/Assets/MigratingToWP.png";
            WPMigration.ApressBookPublishDate = new DateTime(2011, 12, 28);
            WPMigration.ApressBookUserLevel = "Intermediate";

            ApressBook WPRecipes = new ApressBook();
            WPRecipes.ApressBookISBN = "978-1-4302-4137-9";
            WPRecipes.ApressBookName = "Windows Phone Recipes";
            WPRecipes.ApressBookAuthor = "Fabio Claudio Ferracchiati, Emanuele Garofalo";
            WPRecipes.ApressBookDescription = "Are you interested in smartphone development? Windows
            Phone 7.5 (code-named Mango) is packed with new features and functionality that make
            it a .NET developer's dream. This book contains extensive code samples and detailed
            walkthroughs that will have you writing sophisticated apps in no time!";
            WPRecipes.ApressBookImageURI = "/Assets/WPRecipes.png";
            WPRecipes.ApressBookPublishDate = new DateTime(2011, 12, 14);
            WPRecipes.ApressBookUserLevel = "Beginner to Intermediate";

            ApressBook WPAppDev = new ApressBook();
            WPAppDev.ApressBookISBN = "978-1-4302-3936-9";
            WPAppDev.ApressBookName = "Windows Phone App Development";
            WPAppDev.ApressBookAuthor = "Rob Cameron";
            WPAppDev.ApressBookDescription = "Pro Windows Phone 7 Development helps you unlock the
            potential of Microsoft's newest mobile platform and updates—NoDo and Mango—to develop
            visually rich, highly functional applications for the Windows Phone Marketplace.";
            WPAppDev.ApressBookImageURI = "/Assets/WPAppDev.png";
            WPAppDev.ApressBookPublishDate = new DateTime(2011, 12, 26);
            WPAppDev.ApressBookUserLevel = "Intermediate to Advanced";
```

```
        _flipViewDemoVM.FeaturedWindowsPhoneApressBooks.Add(WPMigration);
        _flipViewDemoVM.FeaturedWindowsPhoneApressBooks.Add(WPRecipes);
        _flipViewDemoVM.FeaturedWindowsPhoneApressBooks.Add(WPAppDev);
    }
```

At this point, your data is all set in the form of a collection of books. Now, take out the hard-coded images as the `FlipView` content and replace it with a more realistic-looking template:

```
<FlipView Grid.Row="1" x:Name="demoFlipView">
        <FlipView.ItemTemplate>
            <DataTemplate>
                <StackPanel Orientation="Vertical">
                <Image Source="{Binding ApressBookImageURI}" Width="350" Height="480" />
                    <StackPanel Orientation="Horizontal" Margin="200,0,0,20">
                        <TextBlock Text="Author(s):   " Style="{StaticResource
                        SubheaderTextStyle}"/>
                        <TextBlock Text="{Binding ApressBookAuthor}" Style="{StaticResource
                        SubheaderTextStyle}"/>
                    </StackPanel>
                    <TextBlock Text="{Binding ApressBookDescription}" Style="{StaticResource
                    BodyTextStyle}" Margin="200,0,0,20"/>
                </StackPanel>
            </DataTemplate>
        </FlipView.ItemTemplate>
    </FlipView>
```

As before, a few things to notice in the code:

- You are no longer directly telling the `FlipView` the number of items present in the collection of books. Instead, you go the template route and provide data bindings. The `FlipView` control, inheriting from the `ItemsControl`, allows for complete customization of data binding and controlling the look and feel of every item in the bound collection. The containing `ItemTemplate` defines the data that should make up each `FlipView` content placeholder. The `DataTemplate` inside defines how the data should be displayed and bound to the UI.
- The `DataTemplate` can take on any child controls (notice your use of the `StackPanel` to line up your content).
- The controls inside the `DataTemplate` do not have raw data until runtime; instead, their bindings tell them how to read the `Object` property values of individual items within the collection that they may be bound to.

Now that your `FlipView` UI is all set and waiting for data, provide it in the form of an `ObservableCollection<>` of Apress books, which you have already defined. Notice the way that you use the global data placeholder to bind to your UI:

```
protected override void OnNavigatedTo(NavigationEventArgs e)
        {
            base.OnNavigatedTo(e);

            demoFlipView.ItemsSource = ((App)Application.Current).FlipViewDemoVM.
            FeaturedWindowsPhoneApressBooks;
        }
```

What is being done here is the programmatic association of the `FlipView`'s `ItemSource` to the global collection of books. This provides the bindings that your UI needs. Each object will be reflected upon to find your property matches and the `DataTemplate` controls will be instantiated once per item in the collection. In the example, you bound the UI to the author name, a description, and an image URI for each book. If everything was done right, your new `FlipView` layout is now data bound and rendered, as shown in Figures 4-6 and 4-7.

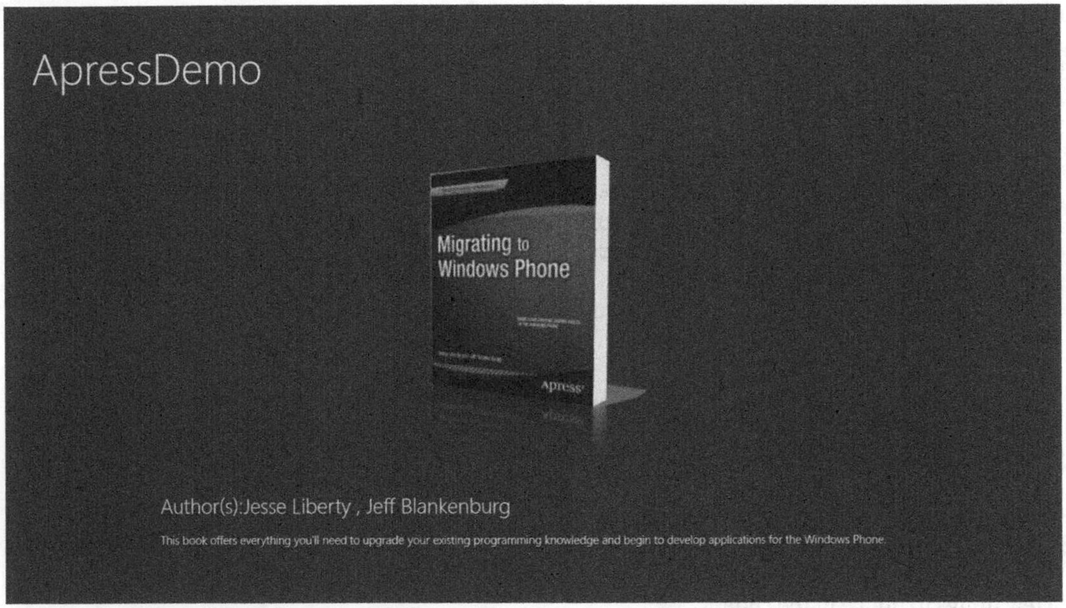

***Figure 4-6.** FlipView demo with data binding showing an item at the start*

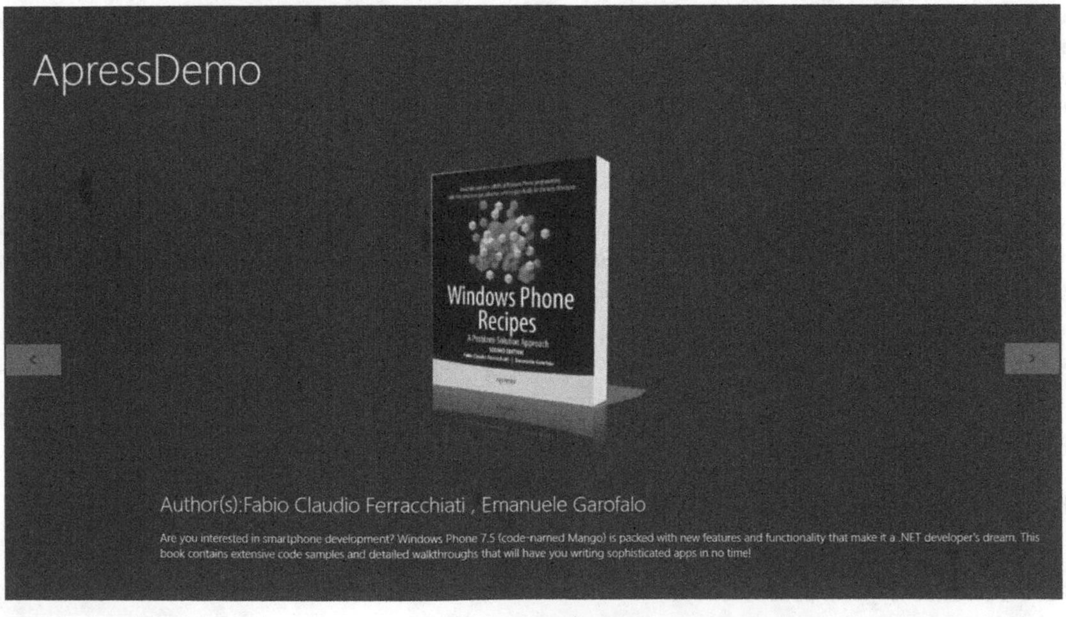

***Figure 4-7.** FlipView demo with data binding showing an item at the middle*

The beauty of using data binding like this is twofold:

- The data display is separate from the data itself.
- Any addition or removal of items to or from your collection automatically updates the UI. Not a code change is required!

Data Binding with ListView

Here's the advantage of the separation of concerns. Let's say that you were suddenly told to switch up your UI—no more flipping through one item at a time. Instead, show a list of books on one page. No problem. Keep your ViewModel intact and simply switch your XAML to use a ListView, like this:

```
<ListView x:Name="demoListView" Grid.Row="1">
        <ListView.ItemTemplate>
            <DataTemplate>
                <StackPanel Orientation="Vertical">
                    <Image Source="{Binding ApressBookImageURI}" Width="80" Height="120"
                    HorizontalAlignment="Left" Margin="200,0,0,0"/>
                    <StackPanel Orientation="Horizontal" Margin="200,0,0,15"
                    HorizontalAlignment="Center">
                        <TextBlock Text="Author(s):   " Style="{StaticResource ItemTextStyle}"/>
                        <TextBlock Text="{Binding ApressBookAuthor}" Style="{StaticResource
                        ItemTextStyle}"/>
                    </StackPanel>
                </StackPanel>
            </DataTemplate>
        </ListView.ItemTemplate>
    </ListView>
```

And now, you'll go back to your App.xaml.cs and change the starting XAML view again. On the next run of the app, you should see a UI like the one shown in Figure 4-8. The points to take home are the complete customization of DataTemplate definitions and the styling and use of margins to get your data to look the way you want.

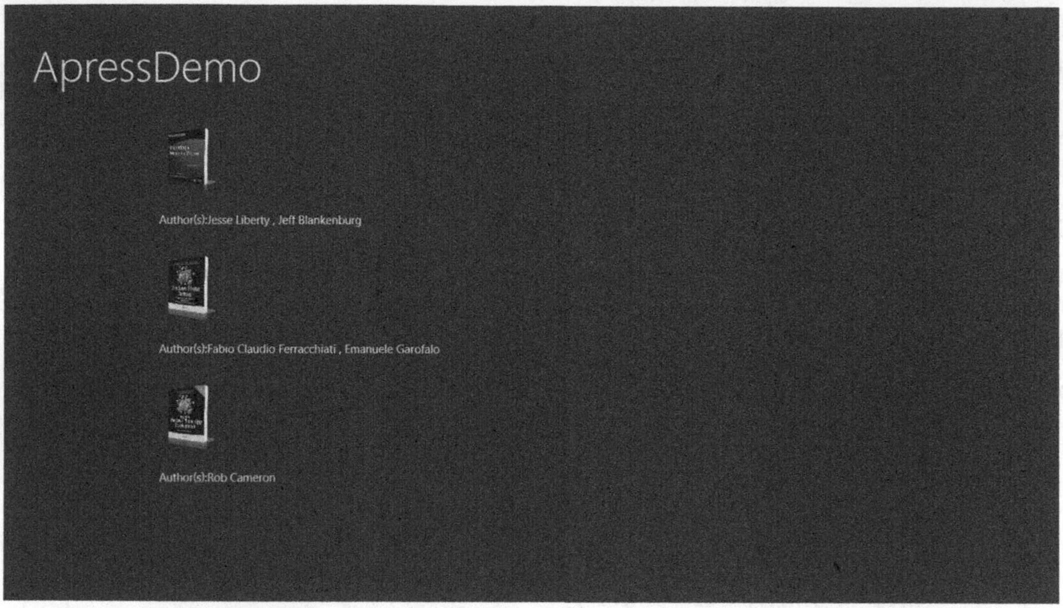

Figure 4-8. *ListView demo*

Selection Controls

As users interact with your Windows 8 Store app, you might need input from them. To make user input easy, you may present a small list of options to the user and ask for a selection to move forward. These types of input elements deserve special controls to exude in the Modern UI look and feel. Do you need the user to make a specific type of data selection? There are options galore to fit your needs. Here are a few controls:

- *CheckBox* and *RadioButton*: As in any XAML UI, these controls allow for the selection/deselection of items. While both allow multiple selections, the common use of `RadioButton` is to enforce mutual exclusivity in a group of items. A sample UI is shown in Figure 4-9.

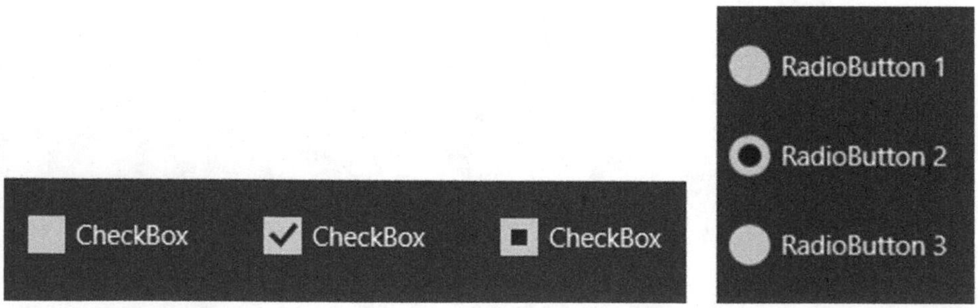

Figure 4-9. *CheckBox and RadioButton controls in Windows 8*

- *ToggleButton* and *ToggleSwitch*: As their names suggest, these controls allow switching between two states and allow the end user to simply exercise choice. A sample UI is shown in Figure 4-10.

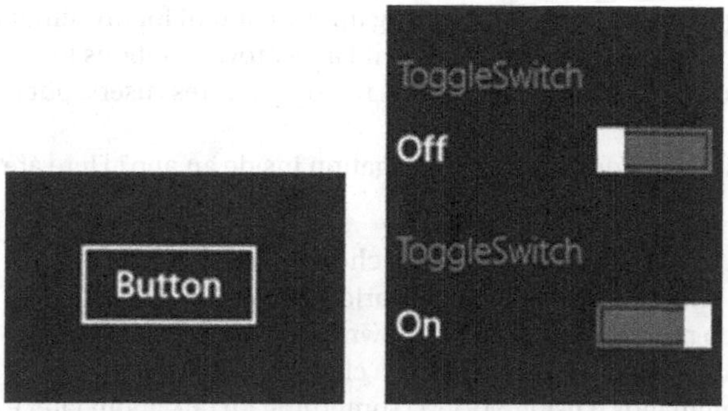

Figure 4-10. *Toggle controls in Windows 8*

- *ListBox* and *ComboBox*: The list box and the combo box let users select one or more values from a set of items that can be adequately represented using single lines of text. As a thumb rule, more than eight items call for `ListBox` or `ComboBox`; otherwise, revert to `CheckBox` or `RadioButton`. A sample UI is shown in Figure 4-11.

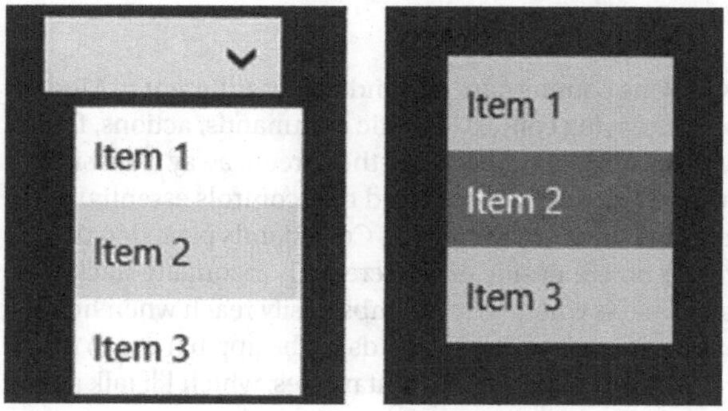

Figure 4-11. *ListBox and ComboBox controls in Windows 8*

- *Slider*: This control allows the user to select from a range of values by moving a finger along a track. The slider can be of great use when selection is not about discrete points, but generally between a range of values, like volume rockers. A sample UI is shown in Figure 4-12.

Figure 4-12. *Slider control in Windows 8*

Filter/Navigation Controls

Once the user is inside a Windows 8 Store app, developers have the opportunity to impress and keep the user hooked to the app. One key aspect of keeping the user engaged is keeping your display simple and not overcrowded. Your content needs breathing room; if a page is getting too busy, consider breaking up the content for presentation in two different pages. Also, when providing a certain data view to the user, you should also provide options for filtering down the data according to what the user wants to see. These customizations not only impress users, but increases user loyalty.

But do you have the right controls at your disposal to do filtering or navigation inside an app? Here are the choices:

- *Button*: The generic XAML control used to navigate, select, filter, choose, and so forth. Buttons are available throughout the Windows 8 ecosystem, in various shapes and sizes. With the display fully customizable, do not forget to inject your own branding for consistency throughout your app. Also, event handlers that respond to button clicks can be wired up in the code-behind or through the use of commands if using MVVM (something I'll talk about later). A sample UI is shown in Figure 4-13.

Figure 4-13. *Button controls in Windows 8*

- *AppBar*: This control, like it's Windows Phone counterpart, is wonderfully adherent to Modern UI design style. It functions as a toolbar displaying context-specific commands, actions, filters, and navigation. It can be tucked away at the bottom or the top of the screen, away from sight but ready to aid the user on an easy swipe. However, keep in mind that controls essential to the user's workflow belong on the canvas, and not in the app bar. Commands placed in the app bar are best organized in category sets on either side of the screen, horizontally stacked on each other. The reason for this is because that is where your thumbs easily reach when holding a tablet in both hands! Other considerations for putting commands in the app bar are to mind for dismissal modes and designing it to support Snapped/Portrait modes, which I'll talk about in the next chapter. A sample UI is shown in Figure 4-14.

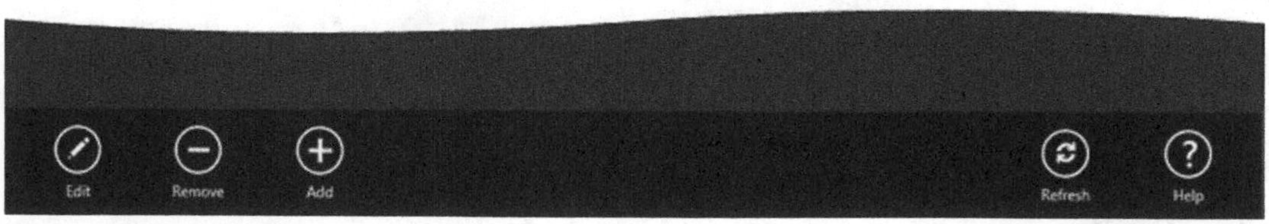

Figure 4-14. *App bar icons in Windows 8*

Let's take a closer look at the app bar because it provides such a unique Windows 8 look and feel. Windows 8 users are already accustomed to using the app bar. So why not extend their comfort by having the same feature in your app? So, how do you go about adding an app bar? It's simple. Take a look at some AppBar code on the XAML view you had for displaying the collection of books in a ListView:

```
<Grid Style="{StaticResource LayoutRootStyle}">
        <Grid.RowDefinitions>
            <RowDefinition Height="140"/>
            <RowDefinition Height="*"/>
        </Grid.RowDefinitions>

        <!-- Top App Bar -->
        <Grid Grid.Row="0">
            <AppBar x:Name="topAppBar" Padding="10,0,10,0">
                <Grid>
                    <StackPanel Orientation="Horizontal" HorizontalAlignment="Left"
                    Margin="20,0,0,0">
                        <Button Content="Windows Phone" Margin="5,0,10,0" BorderBrush="Yellow"
                        BorderThickness="2"/>
                        <Button Content="Windows 8" Margin="5,0,10,0" BorderBrush="Yellow"
                        BorderThickness="2"/>
                        <Button Content="Silverlight" Margin="5,0,10,0" BorderBrush="Yellow"
                        BorderThickness="2"/>
                    </StackPanel>
                </Grid>
            </AppBar>
        </Grid>
.....
</Grid>
<Page.BottomAppBar>
        <AppBar x:Name="bottomAppBar" Padding="10,0,10,0">
            <Grid>
                <StackPanel Orientation="Horizontal" HorizontalAlignment="Left">
                    <Button Style="{StaticResource EditAppBarButtonStyle}" />
                    <Button Style="{StaticResource AddAppBarButtonStyle}" />
                </StackPanel>
                <StackPanel Orientation="Horizontal" HorizontalAlignment="Right">
                    <Button Style="{StaticResource RefreshAppBarButtonStyle}" />
                </StackPanel>
            </Grid>
        </AppBar>
    </Page.BottomAppBar>
```

If you did things right, upon running the app, you first see the book list. Swipe from the top to bottom or right-click on a mouse-and-keyboard system—and voilà, you see the app bar, like the one shown in Figure 4-15.

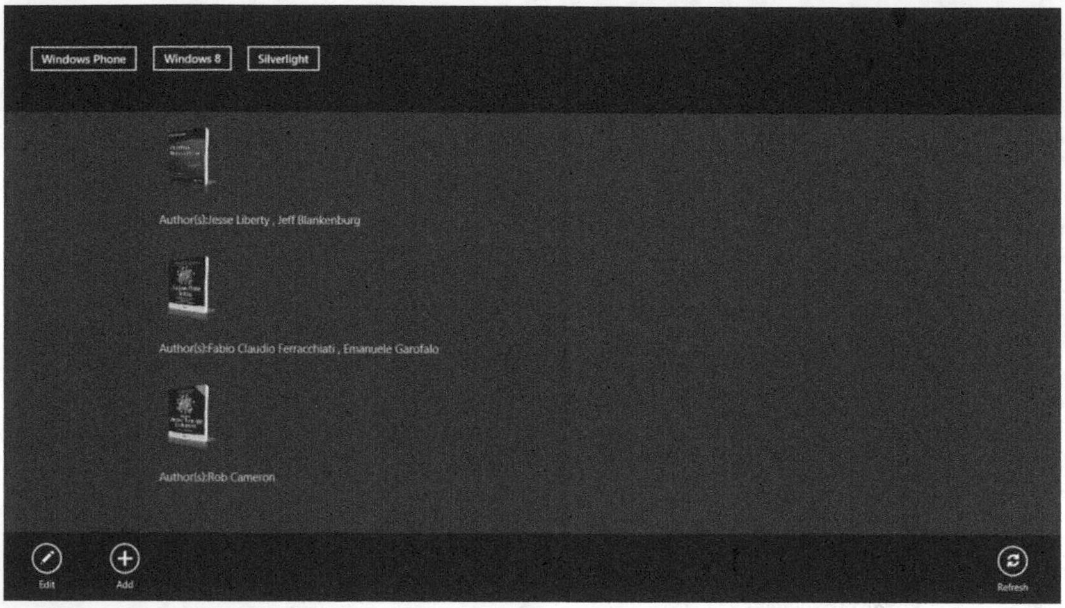

Figure 4-15. *Top and bottom AppBar demo in Windows 8*

The following are several things to note:

- The AppBar control can be used with the <Page.TopAppBar/> /<Page.BottomAppBar/> or you can roll in your own placeholders.
- As you'll notice in the preceding code, you replaced (for demo purposes) the top 140 pixel grid rows to hold the top app bar and used the Page placeholders for the bottom app bar. The Page-level placeholders need to be outside any other container controls.
- Notice how you use StackPanels to align the AppBar icons to the left and right. This is so that they are easier to touch when holding a tablet in both hands, which is more convenient than having the buttons in the center of the screen.
- The AppBar icons are really buttons with click-event handlers that you can associate to some action. They use the styles to look like the Modern UI–style rounded buttons with an icon inside.
- Did you notice how easily you styled the bottom AppBar buttons with StaticResources? The magic is in the Common/StandardStyles.xaml file, which has commented-out styles for a large number of commonly used AppBar icons based on Segoe UI glyphs. Just uncomment the style you need to use, or roll your own icons.
- You can really put whatever you want in the app bars. As an example, you put static buttons on the top app bar to perhaps navigate to different technical areas while browsing Apress books. However, there are some guidelines, with the most prominent rules listed next.

- The bottom app bar is to be used for commanding, filtering, and sorting. It is the view that the user typically sees.
- Among the bottom app bar icons, the global icons should be stacked to the right and remain present throughout the app for user's familiarity. The context-sensitive icons, based on a user selection, may be on stacked on the left edge of the app bar. This is just a simple convention that users may come to expect from your app.
- The top app bar is used for navigation purposes, mostly to take the user out of the context of the existing view to a different section of the app.

Transient UI Controls

Sometimes, you may need to present UI elements that are not constantly on the canvas, but show up on demand. Turns out, the HTML world for creating Windows Store apps has a few more controls than the XAML ones, for now; but UI elements like flyouts and context menus are easily re-creatable in XAML using hidden containers and entrance animations. A few example UI elements are shown in Figure 4-16.

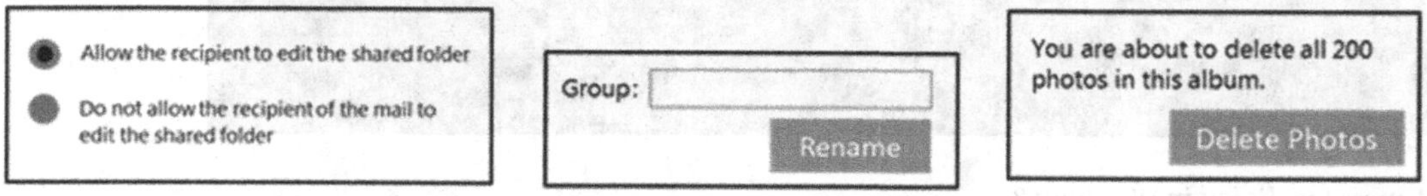

Figure 4-16. *Transient UI controls in Windows 8*

Take a look at some transient controls you have in the XAML UI stack. All of the following controls serve similar purposes, but with differing UI presentation.

- *MessageDialog*: Though not an XAML control by itself, the message dialog UI can be achieved using the `PopupMenu` XAML control. You need to be conservative in the usage of message dialogs because it takes the user out of the immersive experience to a modal dialog; but urgent information, blocking questions, and errors present genuine needs for using a message dialog. A sample UI is shown in Figure 4-17.

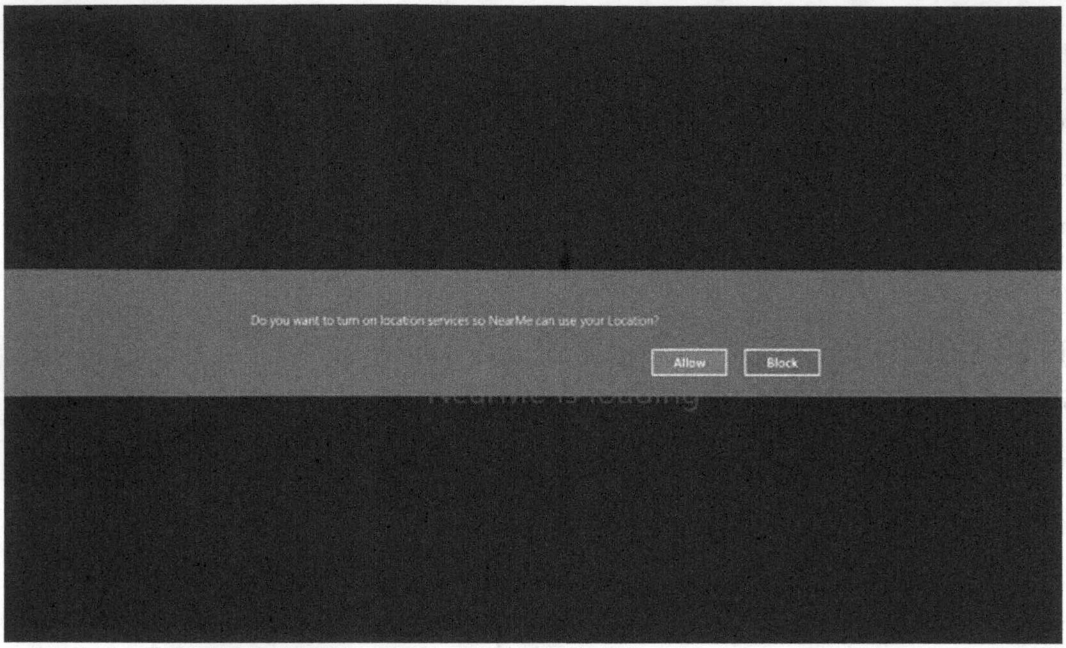

Figure 4-17. *A message dialog in Windows 8*

Did you just try adding a `MessageBox` to your app and then freaked out because you couldn't find the control? No worries. It happens to all of us starting out. Make sure to add the `Windows.UI.Popups` namespace, and then you'll have access to the `MessageDialog` control.

- *ToolTip*: This control displays a pop-up window with information about another UI element. It helps users understand unfamiliar objects that aren't described directly in the UI. The tooltip should only appear if the user does a press-and-hold or a mouse hover over an UI element. It should never be deployed programmatically and dismissed easily. Because the user is not supposed to interact with the control, due diligence needs to put in to make sure its usage is appropriate. A sample UI is shown in Figure 4-18.

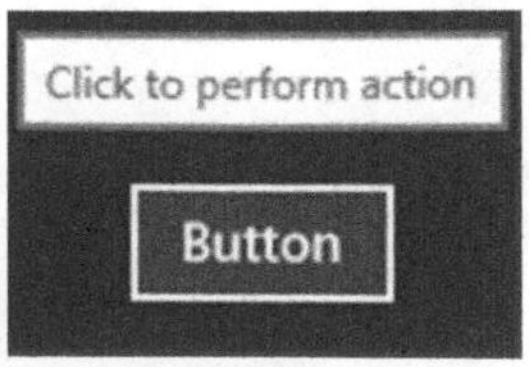

Figure 4-18. *ToolTip control in Windows 8*

- *Progress controls*: Windows Store apps are often doing expensive operations, but the UI can never be locked up (achieved through the `async-await` magic, which I will talk about later). You also need to show visual indication of the progress being made. XAML progress controls come in two flavors: the progress bar and the progress ring. They are both customized to fit Modern UI styling guidelines and have typical use cases. Whereas the `ProgressBar` can be determinate or indeterminate, the `ProgressRing` is always indeterminate. A sample UI is shown in Figure 4-19.

Figure 4-19. *Progress indicator controls in Windows 8*

Summary

So, that's it. A compilation of some of the most commonly used controls to use for developing Windows Store apps. Did I provide enough ammunition for your next Windows 8 dream app? A comprehensive list of available XAML controls is at `http://msdn.microsoft.com/en-US/library/windows/apps/xaml/hh465351#r_section`. Make sure to bookmark this page and visit it often.

If you feel the need to innovate for the sake of a unique experience in your app, there is nothing stopping you. Perhaps you want to combine a bunch of controls into a user control for reusability. Before you reinvent the wheel, make sure to look around for toolkits that already have the control that you are looking for, or look for open-source community contributions. You might also look into third-party vendor DLLs, which often contain fabulous performance-optimized controls. I encourage you to look into controls sets released by Microsoft partners like Telerik, ComponentOne, and Infragistics, to name a few. The mantra is "the right controls for the right UX!"

CHAPTER 5

The Look and Feel

Are you excited about starting your first Windows 8 Store app? Excellent. Let's get cracking! This chapter will be a quick rundown on how to make your Windows 8 Store app look professional right out of the gate. You will implement some of the coveted Windows 8 silhouette and make your app a delight to use from get go.

What if your app presents so much data that it causes navigation headaches for users? Will you be ready when the user does a pinch-and-zoom on your app content? Break no sweat, because I will talk about data binding and Semantic Zoom in detail in this chapter.

Imagery

Let's start with the use of images and logos in your Windows 8 Store app. As they say: a picture is worth a thousand words! Once your Windows 8 app is ready, you might want to package it for Store availability, which I will talk about in later chapters. Apart from a 2GB application packet limit, you really have complete liberty in the use of imagery in your app. So why not take full advantage of this to impress the user—starting with first impression, as you'll see next. Windows 8 supports JPEGs and PNGs; no GIFs, please.

Getting App Logos Right

Start a new Visual Studio project with a Blank/Grid/Split template to follow along. Do you see an `Assets` folder in your solution? Yes, this folder is supposed to house all of your imagery. It is not a necessity, of course, but it is a good convention to have all imagery tucked away nicely in one spot. You may choose to make subfolders for images belonging to different parts of the app.

Now, go ahead and press F5 to run your app, selecting Local Machine/Simulator for installation. Do you notice a few things?

For demo purposes, let's say you have been tasked with building a Windows 8 Store app for browsing through Apress's vast number of publications. You'll build this app (called `ApressDemo`) from the ground up through several chapters in this book. Right now, you have a blank app; run it. Your Windows 8 Start screen should look like Figure 5-1.

Figure 5-1. *Default app logo*

As you know, the Windows 8 Start experience is full of gorgeous app representations called *tiles*, many of which are live tiles pulling in content without the app even running. Ours doesn't look very good against the rest of the apps, does it? Figure 5-2 gives a glimpse of what a temporary splash screen looks like as your app is launched in the simulator and before you see the first page in your app.

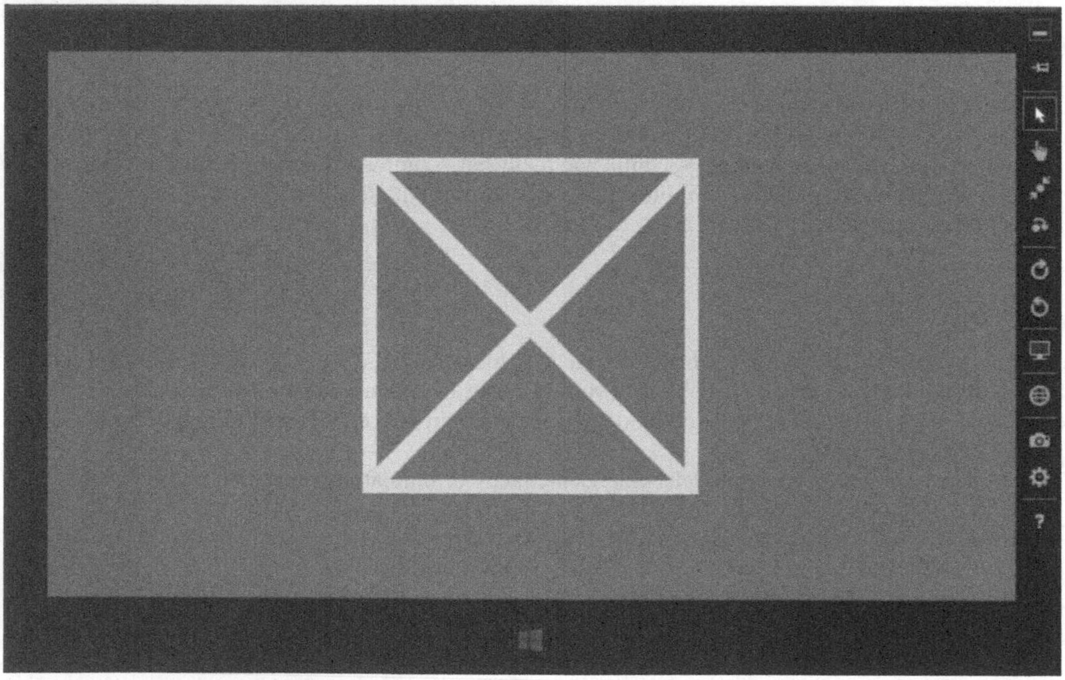

Figure 5-2. *Default splash screen*

Again, not very impressive. What's happening is that you're seeing the default app tile on the Start screen and the default splash screen because you have not had the time to customize the app. Your app's default tile and the initial splash screen provide the first impression to the user. These images and colors establish your app's brand. Needless to say, the more polished the presentation, the higher that the app will pique the user's interest. So it is clear that you need to make imagery count to convey your branding and make a nice entrance to the scene. Here's how.

Let's look inside the `Assets` folder to see the default images; pixel sizes are important. You may replace all of the images, but they need to conform to the exact pixel dimensions. The images are described as follows:

- *Logo.png*: This is the default app tile. It is possibly the most commonly used logo for your app. Size = 150×150 pixels.
- *SmallLogo.png*: This is the logo used whenever your app is presented in a list; for example, in the app list or through the usage of OS Charms. It is also used by the live tiles on the bottom-left corner as branding. Size = 30×30 pixels.
- *StoreLogo.png*: This is the logo that is used to identify your app for Windows Store purposes, such as an app listing or in search results. Size = 50×50 pixels.
- *SplashScreen.png*: This is the image temporarily shown during app launch and as the app is loading resources to take the user to the first page. Size = 620×300 pixels.

These images are the defaults, which you can quickly replace with the images included in the demo code solution. Your next deployment/run of the Apress demo app makes your branding a little better, as shown in Figure 5-3.

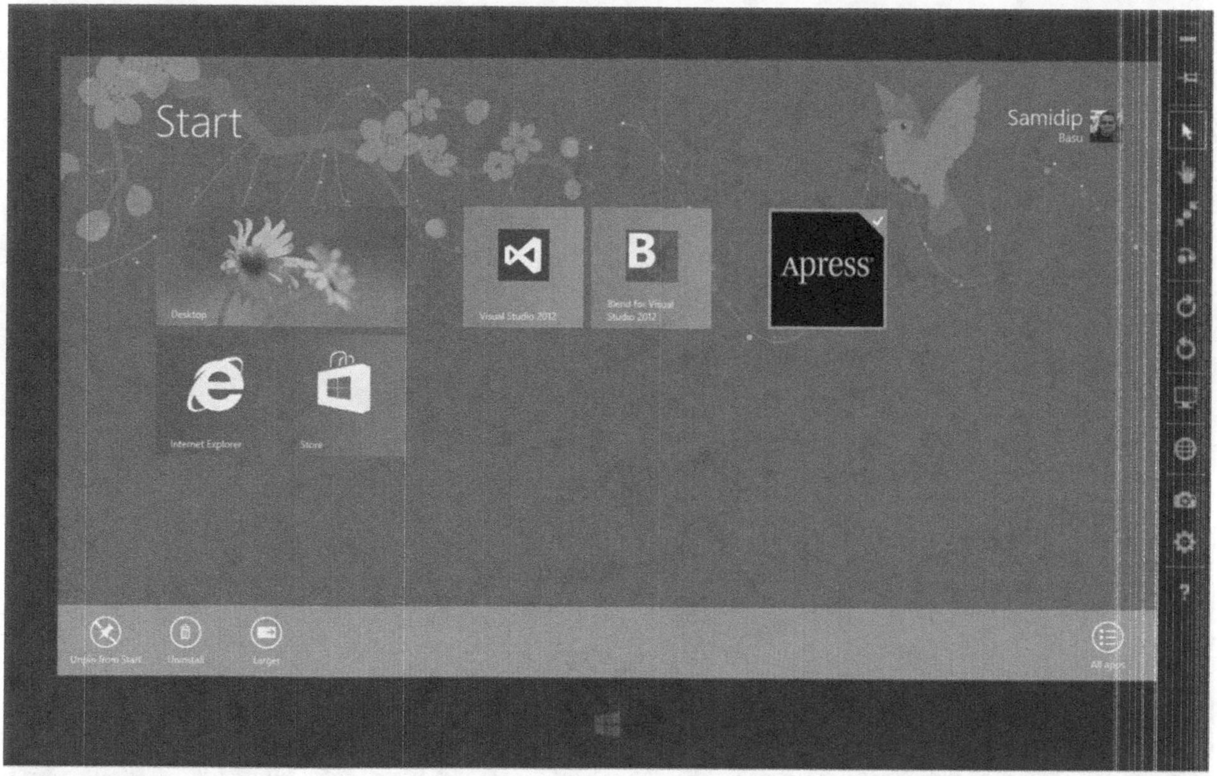

Figure 5-3. *Square app tile*

Your branded app tile now shows up as the default logo for the app. There is another image that you should include, although it is not required. Windows 8 app tiles come in two sizes: one that is square, as seen in Figure 5-3, and one that is a somewhat wider rectangle. This simply allows the user more flexibility in organizing/prioritizing apps on his or her Start screen. The wider tile conveys more information with its extended real estate, especially if it is a live tile. So, let's include a 310×150-pixel `WideLogo.png` in your `Assets` folder, and then update the `PackageAppXManifest` file to point to the new image.

Run your app again. Now right-click the square tile or short-swipe down to expose the app bar at the bottom. Because you included a wider logo, the user now has the option of toggling between the two sizes of your app tiles, resulting in a better branding opportunity. If you did not include a wide tile, the app bar option to resize the app tile is simply not presented to the user. The only way to change that is to include the wide tile in the package manifest and push out an app update if the app is in the Windows Store.

Another thing to note is that wide tiles are definitely good-looking and project branding. However, the user might have expectations of fresh content if a wide tile is in use, so make sure that you are not using it just for kicks. Microsoft has provided a wonderful set of guidelines on how to best use square/wide tiles along with badges, which I discuss later in Chapter 12. The guidelines can be found at `http://msdn.microsoft.com/en-us/library/windows/apps/hh465403`. If you were to use a wide tile, Figure 5-4 shows how the Start screen might look on your demo Apress app.

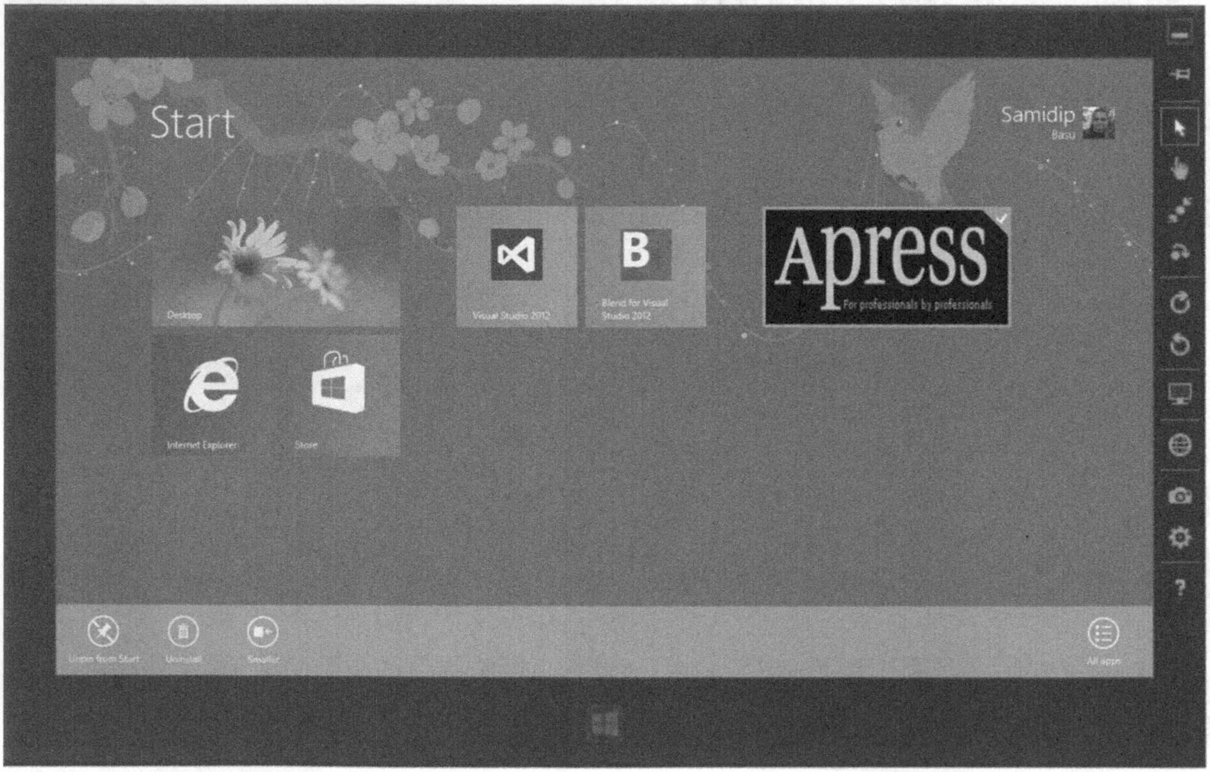

Figure 5-4. *Wide app tile and size toggle*

If your app branding image already conveys the name of the app, a simple square or wide tile might work. Alternatively, you could use a graphic for the logo and have Windows overlay your default app tile with a short name for the app, as shown in Figure 5-5. Please note that the app name should not merely repeat the name of the app if it is already apparent in the tile image, as it is in this case. You may choose to display the app name on square or wide tiles, both, or neither. Alternatively, a small logo on the bottom-left corner may be used as a branding identifier for the app, which I will discuss while talking about live tiles in Chapter 12.

Figure 5-5. *Wide app tile with app name*

All the configuration settings for the use of images and logos, a short name, and the splash screen are conveniently controlled from the app package manifest (`PackageAppXManifest.xml`) file. It is a simple XML file that you can either hand-code or use the visual editor that Visual Studio offers, as shown in Figure 5-6 with settings for the Apress demo app. You'll notice that pixel sizes are enforced in the designer to choose the right imagery. Also, the tile foreground and background colors are important for conveying your app's branding colors for use in store descriptions and any dialogs that the OS needs to present to the user on your app's behalf.

Package.appxmanifest
FeaturedBookList.xaml.cs
FeaturedBookList.xaml
StandardStyles.xaml
App.xaml
The properties of the deployment package for your app are contained in the app manifest file. You can use the Manifest Designer to set o
Application UI
Capabilities
Declarations
Packaging
Display name:
ApressDemo
Entry point:
ApressDemo.App
Default language:
en-US
More information
Description:
ApressDemo
Supported rotations:
An optional setting that indicates the app's orientation preferences.
Landscape
Portrait
Landscape-flipped
Portrait-flipped
Tile:
Logo:
Assets\Logo.png
Required size: 150 x 150 pixels
Wide logo:
Assets\ApressLogoWide.png
Required size: 310 x 150 pixels
Small logo:
Assets\SmallLogo.png
Required size: 30 x 30 pixels
Short name:
Show name:
No Logos
Foreground text:
Light
Background color:
#464646
Notifications:
Badge logo:
Required size: 24 x 24 pixels
Toast capable:
(not set)
Lock screen notifications:
(not set)
Splash Screen:
Splash screen:
Assets\ApressLogo.png
Required size: 620 x 300 pixels
Background color:
black

***Figure 5-6.** Visual Studio app package manifest editor*

Splash Screen

Now, let's talk a little bit more about the splash screen that shows up as your app is launching. It is mandatory for all apps and it presents the next opportunity to impress the user after the app tile. It should not be gaudy just because you have the whole screen real estate. It should be something simple that conveys your app's branding logo and colors and provides a visual indication to the user that the app resources are being loaded. The splash screen for the Apress demo app looks something like Figure 5-7.

Figure 5-7. *Custom splash screen*

There are a couple of things to note about the use of splash screen imagery. First, the image itself is 620×300 pixels, which is smaller than most full-screen resolutions. As you know, Windows 8 devices come in a variety of screen sizes and Microsoft simply wants your app's splash screen to look good no matter what. The splash screen images are positioned at the center of the screen and the remainder of the screen is filled with default background color. It is up to you to override this color in your app package manifest file, as done here to match the Apress logo.

Splash screens can serve another important purpose. What if your Windows 8 app needs to make network calls to pull down fresh content before the first screen is shown? You may need to show progress indicators to let the user know that your app is doing some heavy lifting. This can be done by showing the progress controls on your first page, or alternatively, by leveraging the splash screen before you even get to the first page. This is called the *extended splash screen* and it can be a handy way to keep the user waiting before you load up gorgeous content. The trick is to make a dummy XAML page that looks exactly like the OS splash screen, perhaps with the addition of a progress indicator. To the user, it needs to feel as if the splash screen is just being shown longer, so the use of the same splash screen image and matching background color is highly suggested.

Additionally, your dummy page's code should use the SplashScreen class to position the splash screen image at the same screen coordinates that Windows positions the app logo in the default Splash screen. The SplashScreen class allows you to listen to Windows resize events (if the screen is snapped or rotated) so that your page can respond with the same look and feel as the Windows splash screen. It also lets you know when to dismiss the dummy splash screen to actually take the user to the first page of the app. Detailed guidelines on how to extend the splash screen are at `http://msdn.microsoft.com/en-us/library/windows/apps/xaml/Hh868191(v=win.10).aspx`. Figures 5-8a and 5-8b offer a glimpse of an extended splash screen for your Apress demo app in two screen orientations.

Figure 5-8a. *Extended splash screen orientation, option 1*

Figure 5-8b. *Extended splash screen orientation, option 2*

Now, let's talk about one last important aspect of using imagery.

Perfecting the Resolution

Windows 8 devices widely vary based on what Microsoft and OEM partners come up with in terms of hardware innovation. This means a variety of screen resolutions—and that usually makes developers a little worried. However, Windows does a terrific job with being resolution aware by using vector graphics to scale content up or down based on screen size. Windows 8 looks the same on 10-inch tablets all the way up to 80-inch TVs with touch screens. With adaptive layouts, the more screen real estate there is, the more content is to be seen. All system resources and fonts are automatically scaled up or down to maintain crispness. But images are where Windows can use a little help from us developers.

If imagery is simply scaled up based on higher resolution, they start looking stretched and lose pixel density. If images are very high-resolution and then scaled down, there are jagged edges, high memory usage, and loss in touch target sizes. Therefore, image pixel size is important as Windows adjusts to screen resolution. To simplify things, Windows 8 uses fixed-scale percentages to adjust: 80%, 100%, 140%, and 180%. We developers are required to submit only for the 100%-scale for images; but to be a nicer citizen, we can submit different versions of our images, including 140% and 180% scaling. This ensures that our app imagery looks native and crisp, no matter the scaling required.

So, how are images of differing sizes used? Simple: convention over configuration. You can save multiple versions of an image using a file name or folder-naming convention, as follows:

```
...\image.scale-100.jpg
...\image.scale-140.jpg
...\image.scale-180.jpg
```

With the images in place, you could simply have the XAML source code read something like this:

```
<Image Source = "Assets/image.jpg" />
```

That's it. Windows takes care of the rest and substitutes images as needed based on screen resolution and scaling percentage in use. No need to write conditional code! More information about using the right imagery in your Windows 8 Store apps is in the Microsoft guideline at `http://msdn.microsoft.com/en-us/library/windows/apps/Hh846296.aspx#storelogo`. As you add more imagery to your solution, please remember to mark them appropriately as app *content* to avoid surprises as to why your images are not deployed as part of the app package. Sample image settings are shown in Figure 5-9.

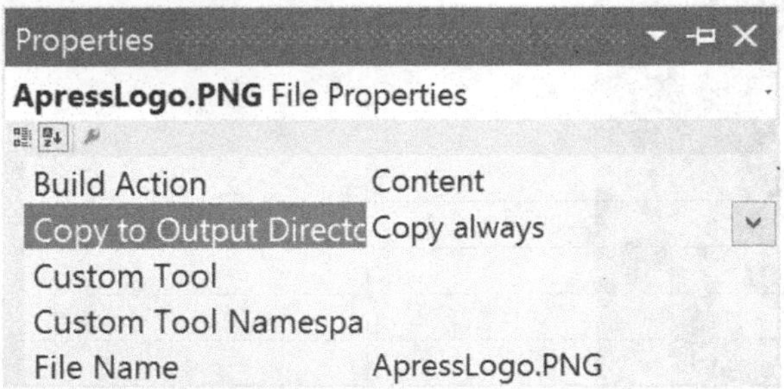

Figure 5-9. *Image configuration properties*

The ball is now back in your court with imagery—go ahead and impress the users of your Windows 8 Store app. Although getting imagery correct is in your control, what about the look and feel of the rest of app? How can you make your Windows 8 Store app inherit the Windows 8 silhouette? Is there any help from Visual Studio? The answer is yes. Read on!

From Template to App

With some of the imagery issues handled and with its own distinct branding, your Windows 8 app is starting to feel very real. So, let's get cracking on code. What are some common ways to present content? If you are following along with a Visual Studio Grid App template, press F5 to run it once. You should be greeted with a starting app page like the one shown in Figure 5-10.

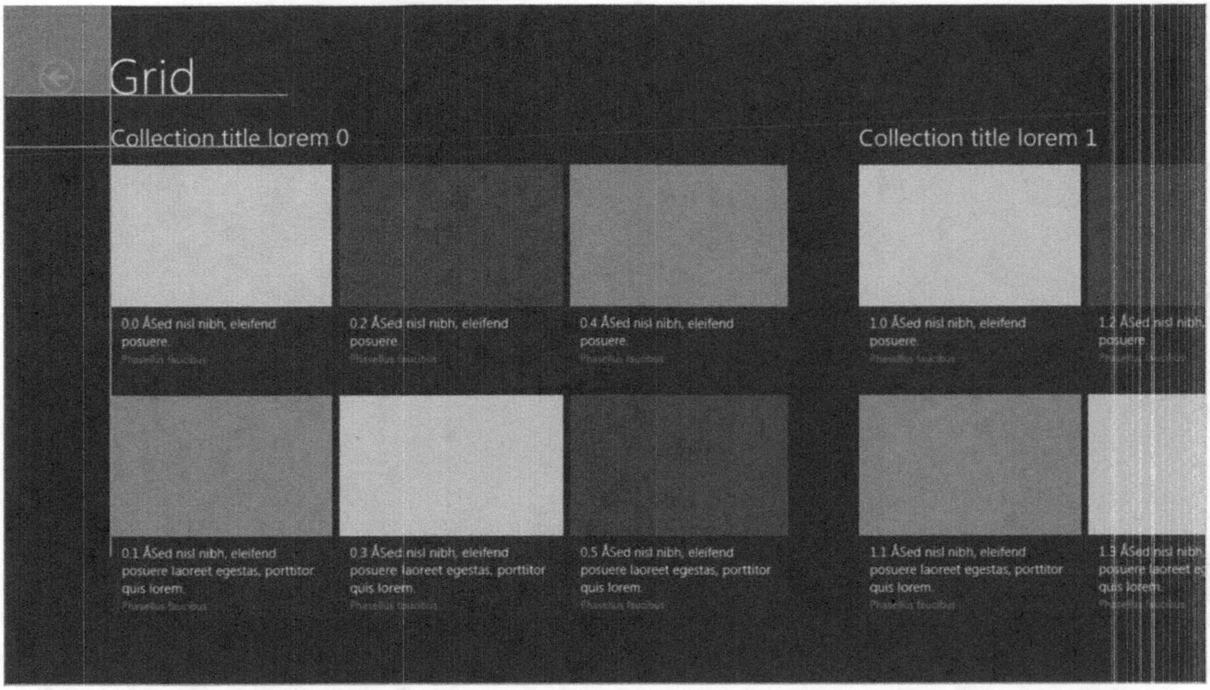

Figure 5-10. *Empty Grid App template showing silhoutte*

The blue overlay shows you what you don't see on screen. With all the Visual Studio templates for Windows 8 Store apps, we developers are getting a couple of UX elements for free:

- *Grid*: Do you remember Modern UI design principles? Everything has to align to the grid for consistency and fluid layout of content. The `GridView` control aligns content perfectly.
- *Typographical ramp*: The text styles already use Segoe UI fonts and the hierarchy of font sizes is built-in to differentiate content areas.

This offers a great start toward making your Windows 8 Store app mimic the look and feel of the Windows 8 silhouette. This is not to say that every Windows Store app has to begin with the given templates. In fact, it is highly suggested that you try doing things your way to provide a unique look and brand. But the templates do help in getting started at a good spot.

If you wanted to make an RSS feed reader Windows Store app, it might look like Figure 5-11.

Figure 5-11. *Data-bound Grid template in app*

Take a look at the two images shown in Figure 5-10 and Figure 5-11. Do you see the similarity? Yet one is an empty template and the other looks like a genuine app! It is the Windows 8 silhouette that's shining through in both. Take the empty template and bind it to your own data—and immediately you have a professional-looking app. Yes, it's that easy. The magic glue is data binding in the XAML UI layer and the use of `GridView` control to display the content. While the essence of it is simple, there is a bit of plumbing required to make data binding work. You'll inspect `GridView` workings and bindings through a real-world scenario next. But first, I'll talk about how `GridViews` and Semantic Zoom can solve a genuine problem. Hang tight here.

Discoverability

Let's envision the RSS feed reader/Headlines app to be a representative app that accentuates the Windows 8 silhouette. It is visually inviting, fast and fluid, and does everything the right way. It is not hard to imagine this app's content being bookshelf items, or shopping lists, or sports events, or movie lists, and so forth. Essentially, a collection of items or a list of some kind can easily use this Windows 8 silhouette to present enticing content. There is one small problem, however.

As nice as it is to pan around a good-looking app for content discoverability, the content itself might present a challenge. What if the collection of items being displayed is huge? Envision a Headlines app with UI as shown in Figure 5-11 when bound to hundreds or more items in the collection. Even if you displayed only the top 500 items, it would probably take a very large number of horizontal swipes to get to the last item. The problem is that the content, although nicely presented, is flattened in a long list, making discoverability less than optimal.

The Solution

Windows 8 presents a new UX paradigm to get around the discoverability problem that comes with a large collection of items. Logically, you would group the items into buckets based on some criteria so that it is a little easier to find a specific item. If the data is being grouped into logical units, why not the UI? This is what Windows 8 calls *Semantic Zoom*, a new UX paradigm particularly suited for touch-based devices.

Are you overwhelmed with a lot of content? Would you rather see a summary view? Simple: pinch in with two fingers on the screen. Pinch out to go back to normal layout. On a PC with a traditional keyboard and mouse setup, hold down the Ctrl key and scroll the mouse wheel up/down or use Ctrl plus +/- to achieve the same result. Semantic Zoom is quite different from optical zoom; unlike changing magnification, the display switches to show a different slice of grouped data.

Semantic Zoom uses data grouping into buckets and simply flips the view to alter the level of detail shown. This is visually delightful UX, if done right, and aids big-time towards discoverability of content. Zoom out to a high-level view, pick what interests you, and dive back in exactly where you desire. If you find your Windows 8 Start screen getting cluttered, just use Semantic Zoom to organize your tiles. Figure 5-12 is a screenshot from my everyday Windows 8 tablet—the Microsoft Surface RT. It shows my Start screen with all the app tiles grouped together in a zoomed-out view using Semantic Zoom.

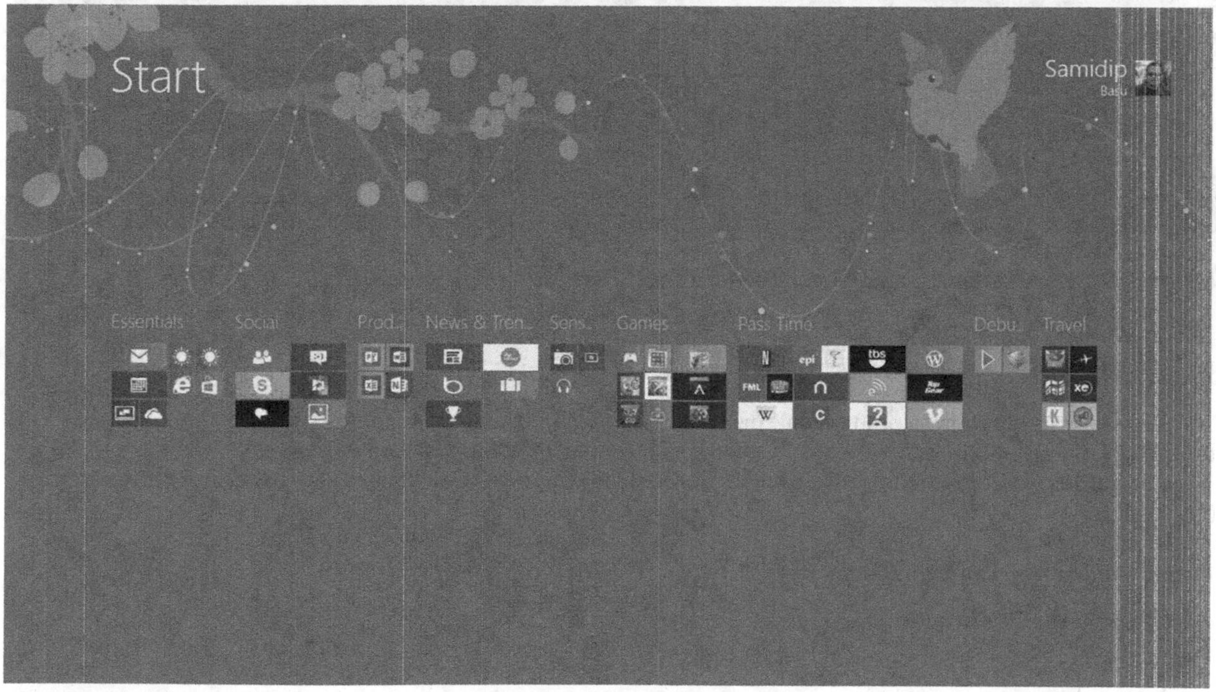

Figure 5-12. *Personal Start screen with zoomed-out view of app groups*

Implementing Semantic Zoom

So, now that you've seen how `GridView` and `SemanticZoom` controls maintain the Windows 8 silhouette, yet making content discoverability a breeze, the developer in you just wants to know: how can I do that in my apps? Let's walk through building a realistic app in your Apress Featured Books Demo app. First, the content needs to be laid out using a `GridView` and then you'll support Semantic Zoom. Let's say Figure 5-13 represents the kind of UI that you want to have—a long scrolling list of books by Apress, grouped by technology area. Let's build this from the ground up.

Figure 5-13. *Proposed start page of Apress Featured Books Demo app*

Data Model

The Apress demo app shows a pretty simple dashboard containing an assortment of Apress books, grouped by technology. But before you can go about presenting your content like this, you need to make sure that your data is set up correctly. Let's begin with the basics. First, in my `Models` folder, I have a class that stands for each individual book (see Listing 5-1).

Listing 5-1. Book Model Definition

```
namespace ApressDemo.Models
{
    public partial class ApressBook
    {
        #region "Properties"

        public string ApressBookISBN { get; set; }
        public string ApressBookName { get; set; }
        public string ApressBookTechnology { get; set; }
        public string ApressBookAuthor { get; set; }
        public DateTime ApressBookPublishedDate { get; set; }
        public string ApressBookDescription { get; set; }
```

```
        public string ApressBookUserLevel { get; set; }
        public string ApressBookImageURI { get; set; }

        public string DisplayablePublishDate
        {
            get
            {
                return ApressBookPublishedDate.ToString("MM/dd/yyyy");
            }
        }

        #endregion
    }
}
```

You could have a large collection of Apress books to show in your app. You need to be able to group them in bundles based on some criteria—the technology focus seems like a good one. Each grouped collection needs an identity of its own along with a count of the number of books that fall into the group. So, you possibly need a dedicated class for grouping (see Listing 5-2).

Listing 5-2. Grouped Book Model Definition

```
namespace ApressDemo.Models
{
    public class GroupedApressBooks : BindableBase
    {
        #region "Members"

        private string _ApressBookGroupName;
        private int _ApressBookGroupCount;

        private ObservableCollection<ApressBook> _bookCollection;

        #endregion

        #region "Properties"

        public string ApressBookGroupName
        {
            get { return _ApressBookGroupName; }
            set { SetProperty(ref _ApressBookGroupName, value); }
        }
        public int ApressBookGroupCount
        {
            get { return _ApressBookGroupCount; }
            set { SetProperty(ref _ApressBookGroupCount, value); }
        }
```

```
        public ObservableCollection<ApressBook> BookCollection
        {
            get { return _bookCollection; }
            set { SetProperty(ref _bookCollection, value); }
        }

        public string ImageURI
        {
            get
            {
                string imageUri = string.Empty;
                switch (ApressBookGroupName)
                {
                    case "Windows Phone":
                        imageUri = "/Assets/WindowsPhoneLogo.png";
                        break;
                    case "Windows Azure":
                        imageUri = "/Assets/WindowsAzureLogo.png";
                        break;
                    case "ASP.NET":
                        imageUri = "/Assets/ASPDotNetLogo.png";
                        break;
                }

                return imageUri;
            }
        }

        #endregion

        #region "Constructor"

        public GroupedApressBooks()
        {
            BookCollection = new ObservableCollection<ApressBook>();
        }

        #endregion
    }
}
```

There are a couple of things to note about your grouping container class. First, it derives from the `BindableBase` class, which in turn implements the `INotifyPropertyChanged` (INPC) pattern. This is done consciously because you are actually going to bind your UI to a collection of this book group's class objects and you want the object properties to raise changed events to the UI layer for automatic updates. Notice how the group `Name` and `Count` properties use *dependency properties* to set the values of the underlying variable; this way, your UI does not need to rebind, but it updates any time the property values change. The grouped class also maintains an `ObservableCollection<T>` of books that fall in the given category; this will also be used in data binding. Finally, each book group has an image URI that you are hard-coding for the sake of this demo. Your real app may retrieve data from a network source or database and get images from the collection source.

ViewModel

At this point, you have your Models lined up with your ApressBook and GroupedApressBooks classes. But you need a ViewModel to abstract this data before handing off to the Views. Also, envision this: you have several Models and need to show object properties pulling from each Model, but not the entire class details. Do you see the benefit of the ViewModel pattern now? It let you mix and match what each view needs and aids in unit testing. So, you need a ViewModel. Let's define one for your Featured Books view (see Listing 5-3).

Listing 5-3. ViewModel Definition

```
namespace ApressDemo.ViewModels
{
    public partial class FeaturedApressBookListViewModel
    {
        #region "Members"

        private ObservableCollection<GroupedApressBooks> _groupedFeaturedApressBooks;

        #endregion

        #region "Properties"

        public ObservableCollection<ApressBook> FeaturedApressBooks { get; set; }

        public ObservableCollection<GroupedApressBooks> GroupedFeaturedApressBooks
        {
            get
            {
                if (_groupedFeaturedApressBooks == null)
                    _groupedFeaturedApressBooks = new ObservableCollection<GroupedApressBooks>();

                // Put Books into Grouped buckets based on Technology.
                var query = from individualApressBook in FeaturedApressBooks
                            orderby individualApressBook.ApressBookTechnology
                            group individualApressBook by individualApressBook.ApressBookTechnology
into g
                            select new GroupedApressBooks
                           {
                               ApressBookGroupName = g.Key,
                               ApressBookGroupCount = g.Count(),
                               BookCollection = new ObservableCollection<ApressBook>(g.ToList())
                           };

                _groupedFeaturedApressBooks = new
ObservableCollection<GroupedApressBooks>(query.ToList());

                return _groupedFeaturedApressBooks;
            }
            set
            {
                _groupedFeaturedApressBooks = value;
            }
```

```
        }

        #endregion
}
}
```

Your ViewModel realizes that you need to display a collection of Apress books, but also present a grouped collection so that you may put the books in their respective logical buckets. This grouping mechanism will also aid in supporting Semantic Zoom later on. Accordingly, your `FeaturedApressBookListViewModel` class holds two collections: the collection of featured Apress books and the same collection grouped by technology focus. Both collections implement the INPC pattern and hence are ready for data binding in the Views.

Did you notice the `Get` definition of the `GroupedFeaturedApressBooks` collection? This is where you do some LINQ magic to actually parse the collection of books and sort them in logical buckets per their technology focus. And once this grouping is done, your data is all set for some easy binding to data elements in your Views. In the demo app, I don't have a real collection of Apress books; I'm simply making up a dummy collection by choosing a few technology areas and sample books from the Apress web site (`www.apress.com`). This is the collection of custom object types that your app might need to handle. It is completely up to you how you hydrate your ViewModels. As for this example, a simple static function fills up the `FeaturedApressBooks` collection with books (see Listing 5-4).

Listing 5-4. Sample Data

```
public void LoadFeaturedBooksDemoVM(FeaturedApressBookListViewModel featuredApressBookListVM)
        {
            featuredApressBookListVM.FeaturedApressBooks = new ObservableCollection<Models.
ApressBook>();

            ApressBook WPMigration = new ApressBook();
            WPMigration.ApressBookISBN = "978-1-4302-3816-4";
            WPMigration.ApressBookName = "Migrating to Windows Phone";
            WPMigration.ApressBookTechnology = "Windows Phone";
            WPMigration.ApressBookAuthor = "Jesse Liberty , Jeff Blankenburg";
            WPMigration.ApressBookDescription = "This book offers everything you'll need to upgrade
your existing programming knowledge and begin to develop applications for the Windows Phone.";
            WPMigration.ApressBookImageURI = "/Assets/MigratingToWP.png";
            WPMigration.ApressBookPublishedDate = new DateTime(2011, 12, 28);
            WPMigration.ApressBookUserLevel = "Intermediate";
        .....
        .....
        .....
        featuredApressBookListVM.FeaturedApressBooks.Add(WPMigration);
        ....
       }
```

The data contained in your `ViewModel` should really be accessible throughout the app in case some other `View` needs access to the same data; this might vary based on how your app is structured. But, the demo app has placeholders defined in the `App.xaml.cs` to make the data globally accessible. Listing 5-5 provides some code in the `App.xaml.cs`.

Listing 5-5. Global Data

```
private FeaturedApressBookListViewModel _featuredBookListVM;
public FeaturedApressBookListViewModel FeaturedBookListVM
        {
            get { return _featuredBookListVM; }
            set { _featuredBookListVM = value; }
        }
....

FeaturedBookListVM = new FeaturedApressBookListViewModel();
FeaturedBookListVM.LoadFeaturedBooksDemoVM(FeaturedBookListVM);
```

The last lines of the code initialize and loads sample data in the ViewModel and this can be done in the `App()` constructor or `Onlaunched()` method in `App.xaml.cs`. This is obviously not the right way to initialize data and you need to handle data caching, fetching fresh content, and so forth, in a real app; but for demo purposes, this will suffice. What you are after is a global list of grouped book collections that you can provide some UI for.

UI Markup

Let's build the UI to display the grouped book collection in a `GridView` control along with support for Semantic Zoom. Let's add a `BasicPage` to the `Views` folder called `FeaturedBookList.xaml`. This will be the dashboard showing the grouped Apress books collection. Start with a clean slate on the UI and clear everything between the `<common:LayoutAwarePage/>` elements. Add the lines of code from Listing 5-6.

Listing 5-6. Page Resources

```
<Page.Resources>

        <!-- Collection of grouped Apress Books displayed by this page -->
        <CollectionViewSource
            x:Name="groupedItemsViewSource"
            Source="{Binding GroupedFeaturedApressBooks}"
            IsSourceGrouped="true"
            ItemsPath="BookCollection"/>

    </Page.Resources>
```

The lines of code in Listing 5-6 use a special dependency object called `CollectionViewSource`. This is a very handy class that serves as a proxy to enable grouping support over a collection of items. You'll notice that the `Source` property of the `CollectionViewSource` has a data-binding declaration. It is not a fluke that the binding matches the named grouped collection of books in your ViewModel. In fact, this is exactly what you need to hand off the grouped collection of books to the UI—group containers with metadata and logical buckets of book collections in each group. You'll notice that the `IsSourceGrouped` property of the `CollectionViewSource` is set to `true` to indicate that your underlying data is already grouped. Also, the `ItemsPath` property is set to the named book collections inside each grouped collection. The reason for this will be apparent very soon.

Before you try to display any data in your app, make sure your View has the data. The `CollectionViewSource` defined in Listing 5-6 knows exactly how to wrap a grouped collection of items; but you haven't really provided any mappings to the data. So, do just that. Open `FeaturedBookList.xaml.cs` and add the little code snippet from Listing 5-7.

Listing 5-7. Data Binding

```
protected override void OnNavigatedTo(NavigationEventArgs e)
        {
            base.OnNavigatedTo(e);

            // Set the Data-Binding context to the Grouped Book collection.
            this.DefaultViewModel["GroupedFeaturedApressBooks"] = ((App)Application.Current).
FeaturedBookListVM.GroupedFeaturedApressBooks;

            // Support zoomed-out semantics.
            var groupedBooks = groupedItemsViewSource.View.CollectionGroups;
            (zoomer.ZoomedOutView as ListView).ItemsSource = groupedBooks;
    }
```

What's going on here? When the user first navigates to the page, the `OnNavigatedTo()` event is raised and you're setting some data-binding context right away. You can see that you are leveraging the globally accessible `FeaturedBookListVM` ViewModel and binding the UI data context to the grouped collection of Apress books, namely `GroupedFeaturedApressBooks`. But how is this one line of code carrying data into the view and what is this `DefaultViewModel`?

Great question! Turns out that this is a tiny bit of plumbing that Windows 8 app templates add to make sure you can easily bind a collection of items to your UI. Take a look at Listing 5-8, which is the code in the XAML file's top declarations section.

Listing 5-8. Data Context

```
<common:LayoutAwarePage
    x:Name="pageRoot"
    x:Class="ApressDemo.Views.FeaturedBookList"
    DataContext="{Binding DefaultViewModel, RelativeSource={RelativeSource Self}}" ....
>
```

These lines of code provide the glue. The page (inherited from a template page called `LayoutAwarePage`) is declaring its `DataContext` as a `Binding` statement and announcing that it knows how to use a placeholder called `DefaultViewModel`. Fill in the `DefaultViewModel` to hand data to the View. Now the code in `OnNavigatedTo()` makes a little more sense. The `DefaultViewModel` can act as a dictionary of name-value pairs and you're simply handing off your grouped book collections to the `DefaultViewModel` with `GroupedFeaturedApressBooks` as the dictionary key. Go back to the `CollectionViewSource` definition and check the source property binding. Yes, the same key is used from the `DefaultViewModel`. No magic—just a little plumbing ☺.

Now add more UI display pieces to present the passed-in data in your page (see Listing 5-9).

Listing 5-9. XAML Markup

```
<Page.Resources>

     <!-- Collection of grouped Apress Books displayed by this page -->
     <CollectionViewSource
         x:Name="groupedItemsViewSource"
         Source="{Binding GroupedFeaturedApressBooks}"
         IsSourceGrouped="true"
         ItemsPath="BookCollection"/>

</Page.Resources>
```

```
<Grid Style="{StaticResource LayoutRootStyle}" Background="Black">
    <Grid.RowDefinitions>
        <RowDefinition Height="140"/>
        <RowDefinition Height="*"/>
    </Grid.RowDefinitions>

    <!-- Page title -->
    <Grid Grid.Row="0">
        <Grid.ColumnDefinitions>
            <ColumnDefinition Width="Auto"/>
        </Grid.ColumnDefinitions>
        <StackPanel Orientation="Horizontal" Margin="20,0,0,0">
            <Image Source="/Assets/ApressLogo.png" Width="200" Height="100"
VerticalAlignment="Center"/>
            <TextBlock x:Name="pageTitle" Grid.Column="1" Text="{StaticResource AppName}"
Style="{StaticResource PageHeaderTextStyle}" VerticalAlignment="Center" Margin="10,10,0,10"/>
        </StackPanel>
    </Grid>

    <SemanticZoom Grid.Row="1" x:Name="zoomer">

        <SemanticZoom.ZoomedInView>
            ....
        </SemanticZoom.ZoomedInView>


    <SemanticZoom.ZoomedOutView>
            ....
        </SemanticZoom.ZoomedOutView>

     </SemanticZoom>
</Grid>
```

Figure 5-14 shows the kind of UI that you're trying to get.

Figure 5-14. *Apress Featured Books Demo app*

The XAML code in Listing 5-9 simply uses a `Grid` as the top-level container control on your page, with two rows taking up the screen real estate. A fixed 140-pixel top row serves as the title bar for your app, and the rest of the page is filled with content. A `SemanticZoom` control has been initialized expecting two different views: a *zoomed-in view* (like the one shown in Figure 5-14 for normal panning of content and a *zoomed-out view* to show summary information based on groupings of data. Let's first try to get the zoomed-in or normal view working. Listing 5-10 provides the code that you add to the zoomed-in view placeholder.

Listing 5-10. Semantic Zoom Zoomed-In View

```
<SemanticZoom.ZoomedInView>
               <GridView
                   x:Name="itemGridView"
                   AutomationProperties.AutomationId="ItemGridView"
                   AutomationProperties.Name="Grouped Items"
                   Margin="30,80,40,46"
                   VerticalAlignment="Center"
                   ItemsSource="{Binding Source={StaticResource groupedItemsViewSource}}"
                   ItemTemplate="{StaticResource Apress277x350BookTemplate}">

                   <GridView.ItemsPanel>
                       <ItemsPanelTemplate>
                           <VirtualizingStackPanel Orientation="Horizontal"/>
                       </ItemsPanelTemplate>
                   </GridView.ItemsPanel>
```

```
                <GridView.GroupStyle>
                    <GroupStyle>
                        <GroupStyle.HeaderTemplate>
                            <DataTemplate>
                                <Grid Margin="1,0,0,6">
                                    <StackPanel Orientation="Horizontal">
                                        <Button AutomationProperties.Name="Group Title"
Content="{Binding ApressBookGroupName}" Style="{StaticResource ApressTextButtonStyle}"
VerticalAlignment="Center"/>
                                        <TextBlock Text="(" Style="{StaticResource
SubheaderTextStyle}" VerticalAlignment="Top" Margin="10,0,5,0"/>
                                        <TextBlock Text="{Binding ApressBookGroupCount}"
Style="{StaticResource SubheaderTextStyle}" VerticalAlignment="Top"/>
                                        <TextBlock Text=")" Style="{StaticResource
SubheaderTextStyle}" VerticalAlignment="Top" Margin="5,0,5,0"/>
                                    </StackPanel>
                                </Grid>
                            </DataTemplate>
                        </GroupStyle.HeaderTemplate>
                        <GroupStyle.Panel>
                            <ItemsPanelTemplate>
                                <VariableSizedWrapGrid Orientation="Vertical"
Margin="0,0,100,0"/>
                            </ItemsPanelTemplate>
                        </GroupStyle.Panel>
                    </GroupStyle>
                </GridView.GroupStyle>
            </GridView>
        </SemanticZoom.ZoomedInView>
```

Aha! The first use of GridView control is here! Take notice of a couple of things. First, the ItemsSource property of the GridView is set to the CollectionViewSource you defined before. This essentially feeds the grouped collection all the way down the GridView items, which defines a GroupStyle section to highlight group headers before presenting the collection of books as items. But what about the ItemTemplate styling—the actual guidance on how the GridView presents each book item? What is this Apress277x350BookTemplate static resource? Good question. Remember, your reusable styles are referenced as static resources and these styles are defined in the Common/StandardStyles.xaml file. Listing 5-11 is the ItemTemplate definition for the GridView items.

Listing 5-11. Zoomed-In Data Template

```
<DataTemplate x:Key="Apress277x350BookTemplate">
    <Grid HorizontalAlignment="Left" Width="277" Height="350">
        <Border Background="{StaticResource ListViewItemPlaceholderBackgroundThemeBrush}">
            <Image Source="{Binding ApressBookImageURI}" Stretch="UniformToFill"/>
        </Border>
        <StackPanel VerticalAlignment="Bottom" Background="{StaticResource
ListViewItemOverlayBackgroundThemeBrush}">
            <TextBlock Text="{Binding ApressBookAuthor}" Foreground="{StaticResource
ListViewItemOverlayForegroundThemeBrush}" Style="{StaticResource TitleTextStyle}" Height="60"
Margin="15,0,15,0"/>
            <TextBlock Text="{Binding ApressBookISBN}" Foreground="{StaticResource
ListViewItemOverlaySecondaryForegroundThemeBrush}" Style="{StaticResource CaptionTextStyle}"
TextWrapping="NoWrap" Margin="15,0,15,10" FontSize="20"/>
```

```
        </StackPanel>
    </Grid>
</DataTemplate>
```

As you can see, the `DataTemplate` is what defines the `ItemTemplate` of each individual `GridView` item. It tells the XAML parser exactly how to bind UI elements to object properties at runtime. And the look and feel of the UI elements can be completely customized to fit your app's branding. In this case, the demo app's `GridView` shows each individual book's image, with an overlay text of the author and ISBN numbers. Any time you see a static resource, like in `CaptionTextStyle/ListViewItemOverlaySecondaryForegroundThemeBrush`, you now know to look inside the `Common/StandardStyles.xaml` file.

In fact, the `Common/StandardStyles.xaml` file has a huge number of styles defined that are used extensively by Windows 8 Store apps and most commonly by the Visual Studio app templates. If you don't like something about a style—well, just change it. But be careful not to mess up any of the existing styles, or you'll end up affecting any of the built-in template/animation needs. Simply copy the style and name it your own before making edits. I urge you to play with different ways of customizing the app display by editing the `Apress277x350BookTemplate` and seeing how the changes affect the look and feel of the book items. For example, work with the height/width of each item's template to see what makes sense in your app. One thing to note here is that varying screen resolutions may have an impact on the density of the content that you present—so choose what works well generically across resolutions.

Are you developing on a machine with limited resolution variations or do you hate changing your default resolution to keep testing your app? No worries—the Windows 8 Simulator provides the easiest solution. Simply debug/deploy App to the Simulator and use the screen resolution icon on the right side (it looks like a monitor) to switch between various resolutions to see how your app layout adjusts. For example, with your given `DataTemplate`, Figure 5-15 shows what the Apress demo app looks like on a very high-resolution screen. When using adaptive layouts, the greater the screen real estate, the more content shown. No need for panning given your small sample size of featured books; the high-resolution view shows the entire collection fully. Do you want to add more books and technology groups to the collection? No problem—your `ItemTemplate` will render more content and the `GridView` happily pans across to show more items.

Figure 5-15. *Apress Featured Books Demo app in high resolution*

Your zoomed-in view is all set displaying its data with a GridView control. Now turn your attention to the zoomed-out view and add the code snippet from Listing 5-12.

Listing 5-12. Semantic Zoom Zoomed-Out View

```
<SemanticZoom.ZoomedOutView>
                <ListView VerticalAlignment="Center" ItemTemplate="{StaticResource
Apress250x250TechTemplate}">
                    <ListView.ItemsPanel>
                        <ItemsPanelTemplate>
                            <StackPanel Orientation="Horizontal" VerticalAlignment="Center"
Margin="100,0,0,0"/>
                        </ItemsPanelTemplate>
                    </ListView.ItemsPanel>
                </ListView>
            </SemanticZoom.ZoomedOutView>
```

In the zoomed-out view, you are using a ListView instead of a GridView control. This is because you are presenting less quantity of content and the view is summary-only or less dense. Again, the ItemTemplate is defined as a static resource in Common/StandardStyles.xaml and it controls the way data is bound to and rendered as individual ListView items. Listing 5-13 is the template in use.

Listing 5-13. Zoomed-Out Data Template

```
<DataTemplate x:Key="Apress250x250TechTemplate">
        <Grid HorizontalAlignment="Left" Width="250" Height="250">
            <Border Background="{StaticResource ListViewItemPlaceholderBackgroundThemeBrush}">
                <Image Source="{Binding Group.ImageURI}" Stretch="UniformToFill" />
            </Border>
            <StackPanel VerticalAlignment="Bottom" Background="{StaticResource
ListViewItemOverlayBackgroundThemeBrush}">
                <TextBlock Text="{Binding Group.ApressBookGroupName}" Foreground="{StaticResource
ListViewItemOverlayForegroundThemeBrush}" Style="{StaticResource TitleTextStyle}" Height="60"
Margin="15,0,15,0"/>
            </StackPanel>
        </Grid>
    </DataTemplate>
```

This template for a zoomed-out view is similar to Listing 5-11 in the use of image and overlay text. Where it differs is in the data binding. This time, the binding is to the grouped collection entities in the CollectionViewSource instead of individual items. This is because the Semantic Zoom zoomed-out view is a high-level summary information mechanism and the group entities in your Apress book collection offer the high-level logical technology bucket. Do you want to see the template in action? Launch the app to see the zoomed-in view and then pinch/zoom to toggle Semantic Zoom states. Ctrl +Scroll or Ctrl and -/+ perform the same action. Figure 5-16 shows a view of your Apress Featured Books Demo app in zoomed-out mode.

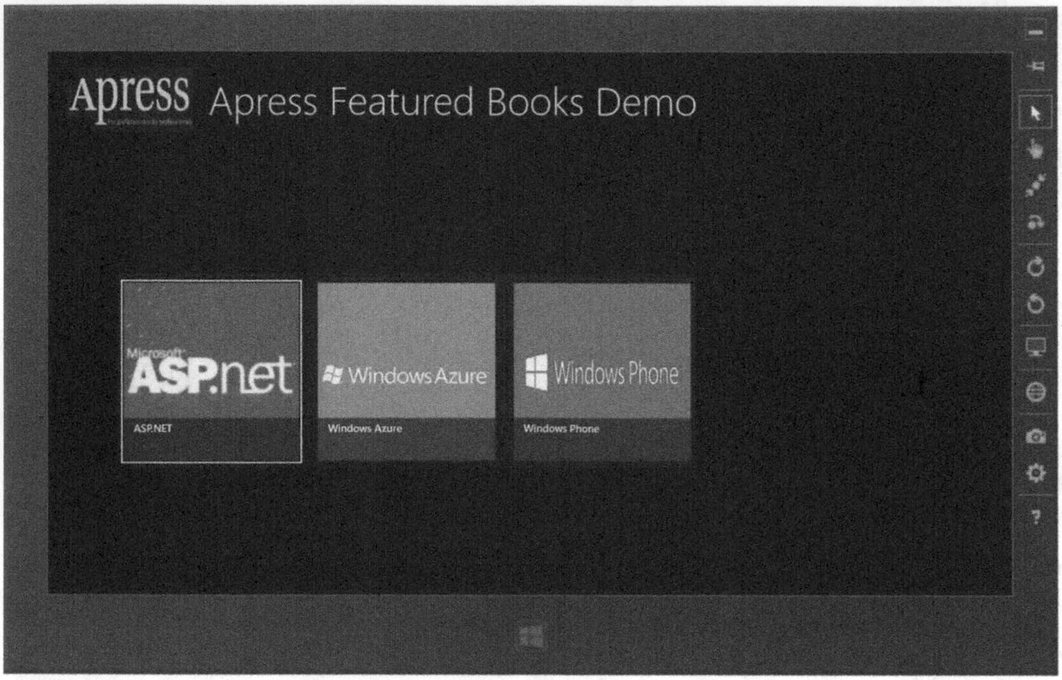

***Figure 5-16.** Apress Featured Books Demo app in zoomed-out view*

As you can see, the details of every book item are gone. Instead, the Semantic Zoom zoomed-out view presents a higher view of data; in this case, presenting the group header information in the form of technology areas. Are you looking through a long list of Windows Azure books but would like to jump to the Windows Phone titles? No problem. Pinch in to the zoomed-out look, select this other group, and swoop right back in at the given group's collection of items.

Summary

Now your data collection is grouped into categories, and through Semantic Zoom, your UI mimics the data in presenting content. According to MSDN, "Semantic Zoom greatly reduces the perception of traveling long distances when navigating through large amounts of content and provides quick and easy access to locations within the content." The zoomed-in and zoomed-out views are great complements to each other, showing two slices of the same data collection and greatly aiding discoverability. The zoomed-out view that groups item views should be kept simple (it should not switch the data content scope being presented and be restricted to a small number of groups), otherwise, it defeats the purpose of the Semantic Zoom. Microsoft's guidelines on using Semantic Zoom in Windows Store apps are at `http://msdn.microsoft.com/en-us/library/windows/apps/hh465319(v=VS.85).aspx`. It's now time to implement Semantic Zoom in your Windows 8 Store app. It is gorgeously Windows 8—and you will be thankful that you did so!

In this chapter, you saw that the look and feel of your Windows 8 Store app is pretty darn important, especially in context of the new design language. Your use of color, imagery, branding, and the implementation of Semantic Zoom all go a long way toward improving the all-important user experience. Buckle down and sweat the details. Take pride in craftsmanship—and it will show in your Windows 8 Store app.

CHAPTER 6

Content Structuring and Navigation

Now that you have a basic idea of how to use the right controls for your Windows 8 Store apps, and you know how to start making your app look professional and infuse it with Windows 8 styling, you probably can't wait to take the next steps toward making your dream Windows 8 Store app a reality, which is where this chapter comes in—unfolding realistic ways to structure your app content and get your ideas flowing. How do you plan to place your precious content in your Windows 8 Store app? Will you have multiple pages, and if so, how will the user navigate? Are there common patterns? How do you handle data? All that and more are covered in this chapter, showing you plenty of real-world code to get the job done.

Planning Your Content Structuring

You're sitting on a million-dollar Windows 8 Store app idea and you just want to get started. Again, before you go to File ➤ New Project in Visual Studio, you need to plan. This little planning phase is critical toward the success of your Windows 8 Store app because it allows you to think through several boundaries for your app: the must-have features in Phase 1, the kind of branding that you're shooting for, and the way you present and persist data. But the planning should also include something more pivotal: the way that you structure the content of your Windows 8 Store app and how it affects the user experience.

I am essentially talking about taking a holistic look at all the content you want to present to the users of your app and deciding how you want to present it. Unless you're writing a very simple Windows 8 Store app, your content will not fit in a single XAML page. So, you really want to think this through by asking yourself how you will break up your content into disparate pages and how does the user navigate between pages? There is a little bit of science behind what each page of your Windows 8 Store app is like, but it boils down to common sense and your app's needs.

If you've done any Windows Phone development, you are already used to the idea of *content structuring*—planning to meticulously break up your app into discrete pages. Although Windows 8 Store apps allow the developer considerably more real estate than Windows Phone apps, the fundamentals remain the same: just because you can, doesn't mean you should. Break up your app content presentation into discrete pages by following these simple rules:

- An app user experience should be made up of multiple pages of content and allow the user to navigate easily between pages.
- Every page should have one and only one purpose. Let the user achieve that one thing while on the page.
- Every page should be clutter-free and encourage discoverability using touch.
- Pages should present continuity in user experience and logically lead the user onto the next thing.
- Pages should present logical data and cache content as appropriate for a better user experience.
- Pages should be able to pass data back and forth between each other within the app or use centralized data.

It is clear that at the start of each Windows 8 Store app, we developers need to sit down and think through how to divvy up our app content into discrete pages. This exercise not only helps us plan what to present in each page and how to handle data, but it also helps us to structure our content, which enhances extending app functionality in the future. This is what designers often call *wireframing*.

What is the best way to do Windows 8 app page planning? Well, it depends on your needs. For a truly professional/enterprise Windows 8 Store app, you may have the luxury of working on a team. You may even have access to a designer. Brainstorming on a chalkboard with a team or sitting down with a designer to decide on app content layout is really the optimal way of planning toward a Windows 8 Store app, but it certainly isn't the only way. A lot of Windows 8 app developers work in silos and build apps themselves. Guess what works for me when I'm working alone? Yes, paper and pencil—and it is free! Start fresh one morning, on a plane ride or in a quiet coffee shop. Envision all that you want your Windows 8 app to do and then break it down into logical pages. While you are at it, take the opportunity to decide on navigation and data handling between pages of your app. Rough sketches on paper work just fine; show it to some family members or friends for feedback, which is often valuable and gets you thinking about user interaction in your own way. Remember to put a little pride aside and listen: ultimately, you are not the user of your app—so it pays to listen to feedback.

There are a couple utilities. If you would like your page sketches to imbibe the Windows 8 silhouette, feel free to invest in the wonderful Windows 8 Stencil Kit; details are at `www.uistencils.com/products/windows-8-stencil-kit`. If you have a Windows 8 slate/tablet already, the free Fresh Paint Windows 8 app (search for it in the Store) is a wonderful companion when you just want to draw your ideas on a PC using your fingers or a digitizer pen. Another possibility is to use the Telerik `AppMock` Windows 8 app to prototype your Windows 8 app quickly; details @ `http://www.telerik.com/products/windows-8/appmock.aspx`. Whatever your method, you are essentially breaking down complex information into manageable chunks. This concept, called the *information architecture* (see Figure 6-1), has widespread usage and is a critical part of planning your Windows 8 Store app. Information architecture often involves *boxology*, which is representing app data/page entities within boxes and then figuring out the relationships between the boxes. Is there a top-level node? What would the subcategories be? Figure 6-1 shows a typical hub-and-spoke model, starting with a high-level data entity or page, and breaking it down to its child elements.

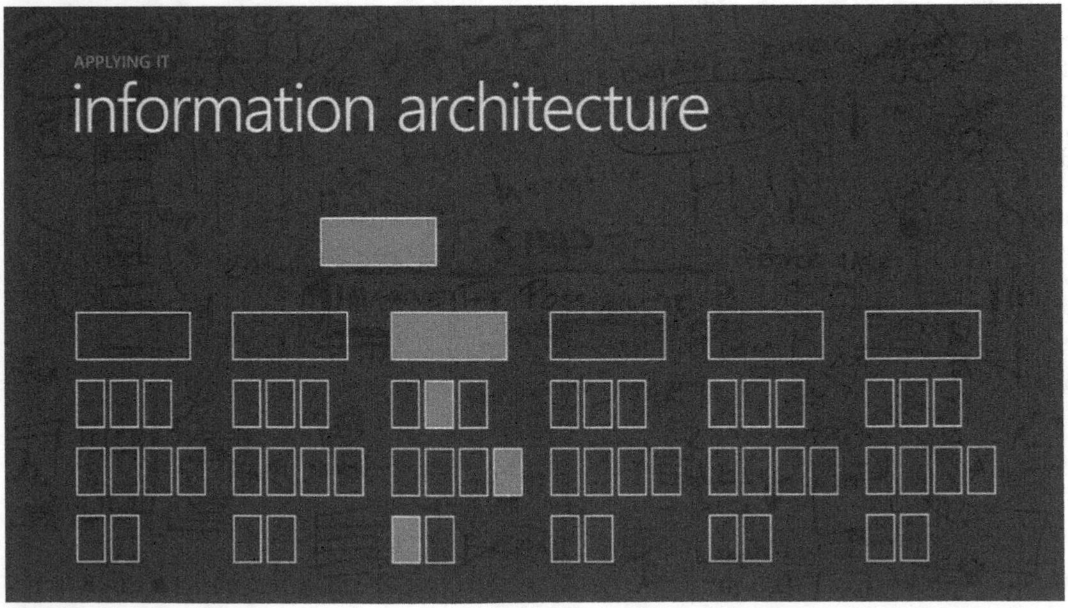

Figure 6-1. *A break down of information architecture*

Page Navigation Within Frame

Once you have planned your Windows 8 Store app and have broken down the information/content that you want to present into discrete pages, the next order of business is to figure out the navigation among pages and how to handle data to enhance the user experience. Let's start exploring navigation inWindows 8 with Figure 6-2.

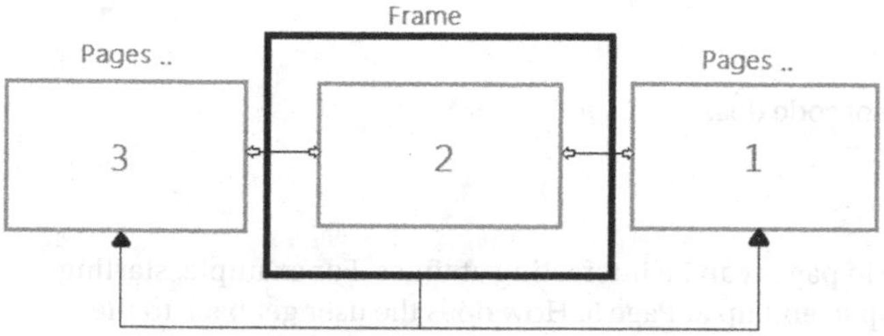

Figure 6-2. Frame and Page setup

The salient points are as follows:

- Windows 8 XAML apps run inside an application frame.
- There isn't a restriction on creating multiple Frames; but most apps stick to one Frame for simplicity.
- The app's content is presented to the user through XAML pages.
- The pages are hosted inside the app frame; one frame houses all the pages in the app and helps in navigation among the pages.
- The app frame loads one page at a time, as instructed programmatically, and maintains a backstack of pages visited, starting from the very first page of the app.
- Pages loaded inside the frame can use a cached mode so that page-level details are persisted as the user comes back to a Page.
- Pages can pass along any parameters among themselves, starting from simple strings/integers to full-fledged objects.

Let's look at some code around page navigation. Do you remember this piece of code from your `App.xaml.cs` file?

```
Frame rootFrame = Window.Current.Content as Frame;

if (rootFrame.Content == null)
{
    if (!rootFrame.Navigate(typeof(PageName)))
    {
        throw new Exception("Failed to create initial page");
    }
}
```

This piece of code loaded up the app frame and handed it the first page of your app. How do you navigate to another page once you already have a handle to the app frame? Turns out, it is exactly the same piece of code with some optional parameters to pass along. Here's a sample to navigate to another page, in case your page inherits from the common `LayoutAwarePage` class:

```
this.Frame.Navigate(typeof(SomeOtherPage), someParameters);
```

It is pretty simple to hop from one page to another and carry along some parameters for context. Sometimes you need to avoid circular navigation. Here's an example of how you may overuse navigation:

Page A ➤ Page B ➤ Page A

In this case, the logical flow from Page B back to Page A does not need to use explicit navigation because you are unconsciously building up a huge page backstack. Instead, this simple piece of code achieves the exact same navigation:

```
this.Frame.GoBack();
```

And of course, I don't need to tell you what this line of code does:

```
this.Frame.GoForward();
```

The depth to which the user is allowed to navigate in pages can be interesting at times. For example, starting from Page 1, a user may click subsequent links in an app to end up at Page 5. How does the user get back to the home page, which happened to be the first page in the backstack? Surely, not by pressing a Back button five times. The answer lies in the frame features. If you have used the BasicPage page template in Visual Studio or any of the Windows 8 project templates, take a peek inside the `LayoutAwarePage.cs` file in the `Common` folder. You'll find the following lines of code:

```
protected virtual void GoHome(object sender, RoutedEventArgs e)
 {
     // Use the navigation frame to return to the topmost page
     if (this.Frame != null)
     {
         while (this.Frame.CanGoBack) this.Frame.GoBack();
     }
 }
```

This is common boilerplate code offered by the base `Page` class of `LayoutAwarePage`. It simply uses a frame feature to see if you can traverse any further back in the page backstack, and accordingly takes you to the top of the navigation stack. Nifty, isn't it? So, have your page inherit from the base class or look around for frame features like these to perform your navigation needs within your Windows 8 Store app. The next section shows examples of carrying data back and forth among the pages, as well as more details on using the frame's backstack features for UI binding.

Let's talk about one last thing before you move from basic navigation. Do this little experiment in a sample project. Create two pages in a Windows 8 Store app and name them Page 1 and Page 2. Put a simple `TextBox` or some other data entry UI element in Page 1 to accept user input. Now add a button to Page 1 and navigate to Page 2 upon user click. If you accepted the BasicPage template for Page 2, it will have a Back button in the page header section prewired to bring you back to the first page of the frame. Let's run the app. On Page 1, start entering some data in the TextBox and then click the button to navigate to Page 2. Now click the Back button on Page 2 to return to Page 1. The data that you entered is lost!

This is an incredibly frustrating user experience and it shows that your app does not respect the user's efforts to remember what he or she was typing. Yet, there is an easy fix to the problem thanks to the app frame. In addition to the page backstack, the frame has built-in caching to remember details on a page as it is being shoved into the navigation backstack. Simply add the following piece of code to the constructor of the page that you want caching turned on:

```
NavigationCacheMode = Windows.UI.Xaml.Navigation.NavigationCacheMode.Enabled;
```

Now enter some data on Page 1, navigating to Page 2, and then come back to Page 1. Voila! The page remembers the exact state of the page when you left it, including unfinished text input in controls. This will surely make for a far better UX than what you had before. The `NavigationCacheMode` can be turned on with an `Enabled` or `Required` setting. `Enabled` first honors the limits of the frame cache size, while `Required` allows for exceeding the cache size in favor of forced caching of page content. This turning on caching mode at the page level is a must-do for pages that are heavy in user data entry. More details about classes, delegates, and enumerations around page navigation are at `http://msdn.microsoft.com/en-us/library/windows/apps/br243300.aspx`.

Hub-and-Spoke Model

When it comes to page navigation patterns in Windows 8 Store apps, you have seen two models, as shown in Figure 6-3. The flat navigation scheme represents when the Windows 8 Store app presents disparate pages and the user does not need the pages to be linked for navigation. This type of navigation is seen in the multiple tabs open in the IE10 Windows 8 browser app. The hierarchical navigation scheme is more common for many Windows 8 Store apps, where there is a home page that acts as a high-level dashboard, followed by closely linked child pages with clear navigation links to traverse up and down the app content tree. This type of navigation is commonly seen in news, travel, photo, and other content aggregator apps.

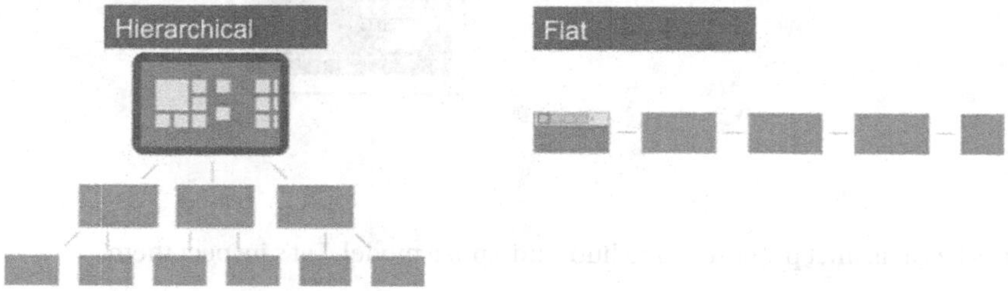

Figure 6-3. *Navigation patterns*

What you see in Figure 6-3's hierarchical navigation model is a theme commonly known as the *hub-and-spoke* model for navigation, which has roots in Windows Phone apps. The idea is to have a home/dashboard-type main page that is visually stunning and brings together all the features that the app provides. From then on, the user is led to any of the possible paths to child pages, which are linked back to the home page. The depth to which your app's tree might allow the user to navigate is completely up to you.

Do you remember the app frame and the navigation backstack discussed in the previous section? As the user navigates away from the home pages onto child pages, the frame is pushing pages visited into its backstack, ready to bring the user traversing up the tree, if desired. Microsoft's own templates recommend a three-level-deep hub-and-spoke model, as shown in Figure 6-3. You are certainly not restricted to that; but remember not to confuse the user with the need to press the Back button several times to return to the home page. You could provide a shortcut link to traverse all the way to the top of the tree.Actually, you are going to spend the rest of the chapter trying to get this three-level hub-and-spoke model of navigation working on your Apress Featured Books Demo app that you are building. Along the way, you should see several tricks on how to accomplish navigation among pages and how to maintain data context. So, download the source code or build your own to follow along. Let's start by inspecting what you get out-of-the-box with the Visual Studio hub-and-spoke template. You will follow up with ways to customize the solution.

The Templated Solution

If you have decided in favor of the hub-and-spoke model for your Windows 8 Store app, let's look at how Visual Studio can help with templates. Start a new dummy project, pick the Grid App template, and allow the solution to load in Visual Studio. You are going to notice three different views or XAML pages dropped in the solution (see Figure 6-4).

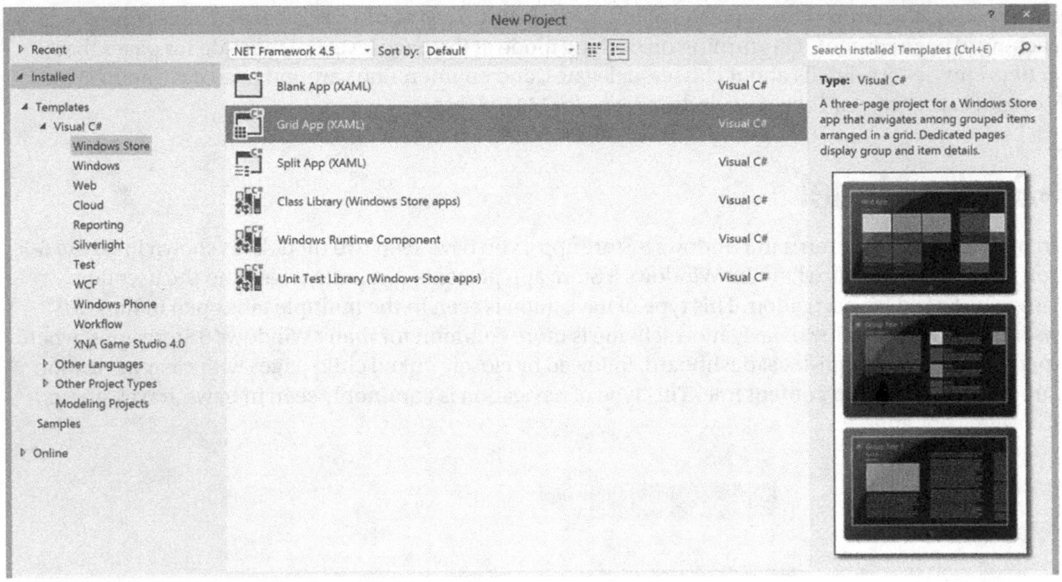

***Figure 6-4.** Grid App template pages*

Every one of the three XAML pages has a distinct purpose in the hub-and-spoke model. Let's inspect them.

- *GroupedItemsPage.xaml/cs*: This is the home page, which shows a collection of grouped items in a `GridView`. It supports panning around for discoverability and should support Semantic Zoom awaiting your implementation.
- *GroupDetailPage.xaml/cs*: This is the Group Details page, which shows a little more information on the grouping mechanism used to sort the collection of items. You get to this page by tapping/clicking the group headers in the `GroupedItemsPage`. Along with the group details, items belonging to the group are also highlighted.
- *ItemDetailPage.xaml/cs*: This is the page that shows details about individual selected items in the collection. You get to this page by tapping/clicking individual items listed in the `GroupedItemsPage` or the `GroupDetailsPage`. Once on a selected item, this page hosts the entire collection of items in the associated group in a `FlipView`, thus allowing the user to easily flip through the items in the given group.

Once Visual Studio loads up the entire solution, press F5 (without changing anything) to run the template project. Things are wired with sample data among the three views, and you can try out the navigation among the pages. From the home page, tap/click the group headers to go the Group Details page. From either page, tap/click individual items to navigate to the Item Details page. Notice the Back buttons in the page headers and how they return you to the home page.

Are you a little confused but you want to use this pattern in your Windows 8 Store app? Would you like to see the inner workings of this template solution? Well, worry no more because you are about to build a custom solution that is heavily inspired by the template, but describes how the inner workings are wired for navigation and data-handling needs.

A Real-World Hub-and-Spoke Solution

Do you remember the Apress Featured Books Demo app that you were building? You had pretty much set up the initial home/splash page, which listed all the featured Apress books, grouped by area of technology. You also added Semantic Zoom support to provide easy discoverability. Figure 6-5 shows what the app home page looks like as of now.

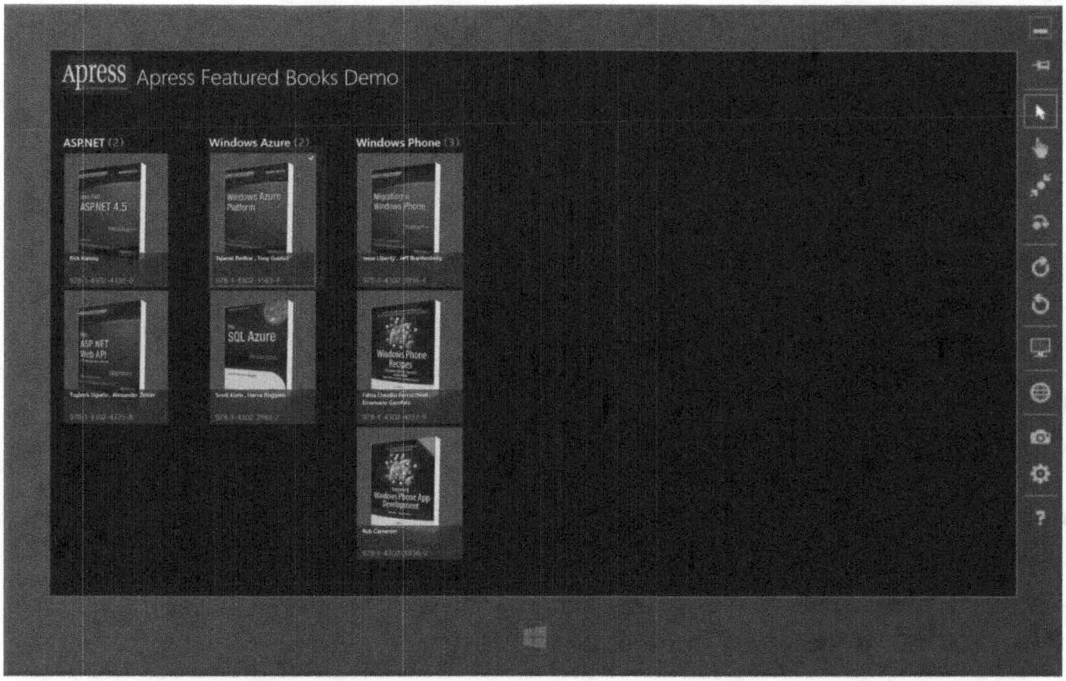

***Figure 6-5.** Home page of Apress demo app*

Now you want to add support for hub-and-spoke model of navigation so that the user may inspect either a technology group or an individual book a little more closely. Accordingly, add the following pages in the `Views` folder, if you are following along in code.

- *FeaturedBooklist.xaml/cs*: This is what already exists as the home page.
- *BookGroupsByTechnology.xaml/cs*: This shows the details of each technology group along with the books that fall in the given technology category.
- *BookDetails.xaml/cs*: This is the page that shows details of a selected Apress book and allows the user to easily flip through other books in the same technology group.

As a little shortcut for demonstration purposes, reuse the same `ViewModel` that you utilized in the FeaturedBookList page for the two new pages (or you can absolutely roll your own). The point is that whatever your `ViewModel` structure, you can choose to have grouped item collection data available globally for easy binding in the two new pages. In your case, your `App.xaml.cs` already held a `FeaturedBookListVM` property exposing the entire `FeaturedApressBookListViewModel` used in the home page UI. The `FeaturedApressBookListViewModel`, in turn, held two collections, as defined here:

```
public ObservableCollection<ApressBook> FeaturedApressBooks { get; set; }

  public ObservableCollection<GroupedApressBooks> GroupedFeaturedApressBooks
  {
      get
      {
          if (_groupedFeaturedApressBooks == null)
              _groupedFeaturedApressBooks = new ObservableCollection<GroupedApressBooks>();
```

```
            // Put Books into Grouped buckets based on Technology.
            var query = from individualApressBook in FeaturedApressBooks
                        orderby individualApressBook.ApressBookTechnology
                        group individualApressBook by individualApressBook.ApressBookTechnology into g
                        select new GroupedApressBooks
                        {
                            ApressBookGroupName = g.Key,
                            ApressBookGroupCount = g.Count(),
                            BookCollection = new ObservableCollection<ApressBook>(g.ToList())
                        };

            _groupedFeaturedApressBooks = new ObservableCollection<GroupedApressBooks>(query.ToList());

            return _groupedFeaturedApressBooks;
        }
        set
        {
            _groupedFeaturedApressBooks = value;
        }

    }
```

Essentially, you have two collections: one simply features the Apress books and the other organizes the books into logical buckets/groups based on technology. The book collection is something you filled with dummy data. This is the sort of collection you want to build from a database or network service call per the business data requirements in your app. And both the `FeaturedApressBooks` and `GroupedFeaturedApressBooks` collections implement the INPC pattern through the use of `ObservableCollection<T>` collection sets—so they are all set for UI data binding.

Setting Up the Spoke Pages

Now that you have your data globally accessible, set up your child pages for the hub-and-spoke navigation model. Take a close look at the home page, as shown in Figures 6-6 and 6-7.

__Figure 6-6.__ Apress demo app showing grouped collections of books, view 1

__Figure 6-7.__ Apress demo app showing grouped collections of books, view 2

It is completely logical that the user might want to know a little bit more about each technology group by clicking/tapping group headers like Windows Azure, Windows Phone, and so forth. So set up a click/tap event handler in the FeaturedBookList.xaml page to handle the navigation to the Group Details page, like so:

```
<GroupStyle.HeaderTemplate>
    <DataTemplate>
        <Grid Margin="1,0,0,6">
            <StackPanel Orientation="Horizontal">
                <Button AutomationProperties.Name="Group Title"
                Content="{Binding ApressBookGroupName}" Style="{StaticResource ApressTextButtonStyle}"
                VerticalAlignment="Center" Click="GroupHeader_Clicked"/>
                <TextBlock Text="(" Style="{StaticResource SubheaderTextStyle}"
                VerticalAlignment="Top" Margin="10,0,5,0"/>
                <TextBlock Text="{Binding ApressBookGroupCount}" Style="{StaticResource
                SubheaderTextStyle}" VerticalAlignment="Top"/>
                <TextBlock Text=")" Style="{StaticResource SubheaderTextStyle}"
                VerticalAlignment="Top" Margin="5,0,5,0"/>
            </StackPanel>
        </Grid>
    </DataTemplate>
</GroupStyle.HeaderTemplate>
```

As you can see, you went into the GroupStyle.HeaderTemplate of the GridView displaying the grouped collection of books and wired up an event handler when the user taps the group header. Here's the code-behind event handler:

```
private void GroupHeader_Clicked(object sender, RoutedEventArgs e)
    {
        // Figure out which Book Group header the user clicked on.
        var bookGroup = (sender as FrameworkElement).DataContext;

        // Navigate to Group Details page and carry along selected Group name.
        this.Frame.Navigate(typeof(BookGroupsByTechnology), ((GroupedApressBooks)bookGroup).
        ApressBookGroupName);
    }
```

You'll notice that you are simply falling back on the UI binding's DataContext to realize which group header the user tapped/clicked. Next, you cast in back to your GroupedApressBooks object and navigate to the Group Details page, carrying along the name of the selected group. Notice how you send over data to another page during navigation to provide the new page with the context of what the user has been up to. Remember, you can send along any objects you want as a parameter to page navigation.

Grouping in the Group Details Page

Now let's set up the Group Details page. Right-click the Views folder to add a new item, as shown in Figure 6-8.

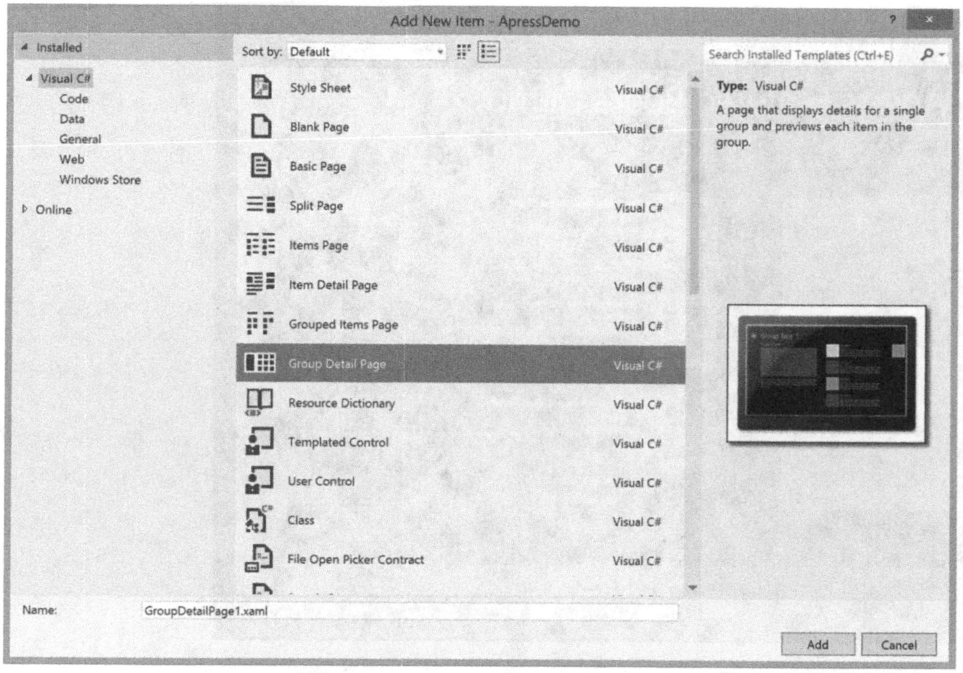

***Figure 6-8.** Group Detail View template*

For the Group Details page, let's say that you want a UI like the ones shown in Figures 6-9 and 6-10.

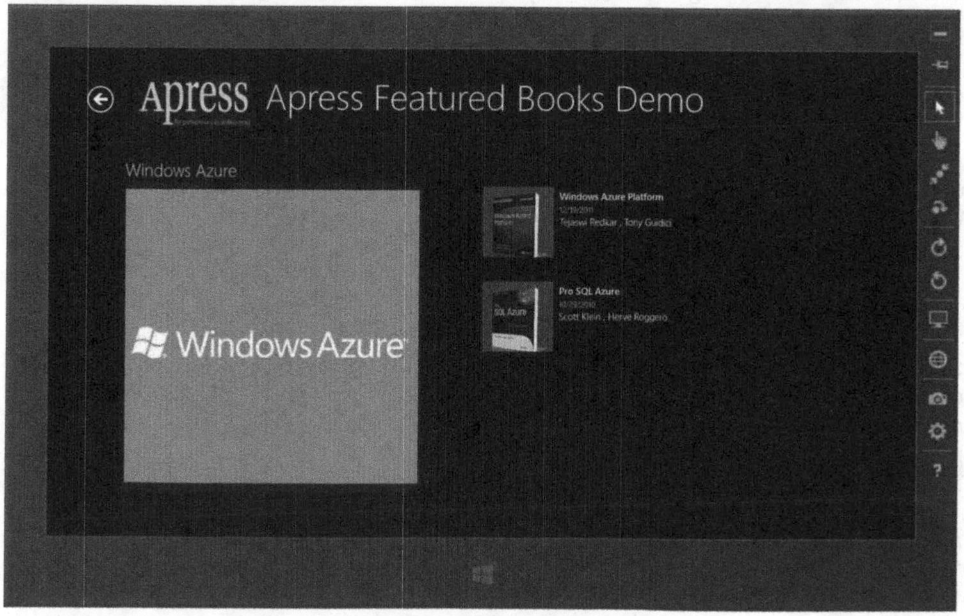

***Figure 6-9.** Apress demo app showing the Group Details page, view 1*

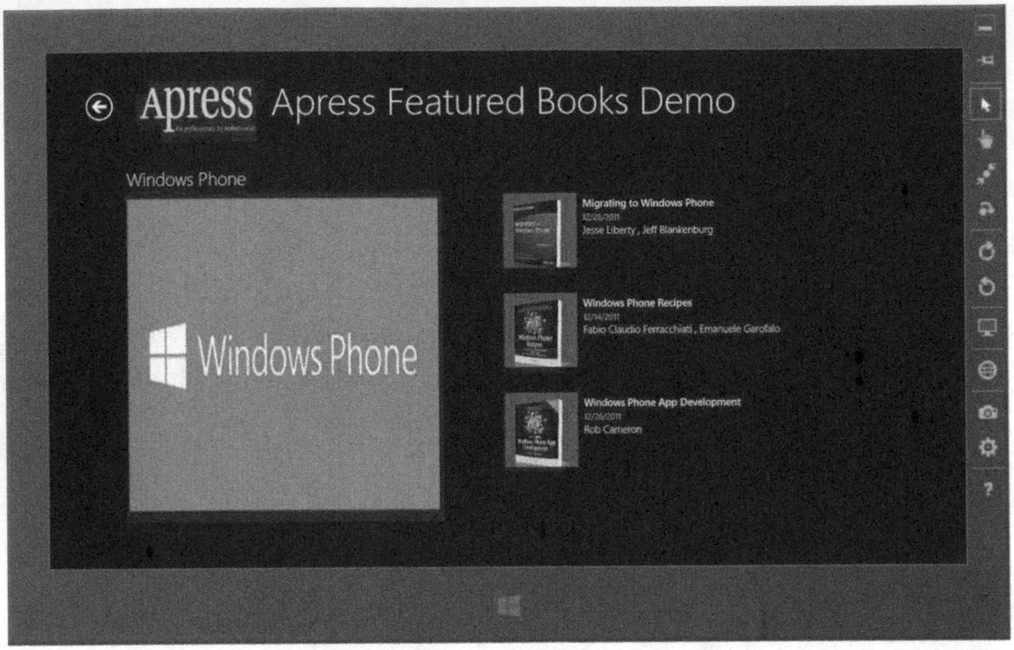

Figure 6-10. *Apress demo app showing the Group Details page, view 2*

This sort of UI makes sense in the Group Details page because you are highlighting the group that has been selected, as well as showing the child book items that belong in the chosen group. This UI is actually taken right from what the template XAML offered—with a few tweaks. So, let's dive into how you got this to work. If you avoid the boilerplate code and some of the `VisualStateManager` stuff (you'll get into this in the next chapter), the XAML code in the `BookGroupsByTechnology.xaml` page is shown in Listing 6-1.

Listing 6-1. XAML Code in the BookGroupsByTechnology.xaml Page

```
<Page.Resources>

    <CollectionViewSource
        x:Name="itemsViewSource"
        Source="{Binding BookItems}"/>

</Page.Resources>

<Grid DataContext="{Binding BookGroup}" Style="{StaticResource LayoutRootStyle}" Background="Black">
    <Grid.RowDefinitions>
        <RowDefinition Height="140"/>
        <RowDefinition Height="*"/>
    </Grid.RowDefinitions>

    <!-- Back button and page title -->
    <Grid Grid.Row="0">
    <StackPanel Orientation="Horizontal" Margin="20,10,0,0">
            <Button x:Name="backButton" Click="GoBack" IsEnabled="{Binding Frame.CanGoBack,
            ElementName=pageRoot}" Style="{StaticResource BackButtonStyle}"/>
```

```
            <Image Source="/Assets/ApressLogo.png" Width="200" Height="100"
            VerticalAlignment="Center" Margin="-10,20,0,0"/>
            <TextBlock x:Name="pageTitle" Text="{StaticResource AppName}" Style="{StaticResource
            PageHeaderTextStyle}" VerticalAlignment="Center" Margin="10,10,0,10"/>
        </StackPanel>
    </Grid>

    <GridView
        x:Name="itemGridView"
        AutomationProperties.AutomationId="ItemGridView"
        AutomationProperties.Name="Items In Group"
        TabIndex="1"
        Grid.RowSpan="2"
        Grid.Row="1"
        Padding="120,60,120,50"
        ItemsSource="{Binding Source={StaticResource itemsViewSource}}"
        ItemTemplate="{StaticResource Apress500x130ItemTemplate}"
        SelectionMode="None"
        IsSwipeEnabled="false"
        IsItemClickEnabled="True"
        ItemClick="bookItem_Click">

        <GridView.Header>
            <StackPanel Width="480" Margin="0,-30,14,0">
                <TextBlock Text="{Binding ApressBookGroupName}" Margin="0,0,18,20"
                Style="{StaticResource SubheaderTextStyle}" MaxHeight="60"/>
                <Image Source="{Binding ImageURI}" Margin="0,0,18,20" Stretch="UniformToFill" />
            </StackPanel>
        </GridView.Header>
        <GridView.ItemContainerStyle>
            <Style TargetType="FrameworkElement">
                <Setter Property="Margin" Value="52,0,0,10"/>
            </Style>
        </GridView.ItemContainerStyle>
    </GridView>
```

There are a few interesting pieces in Listing 6-1. First, you are using a Grid as the primary container in the page and it splits the contents into two: a top header with a Back button and the rest of the page. Did you notice the Back button in the header section? It is conveniently using a little framework instrumentation so that you don't have to write any code to make the back navigation work. First, the button is enabled based on the frame's CanGoBack property, which tells us whether the frame has entries in its navigation backstack to allow back navigation. If the frame can go back, you simply fall back on the LayoutAwarePage's GoBack functionality to navigate backward—no code whatsoever to add in the code-behind.

Next, you are using a GridView to display your group information and book collections inside each group. You'll notice that the GridView is actually using the CollectionViewSource as its source data. The CollectionViewSource is already wired up to your chosen group and the book collections in it. Here's some code from the code-behind:

```
protected override void LoadState(Object navigationParameter, Dictionary<String, Object> pageState)
    {
        // Get the selected Book Group from Navigation parameter and data bind.
        GroupedApressBooks selectedGroup =
        (GroupedApressBooks)((App)Application.Current).FeaturedBookListVM.
        GroupedFeaturedApressBooks.
```

```
First(X => X.ApressBookGroupName == navigationParameter);
            this.DefaultViewModel["BookGroup"] = selectedGroup;
            this.DefaultViewModel["BookItems"] = selectedGroup.BookCollection;
        }
```

Let's unwrap what you are doing here. First, you did an override on the `LoadState` event so that you could add your custom code. This is commonly the method that you want to use as you are hydrating a `View` with data. Next, you read the `navigationParameter` object, which is the exact same parameter that you added onto your navigation mechanism in this page. If you remember, you sent along the selected group's name as the navigation parameter—it is the same value available in this method. You should stop here and debug to verify if this is true.

If everything worked as desired, in your `LoadState` method, you have access to the selected group that the user clicked/tapped. You want to load your UI in that context. However, the new BookGroupsByTechnology page has no other information. In the preceding code, you use a little bit of LINQ to pluck out the matching group from the global collection of book groups. That's it. You now have pertinent data to bind to your UI. The next step is simply to pass along this data to the `DefaultViewModel`, which, as you have seen in the past, is already wired up for use in your XAML. You simply hand over the selected book group and its associated child collection to the `DefaultViewModel` with named keys. This is exactly the glue that allows you to do UI binding in the `CollectionViewSource` and the `Grid` used in your Group Details page.

Items in the Group Details Page

With the steps from the previous section, your page should now light up to show the book group name and its image. But what about the individual books in the group's collection? Notice the `ItemTemplate` usage in the `GridView`. Yes, that's what shows the list of books. Here's the definition of the `ItemTemplate` in the `StandardStyles.xaml` file:

```
<DataTemplate x:Key="Apress500x130ItemTemplate">
    <Grid Height="110" Width="480" Margin="10">
        <Grid.ColumnDefinitions>
            <ColumnDefinition Width="Auto"/>
            <ColumnDefinition Width="*"/>
        </Grid.ColumnDefinitions>
        <Border Background="{StaticResource ListViewItemPlaceholderBackgroundThemeBrush}"
Width="110" Height="110">
            <Image Source="{Binding ApressBookImageURI}" Stretch="UniformToFill"/>
        </Border>
        <StackPanel Grid.Column="1" VerticalAlignment="Top" Margin="10,0,0,0">
            <TextBlock Text="{Binding ApressBookName}" Style="{StaticResource
TitleTextStyle}" TextWrapping="NoWrap"/>
            <TextBlock Text="{Binding DisplayablePublishDate}" Style="{StaticResource
CaptionTextStyle}" TextWrapping="NoWrap"/>
            <TextBlock Text="{Binding ApressBookAuthor}" Style="{StaticResource
BodyTextStyle}" MaxHeight="60"/>
        </StackPanel>
    </Grid>
</DataTemplate>
```

Now you see exactly how you display the book's image and other details. Adding a Group Details page was relatively easy, wasn't it? With a little effort, you are offering the user a nice UX to dig into the collection of items displayed on the home page.

So at this point, you have a home page displaying a grouped collection of books and a Group Details page allowing the user to drill down into each group. What's common between the two pages? Yep, the list of book items. What if the user finds something interesting and actually wants to learn more about a selected book? Now you see the need for having an Item Details page. In line with the Modern UI design principles, you do not want any extra buttons that allow navigating to the Item Details page; the content is the navigation. So, add support to the FeaturedBookList and BookGroupsByTechnology pages so that the user can directly tap/click an individual book item and navigate to the Item Details page.

Here's some XAML code displaying the collection of books, which should be common to both pages and their respective GridViews:

```
<GridView
    x:Name="itemGridView"
    AutomationProperties.AutomationId="ItemGridView"
    AutomationProperties.Name="Grouped Items"
    Margin="30,80,40,46"
    VerticalAlignment="Center"
    ItemsSource="{Binding Source={StaticResource groupedItemsViewSource}}"
    ItemTemplate="{StaticResource Apress277x350BookTemplate}"
    SelectionMode="None"
    IsSwipeEnabled="false"
    IsItemClickEnabled="True"
    ItemClick="bookItem_Click">
....
...
</GridView>
```

The interesting lines of code are the last few declarations in the GridView setup. You are essentially setting SelectionMode to None. This removes the default at-least-one-selected-item check box from your display of the book collection. Next, instead of trying to see where the user tapped the screen, you simply leave it to the GridView to tell us when an associated child item is clicked/tapped. Accordingly, you add an ItemClick event handler after enabling item clicking. Here's the event handler from the code-behind:

```
private void bookItem_Click(object sender, ItemClickEventArgs e)
   {
       // Figure out which Book item the user clicked on.
       var bookItem = e.ClickedItem;

       // Navigate to Book Details page and carry along selected Book's ISBN identifier.
       this.Frame.Navigate(typeof(BookDetails), ((ApressBook)bookItem).ApressBookISBN);
   }
```

You'll notice how you allow the ItemClickEventArgs to determine which book item the user clicked/tapped. Once you have this information, you cast the selection back to an ApressBook object and send along the book's ISBN number to the Book Details page being navigated to. The point is that you can carry along any parameter that helps your new page uniquely figure out the context behind the navigation. And hopefully, you are also seeing a pattern in how to transfer the user to a different page while carrying along the navigation parameter. This is the technique that you'll use for page navigation.

Setting Up the Item Details Page

Next, set up the Item Details page. There is help in adding some boilerplate code and the standard look and feel of a Details page. Right-click your Views folder and add a template view (see Figure 6-11).

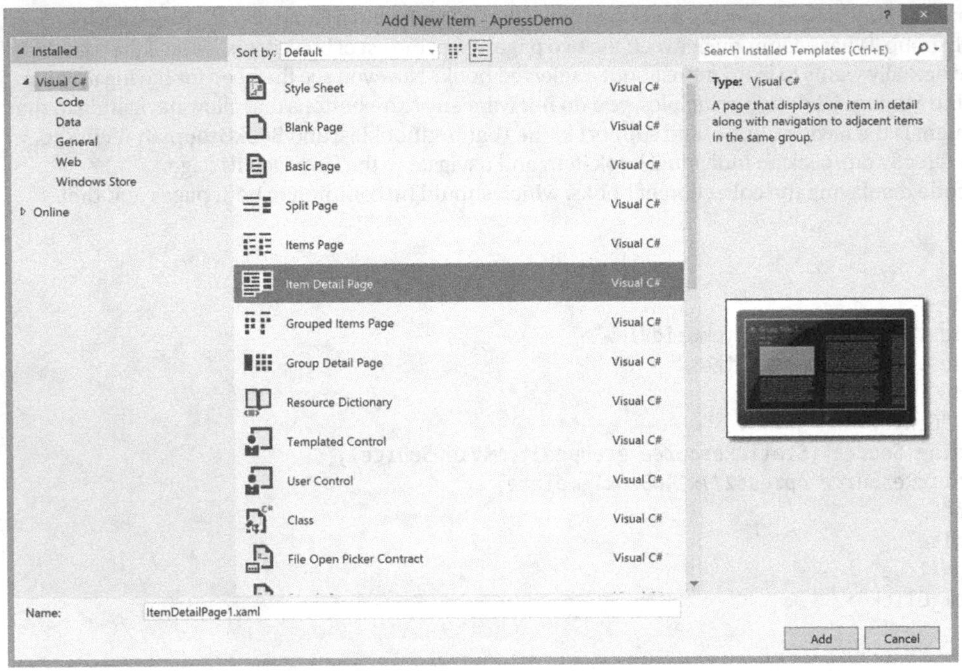

Figure 6-11. *Item Detail template*

Once added, you will start tweaking the XAML and code-behind code to make it work toward your goal. The sort of UI you're striving for is shown in Figures 6-12 and 6-13.

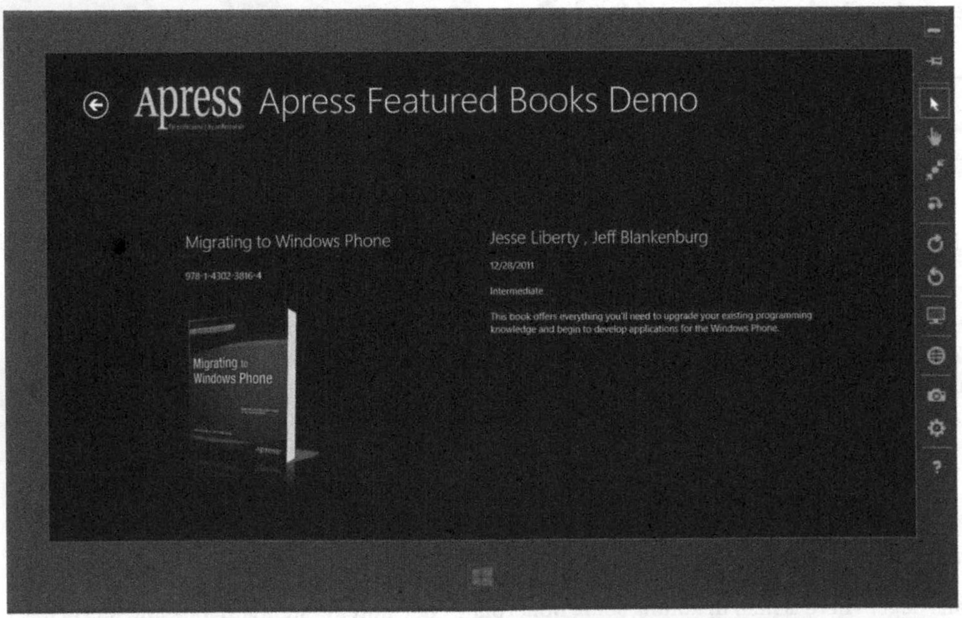

Figure 6-12. *Apress demo app showing Item Details page, view 1*

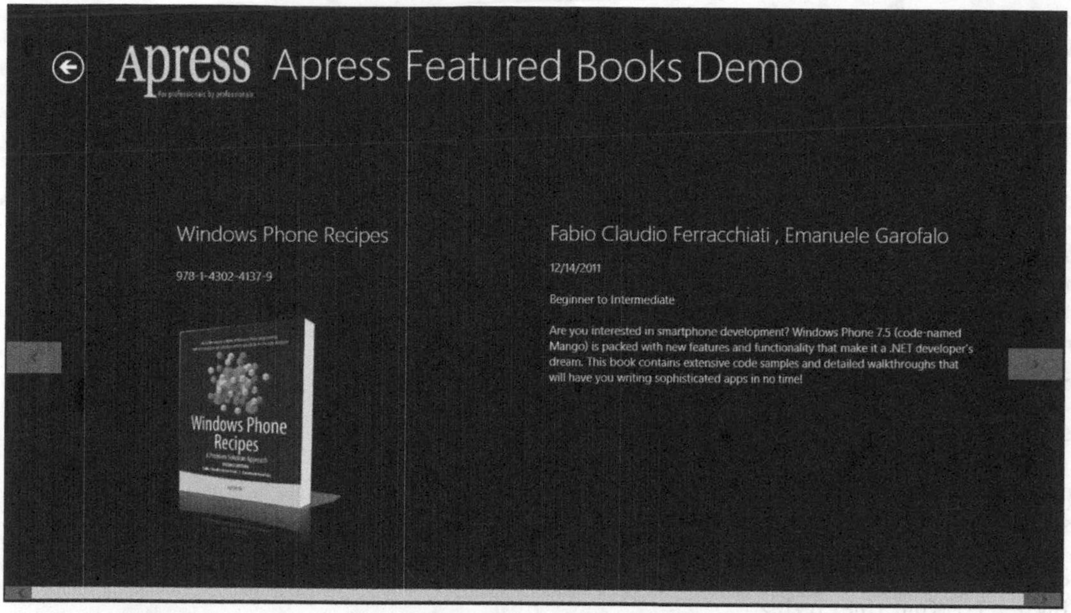

Figure 6-13. *Apress demo app showing Item Details page, view 2*

You'll notice that the Book Details page nicely shows the details of a single book. The point is to fill up this page with all the pertinent details about each individual item. Not just that, the Details page actually lists its contents within a `FlipView` for easy flipping through books that fall in the same technology group. The expectation is that if the user has drilled down to see details of a certain book or item, he or she may also be interested in the other offerings within the same group. Why have the user step back out to select another book? You can allow easy discoverability within the Details page itself.

Listing 6-2 is the markup you add in the XAML Details page.

Listing 6-2. XAML in the Item Details Page

```
<Page.Resources>

    <CollectionViewSource
        x:Name="itemsViewSource"
        Source="{Binding BookItems}"/>

</Page.Resources>

<Grid Style="{StaticResource LayoutRootStyle}" Background="Black">
    <Grid.RowDefinitions>
        <RowDefinition Height="140"/>
        <RowDefinition Height="*"/>
    </Grid.RowDefinitions>

    <!-- Back button and page title -->
    <Grid Grid.Row="0">
        <StackPanel Orientation="Horizontal" Margin="20,10,0,0">
            <Button x:Name="backButton" Click="GoBack" IsEnabled="{Binding Frame.CanGoBack,
            ElementName=pageRoot}" Style="{StaticResource BackButtonStyle}"/>
```

```
            <Image Source="/Assets/ApressLogo.png" Width="200" Height="100"
            VerticalAlignment="Center" Margin="-10,20,0,0"/>
            <TextBlock x:Name="pageTitle" Text="{StaticResource AppName}" Style=
            "{StaticResource PageHeaderTextStyle}" VerticalAlignment="Center" Margin="10,10,0,10"/>
        </StackPanel>
    </Grid>

    <FlipView
        x:Name="flipView"
        AutomationProperties.AutomationId="ItemsFlipView"
        AutomationProperties.Name="Item Details"
        TabIndex="1"
        Grid.Row="1"
        Grid.RowSpan="2"
        ItemsSource="{Binding Source={StaticResource itemsViewSource}}">

        <FlipView.ItemContainerStyle>
            <Style TargetType="FlipViewItem">
                <Setter Property="Margin" Value="0,137,0,0"/>
            </Style>
        </FlipView.ItemContainerStyle>

        <FlipView.ItemTemplate>
            <DataTemplate>

                <UserControl Loaded="StartLayoutUpdates" Unloaded="StopLayoutUpdates">
                    <ScrollViewer x:Name="scrollViewer" Style="{StaticResource
                    HorizontalScrollViewerStyle}" Grid.Row="1">

                        <!-- Content is allowed to flow across as many columns as needed -->
                        <common:RichTextColumns x:Name="richTextColumns" Margin="117,0,117,47">
                            <RichTextBlock x:Name="richTextBlock" Width="500" Style="{StaticResource
                            ItemRichTextStyle}" IsTextSelectionEnabled="False">
                                <Paragraph Margin="100,100,10,0" LineHeight="25">
                                    <Run FontSize="26.667" FontWeight="Light" Text="{Binding
                                    ApressBookName}"/>
                                    <LineBreak/>
                                    <LineBreak/>
                                    <Run FontWeight="Normal" Text="{Binding ApressBookISBN}"/>
                                </Paragraph>
                                <Paragraph LineStackingStrategy="MaxHeight">
                                    <InlineUIContainer>
                                        <Image x:Name="image" Margin="70,20,0,10" Stretch="Uniform"
                                        Source="{Binding ApressBookImageURI}"
                                        AutomationProperties.Name="{Binding Title}"/>
                                    </InlineUIContainer>
                                </Paragraph>
                                <Paragraph Margin="0,100,10,0">
                                    <Run FontSize="26.667" FontWeight="Light" Text="{Binding
                                    ApressBookAuthor}"/>
```

```
                            <LineBreak/>
                            <LineBreak/>
                            <Run FontWeight="Normal" Text="{Binding DisplayablePublishDate}"/>
                            <LineBreak/>
                            <LineBreak/>
                            <Run FontWeight="Normal" Text="{Binding ApressBookUserLevel}"/>
                            <LineBreak/>
                            <LineBreak/>
                            <Run FontWeight="Normal" Text="{Binding ApressBookDescription}"/>
                        </Paragraph>
                    </RichTextBlock>
                    <!-- Additional columns are created from this template -->
                    <common:RichTextColumns.ColumnTemplate>
                    <DataTemplate>
                            <RichTextBlockOverflow Width="560" Margin="80,0,0,0">
                                <RichTextBlockOverflow.RenderTransform>
                                    <TranslateTransform X="-1" Y="4"/>
                                </RichTextBlockOverflow.RenderTransform>
                            </RichTextBlockOverflow>
                        </DataTemplate>
                    </common:RichTextColumns.ColumnTemplate>
                </common:RichTextColumns>
            </ScrollViewer>
        </UserControl>
    </DataTemplate>
  </FlipView.ItemTemplate>
</FlipView>
```

Showing Details in Item Details Page

A lot of the code in Listing 6-2 should look familiar. The way you wire up your Back button in the page header defaults back to the standard way of using the frame's navigation features. You also use a `FlipView` control to house all of your content. This has the unique advantage of showing the details about a selected item with full real-estate usage, but also providing little left/right buttons on either end that allow easy flick/swipe navigation to the other items in the selected group. As you have seen in the past, the `FlipView` is smart enough not to show the left arrow on the first item in the collection or the right arrow on the last item. For anything between, the `FlipView` shows both buttons and leads to a very pleasant UX. Now, for the `FlipView`'s `DataTemplate`, you're using a `UserControl` with `RichTextColumns`. This is simply because the Visual Studio template starts out using such a `UserControl` within the `FlipView` and it is easy to change the binding to display the details about your selected book. You are absolutely free to roll in any UI inside the repeatable `DataTemplate` of the `FlipView` control.

You may be wondering how the `FlipView` knows which book to show details for or how it gets the context of the overall technology group that the selected book belongs to. Good questions. Let's dig into some code. You again use the `CollectionViewSource` for data binding your UI to a grouped collection. Where is this wiring happening? Well, check out this little piece of code in the code-behind file:

```
protected override void LoadState(Object navigationParameter, Dictionary<String, Object> pageState)
        {
            // Get the selected Book Item from Navigation parameter.
            ApressBook selectedBook = (ApressBook)((App)Application.Current).FeaturedBookListVM.
            FeaturedApressBooks.First(X => X.ApressBookISBN == navigationParameter);
```

```
        // Also fetch the corresponding Technology Group.
        GroupedApressBooks selectedGroup = (GroupedApressBooks)((App)Application.Current).
        FeaturedBookListVM.GroupedFeaturedApressBooks.First(X => X.ApressBookGroupName ==
        selectedBook.ApressBookTechnology);

        this.DefaultViewModel["BookGroup"] = selectedGroup;
        this.DefaultViewModel["BookItems"] = selectedGroup.BookCollection;
        this.flipView.SelectedItem = selectedBook;
    }
```

So, you are again overriding the `LoadState` method to provide data for your UI bindings. Here, you essentially read the `navigationParameter` being sent down, which if you remember from your click event handler, is the book's ISBN identifier. Look inside your global collection of books and use LINQ to pluck out the exact book that the user had clicked/tapped to select. This context is good for the detailed view of the selected book, but too narrow for the `FlipView` to work correctly. Although you do need the details about the selected book, you also need the context of the technology group that this selected book is a part of. This helps in UI binding and flipping through other books in the group. Accordingly, you retrieve the appropriate group from the global collection using a match on the selected book's group name. Once you have the book and its group, data binding works like magic with the hydration of the `DefaultViewModel`. Did you notice how you told the `FlipView` control the exact book to start out as the selected item? Yep, it's that easy.

Summary

Now you know how to get a real-world example app to implement the three-level hub-and-spoke information architecture. This allows for a pleasant navigation user experience by simply using the content, and it offers the user easy discoverability. The point is to avoid clutter and prevent overcrowding of information in individual XAML pages. Consider breaking up your object model into discrete pieces and allow each XAML page to fulfill one purpose. Are you coding yet?

PART 3

Into the Groove

You had a vision and you are now on your way toward that awesome, dream Windows 8 Store app. Chapters 7-10 get you into the groove toward making your Windows 8 app a reality.

How do you manage the all-important data in your app? What data strategy should be in place? How should you "play nice" as your app goes through its life cycle? What about integrating with the Windows 8 OS through contracts so that your app feels at home and natural to the user?

All this and more are discussed in the next few chapters on making your app Windows 8 Store-ready.

Hang tight and read well, my friends!

CHAPTER 7

Orientation and View States

Developing applications for tablet form factors is largely considered part of the "mobile" app development family. Ever wonder why? Tablets are lightweight computing form factors that people can carry around, and they also pack a lot more sensors than traditional desktops and laptops. Accordingly, in order to provide the best possible user experience, apps meant for tablets need to be much more responsive to possible changes in visual states and rotational orientations. This is very true for Windows 8 Store apps that run on tablet-like PCs. In fact, such support is required for apps that go live in the Windows Store. How does your app respond as the user flips his or her tablet? Can two apps run side by side? What is the state of each? All this and more are coming up in this chapter—with succinct sample code to show you how to get the job done in your Windows 8 Store app.

Device Orientation

Any time you consider writing software that runs on small mobile devices like smartphones or tablets, device orientation should be taken into consideration for the optimum user experience. What is meant by "orientation"? Quite simply, the way the device is oriented in space—or in other words, the way that the user is holding the device for usage. Does the device have marked top/bottom or left/right edges? What happens when the default orientation changes?

These orientation considerations are very important when we developers make Windows 8 apps meant for the tablet form factor. Sure, our apps can be used on a desktop or laptop that traditionally sits one way; but the same apps will be available on thin and light tablet devices that offer a much more mobile lifestyle. Accordingly, the user will be on the move with such devices and your Windows 8 app will be subject to orientation changes. Let's see what your Windows 8 app can do to respond.

First, consider the Windows 8 tablet form factor, starting with the stock photo of the Surface tablet, as shown in Figure 7-1.

Figure 7-1. A Windows 8 tablet showing the Windows button

As you can see, like most other Windows 8 tablet devices, the Surface has a Windows button that always takes the user back to the Windows 8 Start screen. This Windows button could be capacitive touch, as it is on the Surface, or it could be a hardware button; either way, the Windows button is always at the bottom of the tablet. This gives a device orientation starting point with respect to the one button. As you can intuitively guess, there are four possible rotational orientations on every Windows 8 tablet:

- *Landscape*: The default mode. The Windows button is at the bottom (see Figure 7-1). It is the most common way that users hold their tablets in their hands or dock it on a kickstand.
- *Portrait*: The mode when the tablet is flipped 90 degrees to the left and the Windows button is on the left vertical edge.
- *Landscape, flipped*: The mode when the tablet is flipped 180 degrees on its head and the Windows button is on the top.
- *Portrait, flipped*: The mode when the tablet is flipped 90 degrees to the right and the Windows button is on the right vertical edge.

When users run your app on their Windows 8 tablets, there is nothing stopping them from making any of these orientation changes. Windows 8 has a software lock to prevent screen orientations when the devices are flipped, and some tablets also have a hardware lock to prevent unintentional orientation changes, but the user can turn these off.

Responses to Orientation Changes

When the user flips his/her tablet, causing an orientation change, what does your Windows 8 Store app do? Well, there are two possible responses:

- Your Windows 8 app supports one or more default orientations and it does nothing on change of orientation. This sounds awkward, but it is actually a feasible solution given your use case. If you feel that your app's content is particularly suited to a certain orientation, you can stick to it and ignore that the user flipped her tablet. The content does not flip—it stays the way it started out. The user will realize the supported orientation(s) and flip the tablet back to the default orientations.

- Or, your app can listen to the orientation changes and actually respond by adjusting content to the user flipping the tablet. In this case, the content orients itself to the rotation and realigns direction or gets redrawn based on device orientation.

Let's see how you might support both of these scenarios. If you want to follow along, return to the Apress Featured Books Demo app that you have been building, or you may use any new Windows 8 app based on Visual Studio templates. Figure 7-2 shows where you stopped in your home/dashboard page in the Apress demo app with a grouped collection of featured books.

Figure 7-2. *Apress Featured Books Demo app home screen*

As you can see, yours is the default landscape orientation. Now, try some orientation changes. If you can deploy your app to a Windows 8 tablet device and do not have software/hardware locks to prevent orientation changes, flip the tablet so that the Windows button is on various edges of the tablet. Alternatively, you may use the Windows 8 Simulator to test your app's orientation support. The simulator is a great way to test Windows 8 apps, as you have seen in the past. The Windows 8 Simulator is not a stand-alone virtual machine that has a configuration completely different from the host machine. However, the simulator really shines in testing support for multitouch, checking out app visuals across a variety of resolutions, and responding to device orientation changes. So, try some device orientations on the simulator. Use the left/right rotation buttons on the right-hand control panel to start rotating the device. Figures 7-3, 7-4, and 7-5 show the Apress Featured Books Demo app in various screen orientations.

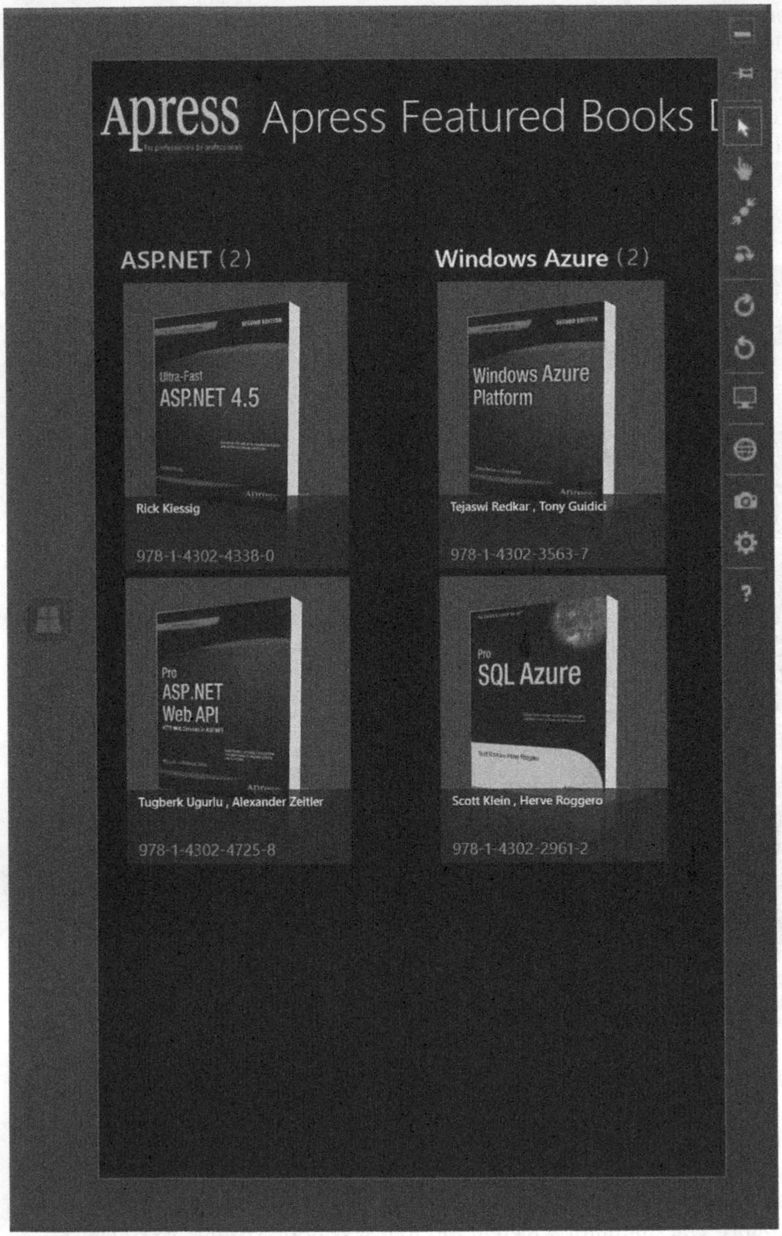

Figure 7-3. Apress demo app in portrait mode

***Figure 7-4.** Apress demo app in landscape-flipped mode*

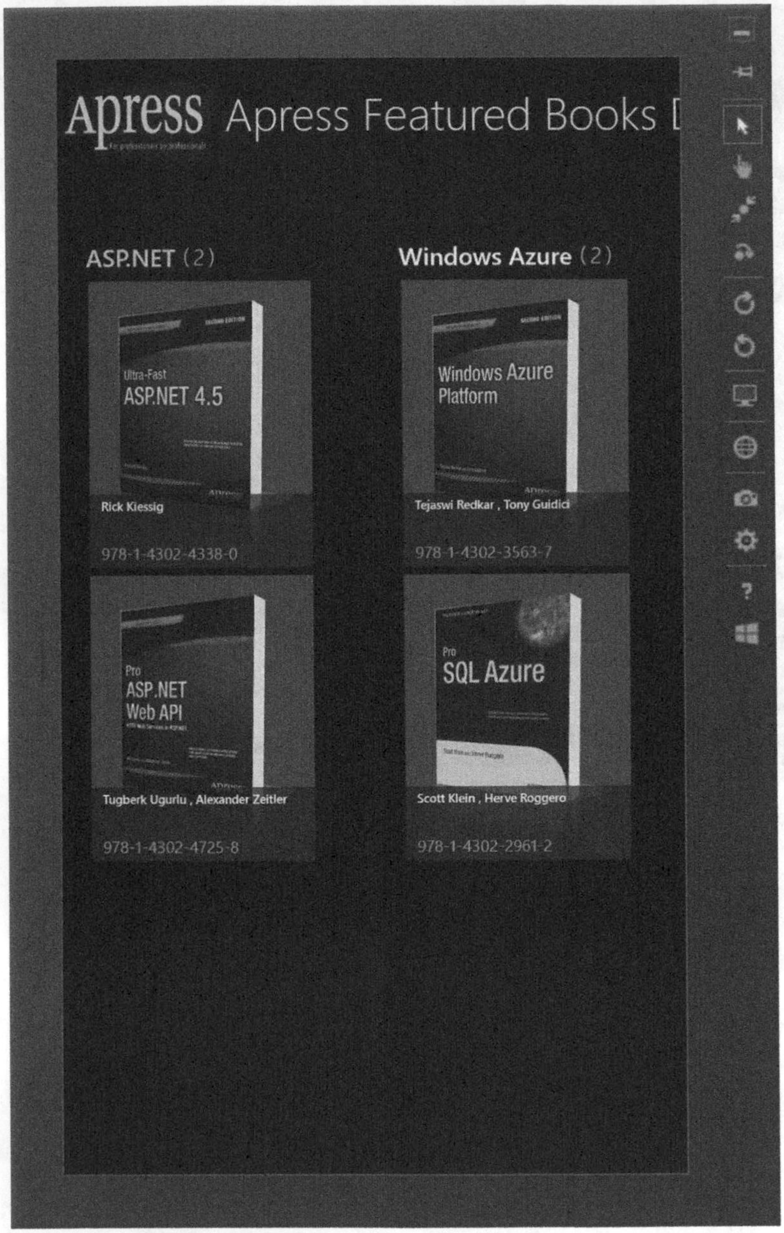

Figure 7-5. *Apress demo app in portrait-flipped mode*

As you can see, the content in your app rotates and gets redrawn as the device orientation changes. How is this happening when you have not taken any explicit action toward supporting orientation? Let's unpack.

Orientation Through Configuration

Remember the `Package.appxmanifest` XML configuration file for your project? Yes, that is the file that holds the key to declaring supported orientations. Double-click to open the file in the Visual Studio designer editor. You should see a section like the one shown in Figure 7-6.

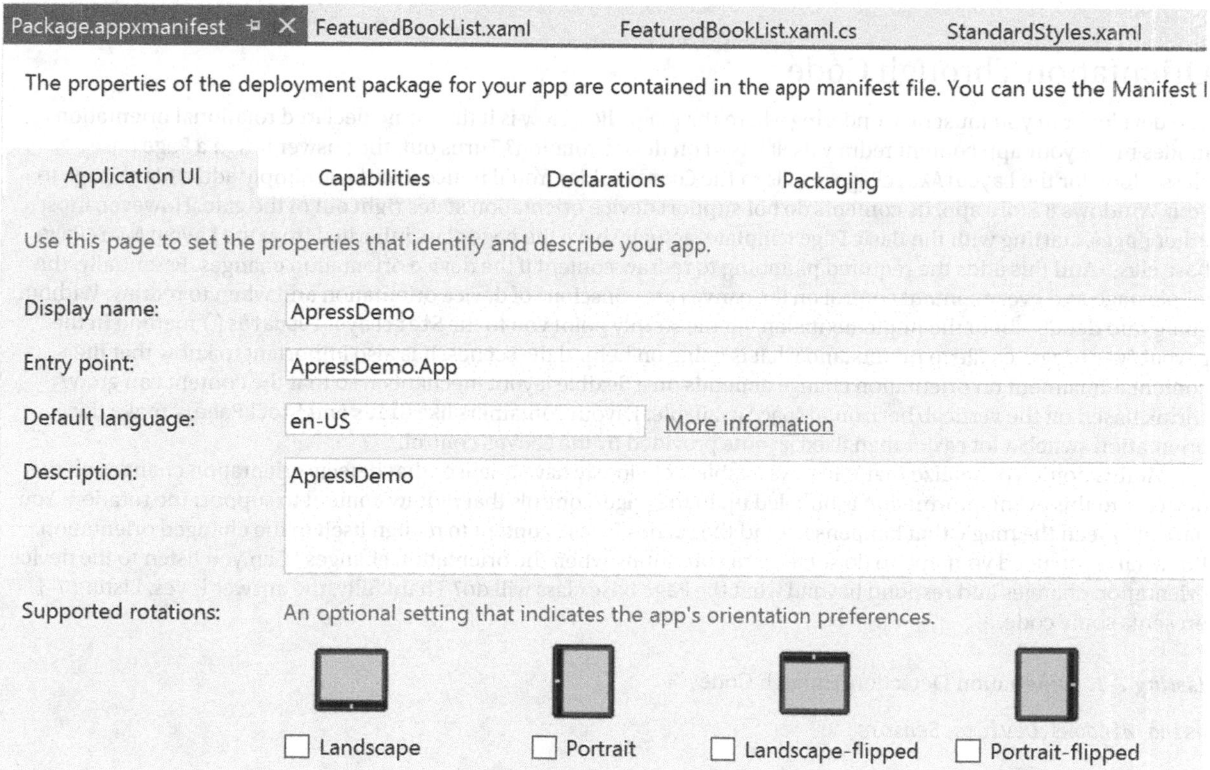

Figure 7-6. *Configuring supported orientations*

The bottom of the *Application UI* tab has the declarations for the app's supported orientations. Now, here is something that may confuse you: the first time you open the `Package.appxmanifest` file, none of the supported rotations are checked, yet your app perfectly supports all orientations! Here's what's going on. All Visual Studio–templated Windows 8 Store apps start out by supporting *all* four rotational orientations. So, even without having any of the check boxes marked, your app content supports rotation due to device orientation.

Supported rotations are the app's initial preference on explicitly declared device orientations. In essence, this is an opt-out model: if nothing is checked, all device orientations are supported; if certain rotations are explicitly checked, the others are not supported. For example, if you checked all four of the check boxes shown in Figure 7-6, and then you opened the `Package.Appxmanifest` file manually to see the XML, you'd see a section like the following:

```
<InitialRotationPreference>
        <Rotation Preference="portrait" />
        <Rotation Preference="landscape" />
        <Rotation Preference="portraitFlipped" />
        <Rotation Preference="landscapeFlipped" />
      </InitialRotationPreference>
```

So, if you just want to support landscape mode, check the Landscape and Landscape-flipped check boxes; portrait orientations will not be supported. Now, there is one caveat to this initial/default rotational preference: on devices that can't be rotated, an app is shown in that device's default orientation, and the app's preferred orientation is ignored. This makes sense when someone is using a desktop monitor (with no rotational support) in portrait mode for running Windows 8, but your app only supports landscape modes. However, an app's preferred rotation orientation will be honored on devices that have the orientation sensor, but on which a rotation lock has been activated.

Orientation Through Code

The developer in you must be wondering where the magic lies. How is it that some declared rotational orientation modes make your app content redraw itself based on device rotation? Turns out, the answer lies in a `Page` base class—look for the `LayoutAwarePage.cs` file in the `Common` folder. You'll notice that if you simply add a blank page to your Windows 8 Store app, its contents do not support device orientation states right out of the gate. However, most other pages, starting with the Basic Page template, actually have the page class inherited from the `LayoutAwarePage` base class. And this adds the required plumbing to redraw content if the device orientation changes. Essentially, the whole page and every content control on the canvas are conscious of device orientation and when to redraw. Without going into details about the implementation, let me simply point you to the `StartLayoutUpdates()` method in the `LayoutAwarePage.cs` file to understand what is going on behind the scenes. It is also important to know that the content adjustment on orientation change depends on a flexible layout mechanism so that the content can grow/shrink based on the vertical/horizontal space available. Layout containers like `Grids` and `StackPanels` make this orientation switch a lot easier than fixed layouts provided by the `Canvas` control.

At this point, you realize that Windows 8 tablets obviously have a sensor that detects orientation changes on the device and this event information is bubbled up to the page/controls that redraw content to support the rotation. You have also seen the magic that happens behind the scenes for the content to realign itself to the changed orientation. But what if you need your app to do some extra computing when the orientation changes? Can you listen to the device orientation changes and respond beyond what the `Page` base class will do? Thankfully, the answer is yes. Listing 7-1 presents some code.

Listing 7-1. Orientation Detection Through Code

```
using Windows.Devices.Sensors;

namespace ApressDemo.Views
{
    public sealed partial class FeaturedBookList : ApressDemo.Common.LayoutAwarePage
    {
        #region "Members"

        private SimpleOrientationSensor _simpleorientation;

        #endregion

        #region "Constructor"

        public FeaturedBookList()
        {
            this.InitializeComponent();
            _simpleorientation = SimpleOrientationSensor.GetDefault();

            // Assign an event handler for the sensor orientation-changed event.
            // Check to make sure the sensor is available on the device first.
```

```
            if (_simpleorientation != null)
            {
                _simpleorientation.OrientationChanged += new
                TypedEventHandler<SimpleOrientationSensor,
                SimpleOrientationSensorOrientationChangedEventArgs>(OrientationChanged);
            }
        }

        #endregion

private async void OrientationChanged(object sender,
SimpleOrientationSensorOrientationChangedEventArgs args)
        {
            await Dispatcher.RunAsync(CoreDispatcherPriority.Normal, () =>
            {
                SimpleOrientation orientation = args.Orientation;
                switch (orientation)
                {
                    case SimpleOrientation.NotRotated:
                        break;
                    case SimpleOrientation.Rotated90DegreesCounterclockwise:
                        break;
                    case SimpleOrientation.Rotated180DegreesCounterclockwise:
                        break;
                    case SimpleOrientation.Rotated270DegreesCounterclockwise:
                        break;
                    case SimpleOrientation.Faceup:
                        break;
                    case SimpleOrientation.Facedown:
                        break;
                    default:
                        break;
                }
            });
        }
}
}
```

Let's dissect this code. First, you'll notice you add a reference to the `Windows.Devices.Sensors` namespace so that you may have access to the orientation sensor. `SimpleOrientationSensor` is your simple API hook into the orientation sensor used by Windows 8 devices. All you need to do is instantiate the sensor to get a handle on its event mechanism. You also double-check that your sensor was initialized properly before using it. This is an opportunity for you to recognize that the Windows 8 device does not actually support the orientation sensor, and accordingly, degrade app functionality gracefully.

Once you have access to the sensor, it is only a matter of listening in on the `OrientationChanged` event and attaching your own event handler to it. In your event handler, you should see another piece of interesting code. This will be pretty standard as you deal with other sensors in future chapters. In Windows 8 Store app development, any time you use the `Windows.*` namespace, you are actually reaching inside WinRT. And for Windows Store apps to remain fast and fluid, the UI thread cannot be locked up, even while some WinRT operation is taking slightly longer to complete. In this case, you are waiting on WinRT to have a proper handle on the `SimpleOrientationSensor` after it is initialized. Because this may be a time-consuming operation, WinRT immediately wants to return control to your code and delegate the job of initializing the orientation sensor to a non-UI thread. This technique is true for any WinRT operation that may take more than 50 milliseconds. Accordingly, you see the usage of the `Async-Await` pattern, followed by the use of a `Dispatcher` object which marshals the other thread back to the main UI thread in your app.

Once everything is in place within your event handler, you start reading the `Orientation` property off the `SimpleOrientationSensorOrientationChangedEventArgs` as the sensor raises the event in response to a device rotation. You'll notice right away that the `SimpleOrientation` enumeration values do not quite match up to the orientations you have seen in the past. No worries, they are the same—only with a mapping layer in between. Figure 7-7 shows MSDN documentation on how the four common orientations match up to the sensor outputs.

Orientation	Corresponding sensor reading
Portrait Up	NotRotated
Landscape Left	Rotated90DegreesCounterclockwise
Portrait Down	Rotated180DegreesCounterclockwise
Landscape Right	Rotated270DegreesCounterclockwise

Figure 7-7. *Mapping between orientation and sensor outputs*

That's it. You now know how to listen to the changing orientations of the user's Windows 8 device and take appropriate action with your app. Within the event handler that you wrote, you have complete access to modify anything in the app UI in response to the orientation-changed event so that your Windows 8 app supports device rotation in a way that makes sense for the given application needs.

View States

Desktop and tablet PCs are vastly different form factors. With a traditional desktop or laptop connected to multiple monitors, you are commonly working with a mouse-keyboard setup. This setup lends itself to getting work done—and you possibly have dozens of windows and browser tabs open to aid your productivity. Tablets are on the other end of the spectrum. Lightweight and portable, tablet PCs lend themselves a lot more toward on-the-go computing. Touch being the only thing needed to navigate, you are much more prone to take a tablet onto the couch or on a cramped airplane. In this mode, you are much less concerned about multitasking and more focused on comfortable computing and getting one thing done at a time.

However, this difference in computing mentality has drawn an unfortunate line between tablets and traditional computer form factors: when you want to have fun or consume content, use your tablet; but when you need to get work done or produce content, head back to your main computer. Is there really no work-fun balance? Could you not carry one device that does it all?

Windows 8 tries to rise to this challenge by having a dual mode built-in. There is a desktop mode that runs all existing Windows applications for productivity (in x86 chipset machines) and a Windows Store app mode where everything is touch-based, optimized for tablet use. We have seen that productivity tools like Microsoft Office can be reengineered for touch-based use on tablet form factors, thus adding to the possibilities of what we can get done on our thin devices.

When using Windows 8 in touch mode, do you feel that you could be more productive than merely focusing on one thing at a time? Of course, you do not want information overload, but many Windows 8 tablets are optimized for landscape use and there is enough horizontal space to fit quite a bit of information. Productivity aside, wouldn't you love to keep an eye on social feeds while watching a Netflix movie at the same time?

This would mean having more than one app run in the foreground. If there is enough room horizontally, why can't you stack two apps side by side and run them both at the same time? Thankfully, Microsoft agrees with this need and Windows 8 supports running apps side by side. One app takes up the bulk of real estate, while the other is stacked to the left or right. This is accomplished by having apps support up to three view states that the user may cycle through. MSDN does the best job explaining this, as demonstrated in Figure 7-8.

Full screen view
App fills entire screen.
Snapped view
App is snapped to a narrow region of the entire screen.
Fill view
App fills remaining screen area not occupied by the app in the snapped state.

Figure 7-8. *Windows 8 app view states*

So, you are essentially seeing that your Windows 8 Store apps need to support three view states: full, filled, and snapped. The full and filled modes are applied when the app has the entire or close to the entire real estate on your tablet screen. The snapped mode is used when your app is the secondary focus on screen and the user has it docked on the left or right edge (always 320 pixels wide). How is this done? For a snapped look, by simply dragging the last app used from the left edge of a Windows 8 tablet and docking it when markers appear; for filled/full looks, by dragging it all the way in.

You might ask if it is necessary for your Windows 8 Store app to support all of the view states. The answer is yes. Windows 8 will always allow snapping of apps side by side; so it is really up to the user to decide how he or she wants to use your app. The only restriction is that the Windows 8 device needs to have at least 1366 horizontal pixel resolution. This protects against a scenario in which the user's screen gets too busy with a low resolution. Most PC device manufacturers know this limitation and you are guaranteed a higher resolution in almost every new Windows 8 device. So, supporting snapping is a necessity. If your app only works in full/filled state, when the user tries to snap your app to the side, it will lead to a rather bad user experience with content getting unceremoniously chopped off.

Designing your Windows 8 Store app to support all three view states takes a little planning. No one other than you can decide what your app's content should look like in snapped mode. The usual goal is to show a different slice of the same data in a different way, and not change context; but this is open to interpretation per what makes sense in your Windows 8 app. The user is essentially going to expect to see a similar slice of data, although with reduced functionality in accordance with the thin real estate. Apps in snapped/filled mode should be equally interactive and provide continuity of functionality. More guidance on planning for these visual states is provided by MSDN at `http://msdn.microsoft.com/en-us/library/windows/apps/hh465371(v=VS.85).aspx`.

So, how are you going to support these visual states in your Windows 8 Store apps? Let's dig into some implementation.

Visual State Manager

Turns out, supporting the three view states on a page is actually rather simple, thanks to the `VisualStateManager` class. Deriving from `DependencyObject`, this class can be used directly in XAML markup as well as code-behind. More details are at `http://msdn.microsoft.com/en-us/library/windows/apps/windows.ui.xaml.visualstatemanager.aspx`.

XAML Markup Adjustments

Let's use the `VisualStateManager` in your Apress Featured Books Demo app to actually walk through an implementation. I'm going to implement snapping in the home/dashboard page only for demonstration. In reality, you should plan on doing this in all of your pages as you see fit in your Windows 8 app. Listing 7-2 shows some revised XAML in the `FeaturedBookList.xaml` page.

Listing 7-2. Revised FeaturedBookList.xaml page

```
<Page.Resources>

        <!-- Collection of grouped Apress Books displayed by this page -->
        <CollectionViewSource
            x:Name="groupedItemsViewSource"
            Source="{Binding GroupedFeaturedApressBooks}"
            IsSourceGrouped="true"
            ItemsPath="BookCollection"/>

    </Page.Resources>

    <Grid Style="{StaticResource LayoutRootStyle}" Background="Black">
        <Grid.RowDefinitions>
            <RowDefinition Height="140"/>
            <RowDefinition Height="*"/>
        </Grid.RowDefinitions>

        <!-- Page title -->
        <Grid Grid.Row="0" x:Name="regularHeader">
            <Grid.ColumnDefinitions>
                <ColumnDefinition Width="Auto"/>
            </Grid.ColumnDefinitions>
            <StackPanel Orientation="Horizontal" Margin="20,0,0,0">
                <Button x:Name="backButton" Click="GoBack" IsEnabled="{Binding
                Frame.CanGoBack, ElementName=pageRoot}" Style="{StaticResource BackButtonStyle}" />
                <Image Source="/Assets/ApressLogo.png" Width="200" Height="100"
                VerticalAlignment="Center" Margin="-120,15,0,0"/>
                <TextBlock x:Name="pageTitle" Grid.Column="1" Text="{StaticResource AppName}"
                Style="{StaticResource PageHeaderTextStyle}" VerticalAlignment="Center"
                Margin="10,10,0,10"/>
            </StackPanel>
        </Grid>
```

```
<Grid Grid.Row="0" x:Name="snappedHeader" Visibility="Collapsed">
    <Grid.ColumnDefinitions>
        <ColumnDefinition Width="Auto"/>
    </Grid.ColumnDefinitions>
    <StackPanel Orientation="Horizontal">
        <Image Source="/Assets/ApressLogo.png" Width="200" Height="100"
        VerticalAlignment="Center" Margin="10,15,0,0"/>
    </StackPanel>
</Grid>

<!-- FullScreen/Filled Mode -->
<SemanticZoom Grid.Row="1" x:Name="semanticZoomer">

    <SemanticZoom.ZoomedInView>
        <GridView
            x:Name="itemGridView"
            AutomationProperties.AutomationId="ItemGridView"
            AutomationProperties.Name="Grouped Items"
            Margin="30,80,40,46"
            VerticalAlignment="Center"
            ItemsSource="{Binding Source={StaticResource groupedItemsViewSource}}"
            ItemTemplate="{StaticResource Apress277x350BookTemplate}"
            SelectionMode="None"
            IsSwipeEnabled="false"
            IsItemClickEnabled="True"
            ItemClick="bookItem_Click">

            <GridView.ItemsPanel>
                <ItemsPanelTemplate>
                    <VirtualizingStackPanel Orientation="Horizontal"/>
                </ItemsPanelTemplate>
            </GridView.ItemsPanel>
            <GridView.GroupStyle>
                <GroupStyle>
                    <GroupStyle.HeaderTemplate>
                        <DataTemplate>
                            <Grid Margin="1,0,0,6">
                                <StackPanel Orientation="Horizontal">
                                    <Button AutomationProperties.Name="Group
                                    Title" Content="{Binding ApressBookGroupName}"
                                    Style="{StaticResource ApressTextButtonStyle}"
                                    VerticalAlignment="Center" Click="GroupHeader_Clicked"
                                    Foreground="White"/>
                                    <TextBlock Text="(" Style="{StaticResource SubheaderTextStyle}"
                                    VerticalAlignment="Top" Margin="10,0,5,0"/>
                                    <TextBlock Text="{Binding ApressBookGroupCount}"
                                    Style="{StaticResource SubheaderTextStyle}"
                                    VerticalAlignment="Top"/>
                                    <TextBlock Text=")" Style="{StaticResource SubheaderTextStyle}"
                                    VerticalAlignment="Top" Margin="5,0,5,0"/>
                                </StackPanel>
                            </Grid>
```

```
                        </DataTemplate>
                    </GroupStyle.HeaderTemplate>
                    <GroupStyle.Panel>
                        <ItemsPanelTemplate>
                            <VariableSizedWrapGrid Orientation="Vertical"
                            Margin="0,0,100,0"/>
                        </ItemsPanelTemplate>
                    </GroupStyle.Panel>
                </GroupStyle>
            </GridView.GroupStyle>
        </GridView>
    </SemanticZoom.ZoomedInView>

    <SemanticZoom.ZoomedOutView>
        <ListView VerticalAlignment="Center" ItemTemplate="{StaticResource
        Apress250x250TechTemplate}">
            <ListView.ItemsPanel>
                <ItemsPanelTemplate>
                    <StackPanel Orientation="Horizontal"
                    VerticalAlignment="Center" Margin="100,0,0,0"/>
                </ItemsPanelTemplate>
            </ListView.ItemsPanel>
        </ListView>
    </SemanticZoom.ZoomedOutView>

</SemanticZoom>

<!-- Snapped Mode -->
<ListView
    x:Name="snappedListView"
    AutomationProperties.AutomationId="ItemListView"
    AutomationProperties.Name="Grouped Items"
    Grid.Row="1"
    Visibility="Collapsed"
    Margin="0,-10,0,0"
    Padding="10,0,0,60"
    ItemsSource="{Binding Source={StaticResource groupedItemsViewSource}}"
    ItemTemplate="{StaticResource ApressSnappedBookTemplate}"
    SelectionMode="None"
    IsSwipeEnabled="false"
    IsItemClickEnabled="True"
    ItemClick="bookItem_Click">

    <ListView.GroupStyle>
        <GroupStyle>
            <GroupStyle.HeaderTemplate>
                <DataTemplate>
                    <Grid Margin="7,7,0,0">
                        <Button
                            AutomationProperties.Name="Group Title"
                            Click="GroupHeader_Clicked"
```

```
                                    Style="{StaticResource TextPrimaryButtonStyle}">
                                    <StackPanel Orientation="Horizontal">
                                        <TextBlock Text="{Binding ApressBookGroupName}"
                                        Margin="3,-7,10,10" Style="{StaticResource
                                        GroupHeaderTextStyle}" Foreground="White" />
                                        <TextBlock Text="{StaticResource ChevronGlyph}"
                                        FontFamily="Segoe UI Symbol" Margin="0,-7,0,10"
                                        Style="{StaticResource GroupHeaderTextStyle}"/>
                                    </StackPanel>
                                </Button>
                            </Grid>
                        </DataTemplate>
                    </GroupStyle.HeaderTemplate>
                </GroupStyle>
            </ListView.GroupStyle>
        </ListView>
```

There are several interesting changes in this XAML markup. First, all of what you plan to show in snapped mode is initially kept hidden until it is needed in a visual state change. In addition to the normal page header, you add a header—called the `snappedHeader`—with smaller header information. Next, the normal view of the page has a `GridView` displaying a grouped collection of books inside a `SemanticZoom` control. To that, you add a simple `ListView` called `snappedListView` and keep it hidden until a snapped state calls for it. The point is that you will still show the same grouped collection of books, you only switch the UI to use a simple `ListView` in order to accommodate the slim snapped-view real estate. The `ListView` is bound to the same grouped data collection that you use for the `GridView`, except it uses a different data template.

The display for each book has to be slimmer than what you did in the `GridView` and not include imagery. So, define the styling in the form of a `DataTemplate` that is fed as an `ItemTemplate` to your `ListView`. This is done in the `StandardStyles.xaml` for reusability:

```
<DataTemplate x:Key="ApressSnappedBookTemplate">
        <Grid Margin="6" Width="320">
            <Border Background="{StaticResource ListViewItemPlaceholderBackgroundThemeBrush}"
            Opacity="1">
                <StackPanel Margin="10,0,0,0">
                    <TextBlock Text="{Binding ApressBookName}" Foreground="#FFCC11"
                    TextWrapping="Wrap" FontSize="16" Width="250" Margin="-55,0,0,0"/>
                    <StackPanel Orientation="Vertical">
                        <TextBlock Text="{Binding ApressBookAuthor}" Foreground="White"
                        FontWeight="SemiBold" TextWrapping="Wrap" Margin="0,10,0,0" Width="300"/>
                        <TextBlock Text="{Binding DisplayablePublishDate}"
                        Foreground="Gray" TextWrapping="NoWrap" Margin="0,10,0,0"/>
                    </StackPanel>
                </StackPanel>
            </Border>
        </Grid>
    </DataTemplate>
```

VisualStateManager Wire-Up

At this point, you know how to support a snapped view state by switching to a `ListView` and using the same data source, albeit with a different data template. But how would you wire this up so that the snapped state shows this changed UI? Here's some code in the XAML markup:

```
<VisualStateManager.VisualStateGroups>

            <!-- Visual states reflect the application's view state -->
            <VisualStateGroup x:Name="ApplicationViewStates">
                <VisualState x:Name="FullScreenLandscape"/>
                <VisualState x:Name="Filled"/>

                <VisualState x:Name="Snapped">
                    <Storyboard>
                        <ObjectAnimationUsingKeyFrames Storyboard.TargetName="snappedListView"
                        Storyboard.TargetProperty="Visibility">
                            <DiscreteObjectKeyFrame KeyTime="0" Value="Visible"/>
                        </ObjectAnimationUsingKeyFrames>
                        <ObjectAnimationUsingKeyFrames Storyboard.TargetName="semanticZoomer"
                        Storyboard.TargetProperty="Visibility">
                            <DiscreteObjectKeyFrame KeyTime="0" Value="Collapsed"/>
                        </ObjectAnimationUsingKeyFrames>
                        <ObjectAnimationUsingKeyFrames Storyboard.TargetName="snappedHeader"
                        Storyboard.TargetProperty="Visibility">
                            <DiscreteObjectKeyFrame KeyTime="0" Value="Visible"/>
                        </ObjectAnimationUsingKeyFrames>
                        <ObjectAnimationUsingKeyFrames Storyboard.TargetName="regularHeader"
                        Storyboard.TargetProperty="Visibility">
                            <DiscreteObjectKeyFrame KeyTime="0" Value="Collapsed"/>
                        </ObjectAnimationUsingKeyFrames>
                    </Storyboard>
                </VisualState>

            </VisualStateGroup>
        </VisualStateManager.VisualStateGroups>
```

You can see how simple this is with the `VisualStateManager`. Your full and filled states are the same and provide the normal `GridView` look with Semantic Zoom. Accordingly, you do nothing on those visual states. However, the moment the user has your app snapped, your special handling of the visual state kicks in. You'll notice that you use simple `Storyboards` to define easing animations so that you can hide the regular content (data + page header) and toggle the visibility of the snapped mode controls to show the updated UI.

Simple enough? Now let's see the results of your efforts.

VisualStateManager in Action

Run the Apress demo app first in full screen mode and then circle through other apps to make your app settle on filled and snapped modes. A shortcut for snapping quickly is Windows logo key + period (.). Figures 7-9, 7-10, 7-11, and 7-12 show your app in various visual states.

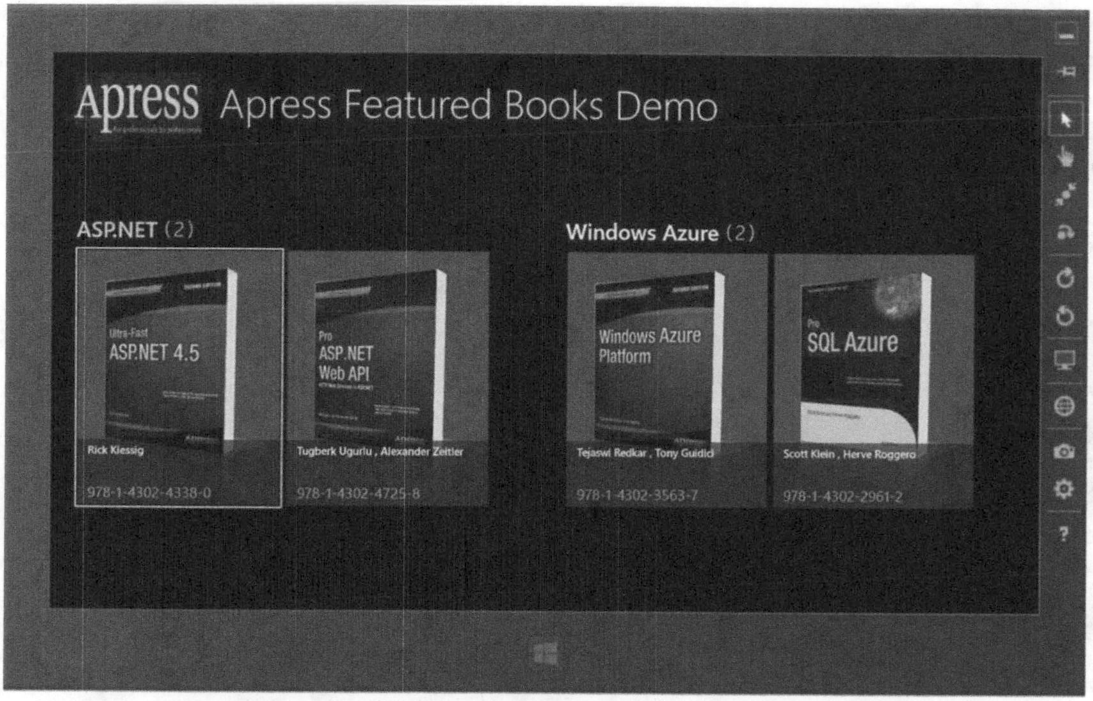

Figure 7-9. *Apress demo app in full-screen mode*

Figure 7-10. *Apress demo app in filled mode*

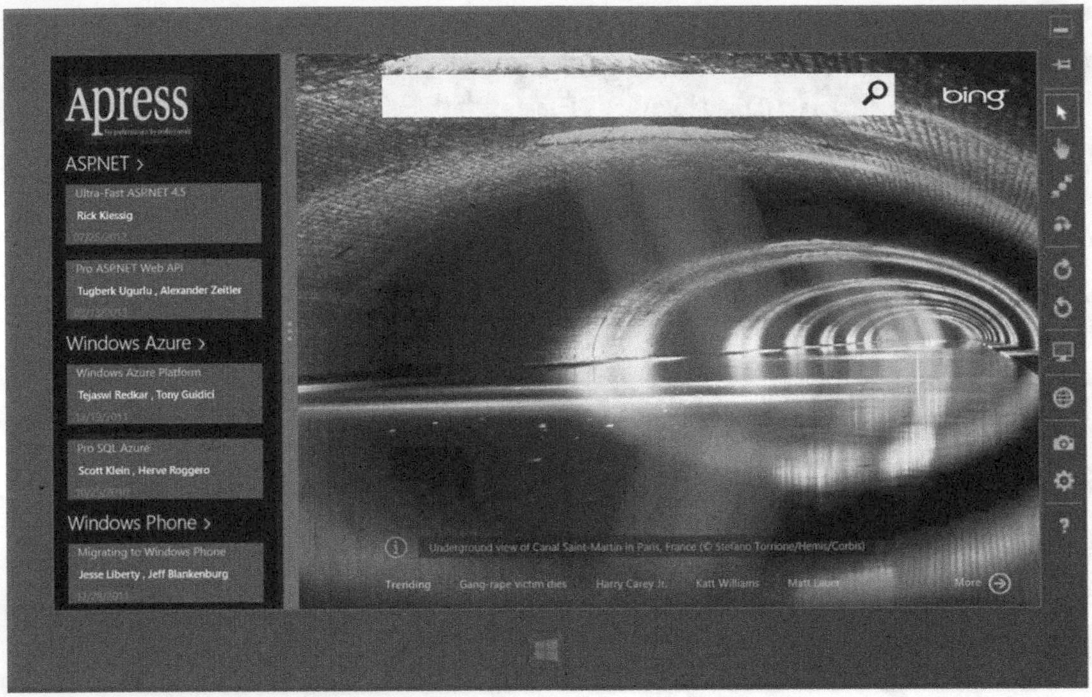

Figure 7-11. *Apress demo app in snapped mode to left*

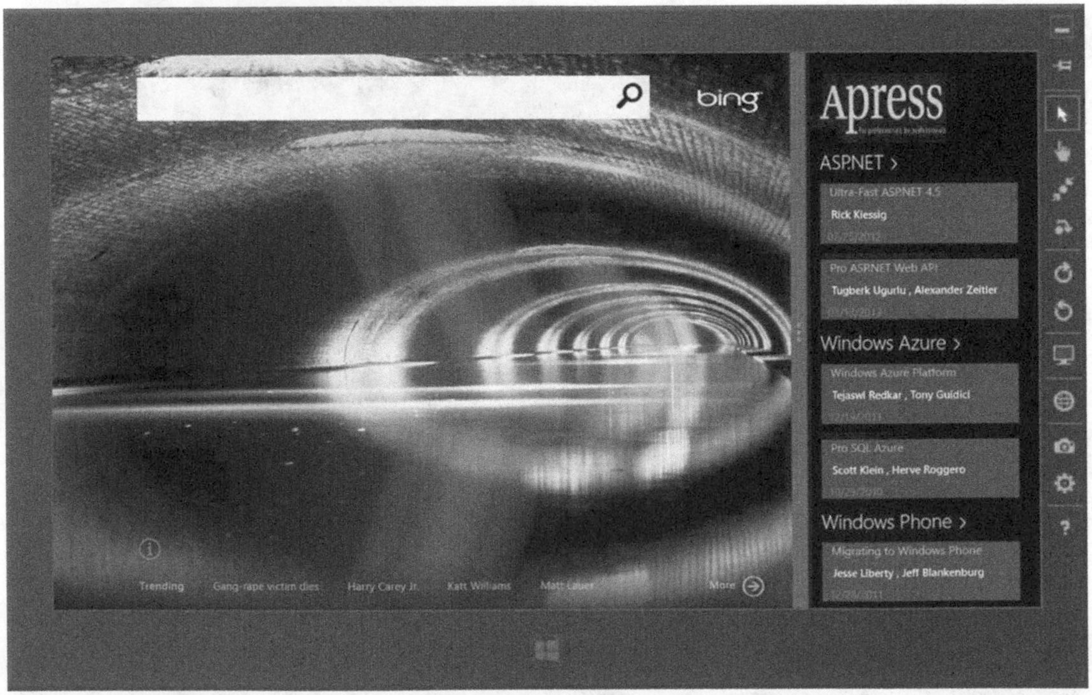

Figure 7-12. *Apress demo app in snapped mode to right*

You can see how your app now changes content based on the following view states: full, filled, snapped left, and snapped right. And, not only did the data display change from `GridView` to `ListView`, but you also flipped to a smaller page header to fit your content in the snapped mode. Grouping books by technology area works the same way. In fact, you can wire up your group headers using the same click/tap event handlers in the code-behind. One nice side effect of designing for the snapped view like this is the fact that it is resilient to changing screen resolutions: the snapped content is still the same and is docked to one side, and the `ListView` simply shows more data when offered a high resolution (see Figure 7-13).

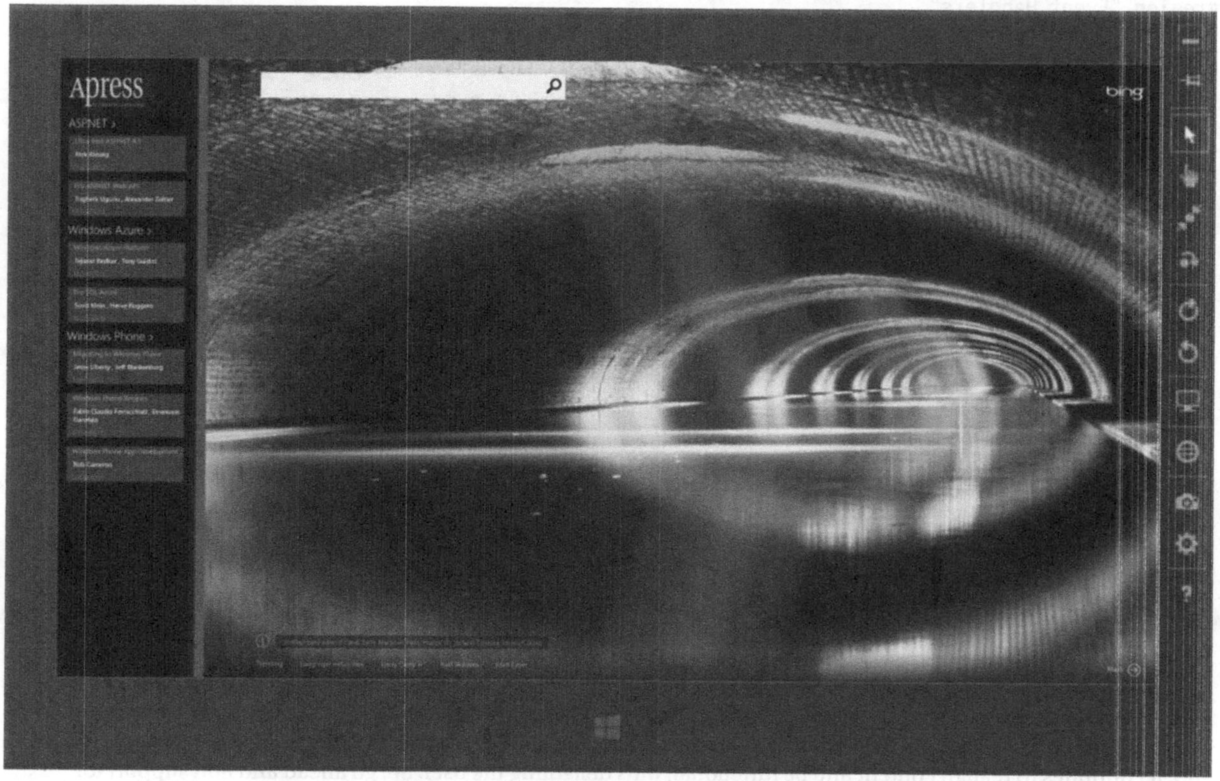

***Figure 7-13.** Apress demo app in snapped mode with high resolution*

So far, you used the VisualStateManager to simply swap your UI controls in response to visual state changes. But what if you had to run some code or adjust some custom UI that was programmatically put on screen? One very common scenario for this is adjusting the app bar control.

Handling View State Changes in Code

Clearly, the number of app bar icons that you can fit on either edge in full/filled mode will not fit in snapped mode. So, it is not uncommon to hide some of the app bar icons in snapped mode in anticipation of streamlined functionality. Yes, you can absolutely do things like this by listening to the view state changes through your own event handlers and writing code to adjust UI pieces accordingly. Here's some code from `FeatureBookList.xaml.cs`:

```
using Windows.UI.ViewManagement;

#region "Constructor"
```

```
        public FeaturedBookList()
        {
            this.InitializeComponent();
            Window.Current.SizeChanged += VisualStateChanged;
        }

        #endregion

#region "Event Handlers"

private void VisualStateChanged(object sender, WindowSizeChangedEventArgs e)
        {
            string visualState = DetermineVisualState(ApplicationView.Value);

            if (visualState == "Snapped")
            {
                // Custom logic, like hiding App Bars if needed.
            }
            else
            {
                // Return to normal UI.
            }
        }

        #endregion
```

You can see how the `Windows.UI.ViewManagement` namespace tapped into the current app Window's `SizeChanged` event. The rest is checking the `ApplicationView` to figure out the visual state and taking any appropriate action in the UI.

Summary

This chapter talked about supporting various device orientations and view state changes in Windows 8 Store apps. The goal is to be a well-behaved citizen on a Windows 8 tablet device—no matter how the user orients or snaps your app, it continues to realign content and be functional, thus delighting the user. So, go ahead and add support for orientation and view state changes in your Windows 8 Store app. When a user brings up your app on a tablet and is able to comfortably use the app any way he or she pleases, you will be thanked with hours of more usage.

CHAPTER 8

Handling Data

What is common across all Windows 8 Store apps? They all present some sort of data. Data is the epicenter of an app's content and plays a crucial role in the end user's experience with any Windows 8 app. Now that you know how to tackle the user interface layouts in your apps and manage visual states to make your app beautiful to use, it's time to turn to a critical aspect of building your Windows 8 Store app: handling data appropriately. You will take a deep dive to know the various types of data and the corresponding persistence strategies. Proper planning around data storage leads to a fast and fluid app user experience across Windows 8 devices and keeps inviting the user back into an app. So, let's dig in toward handling the all-important data correctly.

Data Types

Before I start talking about data persistence in Windows 8 Store apps, let's first dissect the kinds of data you have to deal with. Data in Windows 8 apps can be broadly categorized into two groups:

- *Application data*: This constitutes all the data needed by an app to run smoothly and provide a consistent UX. Examples include settings, files, cache, session state, custom objects/lists, ViewModels, and so forth.
- *User data*: This constitutes all the data that is personally tied to the user, created by the app or the user. Examples include documents, credentials, photos, music, and so forth.

The differentiation in data types actually helps us build robust strategies around handling the data appropriately. Application data is the mutable data that is specifically tied to a Windows 8 Store app. This data is created, read, updated, and deleted when the app is running. Not surprisingly, application data is also tied to the app's lifetime in a Windows 8 device—uninstall the app, and all of its data is gone. User data, on the other hand, is tied to the user and not just a particular app or device. This distinction guides some of your decisions around storage targets given the type of data. It is appropriate to store application data on a Windows 8 device and perhaps even make the data roam with the user if he uses the same app on another device. It is fine for this app-sandboxed data store to be wiped along with the app removal. User data, on the other hand, needs to be persisted carefully across apps/devices and cannot be stored in targets that may be wiped without the user's explicit permission.

Next, I'll talk about possible containers to persist your data in.

Data Containers

Data is obviously the crux of every Windows 8 Store app and it needs to be persisted correctly for a consistent UX. But each app shares a big responsibility: to not undermine the faith that a Windows 8 user has in the app's ability to manage its own data. Data leakage or possible corruption of application data is a major threat to any operating system and invites bigger problems around the security of the ecosystem.

To avoid such threats and to reduce the burden on Windows 8 Store apps to protect themselves, Windows 8 as an OS takes an important stance: apps run in their own sandboxes. Every Windows 8 Store app gets its own private data repository—to read and write data to its heart's content. No other app is allowed access to this sandbox directly; if content needs to be shared between apps, Windows 8 offers to broker that through *contracts* (you'll devote substantial time to this in an upcoming chapter). This protection is a key part of the security that Windows 8 offers to its end users. No app available in the Windows Store is allowed to go rogue and consume APIs or do damage to the user's machine. However, even if something unforeseen was to happen, the sandboxed model offers immediate protection—damage is contained to the app's own storage without affecting the integrity of the OS or the user's personal data. Data corruptions, potential malware, or other application catastrophes are much less of a threat to a Windows 8 user because of this model.

Here are the options for data containers for Windows 8 Store apps, with sample code to follow:

- Data can be persisted, as *application settings* in key-value pairs, with the keys/values being set per application needs. Simple settings, strings/integers, and all the way up to serialized objects can be persisted. This type of data is usually stored in the system registry, but the actual mechanism of storage is transparent to developers. Within the app data store, each app gets its *root container* to store information, with the flexibility of supporting custom-nested containers. Application settings call for the storage of small bits of data for very quick reads/writes. The OS matches the data space allocation according to the data type, but no validations are done on the data itself.
- Larger data can be saved as *application files*, which are stored in the sandboxed file system access that apps have on the Windows 8 device hard-drive. While a predefined root directory is present, any nesting of folder/directory structures are supported for better organization of data.

Now that you know how to store data in the appropriate containers, let's look at some of the options that you have for where to persist your data.

Storage Targets

WinRT `ApplicationData` APIs expose three possible options for data storage targets, with external storage options available to all Windows 8 Store apps.

- *Local*: This option allows storage of data on a given Windows 8 device, no matter what the form factor. The data to be persisted can be in the form of settings or files and is very much tied to the app handling the sandbox. This form of storage, collectively called *isolated storage*, is easy to manage, useful for data needed across app sessions, and has become quite popular since the advent of Windows Phone on the Microsoft stack.
- *Roaming*: You've heard the buzzword about Windows 8 being a cloud-ready OS. This storage target is one of the reasons why. In your connected lifestyles, you may be using multiple PCs—perhaps a desktop or laptop at work and a tablet or ultrabook for casual computing at home. One way to log into a PC is to use a Microsoft account—so the device obviously knows who the user is. Wouldn't it be nice to sync settings and other app data across devices? This is where the roaming data storage comes in, allowing for saving small pieces of data as settings/files that are tied to the user and synced across multiple devices that have the same app installed. Roaming data is kept in sync by Microsoft across Windows 8 devices and the cloud infrastructure, thus eliminating app setup work on successive devices and allowing continuation of tasks across devices.

- *Temporary*: Windows 8 app data may also be stored in temporary storage, using it as a caching mechanism during an app session. This type of storage does not guarantee data persistence because the disk location may be claimed by the system during maintenance or cleanup. However, such temporary storage may come in handy to offload some of the data that an app may have to carry around in memory during its execution.
- *SkyDrive*: Although it will be covered later in this book, it is important to keep SkyDrive in mind as a data storage target. It is the Microsoft-hosted personal cloud space for every user, armed with a Microsoft account. This cloud storage is substantial in size, starting at 7GB for the free quota. It makes total sense to use SkyDrive for hosting a user's personal data—things like documents, photos, and media. As an added advantage, SkyDrive content is always accessible to the user through the browser and is kept in sync across the user's multiple variant devices with the help of dedicated SkyDrive apps.
- *Internal/external storage*: This type of data storage target is available to all types of applications across platforms, and encompasses files on the user's hard drive (outside the app sandbox) or external storage on a cloud-based database or service. Data storage through such means, although not primarily meant for Windows 8 Store apps, should not be neglected. In fact, such storage may be the only option in some use cases, such as document creation or sharing data across users through a centralized web service.

Storage Through Application Settings

Enough talking, right? Let's get coding and see some of the data storage mechanisms in action. In reality, you can chose to save data from any point in your Windows 8 Store app. I will talk about some predefined checkpoints to persist data in the next chapter. For the time being, go back to the Apress Featured Book Demo app and use the `App.xaml.cs` file as your playground to figure out how the various data persistence techniques work.

Application Settings in Local Storage

You begin with the simplest case—using local storage to save application settings. Here's some code on how to get a reference API handle to store your key-value-pair type data:

```
// Reference to Local Application Settings.
        Windows.Storage.ApplicationDataContainer localSettings =
Windows.Storage.ApplicationData.Current.LocalSettings;

// Persisting simple Application Settings.
           localSettings.Values["CurrentReadingBook"] = "Migrating to Windows Phone";
```

Simple, right? You essentially provide a key for the `LocalSettings` to identify your data and set the value to whatever you need. Do you want to read the saved data back into your app? Here's how:

```
// Reading settings back.
           string currentBook = string.Empty;

  if (localSettings.Values["CurrentReadingBook"] != null)
          currentBook = localSettings.Values["CurrentReadingBook"].ToString();
```

Did you notice that you checked whether the key actually existed before trying to read its value? This is just a simple precaution against getting null reference exceptions. Now, what if you are using lots of small pieces to save as data to be persisted and `LocalSettings` becomes one huge dictionary of key-value pairs? Well, you can get a little organized around the data that your app is trying to save. Although `LocalSettings` offers a root container to save app data, you can also create your own *containers* to arrange your data into logical buckets. Here's how you create custom containers and push data into them:

```
// Organizing settings in containers.
            Windows.Storage.ApplicationDataContainer container = localSettings.CreateContainer
("FavoriteBooks", Windows.Storage.ApplicationDataCreateDisposition.Always);
            if (localSettings.Containers.ContainsKey("FavoriteBooks"))
            {
                localSettings.Containers["FavoriteBooks"].Values["FavoriteWindowsPhoneBook"] =
"Windows Phone Recipes";
            }
```

And the following shows how you read the data back out from the `LocalSettings` custom container. Note that you double-check the existence of both the container and the key before trying to read the data. You may call me paranoid, but defensive code never hurts.

```
bool hasFavoritesContainer = localSettings.Containers.ContainsKey("FavoriteBooks");
            string favoriteWindowsPhoneBook = string.Empty;

            if (hasFavoritesContainer)
            {
                if (localSettings.Containers["FavoriteBooks"].Values.ContainsKey
("FavoriteWindowsPhoneBook"))
                    favoriteWindowsPhoneBook = localSettings.Containers["FavoriteBooks"].Values
["FavoriteWindowsPhoneBook"].ToString();
            }
```

Do you need to free up space once no longer needed? Here's how:

```
// Deleting Settings from Storage.
            localSettings.Values.Remove("CurrentReadingBook");
            localSettings.DeleteContainer("FavoriteBooks");
```

Now, let's talk about saving data as application settings, but with the roaming storage as the target.

Application Settings in Roaming Storage

The use of `RoamingSettings` will look incredibly similar to the use of `LocalSettings`, except now the data is being persisted and synced by Microsoft across multiple devices and the cloud. Don't you love it when APIs are this simple? Listing 8-1 shows how to get a handle on where to save the roaming data.

Listing 8-1. Roaming Application Settings

```
// Reference to Roaming Application Settings.
        Windows.Storage.ApplicationDataContainer roamingSettings =
Windows.Storage.ApplicationData.Current.RoamingSettings;
```

And here is how you will use key-value pairs to read/write/delete app data from `RoamingSettings`:

```
// Persisting simple Application Settings.
         roamingSettings.Values["LastPageReadOnCurrentBook"] = 20;

// Reading settings back.
         int lastPageReadOnCurrentBook;

         if (roamingSettings.Values["LastPageReadOnCurrentBook"] != null)
             lastPageReadOnCurrentBook = Convert.ToInt32(roamingSettings.Values
["LastPageReadOnCurrentBook"]);

// Deleting Settings from Storage.
         roamingSettings.Values.Remove("LastPageReadOnCurrentBook");
```

As you have seen, you check for the presence of a given key before trying to read the corresponding data. Also, the key-value simply stores the data as is, within the wrapper of a generic object. The data type will be preserved, but while reading the contents back, you have to cast the data to the type you used to save it, as shown earlier with your casting the object to an integer. `RoamingSettings` also support the organization of storage into custom containers to hold any given data.

Now, let's stop here for just a bit and explore some caveats to keep in mind while using `RoamingSettings` to store data. The roaming data containers offer a very simple API, but are incredibly powerful. With just one line of code, you are saving data from your app in the local device as well as making it available for syncing through duplication in the cloud infrastructure. The user picks up another Windows 8 device and downloads your app—and boom, all the customizations and application settings are synced down through the cloud into the new device and it starts working backward as well. Roaming data truly provides a great opportunity for app developers to provide the continuity of the user experience across Windows 8 devices and it should be leveraged with care. The following are points to keep in mind:

- Do not undermine the trust of the user in a cloud-based Microsoft account data-sync. Use roaming data only when needed, following apt guidelines. Application data on another device that the user does not have any use in knowing is better left local.
- Provide the continuity of experiences so that the user can begin a task on one device and continue on another device from where he left off. Bookmarks, game scores/progress, and so forth, are prime examples on where to use roaming settings.
- There is a size limitation for each app that counts toward the amount of data that can be roamed. This makes sense given the multitude of apps that the user may have installed, as well as the cloud infrastructure it takes to move such data around and download to each new device toed to the Microsoft account. The `ApplicationData.RoamingStorageQuota | roamingStorageQuota` property tells the developer how much of the roaming storage quota can be used. If your app hits this limit, none of the roaming application data will be replicated to the cloud until the app's total roamed application data is less than the limit again. So, you get the hint: roam the small stuff for user convenience, not huge data models.
- Application design should not count on the roaming of settings to happen instantaneously. Windows roams app data opportunistically based on complex algorithms/triggers and doesn't guarantee an instant sync. So, based on other higher priority OS tasks, syncing of app data may be postponed until conditions are more suitable. Your app should be ready for the delayed sync. If you are looking for a time-critical settings sync, only one roaming setting per app can be marked "`HighPriority`" and limited to 8KB for a faster sync.

Detailed considerations on the use of roaming data can be found in MSDN documentation at `http://msdn.microsoft.com/en-us/library/windows/apps/hh465094.aspx`.

The last point on possible non-instant roaming app data sync is a nice segue to our next conversation. Envision this: your app uses roaming data storage and the user has just triggered some data changes on a device. Opportunistically, Windows tries to sync this roaming data by copying it from the local device to the cloud, ready for it to be pushed down to another device if the user switches machines. Let's suppose that by the time the user grabs a different device and launches your app, the cloud copy of the roaming data has changed, but the second device is still showing the stale data. We developers need a hook or an event to know that roaming data has changed in the cloud and your local storage needs to be refreshed. The following shows how to do this in code; it is most commonly added to the `App.xaml.cs` file:

```
#region "Constructor"

        public App()
        {
            . . .

            Windows.Storage.ApplicationData.Current.DataChanged += new
TypedEventHandler<ApplicationData, object>(DataChangeHandler);
        }

        #endregion

private void DataChangeHandler(Windows.Storage.ApplicationData appData, object someObject)
        {
            // Refresh local data here.
        }
```

As you can see, you simply listen to the `DataChanged` event to know that roaming data in the cloud has changed and you need to do a local data refresh. Nifty, isn't it?

There is one other point to note about roaming data storage. Unlike local data storage, roaming data in the cloud is not erased immediately just because the user uninstalled the concerned app from one/all of his or her devices. There is a threshold time (at present, it is 30 days) until which roaming app data is preserved in the cloud, even if orphaned by the concerning app in the user's devices. If the user has not needed the roaming data within the threshold, cloud data is erased. This means that if the user reinstalls the concerned app again within the time period, cloud sync of roaming data will kick in again based on what was saved before.

Storage Through Files

So far, you have seen the use of application settings to store data in both local and roaming containers. Much of this data, however, has been in the form of key-value pairs and limited to small bytes. What if you actually wanted to persist more-complex objects or store large quantities of data?

This is when you fall back to the use of the file system, which the Windows 8 Store app has access to. Please remember, however, that the sandboxing continues—each app gets a dedicated storage area to save files in the file system; no other app has access. Within its app file data store, each app gets system-defined root directories: one for local files, one for roaming files, and one for temporary files. And the developer is free to add directories to improve file organization. The internals of the file storage mechanism is hidden behind a simple API; but you can look into the file system, as you shall see in a bit. First, write some code to save data into the local data storage (see Listing 8-2).

Listing 8-2. Local Storage File Persistence

```
// Reference to Local Folder.
        Windows.Storage.StorageFolder localFolder =
Windows.Storage.ApplicationData.Current.LocalFolder;

private async void DemoDataPersistenceCodeThroughFiles()
        {
            StorageFile localFileToWrite = await localFolder.CreateFileAsync("FileTest.txt",
CreationCollisionOption.ReplaceExisting);
            await FileIO.WriteTextAsync(localFileToWrite, "This is a sample file!");

            StorageFile localFileToRead = await localFolder.GetFileAsync("FileTest.txt");
            string textRead = await FileIO.ReadTextAsync(localFileToRead);

            StorageFile localFileToDelete = await localFolder.GetFileAsync("FileTest.txt");
            await localFileToDelete.DeleteAsync();
        }
```

Several things happened in Listing 8-2. First, you used the `ApplicationData` API to get a handle on where you might save your file. Turns out, you do not need to care about the implementation of this file system access; all you can work with is a reference to a folder where you get to write your files, in this case the `LocalFolder`. Next, you created your file (of the type `StorageFile`, which is a WinRT API) by giving it a name and adding some content, followed by the `FileIO` operation to write the file to the local folder. Did you notice the use of the `async-await` C# pattern? Since the file operation might take longer than 50 milliseconds, WinRT requires that you do this asynchronously so that the UI thread is never hampered from user interactivity. Do you need to read a file from the local folder or delete a file when done with it? You see the same techniques: you get a handle on the file based on its name and then take appropriate action asynchronously.

The curious developer in you must be wondering where these files are written out in the file system. Is it some secret isolated storage that you can never see? Turns out, you can. Simply debug the lines of code in Listing 8-2 and stop to inspect the `Path` property file written to the `LocalFolder`. You should see something like the screenshot shown in Figure 8-1.

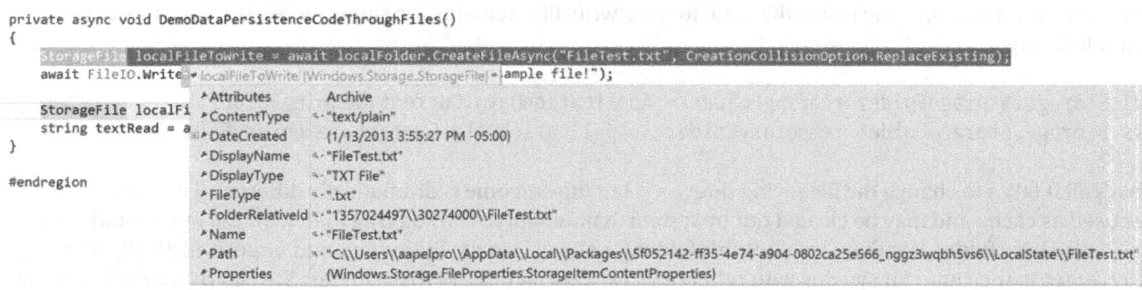

Figure 8-1. *Debugging a file-save to local storage*

As you can see, the file path is specific to the user and follows the app package GUID-name folder structure. You can actually navigate to the folder in Windows Explorer and see the contents of the file that your app has just written, which should look something like the screenshot shown in Figure 8-2.

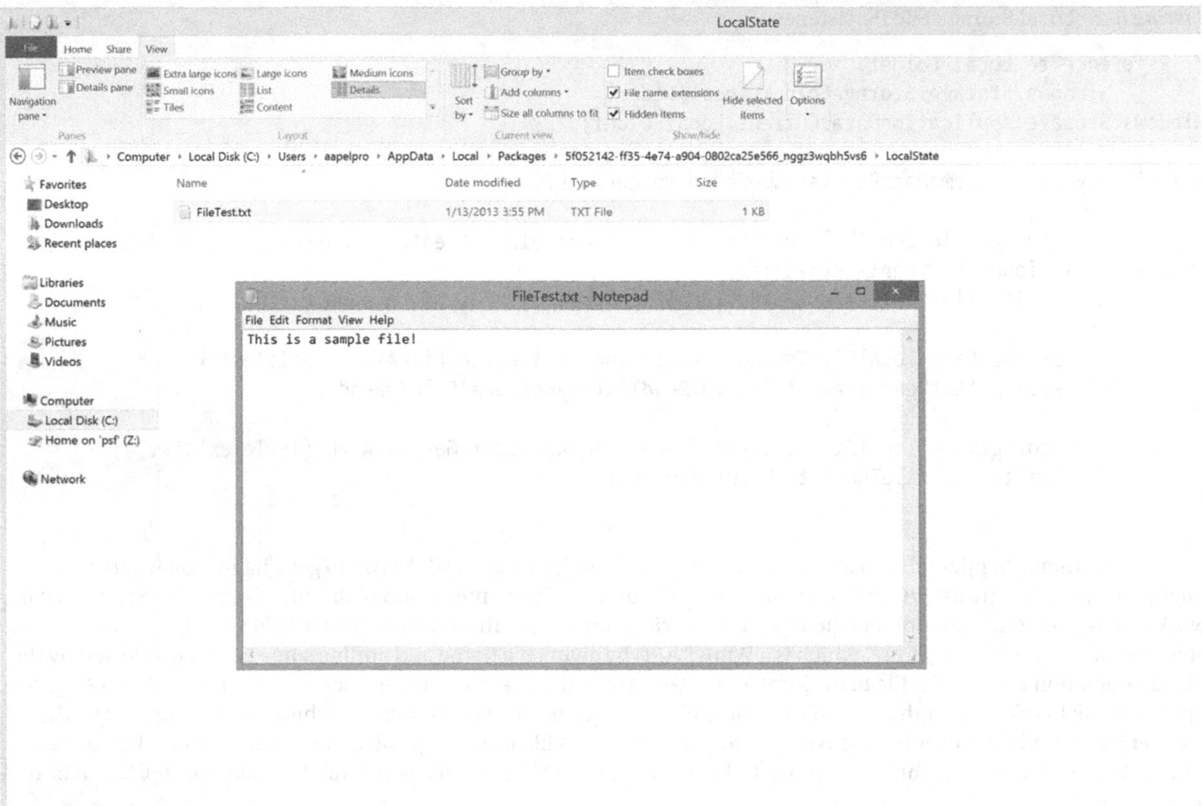

Figure 8-2. *Sample file on local hard drive*

At this point, you know how to read/write/delete files in the local app data store. But what if you wanted to use the same techniques to write files to temporary or roaming storage? Turns out, you simply need to change the folder you get the handle on—the rest of the code to read/write files remains the same. Here's the code to switch to a different folder target:

```
Windows.Storage.StorageFolder roamingFolder = ApplicationData.Current.RoamingFolder;
Windows.Storage.StorageFolder temporaryFolder = ApplicationData.Current.TemporaryFolder;
```

That's all it takes to change the file saving directory, but the outcome is dramatically different. The `Temporary` folder is used as cache and may be cleared out by system maintenance. The `Roaming` folder, on the other hand, acts like a mini SkyDrive folder. Windows watches this folder for changes in the file system and opportunistically writes out the changes to the cloud for syncing with other devices. Also, all three of these folders are clearly marked for their appropriate roles in the app package root directory, as shown in Figure 8-3.

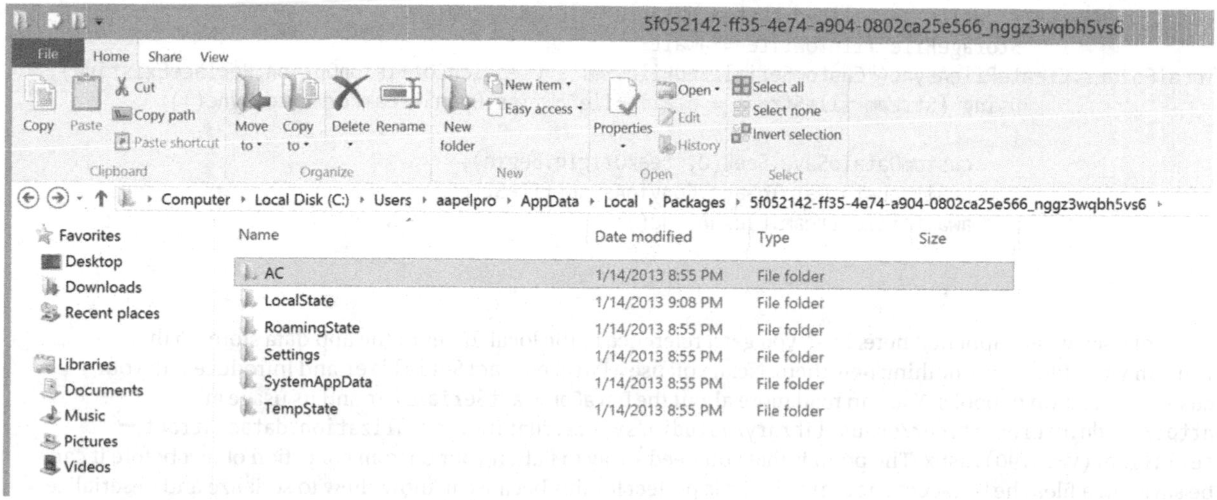

Figure 8-3. *Root storage directory of app package*

OK, so data storage through files isn't very difficult. But I know what you are thinking: can you write something a little more advanced, more like a real-world Windows 8 Store app might need? Why, of course you can ☺.

Persisting Custom Data

Take your Apress Featured Books Demo app, for example. At the crux of the app's data is a collection of books of the type `ApressBook`, a custom object type. This is a somewhat more real-world scenario—your apps may often deal with the collection of custom objects of some kind. Maybe it's a product catalog, a list of contacts, or a collection of news items and so forth. The point is that you need to know how to easily persist large datasets as files for storage. This is critical for your apps to have hydrated data models (read ViewModels) on successive app user sessions.

Given your collection of Apress books in the `FeaturedBookListVM` view model, try your hand at persisting the collection. Keep in mind that your collection of books is already full with the sample books that you loaded. Your collections will similarly be filled, either locally or through network calls, to fetch data. Listing 8-3 shows the code.

Listing 8-3. Custom Data Persistence

```
// Reference to Local Folder.
        Windows.Storage.StorageFolder localFolder = Windows.Storage.ApplicationData.Current.
LocalFolder;

private async void SaveCustomData()
        {
            MemoryStream customDataToSave = new MemoryStream();
            DataContractSerializer serializer = new DataContractSerializer
(typeof(ObservableCollection<ApressBook>));
            serializer.WriteObject(customDataToSave, FeaturedBookListVM.FeaturedApressBooks);
```

```
            // Write serialized custom data to File on HardDisk.
            StorageFile fileToWrite = await
localFolder.CreateFileAsync("CustomSerializedFile.xml", CreationCollisionOption.ReplaceExisting);
            using (Stream fileStream = await fileToWrite.OpenStreamForWriteAsync())
            {
                customDataToSave.Seek(0, SeekOrigin.Begin);
                await customDataToSave.CopyToAsync(fileStream);
                await fileStream.FlushAsync();
            }
        }
```

Let's see what happened here. First, you get a reference to the local folder in the app data store, so that you can write files to it—nothing new there. Next, you use a `DataContractSerializer` and introduce it to your custom collection of books. You can read more about the `DataContractSerializer` and its usage at `http://msdn.microsoft.com/en-us/library/vstudio/system.runtime.serialization.datacontract` ↩ `serializer(v=vs.90).aspx`. The point is that you need a way to flatten your custom collection object before it can be saved in a file. The `DataContractSerializer` is perfect for this because it knows how to serialize and deserialize object types into an XML stream, written to a MemoryStream in your case. Your `ApressBook` class did not use any complex properties; if needed, you may need to decorate your custom class with `DataContractSerializer` attributes for the serialization to work properly. Or you may also look into other techniques or formats for data serialization/deserialization.

With your custom book collection now flattened as XML, the next steps are simple: you name a custom file and use a `Stream` object to write its contents asynchronously into the designated storage folder—the local folder in your code example. Do you want to see if this worked? Pop open the same app package location and you should see something like the screenshot shown in Figure 8-4.

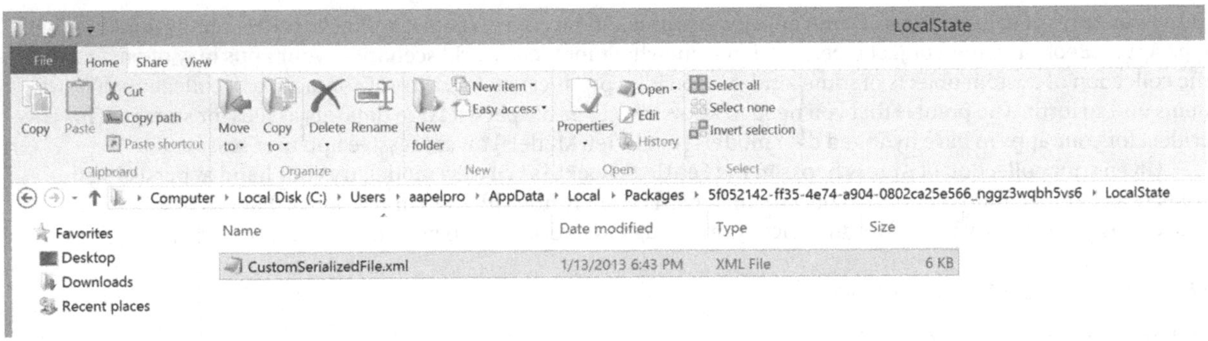

Figure 8-4. *Custom file on local hard drive*

The file has been written out, but have the contents of your book collection been properly serialized into XML? Open the file and, hopefully, you will see something like the screenshot shown in Figure 8-5.

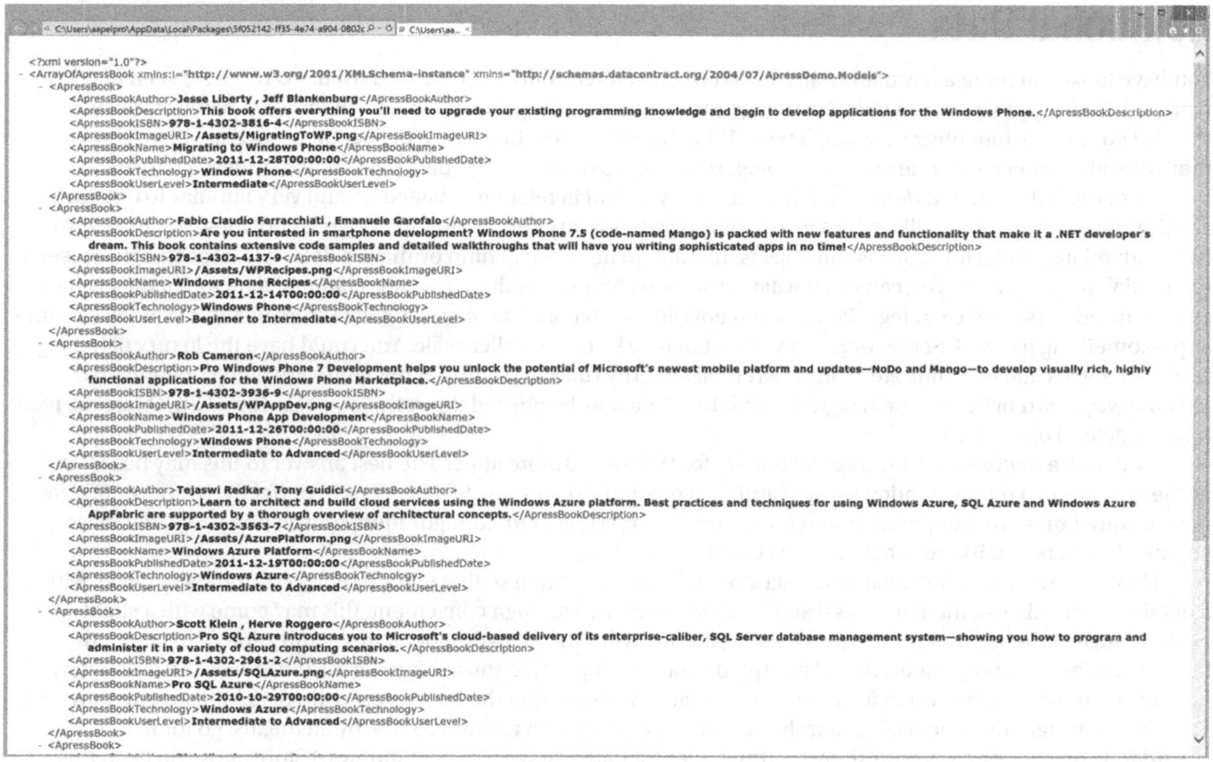

Figure 8-5. *Serialized XML in local file*

Voilà. Pure XML built from your custom collection of Apress books. So serialization does work and it makes persisting large datasets through files quite a breeze. You really do not even have to write the little code snippet. It gets even easier, as you shall see in the next chapter. Now, suppose that the preceding collection was cached and you wanted to read/rehydrate your Apress book collection on a subsequent app session. Could you read back this flattened XML and magically have your collection object filled? Well, sure. That's the job of deserializers. Listing 8-4 presents code to read such a flattened XML file, deserialize the content using `DataContractSerializer`, and rehydrate the object collection.

Listing 8-4. Reading Custom Data Out of Persistence

```
private async void ReadCustomData()
        {
            StorageFile fileToRead = await localFolder.GetFileAsync("CustomSerializedFile.xml");
            using (IInputStream inStream = await fileToRead.OpenSequentialReadAsync())
            {
                // Read data from File & Deserialize.
                DataContractSerializer serializer = new
DataContractSerializer(typeof(ObservableCollection<ApressBook>));
                FeaturedBookListVM.FeaturedApressBooks = (ObservableCollection<ApressBook>)
serializer.ReadObject(inStream.AsStreamForRead());
            }
        }
```

Relational Data

You have looked at quite a few data strategies so far and written code on how to persist data. You have seen how the type and quantity of data may guide the storage mechanism and target used. But, all of this data being stored was simple settings, custom objects, or collections. What if you were dealing with a collection of several object types and they were all connected to one another through relationships? Would your data persistence strategy change?

This is called *relational data*, much like the kind you find in relational databases and very familiar to enterprise application developers. Just like tables in a database with primary key and foreign key relationships, you may have data with related collections of custom objects. In order to not leave behind orphaned data, it is important to preserve referential integrity. Sure, you can use the data storage techniques in this case, but relational data might only call for an optimized persistence strategy. Perhaps you envision a relational database as a data store inside a Windows 8 Store app—something like SQL Server or SQL Express, but may be on a smaller scale. You could have the luxury of having relational tables laid out, thus enforcing referential integrity rules as records in the tables are being manipulated. In some ways, part of the business logic of validating data may be pushed down the database level CRUD (create, read, update, delete) operations.

So, could a database be a storage technique for Windows 8 Store apps? The best answer to this may be SQLite. In the absence of a native Windows way of adding a relational data store, SQLite steps in perfectly. In short, "*SQLite* is a software library that implements a self-contained, serverless, zero-configuration, transactional SQL database engine." Furthers details are at `http://sqlite.org`.

There is one caveat. Any relational data store adds orchestration so that you can house your data in tables within a database, but still use the Windows 8 app data store targets. Although convenient, this may come with a slight performance hit because of the extra processing for the hydration, dehydration, and organization of data. But the benefit may be a true representation of the app data at a storage layer, thus enforcing business logic. Also, you may have more fine-tuned control in fetching only the data you need from the database. So, there are pluses and minuses. You need to weigh the benefits. If you truly feel you are dealing with relational data, by all means, go for it. But again consider if you can get away with simple settings/files for data storage—most Windows 8 Store apps will be in this category. If you are truly in an enterprise setting and have complex data structures feeding your app, SQLite may be the data storage strategy to consider.

If you have made up your mind to use SQLite as a relational data store for your Windows 8 Store app, let's get to the business of implementing it. You are going to continue using the Apress Featured Books Demo app to demonstrate the use of a relational data store. First, since this is not a part of the SDK or WinRT, some tools need to be installed. Get the SQLite bits that are compatible. In Visual Studio, you can select Tools ➤ Extensions And Updates, and then search for and install the SQLite package (see Figure 8-6).

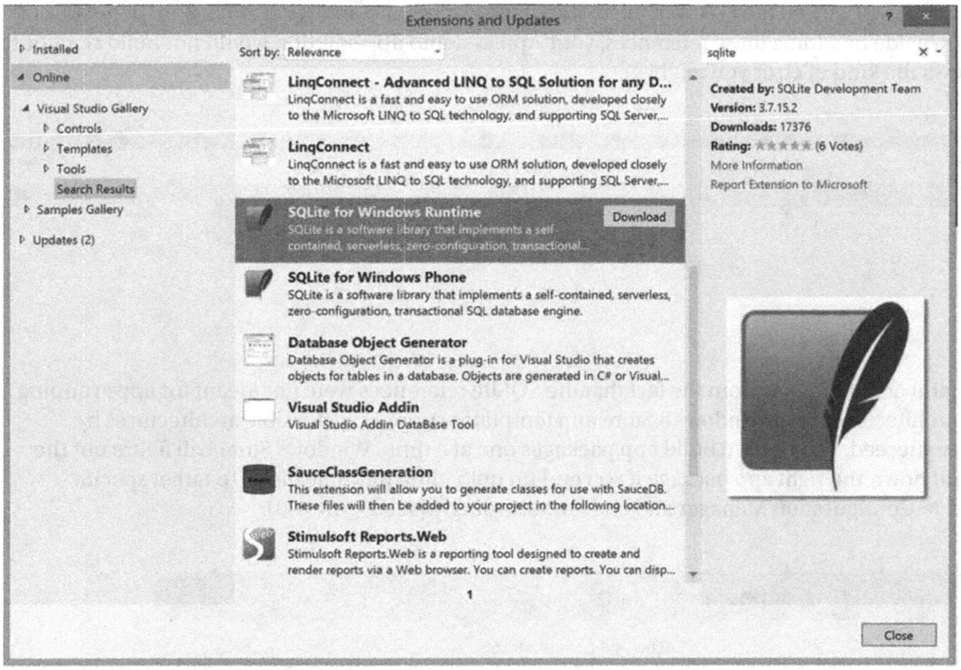

Figure 8-6. *Installing SQLite*

Next, add the appropriate references to your Apress demo app solution, as shown in Figure 8-7.

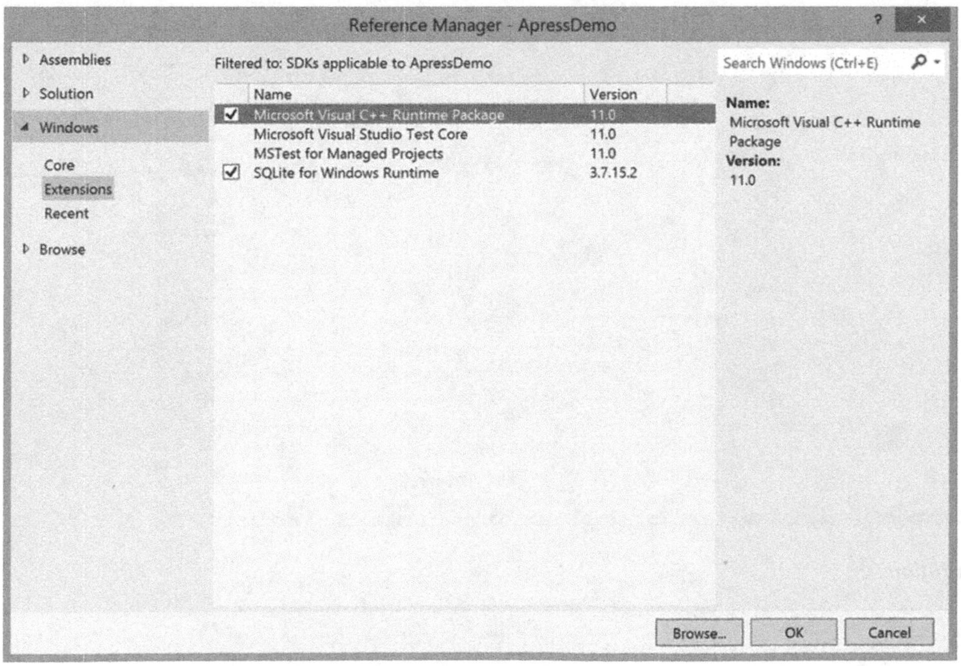

Figure 8-7. *Adding project references*

Note how you added both SQLite and the C++ reference, since some internal workings of SQLite are dependent on C++ interfaces. As a downside to adding these references, your Apress demo app solution would not build right out of the gate. Figure 8-8 shows the kind of error you might get.

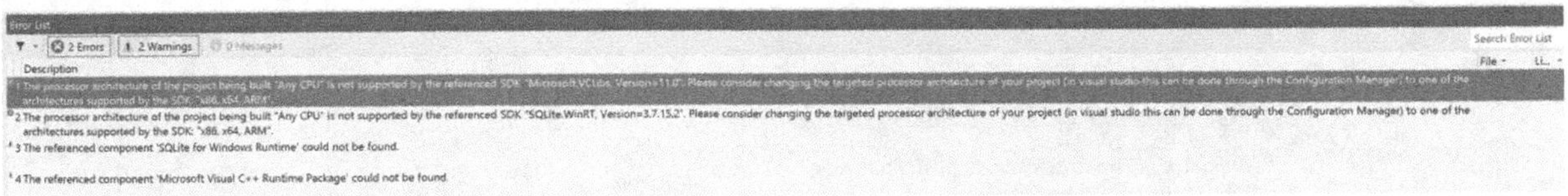

***Figure 8-8.** Compile error*

This compiler complaint actually stems from the fact that the SQLite references were not meant for apps running on a variety of processor architectures, and Windows 8 Store app templates support all possible architectures by default. For compilation to succeed, you need to build app packages one at a time. Windows Store will figure out the user's device type and send down the right app package if you end up uploading multiple ones. To target specific architectures, select Build ➤ Configuration Manager and choose accordingly (see Figure 8-9).

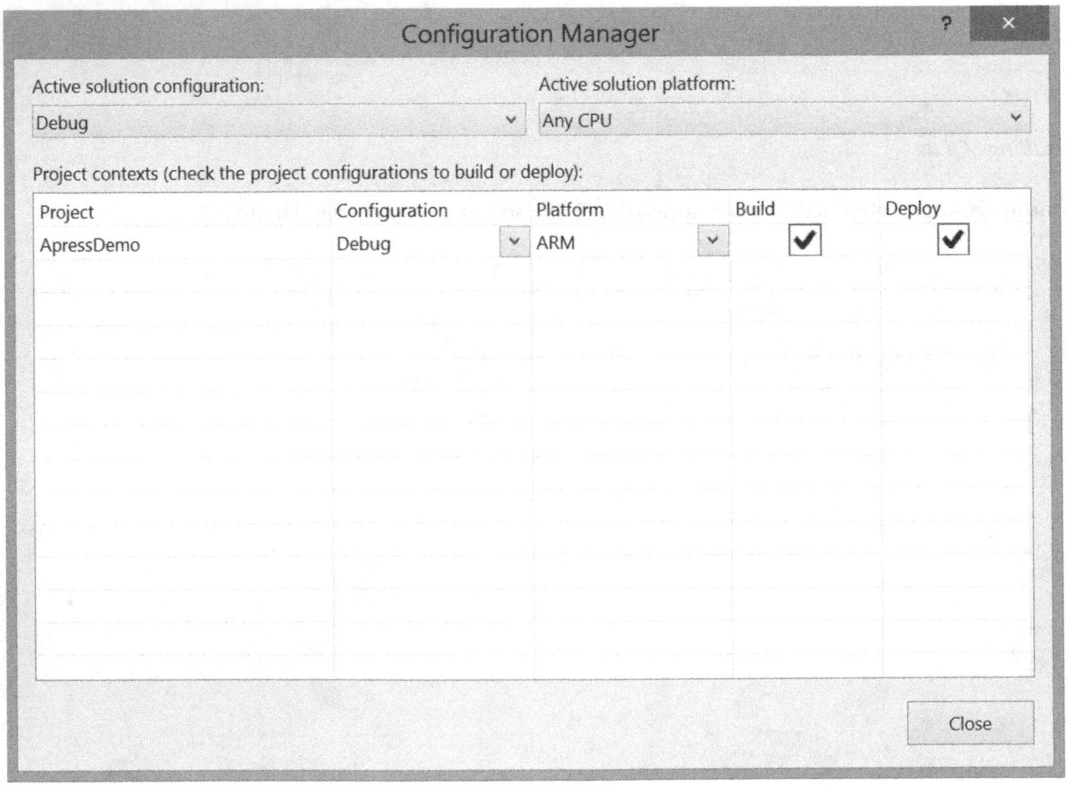

***Figure 8-9.** Build configuration*

Your project now builds and you are back in business. You have the infrastructure to host a relational database and use it as a data store. Before moving on, however, take a look at one more tool that makes life easier while retrieving/updating data from the database: the sqlite-net NuGet package. This package helps refer to database records using LINQ-to-SQL–like syntax and makes data manipulation a breeze. Select Tools ➤ Library Package Manager ➤ Manage NuGet Packages For Solution and search among online packages. Figure 8-10 shows a visual representation of how to do this.

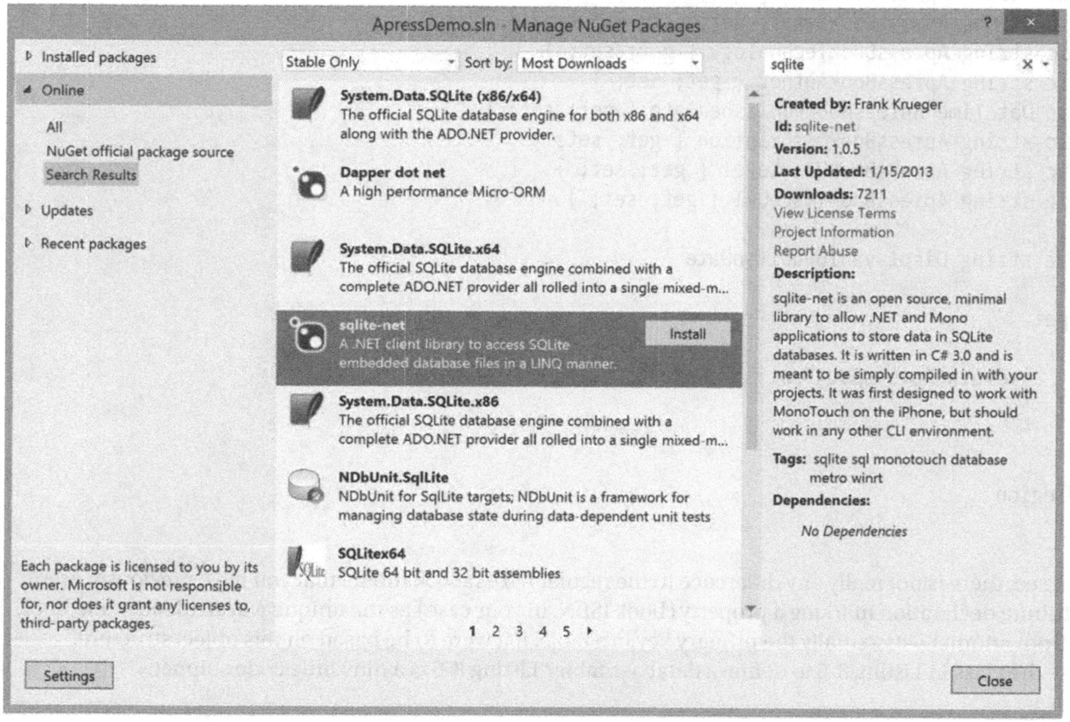

Figure 8-10. *Installing sqlite-net*

Persisting Relational Data

Armed with your new tool sets, proceed to implement the relational data store. Instead of building your relational database by hand, SQLite supports a nifty way of adding a database and dropping structured relational tables in it. Forget that you need to build a database and just define the classes that are needed in your data models. With proper decorative attributes, SQLite can reflect on these POCO (plain-old CLR objects) and figure out the structure of tables to add to a database. If you have ever played with the Entity Framework, this will sound very similar to the code-first method of generating databases.

Let's suppose that you envision the Apress demo app needing relational data support. Maybe you will have business objects like books, customers, authors, technologies, and so forth, which are all related to each other. It makes sense to add an underlying database and serialize objects to store them as table records. Listing 8-5 shows how you can get started. Let's redefine the `ApressBooks` model, this time with an SQLite twist.

Listing 8-5. Relational App Data

```
public partial class RelationalApressBookModel
    {
        #region "Properties"

        [SQLite.PrimaryKey]
        public string ApressBookISBN { get; set; }
        public string ApressBookName { get; set; }
        public string ApressBookTechnology { get; set; }
        public string ApressBookAuthor { get; set; }
        public DateTime ApressBookPublishedDate { get; set; }
        public string ApressBookDescription { get; set; }
        public string ApressBookUserLevel { get; set; }
        public string ApressBookImageURI { get; set; }

        public string DisplayablePublishDate
        {
            get
            {
                return ApressBookPublishedDate.ToString("MM/dd/yyyy");
            }
        }

        #endregion
    }
```

As you can see, there is not really any difference to the regular ApressBook model that you have previously used. It's just one attribute declaration marking a property (book ISBN, in your case) as the unique way to identify one book object/record from another—essentially the primary key in a table, if it were to be based on this object structure. How do you use the class in Listing 8-5 to define a database table? Listing 8-6 is a nifty little code snippet.

Listing 8-6. Relational Data Persistence Using SQLite

```
private void SQLiteDemo()
        {
            string sqliteDBPath = Path.Combine
(Windows.Storage.ApplicationData.Current.LocalFolder.Path, "ApressBookDB.sqlite");

            using (var DB = new SQLite.SQLiteConnection(sqliteDBPath))
            {
                // Create Table from Class.
                DB.CreateTable<RelationalApressBookModel>();

                // Instantiate & add record to table.
                RelationalApressBookModel WPMigration = new RelationalApressBookModel();
                WPMigration.ApressBookISBN = "978-1-4302-3816-4";
                WPMigration.ApressBookName = "Migrating to Windows Phone";
                WPMigration.ApressBookTechnology = "Windows Phone";
                WPMigration.ApressBookAuthor = "Jesse Liberty , Jeff Blankenburg";
```

```
                WPMigration.ApressBookDescription = "This book offers everything you'll need to
upgrade your existing programming knowledge and begin to develop applications for the Windows
Phone.";
                WPMigration.ApressBookImageURI = "/Assets/MigratingToWP.png";
                WPMigration.ApressBookPublishedDate = new DateTime(2011, 12, 28);
                WPMigration.ApressBookUserLevel = "Intermediate";

                DB.Insert(WPMigration);

                // Read record from table using LINQ-like syntax.
                var apressBookFromDB = (DB.Table<RelationalApressBookModel>().Where(book =>
book.ApressBookISBN == "978-1-4302-3816-4")).Single();
            }
        }
```

What's going on in Listing 8-6? First, recall that I told you that relational data stores are an abstraction/orchestration—the underlying data storage remains the same. The first line of code establishes the handle to the local folder storage in the app's isolated storage root—the same path where you saved normal files. The SQLite engine treats this path as a database connection string for initial database creation and subsequent data access. An SQLite database is a single file and it should take the name `ApressBookDB.sqlite`, as you have defined. Do you want to double-check whether SQLite actually created the database? Let's head over to the app package root directory in Windows Explorer. You should see the single database file shown in Figure 8-11.

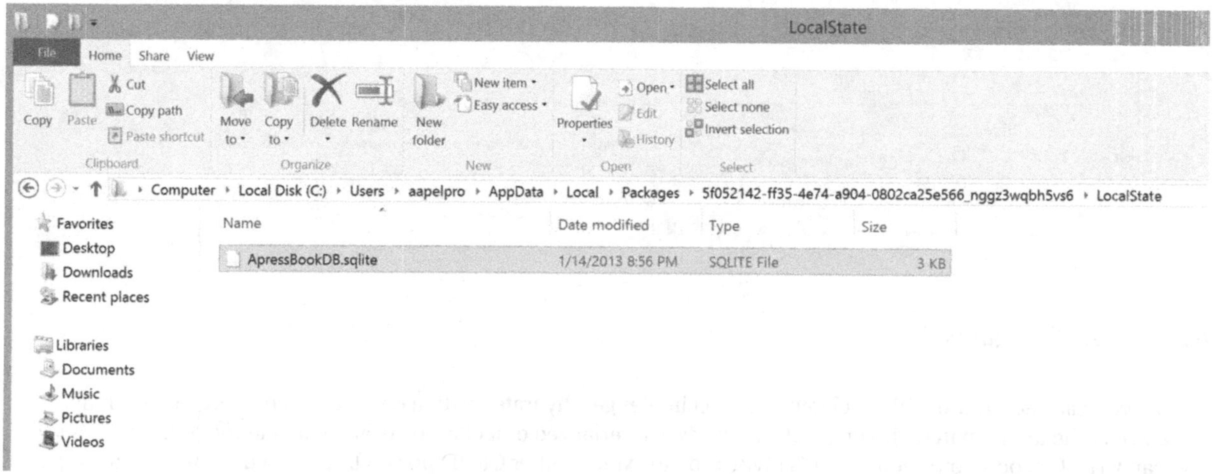

***Figure 8-11.** SQLite database file on local storage*

Next, the `DB.CreateTable()` method takes in the signature of your custom POCO class and tries to create a table in the new database. The goal is to match the table schema to the property-structure of the corresponding object—the properties of the object become the columns of the table, whereas the object itself is flattened into record for storage. Then, you saw how you created a custom `RelationalApressBookModel` object and simply pushed it into the database using `DB.Insert()`, which is self-explanatory. No more SQL to write to add/update/delete records from a database—you can simply write C# code and allow the underlying plumbing to take care of database commands.

At this point, you have an underlying database with a structured table, and you have managed to push a record into the table. Try out the earlier theory of using LINQ-like syntax to retrieve/update database records. Again, here is the last line of code from Listing 8-6:

```
// Read record from table using LINQ-like syntax.
var apressBookFromDB = (DB.Table<RelationalApressBookModel>().Where(book => book.ApressBookISBN ==
"978-1-4302-3816-4")).Single();
```

You are essentially pointing at the given table (using the same connection path) and trying to pluck out a record that matches the given predicate, an ISBN number match in your case. Again, you did not have to write SQL, only C# with a LINQ-like query. The `Single()` method at the end essentially tells the database to return the first matching record and stop processing. You may choose to return all possible records that matched your query. Let's debug and see if this actually works (the results are shown in Figure 8-12).

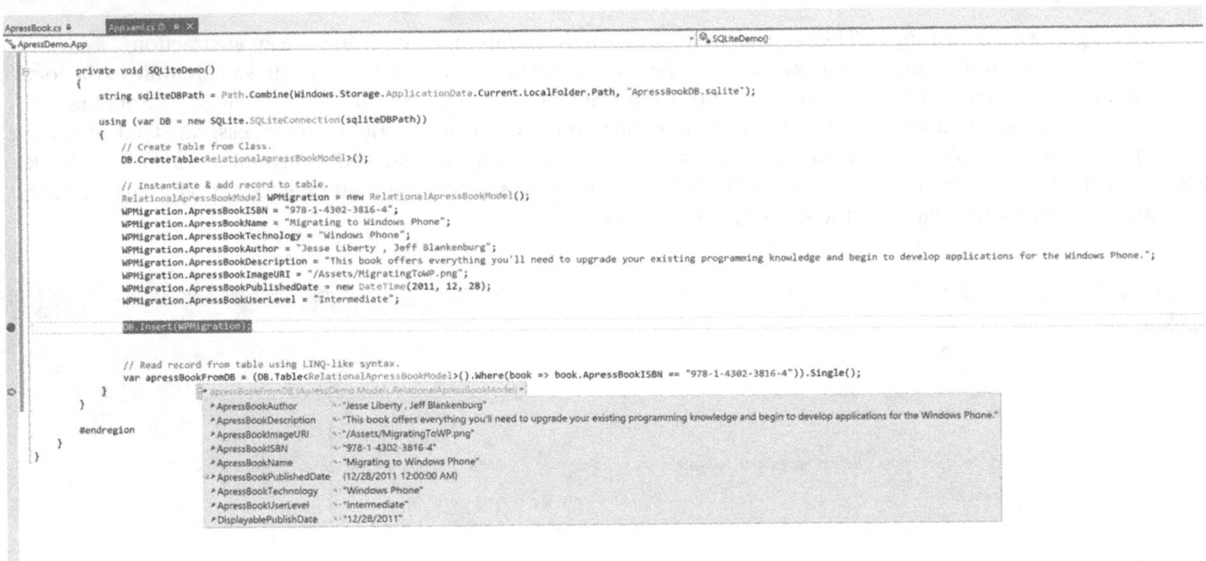

Figure 8-12. *Debugging SQLite code*

As you can see, your freshly declared `var` placeholder gets hydrated with a database record, fetched from the table where the query matched. The result is already a deserialized object in the exact type that the object belongs to. You can write C# code from then on. This invites you to explore other CRUD possibilities with the database records. Once you know how to fetch an individual record, updates/deletes are easy. Simply manipulate your object and call `DB.Update()` or `DB.Delete()`. I leave that exercise for your needs.

Summary

In this chapter, you saw a variety of ways that data can be handled in Windows 8 Store apps. Data can be of varying types and each scenario/app might demand a specific data storage strategy. This chapter gave you a taste for the assortment of data storage techniques and targets available. No one mechanism is ideal; it all depends on your app and the user's needs. You are well equipped as a developer, at least. Think hard about the current and future requirements of your Windows 8 app, and devise a data storage strategy that is appropriate. Best wishes for your data!

CHAPTER 9

Application Life-Cycle Management

No matter how feature-rich the Windows 8 Store app is or how sophisticated the design, the user experience provided by the app will fall flat on its face if application life-cycle management isn't done right. What does that mean? Well, basically, knowing how a Windows 8 Store app cycles through several stages in its process life cycle, across sessions from installation to removal. Does Windows offer events you could listen to at various phases in the life cycle and take appropriate action? What do suspend, resume, and termination mean? How about knowing when to save application data or a session state? Can there be any processing done in the background? All of these questions are answered in this important chapter. Handling the process life cycle correctly truly makes an app feel all grown up and ready for the Windows Store. The goal is simple: provide continuity of experience across uses of the Windows 8 Store app and consistently delight the user.

Process Life Cycle

So, you download a Windows 8 app from the Store or have a line-of-business app side-loaded onto your Windows 8 device. At this point, you have acquired the app, which is ready for use after installation and registered with your Windows 8 OS. You launch the app, use it for a while, and move on to other tasks/apps. Perhaps you even take the time to manually close the app (a swipe gesture from the top to the bottom of the screen) between multiple sessions. No matter how you use a Windows 8 app, have you noticed some trends? The user experience is consistent as you jump back into the app every time—it somehow seems to remember what you were up to last time. A little spooky at first, but you begin to appreciate that Windows 8 apps are designed with the user's workflow in mind.

Here's what is happening behind the scenes. A Windows 8 Store app cycles between different states during its application life cycle, based on how the app was launched, used, or closed. Apps that are good citizens in the Windows 8 world handle these life-cycle states smoothly and manage user data, giving the user the illusion that he or she never really left the app. Throughout the life-cycle stages, Windows 8 apps provide appropriate checkpoints (read events) that can be leveraged by app developers to manage data and session states for a smooth user experience. But first, you'll dive into the different life-cycle stages for every Windows 8 Store app. A picture is worth a thousand words, right? So, you'll begin with the Windows 8 app life-cycle visual shown in Figure 9-1.

Figure 9-1. Application life cycle

Let's unpack what happens as you run a Windows 8 Store app:

1. On a fresh app launch, Windows 8 applications will display a splash screen and start showing the first page of the app. This initial launch of the app is mostly from the user tapping/clicking the main/secondary app tile on the Windows 8 Start screen.

2. During the time the splash screen shows, the app's custom UI, data bindings, and registering of event handlers are happening at a frantic pace. Because you will only get a few seconds to show the first page, heavy operations should be avoided to quicken application load time. Once done, the splash screen is torn down and the app enters the *running* state.

3. In addition to the normal launching of an app by tapping the Start screen tile, Windows 8 apps may also be launched through several *contract implementations* (like Search, Share Target, File Opener, etc.). Each one of these could start a nonrunning Windows 8 app and the app activations are handled through specially marked entry points for taking appropriate action. I will talk about Windows 8 app contracts and activations in detail in the next chapter.

4. Once an app is running, the user may step away from it, thus putting it in the background. This stepping away can be the result of coming back to the Start screen or stepping into another app in response to a toast or using the application backstack to navigate to the last app in use. When the user moves an app to the background, Windows waits a few seconds to see whether the user will immediately switch back to the app. If the user does not switch back, Windows suspends the app. This triggers the app to go into a *suspended* state immediately.

5. While in a suspended state, the app, with all its contents, is just being held in memory by Windows. The app does not get CPU cycles (except for background tasks). This is to support fast application switching so that when the user comes back to your app through the application backstack, the app is immediately rehydrated and running again. This is called *app resume*, and it is meant to provide Windows 8 users a lot of flexibility in endlessly switching between apps, without sacrificing performance.

6. Many Windows 8 apps in suspension eventually stretch system resources, at which point Windows decides to *terminate* suspended apps. This is when apps are truly killed and all resources are freed up. Windows 8 apps enter a *not running* state upon termination. As you shall see in a bit, Windows 8 does not provide a mechanism for apps to get notified before termination. This is why handling the app suspension correctly becomes all the more important: you never know when your Windows 8 app may be terminated.

7. Although users generally do not need to close Windows 8 apps, they can choose to do so through a swipe-down touch gesture from the top of the screen or by pressing Alt+F4. Or, a running application may have crashed due to unforeseen circumstances, bringing the user back to the Start screen. In both cases, the app is terminated and enters the not running state.

Events

Surely, you expect your own Windows 8 Store app to let you, as the developer, know when it is cycling through the different application life-cycle stages. What good would come from a detailed process life-cycle plan if you cannot get hooks into knowing when an app changes state? We developers have complete visibility into the life cycle of our Windows 8 Store apps. It is highly suggested that you leverage this opportunity to provide optimum continuity in the user experience.

But first, let's inspect the hooks that developers have access to when it comes to app life-cycle stage switching. Then you can start making sense of the best opportunity to perform an appropriate action. Here are some application life-cycle events that can act as hooks telling you what's going on with your app:

- *OnLaunched*: This event is triggered when a Windows 8 app is activated from a cold start. It most commonly means the app is being started from the Start screen tile. This is your first opportunity to run custom code in response to a Windows 8 system event and take appropriate action before the first page of your app is shown to the user. Please note that this event is not raised if the app is resuming from suspension.
- *Suspending*: This event is triggered when the Windows 8 app has been pushed off the screen by the user and Windows has waited its customary few seconds to see if the user wants to switch back. The `Suspending` event is raised just before Windows 8 is about to put an app in suspended mode. This means that the app, with all its hydrated custom objects, will be held in memory by Windows 8, but the app will not be given any more computational cycles. It is your best opportunity as a developer to try to save state so that the user can be brought right back to his or her experience. Although Windows will save most of the current state of the app in memory, user/application data cannot be risked by just being in memory. What if the app stays in suspension and eventually gets terminated? Windows does *not* provide a notification to apps as they are being terminated. So the `Suspending` event is your best shot to save appropriate data and provide the user experience of continuity.
- *Resuming*: This event, as the name suggests, is simply raised when the app is coming back to the foreground through user action. It most commonly means that an app was in a suspended state and is coming back to being in a running state. Most times, app developers do not need to do much because the app was held in memory in its entirety; but certain application requirements may force you to take action on this event (for example, refreshing a news feed if the app has been suspended long enough).

So, enough talking. Shall you write some code? All of the app life-cycle events come to us as a courtesy of your app being a part of the `frame`-rendering mechanism that runs Windows 8 Store apps. Although life-cycle events are at an application level, they are exposed to every XAML page, as you shall see in a bit. First, go back to your Apress Featured Books Demo app for some sample code. Look inside the `App.xaml.cs` file for some application-level event handling. You should see some boilerplate code that looks like Listing 9-1.

Listing 9-1. The OnLaunched Event Handler

```
protected override async void OnLaunched(LaunchActivatedEventArgs args)
        {
            Frame rootFrame = Window.Current.Content as Frame;

            // Do not repeat app initialization when the Window already has content,
            // just ensure that the window is active

            if (rootFrame == null)
            {
                // Create a Frame to act as the navigation context and navigate  to the first page
                rootFrame = new Frame();
                //Associate the frame with a SuspensionManager key
                SuspensionManager.RegisterFrame(rootFrame, "AppFrame");

                if (args.PreviousExecutionState == ApplicationExecutionState.Terminated)
                {
                    // Restore the saved session state only when appropriate.
```

```
                try
                {
                    await SuspensionManager.RestoreAsync();
                }
                catch (SuspensionManagerException)
                {
                    //Something went wrong restoring state.
                    //Assume there is no state and continue
                }
            }
            else
            {
            }

            // Place the frame in the current Window
            Window.Current.Content = rootFrame;
        }
        if (rootFrame.Content == null)
        {
            // When the navigation stack isn't restored navigate to the first page,
            // configuring the new page by passing required information as a navigation
            // parameter
            if (!rootFrame.Navigate(typeof(FeaturedBookList)))
            {
                throw new Exception("Failed to create initial page");
            }
        }
        // Ensure the current window is active
        Window.Current.Activate();
    }
```

As you can see, the OnLaunched application event is overridable and you have a chance to do custom processing in addition to what's needed to show the current frame on screen. In just a bit, you will return to the code that you can add here. First, take a look at the modified app constructor method:

```
public App()
{
    this.InitializeComponent();
    this.Suspending += OnSuspending;
    this.Resuming += OnResuming;
}
```

Notice how you choose to listen in on the Suspending and Resuming events at the app level. Next, you can write event handlers in response to those events, like in the following:

```
private async void OnSuspending(object sender, SuspendingEventArgs e)
{
}

private void OnResuming(object sender, object e)
{
}
```

All of this code is at the application level and within App.xaml.cs. Could individual XAML pages not choose to listen in? Go back to the FeaturedBookList.xaml.cs file in your Apress demo to do some page-level event handling. Listing 9-2 presents the code.

Listing 9-2. Life-Cycle Event Handlers Within XAML Pages

```
protected override void OnNavigatedTo(NavigationEventArgs e)
        {
            base.OnNavigatedTo(e);

            Application.Current.Suspending += new SuspendingEventHandler(App_Suspending);
            Application.Current.Resuming += new EventHandler<Object>(App_Resuming);
        }

        protected override void OnNavigatedFrom(NavigationEventArgs e)
        {
            base.OnNavigatedFrom(e);

            Application.Current.Suspending -= App_Suspending;
           Application.Current.Resuming -= App_ Resuming;
        }

        protected void App_Suspending(Object sender, Windows.ApplicationModel.SuspendingEventArgs e)
        {

        }

        protected void App_Resuming(Object sender, Object e)
        {

        }
```

As you can see, you tapped into two events during a XAML page's life cycle—OnNavigatedTo and OnNavigatedFrom—to add to your application life-cycle code. You simply listen in on the current application's Suspending and Resuming events, with matching event handlers to take appropriate action accordingly. Pretty simple, isn't it? One quick thing to note is about the wiring/unwiring of event handlers within a XAML page's own life cycle: it is normally considered good practice to unwire event handlers from events while navigating away from pages, as you can see in Listing 9-2.

Timing and Debugging

At this point, you have a fair understanding of the Windows 8 Store app life cycle and the events that occur along the way that we developers can tap into to get our custom application logic in. Your next question might be: *When* do I know it's time to do *what* in my Windows 8 app?

While the application life cycle offers couple different events and opportunities to save/load session state, the timing of actions is important. Here are a few guidelines:

- Application data should be hydrated for the first time in the OnLaunched event handler and saved in the OnSuspending event handler. This should be global data within your Windows 8 Store app. It can be done in the App.xaml.cs.
- Although OnSuspending is the one event to save session/application data, you should not wait for this one opportunity to save all the data required by the app. The point is to save incrementally so that you are not doing everything in one go. During app execution, if you feel some application/user data can be persisted right away, you should absolutely do that.

- Any data that is not considered application or global level should be left to individual pages to save and load. Even if the user comes back to a page in your app after it has been terminated, you should bring the user back to exactly where he or she left off for continuity of user experience. Any typing or selections the user has done on input UI controls should absolutely be retained.

Responding to Life-Cycle Events

Now, with some of those guidelines in mind, let's look at some sample code. Suppose that you want to keep track of the last time the user viewed the Featured Books page in your Apress demo app. Listing 9-3 provides some code toward that goal.

Listing 9-3. Resume/Suspend Event Handlers

```
protected override void OnNavigatedTo(NavigationEventArgs e)
        {
            base.OnNavigatedTo(e);

            Application.Current.Suspending += new SuspendingEventHandler(App_Suspending);
            Application.Current.Resuming += new EventHandler<Object>(App_Resuming);
        }

        protected override void OnNavigatedFrom(NavigationEventArgs e)
        {
            base.OnNavigatedFrom(e);

            Application.Current.Suspending -= App_Suspending;
            Application.Current.Resuming -= App_Resuming;
        }

        protected void App_Suspending(Object sender, Windows.ApplicationModel.SuspendingEventArgs e)
        {
            // Reference to Local Application Settings.
            Windows.Storage.ApplicationDataContainer localSettings =
Windows.Storage.ApplicationData.Current.LocalSettings;

            localSettings.Values["lastViewedTimeStamp"] = DateTime.Now.ToString();
        }

        protected void App_Resuming(Object sender, Object e)
        {
            // Reference to Local Application Settings.
            Windows.Storage.ApplicationDataContainer localSettings =
Windows.Storage.ApplicationData.Current.LocalSettings;

            string lastViewedTimeStamp = (string)localSettings.Values["lastViewedTimeStamp"];
        }
```

As you can see, you are simply saving the current timestamp in a local settings placeholder during the app's suspension and reading it back upon resuming. As you run the code in Listing 9-3 in your app, you may feel the need to validate that it is working correctly. Short of throwing test UI controls to read/write timestamps, you are looking for ways to debug application life-cycle code. Let's look at how this is possible.

To properly test application life-cycle code, we developers have to constantly run our Windows 8 Store app, put it in suspension, and hope that we can tax the system enough to trigger an app termination. Sounds difficult and begs for an easier way. And, of course, Visual Studio obliges. So, in your Visual Studio setup, go to the Windows Toolbars options. You need to enable the Debug Location menu. Figure 9-2 shows how to enable life-cycle debugging after you right-click the Visual Studio menu toolbar.

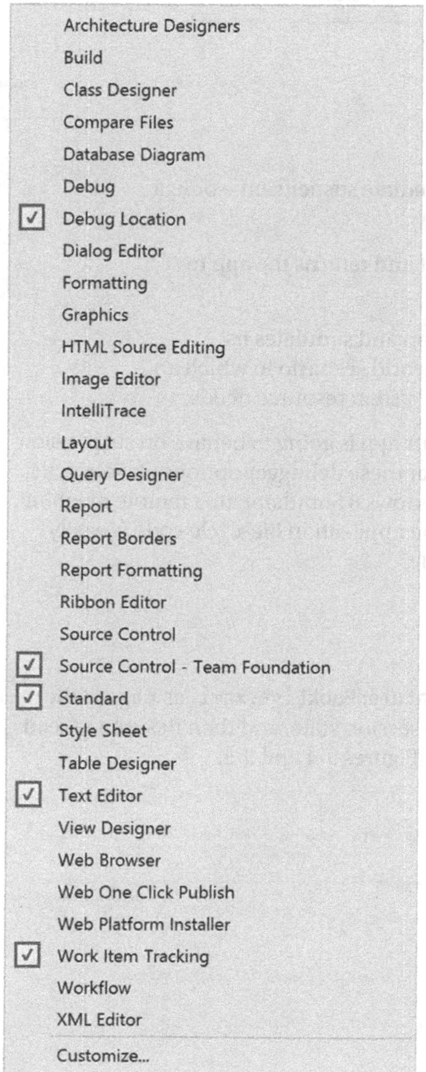

Figure 9-2. *The Debug Location menu option*

Once enabled, you should see the Debug Location toolbar options (see Figure 9-3) for the Apress demo app in Visual Studio.

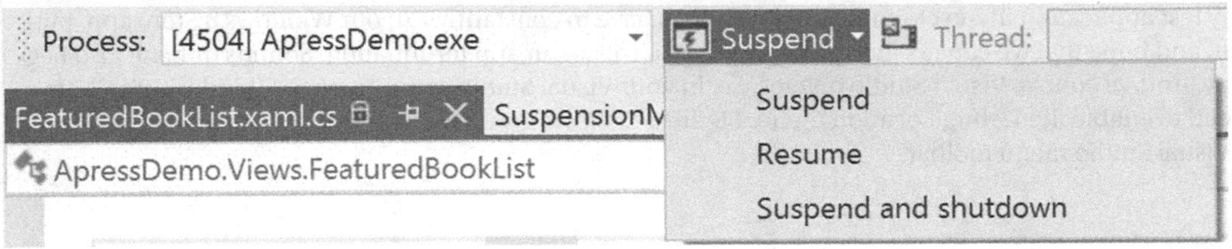
Process: [4504] ApressDemo.exe
Suspend
Thread:
FeaturedBookList.xaml.cs
ApressDemo.Views.FeaturedBookList
Suspend
Resume
Suspend and shutdown

Figure 9-3. *Debug options*

Here's what the three options mean:

- *Suspend*: This simply puts a running Windows 8 Store app in immediate suspension—or in a not running state.
- *Resume*: This immediately brings a suspended app to the forefront and returns the app to running state.
- *Suspend and shutdown*: This option takes a running Windows 8 app and simulates its suspension with immediate termination. This is close to the real-world scenario in which an app is suspended for a while and then gets terminated because of system resource needs.

These three debugger options are very powerful in testing exactly how your app is going to behave on suspension and reactivation from suspension, or after termination. And the best part is that these debugger options work exactly the same way whether the developer is debugging on a local machine, the Windows 8 Simulator, or a remote machine. In short, it provides complete flexibility for the developer to make sure all of the application life-cycle code is easily testable through simulation of the app running at various phases in its life cycle.

Debugging Through Life-Cycle Events

Armed with the debugger options, try debugging the code you wrote in the `FeaturedBookList.xaml.cs` page of the Apress demo app. Once the app is running, you can press Suspend to save the session state, and then Resume to read back any saved data. The debugger happily hits your breakpoints, as shown in Figures 9-4 and 9-5.

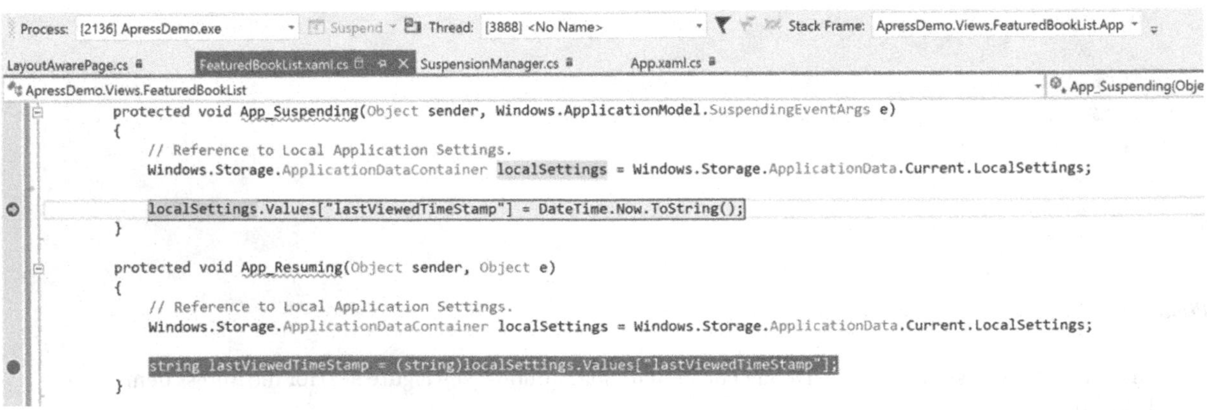
Process: [2136] ApressDemo.exe
Thread: [3888] <No Name>
Stack Frame: ApressDemo.Views.FeaturedBookList.App
LayoutAwarePage.cs
FeaturedBookList.xaml.cs
SuspensionManager.cs
App.xaml.cs
ApressDemo.Views.FeaturedBookList
App_Suspending(Obje
protected void App_Suspending(Object sender, Windows.ApplicationModel.SuspendingEventArgs e)
{
// Reference to Local Application Settings.
Windows.Storage.ApplicationDataContainer localSettings = Windows.Storage.ApplicationData.Current.LocalSettings;
localSettings.Values["lastViewedTimeStamp"] = DateTime.Now.ToString();
}
protected void App_Resuming(Object sender, Object e)
{
// Reference to Local Application Settings.
Windows.Storage.ApplicationDataContainer localSettings = Windows.Storage.ApplicationData.Current.LocalSettings;
string lastViewedTimeStamp = (string)localSettings.Values["lastViewedTimeStamp"];
}

Figure 9-4. *Debugging suspension*

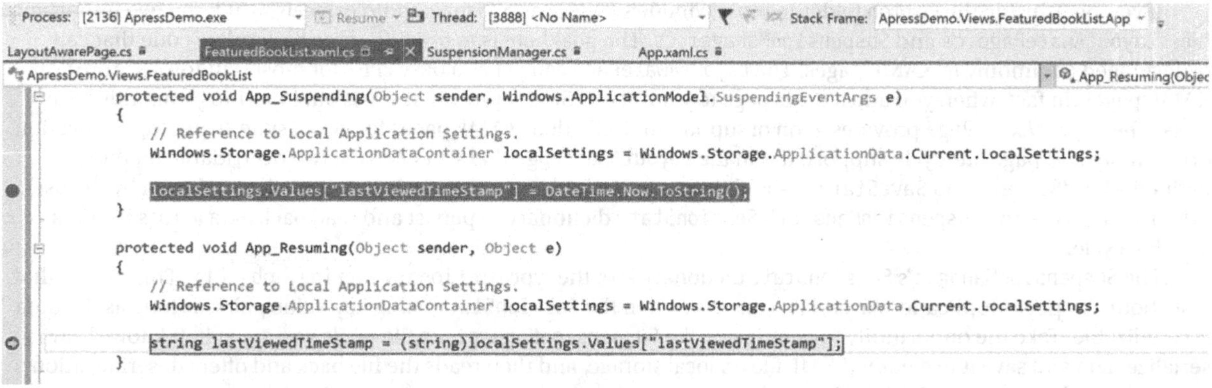
Process: [2136] ApressDemo.exe
Resume
Thread: [3888] <No Name>
Stack Frame: ApressDemo.Views.FeaturedBookList.App
LayoutAwarePage.cs
FeaturedBookList.xaml.cs
SuspensionManager.cs
App.xaml.cs
ApressDemo.Views.FeaturedBookList
App_Resuming(Objec
protected void App_Suspending(Object sender, Windows.ApplicationModel.SuspendingEventArgs e)
{
// Reference to Local Application Settings.
Windows.Storage.ApplicationDataContainer localSettings = Windows.Storage.ApplicationData.Current.LocalSettings;
localSettings.Values["lastViewedTimeStamp"] = DateTime.Now.ToString();
}
protected void App_Resuming(Object sender, Object e)
{
// Reference to Local Application Settings.
Windows.Storage.ApplicationDataContainer localSettings = Windows.Storage.ApplicationData.Current.LocalSettings;
string lastViewedTimeStamp = (string)localSettings.Values["lastViewedTimeStamp"];
}

Figure 9-5. *Debugging resume*

Not every developer will know, right out of the gate, how to latch onto the app's `Suspending` and `Resuming` events to hydrate or dehydrate the object model or the user data on every page. To make this a little easier, let's take a look at some boilerplate code that gets added to a Basic page's code-behind:

```
protected override async void LoadState(Object navigationParameter, Dictionary<String, Object>
pageState)
        {
        }

        protected override void SaveState(Dictionary<String, Object> pageState)
        {
        }
```

So, it seems like you already have two hooks built in place in every page to save/load data as the user moves in and out of the page. And they seem like overrides. Where do you think this comes from?Figure 9-6 tries to explain, as you can see if you look under Solution Explorer in your Visual Studio project structure.

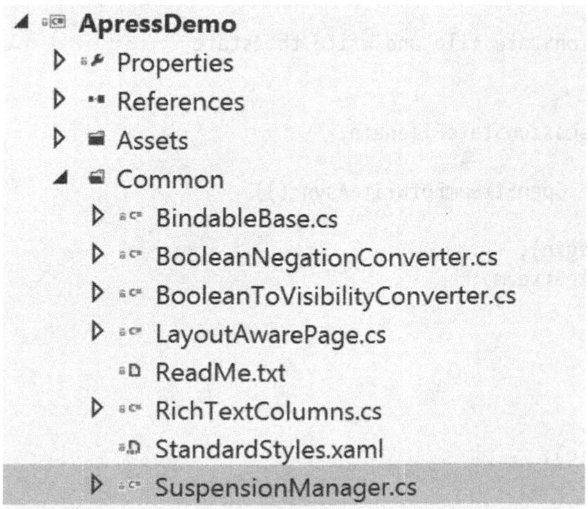
ApressDemo
Properties
References
Assets
Common
BindableBase.cs
BooleanNegationConverter.cs
BooleanToVisibilityConverter.cs
LayoutAwarePage.cs
ReadMe.txt
RichTextColumns.cs
StandardStyles.xaml
SuspensionManager.cs

Figure 9-6. *App Suspension plumbing*

If you peek inside the Common folder in most Windows 8 Store app Visual Studio projects, you'll see two important files: LayoutAwarePage.cs and SuspensionManager.cs. The goal here is to provide some boilerplate code that can be leveraged commonly in XAML pages. The LayoutAwarePage can act as a base class for most Windows 8 Store app XAML pages. In fact, when you add a Basic page to your Visual Studio project, it starts out inheriting from this base class. The LayoutAwarePage provides a ton of support for individual XAML pages for visual state switching, navigation, orientation, and page life-cycle support. It is in the LayoutAwarePage that you have the two overridable methods defined—LoadState() and SaveState()—and they are prewired to the page being navigated to and from by the user. Both methods use the SuspensionManager's SessionState dictionary to persist and read back data across a page's own life cycle.

The SuspensionManager's SessionState dictionary is of the type Dictionary<string, object>. This means that just about any page/application/user data can be saved in the SessionState using key-value pairs, as long as the data is serializable. Take the opportunity to peek inside the SuspensionManager.cs file while you are at it. It knows how to serialize data and save it to a named XML file on local storage, and then reads the file back and offers deserialization to rehydrate object models. Let's look at some code in the SuspensionManager (see Listing 9-4).

Listing 9-4. Asynchronous Save and Restore

```
private static Dictionary<string, object> _sessionState = new Dictionary<string, object>();
        private static List<Type> _knownTypes = new List<Type>();
        private const string sessionStateFilename = "_sessionState.xml";

public static async Task SaveAsync()
        {
            try
            {
            ....

            // Serialize the session state synchronously to avoid asynchronous access to shared
state.
            MemoryStream sessionData = new MemoryStream();
            DataContractSerializer serializer = new
DataContractSerializer(typeof(Dictionary<string, object>), _knownTypes);
            serializer.WriteObject(sessionData, _sessionState);

                // Get an output stream for the SessionState file and write the state
asynchronously.
                StorageFile file = await
ApplicationData.Current.LocalFolder.CreateFileAsync(sessionStateFilename,
CreationCollisionOption.ReplaceExisting);
                using (Stream fileStream = await file.OpenStreamForWriteAsync())
                {
                    sessionData.Seek(0, SeekOrigin.Begin);
                    await sessionData.CopyToAsync(fileStream);
                    await fileStream.FlushAsync();
                }
            }
            catch (Exception e)
            {
                throw new SuspensionManagerException(e);
            }
        }
```

```
        public static async Task RestoreAsync()
        {
            _sessionState = new Dictionary<String, Object>();

            try
            {
                // Get the input stream for the SessionState file
                StorageFile file = await
ApplicationData.Current.LocalFolder.GetFileAsync(sessionStateFilename);
                using (IInputStream inStream = await file.OpenSequentialReadAsync())
                {
                    // Deserialize the Session State
                    DataContractSerializer serializer = new
DataContractSerializer(typeof(Dictionary<string, object>), _knownTypes);
                    _sessionState = (Dictionary<string,
object>)serializer.ReadObject(inStream.AsStreamForRead());
                }
            }
...
            catch (Exception e)
            {
                throw new SuspensionManagerException(e);
            }
        }
```

Listing 9-4 shows two methods offered for reuse by the SuspensionManager: SaveAsync and RestoreAsync. As their names suggest, these two methods are good at saving and restoring data, and they do it completely asynchronously using the new C# 5.0 async-await pattern so that UI threads are never blocked. Essentially, the use of DataContractSerializer flattens/unflattens data into XML and then saves/reads it from disk. If you trace your Windows 8 Store app's local data storage in the AppData/Packages directory, you can actually see the SessionState XML file being written. The point is that any custom data (as long as it is serializable) can be added to the KnownTypes list so that the DataContractSerializer knows how to serialize/deserialize. So, you can write custom code to save/read, or simply use the SuspensionManager's help.

Dictionaries and Deferrals

Now, turn your attention back to the App.xaml.cs file and add some code to the application's Suspending/Resuming event handlers:

```
private async void OnSuspending(object sender, SuspendingEventArgs e)
        {
            var deferral = e.SuspendingOperation.GetDeferral();

            // Save regular settings or App level data.
            SuspensionManager.SessionState["LastViewedTimeStamp"] = DateTime.Now.ToString();
            await SuspensionManager.SaveAsync();

            deferral.Complete();
        }
```

```
        private void OnResuming(object sender, object e)
        {
            string lastViewTimeStamp =
(string)SuspensionManager.SessionState["LastViewedTimeStamp"];
        }
```

In this code, you are leveraging the SuspensionManager's SessionState dictionary to quickly save the current timestamp during suspension, and then read it back during resume. Do you see the use of the SaveAsync() method from the SuspensionManager? This is where you get to serialize your custom data for writing to an XML file. Simply add your type to the SuspensionManager's KnownTypes for the DataContractSerializer to work with. Now, once the Suspending event kicks in, Windows 8 will give the app a few seconds to save state before putting it in suspension. Anything longer than 5 seconds will not be run by the OS. This is where the deferral mechanism kicks in. It's a way for us to tell the OS to completely finish the data save asynchronously before moving on; deferral.Complete() is an indication that you're done saving.

AppExecutionStates

Look into some boilerplate code in the App.xaml.cs file's OnLaunched event handler:

```
if (args.PreviousExecutionState == ApplicationExecutionState.Terminated)
                {
                    // Restore the saved session state only when appropriate.
                    try
                    {
                        await SuspensionManager.RestoreAsync();
                    }
                    catch (SuspensionManagerException)
                    {
                        //Something went wrong restoring state.
                        //Assume there is no state and continue
                    }
                }
```

You can now see the full picture. Upon app launch, you have the option of using the SuspensionManager's RestoreAsync() method to read the session state back from the serialized data in file. This code also introduces you to an interesting API: the ApplicationExecutionState. It is available for use anywhere and it is your one-stop answer to the question: What was the app state before its present state? Figure 9-7 shows the enumeration values from an MSDN screen grab. The enumeration key-values should be pretty self-explanatory. It is very handy for developers to check the last application state before taking action.

Members

The **ApplicationExecutionState** enumeration has these members.

Member	Value	Description
NotRunning | notRunning	0	The app is not running.
Running | running	1	The app is running.
Suspended | suspended	2	The app is suspended.
Terminated | terminated	3	The app was terminated after being suspended.
ClosedByUser | closedByUser	4	The app was closed by the user.

Figure 9-7. *ApplicationExecutionState enumerations*

Async-Await and Race Conditions

Since you are talking about saving/loading data as needed during the app's life cycle, this may be a good time to actually take a closer look at some of the asynchronous operations you have been doing. Asynchronous programming is nothing new, but it hasn't always been easy. Take a look at how coding for asynchronicity evolved over time.

- *Asynchronous Programming Model (APM)*: This is the initial traditional asynchronous programming pattern where expensive operations are invoked through `BeginXXX`/`EndXXX` pairs. Essentially, you fire off a long-running operation after assigning an `Async` callback handler, which provides the result handle to receive context when execution is completed. More information is at `http://msdn.microsoft.com/en-us/library/ms228963.aspx`.
- *Event-based Asynchronous Programming (EAP)*: This is the more sophisticated brother of APM, in which the operation completion callbacks are wired through event handling. Remember the times when you did a *DoSomethingComplete += ExecutionEndFunction();* ? Yep, that is an EAP pattern. More information is at `http://msdn.microsoft.com/en-us/library/wewwczdw.aspx`.
- *Async-Await*: While the APM and EAP patterns of asynchronous programming work, the complexities of wiring callbacks or marshaling context from non-UI threads did not make things easy for developers. So, C# 5.0, which is what you use to develop Windows 8 Store apps, introduces two keywords to make life easier: `async` and `await`. The point is in-line asynchrony, with the developer released from having to wire completion callbacks. More information is at `http://msdn.microsoft.com/en-us/library/hh191443.aspx`.

Take a very simple example pattern of asynchronous programming to understand what `Async-Await` is doing under the covers. Suppose that you have a method like the following:

```
public async void DoSomething()
{
        Code Line 1
        SomeValue = await SomeHeavyOperation();
        Code Line 2, works with SomeValue
        Code Line 3
}
```

Essentially, before you use the Await keyword inside a method, the method needs to use the keyword Async in its declaration. Marking a method Async does not automatically make the method perform its executables asynchronously; instead, it is just an indication/declaration to the compiler that this method may contain heavy, time-consuming operations. The compiler then looks out for the first occurrence of the Await keyword, and then the magic begins. The preceding method gets broken into two pieces called *state machines*—things before and after the Await operation. First, all the code leading up to the first Await command is executed as usual. Then, the Await operation simply puts the rest of the method on hold until the operation completes. Once the results of the expensive operation are available, the rest of the code in the method executes and you are free to use results from the Await operation in your code.

You are probably wondering how the async-await operation supports asynchronous operations since the execution of the method stops at the first Await keyword. The magic under the covers lies in the fact that this pausing of code execution until some operation finishes is completely invisible to the developer. When code execution control hits the first Await, execution of code pauses for as long it takes to finish the operation. In the meantime, a Task is immediately returned in response to the Await operation and the compiler wires callbacks (the rest of the method) and returns the execution to the caller. This means that whichever part of the code invoked your little *DoSomething()* method gets control, and program execution continues along merrily as if no heavy operations needed to be performed. The whole trick of executing the rest of the method upon completion of the Await operation is hidden and handled at runtime. You can read more about the Task Parallel Library (TPL), which powers the async-await pattern, at http://msdn.microsoft.com/en-us/library/dd460717(v=VS.110).aspx.

The async-await pattern has the distinct advantage of having developers write asynchronous code that looks just like synchronous code—simple, inline, and code segments one after another without any waiting/callbacks. Such asynchronous programming is obviously much needed for touch-friendly Windows 8 Store apps, where the main UI application thread can never be blocked. In fact, Windows 8 Store XAML/C# app development is actually going to enforce asynchrony by not allowing developers to write synchronous/blocking code. Any network operations, file system access, or operations with WinRT APIs that take more than 50 milliseconds are all written in an asynchronous programming model using Async-Await.

Amid all the goodness you derive from the use of the latest C# feature of the async-await pattern, there may be a potential risk area in Windows 8 Store app development that I want to spend a little time on. Developers may use Async-Await in the right way; but not be conscious of potential race conditions that are being built up in the code. The fact that the Async-Await pattern immediately returns code control to the calling method, without executing a whole method, may catch a few developers off guard. Let's dig in with an example.

Remember the code on how to save/load custom object data, serialized as XML (from the last chapter)? Listing 9-5 is a recap of where you save and read custom data in the Apress demo's App.xaml.cs file to hydrate/dehydrate your FeaturedApressBooks collection:

Listing 9-5. Custom Data Persistence

```
private async void SaveCustomData()
        {
            MemoryStream customDataToSave = new MemoryStream();
            DataContractSerializer serializer = new
DataContractSerializer(typeof(ObservableCollection<ApressBook>));
            serializer.WriteObject(customDataToSave, FeaturedBookListVM.FeaturedApressBooks);

                // Write serialized custom data to File on HardDisk.
                StorageFile fileToWrite = await
localFolder.CreateFileAsync("CustomSerializedFile.xml", CreationCollisionOption.ReplaceExisting);
                using (Stream fileStream = await fileToWrite.OpenStreamForWriteAsync())
                {
                    customDataToSave.Seek(0, SeekOrigin.Begin);
```

```
                await customDataToSave.CopyToAsync(fileStream);
                await fileStream.FlushAsync();
            }
        }

        private async void ReadCustomData()
        {
            StorageFile fileToRead = await localFolder.GetFileAsync("CustomSerializedFile.xml");
            using (IInputStream inStream = await fileToRead.OpenSequentialReadAsync())
            {
                // Read data from File and Deserialize.
                DataContractSerializer serializer = new
DataContractSerializer(typeof(ObservableCollection<ApressBook>));
                FeaturedBookListVM.FeaturedApressBooks =
(ObservableCollection<ApressBook>)serializer.ReadObject(inStream.AsStreamForRead());
            }
        }
```

Since this saving/loading of data involves file system access through WinRT, you obviously revert to using the `Async-Await` pattern for deferred reads/writes. Listing 9-5 is also very similar to the `SaveAsync()` and `RestoreAsync()` methods you saw in the `SuspensionManager` class. You can very well reuse what the `SuspensionManager` offers or roll your own. Now, envision application life-cycle code like Listing 9-6.

Listing 9-6. Persistence During Life-Cycle Events

```
private async void OnSuspending(object sender, SuspendingEventArgs e)
        {
            var deferral = e.SuspendingOperation.GetDeferral();

            // Save custom data.
            this.SaveCustomData();

            deferral.Complete();
        }

protected override async void OnLaunched(LaunchActivatedEventArgs args)
        {
        if (args.PreviousExecutionState == ApplicationExecutionState.Terminated ||
args.PreviousExecutionState == ApplicationExecutionState.NotRunning)
                {
                    // Restore the saved session state only when appropriate.
                    try
                    {
                        // Hydrate from saved custom data.
                        this.ReadCustomData();
                    }
                    catch (SuspensionManagerException)
                    {
                        //Something went wrong restoring state.
                        //Assume there is no state and continue
                    }
                }
```

```
            else
            {
                // Hydrate with sample data.
                FeaturedBookListVM.LoadFeaturedBooksDemoVM(FeaturedBookListVM);
            }
        }
```

As your Apress demo app is suspending in Listing 9-6, you serialize and save the entire collection of featured books. When the app is launched next time, you check its `PreviousExecutionState` to see if you want to rehydrate the book collection with sample data (read from network or some database in the real world) or actually read what has been saved in local storage during suspension. This should be pretty standard code and indicative of what many Windows 8 Store apps need to do to support caching across application life cycles.

If you run the code as is, however, you'll see a potential problem: you have unconsciously built a race condition in your code. Run the Apress demo app once, and then close/terminate it. Upon the next launch, you may see an error getting to the first page of the app. Here's the problem: your code looks good, but your `OnLaunched` event handler is trying to hydrate the `FeaturedApressBooks` collection by using the `ReadCustomData()` method. As you know, this involves file system access and it is leveraging the `Async-Await` pattern. Accordingly, code control execution is returned immediately to the `OnLaunched` event handler and the app proceeds with what's next: displaying the first page that shows a grouped collection of featured Apress books. The trouble is, since the `Await` operation inside `ReadCustomData()` may take a little while to finish and execute the rest of the method, code control execution may have already reached the code in the first XAML page, which will attempt data binding on the `FeaturedApressBooks` collection. The big problem is that your book collection may still be empty because the `Await`-powered hydration from deserialized file data may not have complete yet! The result is a bad app crash and difficulty for the developer to figure out where the cause of the problem lies. The lengthy `Await` operation simply has not finished before you try to act on the data returned.

Is there a solution without having to revert to block code execution until data rehydration completes? The answer lies in a careful implementation of the `Async-Await` pattern and leveraging the `Task` return type—a promised placeholder of future results of an operation. Let's look at some code. First, rewrite your reading of the book collection from the file system:

```
public async Task<ObservableCollection<ApressBook>> ReadCustomDataAsync()
        {
            StorageFile fileToRead = await localFolder.GetFileAsync("CustomSerializedFile.xml");
            using (IInputStream inStream = await fileToRead.OpenSequentialReadAsync())
            {
                // Read data from File and Deserialize.
                DataContractSerializer serializer = new
DataContractSerializer(typeof(ObservableCollection<ApressBook>));
                return (ObservableCollection<ApressBook>)serializer.ReadObject
(inStream.AsStreamForRead());
            }
        }
```

So, instead of the collection of books, you simply return a `Task`—a container for the future collection of books. While this is a good first step, the real problem is that the UI rendering will try to bind itself to the grouped collection of books without actually having a collection in the first place. Can you not delay the UI data binding until after the data is ready? Well, of course. Here's some code in the `FeaturedBookListViewModel.cs` file:

```
public async Task<ObservableCollection<GroupedApressBooks>> GetAwaitableGroupedFeaturedApressBooks()
        {
            this.FeaturedApressBooks = await ((App)Application.Current).ReadCustomDataDeferred();
```

```
            // Put Books into Grouped buckets based on Technology.
            var query = from individualApressBook in FeaturedApressBooks
                        orderby individualApressBook.ApressBookTechnology
                        group individualApressBook by
individualApressBook.ApressBookTechnology into g
                        select new GroupedApressBooks
                        {
                            ApressBookGroupName = g.Key,
                            ApressBookGroupCount = g.Count(),
                            BookCollection = new ObservableCollection<ApressBook>(g.ToList())
                        };

            if (_groupedFeaturedApressBooks == null)
                _groupedFeaturedApressBooks = new ObservableCollection<GroupedApressBooks>();

            _groupedFeaturedApressBooks = new
ObservableCollection<GroupedApressBooks>(query.ToList());

            return _groupedFeaturedApressBooks;
        }
```

In this case, instead of simply returning the grouped collection of books from the ViewModel property, you have made a separate method that returns the collection in a deferred way. Notice how you hydrated your FeaturedApressBooks collection using an Await keyword on ReadCustomDataDeferred(). The rest of the method can directly work with the book collection, knowing that these pieces of code will not execute until the Await operation completes.

But what about your UI binding? Will that wait for data to be available? Sure, here's some code:

```
// Set the Data-Binding context to the Grouped Book collection.
            if (((App)Application.Current).FeaturedBookListVM.FeaturedApressBooks != null)
                this.DefaultViewModel["GroupedFeaturedApressBooks"] =
((App)Application.Current).FeaturedBookListVM.GroupedFeaturedApressBooks;
            else
                // Allow for awaitable Data Binding.
                this.DefaultViewModel["GroupedFeaturedApressBooks"] = await
((App)Application.Current).FeaturedBookListVM.GetAwaitableGroupedFeaturedApressBooks();
```

That's it. Now, if your book collection is empty because the Await operation is not complete yet, the app will still render the first page, but the UI binding will wait it out until data becomes available and then automatically push out data on the screen. Race conditions solved. Also, as you write more and more Async-Await code, you may want to pay attention to how you handle exceptions. A great writeup on handling unhandled exceptions is at www.markermetro.com/2013/01/technical/handling-unhandled-exceptions-with-asyncawait-on-windows-8-and-windows-phone-8/.

Background Agents

Even with the all the options that developers have to execute custom code at various phases in a Windows 8 Store app's life cycle, you may still find yourself asking for more. Part of this may be because your Windows 8 app needs to have functionality that cannot be tied directly to the app's life cycle, or in particular, have code that would wait to execute during for the next time the app gets back into the running state. If this is the case, what you are looking for is slightly outside the app's life cycle. It's a little magic wand called a background agent.

A *background agent*, in short, is a part of your app's code that executes functionality when your app is not actually running. There are numerous examples where you can see why this type of flexibility is needed. What if your app wanted to play music in the background while the user is on a different app? What if you wanted to fetch the next news/sports feed and have it ready for the user upon app usage? Although I have yet to talk about app tiles/toasts/badges in detail, background agents are invariably helpful in updating these notification mechanisms while the actual app is not running. The point is that there is a genuine need to support background agents running from time to time, regardless of the app.

Making your app have a background agent is actually pretty simple. You need to define a task that can run in the background, register it with the OS, and set up triggers/conditions that will make the background agent run.

Adding a Background Agent

Start by setting up a background agent for your Apress demo app. Figure 9-8 shows how to take the first step. Right-click your Visual Studio solution and add a new project.

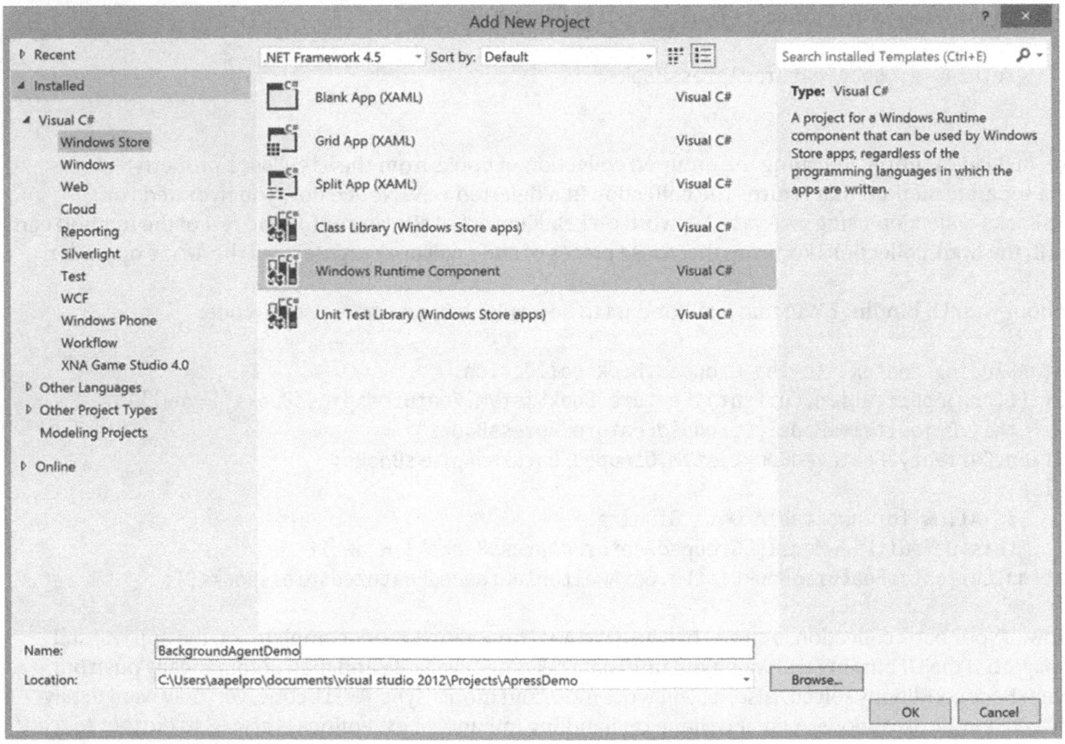

Figure 9-8. *Background agent addition*

As you can see, you added a new project to your solution to house your background agent. Although the project can really be anything that can hold a class, the output of the project needs to be a WinMD file, which is why you start with the Windows Runtime component project. After renaming the default class to something more friendly sounding, your project should look something like Figure 9-9. You simply need one class as a placeholder.

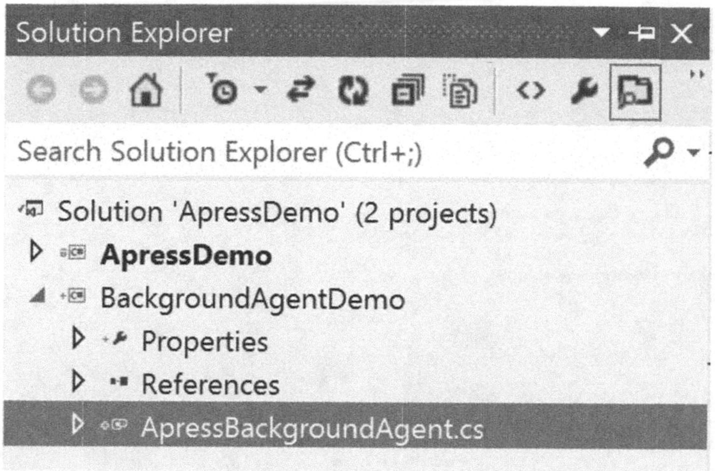

Figure 9-9. *Background agent project added to solution*

The code inside the `ApressBackgroundAgent.cs` starts out simple, as follows:

```
namespace BackgroundAgentDemo
{
    public sealed class ApressBackgroundAgent : IBackgroundTask
    {
        public void Run(IBackgroundTaskInstance taskInstance)
        {

        }
    }
}
```

Essentially, you need to implement an interface called `IBackgroundTask` for your background agent to be set up correctly. This works out easily because there is only one method to support, called `Run(IBackgroundTaskInstance)`, in which you declare what you actually want your background agent to execute.

Wiring the Background Agent

Before you start adding code here, a little plumbing is necessary so that Windows 8 OS knows your app will have a background agent running outside of the app life cycle. This is a two-step process: first, declare that the app will need a background agent and register the agent with the OS. For the declaration part, pop open the `Package.Appxmanifest` file and edit the Declarations tab, as shown in Figure 9-10.

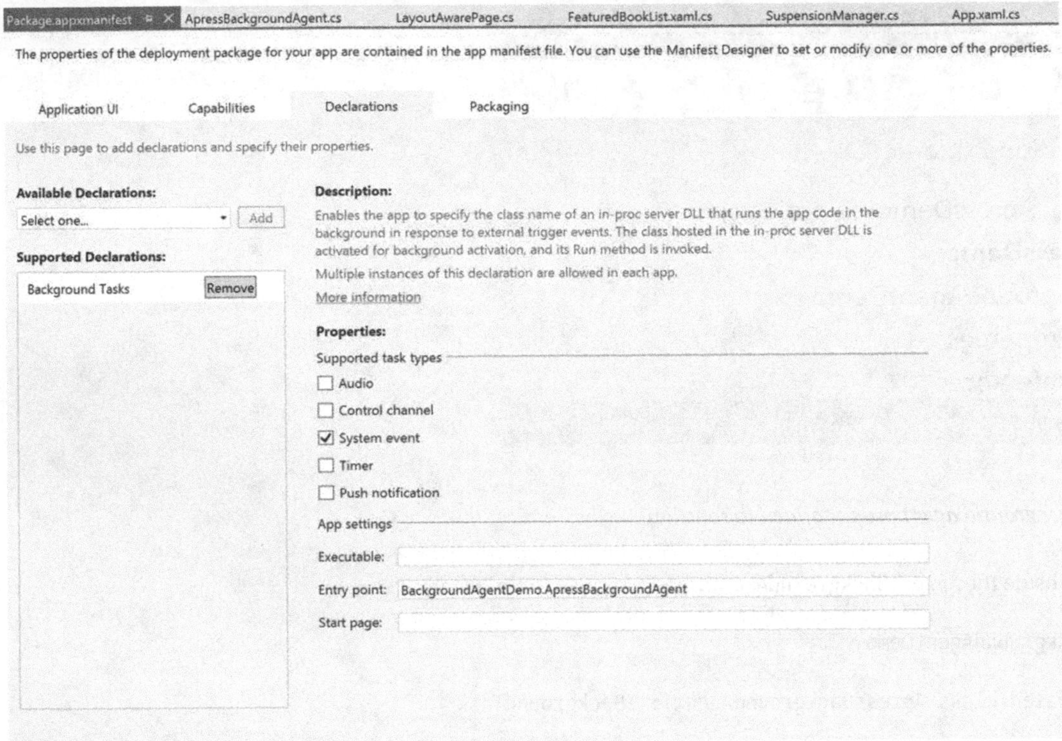

Figure 9-10. *Package.Appxmanifest background agent declaration*

So, you just declared your app's intention to support a background agent and specified an entry point. If you notice, this entry point matches your namespace and class declaration in the separate background agent project. This simply means you are pointing the OS at the right background task/agent to use. The `IBackgroundTask` interface takes care of the rest of the plumbing to execute whatever is defined in the `Run()` method. Do you wonder what the preceding change in the `Package.Appxmanifest` resulted in? Open the XML file without the designer and you should see something like that shown in Figure 9-11.

Package.appxmanifest ApressBackgroundAgent.cs LayoutAwarePage.cs FeaturedBookList.xaml.cs SuspensionManager.cs App.xaml.cs

```
<?xml version="1.0" encoding="utf-8"?>
<Package xmlns="http://schemas.microsoft.com/appx/2010/manifest">
  <Identity Name="5f052142-ff35-4e74-a904-0802ca25e566" Publisher="CN=aapelpro" Version="1.0.0.0" />
  <Properties>
    <DisplayName>ApressDemo</DisplayName>
    <PublisherDisplayName>aapelpro</PublisherDisplayName>
    <Logo>Assets\StoreLogo.png</Logo>
  </Properties>
  <Prerequisites>
    <OSMinVersion>6.2.1</OSMinVersion>
    <OSMaxVersionTested>6.2.1</OSMaxVersionTested>
  </Prerequisites>
  <Resources>
    <Resource Language="x-generate" />
  </Resources>
  <Applications>
    <Application Id="App" Executable="$targetnametoken$.exe" EntryPoint="ApressDemo.App">
      <VisualElements DisplayName="ApressDemo" Logo="Assets\Logo.png" SmallLogo="Assets\SmallLogo.png" Description="ApressDemo"
        <DefaultTile WideLogo="Assets\ApressLogoWide.png" />
        <SplashScreen Image="Assets\ApressLogo.png" BackgroundColor="black" />
        <InitialRotationPreference>
          <Rotation Preference="portrait" />
          <Rotation Preference="landscape" />
          <Rotation Preference="portraitFlipped" />
          <Rotation Preference="landscapeFlipped" />
        </InitialRotationPreference>
      </VisualElements>
      <Extensions>
        <Extension Category="windows.backgroundTasks" EntryPoint="BackgroundAgentDemo.ApressBackgroundAgent">
          <BackgroundTasks>
            <Task Type="systemEvent" />
          </BackgroundTasks>
        </Extension>
      </Extensions>
    </Application>
  </Applications>
  <Capabilities>
    <Capability Name="internetClient" />
  </Capabilities>
</Package>
```

Figure 9-11. *Package.Appxmanifest background agent XML extension*

As you can see in Figure 9-11, your changes added a new extension to your app manifest, declaring the background agent that was just declared. Do not forget to reference the background task/agent project in your main app project. This makes sure that the background agent gets packaged together with the app and makes it easy to debug. Right-click the `References` folder in the main app to add a new reference to your project (see Figure 9-12). The main app should refer back to the background agent that you just created.

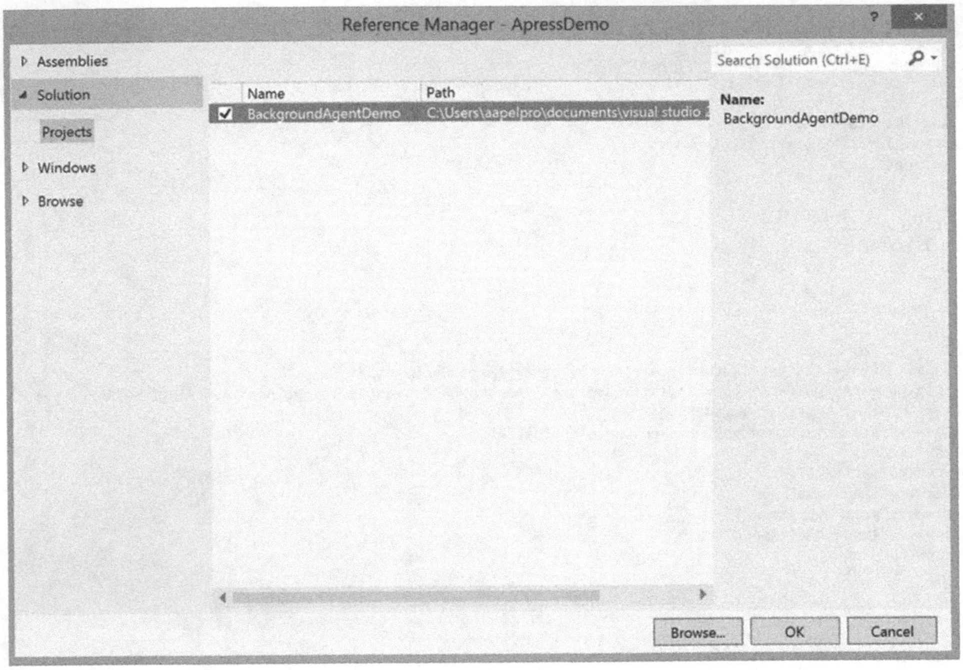

Figure 9-12. *Adding a background agent reference*

Background Agent Registration

This is the last step toward setting up the background task/agent: registering with the OS so that your background agent gets CPU cycles if the conditions for its running are met. Here's some code on registration from your Apress demo app's `App.xaml.cs` file:

```
private void BackgroundAgentRegistration()
        {
            // Background Agent Registration.
            bool isBackgroundAgentRegistered = false;
            foreach (var task in BackgroundTaskRegistration.AllTasks)
            {
                if (task.Value.Name == "ApressBackgroundAgent")
                {
                    isBackgroundAgentRegistered = true;
                    break;
                }
            }
            if (!isBackgroundAgentRegistered)
            {
                var builder = new BackgroundTaskBuilder();

                builder.Name = "ApressBackgroundAgent";
                builder.TaskEntryPoint = "BackgroundAgentDemo.ApressBackgroundAgent";
                builder.SetTrigger(new SystemTrigger(SystemTriggerType.InternetAvailable, false));
```

```
            BackgroundTaskRegistration backgroundAgent = builder.Register();
        }
    }
```

This code shows that you cycle all background tasks/agents through the `BackgroundTaskRegistration` API and skip registration if the named background task/agent is already registered. The entry point declaration is the same endpoint for your custom background agent class. The trigger uses a system enumeration to pinpoint when your background agent will run. Figure 9-13 shows a smattering of other system events that could be used as triggers to run your background agent.

Members

The **SystemTriggerType** enumeration has these members.

Member	Value	Description
Invalid | invalid	0	Not a valid trigger type.
SmsReceived | smsReceived	1	The background task is triggered when a new SMS message is received by an installed mobile broadband device.
UserPresent | userPresent	2	The background task is triggered when the user becomes present. **Note** An app must be placed on the lock screen before it can successfully register background tasks using this trigger type.
UserAway | userAway	3	The background task is triggered when the user becomes absent. **Note** An app must be placed on the lock screen before it can successfully register background tasks using this trigger type.
NetworkStateChange | networkStateChange	4	The background task is triggered when a network change occurs, such as a change in cost or connectivity.
ControlChannelReset | controlChannelReset	5	The background task is triggered when a control channel is reset. **Note** An app must be placed on the lock screen before it can successfully register background tasks using this trigger type.
InternetAvailable | internetAvailable	6	The background task is triggered when the Internet becomes available.
SessionConnected | sessionConnected	7	The background task is triggered when the session is connected. **Note** An app must be placed on the lock screen before it can successfully register background tasks using this trigger type.
ServicingComplete | servicingComplete	8	The background task is triggered when the system has finished updating an app.
LockScreenApplicationAdded | lockScreenApplicationAdded	9	The background task is triggered when a tile is added to the lock screen.
LockScreenApplicationRemoved | lockScreenApplicationRemoved	10	The background task is triggered when a tile is removed from the lock screen.
TimeZoneChange | timeZoneChange	11	The background task is triggered when the time zone changes on the device (for example, when the system adjusts the clock for daylight saving time).
OnlineIdConnectedStateChange | onlineIdConnectedStateChange	12	The background task is triggered when the Microsoft account connected to the account changes.

Figure 9-13. *SystemTriggerType enumeration*

Executing Code in Background

At this point, you are all set with your background task/agent. It hooks/triggers into the Windows 8 OS. It's time to do something for when your background task actually executes. Here's some sample code:

```
public sealed class ApressBackgroundAgent : IBackgroundTask
    {
        public void Run(IBackgroundTaskInstance taskInstance)
        {
            Windows.Storage.ApplicationDataContainer localSettings =
Windows.Storage.ApplicationData.Current.LocalSettings;
            localSettings.Values["LastBackgrounAgentRunTimestamp"] = DateTime.Now.ToString();

            BackgroundTaskDeferral deferral = taskInstance.GetDeferral();
            // Do asynchronous stuff here using Async-Await
            deferral.Complete();
        }
    }
```

Just like in any other part of your app, this sample code shows how, from a background task, you are able to edit a local setting using the same APIs as in the app. In fact, code in the background agent has the same rights and privileges as the code in the app itself. You use `deferrals` to indicate any long-running asynchronous operations that might happen inside your background task/agent, such as during saving or in the loading session state. Windows 8 might (opportunistically and based on triggers) offer short CPU cycles to such background tasks. `deferral.Complete()` indicates to the OS that your task has completed its actions. Background agents are really popular to update an app tile/toast with new information, even when the app isn't running. This creates an inviting and exploratory user experience.

Debugging Background Agents

How do I already know your next question? Because I am a developer and we love to debug to figure out if our code is doing what we intended it to do. Can the background task/agent code be debugged? Sure. All you have to do is make sure your references and registration of the background task with the Windows 8 OS is successful. Pop open your Debug Location menu item. You should see something like Figure 9-14. Simply put a breakpoint in the `Run()` method of the background task/agent and select the named agent/task option from the menu. Voilà. Your breakpoint hits and you are debugging inside a background task/agent. Developers are also encouraged to play with different system trigger settings to see which ones can be triggered manually to run the registered background task/agent. MSDN has a detailed writeup on how to debug background tasks/agents (`http://msdn.microsoft.com/en-us/library/windows/apps/xaml/jj542416.aspx`).

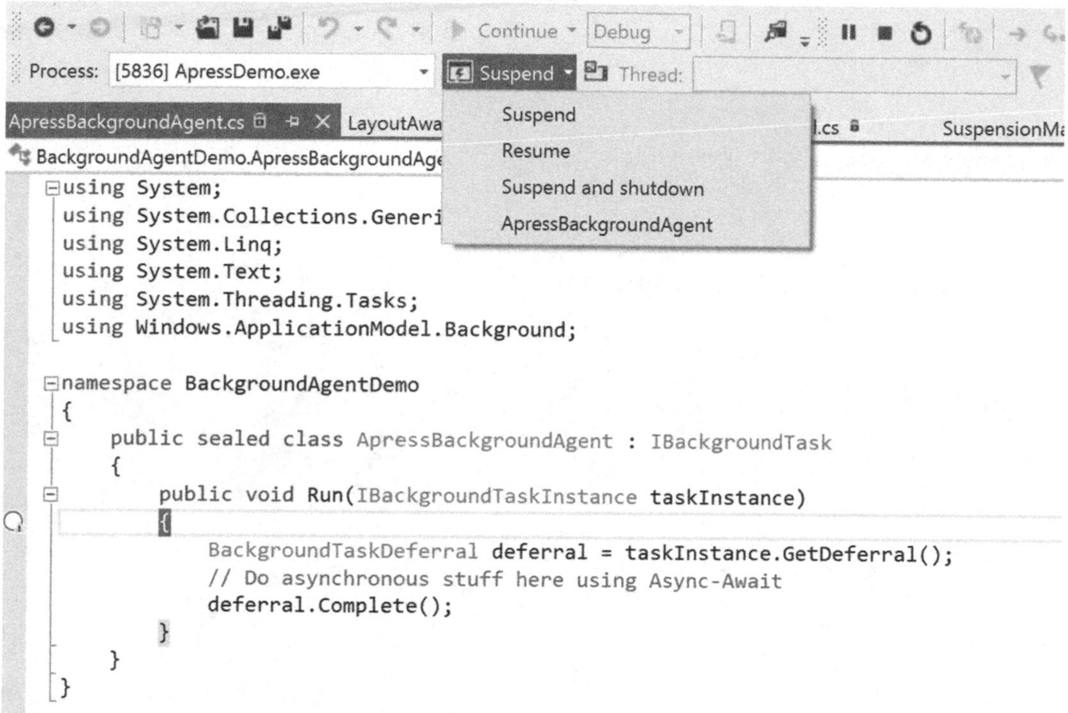

***Figure 9-14.** Debugging background agents*

Summary

This chapter talked about the Windows 8 Store app life cycle in detail. You saw all the phases that an app goes through, along with events at each step that we developers can listen in on. You also saw sample code showing the use of boilerplate code to save/restore state versus rolling your own techniques. In addition, we talked about some best practices on how and where to save/load data, along with options on how to debug life-cycle event handlers. A discussion on the `Async-Await` pattern was much called for, along with how to avoid common mistakes like the introduction of race conditions. We ended with a bang, talking about how to set up, register, run, and debug background tasks/agents. You are all set now. Knowing storage mechanisms and implementing application life-cycle management truly makes your Windows 8 Store app feel professional and offers the best possible user experience.

CHAPTER 10

Contracts

If you are building a Windows 8 Store app as you read the chapters, by now, your app is mostly functional in what it is meant to do. However, remember the promise of the one Windows 8 ecosystem? As the user is using your Windows 8 Store app, you do not want the experience to be jarring, or worse—making the user jump through hoops to get something done. What we developers should do is integrate our Windows 8 Store apps as closely as possible with the operating system (OS) so that users have a seamless experience. Wouldn't you like your app's data to be searchable, even if the user is not explicitly running your app? How about talking to other apps so that you do not reinvent the wheel for a feature? All of this is accomplished through what we call Windows 8 app *contracts*. You will take a deep dive into several must-implement contracts, like Search, Share, Settings, and File Picker. You will start simple and take a look at lot of code to get contracts integration working end-to-end for your dream Windows 8 app. This chapter will be a tad long, but hang tight and pick the pieces you need. Implement some of these contracts and rest assured, your Windows 8 Store app will shine with OS integration that leads to increased usage—and ultimately a happier you.

Contracts and Extensions

As you have seen in the past, Windows 8 Store apps run within a silo with user's protection in mind. What this boils down to is data security—having Windows 8 apps do all data storage/retrieval needed from within an isolated storage area so that the external impact is minimized to the local app. In terms of features, though, you want your Windows 8 Store apps to be anything but siloed. You want integration with OS features so that the users get to spend more time in your app. You want apps to talk to each other to leverage features; but this talking cannot happen directly for safety reasons. Windows 8 is happy to act as a broker between apps. Let's look at how Windows 8 contracts/extensions make handshaking between apps and the OS possible.

Defined at MSDN, "A *contract* is like an agreement between one or more apps. Contracts define the requirements that apps must meet to participate in these unique Windows interactions." (`http://msdn.microsoft.com/en-us/library/windows/apps/hh464906.aspx`.) It seems like a straightforward and wonderful way to lead developers into OS integration. Windows defines the contracts between apps and then brokers the mediation between them. In essence, Windows 8 makes participating apps talk the same language without having the apps know anything about each other. Participating apps have the confidence that Windows will support the workflow end to end, if the contract is followed correctly.

Defined at MSDN, "An *extension* is like an agreement between an app and Windows. Extensions let app developers extend or customize standard Windows features primarily for use in their apps and potentially for use in other apps." (`http://msdn.microsoft.com/en-us/library/windows/apps/hh464906.aspx`.) Unlike contracts, extensions let an app to closely integrate with Windows and offer unique customizations to the user. If your Windows 8 app offers a feature (like handling a file type or taking a picture, etc.), extensions simply provide a way for the developer to announce that feature to the OS through a declaration. Windows 8 takes care of the rest and exposes your app to the user as appropriate.

These contracts and extensions are really golden to Windows 8 Store app developers. This is the first time in the history of Windows that third-party apps get to be so intimate with the OS in offering unique experiences to the user. Now, there are a lot of contracts and extensions. I will cover some of the most popular and the hardest to implement. For a complete listing, as well as how-to's, please visit MSDN at `http://msdn.microsoft.com/en-us/library/windows/apps/hh464906.aspx`.

Share

People like to share. Period. Our generation leads a very connected lifestyle and wants to share stories/experiences/places socially with friends or family. Windows 8 understands the need for technology that allows users to easily share information, so it steps in with what is called the Share contract. Envision this: you wrote a photoediting Windows 8 app and the user wants to share the work he or she did in your app. Previously, this meant that developers had to know how to write network code and integrate with social media services like Twitter and Facebook. This is reinventing the wheel because every app has to do so—not to mention that social media integration may not be the easiest thing to code for and it takes away focus from what the app is intended to do. If your photoediting app could simply talk to another app that knew how to post content to social sites, life would be whole lot easier as a developer.

Windows 8 steps in here with the app Share contract. This contract is meant to level the playing field. It provides a way for Windows 8 apps to easily share and exchange content. While using the clipboard or handling files between apps are ways of sharing, you'll next take a look at the Share contract implementation that the user is most likely to use—through the Share charm.

Charms Bar Integration

Swipe from the right edge of a touch-enabled Windows 8 device or mouse-hover on the right edge. What you see is the Windows 8 charms bar. And Share features prominently as a menu option. Let's take a look at that in Figure 10-1 while you're running your Apress Featured Books Demo app.

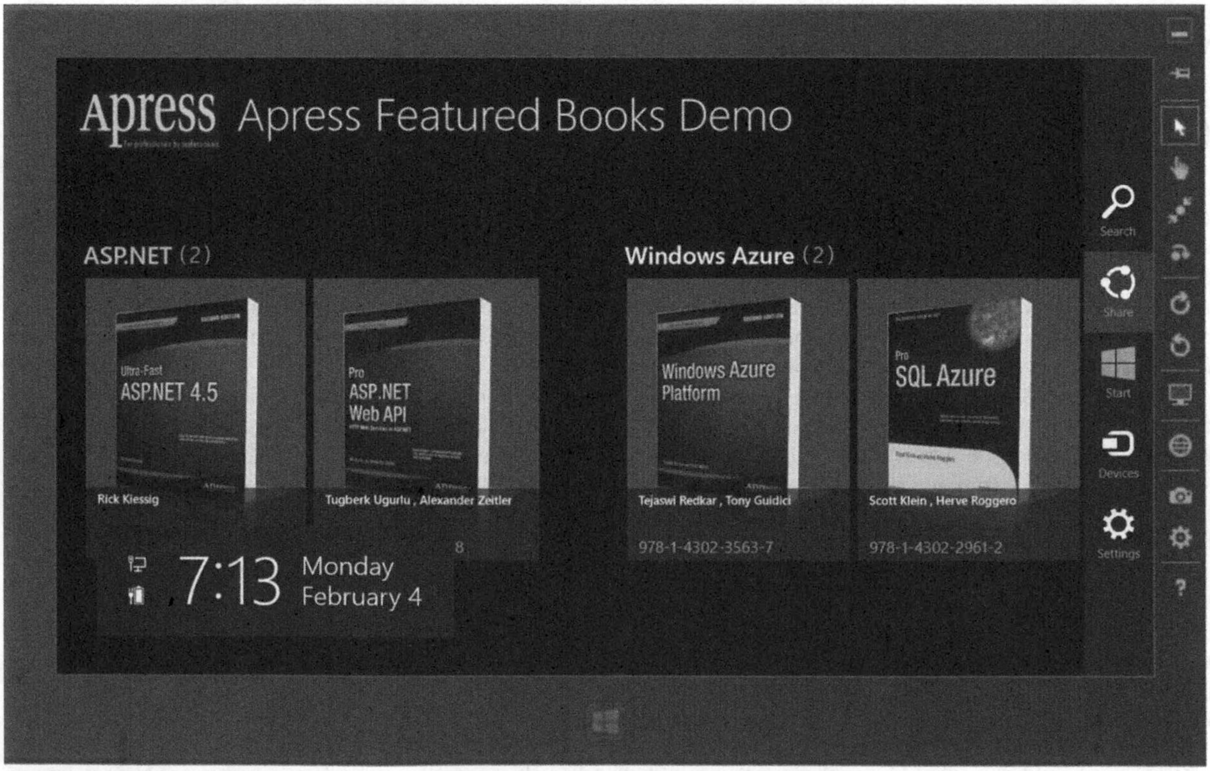

Figure 10-1. Share charms menu

This charms bar is always accessible to the user. No matter where the user is while running Windows 8, sharing is always a click or swipe away. Go ahead and select the Share menu option in your app. Your screen should look similar to what you see in Figure 10-2.

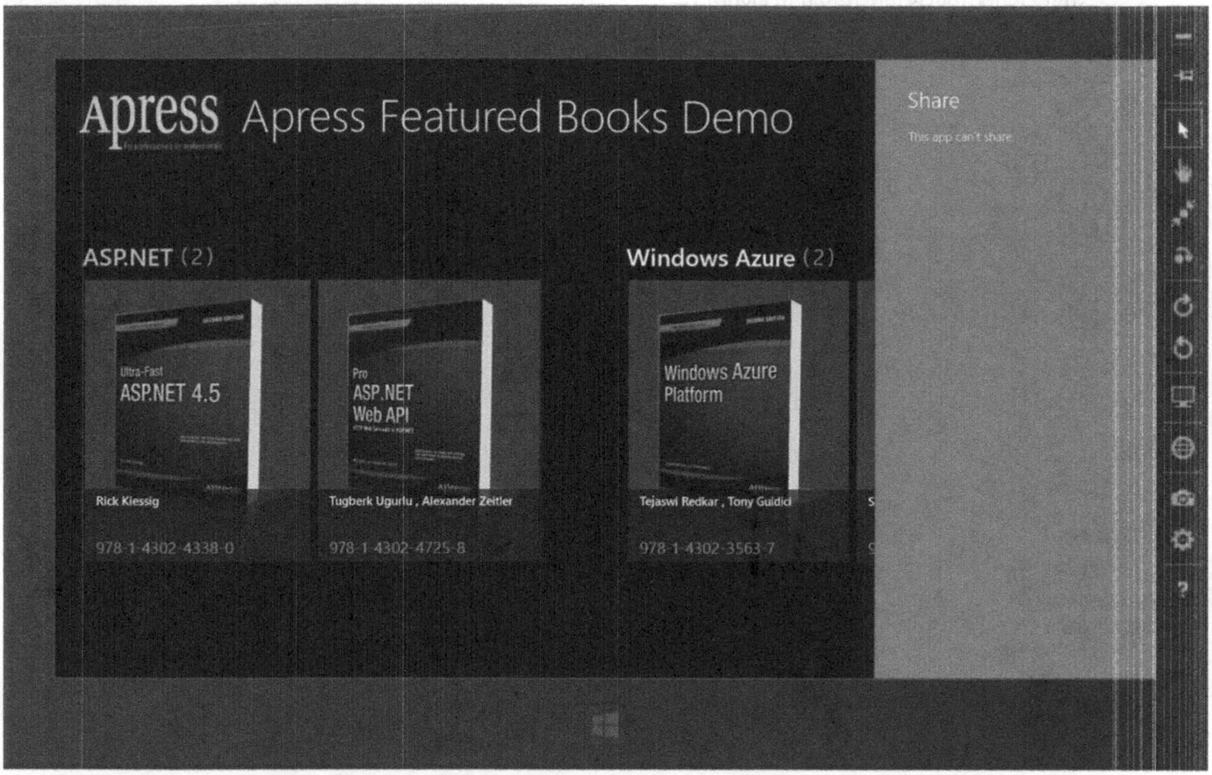

Figure 10-2. *Share not implemented*

Oops! Let's see what happened here. The user invoked the omnipresent charms bar and chose to share something. Windows 8 turned around and asked your app if it had anything to share, but without supporting the Share contract, your app obviously said no. Hence, Windows 8 simply reports to the user that the app cannot share, which is a pretty bad user experience if the user did wanted to share something. Just be aware that unless you implement the Share contract in your app, the user will always see this negative message when trying to share from your app. So, let's fix this. But first, you need to understand the Share contract anatomy (see Figure 10-3) to make sure you are handling sharing correctly.

Anatomy of a Share Contract

The Share contract involves three participants:

- *Share source*: This is the Windows 8 app in use that wants to share some data.
- *Share target*: This is the app that knows how to handle specific types of data and allow the user to share the data to the outside world (through e-mails, social media updates, etc.).

- *The Broker*: This is Windows 8 acting as a middleman in the Share contract so that the share source and share target do not need to talk to each other directly. Windows 8 facilitates the exchange of information through a common `DataPackage` and carries messages between the source and the target. The interaction between the OS and the source/target during the share workflow is illustrated in Figure 10-3.

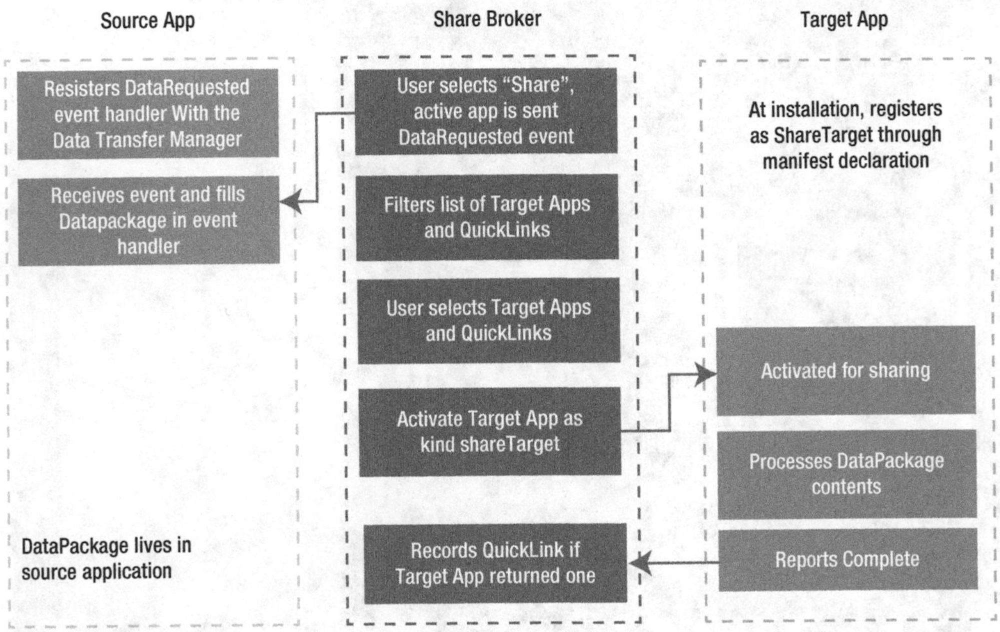

Figure 10-3. *Anatomy of a Share contract*

Let's break down the Share contract workflow a little. When the user shows the intention to share through the charms menu, Windows 8 asks the share source app to build up a data package with what it wants to pass along. Next, based on the type of data in the package, Windows 8 presents the user with a list of existing/preinstalled apps that have already declared to the OS that they can handle the given type of data. The user's chosen share target app is then activated and handled over the data package, beyond which the target is simply expected to process/act on the data and report completion back to the OS. All this handshaking is completely hidden from the end user, who was simply looking at something interesting in the source app and clicks/taps the charms to share through the target app.

So, what type of data can be shared? Well, that depends squarely on the `DataPackage` object that is at the core of the share workflow. Here are the types of data that can be set in the `DataPackage`:

- Plain text
- Uniform Resource Identifiers (URI) links
- HTML
- Bitmaps
- Files
- Custom data with defined schema

Implementing the Share Source

Let's look at some code to show solid examples of how you can handle the Share contract interactions through the use of the DataPackage. You begin with trying to support share as a share source app. As usual, you go back to your Apress demo app for code samples. Suppose you were browsing for Apress books in the app and found an interesting book. Want to share it? Let's support a couple different data types to get the hang of implementing the Share contract.

In the BookDetails.xaml.cs page, which displays details of every featured Apress book, add the following code:

```
using Windows.ApplicationModel.DataTransfer;
DataTransferManager dataTransferManager = DataTransferManager.GetForCurrentView();

protected override void OnNavigatedTo(NavigationEventArgs e)
        {
            base.OnNavigatedTo(e);

            // Listen in on when the user invokes the Share charm.
            dataTransferManager.DataRequested += new TypedEventHandler<DataTransferManager,
            DataRequestedEventArgs>(dataTransferManager_DataRequested);
        }

        protected override void OnNavigatedFrom(NavigationEventArgs e)
        {
            base.OnNavigatedFrom(e);

            // Unwire event handler.
            dataTransferManager.DataRequested -= new TypedEventHandler<DataTransferManager,
            DataRequestedEventArgs>(dataTransferManager_DataRequested);
        }
```

The DataTransferManager API is used by the Share contract for Windows 8 to request DataPackage information from the share source. So, in the preceding code you get a reference to the DataTransferManager and listen in on the DataRequested event. Notice how you wire and unwire the event handler in response to the DataRequested event during the XAML page's OnNavigatedTo and OnNavigatedFrom life-cycle events. This kind of code is actually good practice in Windows 8 app development. To avoid unintended consequences, all wired event handlers should be unwired if going out of scope. So now, what about actually adding some code in the event handler you registered for? Here goes:

```
private void dataTransferManager_DataRequested(DataTransferManager sender,
DataRequestedEventArgs args)
        {
            if (this.flipView.SelectedItem != null)
            {
                ApressBook selectedBook = (ApressBook)this.flipView.SelectedItem;

                // Set what to share.

                //string textToShare = "Currently Reading Book: Name:
                " + selectedBook.ApressBookName + " | Author: " + selectedBook.ApressBookAuthor +
                " | Published: " + selectedBook.DisplayablePublishDate + ".";
                //args.Request.Data.Properties.Title = "Apress Featured BookShare:";
                //args.Request.Data.SetText(textToShare);
}
    }
```

Let's inspect what you did in the preceding code. If you remember your `BookDetails` page from earlier chapters, it used a `FlipView` controls to show featured Apress books one at a time. So clearly, if the user is looking at one such `FlipView` page, you know which book is being looked at. This is good because it now gives a context to share if the user invoked the Share menu through the charms. Do you see the `DataRequestedEventArgs` arguments that are passed in as a parameter to your event handler? That is your opportunity to pass along what the user wants to share. The `Request.Data` property of the `DataRequestedEventArgs` is actually the `DataPackage` that the share source app is supposed to fill in. As you can see in this case, you're building a simple string and using the `SetText()` method to fill in the `DataPackage`. Do you think you might have better luck if the user tries to share now? Let's look at the results, shown in Figure 10-4.

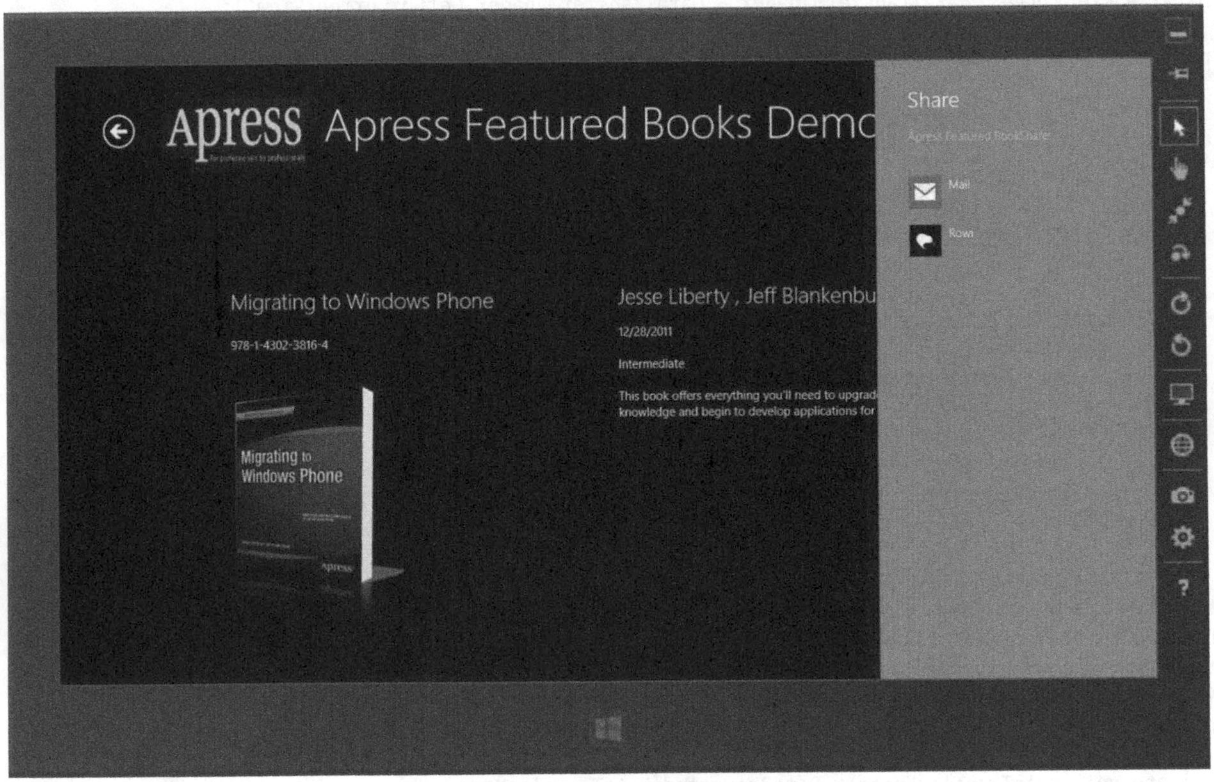

***Figure 10-4.** Text share*

This is already looking better. Seems like Windows 8 realized that your app filled in the `DataPackage` with some text and is offering the user choice in matching share target apps that can handle such data. On my virtual machine, I just have two apps. You should get lot more options on your full Windows 8 device. Select Rowi—a great Twitter client—from the list and try sharing. You should see that the string you made about the Apress book that the user was looking at makes it to the Rowi app as is, and is now one tap away from sharing with the world (see Figure 10-5). Envision the same kind of functionality as the user is reading/viewing something interesting in her Windows 8 apps—news, sports, movies, social feeds, and so forth. Sharing is simply a tap away and it is imperative that app developers support the Share source contracts for an optimal user experience.

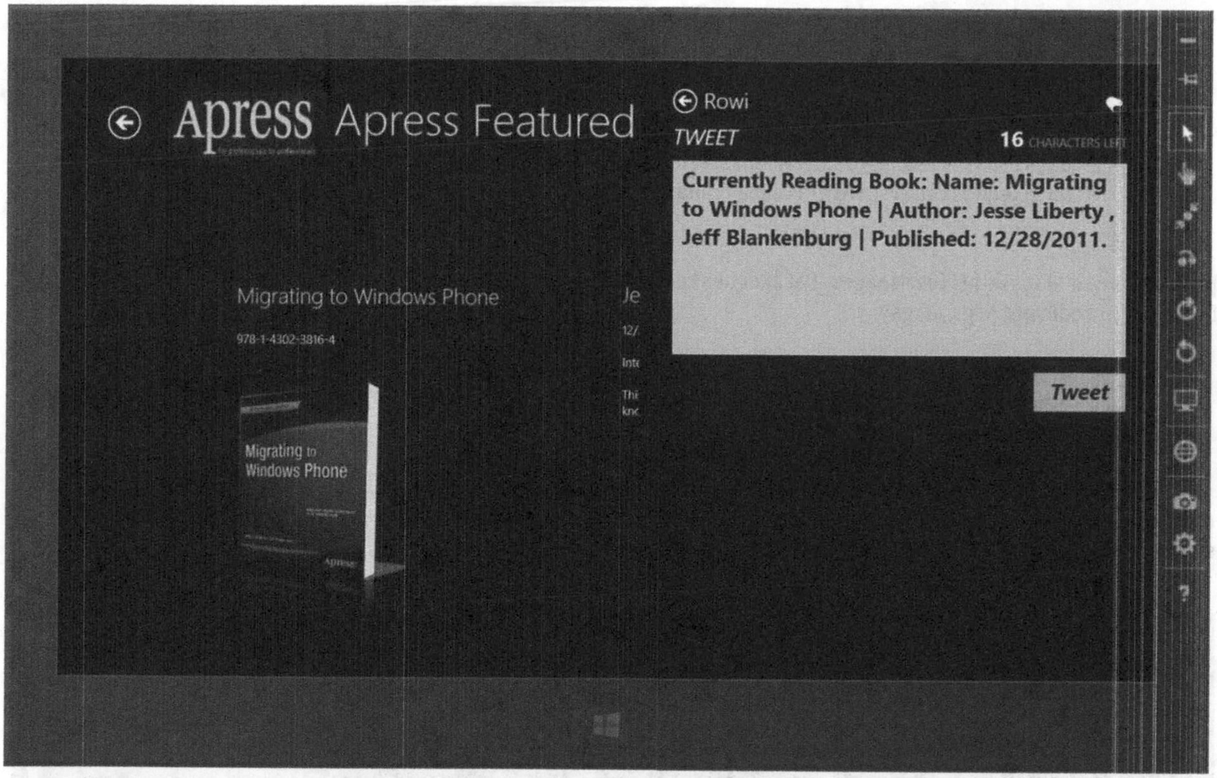

Figure 10-5. *Shared text in share target app*

The preceding scenario of sharing text through a Share contract works fine on your `BookDetails` page, but did you notice that the code you added was very much tied to the particular page? This is by design, because not every page or content in your app may be suitable for users to share. But wouldn't it be nice to indicate to the user that a particular page/interaction cannot share content, but other parts of the app can? This gets us around Windows 8 bluntly telling the user that the app simply cannot share.

User-Friendly Non-support of Share

Let's add some code to the `FeaturedBookList.xaml.cs` file—the main dashboard page in the app:

```
using Windows.ApplicationModel.DataTransfer;

DataTransferManager dataTransferManager = DataTransferManager.GetForCurrentView();

protected override void OnNavigatedTo(NavigationEventArgs e)
      {
          base.OnNavigatedTo(e);

          // Listen in on when the user invokes the Share charm.
          dataTransferManager.DataRequested += new TypedEventHandler<DataTransferManager,
          DataRequestedEventArgs>(dataTransferManager_DataRequested);
      }
```

```
        protected override void OnNavigatedFrom(NavigationEventArgs e)
        {
            base.OnNavigatedFrom(e);

            // Unwire event handler.
            dataTransferManager.DataRequested -= new TypedEventHandler<DataTransferManager,
            DataRequestedEventArgs>(dataTransferManager_DataRequested);
        }

private void dataTransferManager_DataRequested(DataTransferManager sender,
DataRequestedEventArgs args)
        {
            args.Request.FailWithDisplayText("The App cannot Share anything without
            a specific Book selection.");
        }
```

This code is similar code to what you saw before, except you let sharing through the charms bar fail with a custom message telling the user that other parts/scenarios in your app can actually support the Share contract. Figure 10-6 shows how sharing from the charms bar looks after your code changes.

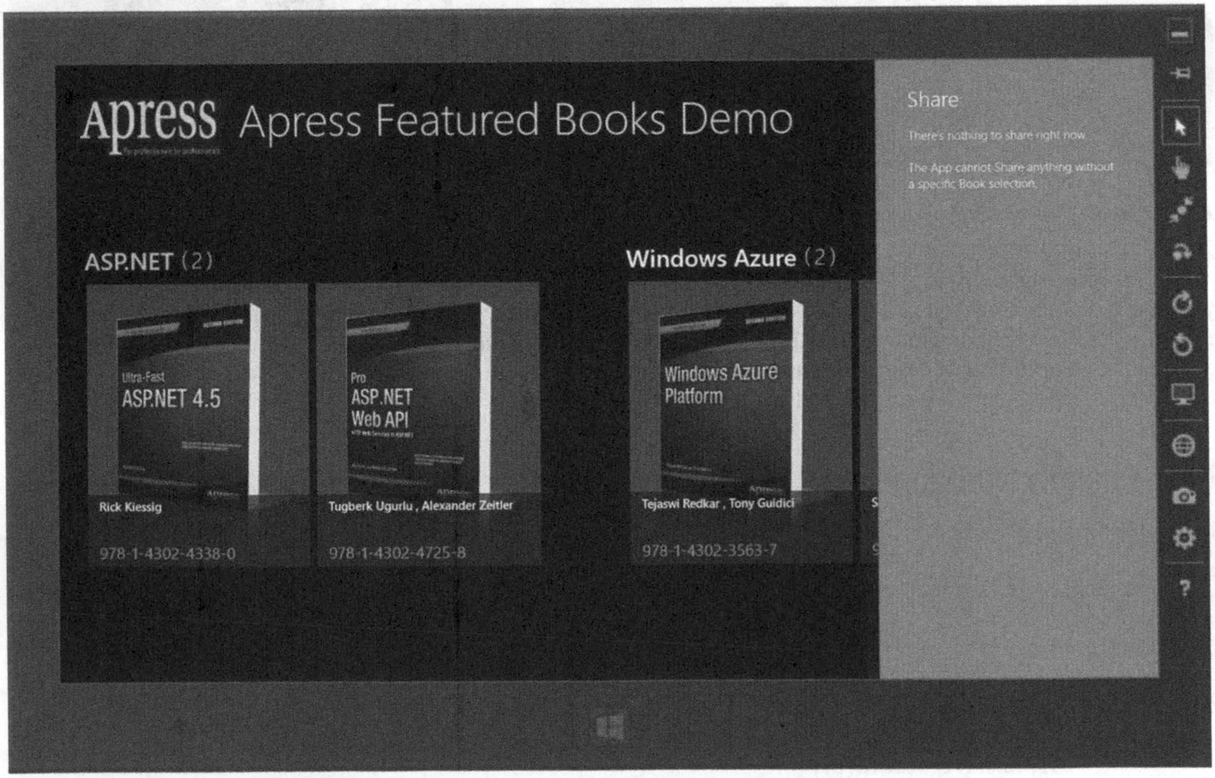

Figure 10-6. Handling nothing to share

Sharing a URI Link

What about sharing other types of data? Here's how you would share a URI link through the DataPackage:

```
private void dataTransferManager_DataRequested(DataTransferManager sender,
DataRequestedEventArgs args)
        {
args.Request.Data.Properties.Title = "Apress Featured BookShare:";
args.Request.Data.SetUri(new Uri("http://www.msn.com"));
        }
```

And here's the resulting UI from the Share menu selection off the charms bar (see Figure 10-7). As an added bonus, if the user shares URI links, Windows actually provides a little preview of the web site (through thumbnails, etc.) at the shared URI address as the user is getting ready to share.

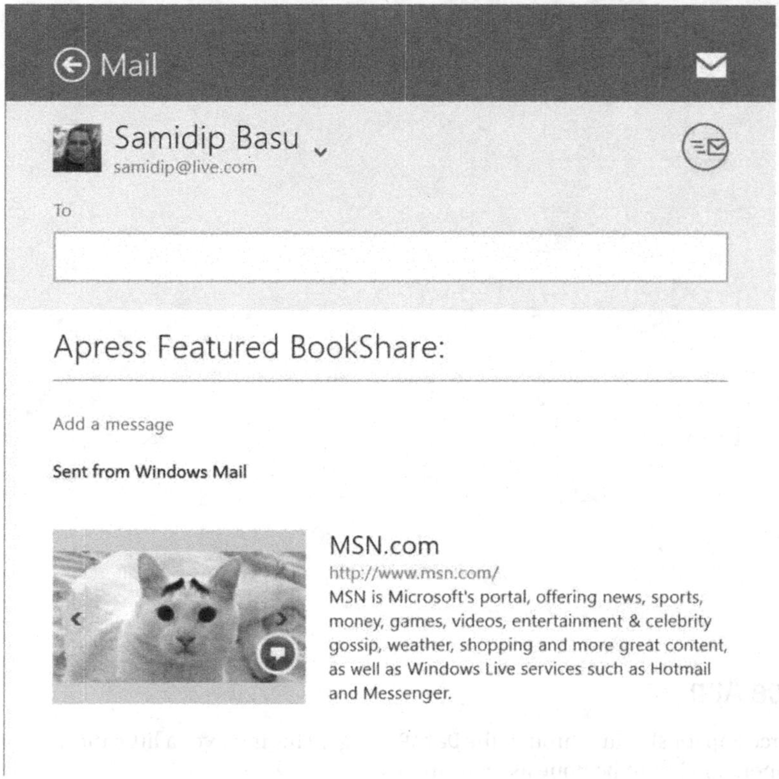

Figure 10-7. *URI share*

Sharing HTML

Now share some HTML or formatted content. Here's the code and a sample of how the Share dialog looks if sharing via e-mail (see Figure 10-8):

```
private void dataTransferManager_DataRequested(DataTransferManager sender,
DataRequestedEventArgs args)
        {
    args.Request.Data.Properties.Title = "Apress Featured BookShare:";
               string someHTML = "<strong>Bold Text</strong><em>Emphasized Text</em>";
               args.Request.Data.SetHtmlFormat(HtmlFormatHelper.CreateHtmlFormat(someHTML));
}
```

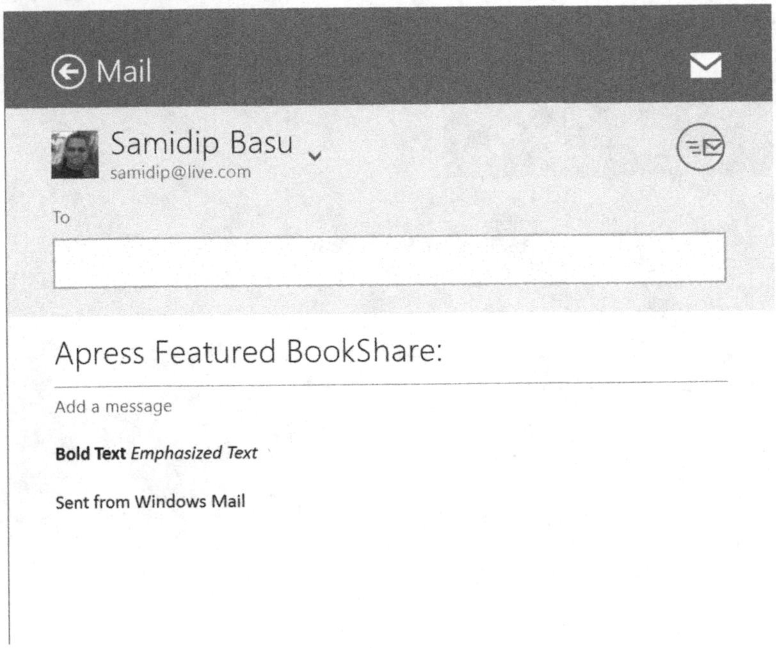

Figure 10-8. *HTML share*

Sharing Files from Share Source App

You can also offer files from your share source app for sharing through the `DataPackage`. This involves a little more code, however, because the local file read operation has to be done asynchronously:

```
private void dataTransferManager_DataRequested(DataTransferManager sender,
DataRequestedEventArgs args)
        {
    DataRequestDeferral deferral = args.Request.GetDeferral();
               try
{
                 // Reference to Local Folder.
                 Windows.Storage.StorageFolder localFolder =
                 Windows.Storage.ApplicationData.Current.LocalFolder;
```

```
            StorageFile storageFile = await localFolder.GetFileAsync("CustomSerializedFile.xml");
        List<IStorageItem> storageItems = new List<IStorageItem>();
        storageItems.Add(storageFile);

        args.Request.Data.Properties.Title = "Apress Featured BookShare:";
        args.Request.Data.SetStorageItems(storageItems);
    }
    finally
    {
        deferral.Complete();
    }
}
```

You are simply offering a local file read from storage as a DataPackage content for the Share contract. Notice the use of DataRequestDeferral, which makes sure Windows 8 waits for the file to be available and read in memory as a StorageFile before offering it for sharing. The resulting UI for the share workflow is shown in Figure 10-9 (when sharing through the built-in Mail client app).

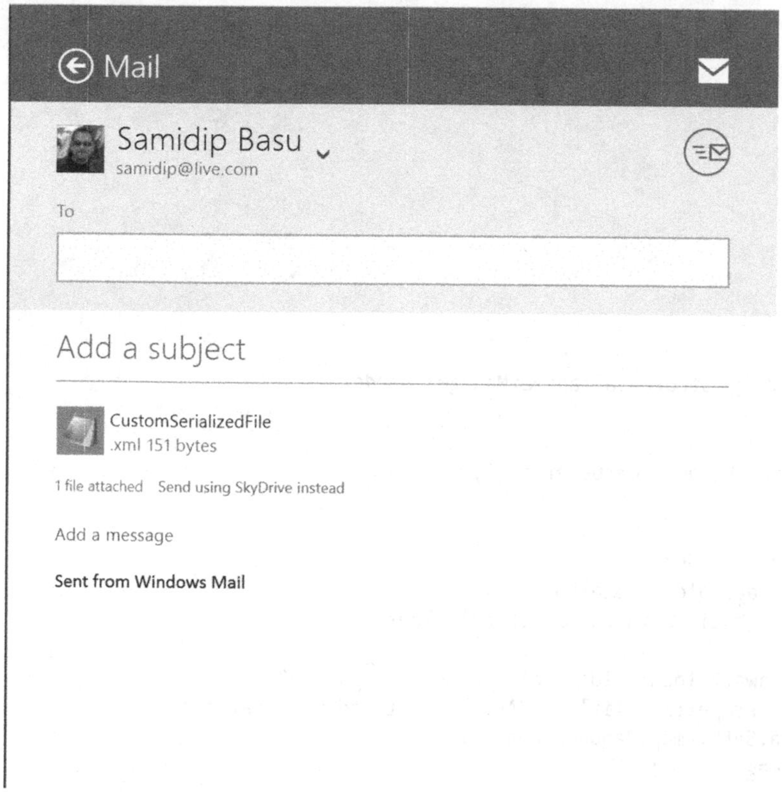

Figure 10-9. *File share*

Sharing Photos Through Share Source

Do you want your users to share photos from your Windows 8 app? Simple and very similar to sharing files, you will only change the data type being set. First, navigate to your local app package repository and drop an image file (see Figure 10-10). Next, you're going to write code to share this image file.

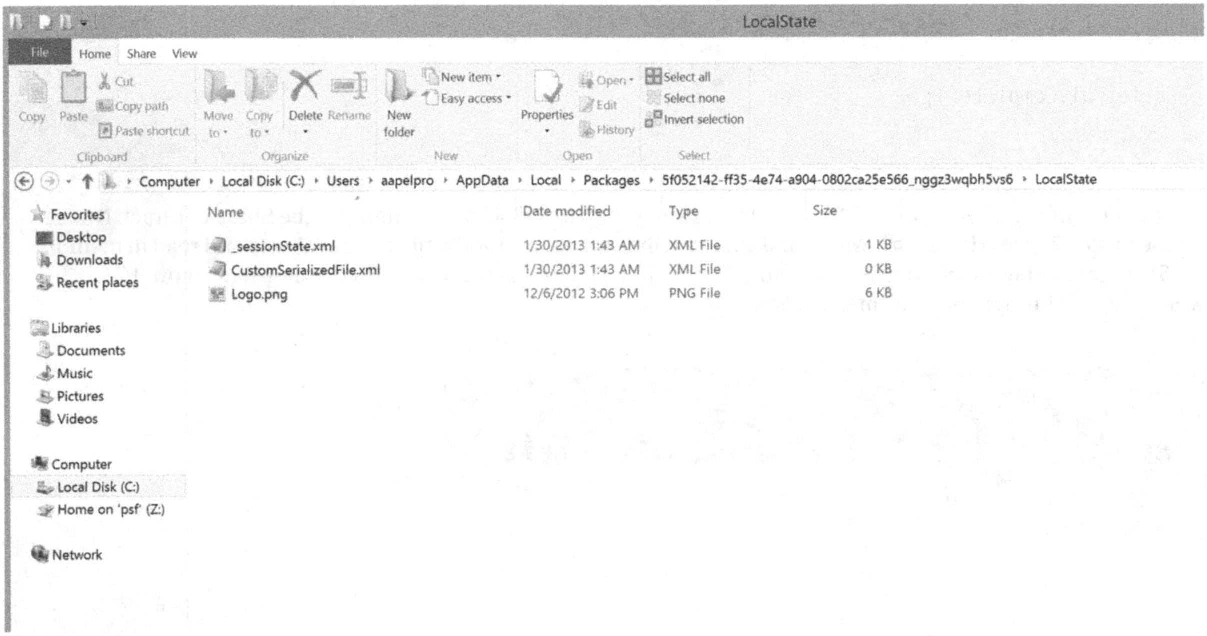

Figure 10-10. *Image share*

```
private void dataTransferManager_DataRequested(DataTransferManager sender,
DataRequestedEventArgs args)
        {
    DataRequestDeferral deferral = args.Request.GetDeferral();
               try
                {
                  // Reference to Local Folder.
                  Windows.Storage.StorageFolder localFolder =
                  Windows.Storage.ApplicationData.Current.LocalFolder;

             StorageFile imageFile = await localFolder.GetFileAsync("Logo.png");
                    args.Request.Data.Properties.Title = "Apress Featured BookShare:";
                    args.Request.Data.SetBitmap(RandomAccessStreamReference.
                    CreateFromFile(imageFile));
                }
                finally
                {
                    deferral.Complete();
                }
}
```

You have now covered most of the data types that a user might like to share from your app. You have also seen various ways of filling the Share `DataPackage`. For more information on making your app a share source, including the use of custom data types, please visit MSDN at `http://msdn.microsoft.com/en-us/library/windows/apps/xaml/Hh871368(v=win.10).aspx`.

Share Target

Let's talk about supporting the Share Target contract. Let's say you are writing a social media Windows 8 app or an app that is capable of handling a specific custom data type. You would absolutely want to support the Share Target contract to provide the users with a way of leveraging your app while sharing content. This simply increases your app's usage since Windows lists your app anytime the user is about to share a data type that your app can handle. So, let's show you how. It is easier than you think.

First, make a separate Windows 8 demo app called **ApressShareTargetDemo** so that you can see the interaction between the share source and share target. You start with a Blank template, as shown in Figure 10-11.

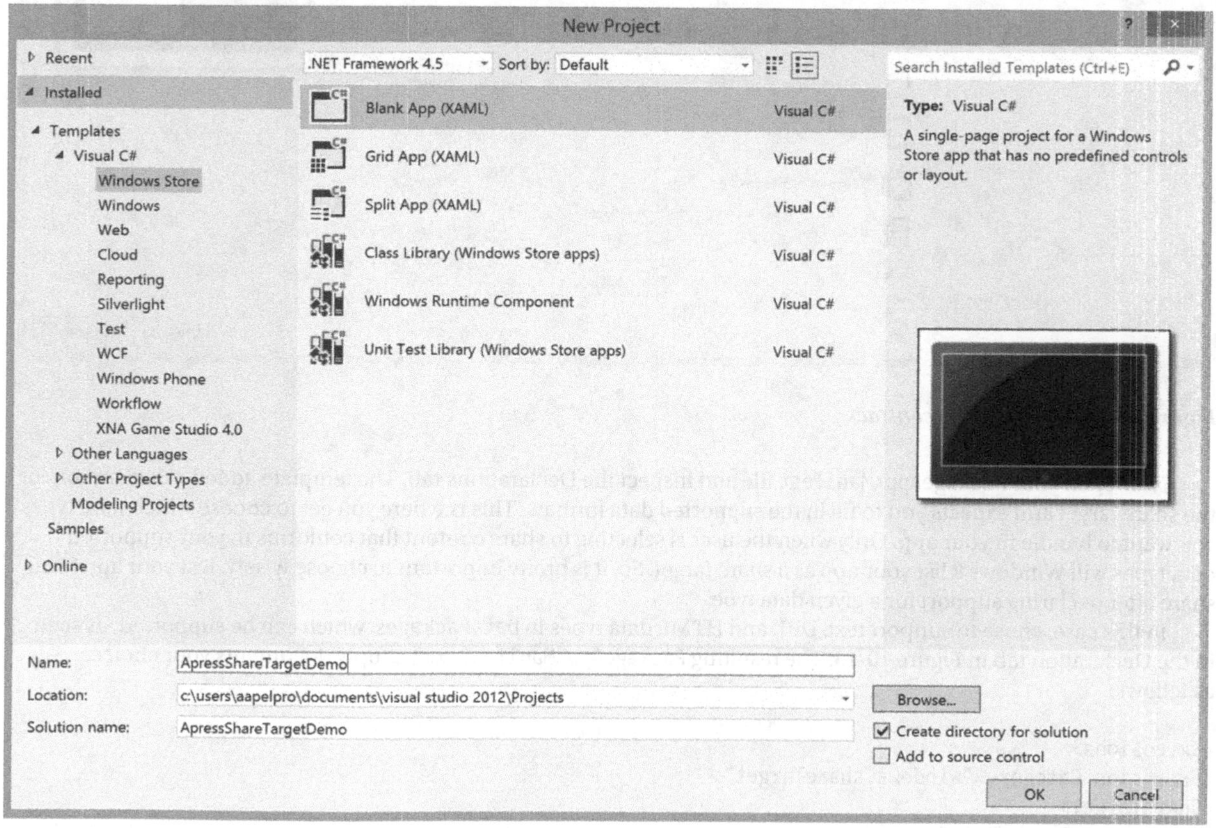

***Figure 10-11.** Blank template to start share target app*

The first step toward being a share target is to declare your app's intentions to Windows 8. Accordingly, use a Visual Studio template that does a little work for you (see Figure 10-12). The Share Target Contract template provides a XAML page ready to receive shared content and a `PackageAppXManifest` setting declaring support for the Share Target contract.

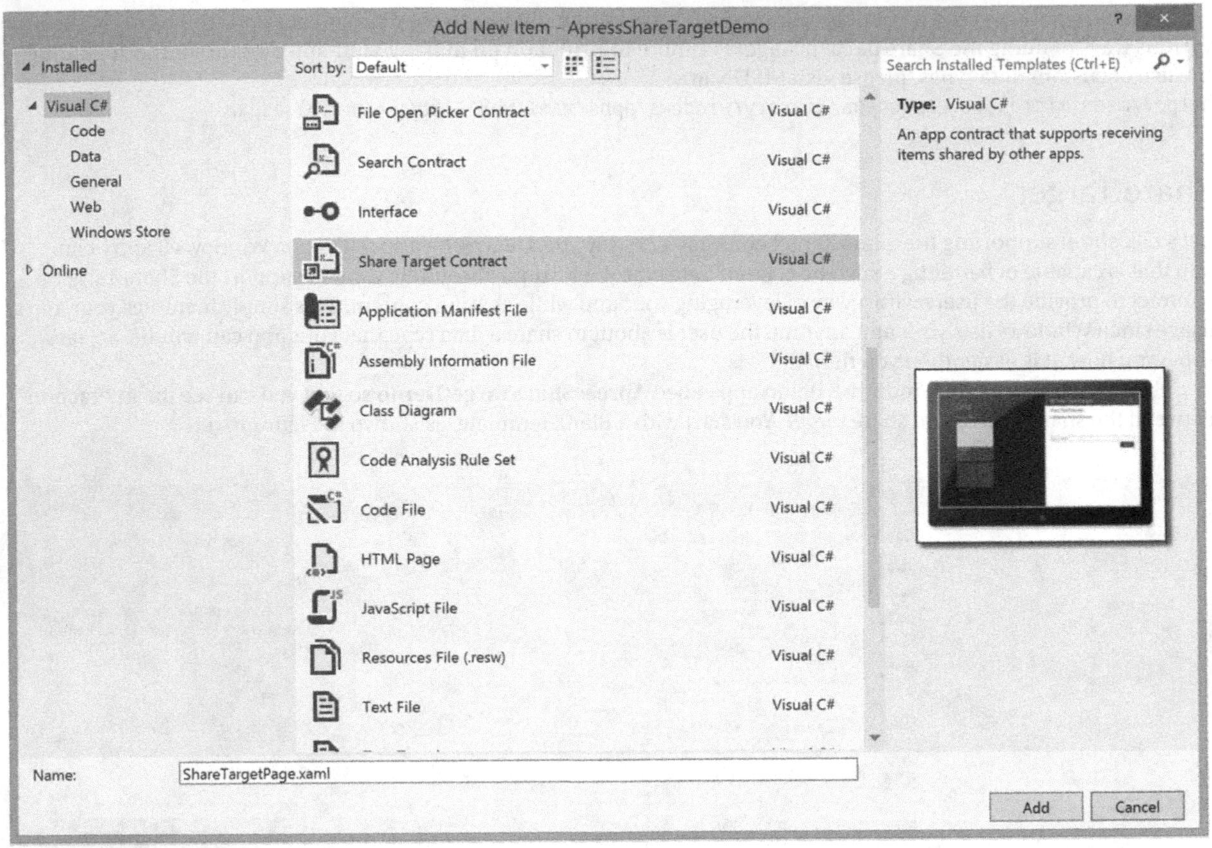

Figure 10-12. *Share Target contract*

Now open your `PackageAppXManifest` file and inspect the Declarations tab. The template added a declaration for the share target and expects you to fill in the supported data formats. This is where you get to choose which data types you want to handle in your app. Only when the user is selecting to share content that conforms to your supported data types will Windows 8 list your app as a share target. So, it is pretty important to choose wisely, lest your app fail to share after declaring support for a given data type.

In this case, chose to support text, URI, and HTML data types in `DataPackages`, which can be supported, as seen in the Declaration tab in Figure 10-13. The resulting `PackageAppXManifest.xml` simply documents your choices, as follows:

```
<Extensions>
<Extension Category="windows.shareTarget">
<ShareTarget>
<DataFormat>text</DataFormat>
<DataFormat>uri</DataFormat>
<DataFormat>html</DataFormat>
</ShareTarget>
</Extension>
</Extensions>
```

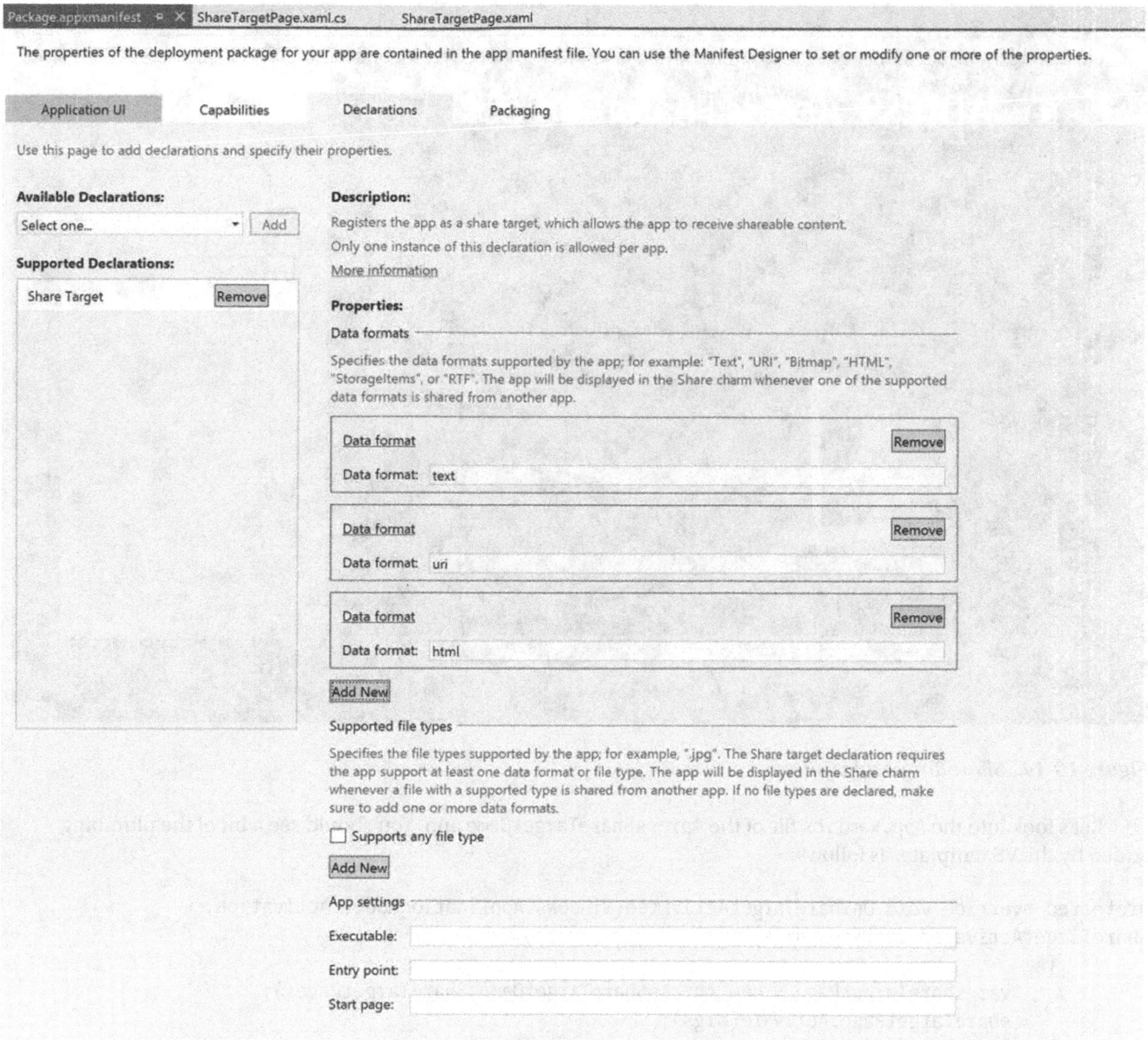

Package.appxmanifest
ShareTargetPage.xaml.cs
ShareTargetPage.xaml
The properties of the deployment package for your app are contained in the app manifest file. You can use the Manifest Designer to set or modify one or more of the properties.
Application UI
Capabilities
Declarations
Packaging
Use this page to add declarations and specify their properties.
Available Declarations:
Select one...
Add
Supported Declarations:
Share Target
Remove
Description:
Registers the app as a share target, which allows the app to receive shareable content.
Only one instance of this declaration is allowed per app.
More information
Properties:
Data formats
Specifies the data formats supported by the app; for example: "Text", "URI", "Bitmap", "HTML", "StorageItems", or "RTF". The app will be displayed in the Share charm whenever one of the supported data formats is shared from another app.
Data format
Remove
Data format: text
Data format
Remove
Data format: uri
Data format
Remove
Data format: html
Add New
Supported file types
Specifies the file types supported by the app; for example, ".jpg". The Share target declaration requires the app support at least one data format or file type. The app will be displayed in the Share charm whenever a file with a supported type is shared from another app. If no file types are declared, make sure to add one or more data formats.
Supports any file type
Add New
App settings
Executable:
Entry point:
Start page:

***Figure 10-13.** Share Target declaration*

You haven't really written any code to do anything with the Share `DataPackages` you are about to receive, but even with the declarations in, you can test whether Windows 8 understands your share target support. First, install the `ApressShareTargetDemo` app and then run the actual `ApressDemo` app, which acts as a share source. If you did everything right, the `ApressShareTargetDemo` app should be listed as a potential share target to handle the declared types of data. So, try your luck by sharing text, URI, or HTML from the `ApressDemo` app and see the choices presented by Windows 8, as shown in Figure 10-14.

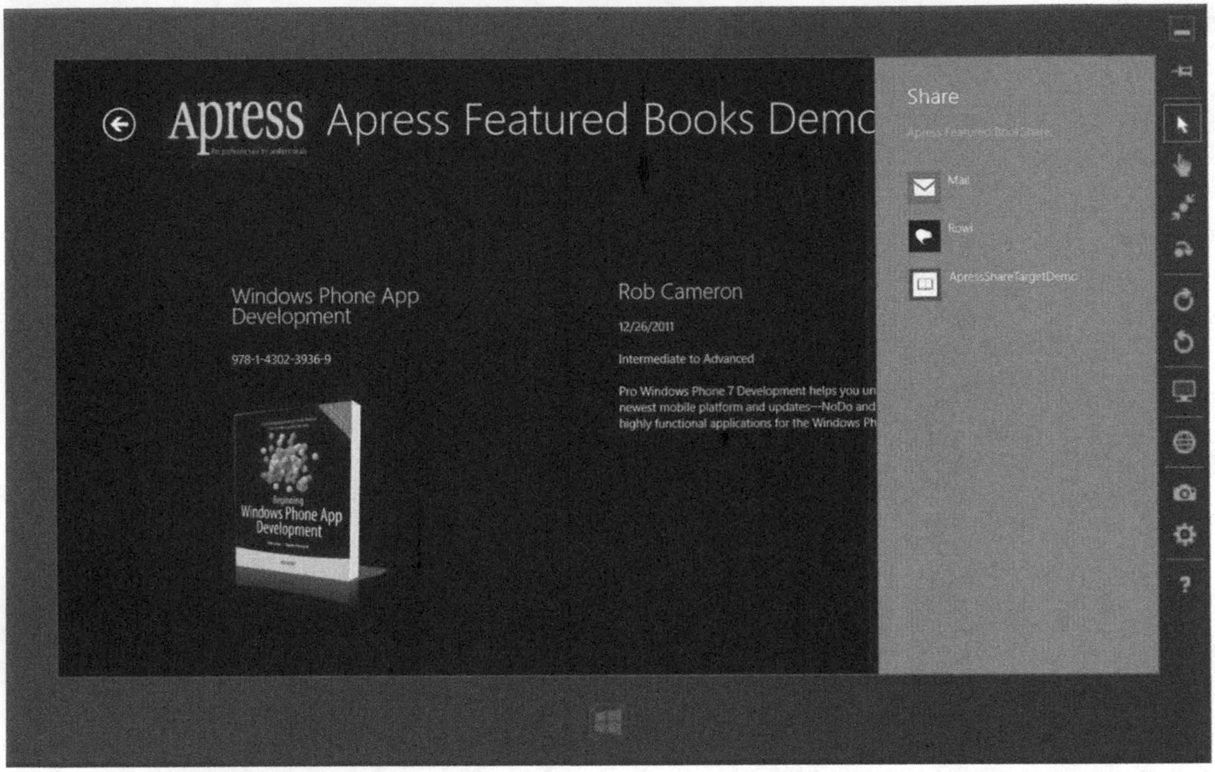

***Figure 10-14.** Share Target app listing*

Let's look into the `App.xaml.cs` file of the `ApressShareTargetDemo` app. You should see a bit of the plumbing added by the VS template, as follows:

```
protected override void OnShareTargetActivated(Windows.ApplicationModel.Activation.
ShareTargetActivatedEventArgs args)
        {
            var shareTargetPage = new ApressShareTargetDemo.ShareTargetPage();
            shareTargetPage.Activate(args);
        }
```

This code is simply an indication to the `ApressShareTargetDemo` app that it may be activated at any time, not just through the user launching the app, but also as a share target while the user is trying to share something pertinent from a completely different app. The `App.xaml.cs` file registers an `OnShareTargetActivated` event handler for such cases and forwards the received arguments to the specialized `ShareTarget` page that can handle the data for sharing.

Now, look into the `ShareTargetPage.xaml.cs` to handle the receipt of the Share `DataPackages`. I will not go into the exact XAML or what you do once you receive the data, because this is completely up to your app and its functionality. Simply look at how you can receive the Share `DataPackages` and peek inside its content. Here's some code:

```
private Windows.ApplicationModel.DataTransfer.ShareTarget.ShareOperation shareOperation;

public async void Activate(ShareTargetActivatedEventArgs args)
        {
            this.shareOperation = args.ShareOperation;
```

```
        // Plain Text.
        if (shareOperation.Data.Contains(StandardDataFormats.Text))
        {
            string text = await shareOperation.Data.GetTextAsync();
        }
        // Some URI.
        if (shareOperation.Data.Contains(StandardDataFormats.Uri))
        {
            Uri uri = await shareOperation.Data.GetUriAsync();
        }
        // Formatted HTML Content.
        if (shareOperation.Data.Contains(StandardDataFormats.Html))
        {
            string html = await shareOperation.Data.GetHtmlFormatAsync();
        }
    ....
   ....
}
```

On the `Activate()` method, you get the `ShareTargetActivatedEventArgs`, passed down from the `OnShareTargetActivated` event. The `ShareOperation` inside the arguments contains the Share `DataPackages`, as filled in by the share source. Once you have that, the rest, as they say, is easy. You'll notice a `StandardDataFormats` enumeration that allows for peaking inside the `DataPackage` to tell you what the data type is. What you do from here with your share target app is completely up to you.

There's one last step. As a courtesy, your share target app should let Windows know when you are about to begin truly sharing the contents of the Share `DataPackage`, as well as reporting completion, like so:

```
this.shareOperation.ReportStarted();
// Do actual sharing.
this.shareOperation.ReportCompleted();
```

For more information on supporting the Share Target contract, please visit MSDN at `http://msdn.microsoft.com/en-us/library/windows/apps/xaml/hh871367.aspx`.

Search

Search is ubiquitous. Most commonly, you see extensive use of searching on the Internet. But desktop/laptop operating systems are not to be left behind. Windows 7 and Mac OS X support searching within the OS for apps, files, and so forth. And Windows 8 simply elevates search to the next level by allowing easy searches through Apps, Files, or Settings and user-friendly results display. Most importantly, the entire search workflow is touch-friendly, which means search is now a first-class citizen in tablet form factors. Also, Windows 8 search extends the search metaphor to contents inside an app and allows apps to offer suggestions or result recommendations, even when the app is not running. Altogether, this can be a powerful search experience for the user, and your app needs to participate.

So, the next question is how does a Windows 8 app participate in the OS-level search? The answer is the Search contract. Through the Search menu on the charms bar, searching is always a swipe or hover away for Windows 8 users (see Figure 10-15). Windows 8 users have muscle memory to use search through the charms. The search workflow gets fired up in response to the Search menu selection, for a consistent and predictable user experience. Apps that implement the Search contract get to play a critical role. This is a great way for your Windows 8 app to get highlighted by Windows 8 (frequently searched apps get higher priority in an app list), leading to increased traffic and usage as well as increased user intimacy because users can now search for your app's content from outside the app. Let's dig in.

Figure 10-15. Search charms menu option

How Should the User Search?

Begin with where and how you should support search in your app. Microsoft's guidelines indicate that since the charms bar already has a Search option, you should not add a search mechanism within your app. This only makes sense because the user is already very familiar with searching through the charms bar, and you do not want repetitive UI. However, if your app revolves around a strong search functionality or if you want to show extended search results, there is nothing stopping you from adding search functionality in your app canvas; the Bing Windows 8 Store app does so. And even if you do add a search mechanism in your app, consider using the Search menu on the charms bar for the user to actually do his or her search. In this case, you are simply nudging the user in the right direction. Confused? Look at the example shown in Figure 10-16.

Figure 10-16. *Search option in app bar*

So, with the Apress Featured Books Demo app, I just added a small Search icon in the app bar. Curious about how to do this? It takes a just a few lines of XAML, as follows:

```
<Page.BottomAppBar>
<AppBar x:Name="bottomAppBar" Padding="10,0,10,0">
<Grid>
<StackPanel Orientation="Horizontal" HorizontalAlignment="Right">
<Button Style="{StaticResource SearchAppBarButtonStyle}" x:Name="searchButton"
Click="searchButton_Click"/>
</StackPanel>
</Grid>
</AppBar>
</Page.BottomAppBar>
```

Now, in your case, the search within the app is to simply help the user find an Apress book quickly. This is nothing spectacular and you should fall back on the ubiquitous OS search to add the search functionality. The Search menu in the charms bar leads to a pane for searching, called the *Search pane*, and it turns out that you can invoke that programmatically. Here's a little code in response to your app bar Search icon click/tap:

```
private void searchButton_Click(object sender, RoutedEventArgs e)
        {
            Windows.ApplicationModel.Search.SearchPane.GetForCurrentView().Show();
        }
```

You can see how to get a handle on the Windows Search pane and show it programmatically. So, when the user hits your app bar Search icon, the Search pane is actually the one that opens, thus offering the Windows search workflow to the user (see Figure 10-17).

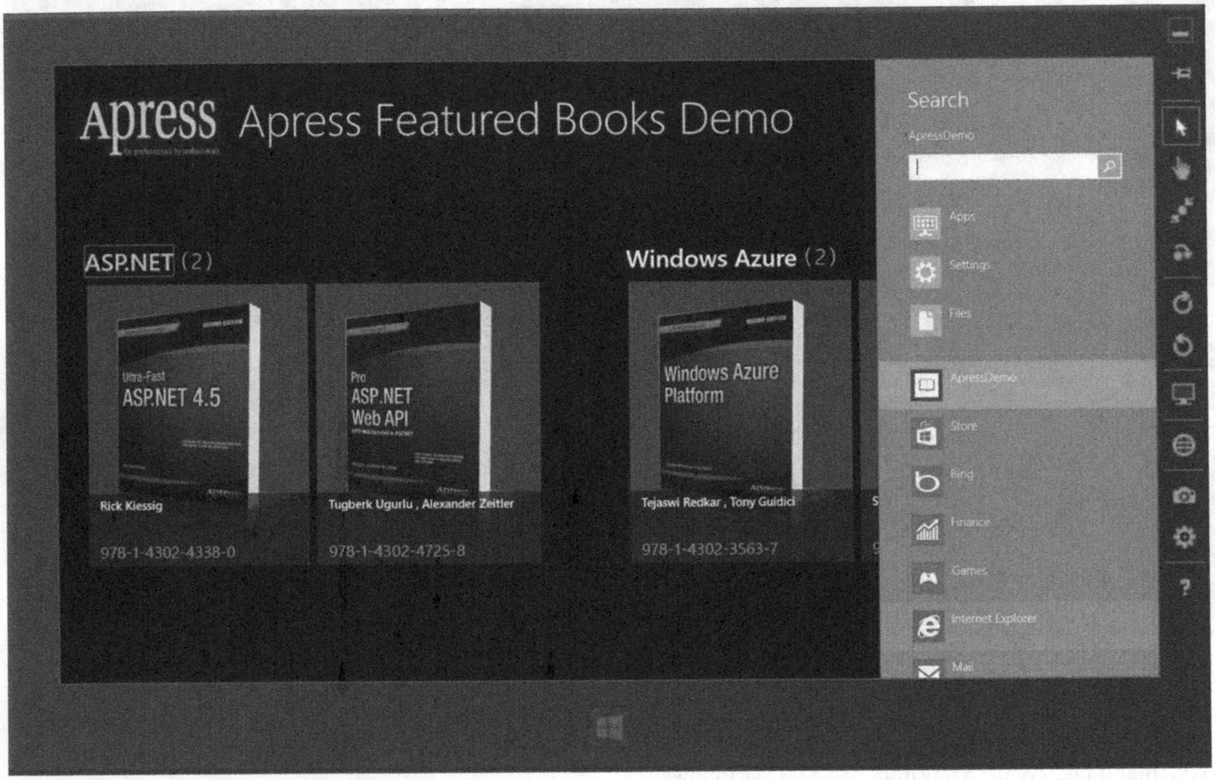

Figure 10-17. *Search contract implemented*

Implementing the Search Contract

Now, let's talk about implementing the Search contract in your app. Sure enough, Visual Studio has a template to help us out and add boilerplate code/settings. First, add a template XAML page to support the Windows 8 Search contract, as shown in Figure 10-18.

Figure 10-18. *Search contract template*

As with other VS templates to support contracts, the Search template makes a few changes in your app. First, your app needs to declare to Windows 8 that you are participating in the Search contract. Accordingly, a setting gets added to the Declarations tab of the `PackageAppXManifest` file, as shown in Figure 10-19.

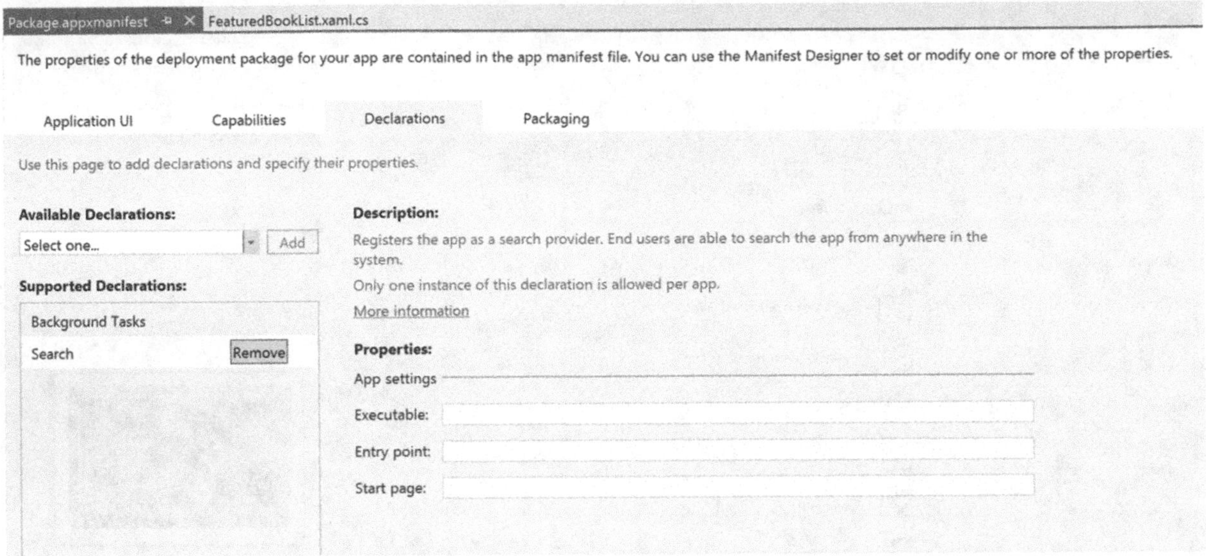

Figure 10-19. *Search declaration*

Next, open the `App.xaml.cs` file and you will notice that a `OnSearchActivated` event handler has been added. Again, this is the hook for the OS to activate your app for searching, even when it is not running. Here's some sample code:

```
protected async override void
OnSearchActivated(Windows.ApplicationModel.Activation.SearchActivatedEventArgs args)
        {
            // TODO: Register the
            Windows.ApplicationModel.Search.SearchPane.GetForCurrentView().QuerySubmitted
            // event in OnWindowCreated to speed up searches once the application is already running

            // If the Window isn't already using Frame navigation, insert our own Frame
            var previousContent = Window.Current.Content;
            var frame = previousContent as Frame;

            // If the app does not contain a top-level frame, it is possible that this
            // is the initial launch of the app. Typically this method and OnLaunched
            // in App.xaml.cs can call a common method.
            if (frame == null)
            {
                // Create a Frame to act as the navigation context and associate it with
                // a SuspensionManager key
                frame = new Frame();
                ApressDemo.Common.SuspensionManager.RegisterFrame(frame, "AppFrame");

                if (args.PreviousExecutionState == ApplicationExecutionState.Terminated)
                {
                    // Restore the saved session state only when appropriate
                    try
                    {
                        await ApressDemo.Common.SuspensionManager.RestoreAsync();
                    }
```

```
                catch (ApressDemo.Common.SuspensionManagerException)
                {
                    //Something went wrong restoring state.
                    //Assume there is no state and continue
                }
            }
        }

        frame.Navigate(typeof(SearchResultsPage), args.QueryText);
        Window.Current.Content = frame;

        // Ensure the current window is active
        Window.Current.Activate();
    }
```

OK, so that was a good chunk of code. Don't fret—you do not need to change most of it. What was done here makes sure that if your app gets activated through the search activation route, the application frame is loaded correctly. Also, do you see the use of `SuspensionManager.RestoreAsync()`? If your app needs an object model to function, you would want to make sure that it is hydrated correctly in the `OnSearchActivated` event handler. Beyond that, you simply carry over the `SearchActivatedEventArgs` to the dedicated `SearchResultsPage`.

At this point and without writing any other code, go ahead and run the Apress demo app. You will fire up search through the charms bar and be directed to the `SearchResultsPage`, as shown in Figure 10-20.

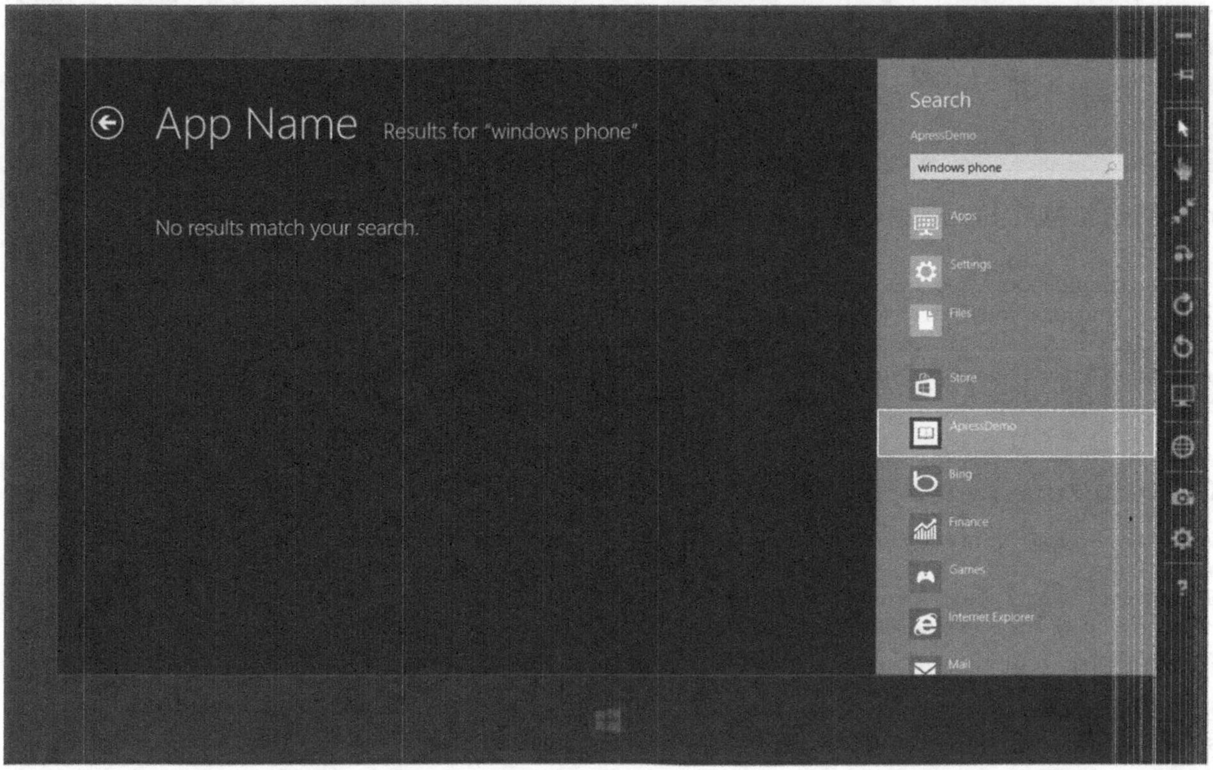

Figure 10-20. *An out-of-the-box search*

Not running your Apress demo app, fire up search through the charms bar again. You should see something like what is shown in Figure 10-21.

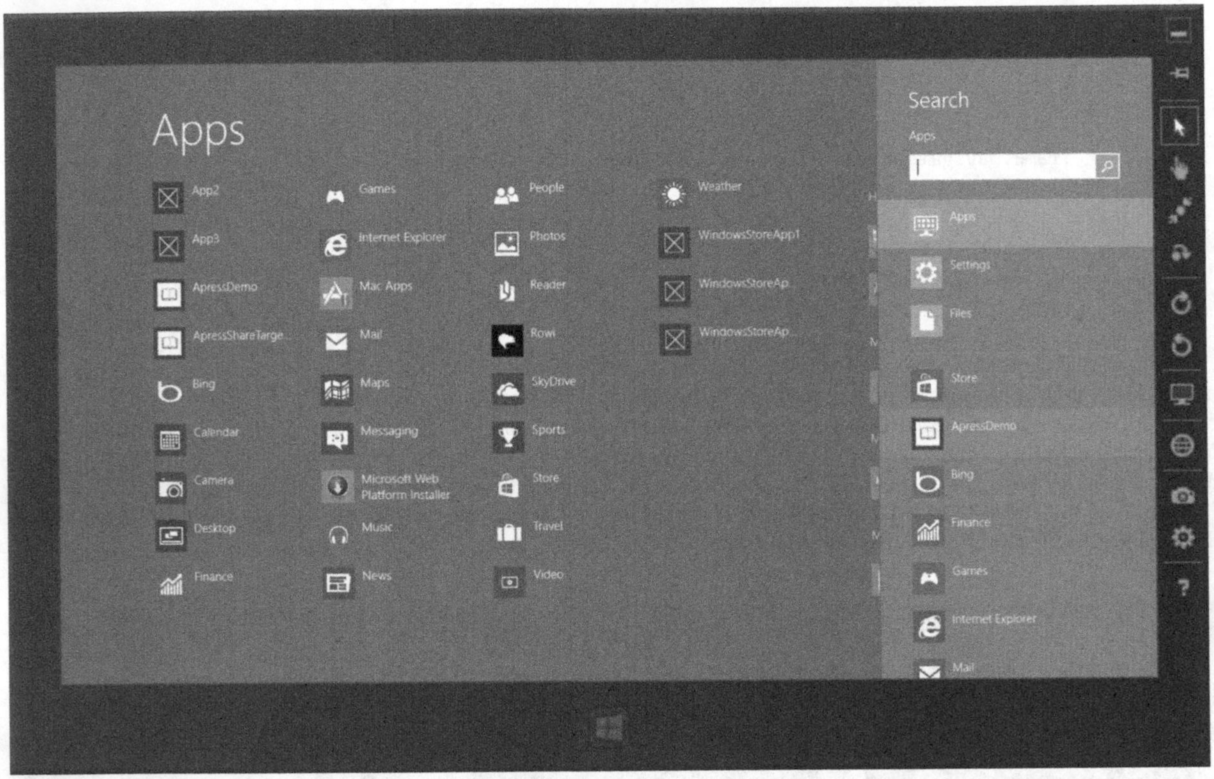

Figure 10-21. *App listing with Search contract implementations*

You should already see some promise in what's happening. Just by adding your search results page through the template, you have your `SearchActivation` event handled, your app listed in the Search pane, and search queries carried into the `SearchResultsPage`. Because of your declaration to support search, your Apress demo app gets listed in the Search pane, even when your app is not running. Let's wire up some UI on the `SearchResultsPage` to customize the search experience.

Customizing Your Search Experience

While it is true that the user's search term gets passed down to this page in your app, you may want to offer a few more search filters to further help users find the items that they are looking for. If you look through the boilerplate code in `SearchResultsPage.xaml.cs`, you will see some `Filter` objects and a `Filter_SelectionChanged()` event handler to respond to when the user changes filters. You can define custom filters and respond to the event to update the search results.

But, let's say you wanted to roll your own filtering mechanism and a custom results view. You will spend a little time doing so because it shows the internal workings of Search. First, customize your `SearchResultsPage` to look something like Figure 10-22.

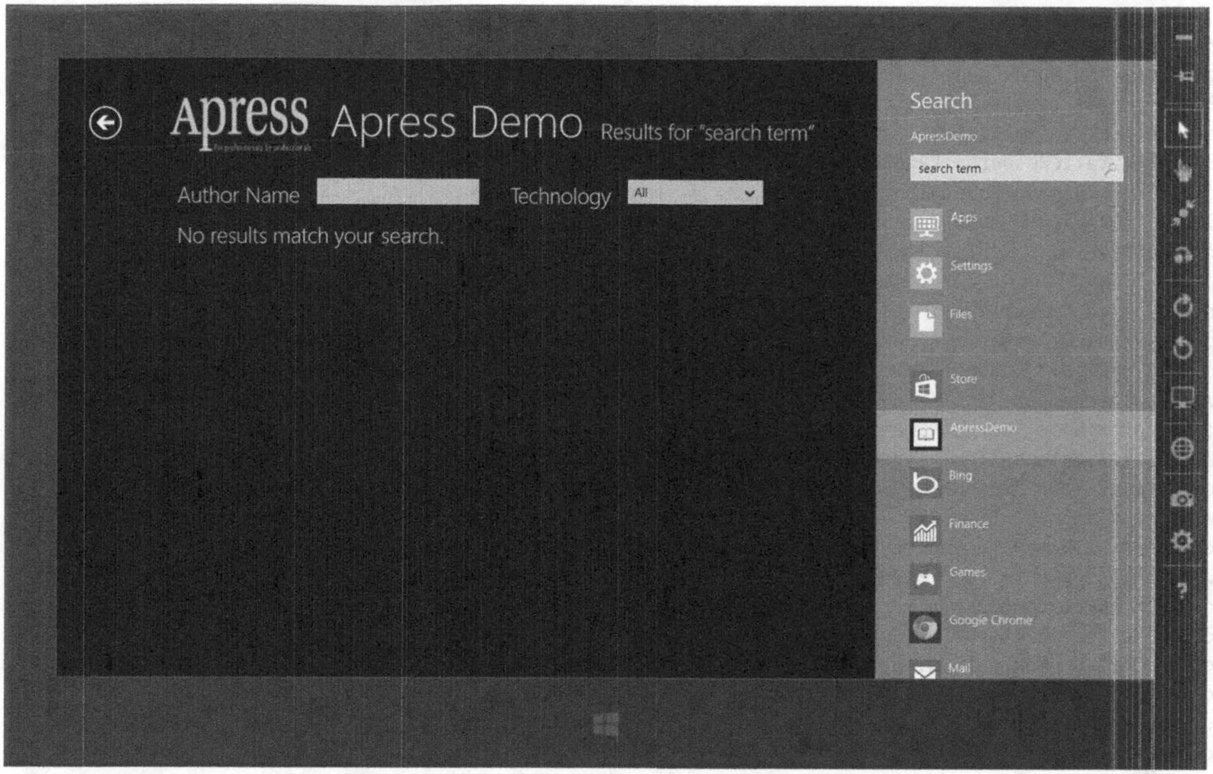

Figure 10-22. *Custom search filters*

Essentially, what you want to do is have three rows in your page to accommodate the following: a header with a Back button, a collection of custom search filters, and a grid showing the search results. Listing 10-1 shows the XAML to power the custom SearchResultsPage.

Listing 10-1. Search Page XAML Markup

```
<Page.Resources>
<CollectionViewSource x:Name="resultsViewSource" Source="{Binding Results}"/>
</Page.Resources>

<Grid Style="{StaticResource LayoutRootStyle}" Background="Black">
<Grid.RowDefinitions>
<RowDefinition Height="140"/>
<RowDefinition Height="100"/>
<RowDefinition Height="*"/>
</Grid.RowDefinitions>

<!-- Back button, page title and subtitles-->
<StackPanel Orientation="Horizontal" Grid.Row="0">
<Button x:Name="backButton" Click="GoBack" IsEnabled="{Binding Frame.CanGoBack,
ElementName=pageRoot}" Style="{StaticResource BackButtonStyle}"/>
```

```
<Image Source="/Assets/ApressLogo.png" Width="200" Height="100" VerticalAlignment="Center"
Margin="10,25,0,0"/>
<TextBlock x:Name="pageTitle" Grid.Column="1" Text="Apress Demo" Style="{StaticResource
PageHeaderTextStyle}" VerticalAlignment="Center" Margin="10,25,20,10"/>
<TextBlock x:Name="resultText" Grid.Column="2" Text="Results for " IsHitTestVisible="false"
Style="{StaticResource PageSubheaderTextStyle}"/>
<TextBlock x:Name="queryText" Grid.Column="3" Text="{Binding QueryText}" IsHitTestVisible="false"
Style="{StaticResource PageSubheaderTextStyle}"/>
</StackPanel>

<!-- Search Criteria -->
<StackPanel Orientation="Horizontal" Margin="150,10,0,0" x:Name="searchFilters" Grid.Row="1">
<TextBlock Text="Author Name" Style="{StaticResource PageSubheaderTextStyle}"
VerticalAlignment="Top"/>
<TextBox x:Name="authorNameTextBox" Width="200" Margin="20,0,0,0" Height="30"
VerticalAlignment="Top" TextChanged="authorNameTextBox_TextChanged"/>
<TextBlock Text="Technology" Style="{StaticResource PageSubheaderTextStyle}" Margin="40,0,0,0"
VerticalAlignment="Top"/>
<ComboBox x:Name="technologyDropdown" Margin="20,0,0,0" Width="170" Height="30"
VerticalAlignment="Top" SelectionChanged="technologyDropdown_SelectionChanged">
<ComboBoxItem Content="All" IsSelected="True"/>
<ComboBoxItem Content="Windows Phone"/>
<ComboBoxItem Content="Windows Azure"/>
<ComboBoxItem Content="ASP.NET"/>
</ComboBox>
</StackPanel>

<Grid x:Name="resultsPanel" Grid.Row="2" Margin="0,10,0,0">

<Grid x:Name="typicalPanel">
<Grid.RowDefinitions>
<RowDefinition Height="*"/>
</Grid.RowDefinitions>

<GridView
                x:Name="resultsGridView"
                AutomationProperties.AutomationId="ResultsGridView"
                AutomationProperties.Name="Search Results"
                TabIndex="1"
                Grid.Row="1"
                Margin="150,10,110,46"
                SelectionMode="None"
                IsSwipeEnabled="false"
                IsItemClickEnabled="True"
                ItemsSource="{Binding Source={StaticResource resultsViewSource}}"
                ItemTemplate="{StaticResource ApressSearchResultsItemTemplate}">

<GridView.ItemContainerStyle>
<Style TargetType="Control">
<Setter Property="Height" Value="70"/>
```

```
<Setter Property="Margin" Value="0,0,38,8"/>
</Style>
</GridView.ItemContainerStyle>
</GridView>
</Grid>

</Grid>

<TextBlock
        x:Name="noResultsTextBlock"
        Grid.Row="1"
        Margin="150,60,0,0"
        Visibility="Collapsed"
        Style="{StaticResource SubheaderTextStyle}"
        Text="No results match your search." />
```

The XAML should be self-explanatory, given the three rows you wanted to have in your page. You should notice the search criteria StackPanel, where you use a TextBox and a ComboBox to filter results on the Apress author name and the technology just for demo purposes.

Now, searching in Windows 8 is contextual within each app. What your app allows the user to search on is completely up to your app and its functionality. In case of your Apress demo app, it makes sense to make the search work for book names to facilitate the user finding something quickly. So, display search results in response to a user search. Here is some code from the SearchResultsPage.xaml.cs file:

```
protected override void LoadState(Object navigationParameter, Dictionary<String, Object> pageState)
     {
        this.searchQueryText = navigationParameter as String;

        // Communicate results through the view model
        this.DefaultViewModel["QueryText"] = '\u201c' + searchQueryText + '\u201d';

        // Apply search filter on Book Name based on search query.
        IEnumerable<ApressBook> searchResults = from book in
        ((App)Application.Current).FeaturedBookListVM.FeaturedApressBooks
                                                where
        book.ApressBookName.ToLower().Contains(searchQueryText.ToLower())
                                                select book;

        this.DefaultViewModel["Results"] = searchResults;

        if (searchResults.Count() > 0)
            VisualStateManager.GoToState(this, "ResultsFound", true);
        else
            VisualStateManager.GoToState(this, "NoResultsFound", true);
     }
```

To break this down, on the page's LoadState() event, you try to first read the incoming navigationParameter. This, if you remember, is the SearchActivatedEventArgs from the SearchActivated event and represents the search query that the user typed in. Next, you will need to filter out some data per the search query and hand off the results to the XAML view through the DefaultViewModel. In this case, you simply look through your global collection of featured Apress books and extract the ones that contain the search query in the book name. Notice the use of

CollectionViewSource from the XAML markup as you simply hand-off the results to the DefaultViewModel. Feeling lucky? Let's run the Apress demo app once again and fire up search through the charms bar. You should see results like those in Figure 10-23.

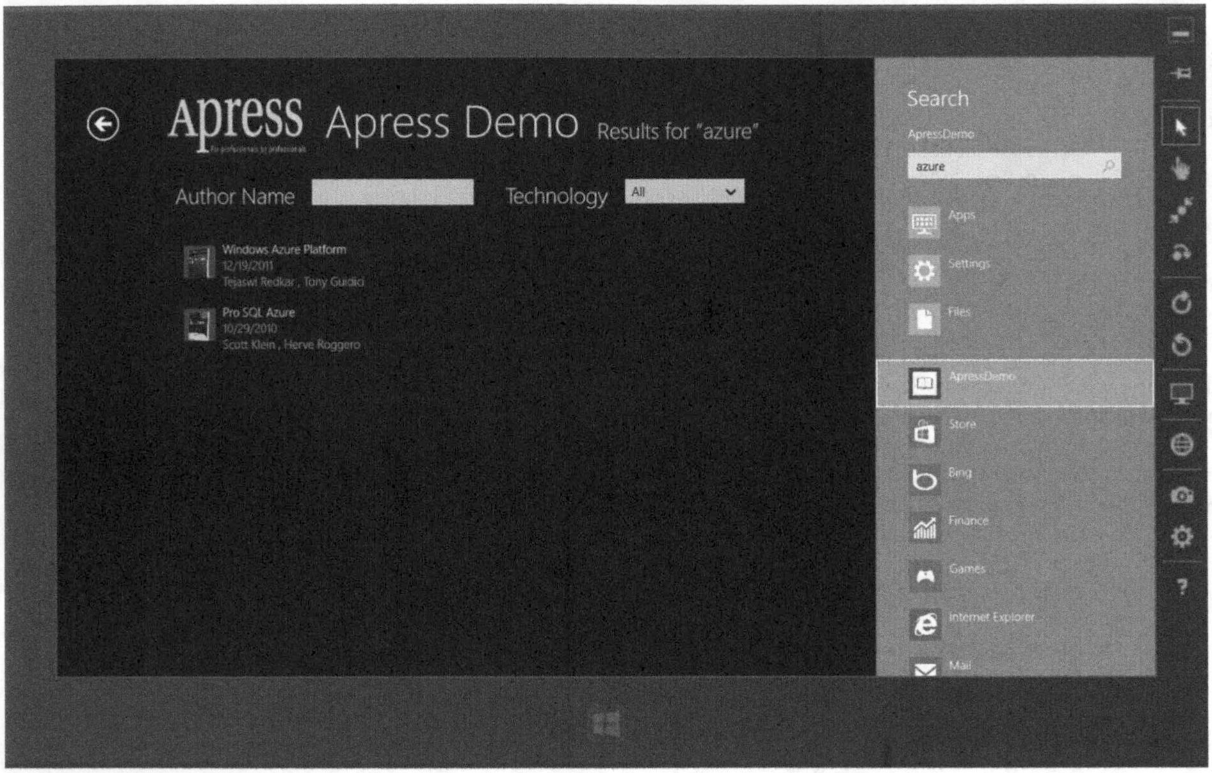

Figure 10-23. *Working search*

How cool is that? You can see the search query being handed down by Windows 8, making it all the way down to your page, and the filtered results showing only what matched the search criteria. Do you care to know how the results grid displays each matching book? A simple style template suffices, like in the following:

```
<DataTemplate x:Key="ApressSearchResultsItemTemplate">
<Grid Width="294" Margin="6">
<Grid.ColumnDefinitions>
<ColumnDefinition Width="Auto"/>
<ColumnDefinition Width="*"/>
</Grid.ColumnDefinitions>
<Border Background="{StaticResource ListViewItemPlaceholderBackgroundThemeBrush}" Margin="0,0,0,10"
Width="40" Height="40">
<Image Source="{Binding ApressBookImageURI}" Stretch="UniformToFill"/>
</Border>
<StackPanel Grid.Column="1" Margin="10,-10,0,0">
<TextBlock Text="{Binding ApressBookName}" Style="{StaticResource BodyTextStyle}"
TextWrapping="NoWrap"/>
```

```
<TextBlock Text="{Binding DisplayablePublishDate}" Style="{StaticResource BodyTextStyle}"
Foreground="{StaticResource ApplicationSecondaryForegroundThemeBrush}" TextWrapping="NoWrap"/>
<TextBlock Text="{Binding ApressBookAuthor}" Style="{StaticResource BodyTextStyle}"
Foreground="{StaticResource ApplicationSecondaryForegroundThemeBrush}" TextWrapping="NoWrap"/>
</StackPanel>
</Grid>
</DataTemplate>
```

One other benefit of implementing search the way you did is that search would work even if the user did not type in anything. Empty search queries should allow the user to see everything—or unfiltered data, like in Figure 10-24.

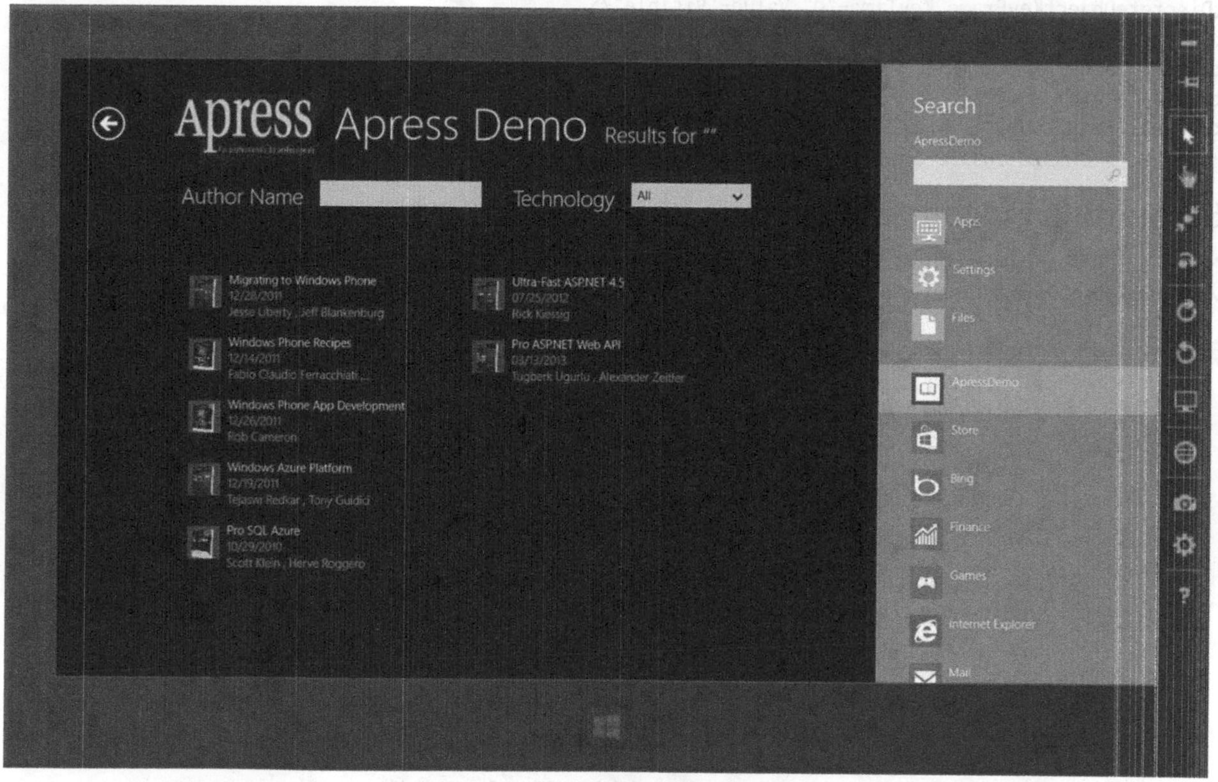

Figure 10-24. *Empty search*

Handling No Results

All of this is good if your search query matches some data, but what if there are no matches? Here's the last piece of code that you saw during data binding, along with the `VisualState` XAML markup showing the flip between showing results or informational text:

```
if (searchResults.Count() > 0)
                VisualStateManager.GoToState(this, "ResultsFound", true);
            else
                VisualStateManager.GoToState(this, "NoResultsFound", true);
```

```
<VisualStateGroup x:Name = "ResultStates">
<VisualState x:Name="ResultsFound" />
<!-- When there are no results, the results panel is replaced with an informational TextBlock -->
<VisualState x:Name="NoResultsFound">
<Storyboard>
<ObjectAnimationUsingKeyFrames Storyboard.TargetName="resultsPanel"
Storyboard.TargetProperty="Visibility">
<DiscreteObjectKeyFrame KeyTime="0" Value="Collapsed"/>
</ObjectAnimationUsingKeyFrames>
<ObjectAnimationUsingKeyFrames Storyboard.TargetName="noResultsTextBlock"
Storyboard.TargetProperty="Visibility">
<DiscreteObjectKeyFrame KeyTime="0" Value="Visible"/>
</ObjectAnimationUsingKeyFrames>
</Storyboard>
</VisualState>
</VisualStateGroup>
```

Supporting Custom Filters

Now, handle your custom filters. Each is meant to offer additional filtering on top of the search query results. Start with the Author Name filter. Here's the code:

```
private void authorNameTextBox_TextChanged(object sender, TextChangedEventArgs e)
        {
            if (authorNameTextBox.Text.Trim() != string.Empty)
            {
                // Apply search filter on Book Name based on search query and then Author Name.
                IEnumerable<ApressBook> searchResults = from book in
                ((App)Application.Current).FeaturedBookListVM.FeaturedApressBooks
                                                        where
                book.ApressBookName.ToLower().Contains(searchQueryText.ToLower())
                && book.ApressBookAuthor.ToLower().Contains(authorNameTextBox.Text.Trim().ToLower())
                                                        select book;

                this.DefaultViewModel["Results"] = searchResults;

                if (searchResults.Count() > 0)
                    VisualStateManager.GoToState(this, "ResultsFound", true);
                else
                    VisualStateManager.GoToState(this, "NoResultsFound", true);
            }
        }
```

The result of implementing an Author Name filter on top of the search is shown in Figure 10-25.

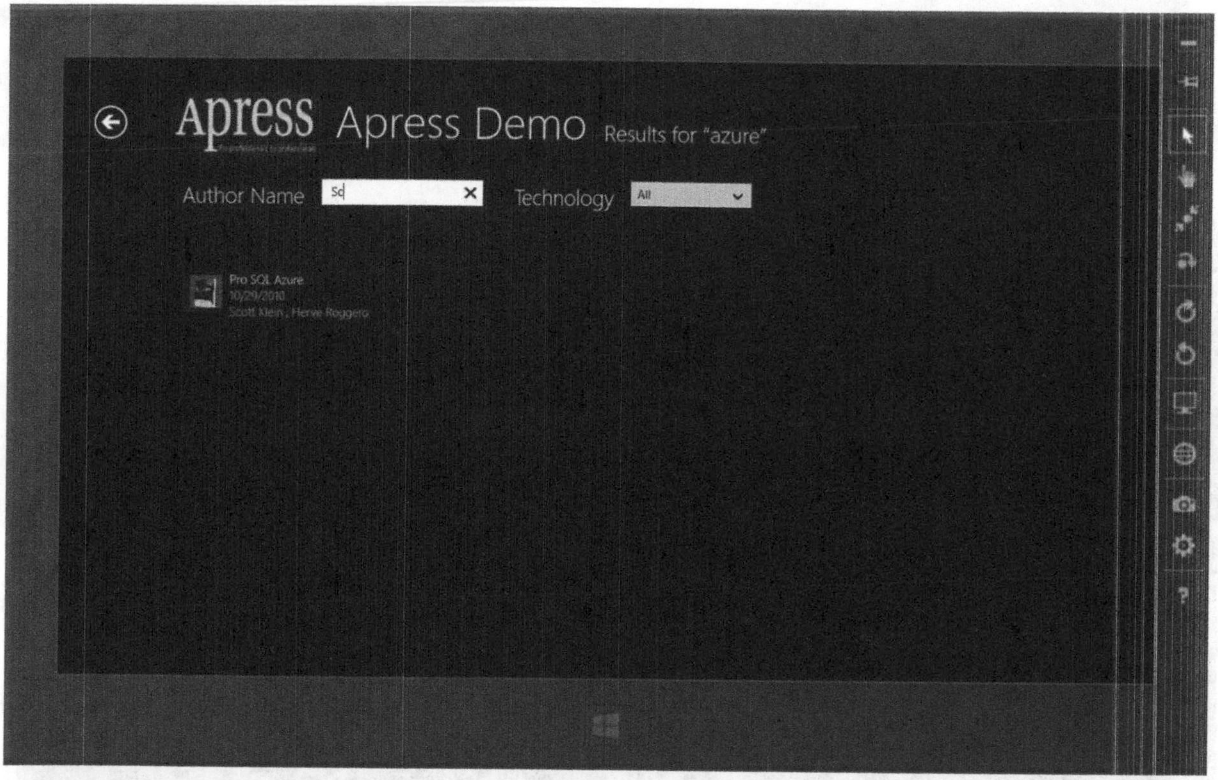

Figure 10-25. *Text search filter*

And now support the search result filtering when the selected technology changes from the drop-down menu. Here's the code, followed by the results of it in action, as shown in Figure 10-26.

```
private void technologyDropdown_SelectionChanged(object sender, SelectionChangedEventArgs e)
        {
            if (technologyDropdown != null && technologyDropdown.SelectedValue.ToString() != "All")
            {
                ComboBoxItem selectedTech = (ComboBoxItem)technologyDropdown.SelectedItem;

                // Apply search filter on Book Name based on search query and selected Technology.
                IEnumerable<ApressBook> searchResults = from book in
                ((App)Application.Current).FeaturedBookListVM.FeaturedApressBooks
                                                        where
                book.ApressBookName.ToLower().Contains(searchQueryText.ToLower())
                && book.ApressBookTechnology == selectedTech.Content.ToString()
                                                        select book;

                this.DefaultViewModel["Results"] = searchResults;
```

```
            if (searchResults.Count() > 0)
                VisualStateManager.GoToState(this, "ResultsFound", true);
            else
                VisualStateManager.GoToState(this, "NoResultsFound", true);
        }
    }
```

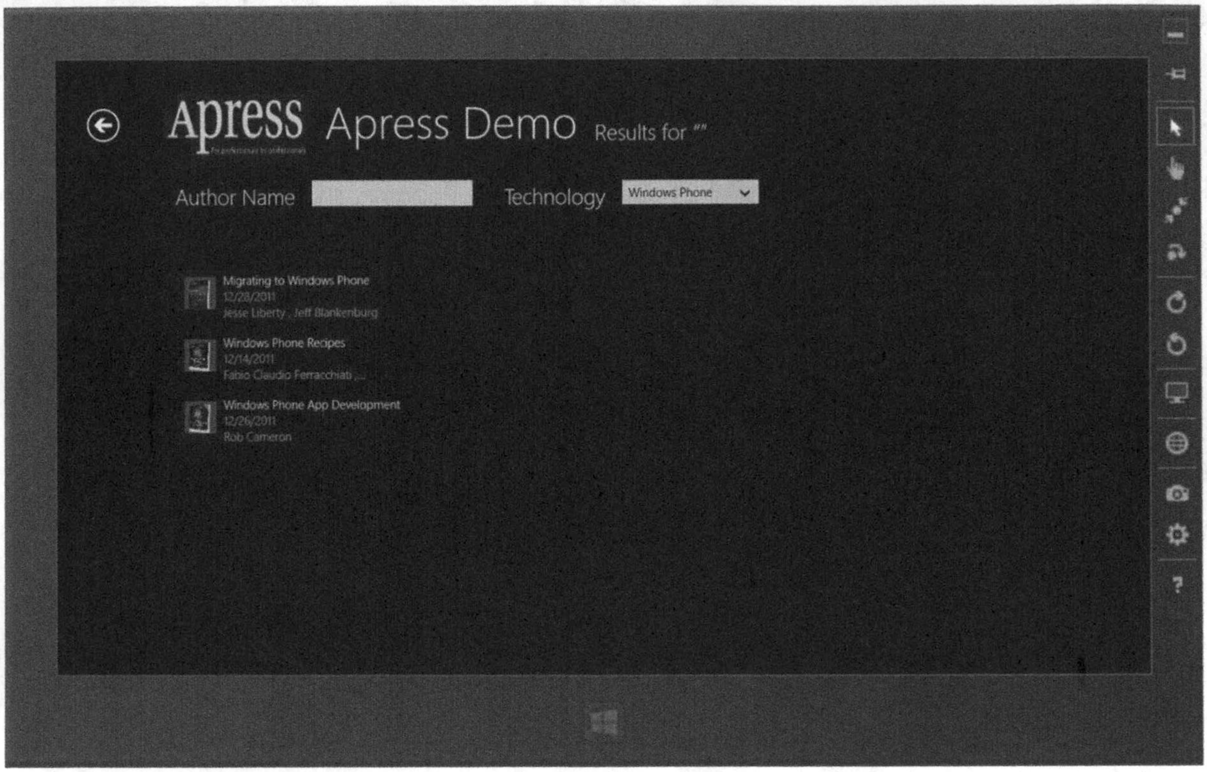

Figure 10-26. *Drop-down search filter*

Search Suggestions

At this point, you are able to make search work from end to end and it truly contributes toward a wonderful user experience. How about sweetening the deal? Wouldn't it be nice if you could recommend suggestions to the user as he or she is typing in the Search pane? These suggestions can be in two forms:

- *Query suggestions* are autocompletions of the user's query text. They provide queries that the user might want to search.
- *Result suggestions* are strong or exact or matches to the user's query that the user may want to view immediately.

Let's see how you may implement query suggestions first.

Query Suggestions

You essentially need to inspect keystrokes as the user is typing in the Search pane and offer text suggestions toward what the user wants to search. This is easier to do than it sounds. Here's a little code:

```
protected override void OnNavigatedTo(NavigationEventArgs e)
        {
            base.OnNavigatedTo(e);

            SearchPane searchPane = SearchPane.GetForCurrentView();
            searchPane.SuggestionsRequested += searchPane_SuggestionsRequested;
        }

        protected override void OnNavigatedFrom(NavigationEventArgs e)
        {
            base.OnNavigatedFrom(e);

            SearchPane searchPane = SearchPane.GetForCurrentView();
            searchPane.SuggestionsRequested -= searchPane_SuggestionsRequested;
        }

private async void searchPane_SuggestionsRequested(SearchPane sender,
SearchPaneSuggestionsRequestedEventArgs args)
        {
            args.Request.SearchSuggestionCollection.AppendQuerySuggestions((from book in
            ((App)Application.Current).FeaturedBookListVM.FeaturedApressBooks
                                                                          where
            book.ApressBookName.ToLower().StartsWith(args.QueryText.ToLower())
                                                                          select
            book.ApressBookName).Take(5));

}
        }
```

Let's look into what the preceding code just did. You essentially get a handle on the Search pane and listen to the `SuggestionsRequested` event. As is good practice, you wire and unwire event handlers during the life cycle of the page. Next, in the event handler, you simply do a match on the `QueryText` as it currently is and see if any of the book names start with what the user is typing. If so, you simply offer that book name as a suggestion and add it to the `SearchSuggestionCollection` for Windows 8 to display in the Search pane. The result is shown in Figure 10-27.

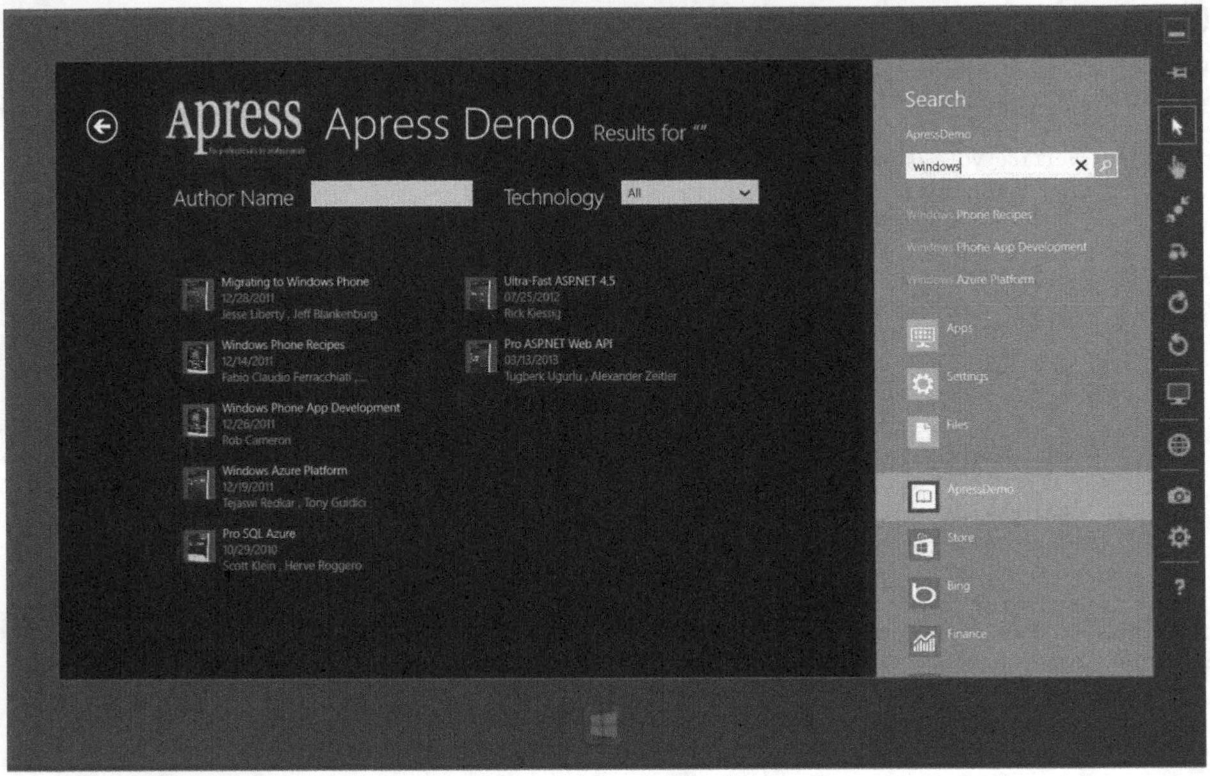

Figure 10-27. *Search query suggestions*

The nice thing about search suggestions is the fact that they work even if the app is not running. So, in effect, you are providing a glimpse of your app's data from outside the app through the search workflow. Now, let's get the result suggestions to work.

Result Suggestions

Result suggestions are meant to be very close search matches to an exact item within the app. Accordingly, you only offer a result suggestion when you have been able to match at least five of the first letters that the user has typed in the search query. Here's the code:

```
private async void searchPane_SuggestionsRequested(SearchPane sender,
SearchPaneSuggestionsRequestedEventArgs args)
        {
            args.Request.SearchSuggestionCollection.AppendQuerySuggestions((from book in
            ((App)Application.Current).FeaturedBookListVM.FeaturedApressBooks
                                                                              where
            book.ApressBookName.ToLower().StartsWith(args.QueryText.ToLower())
                                                                              select
            book.ApressBookName).Take(5));
```

```
            IEnumerable<ApressBook> recommendedBooks = from book in
            ((App)Application.Current).FeaturedBookListVM.FeaturedApressBooks
                                                            where
            book.ApressBookName.Substring(0, 5).ToLower() == args.QueryText.ToLower()
                                                            select book;

            if (recommendedBooks.Count() > 0)
            {
                ApressBook firstRecommendedBook = null;
                foreach (ApressBook book in recommendedBooks)
                {
                    firstRecommendedBook = book;
                    break;
                }

                StorageFile imageToRead = await localFolder.GetFileAsync("MigratingToWP.png");

args.Request.SearchSuggestionCollection.AppendResultSuggestion(firstRecommendedBook.ApressBookName,
firstRecommendedBook.DisplayablePublishDate, firstRecommendedBook.ApressBookISBN,
RandomAccessStreamReference.CreateFromFile(imageToRead), string.Empty);
            }
        }
```

When offering a result suggestion, you are supposed to provide a thumbnail view (choose a random file from the disk just for demos) of the matching item, along with a title and some description. This gets listed out in the Search pane under the suggestions. If the user selects the suggested result, a `resultsuggestionchosen` event is fired. When your app handles this event, it can get the tag of the chosen result suggestion from the `searchPaneResultSuggestionChosenEventArgs.tag` property (that you filled in the selected book's ISBN) and this allows you to take the user directly to the details of the selected item. Figure 10-28 shows the result suggestions in action. Remember, with power comes responsibility, so use the search suggestions carefully to augment the user's search experience.

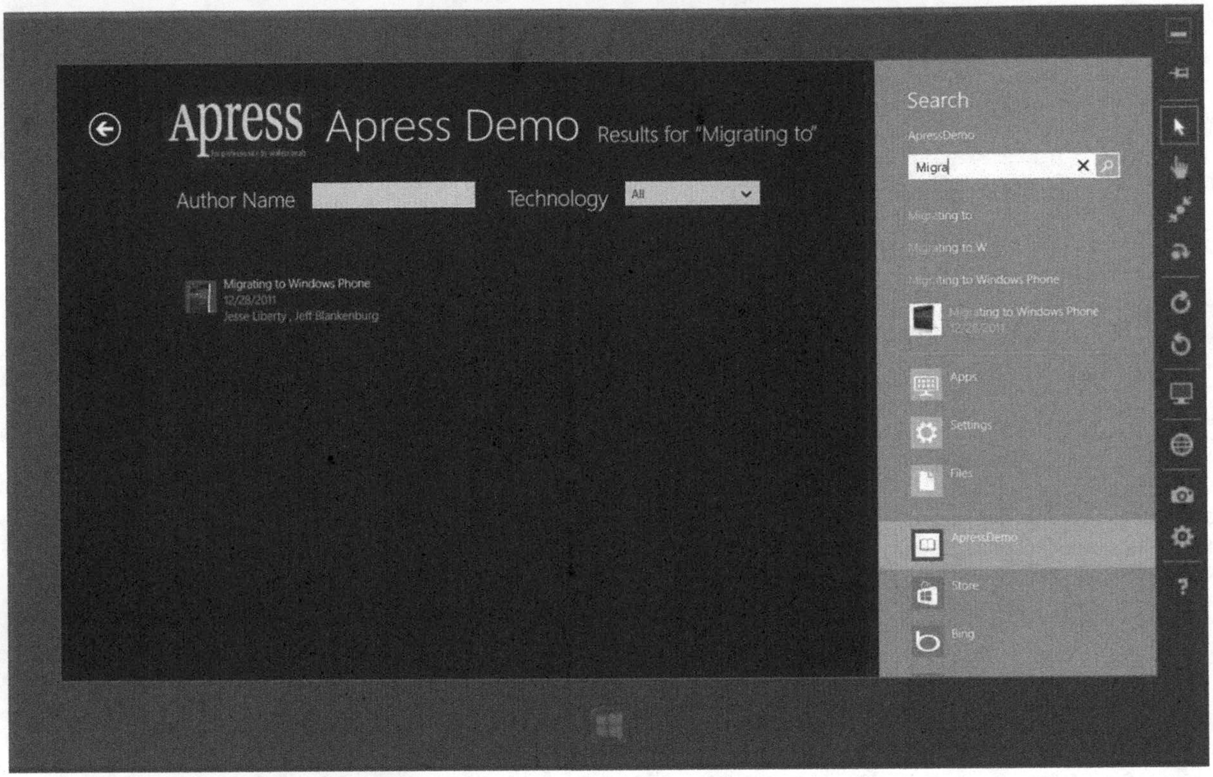

Figure 10-28. *Search result suggestions*

Settings

Every OS and every app across the ecosystem needs to support settings for the various ways a user may configure functionality toward his or her preferences. Windows 8 is no exception. It offers a smooth and consistent user experience with settings, which is carried over to each app and its settings. Swipe or hover from the right-hand screen edge to expose the charms bar. Settings is the last menu option. No matter where you are in Windows 8, the charms bar Settings menu option is always available. It provides a one-stop shop for all settings, but caters to context. Figure 10-29 shows the Settings menu option in the charms bar and Figure 10-30 shows the Settings options while running the Internet Explorer 10 app in Windows 8.

Figure 10-29. *Settings charms bar menu*

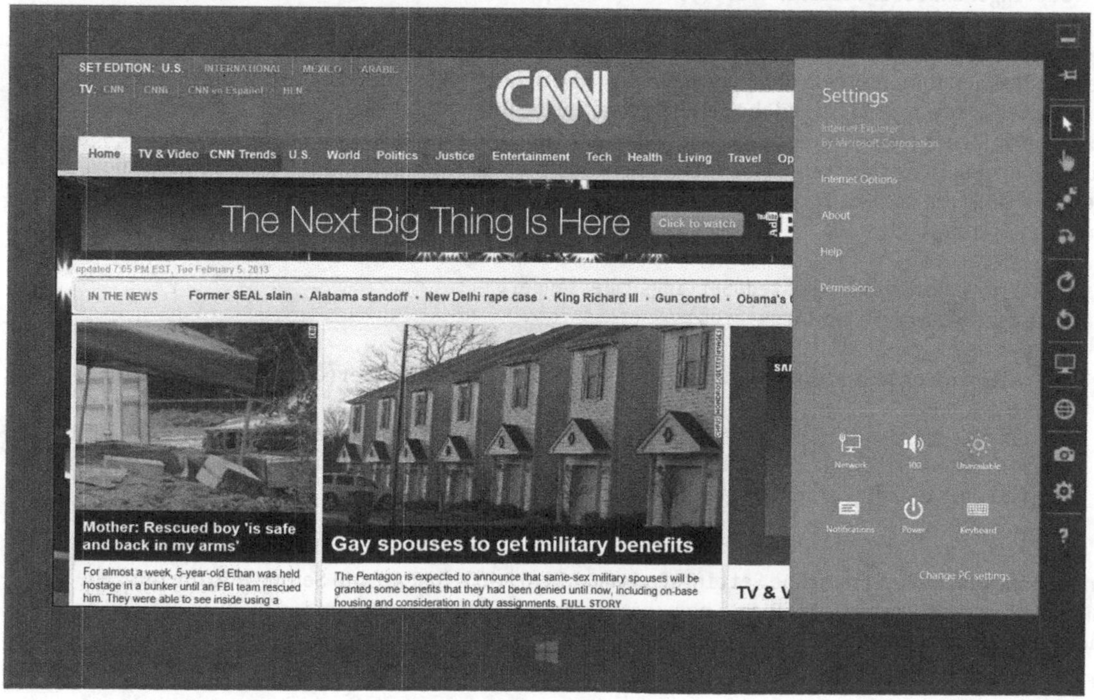

Figure 10-30. *The IE settings*

So, it is obvious that app settings belong in the charms bar, after the Settings menu invocation. This is simply in line with the user's muscle memory for using the charms bar and caters to his or her expectations of consistency from every Windows 8 Store app. So, implement that in your Apress demo app.

First, a little caveat: folks doing Windows 8 app development in HTML/JavaScript have it a little easy here with a built-in `SettingsFlyout` control. This is not yet available in the XAML stack natively, but certainly does not prevent you from getting app settings to work. If you are looking for some help with a ready-made control from a third-party library, look no further than Callisto by Tim Heuer for settings flyout controls and other goodies. Further details are at `http://visualstudiogallery.msdn.microsoft.com/0526563b-7a48-4b17-a087-a35cea701052`.

But, you like to fly solo, right? Knowing how to implement settings on your own gives you insight into how app settings work and makes sure that you are doing things right.

Implementing Settings

Let's pick the main dashboard page `FeaturesBookList.xaml` in your Apress demo to see how you can make app settings work. Here's some code to start:

```
// Used to determine the correct height to ensure our custom UI fills the screen.
        private Rect windowBounds;

protected override void OnNavigatedTo(NavigationEventArgs e)
        {
            base.OnNavigatedTo(e);
            windowBounds = Window.Current.Bounds;

            // Listen to Settings Pane events.
            SettingsPane.GetForCurrentView().CommandsRequested += Settings_CommandsRequested;
        }
```

Just like search, when the settings flyout comes into play, the right-hand extended pane is the one that shows contents from the OS or any app. It is called the *Settings pane*. So, the first step is to get a handle on the Settings pane and listen in on when the user invokes the Settings menu option from the charms bar. Since you are creating settings by hand, you want to make sure that your UI looks consistent and that the Settings options fill the entire vertical screen real-estate—thus, the use of `Window.Current.Bounds`. Next, see what you can do when the user hits the Settings menu. Here's some code:

```
private void Settings_CommandsRequested(SettingsPane sender,
SettingsPaneCommandsRequestedEventArgs args)
        {
            UICommandInvokedHandler handler = new UICommandInvokedHandler(onSettingsCommand);

            SettingsCommand settingsCommand = new SettingsCommand("ApressSettings",
            "Apress Demo Settings", handler);
            args.Request.ApplicationCommands.Add(settingsCommand);
        }
```

You can see that you are leveraging the `SettingsCommand` API to add a custom app Setting into the mix. The results of this can be seen in Figure 10-31. Please note that the Permissions menu option is system-controlled and driven by the declarations in your app's `PackageAppxManifest` file.

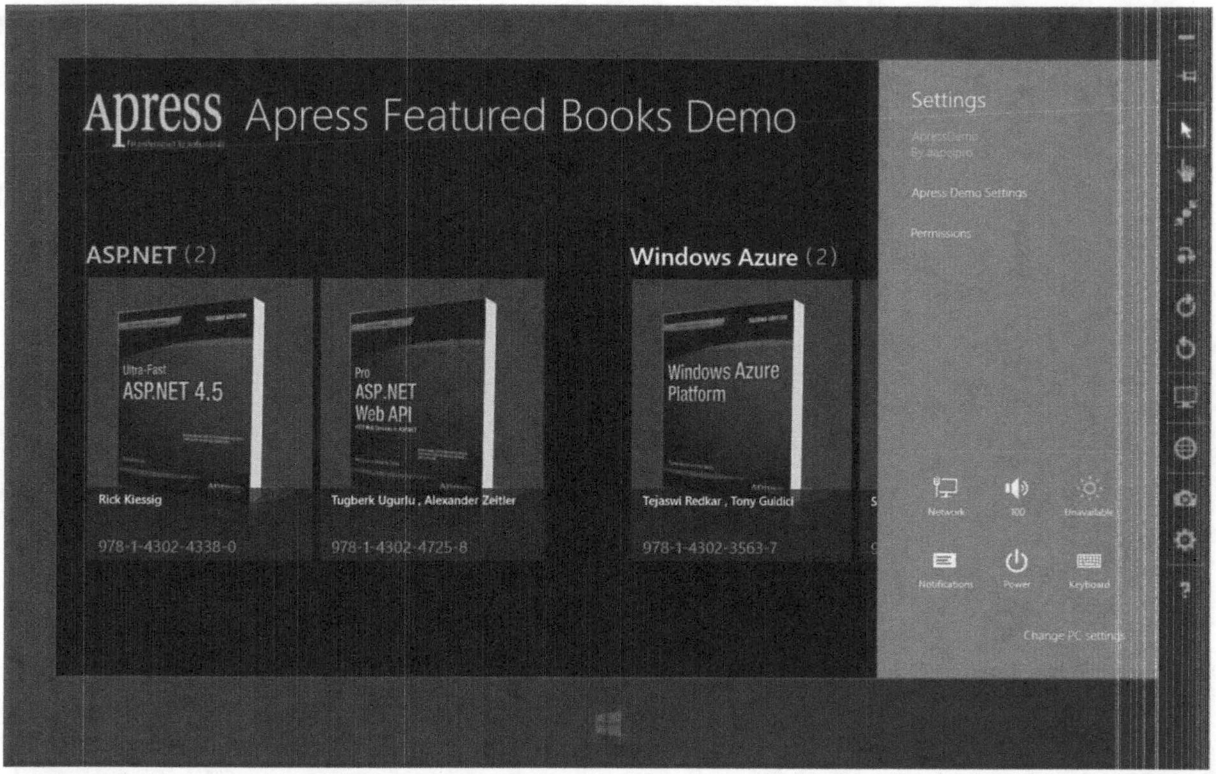

Figure 10-31. Custom Settings menu

Custom Settings User Control

You are one step closer to having a custom app setting through the custom menu option that you made. But what happens when the user selects the custom menu? Well, Windows 8 will expect a settings flyout, which animates from the right edge and offers the user whatever settings your app needs to support. This is the part that you have to do by hand—and it's actually not that difficult. First, define a user control (see Figure 10-32) that will hold all of your app settings.

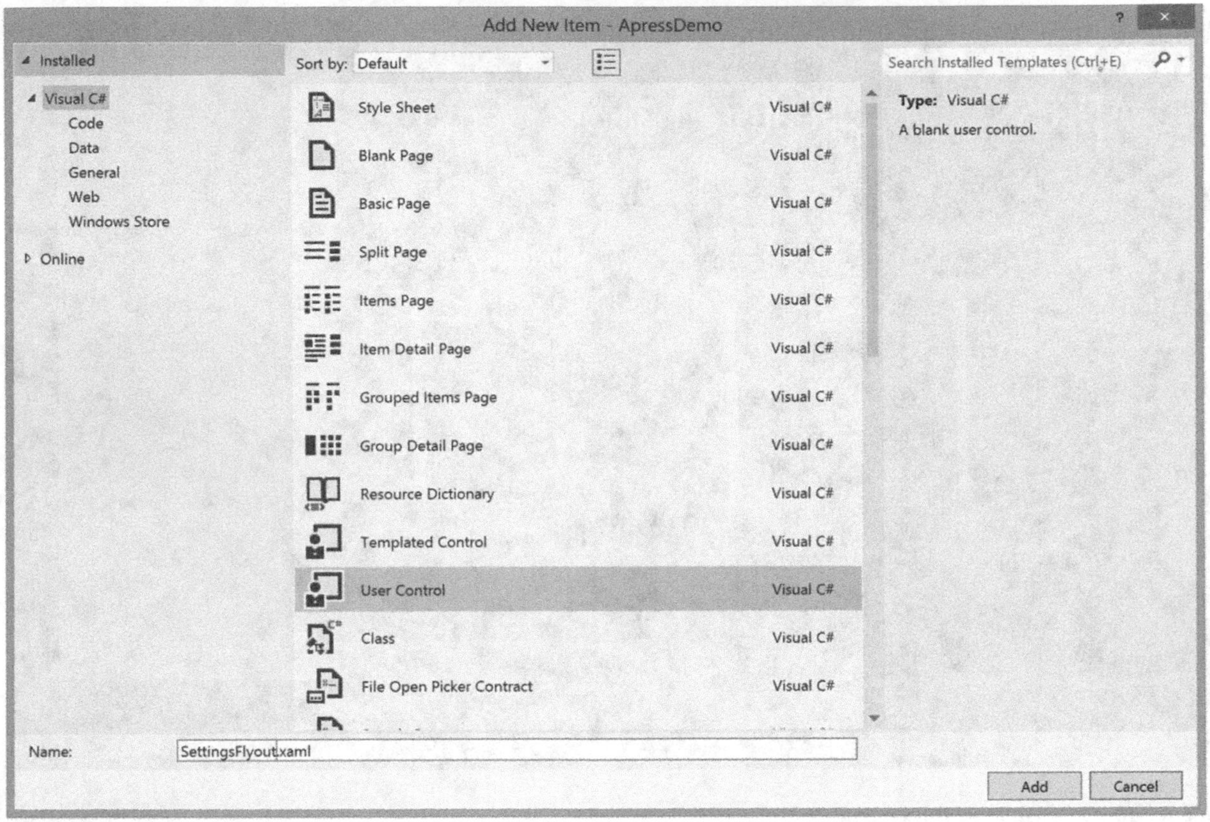

Figure 10-32. *User control for settings flyout*

Your goal in the `SettingsFlyout` user control is to build up whatever UI that is needed to support all of the app's settings. In the Apress demo app, I just threw in a couple dummy On/Off settings through `ToggleSwitch` controls. Here's my XAML markup:

```
<Grid Style="{StaticResource LayoutRootStyle}" Background="Black">
<Grid.RowDefinitions>
<RowDefinition Height="160"/>
<RowDefinition Height="*"/>
</Grid.RowDefinitions>

<!-- Logo Area -->
<Grid Grid.Row="0">
<StackPanel Orientation="Horizontal">
<Button x:Name="backButton" Click="MySettingsBackClicked" Style="{StaticResource BackButtonStyle}"
Margin="40, 0, 25, 0"/>
<Image x:Name="Logo" Source="/Assets/ApressLogo.png" Width="180" Height="80" Margin="2, 80, 40, -30"
VerticalAlignment="Center" HorizontalAlignment="Left"/>
</StackPanel>
</Grid>
```

```
<!-- App Settings -->
<Grid x:Name="settingsContent" Grid.Row="1" Margin="50">
<StackPanel Margin="0, 40, 0, 0" Orientation="Vertical">
<TextBlock Text="App Settings go here:" TextWrapping="Wrap" Style="{StaticResource BasicTextStyle}"
HorizontalAlignment="Left" FontSize="24" Foreground="Orange"/>
<ToggleSwitch Margin="0,25, 0, 0" Header = "Download updates" HorizontalAlignment="Left"
HorizontalContentAlignment="Left" FontSize="24" Foreground="Orange"/>
<ToggleSwitch Margin="0, 25, 0, 0" Header = "Push Notifications" HorizontalAlignment="Stretch"
FontSize="24" Foreground="Orange"/>
</StackPanel>
</Grid>
</Grid>
```

And here is some code back in your app page code-behind, where you were supporting the SettingsPane activation event:

```
        private Popup settingsPopup;

        // Desired width for the settings UI. UI guidelines specify this should be 346 or
        646 depending on your needs.
        private double settingsWidth = 346;

void onSettingsCommand(IUICommand command)
        {
            // Create a Popup window which will contain our flyout.
            settingsPopup = new Popup();
            settingsPopup.Closed += OnPopupClosed;
            Window.Current.Activated += OnWindowActivated;
            settingsPopup.IsLightDismissEnabled = true;
            settingsPopup.Width = settingsWidth;
            settingsPopup.Height = windowBounds.Height;

            // Add the proper animation for the panel.
            settingsPopup.ChildTransitions = new TransitionCollection();
            settingsPopup.ChildTransitions.Add(new PaneThemeTransition()
            {
                Edge = (SettingsPane.Edge == SettingsEdgeLocation.Right) ?
                        EdgeTransitionLocation.Right :
                        EdgeTransitionLocation.Left
            });

            // Create a SettingsFlyout the same dimensions as the Popup.
            SettingsFlyout mypane = new SettingsFlyout();
            mypane.Width = settingsWidth;
            mypane.Height = windowBounds.Height;

            // Place the SettingsFlyout inside our Popup window.
            settingsPopup.Child = mypane;
```

```
        // Let's define the location of our Popup.
        settingsPopup.SetValue(Canvas.LeftProperty, SettingsPane.Edge ==
        SettingsEdgeLocation.Right ? (windowBounds.Width - settingsWidth) : 0);
        settingsPopup.SetValue(Canvas.TopProperty, 0);
        settingsPopup.IsOpen = true;
    }
```

There were a few moving pieces in the preceding code; let's break it down. The key trick here is to use a PopUp XAML control and house your SettingsFlyout user control inside it. This is done with precise dimensions so that the pop-up's height, width, and location are exactly where you expect a settings flyout to be. The SettingsFlyout user control simply inherits the pop-up's dimensions and thus looks indistinguishable when the settings open. The other little trick is to mimic some Windows 8–style animation from the edge, so that the settings do not appear abruptly on screen but rather slide in from the edge. Notice how you account for Windows 8 localization settings. For languages that read right to left, the settings flyout moves in from the left, as compared to the typical right edge. Figure 10-33 shows the custom settings flyout in action, housed inside an invisible PopUp control.

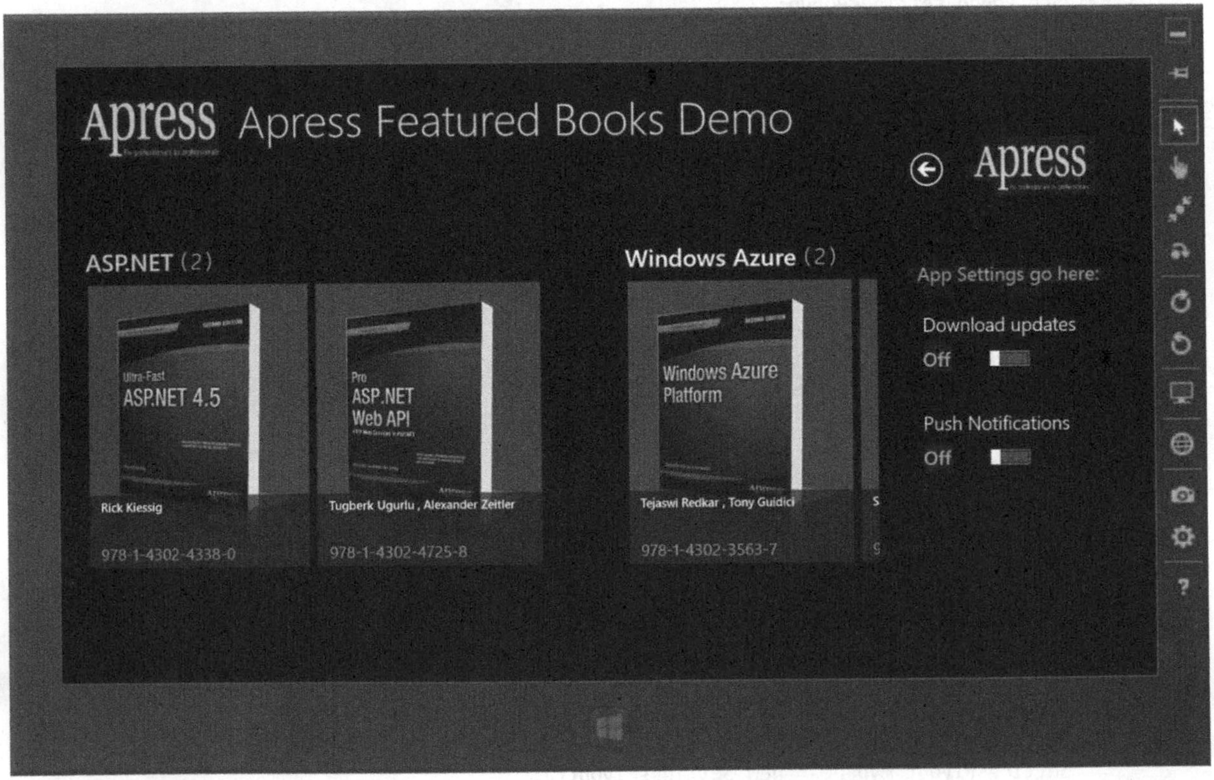

Figure 10-33. *Custom settings flyout*

I am not showing what your app is supposed to do as the user manipulates the Settings options. The ideal thing to do is save the settings immediately, as the user is changing them. Honor the input from the user. The saving of settings can happen locally or through roaming storage for syncing across devices. Essentially, any of the techniques you used in Chapter 8 can be used to persist app/user settings, depending on the needs of your app.

Settings Flyout Dismissal

One other thing: just like any other flyout menu in Windows 8, the settings flyout is supposed to support light dismiss. This means that the user should be able to tap/click outside the flyout menu and make it disappear. Let's add a little more code to support this:

```
void OnPopupClosed(object sender, object e)
        {
            Window.Current.Activated -= OnWindowActivated;
        }

        private void OnWindowActivated(object sender, Windows.UI.Core.WindowActivatedEventArgs e)
        {
            if (e.WindowActivationState == Windows.UI.Core.CoreWindowActivationState.Deactivated)
            {
                settingsPopup.IsOpen = false;
            }
        }
```

Essentially, when the main app window gets tapped or activated, you simply go ahead and close the `settingsPopup` and its child `SettingsFlyout` user control, along with unwiring the event handler. Also, the user may want to press the Back button from your custom settings flyout to get back to the Settings menu, as it is from the charms bar; so, you add a little code in the settings flyout code-behind to enable this, as shown in the following:

```
private void MySettingsBackClicked(object sender, RoutedEventArgs e)
        {
            // First close our Flyout.
            Popup parent = this.Parent as Popup;
            if (parent != null)
            {
                parent.IsOpen = false;
            }

            // If the app is not snapped, then the back button shows the Settings pane again.
            if (Windows.UI.ViewManagement.ApplicationView.Value !=
            Windows.UI.ViewManagement.ApplicationViewState.Snapped)
            {
                SettingsPane.Show();
            }
        }
```

That's it! Just a little bit of work and you now have complete control over your own app's custom settings. Throw in anything that is configurable in your app and offer it as a setting that the user can change through the Settings menu on charms bar. And do not forget to save the user's changes immediately. Your users will be thankful for the consistency and ease of use in managing app settings.

File Contracts

Last but not the least, let's talk about the contracts around access (read/write) to files on the user's device. Windows did not always make it very easy to gain access to files on the user's system—there could be complicated pop-ups and inconsistencies between applications. Windows 8 makes file access dead simple through the use of contracts and it takes over some of the UI for consistency.

Dissecting the File Picker Contract

First, focus on the File Picker contract. How does this Windows 8 contract help when your app simply needs access to file(s) on the user's device? Let's take a look at how your app could integrate with the File Picker contract. For your Apress demo app, suppose that you want to provide the user a way to pick through images on his device—to set an account picture for him or herself, for example. The first course of action, like with other contracts, is to declare to Windows 8 that your app wants to participate in a contract. The declaration for the File Picker contract is shown in Figure 10-34.

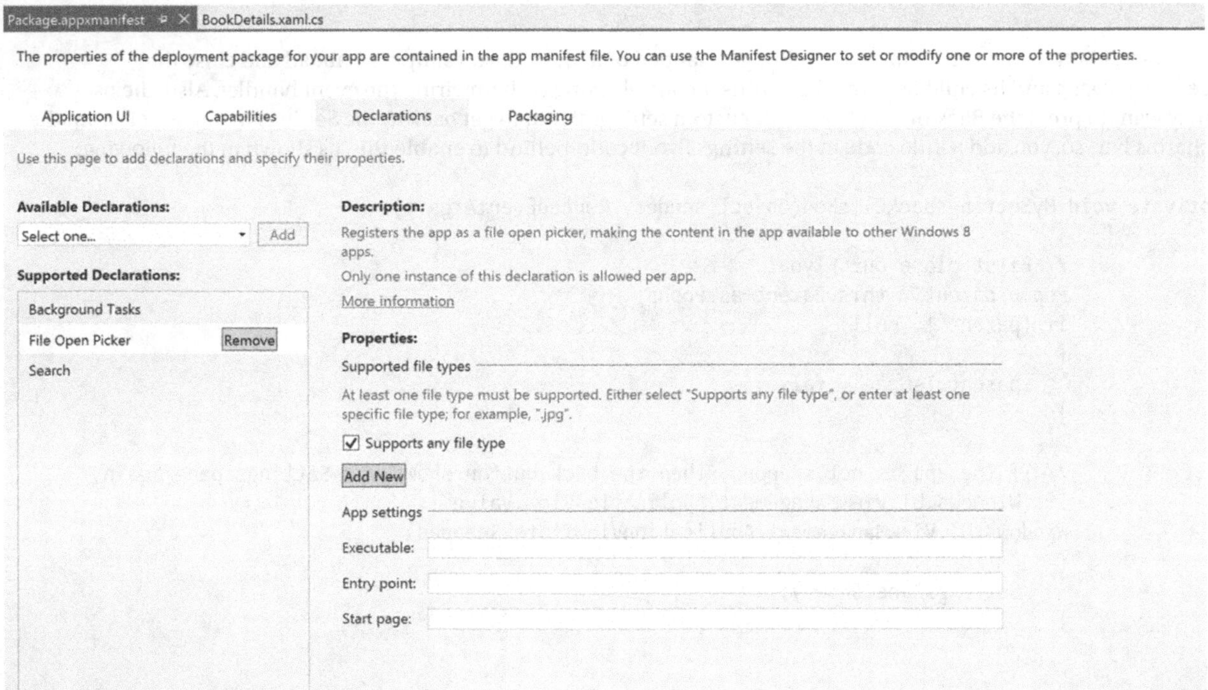

Figure 10-34. *File Picker declarations*

Next, add a little App Bar icon to your Featured Apress Books Demo dashboard (see Figure 10-35) so that you can write some sample code against it.

Figure 10-35. *App Bar icon for picking files*

The XAML markup is simply two App Bar buttons stacked next to each other. The following is the little code:

```
<Page.BottomAppBar>
<AppBar x:Name="bottomAppBar" Padding="10,0,10,0">
<Grid>
<StackPanel Orientation="Horizontal" HorizontalAlignment="Right">
<Button Style="{StaticResource SearchAppBarButtonStyle}" x:Name="searchButton"
Click="searchButton_Click"/>
<Button Style="{StaticResource PicturesAppBarButtonStyle}" x:Name="loadButton"
Click="loadButton_Click"/>
</StackPanel>
</Grid>
</AppBar>
</Page.BottomAppBar>
```

Using File Picker

Respond to a button click from the user and see if you can make the user choose a file from his system. Here's the code you add in the code-behind:

```
using Windows.Storage.Pickers;
using Windows.Storage;

private async void loadButton_Click(object sender, RoutedEventArgs e)
        {
            FileOpenPicker picker = new FileOpenPicker();
            picker.FileTypeFilter.Add(".png");
            picker.FileTypeFilter.Add(".jpg");
            picker.SuggestedStartLocation = PickerLocationId.PicturesLibrary;
            StorageFile pickedImageFile = await picker.PickSingleFileAsync();
        }
```

You are using a File Picker contract here. Right away you see how simple it is to integrate with the OS-level file system access. You can specify file-type filters to only allow selection of specific file types. Also, the File Picker offers a `SuggestedStartLocation` property that takes in the `PickerLocationId` enumeration value. Do you want to know the choices? Well, it can be any of the following:

- `DocumentsLibrary`
- `ComputerFolder`
- `Desktop`
- `Downloads`
- `HomeGroup`
- `MusicLibrary`
- `PicturesLibrary`
- `VideosLibrary`

The enumeration values are self-explanatory; essentially, you want to provide a starting location in the user's hard drive where he or she can start looking for the file of choice. Now, please note that the `SuggestedStartLocation` isn't meant to always work as specified. To give the user a sense of consistency, the File Picker remembers the last location that the user navigated to and will generally start at that location. Are you curious to see the preceding code in action? Simply click/tap the App Bar icon and you should be greeted with a full-screen interface, as shown in Figure 10-36.

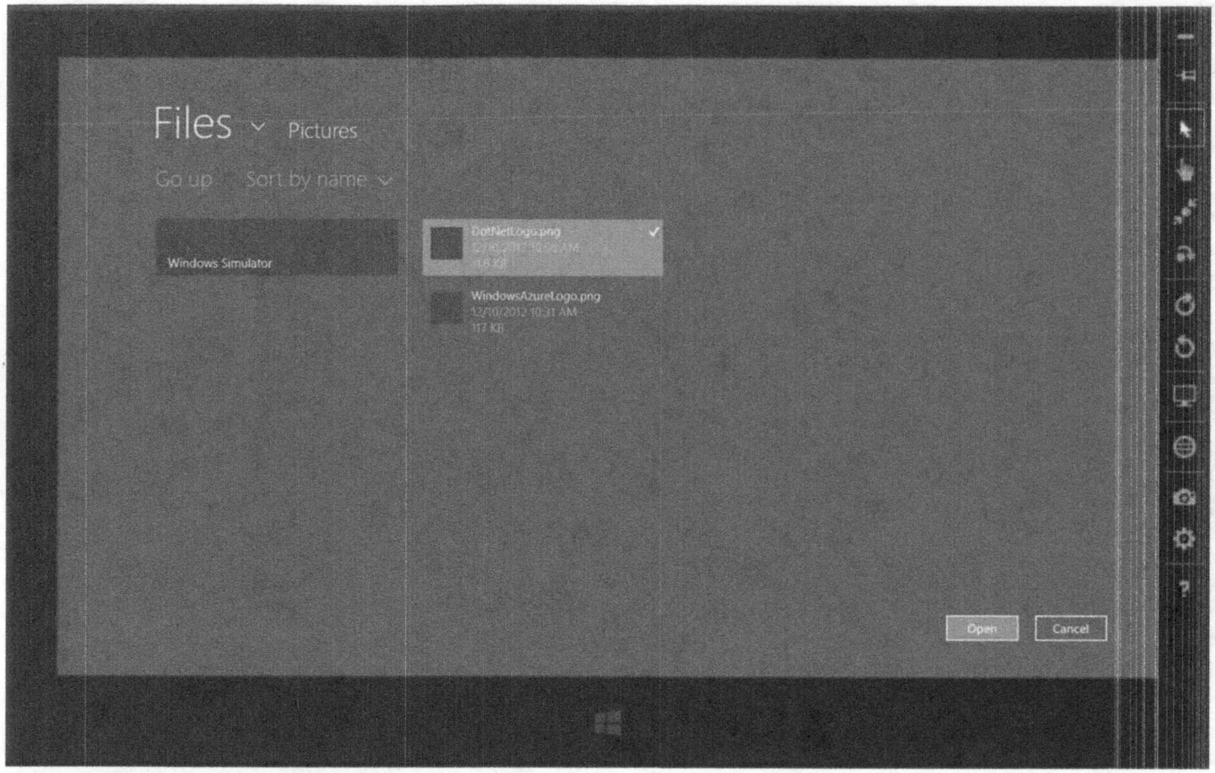

Figure 10-36. *Single file select from list*

You can start appreciating where Windows 8 takes over control and provides a consistent UI for file picking. Do you want your user to see a little more about the files being displayed? Consider switching the display to show thumbnails by using the following code. Accordingly, you should see the UI change to show thumbnails of files at a given location, as shown in Figure 10-37.

```
picker.ViewMode = PickerViewMode.Thumbnail;
```

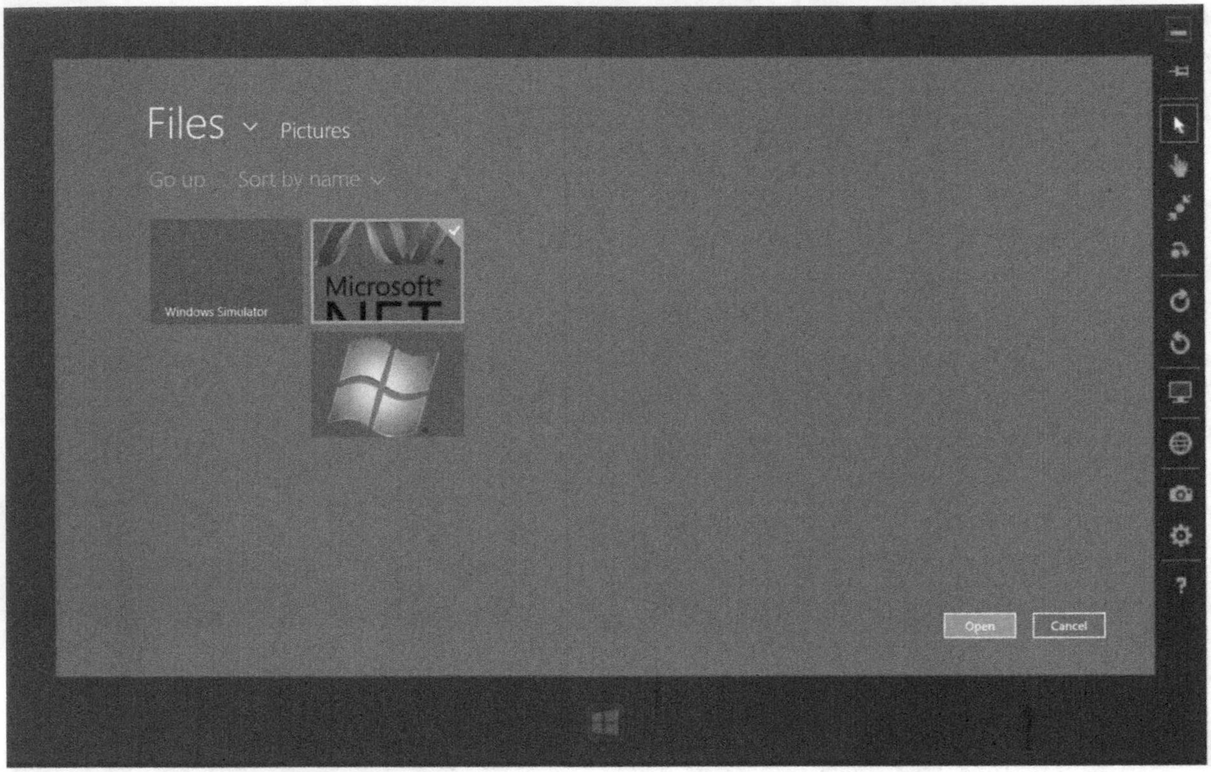

Figure 10-37. *Single file select from thumbnails*

Given the File Picker setup, the key is the `picker.PickSingleFileAsync()` method. It simply waits for the user to select a file before returning control to the rest of the method. What you get returned is a handle on a `StorageFile` that the user has chosen. Beyond that, it is up to however your app uses the file.

Multiple File Support

Want the user to select multiple files at once? No problem—simply a one-line code change from the preceding snippet will achieve the result, like so:

```
IReadOnlyList<StorageFile>selectedFiles = await picker.PickMultipleFilesAsync();
```

And the UI changes accordingly with support for multiple file selections, as shown in Figure 10-38. What is really cool is the fact that the File Picker maintains a list of the files selected thus far and displays a small thumbnail collection at the bottom of the screen. These selected files could come from the `SuggestedStartLocation`, the same folder, or even multiple folders. They are all stacked together and your code returns a collection of `StorageFiles`.

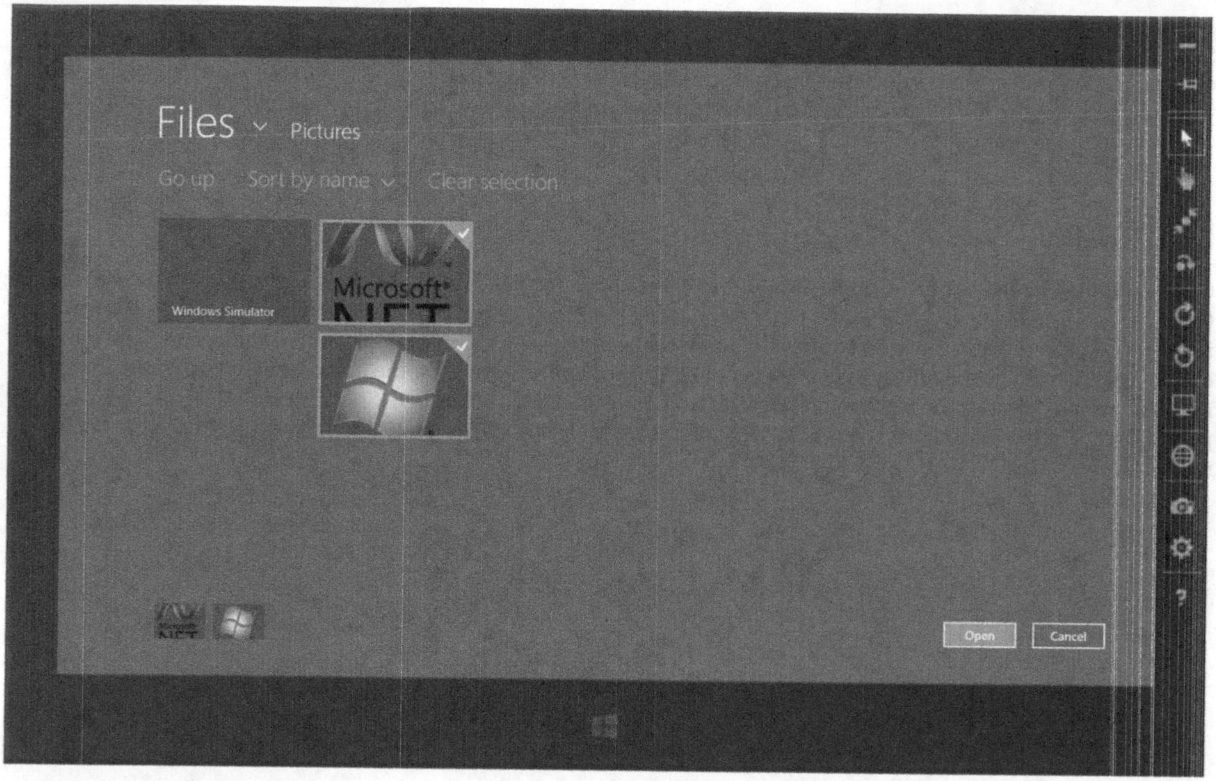

Figure 10-38. *Multiple file select*

Using File Save Picker

Want to save a file on the user's device? It is almost the reverse process. Declare the intention (File Saver Picker) in the `PackageAppXManifest` file and write some code, like the following:

```
FileSavePicker fileSaver = new FileSavePicker();
fileSaver.SuggestedStartLocation = PickerLocationId.Desktop;
fileSaver.FileTypeChoices.Add("Text File", new List<string>() { ".txt" });
fileSaver.SuggestedFileName = "SampleFile";
StorageFile file = await fileSaver.PickSaveFileAsync();

if (file != null)
{
    CachedFileManager.DeferUpdates(file);
    await FileIO.WriteTextAsync(file, "Sample Text");
    FileUpdateStatus status = await CachedFileManager.CompleteUpdatesAsync(file);
}
```

In this code, you are trying to suggest that the user save a file named `SampleFile.txt` on the desktop. The `SuggestedStartLocation` and `FileTypeChoices` provide the starting choices for the user, but he or she is free to change this, of course. Once selections are made, the `CachedFileManager.DeferUpdates(file)` call makes sure that your app gets to write the file to disk without interruptions and `CachedFileManager.CompleteUpdatesAsync(file)` completes the operation.

Summary

Contracts and extensions are a wonderful addition to Windows 8 and they are sure-shot ammunition to please users. Covering every contract in detail would make this a really long chapter, but be assured that you covered the most important, common, and must-do contracts. You must absolutely look to implement Search, Share, and Settings contracts and leverage the others as your apps demand. The chapter covered some of the hardest issues regarding implementing contracts; the rest should be easier from here on. For a complete listing of all contracts and extensions, please start at `http://msdn.microsoft.com/en-us/library/windows/apps/hh464906.aspx` and choose the ones you need. Happy coding!

PART 4

The Bling

Give yourself a little pat on the back. If you have been coding along, your dream Windows 8 Store app is functional at this point! The app is almost feature-complete and you are managing data and the application life cycle, as well as integrating with the OS where possible.

But, the job isn't done. Chapters 11 and 12 show you how to add bling to your app. It sounds cheesy, but the proper use of multimedia and tapping into the loaded sensors in today's devices helps entice users back to your app. And don't forget custom tiles, toasts, or badges to allow for richer customization and immersion into the app's user experience.

Remember alive and connected apps? This is it! We are not looking for app after app, but experiences over apps. With diligence, you can do it!

CHAPTER 11

Media and Sensors

Today's computers—especially the new breed of tablets and hybrids—are sophisticated devices. Not only do they push the boundaries of computing, but they also come loaded with various device sensors. And, pictures, audio, and video are worth a thousand words. Don't you want to provide the users of your Windows 8 Store app with an immersive rich user experience? If yes, leverage multimedia capabilities to provide a personal visual experience through your app so that the user feels intimate and comfortable enough to settle down on a couch to enjoy it. Also, if you know the user's device has supported sensors, you have a clear opportunity to tap into these sensors' input to augment the experience of using your app. Use sensor feedback from the device to enable unique experiences that make your Windows 8 app "unputdownable." Ready? This chapter will give you a preview of all that is possible with media and sensors in Windows 8 Store apps.

Remote Debugging

Most developers like having beefy machines for their core development tasks and these often end up being high-powered but bulky desktops and laptops. While such PCs are great for development, they will often lack the multimedia capabilities and device sensors commonly found in lightweight ultrabooks or tablet/hybrid/ARM-processor-based PCs. Even if you have access to any such modern lightweight device, you might still like developing on powerful hardware, but use the lighter devices for testing. Is this possible—and easily doable? Yes. Visual Studio 2012 has an answer and it is called remote debugging.

Although I have talked about remote debugging before and have provided links on how to do it, this chapter begs for a more hands-on discussion. Nothing demands more need for remote debugging on lighter devices and tablets than the use of motion sensors, which, for the most part, are absent on powerful desktops and laptops. So, let's spend a little time learning how to enable remote debugging from Visual Studio. The promise is simple: develop your Windows 8 Store apps on one PC with Visual Studio, and then remotely deploy app over network to another device for testing. And what about the ability to debug code while it is executing on the other device? Yes, that's possible too. Let's see how.

Install Remote Debugging Tools

First, on your Windows 8 tablet/hybrid device, you want to head to `www.microsoft.com/en-us/download/details.aspx?id=30674` to install Remote Tools for Visual Studio 2012. It is meant to enable lighter Windows 8 devices (which are not running Visual Studio) to accept app deployment from another PC and enable debugging and testing. Figure 11-1 shows the download page.

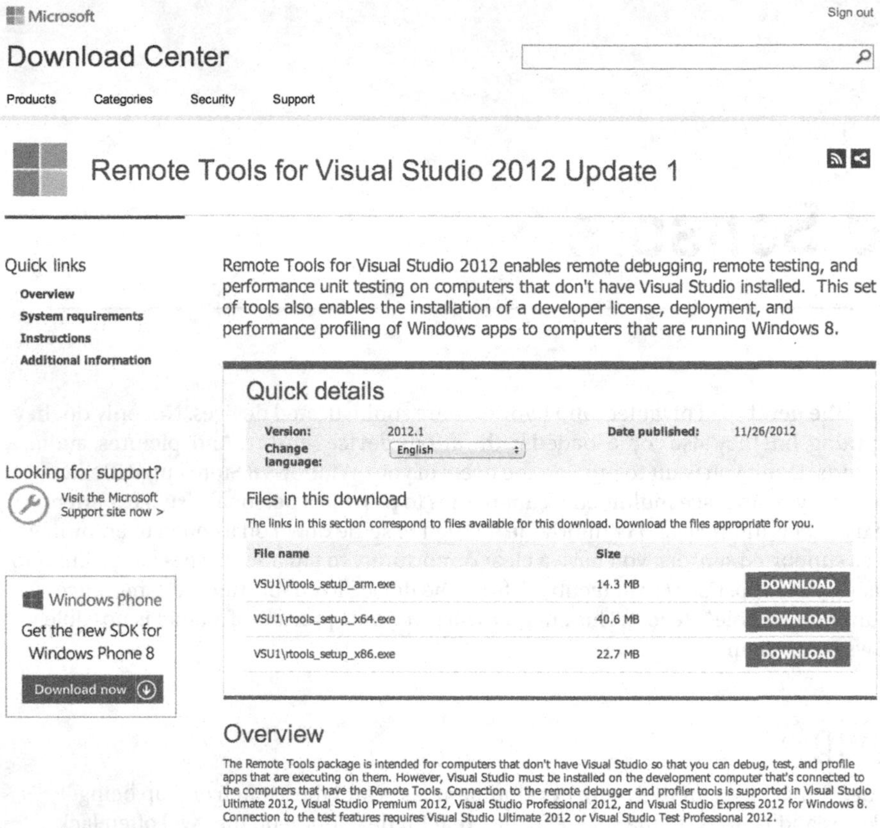

Figure 11-1. *Remote Tools for Visual Studio 2012*

There are different installers, depending upon whether your lightweight Windows 8 device is a 32-bit/64-bit machine or one sporting an ARM processor. So, obviously, you need to choose the one that fits your device. Once installed, you should see app tiles, like in the Debug group on my ARM-based MSFT Surface RT device, shown in Figure 11-2.

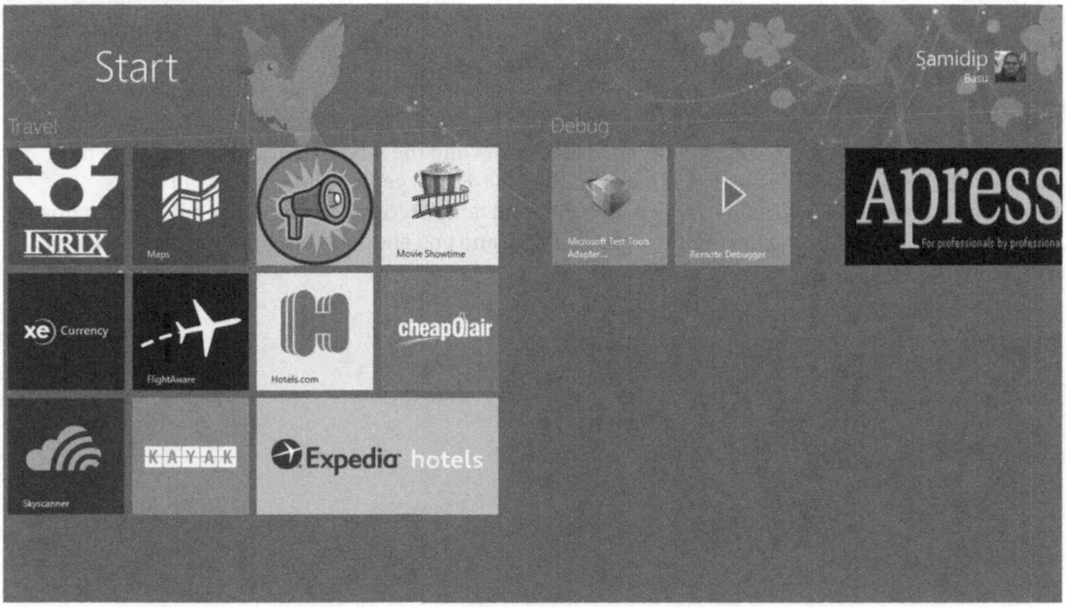

Figure 11-2. *Remote debugger*

Tap on the Remote Debugger tile to launch the app. It runs on the desktop side of Windows 8. This essentially gives a handshake to Visual Studio running on your development machine and prepares your tablet device for remote deployment. You should see an interface like the one shown in Figure 11-3.

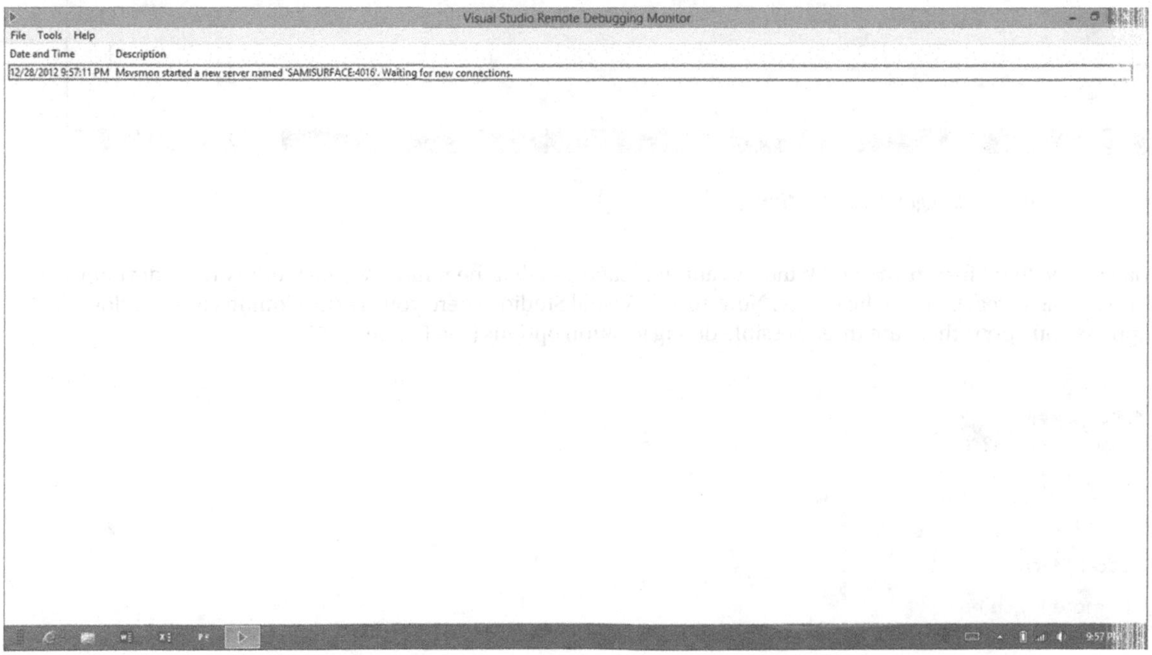

Figure 11-3. *Remote debugger running*

Your remote debugger app is now running, but it needs a little configuration before a remote Visual Studio can talk to it.

Configure Your Remote Debugger

Ideally, you want the development machine that's running Visual Studio and the tablet/hybrid that's running the remote debugger to be on the same network—such as a home/office Wi-Fi—to get around any firewall issues. Even so, there is security on the Windows 8 tablet, which I recommend temporarily disabling for remote debugging to work easily. So, click Tools ➤ Options on the remote debugger app, and you should see a configuration window, like the one shown in Figure 11-4.

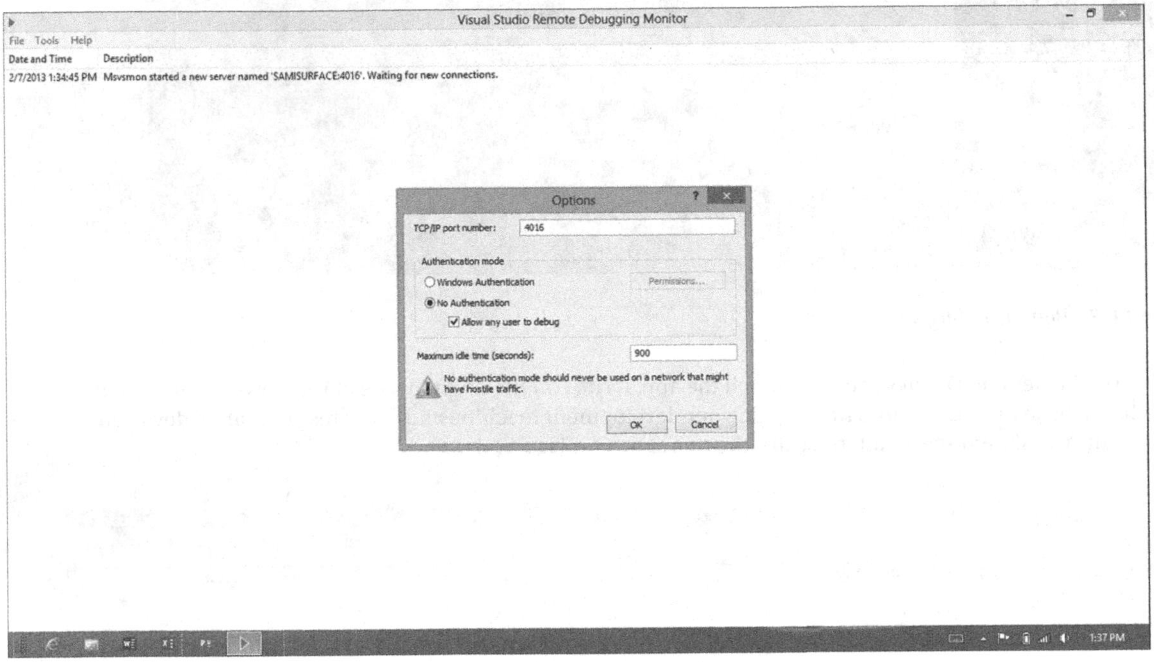

Figure 11-4. *Remote debugger configuration*

You can see that I have turned off Windows authentication so that the remote Visual Studio on the development machine can easily reach out to the device. Now, turn to Visual Studio, where you are developing your Windows 8 Store app. As you know, there are three possible debug location options (see Figure 11-5).

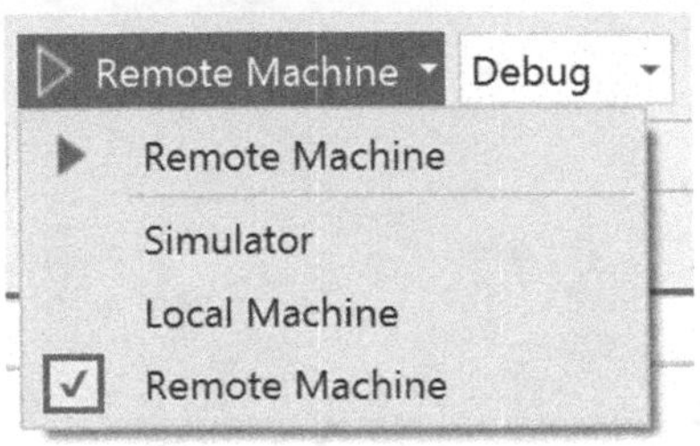

Figure 11-5. *Debug locations*

You would obviously pick Remote Machine for deployment and debugging. But the first time you select this option and try running your Windows 8 app, you will be presented with a Visual Studio dialog box asking where to debug; mine is shown in Figure 11-6. As you can see, I simply tell Visual Studio the name of my tablet/hybrid Windows 8 device along with the port number based on my earlier app configuration, and then match the authentication mode.

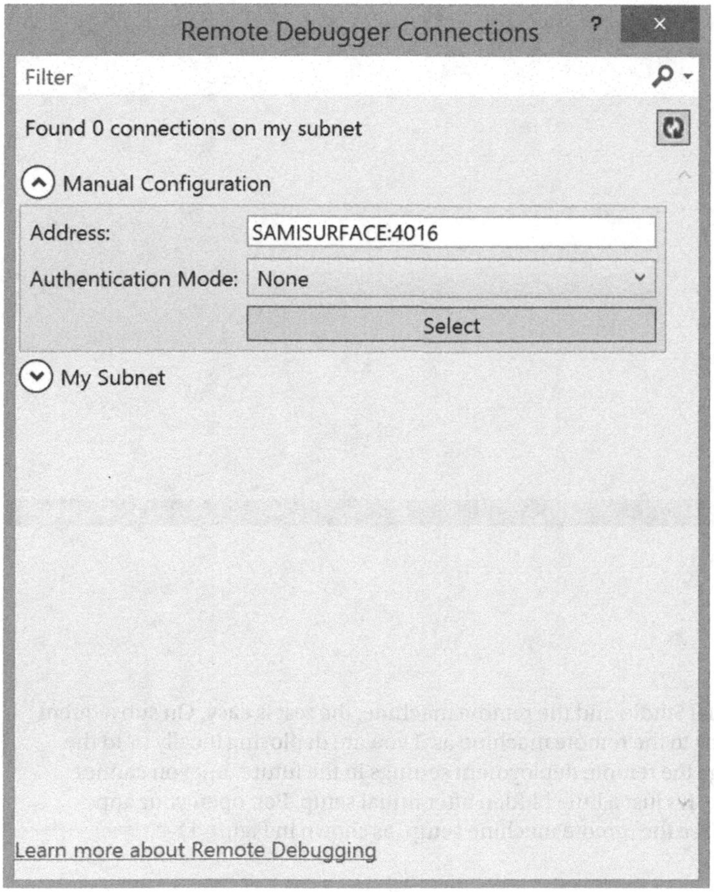

Figure 11-6. *Remote debug connections*

One last thing: make sure that your Windows 8 Store app's build configuration supports all processors or matches that of the device you are deploying to (x86 for 32-bit, x64 for 64-bit or ARM). That's all you need. Press F5 or Control + F5 to deploy the Windows 8 app to the remote device. If everything is successful, you should see a connection established on your remote debugger tool that goes back to your main development machine (see Figure 11-7). And your Windows 8 Store app should create a tile on the remote Start screen and start running. This is so cool, isn't it?

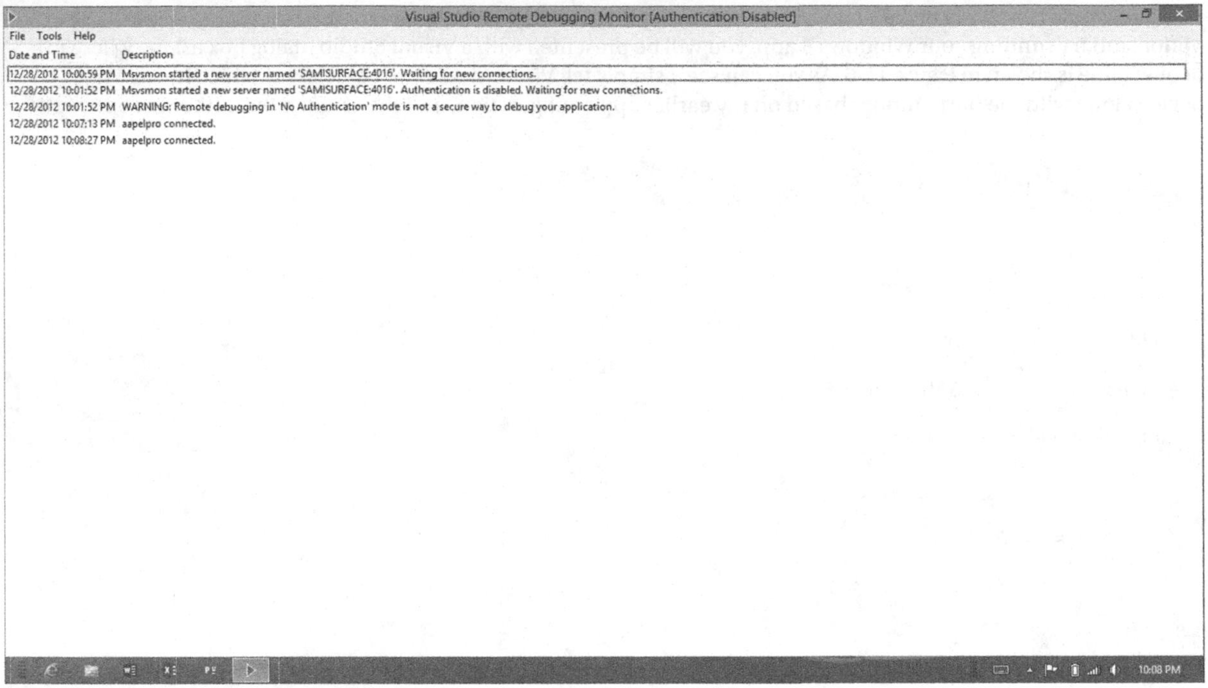

Figure 11-7. *Remote debugger connected*

Deploy to Remote Debugger

Once the connection is established between Visual Studio and the remote machine, the rest is easy. On subsequent builds of your Windows 8 Store app, simply deploy to the remote machine as if you are deploying locally or to the Simulator. Do you think that you'll want to change the remote deployment settings in the future, but you cannot find the configuration pop-up? Fear not, it's there. It's just a little hidden after initial setup. Pop open your app Settings/Properties in Visual Studio and you will see the remote machine setup, as shown in Figure 11-8.

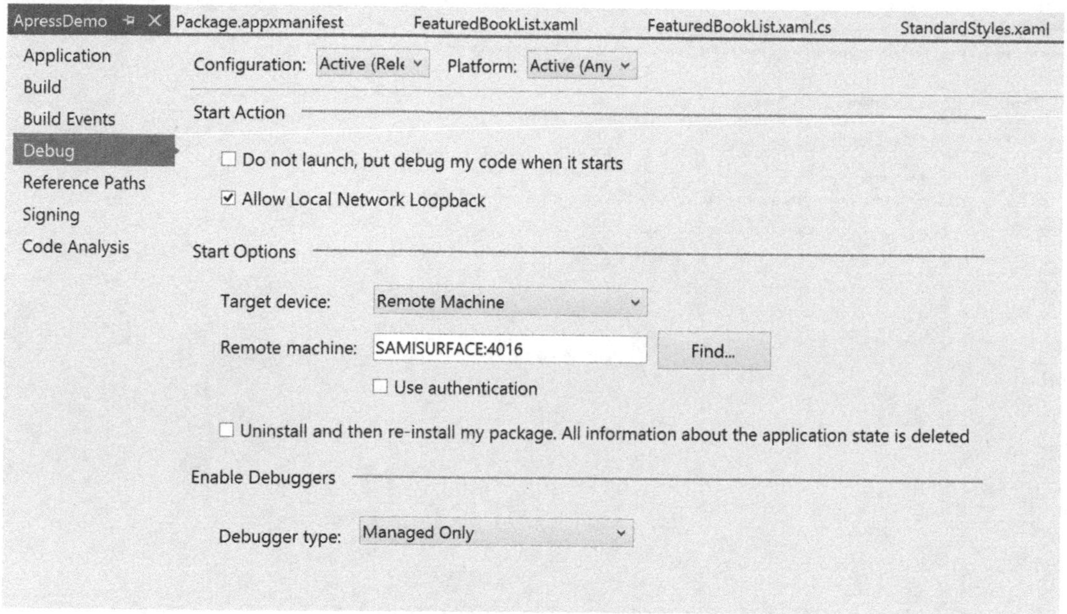

Figure 11-8. *Changing remote debug connections*

Camera

Are you happily deploying your Windows 8 app locally to the Simulator or to a remote machine? Good for you! Now it's time to get down to business and see where you can leverage multimedia capabilities and the all-new device sensors in Windows 8 machines. Let's begin with the simple camera sensors.

Most Windows 8 PCs, especially tablets, have some sort of camera or webcam on the device—front facing, rear facing, or both. Let's see how you can capture data from the camera.

Capture Photos from the Camera

The first step is to declare to Windows 8 that your app is about to use the device camera, unless you want to get a rude error. Open the `Package.Appxmanifest` file and make sure that you declare Webcam as a capability need in your app (see Figure 11-9).

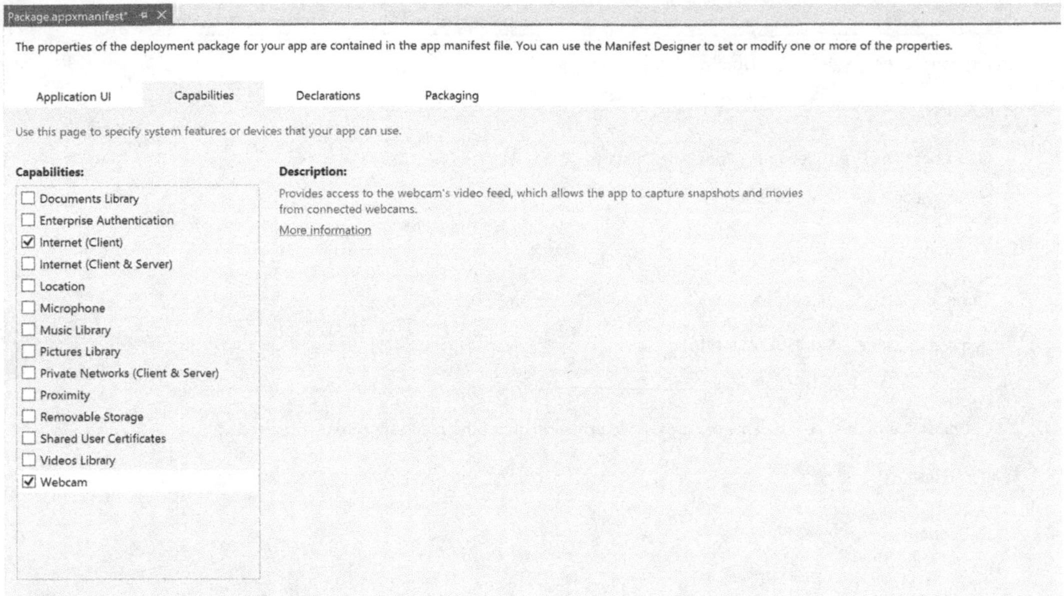

Figure 11-9. *Webcam declaration*

The first simple task is to allow the user to take a picture with the camera and show the result in your app. Go back to your Apress Featured Books Demo app and see if you can enable this functionality. How about a scenario where the user can take a picture of himself/herself to create an account in the app? Sounds plausible, so let's get started. With the capability declaration out of the way, add a new app bar icon on the main dashboard page to enable use of the webcam (see Figure 11-10). Are you wondering how to do this? The little XAML markup is here:

```
<Page.BottomAppBar>
<AppBar x:Name="bottomAppBar" Padding="10,0,10,0">
<Grid>
<StackPanel Orientation="Horizontal" HorizontalAlignment="Right">
<Button Style="{StaticResource SearchAppBarButtonStyle}" x:Name="searchButton"
Click="searchButton_Click"/>
<Button Style="{StaticResource PicturesAppBarButtonStyle}" x:Name="loadButton"
Click="loadButton_Click"/>
<Button Style="{StaticResource WebcamAppBarButtonStyle}" x:Name="accountButton"
Click="accountButton_Click"/>
</StackPanel>
</Grid>
</AppBar>
</Page.BottomAppBar>
```

Figure 11-10. Updated app bar

To demonstrate the use of the camera, create a new Basic page called AccountPage.xaml, with the intention of having the user take a picture to set up an account. The little XAML markup you add on the page looks like this:

```
<!-- Page title -->
<Grid Grid.Row="0">
<StackPanel Orientation="Horizontal" Margin="20,10,0,0">
<Button x:Name="backButton" Click="GoBack" IsEnabled="{Binding Frame.CanGoBack,
ElementName=pageRoot}" Style="{StaticResource BackButtonStyle}"/>
<Image Source="/Assets/ApressLogo.png" Width="200" Height="100" VerticalAlignment="Center"
Margin="-10,20,0,0"/>
<TextBlock x:Name="pageTitle" Text="{StaticResource AppName}" Style="{StaticResource
PageHeaderTextStyle}" VerticalAlignment="Center" Margin="10,10,0,10"/>
</StackPanel>
</Grid>

<!-- Page Content -->
<StackPanel Grid.Row="1" Orientation="Vertical" Margin="150,70,70,70">
<StackPanel Orientation="Horizontal">
<TextBlock Text="Grab your picture to create an account:" Style="{StaticResource
SubheaderTextStyle}"/>
<Button Content="Say Cheese!" Click="Camera_Click" Margin="20,0,0,0"/>
</StackPanel>
<Image x:Name="cameraFeed" Margin="50" Height="400" Width="400"/>
</StackPanel>
```

And the simple UI is shown in Figure 11-11.

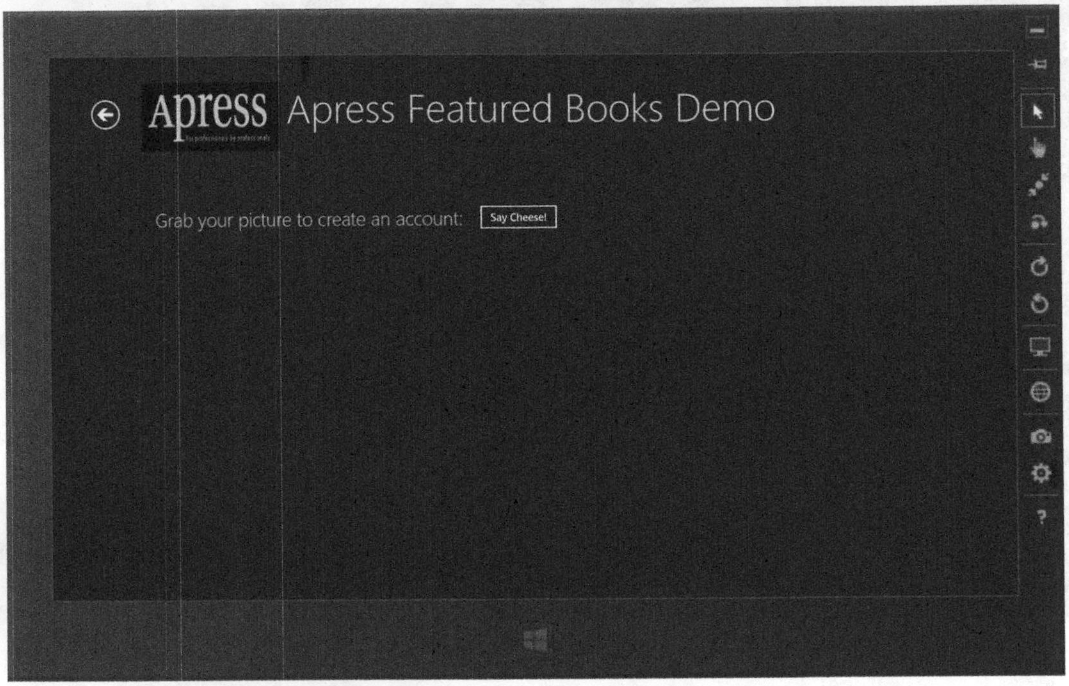

Figure 11-11. *Webcam template page*

So, you essentially want the user to click a button, grab a picture from the webcam, and bring it back to your app. Add some code for the button's `Click` event handler, shown in Listing 11-1.

Listing 11-1. CameraCapture UI Code

```
private async void Camera_Click(object sender, RoutedEventArgs e)
        {
            CameraCaptureUI webCam = new CameraCaptureUI();
            webCam.PhotoSettings.CroppedAspectRatio = new Size(16, 9);
            StorageFile capturedPhoto = await webCam.CaptureFileAsync(CameraCaptureUIMode.Photo);

            if (capturedPhoto != null)
            {
                BitmapImage imageBitmap = new BitmapImage();
                using (IRandomAccessStream stream = await capturedPhoto.OpenAsync(FileAccessMode.Read))
                {
                    imageBitmap.SetSource(stream);
                }

                cameraFeed.Source = imageBitmap;
            }
}
```

To break down the code, you are using a new API called CameraCaptureUI, setting the aspect ratio on the photo to be captured and expecting a StorageFile in response to an asynchronous capture-photo operation. Once you have a StorageFile back, you read the file as a stream and create a bitmap out of it, which would be bound to the UI placeholder. Sounds simple. Let's run this and see your code in action. The first time the user clicks the button, however, there is a pop-up message, as shown in Figure 11-12.

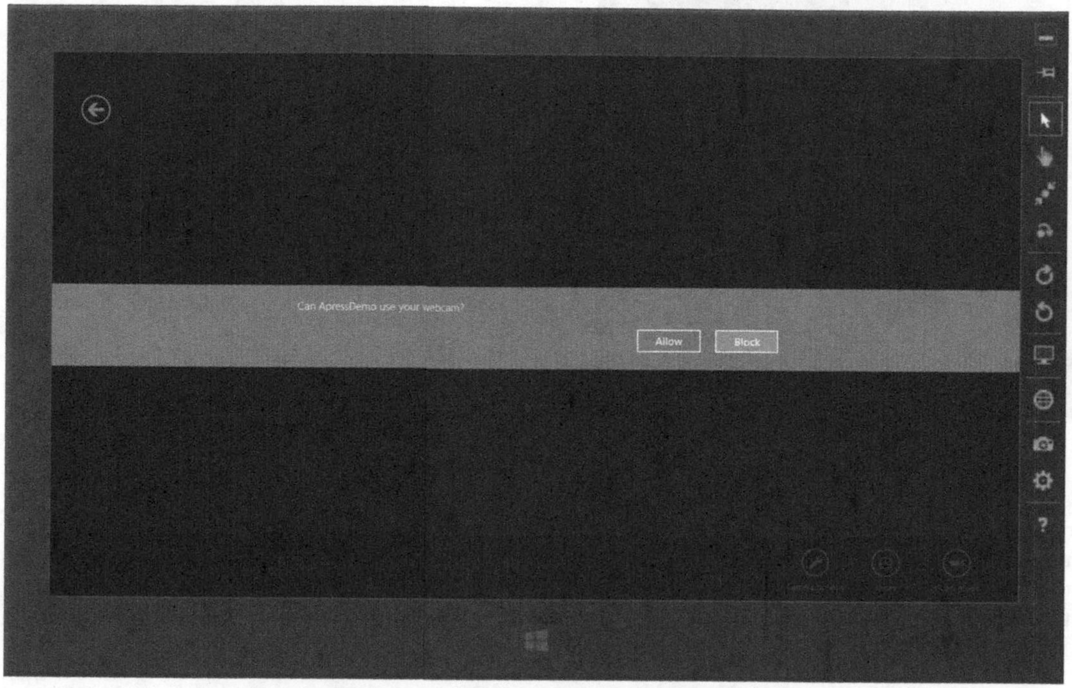

Figure 11-12. *The first webcam usage warning*

Even though your Windows 8 app has a declared capability of using the webcam, this is the first time the user is experiencing the feature; so, it is a privacy protection warning. If the user allows the app access to the webcam, the app can proceed as usual. If the user denies access, the camera access portion of the app will simply not work. The user, however, will get a friendly message asking him to turn on the camera access in the app settings. You will see this in just a bit; but for now, assume the user allowed the app access to the webcam. With permission granted, your app uses the CameraCaptureUI to show the user a preview of what his or her camera is about to capture, such as in Figure 11-13.

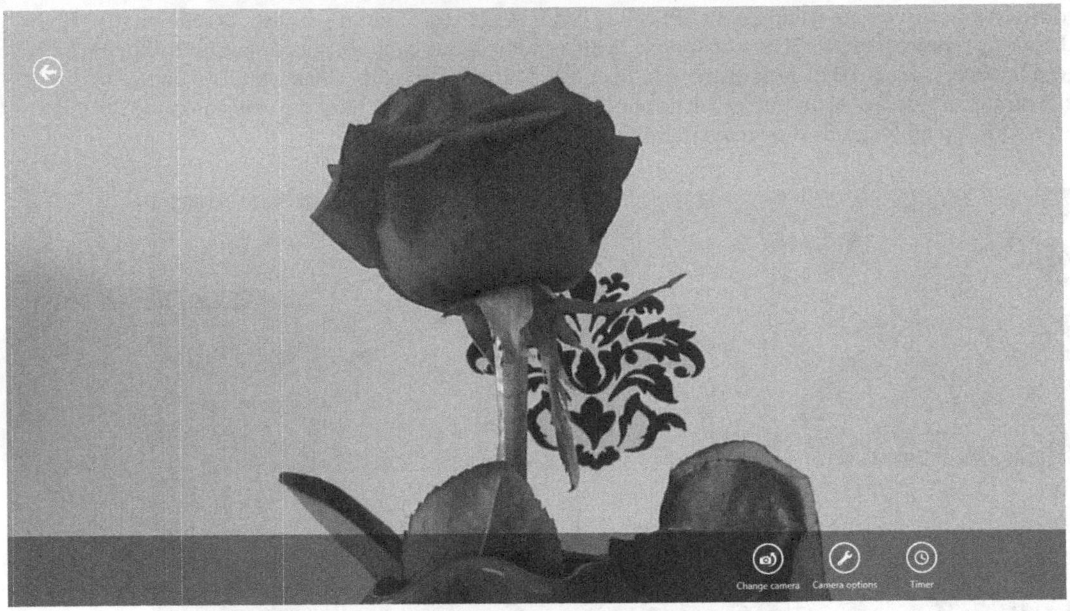

Figure 11-13. *Webcam photo preview*

In case you were wondering, Figure 11-13 does not show me through the front-facing camera, but rather a rose sitting on a dining table. The camera preview shows a few extra add-ons: you can toggle the camera from front to back on devices with both options, use a timer to take picture, and tinker with other camera options. Tapping the screen allows you to take a picture, but not before a cropping opportunity (by scaling or repositioning using the white-dotted surface area), as seen in Figure 11-14.

Figure 11-14. *Webcam photo cropping*

Finally, when the user is happy with the image capture, your code gets the `StorageFile` back and the UI placeholder is bound to the resulting bitmap, as shown in Figure 11-15.

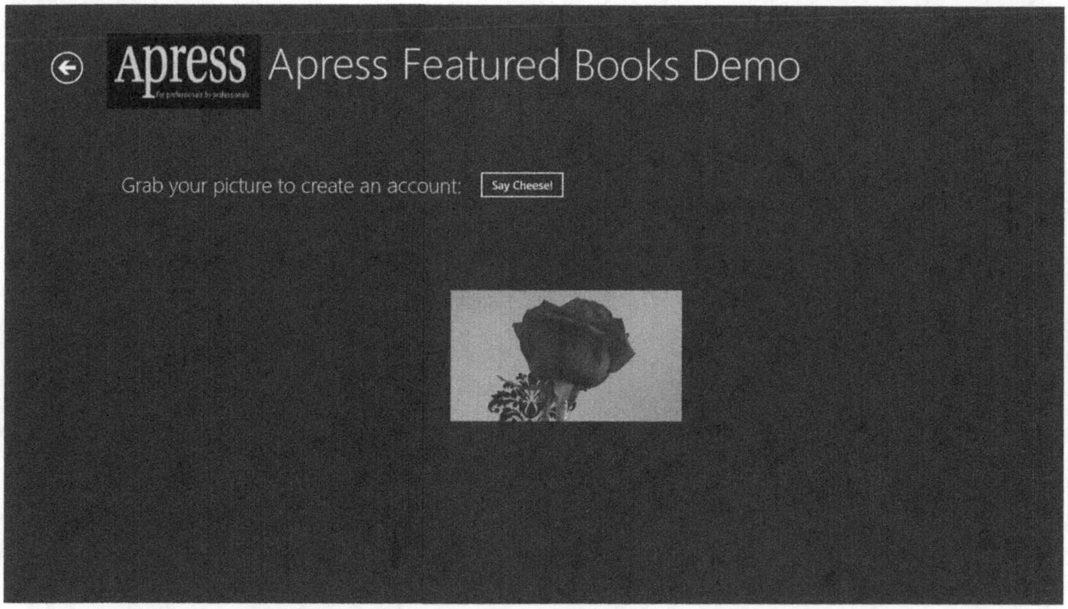

Figure 11-15. *Webcam photo back in app*

Capture Video Through the Webcam

Do you want the user to capture video through the webcam and bring it back to the app? Thankfully, the process is very similar to capturing a photo. But first, you need to declare a capability to leverage the microphone on the device (see Figure 11-16).

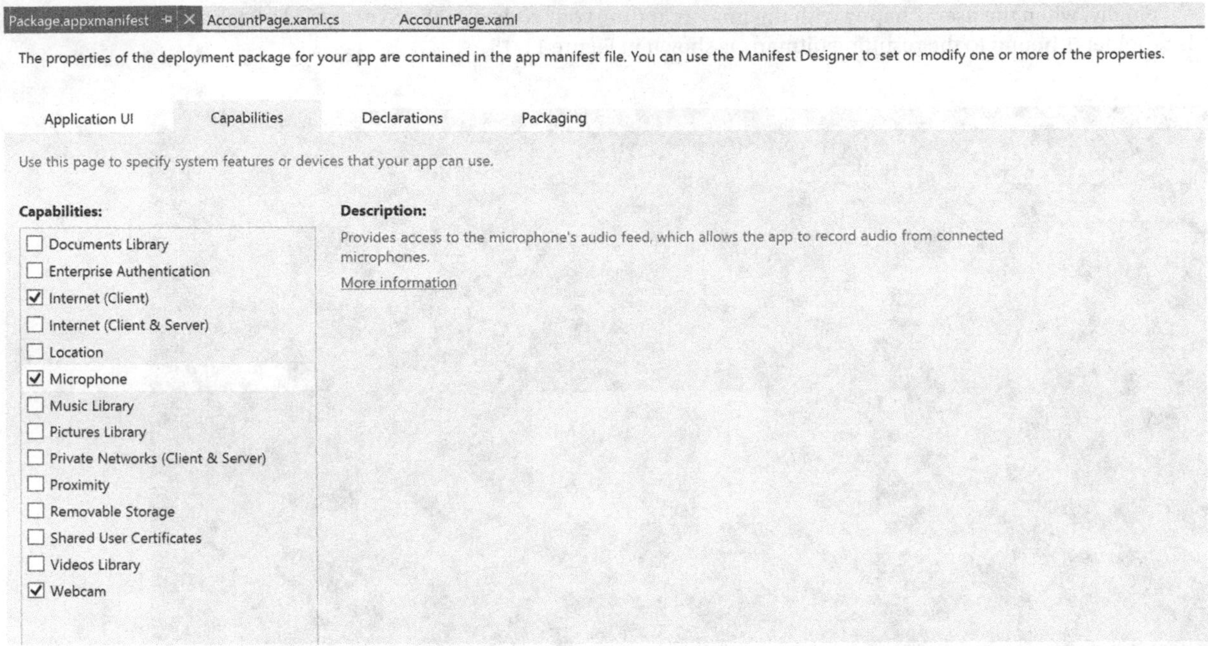

Figure 11-16. *Webcam and microphone declaration*

With the declaration out of the way, you can use the CameraCaptureUI the same way, but with different settings to allow the user to capture video. Here's a little code:

```
CameraCaptureUI videoCapture = new CameraCaptureUI();
videoCapture.VideoSettings.Format = CameraCaptureUIVideoFormat.Mp4;
videoCapture.VideoSettings.AllowTrimming = true;
videoCapture.VideoSettings.MaxDurationInSeconds = 60;
videoCapture.VideoSettings.MaxResolution = CameraCaptureUIMaxVideoResolution.HighestAvailable;
StorageFile video = await videoCapture.CaptureFileAsync(CameraCaptureUIMode.Video);
```

As you can see, you were able to set several settings on the video to be captured before the CameraCaptureUIMode was flipped to Video. This allows the user to capture video with sound using his device, trim it, if necessary, and the resulting StorageFile finally gets returned to your app. CameraCaptureUI is a powerful API; read more details at http://msdn.microsoft.com/en-us/library/windows/apps/windows.media.capture.cameracaptureui.aspx. Also, the first time you run this code, you will be greeted with another warning (see Figure 11-17).

Figure 11-17. *Webcam and microphone first usage warning*

Do you remember that you added another capability?

Permissions Settings from Capabilities

Back in your Apress demo app, swipe/mouse-hover from the right edge to see the charms bar, and then tap/click Settings. You should see something like the screenshot shown in Figure 11-18.

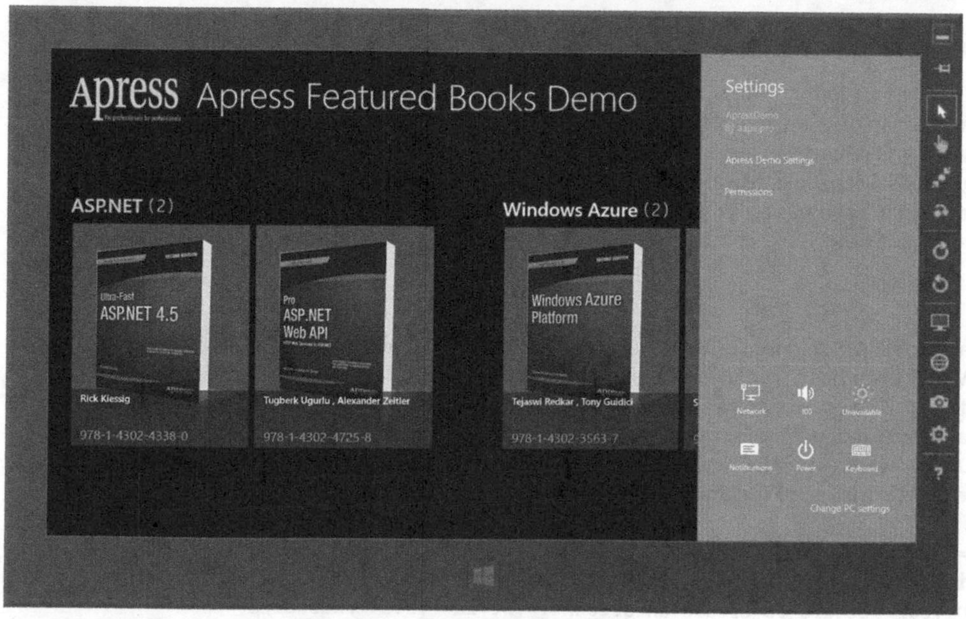

Figure 11-18. *App permissions*

Now, if you look back through Chapter 10, you will realize that you added only one custom app setting. So where is this Permissions setting (seen in the charms bar in Figure 11-18) coming from? Turns out, it is present in all Windows 8 Store apps and it is driven entirely by the app developer's declarations of needed hardware usage in the `PackageAppXManifest` file. Go ahead and tap/click the Permissions setting. You should see something like Figure 11-19, based on your declarations.

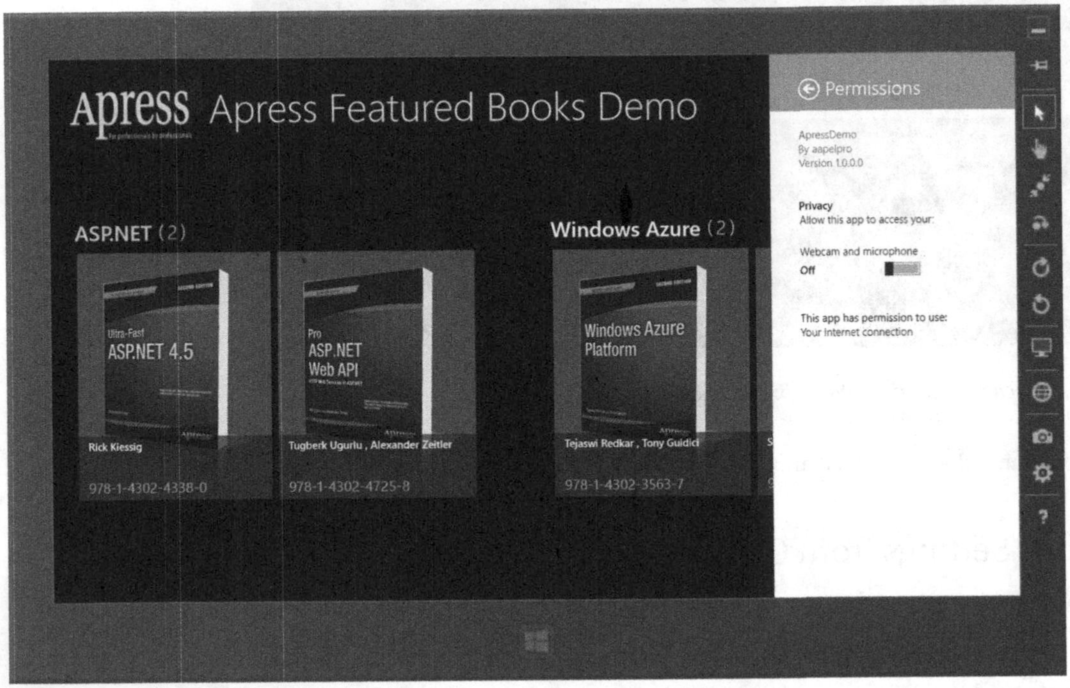

Figure 11-19. *App permissions driven by declarations*

You did not write any code to offer the Permissions UI—it is autobuilt for every app by Windows 8 based on available declarations. So, for most hardware declarations, the user gets a toggle switch in the app permissions to turn usage on or off. If the app needs a sensor/hardware piece to work, and the user has the permissions turned off, the user is gently reminded to turn the settings on from the permissions flyout.

MediaCapture

I discussed the `CameraCaptureUI` API, but that is not the only option in terms of photo/audio/video capture in Windows 8. Turns out, WinRT layer has a whole namespace, called `Windows.Media.Capture`, dedicated to this. Further information is at `http://msdn.microsoft.com/en-us/library/windows/apps/xaml/windows.media.capture.aspx`. There is another great option for capturing media, in the form of the `MediaCapture` API, and it often leads to succinct code. Do you want to preview a video from the webcam in your app's screen? Let's write some code. First, you will change the XAML markup to include a new control, like so:

```
<StackPanel Grid.Row="1" Orientation="Vertical" Margin="150,70,70,70">
<StackPanel Orientation="Horizontal">
<TextBlock Text="Grab your picture to create an account:" Style="{StaticResource
SubheaderTextStyle}"/>
```

```
<Button Content="Say Cheese!" Click="Camera_Click" Margin="20,0,0,0"/>
</StackPanel>
<CaptureElement x:Name="videoFeed" Margin="50" Height="400" Width="400" />
</StackPanel>
```

The CaptureElement is designed to work with input from the MediaCapture API. Now, write some code as the user clicks the button:

```
private async void Camera_Click(object sender, RoutedEventArgs e)
        {
            MediaCapture captureMgr = new MediaCapture();
            await captureMgr.InitializeAsync();
            videoFeed.Source = captureMgr;

            await captureMgr.StartPreviewAsync();
      }
```

Go ahead and run the code. Just a few lines of code—and voilà, you have a live preview of video on your app's page, straight from the device webcam. Now, here is something I haven't talked about: many Windows 8 devices may have both front-facing and rear-facing cameras. The user can always toggle—but could you, the developer, choose either one programmatically? For video instant messenger apps (such as Skype), it totally makes sense to default usage to a front-facing camera and then allow the user to toggle if needed. How should you do this? Turns out, there is a bigger DeviceInformation API that cycles through all devices/sensors available in a Windows 8 machine. If the OEMs (original equipment manufacturers) have done their job right, you should be able to inspect all devices on a Windows 8 PC and choose the one you would like to use. Let's look at the code in Listing 11-2.

Listing 11-2. Windows 8 Device Inspection

```
var devices = await DeviceInformation.FindAllAsync(DeviceClass.VideoCapture);

DeviceInformation frontCamera = devices.FirstOrDefault(x => x.EnclosureLocation != null &&
x.EnclosureLocation.Panel == Windows.Devices.Enumeration.Panel.Front);

DeviceInformation backCamera = devices.FirstOrDefault(x => x.EnclosureLocation != null &&
x.EnclosureLocation.Panel == Windows.Devices.Enumeration.Panel.Back);

            MediaCapture specificCamera = new MediaCapture();
            await specificCamera.InitializeAsync(
                new MediaCaptureInitializationSettings
                {
                    VideoDeviceId = frontCamera.Id
                });
```

As you can see, you first fetch a list of all available devices and then try to detect the front/back facing cameras using the EnclosureLocation.Panel API. If you find a specific camera, you could initialize your MediaCapture with the unique DeviceID of the attached camera. Nifty, isn't it?

Media Playback

What about some media playback on your Windows 8 app to immerse the user in an audio-visual experience? You may be writing an app that allows the user to play music or videos locally available on the device or streamed from the Internet. Let's look at some API options. First, go back to your Apress demo app so that you can write some code. An app that lists books by Apress probably does not need to play media, but for the purpose of the demo, add a fresh new page to your app, accessible from the updated app bar on the main dashboard (see Figure 11-20).

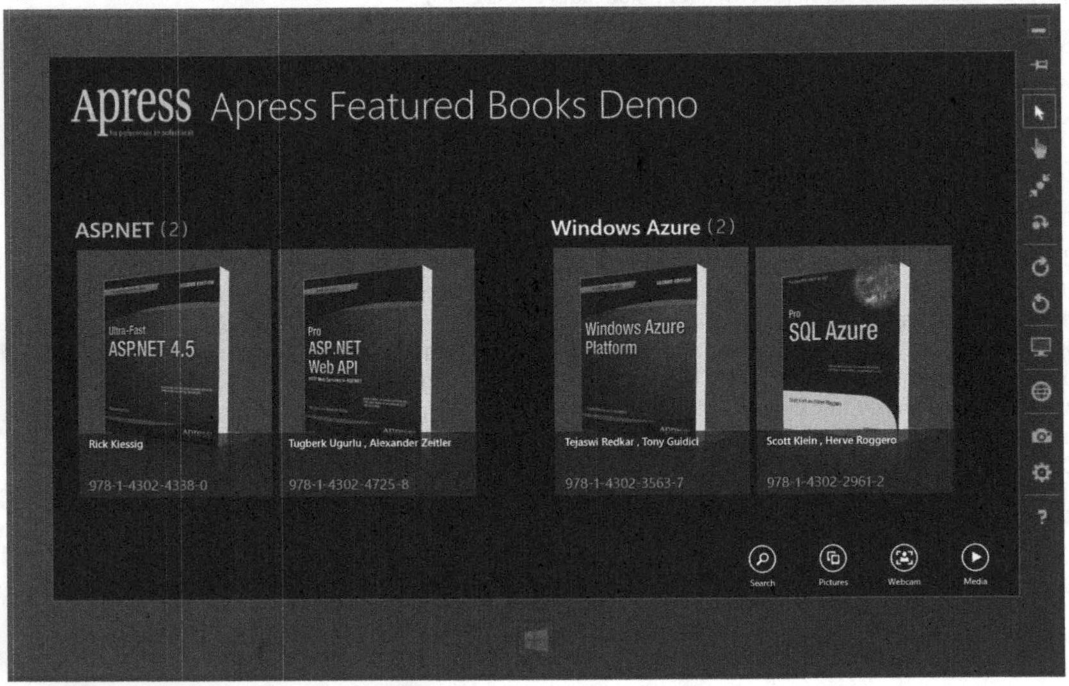

Figure 11-20. *Updated app bar*

The following shows the little XAML markup needed to get this done. When the user clicks/taps the media app bar icon, you simply take them to a fresh page.

```
<Page.BottomAppBar>
<AppBar x:Name="bottomAppBar" Padding="10,0,10,0">
<Grid>
<StackPanel Orientation="Horizontal" HorizontalAlignment="Right">
<Button Style="{StaticResource SearchAppBarButtonStyle}" x:Name="searchButton"
Click="searchButton_Click"/>
<Button Style="{StaticResource PicturesAppBarButtonStyle}" x:Name="loadButton"
Click="loadButton_Click"/>
<Button Style="{StaticResource WebcamAppBarButtonStyle}" x:Name="accountButton"
Click="accountButton_Click"/>
```

```
<Button Style="{StaticResource PlayAppBarButtonStyle}" x:Name="mediaButton"
Click="mediaButton_Click"/>
</StackPanel>
</Grid>
</AppBar>
</Page.BottomAppBar>
```

Building the Media Page

Next, you add a simple `Media.xaml` page to contain some placeholders as you dabble into multimedia and later some sensors. You are shooting for an oversimplified UI that allows the user to pick a local media file and play it in your app. Start by trying to play a local video file; audio playback is going to be the same and simpler. Because you expect the user to pick a local media file, it is not unusual to expect that such files would be in the user's media library; so, that is a recommended location to pick media files from. Also, while file read access is free, if your app wants to write/update files in the media libraries, declared access is needed. Figure 11-21 shows my `PackageAppXManifest` with the new capabilities, although you are not editing files in this demo.

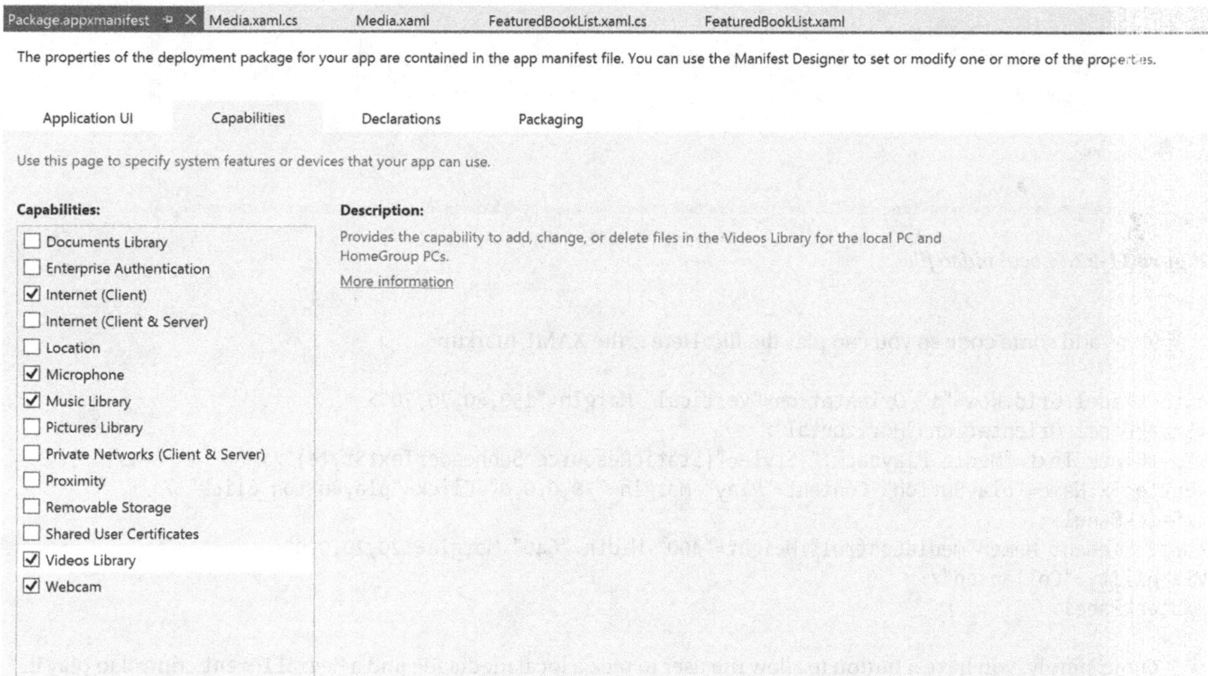

Figure 11-21. *Media library access declaration*

Before you write any code, let me put a sample video file in my Video Library. Turns out, I had a Windows Phone promotional MP4 file at hand (see Figure 11-22). You can see that I added the file to the `My Videos` folder, which is the default OS video library.

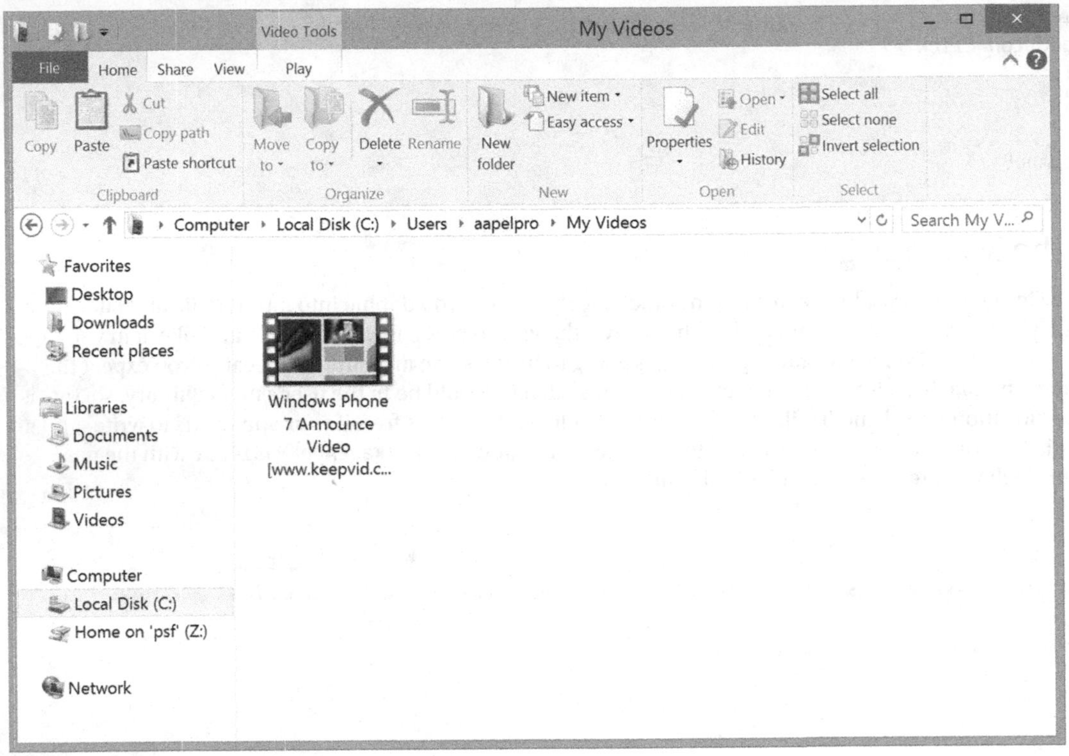

Figure 11-22. *Local video file*

Now, add some code so you can play the file. Here is the XAML markup:

```
<StackPanel Grid.Row="1" Orientation="Vertical" Margin="150,40,70,70">
<StackPanel Orientation="Horizontal">
<TextBlock Text="Media Playback:" Style="{StaticResource SubheaderTextStyle}"/>
<Button x:Name="playButton" Content="Play" Margin="20,0,0,0" Click="playButton_Click" />
</StackPanel>
<MediaElement Name="mediaControl" Height="400" Width="640" Margin="20,20,0,0"
Visibility="Collapsed"/>
</StackPanel>
```

Quite simply, you have a button to allow the user to pick a local media file and a `MediaElement` control to play it. This `MediaElement` control is very powerful and the class has tons of properties/methods to support a variety of media playback, along with mechanisms to control the playback. Further details about the `MediaElement` control are found at `http://msdn.microsoft.com/en-us/library/windows/apps/windows.ui.xaml.controls.mediaelement.aspx`.

Playing Media

Next, add the all-important code to allow the user to pick a file from his/her media libraries and provide the file handle back to your app, and your `MediaElement` control will play it back to the user (see Listing 11-3).

Listing 11-3. Media Playback Code

```
private async void playButton_Click(object sender, RoutedEventArgs e)
        {
            FileOpenPicker mediaFilePicker = new Windows.Storage.Pickers.FileOpenPicker();
            mediaFilePicker.SuggestedStartLocation =
            Windows.Storage.Pickers.PickerLocationId.VideosLibrary;

            mediaFilePicker.FileTypeFilter.Add(".wmv");
            mediaFilePicker.FileTypeFilter.Add(".mp4");

            StorageFile file = await mediaFilePicker.PickSingleFileAsync();
            var stream = await file.OpenAsync(Windows.Storage.FileAccessMode.Read);

            mediaControl.SetSource(stream, file.ContentType);
            mediaControl.Visibility = Windows.UI.Xaml.Visibility.Visible;
            mediaControl.Play();
        }
```

At the core of this interaction is a `FileOpenPicker`, on which you are able to set a default start location and add some filters for the file types you want the user to pick. The rest is easy: you get a `StorageFile` handle once the user has chosen a media file, grab the stream off the file, and hand it off to your `MediaElement` control for playback.
As you run the code in Listing 11-3, you should first see the `FileOpenPicker` in action (see Figure 11-23) followed by the media playback in your app (see Figure 11-24).

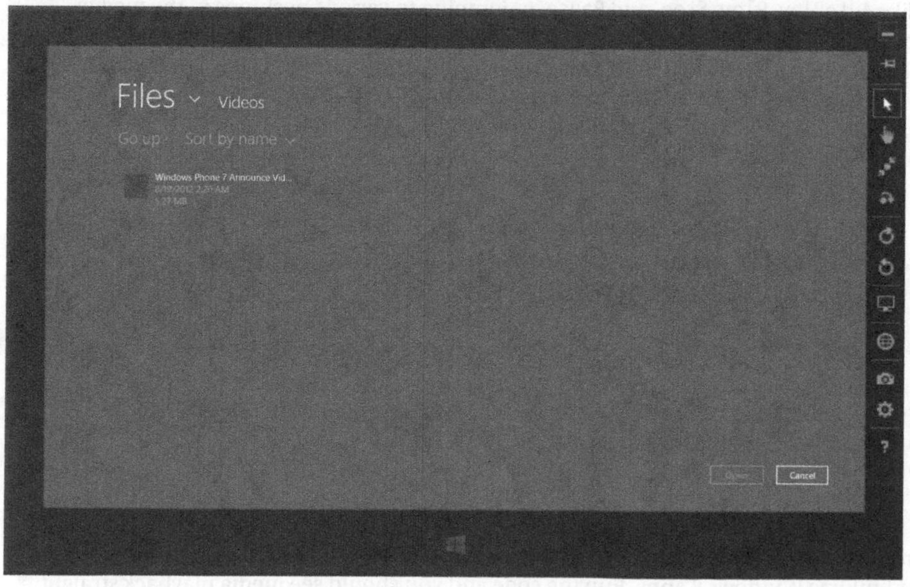

Figure 11-23. *Local media picker*

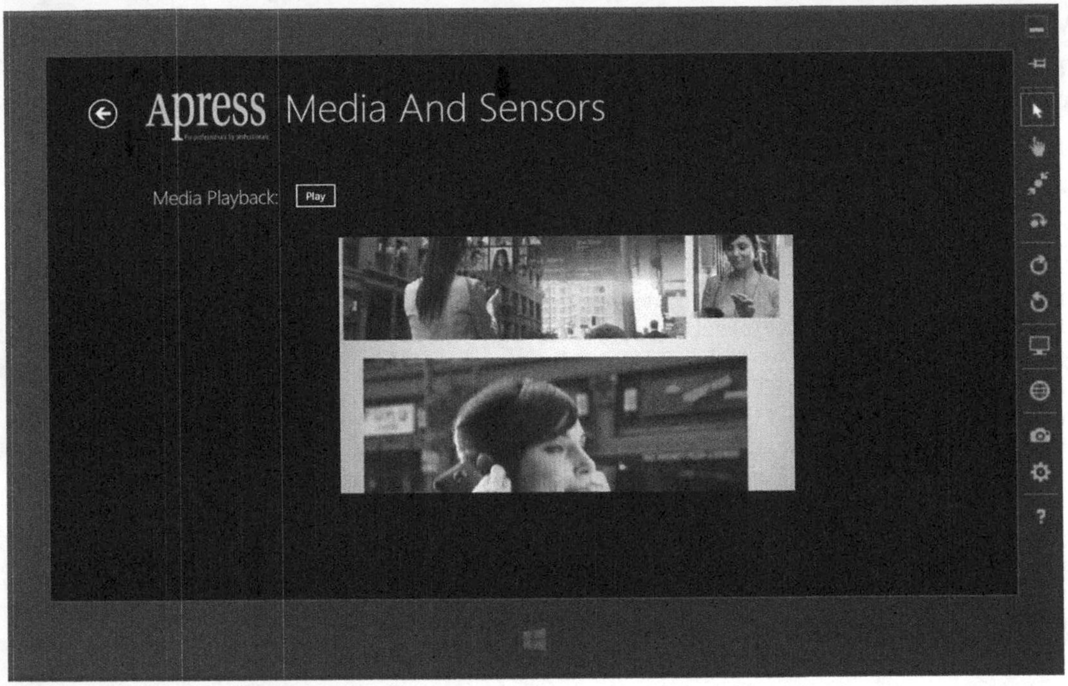

Figure 11-24. Local media playback

And there you have it—your MediaElement control happily plays a local video file from the user's library. You would obviously want the experience to be a little friendlier, with perhaps full-screen playback and such. One other thing to note: the MediaElement control does not automatically add media playback control functions, but it does support methods/properties like AutoPlay, Play, Stop, and Pause, or jumping to various positions in the media file during playback. It is up to the developer to add buttons or controls on the canvas to allow the user to control the media playback. The app bar also serves as a great placeholder for media control-button icons. For detailed walkthroughs on how to play different types of local media, please feel free to check out MSDN documentation at http://msdn.microsoft.com/en-us/library/windows/apps/xaml/hh465154.aspx.

Streaming Media

What if your Windows 8 app wanted to stream media from the Internet for the user to consume? No worries, you can have the same setup as if playing local media and change your code a little, like so:

```
private async void playButton_Click(object sender, RoutedEventArgs e)
        {
        mediaControl.Source = new Uri("http://media.ch9.ms/ch9/b5a6/9b11ab16-bcc5-41b7-b727-
        a593951db5a6/kona_Source.wmv", UriKind.Absolute);
        mediaControl.Play();
        }
```

So essentially, you are simply feeding a network URI link as the media source for your MediaElement control, in this case a Channel 9 video for building Windows 8 apps. Run the code and you should see media playback straight from the Internet (see Figure 11-25).

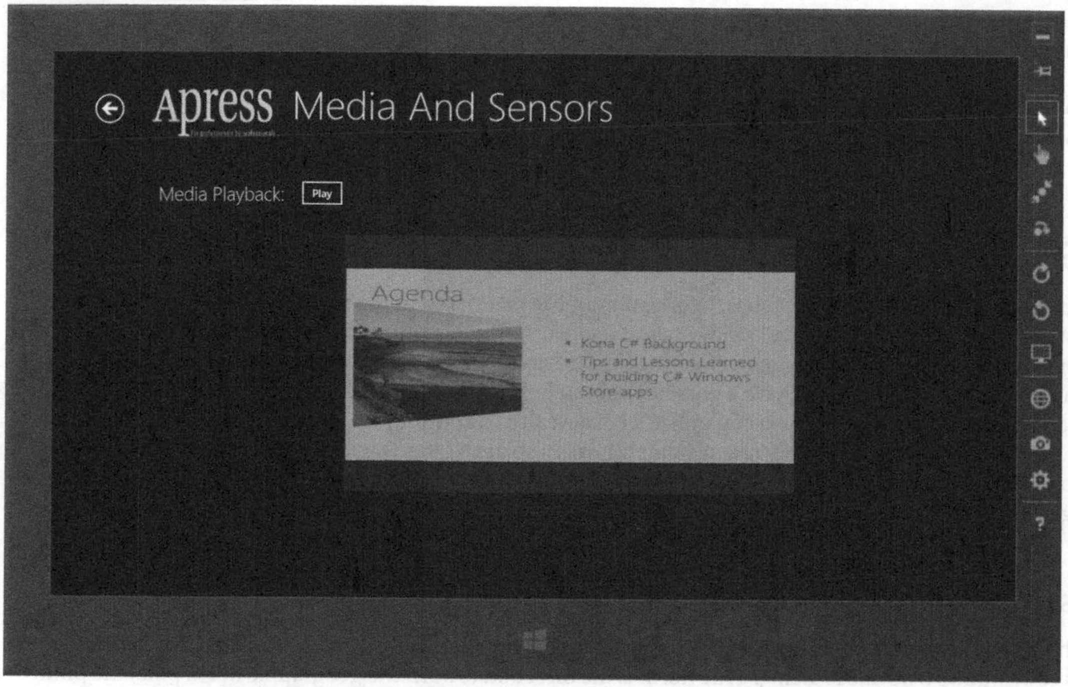

Figure 11-25. Remote media playback

Now, just a little caveat before you start pointing your `MediaElement` control to all kinds of links on the Internet: there are some restrictions on the media playback format. For example, YouTube videos meant for Flash playback will simply not work. For a complete list of supported audio/video formats for Windows 8 Store apps, please see MSDN documentation at `http://msdn.microsoft.com/en-us/library/windows/apps/hh986969.aspx`. Also, there is a very nifty Play To OS contract that your app can participate in. This contract enables users to easily stream audio, video, and images from their Windows 8 device to other devices in their home network. This could be a superb addition that augments the user experience offered by your Windows 8 Store app. Everybody loves a big screen and sharing with family. Your app is catering to that need during media playback. For more information on supporting the Play To contract, please visit `http://msdn.microsoft.com/en-us/library/windows/apps/xaml/hh465183.aspx`.

One other consideration during media playback is the Windows 8 device display. Normally, a Windows 8 device will dim the display (and eventually turn it off) to save battery life when the user is away, but media playback apps might need to keep the screen on so that the user can continue enjoying the audio/video playback despite extended periods of noninteraction with the screen. How do you achieve this? Simple: an API is there to help.

```
private DisplayRequest dispRequest = null;

// Before media playback starts ..
if (dispRequest == null)
{
        dispRequest = new DisplayRequest();
        dispRequest.RequestActive();
}
```

```
// When media playback pauses or stops ..
if (dispRequest != null)
{
        dispRequest.RequestRelease();
        dispRequest = null;
}
```

Sensors

Device sensors set apart today's modern tablets/hybrid/ultrabooks compared to the laptops of yesteryear. These nimble yet fast devices come loaded with all kinds of device sensors, which readily provide feedback about the device's motion, orientation in space, angular velocity, compass, and so forth. Combine all of these, and as the developer of a Windows 8 Store app, you have a good idea about how the user is holding his or her device. It is up to you and your app's needs to decide how you can utilize such a wealth of information to provide unique experiences for your users. Game developers for Windows 8 absolutely love these device sensors, but there is no reason why regular Windows 8 apps could not use sensor feedback in some way. So, let's dig in to see some examples of sensors and their usage.

Compass

Let's start with the simple compass sensor. This sensor is meant to point to the earth's true north in degrees, based on the direction the Windows 8 device is facing. True north is the direction toward the geographic north pole, the point on the globe exactly 90 degrees north of the equator. The compass sensor, based on device support, can also offer a reading of magnetic north, which is the direction toward the earth's magnetic north pole, skewed by a few degrees.

So, how do you read the compass sensor in your Windows 8 Store app? The `Windows.Devices.Sensors` namespace offers a very simple API: an event handler wired up to the compass sensor. In fact, every device sensor in Windows 8 is read using the same technique, which really brings down the learning curve for developers. So, you will write some code to handle the compass and then repeat for other sensors, each time seeing only what needs to be changed.

First, let's add a little XAML markup in the form of simple `TextBlocks` in your `Media.xaml` page so that you can see the output of the compass sensor. Here's what you add:

```
<StackPanel Orientation="Horizontal" Margin="0,40,0,0">
<TextBlock Text="Compass Magnetic North:" Style="{StaticResource SubheaderTextStyle}"
VerticalAlignment="Top"/>
<TextBlock x:Name="compassMagNorth" Margin="20,10,0,0" FontSize="20" Text="No Data"
VerticalAlignment="Bottom"/>
<TextBlock Text="Compass True North:" Style="{StaticResource SubheaderTextStyle}"
VerticalAlignment="Top" Margin="60,0,0,0"/>
<TextBlock x:Name="compassTrueNorth" Margin="20,10,0,0" FontSize="20" Text="No Data"
VerticalAlignment="Bottom"/>
</StackPanel>
```

Next, Listing 11-4 shows the code in the code-behind file:

Listing 11-4. Typical Sensor-Handling Code

```
Compass compassSensor = Compass.GetDefault();
protected override void OnNavigatedTo(NavigationEventArgs e)
        {
            base.OnNavigatedTo(e);
```

```
            if (compassSensor != null)
                compassSensor.ReadingChanged += compassSensor_ReadingChanged;
        }

protected override void OnNavigatedFrom(NavigationEventArgs e)
        {
            base.OnNavigatedFrom(e);

            if (compassSensor != null)
                compassSensor.ReadingChanged -= compassSensor_ReadingChanged;
        }
```

In Listing 11-4, you first instantiate a Compass sensor object. The GetDefault() method has the OS return your app a handle to the internal compass sensor. Next, in the overridden OnNavigatedTo() event handler, you check to see if your compass object is actually null. This is a critical step and it should never be skipped. In older devices running Windows 8, there may not be a compass sensor, in which case your handle would be null. This simple check makes your code backward compatible and fail graciously if a device sensor is not available. Next, you listen in on the ReadingChanged event off the compass sensor with your own event handler. This is your opportunity to read compass sensor input as it changes. Now, in the overridden OnNavigatedFrom() event, you unwire the ReadingChanged event handler to prevent multiple handlers listening in on the same event. This, as you have seen, is standard practice in XAML pages that make up a Windows 8 Store app.

So, let's recap this pattern one more time: initialize the sensor with a GetDefault() call, check for null, wire up a custom event handler to the ReadingChanged event, and unwire the same during appropriate page life-cycle events. This is a pattern that you will repeat for each Windows 8 device sensor while reading its input. These steps are crucial for errorless code. You will not repeat the same code in the following sections.

Now, look at the custom event handler for reading the compass sensor input:

```
private async void compassSensor_ReadingChanged(Compass sender, CompassReadingChangedEventArgs args)
        {
            await Dispatcher.RunAsync(CoreDispatcherPriority.Normal, () =>
            {
                CompassReading reading = args.Reading;

                if (reading.HeadingMagneticNorth != null)
                    compassMagNorth.Text = String.Format("{0,5:0.00}",
                    reading.HeadingMagneticNorth);

                if (reading.HeadingTrueNorth != null)
                    compassTrueNorth.Text = String.Format("{0,5:0.00}", reading.HeadingTrueNorth);
            });
        }
```

Let's inspect what you did here. Guess what the await Dispatcher.RunAsync() code does? Because you are reaching inside WinRT to fetch the compass sensor input, this ends up being an asynchronous operation and, consequently, may not execute on the main UI thread. If on a different thread, you need a way to marshal back the results to the UI thread so that you may update your controls with values from the device sensor. Take note here: this is a very common technique for merging asynchronous operations back onto the UI thread; without this line of delegate code, you would get nasty cross-thread security errors. The rest is easy: you read the Reading off of the CompassReadingChangedEventArgs args, which is already of the type CompassReading. Next, you check for null and read values from the sensor and update your UI.

Let's run this code. Figure 11-26 shows the result from my Windows 8 machine running the app in the Simulator.

Figure 11-26. *No sensor support*

Hmm, so what happened here? Clearly, your compass sensor variable was null and you never got to read any sensor input. What's happening is normal—my current Windows 8 installation is a virtual machine running on a MacBook Pro laptop, which is devoid of any such fancy device sensors like the compass. So, without a valid sensor to read input from, you fail graciously, which should be acceptable. Now, this is where remote debugging comes into play. Deploying the same app code to a Surface RT device makes the device compass sensor come alive with support. Figure 11-27 is a screenshot of the same app, now reading input from the compass sensor. True north data may not be present on many devices.

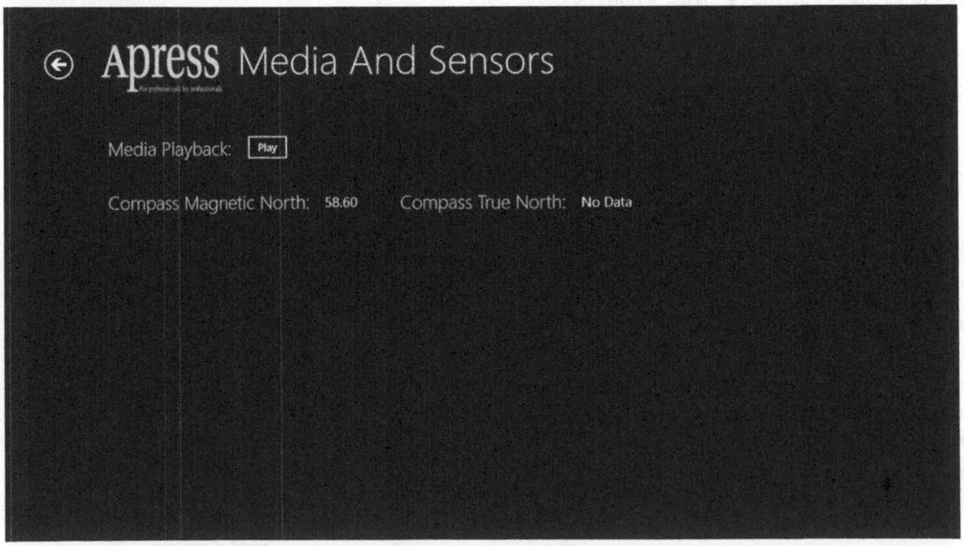

Figure 11-27. *Compass sensor input*

Accelerometer

Next up is the accelerometer device sensor. This device sensor measures acceleration across three axes: X, Y, and Z. The acceleration is measured in terms of g-force or earth's gravitational pull; so you can guess values when your Windows 8 tablet is laying horizontal on a table or standing vertically.

First, add some XAML markup to have placeholders for displaying sensor input, like so:

```
<StackPanel Orientation="Horizontal" Margin="0,40,0,0">
<TextBlock Text="Accelerometer Inputs (X, Y, Z):" Style="{StaticResource SubheaderTextStyle}"
VerticalAlignment="Top"/>
<TextBlock x:Name="xAxis" Margin="20,10,0,0" FontSize="20" Text="X = " VerticalAlignment="Bottom"/>
<TextBlock x:Name="yAxis" Margin="20,10,0,0" FontSize="20" Text="Y = " VerticalAlignment="Bottom"/>
<TextBlock x:Name="zAxis" Margin="20,10,0,0" FontSize="20" Text="Z = " VerticalAlignment="Bottom"/>
</StackPanel>
```

Next, some code in the code-behind following the sensor-reading pattern that you saw earlier; this should be self-explanatory:

```
Accelerometer accelerometerSensor = Accelerometer.GetDefault();
if (accelerometerSensor != null)
            accelerometerSensor.ReadingChanged += accelerometerSensor_ReadingChanged;
private async void accelerometerSensor_ReadingChanged(Accelerometer sender,
AccelerometerReadingChangedEventArgs args)
      {
          await Dispatcher.RunAsync(CoreDispatcherPriority.Normal, () =>
          {
              AccelerometerReading reading = args.Reading;

              xAxis.Text = String.Format("{0,2:0.00}", reading.AccelerationX.ToString());
              yAxis.Text = String.Format("{0,2:0.00}", reading.AccelerationY.ToString());
              zAxis.Text = String.Format("{0,2:0.00}", reading.AccelerationZ.ToString());
          });
      }
```

Let's run the code on a Windows 8 tablet and hold the device in various orientations. You should start seeing the X, Y, and Z acceleration values change very quickly, like in the screenshot shown in Figure 11-28.

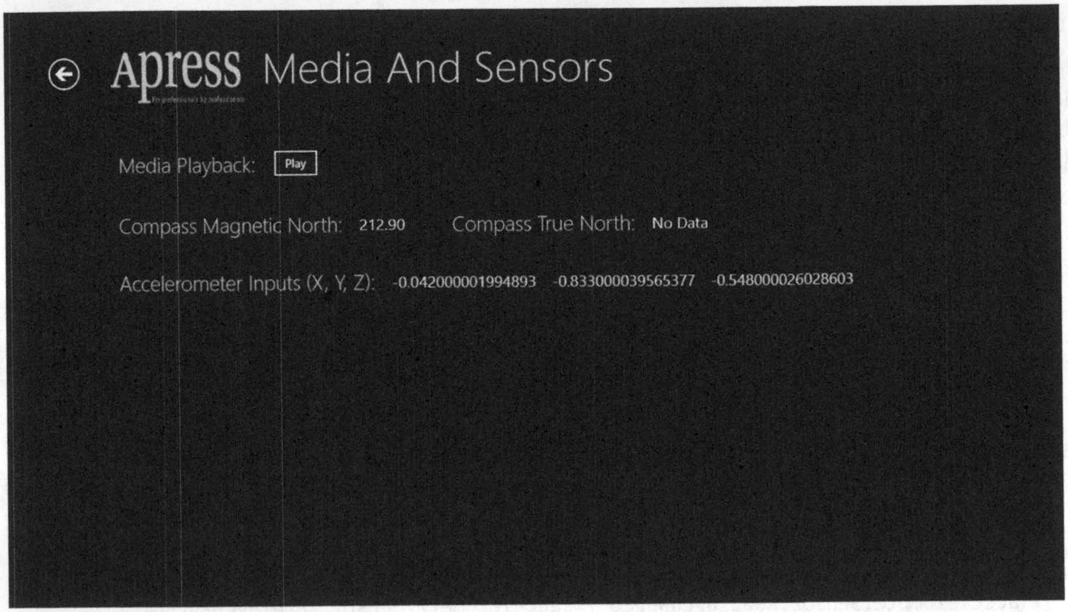

***Figure 11-28.** Accelerometer sensor input*

Inclinometer

The inclinometer is one of the coolest Windows 8 device sensors. Essentially, it provides three device values: yaw, pitch, and roll. What do these mean? They essentially indicate the device rotation across three principle axes: X, Y, and Z. The terms yaw, pitch, and roll are commonly used in the aviation industry to describe rotation in terms of an aircraft, across its vertical, lateral, and longitudinal axes. The Wikipedia article at `http://en.wikipedia.org/wiki/Aircraft_principal_axes` does a great job explaining these rotations across axes.

Now, let's write some code, starting with XAML markup to show sensor input:

```
<StackPanel Orientation="Horizontal" Margin="0,40,0,0">
<TextBlock Text="Inclinometer Inputs (Yaw, Pitch, Roll):" Style="{StaticResource
SubheaderTextStyle}" VerticalAlignment="Top"/>
<TextBlock x:Name="yawDegrees" Margin="20,10,0,0" FontSize="20" Text="X = "
VerticalAlignment="Bottom"/>
<TextBlock x:Name="pitchDegrees" Margin="20,10,0,0" FontSize="20" Text="Y = "
VerticalAlignment="Bottom"/>
<TextBlock x:Name="rollDegrees" Margin="20,10,0,0" FontSize="20" Text="Z = "
VerticalAlignment="Bottom"/>
</StackPanel>
```

And now some familiar code-behind logic:

```
Inclinometer inclinometerSensor = Inclinometer.GetDefault();
if (inclinometerSensor != null)
            inclinometerSensor.ReadingChanged += inclinometerSensor_ReadingChanged;

private async void inclinometerSensor_ReadingChanged(Inclinometer sender,
InclinometerReadingChangedEventArgs args)
```

```
{
    await Dispatcher.RunAsync(CoreDispatcherPriority.Normal, () =>
    {
        InclinometerReading reading = args.Reading;

        yawDegrees.Text = String.Format("{0,2:0.00}", reading.YawDegrees.ToString());
        pitchDegrees.Text = String.Format("{0,2:0.00}", reading.PitchDegrees.ToString());
        rollDegrees.Text = String.Format("{0,2:0.00}", reading.RollDegrees.ToString());
    });
}
```

Run the preceding code again on a Windows 8 tablet and try rotating the device across three axes to see quickly changing values, as captured in the screenshot in Figure 11-29.

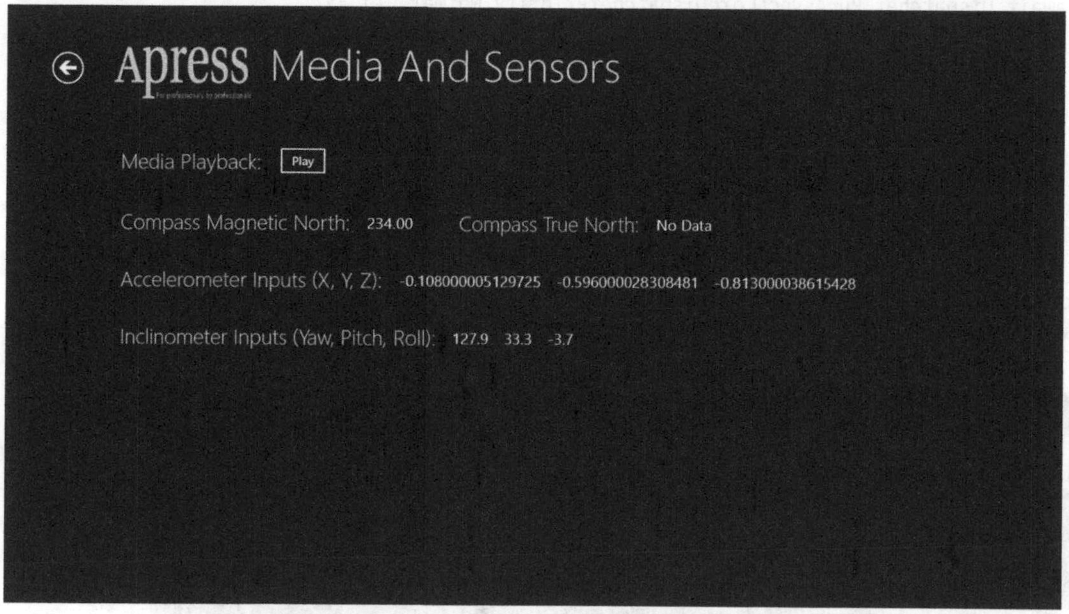

Figure 11-29. *Inclinometer sensor input*

Gyrometer

The gyrometer (also called a gyroscope) is a Windows 8 device sensor that measures rotational/angular velocity across the three axes X, Y, and Z. The entire function of a gyroscope sensor is well explained in the Wikipedia article at `http://en.wikipedia.org/wiki/Gyroscope`.

Add your usual XAML markup to display the gyrometer sensor input:

```
<StackPanel Orientation="Horizontal" Margin="0,40,0,0">
<TextBlock Text="Gyrometer Velocity Inputs (X, Y, Z):" Style="{StaticResource SubheaderTextStyle}"
VerticalAlignment="Top"/>
<TextBlock x:Name="xAxisVel" Margin="20,10,0,0" FontSize="20" Text="X = "
VerticalAlignment="Bottom"/>
```

```
<TextBlock x:Name="yAxisVel" Margin="20,10,0,0" FontSize="20" Text="Y = "
VerticalAlignment="Bottom"/>
<TextBlock x:Name="zAxisVel" Margin="20,10,0,0" FontSize="20" Text="Z = "
VerticalAlignment="Bottom"/>
</StackPanel>
```

And the code-behind follows with a similar custom event handler:

```
Gyrometer gyrometerSensor = Gyrometer.GetDefault();
if (gyrometerSensor != null)
                gyrometerSensor.ReadingChanged += gyrometerSensor_ReadingChanged;
private async void gyrometerSensor_ReadingChanged(Gyrometer sender,
GyrometerReadingChangedEventArgs args)
        {
            await Dispatcher.RunAsync(CoreDispatcherPriority.Normal, () =>
            {
                GyrometerReading reading = args.Reading;

                xAxisVel.Text = String.Format("{0,2:0.00}", reading.AngularVelocityX.ToString());
                yAxisVel.Text = String.Format("{0,2:0.00}", reading.AngularVelocityY.ToString());
                zAxisVel.Text = String.Format("{0,2:0.00}", reading.AngularVelocityZ.ToString());
            });
        }
```

Now, if you deploy the code to a modern Windows 8 tablet with gyrometer sensor support, you will see quickly changing sensor input if you keep flipping the device across X, Y, and Z axes, as captured in Figure 11-30.

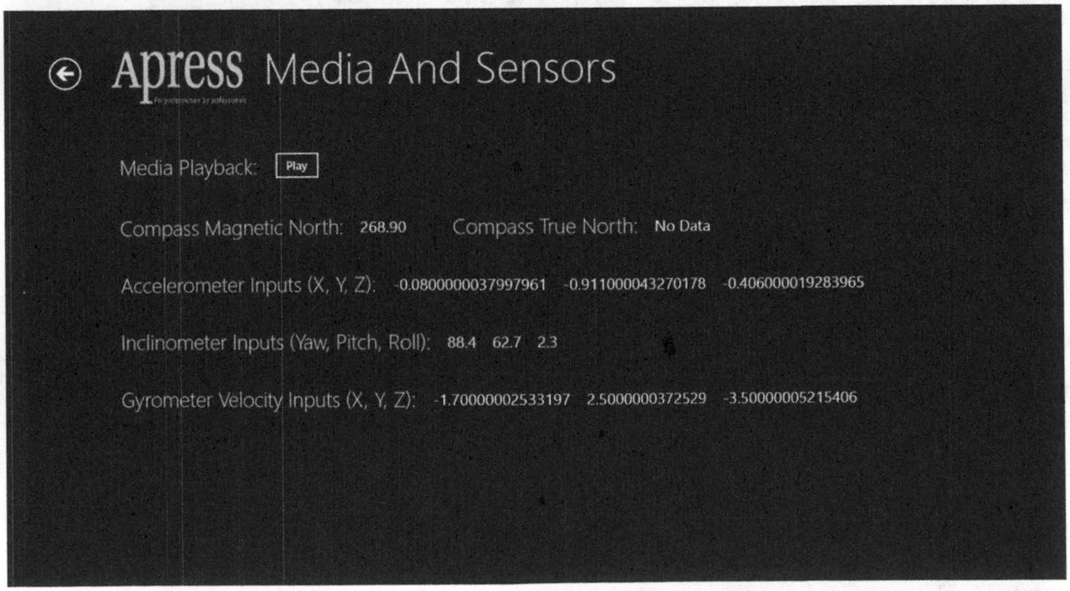

Figure 11-30. *Gyrometer sensor input*

Light Sensor

The last device sensor you will cover is the light sensor, but by no means, is it the least. In fact, proper use of the light sensor may result in immediate high usage of your Windows 8 app. The light sensor quite simply measures ambient light on the Windows 8 device; in other words, the brightness of the surroundings. This can be a critical piece of device sensor feedback because you can immediately adjust your app's content to fit the illumination by tweaking the brightness of colors, contrast, and so forth. This will be highly appreciated by the user when he or she is moving between areas with different lighting. The light sensor provides its input in terms of the unit of measurement called *lux*, which is a way to measure illumination. Wikipedia also has a great article on lux at `http://en.wikipedia.org/wiki/Lux`.

Let's add your usual XAML markup, followed by the custom event handler:

```
<StackPanel Orientation="Horizontal" Margin="0,40,0,0">
<TextBlock Text="LightSensor Input (Lux):" Style="{StaticResource SubheaderTextStyle}"
VerticalAlignment="Top"/>
<TextBlock x:Name="illumination" Margin="20,10,0,0" FontSize="20" Text="X = "
VerticalAlignment="Bottom"/>
</StackPanel>

LightSensor lightSensor = LightSensor.GetDefault();
if (lightSensor != null)
            lightSensor.ReadingChanged += lightSensor_ReadingChanged;

private async void lightSensor_ReadingChanged(LightSensor sender,
LightSensorReadingChangedEventArgs args)
    {
        await Dispatcher.RunAsync(CoreDispatcherPriority.Normal, () =>
        {
            LightSensorReading reading = args.Reading;

            illumination.Text = String.Format("{0,2:0.00}",
reading.IlluminanceInLux.ToString());
        });
    }
```

Run the preceding code in a Windows 8 tablet that supports the light sensor, and try moving between dark and well-lit rooms to see the changing illuminance values in terms of lux, as captured in the Figure 11-31 screenshot.

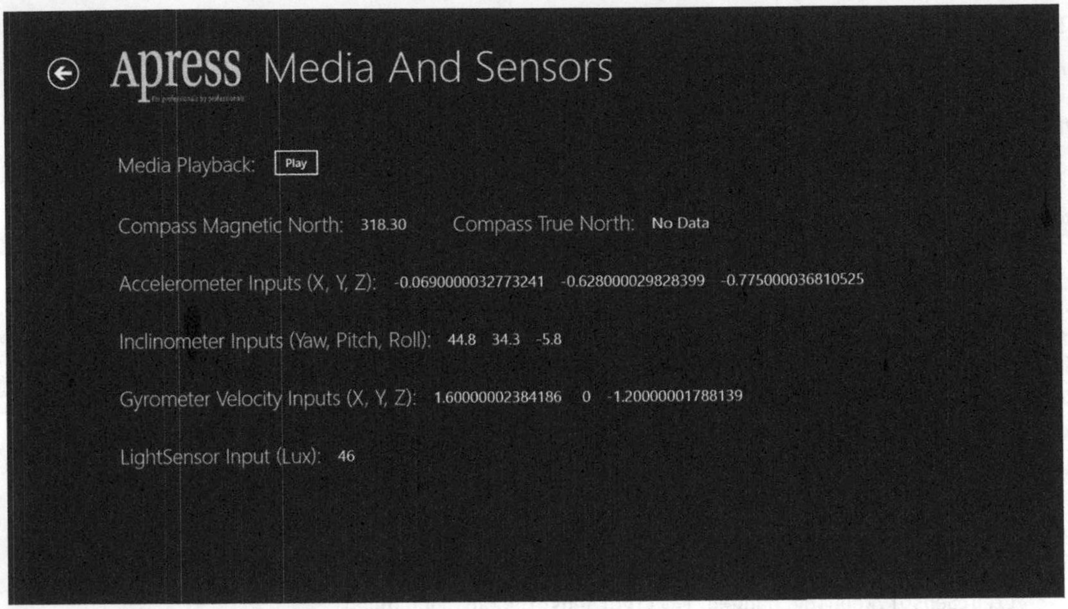

***Figure 11-31.** Light sensor input*

Summary

That's a wrap. This chapter gave you a brief look at all that is possible when you incorporate multimedia and tap into device sensors for your Windows 8 Store apps. Feel free to use the device webcam and microphone whenever appropriate. It adds big-time points toward personalization of the app's user experience. Windows 8 devices have a very capable media player setup—so entertain the user wherever possible. And then look to leverage as many device sensors as needed to provide a unique user experience in your app. You learned about most sensors, but a more complete listing of all device sensors supported in Windows 8 is at `http://msdn.microsoft.com/en-us/library/windows/apps/br206408.aspx`. Feel free to check out the `SensorQuaternion` device sensor that combines the input of multiple sensors into a matrix for complex space-motion inputs, often needed in games.

The key takeaway from this chapter is to have fun with multimedia and sensors. Your users will not mind.

CHAPTER 12

Tiles, Badges, and Toasts

Have you ever decorated the front door of your home so guests feel welcome? Have you ever been pleasantly surprised when a gift arrived in the mail? Have you ever considered how convenient it would be to know what's going on inside your home (like through a live video feed) when you are out of town? But wait—how does all this relate to Windows 8 app development? Turns out, these real-world scenarios are very apt when it comes to usage of tiles, badges, toasts, and lock screen apps in your Windows 8 Store apps.

In short, what you are shooting for here is to have a robust notification mechanism from your Windows 8 app for the user, even when the app may not be running. The goal of using live tiles, badge updates, and toast/lock screen notifications is simple: make the user of the app feel connected at all times. A Windows Store app that feels alive and connected, and communicates fresh information to the user, can garner increased usage of the app as the user starts building loyalty from timely notifications from the app. Ready to do it yourself? Then, this chapter will be your one-stop shop to get tiles, badges, and toasts working for your Windows Store apps. Do these right, and you will keep inviting your users back into your app through timely and appropriate notifications.

Notification Delivery

Now, before starting the in-depth conversation about tiles, badges, and toasts, I think it would be pertinent to know all the techniques available for providing notification updates. Essentially, these are the live representations of Windows 8 apps on the Start screen. Badges are overlay information on top of tiles. Tiles can start as defaults, as the user installs a Windows Store app, with possibilities of updates later on. Toasts, on the other hand, are transient pieces of information that appear on the top corner of the user's screen, informing the user of something important from a concerned app. But tiles, badges, and toasts are essentially notifications for the app user. So, as a developer, what options do you have to deliver such notifications? Turns out, there are four:

- *Local*: This delivery mechanism necessitates the Windows 8 app being run by the user, and generating a notification update from inside the app. There are well-defined APIs in Windows that allows us developers to send out such notifications while our apps are running. This works for tile, toast, and badge updates. In fact, this where you will spend most of your time in this chapter.
- *Scheduled*: This delivery mechanism is similar to local updates, except that the notification delivery is scheduled in the future at a precise date and time. This works for tile and toast updates.
- *Periodic*: This delivery mechanism is meant to set up a periodic schedule where an external source (web site or cloud service) is polled at defined intervals to pull down the latest content for notification delivery. This works for tiles and badges.

- *Push*: This is the truest form of an external content/notification delivery mechanism, since nothing is initialized from the client Windows 8 app. Some service on the Internet does a little handshaking with the Windows Push Notification Service to route notification messages to subscribing clients. This delivery mechanism can happen any time (ideal for real-time scenarios), and works with tile, badge, or toast notifications, as well as being capable of delivering raw messages in a chosen format directly for the Windows 8 app to process (this only works if the app is running). I will discuss push notifications in detail in Chapter 13.

Tiles

App tiles are the front doors to your Windows 8 Store apps and your first opportunity to make a good impression with the user. Tiles are representations of your Windows 8 apps on the Start screen and most commonly, the launchpad where the user starts your app. So, an app tile that exudes branding and purpose is obviously desirable for Windows 8 apps.

Default tiles, as you have seen in Chapter 5, can come in two sizes: square or wide. For your Apress Featured Books Demo app, the two app tile sizes are shown in Figures 12-1 and 12-2.

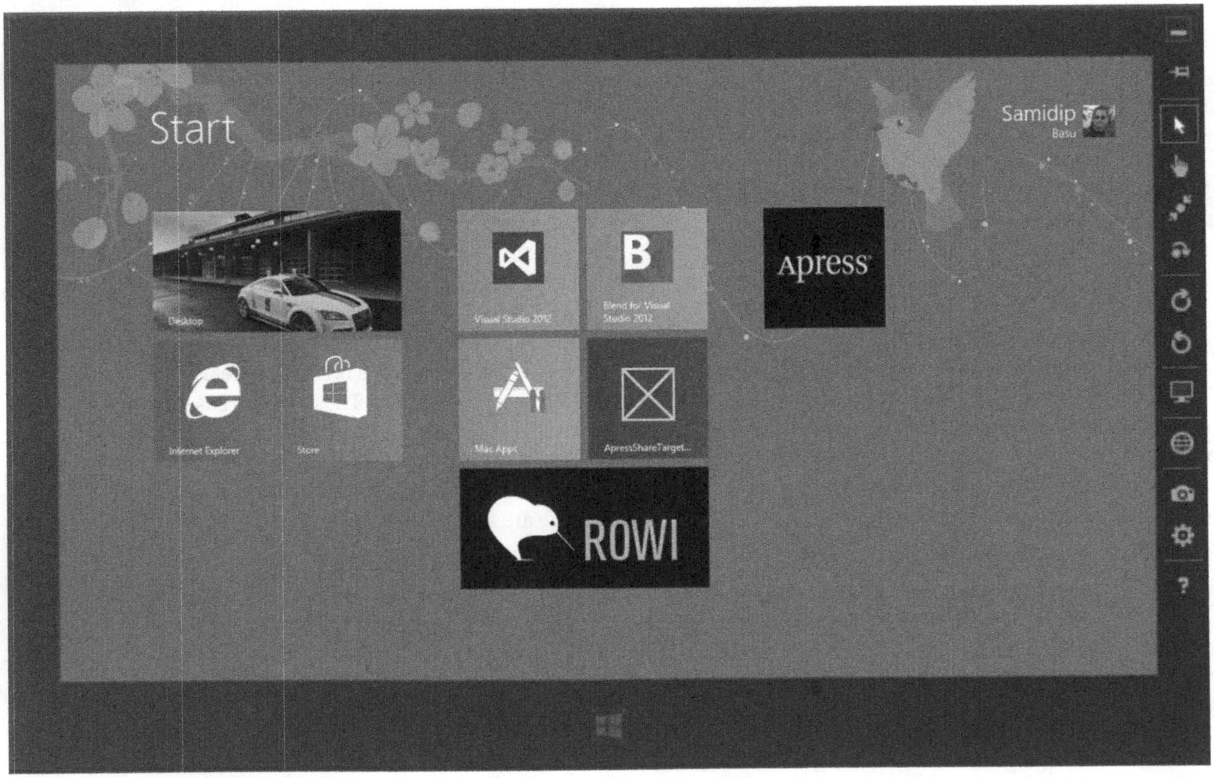

Figure 12-1. *Default square app tile*

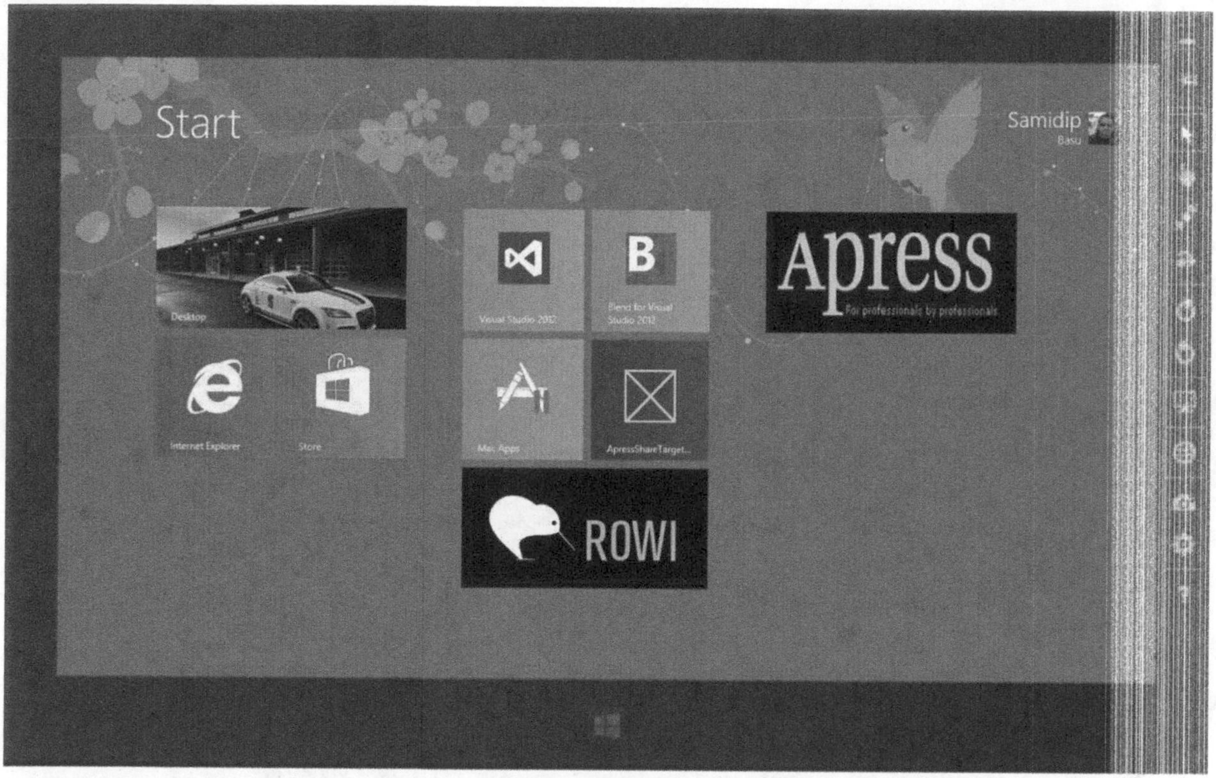

Figure 12-2. *Default wide app tile*

As you can see, both tile sizes have their place on the user's Start screen, simply allowing for greater customization in the arrangement of tiles around what is important to the user. These default tiles begin as static images (of predefined sizes) that you could choose and configure, as seen in the `PackageAppXManifest` configuration in Figure 12-3. The bottom-line: choose your tile images to be inviting and vibrant, and to highlight your app and branding.

Figure 12-3. *Tile image configurations*

The square tile is the default size. If your Windows 8 app does not have support for the wide tile, the option to toggle between the two sizes will simply not be offered to the user. Please be aware, though, that if your Windows 8 app does not support a wide tile as it first goes live in the Windows Store, the only way to fix it is to submit an app update. While the wide tile offers double the size of the square tile, it also comes with the added responsibility of impressing the user. Since the user is approving your app tile to have such a big real estate on his/her Start screen, the onus falls back on the developer to honor the user's loyalty by pushing out live content updates to the wide tile, as you shall explore in this chapter.

Live Tiles

Do you know what's better than a great app tile for a Windows 8 Store app? Yes, a live tile. The live attributes come from the fact that the app tile can get updated from the default tile, has the ability to show information from within the app on the Start screen, does peek animation flips with content, and generally is always inviting the user back into the app. Both the square and wide tile sizes can display any combination of text, images, app branding (logo or app name), and notification badges. Figure 12-4 shows a smattering of some of the tile options possible by mixing-and-matching text, images, and badges to create dramatic tile combinations. Live tiles are immediately vibrant with color, present relevant content right on the Start screen, and continuously tempt the user to tap/click to get inside the app. And when the tiles display fresh information without the user even running the app, it does feel like the tiles have a mind of their own—like they are alive.

Figure 12-4. *Live tile assortment*

So, you must now be wondering how there is any semblance of standardization when live tiles can be so varied? Well, fear not: however much variety there might be in permutations and combinations of putting text, images, and badges on a tile, it is all controlled through simple XML payloads. Figure 12-5 shows a simple live tile example from an MSDN screen capture.

TileSquareBlock
One short string of large block text over a single, short line of bold, regular text.

Example

Example XML

```
<tile>
  <visual>
    <binding template="TileSquareBlock">
      <text id="1">Text Field 1</text>
      <text id="2">Text Field 2</text>
    </binding>
  </visual>
</tile>
```

Figure 12-5. *Anatomy of a live tile*

So, the live tile example in Figure 12-5 shows that updates to a tile have predefined names (`TextSquareBlock` in this case) and an XML template that defines the content. These XML packets are not extensible, and your live tile update must adhere to a predefined format. Can you guess why? The simple reason for predefining the XML schema is due to the fact that the Windows 8 OS is actually the one processing the XML payload to update the live tiles. A live tile update in the form of XML payload may happen anytime, even if the concerned Windows 8 app is not running or in a suspended state. In the absence of custom app code that can process live tile updates, the OS is the one to parse the XML and figure out how to repaint the tile with the given combination of images and text. If every Windows 8 app were at liberty to define its own XML schema for live tile updates, the OS would have no clue about how to parse it. Do you see the reason for system-defined templates now?

Now, there are about 45 such system-defined XML templates for use in live tile updates. You get to choose any combination of square/wide, with/without peeking templates to use in your Windows 8 app tile update. And no one can do a better job at listing out the options with the XML templates than the MSDN tile template catalog for Windows 8 app tiles. You can find the entire catalog at `http://msdn.microsoft.com/en-us/library/windows/apps/hh761491.aspx#TileWideText01`. Bookmark and choose one or more of the live tile templates appropriate for your Windows 8 app. The tile template catalog also provides some examples on what types of live tile templates are appropriate, given the context of your Windows 8 app. A full detailed guideline on app tile design can be found at `http://msdn.microsoft.com/en-us/library/windows/apps/hh465403.aspx`. Read well, my friends.

Local Tile Updates

Now that you understand the anatomy of what makes up a live tile, let's explore some options to send out local updates to your default app tile. This will also be an opportunity to take a close look at the API used to update tiles and to see some edge conditions in action.

First, let's get an important caveat out of the way. If your Windows 8 Store app only supports a square app tile, the user never gets to see the tile size-changing toggle UI, and accordingly, it is OK to send out a tile update just for the square tile. However, if your Windows 8 app also supports a wide tile, the user is entirely in control. The user can, at any time, toggle between seeing the square or wide tile versions of your app's tile and you, the developer, have no way of knowing which tile size the user is viewing. So in such cases, while sending out a live tile update, you cannot choose just the square or wide tile templates, since you do not know the size beforehand and the live tile update will simply be ignored by the OS. You must send out live tile updates supporting both square and wide templates so that the user sees the update, regardless of which tile size he or she has on the Start screen. I just saved you a whole bunch of debugging frustration, didn't I?

Text Tile Templates

Now, let's see some code. Given your default app tiles in the Apress demo app, suppose you are trying to update them to convey some information to the user. This would be done locally as the app is running, and `app.xaml.cs` is often a good place for code to update tiles. Let's begin with some text-only tile updates. For the wide tile update, you are going to pick the `TileWideText03` template, which puts out large text in wrapped format. The XML template is as follows:

```
<tile>
  <visual>
    <binding template="TileWideText03">
      <text id="1">Text Header Field 1</text>
    </binding>
  </visual>
</tile>
```

For the square tile update, let's pick `TileSquareText03`, which puts out up to four regular texts without wrapping. Here's the XML template:

```
<tile>
  <visual>
    <binding template="TileSquareText03">
      <text id="1">Text Field 1</text>
      <text id="2">Text Field 2</text>
      <text id="3">Text Field 3</text>
      <text id="4">Text Field 4</text>
    </binding>
  </visual>
</tile>
```

Either one of these XML templates would have been fine if you were just targeting square or wide live tile updates. But as I said before, you really do not have an option to just send one if your app supports a wide tile. So, how do you include both templates into one payload? Simple—merge them like so:

```
<tile>
  <visual>
    <binding template="TileWideText03">
      <text id="1">Text Header Field 1</text>
    </binding>
    <binding template="TileSquareText03">
      <text id="1">Text Field 1</text>
      <text id="2">Text Field 2</text>
      <text id="3">Text Field 3</text>
      <text id="4">Text Field 4</text>
    </binding>
  </visual>
</tile>
```

Now, let's write some code to build up the needed merged XML template and try sending out your first live tile update. Here goes:

```
using Windows.UI.Notifications;
using Windows.Data.Xml.Dom;

XmlDocument wideTileXml = TileUpdateManager.GetTemplateContent(TileTemplateType.TileWideText03);
            XmlDocument squareTileXml =
TileUpdateManager.GetTemplateContent(TileTemplateType.TileSquareText03);

            XmlNodeList wideTileTextAttributes = wideTileXml.GetElementsByTagName("text");
            wideTileTextAttributes[0].InnerText = "Hello Apress!";

            XmlNodeList squareTileTextAttributes = squareTileXml.GetElementsByTagName("text");
            squareTileTextAttributes[0].InnerText = "Line 1";
            squareTileTextAttributes[1].InnerText = "Line 2";
            squareTileTextAttributes[2].InnerText = "Line 3";

IXmlNode node = wideTileXml.ImportNode(squareTileXml.GetElementsByTagName("binding").Item(0), true);
            wideTileXml.GetElementsByTagName("visual").Item(0).AppendChild(node);
            TileNotification tileNotification = new TileNotification(wideTileXml);

            tileNotification.ExpirationTime = DateTimeOffset.UtcNow.AddDays(1);
            TileUpdateManager.CreateTileUpdaterForApplication().Update(tileNotification);
```

Inspect the preceding code a little closely because there are patterns in it that you will repeat many times to send out various types of live tile updates. First, you use the `TileUpdateManager`'s `GetTemplateContent` method to go fetch the named XML template. This returns an `XmlDocument` and the initial placeholder for the given template. Next, your code tries to manipulate the XML DOM (Document Object Model) to insert nodes and node values where required. Next, notice how you fetched both the wide and square templates and merged them? The square tile template is essentially added as a child `<binding>` node to the `<visual>` node. Then, you create the `TileNotification` object and hand it your consolidated XML. You can set additional properties on the `TileNotification` object, like an expiration timestamp. This expiration timestamp tells Windows 8 how long to show the updated tile before reverting back to the default tile. For example, you may want to show the day's news headline as tile data for the given day only. Once everything is set, you use the `TileManager`'s `CreateTileUpdaterForApplication().Update()` method to flush out your updated content. At this point, it is up to Windows 8 to parse the included XML template and update your app tile appropriately.

Do you want to see what the code did? Let's run it for your Apress demo app. Voilà! You should be seeing updates for both square and wide app tiles on the Start screen, as shown in Figures 12-6 and 12-7.

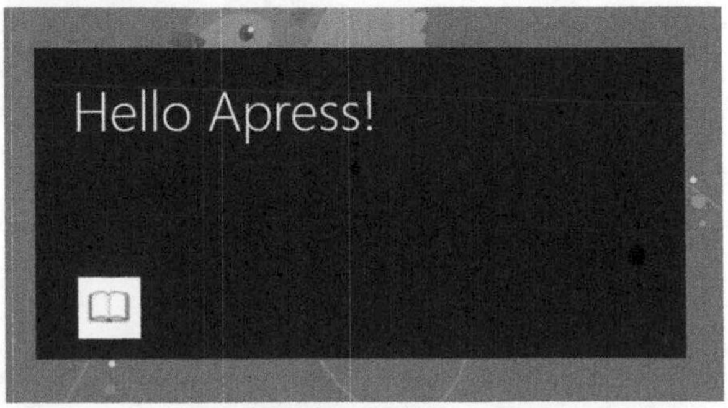

***Figure 12-6.** Wide tile update*

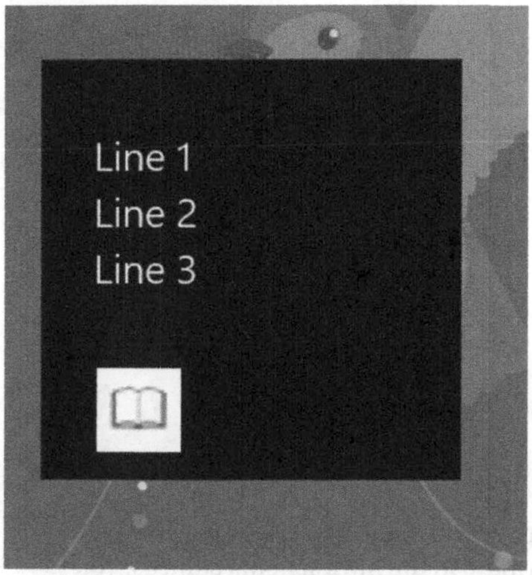

Figure 12-7. *Square tile update*

Did you notice anything interesting? Your square and wide live tiles updated per your XML template, but there is an additional logo on the bottom-left corner. Wonder where this is coming from? That logo is part of the app branding on tile updates and is fetched from your `PackageAppxManifest` configuration. The 30×30-pixel small logo is being displayed.

If you did not want an app logo, but instead wanted to see the app name in the tile's branding area, this is possible too. Simply switch up some configuration in the `PackageAppxManifest` file (see Figure 12-8), and you will see the app name instead, like in the wide tile in Figure 12-9.

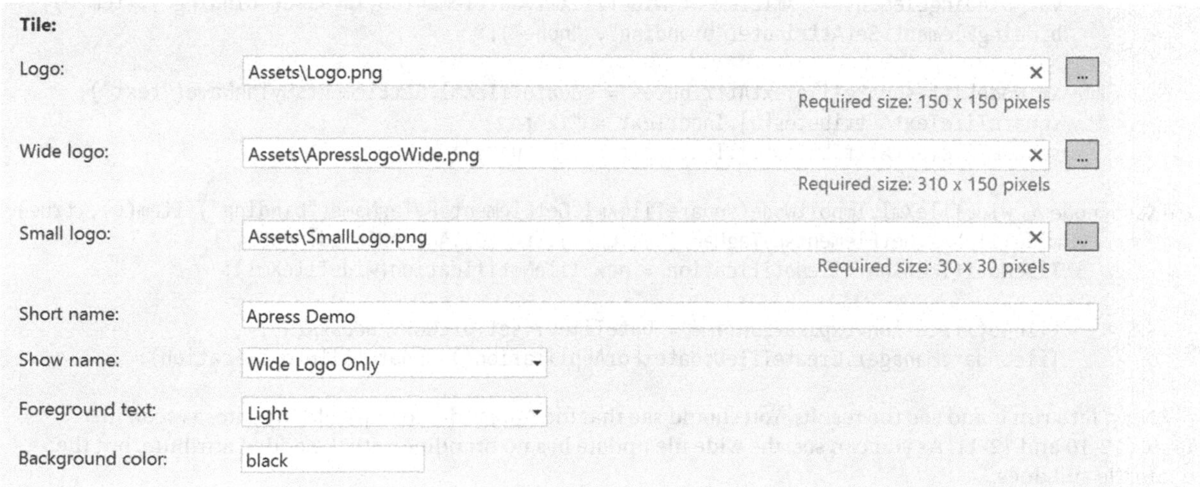

Figure 12-8. *App name configuration*

Figure 12-9. *Wide tile with app name*

Now, what if your tile content had enough branding and you wanted to get rid of the branding area entirely? Sure, you don't have to display the logo or the app name. Turns out, an extra attribute in the XML schema suffices; you simply need to set "branding = none" on the <binding> node. Before you make that code change, however, why not utilize the opportunity to play with another set of square/wide text-based XML templates? Here's some code:

```
XmlDocument wideTileXml = TileUpdateManager.GetTemplateContent(TileTemplateType.TileWideText09);
            XmlDocument squareTileXml =
TileUpdateManager.GetTemplateContent(TileTemplateType.TileSquareBlock);

            XmlNodeList wideTileTextAttributes = wideTileXml.GetElementsByTagName("text");
            wideTileTextAttributes[0].InnerText = "Hello Apress!";
            wideTileTextAttributes[1].InnerText = "This is our first Tile update";

            var bindingElement = (XmlElement)wideTileXml.GetElementsByTagName("binding").Item(0);
            bindingElement.SetAttribute("branding", "none");

            XmlNodeList squareTileTextAttributes = squareTileXml.GetElementsByTagName("text");
            squareTileTextAttributes[0].InnerText = "12";
            squareTileTextAttributes[1].InnerText = "February";

IXmlNode node = wideTileXml.ImportNode(squareTileXml.GetElementsByTagName("binding").Item(0), true);
            wideTileXml.GetElementsByTagName("visual").Item(0).AppendChild(node);
            TileNotification tileNotification = new TileNotification(wideTileXml);

            tileNotification.ExpirationTime = DateTimeOffset.UtcNow.AddDays(1);
            TileUpdateManager.CreateTileUpdaterForApplication().Update(tileNotification);
```

Now, let's run it and see the results. You should see that the Apress demo app's tiles update, as seen in Figures 12-10 and 12-11. As you can see, the wide tile update has no branding with the added attribute, but the square tile still does.

***Figure 12-10.** Wide tile update without branding*

***Figure 12-11.** Square tile update with branding*

Image Tile Templates

Plain text can only be fun for so long. Let's try sending out images as a part of the live tile updates. The process is very similar: you simply grab a template that supports images and fill in the text/image nodes appropriately in the XML template. The rest of tile update code remains the same, but for brevity, it is not shown here. Here's some code:

```
XmlDocument wideTileXml =
TileUpdateManager.GetTemplateContent(TileTemplateType.TileWideImageAndText01);
            XmlDocument squareTileXml =
TileUpdateManager.GetTemplateContent(TileTemplateType.TileSquareImage);

            XmlNodeList wideTileTextAttributes = wideTileXml.GetElementsByTagName("text");
            wideTileTextAttributes[0].InnerText = "Woot - Image + Text!";

            XmlNodeList wideTileImageAttributes = wideTileXml.GetElementsByTagName("image");
            ((XmlElement)wideTileImageAttributes[0]).SetAttribute("src",
"ms-appx:///Assets/ApressBooth.png");
            ((XmlElement)wideTileImageAttributes[0]).SetAttribute("alt", "apress booth");
```

```
            var bindingElement = (XmlElement)wideTileXml.GetElementsByTagName("binding").Item(0);
            bindingElement.SetAttribute("branding", "none");

            XmlNodeList squareTileImageAttributes = squareTileXml.GetElementsByTagName("image");
            ((XmlElement)squareTileImageAttributes[0]).SetAttribute("src",
"ms-appx:///Assets/HappyHolidays.png");
            ((XmlElement)squareTileImageAttributes[0]).SetAttribute("alt", "apress booth");
```

What changed? Of course, you grabbed two new tile XML templates and manipulated the image nodes, in addition to the text ones. Now, as for the image sources, they could come from the app's package, the app's local storage, or the Internet. Do you see the preceding code where you set the "src" attribute of the image node? The "ms-appx:///Assets/ApressBooth.png" indicates to Windows 8 that this is an image out of the Assets folder in the app package. Notice how you also set the image's alternate text for accessibility purposes. Want to use a photo from the app's local storage in file system? No problem, simply add a "ms-appdata:///local/" prefix before the image name. And for web images in the tile template, simply use the HTTP URI as the image node's "src" attribute value. Yes, it's that simple. Do you want to see the preceding code in action? Fire up the Apress demo app one more time. You should see that the tile updates for both square and wide tiles, as seen in Figures 12-12 and 12-13.

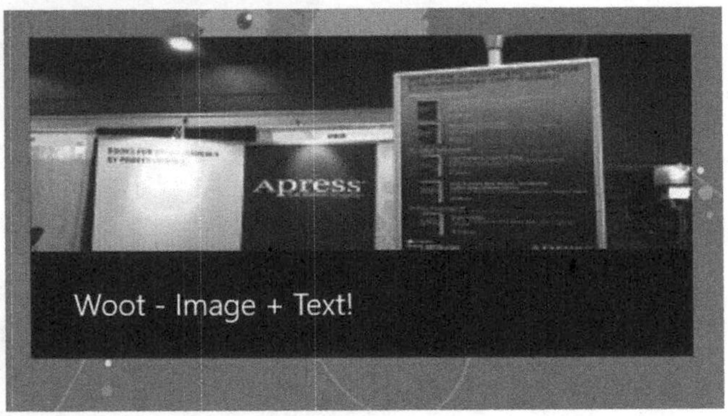

Figure 12-12. *Wide tile with image and text*

Figure 12-13. *Square tile with image*

Peek Tile Templates

In addition to tile templates containing text and images, there is another type of template that truly lights up the Windows 8 Start screen. Yes, the peek templates! These XML tile templates have two faces—usually one with images and one with text. The bling is in the form of a neat peek animation that shows the two faces in cycles, with each face covering the other in a smooth transition. This type of tile template is a huge contributor toward the user's perception of the Windows 8 Start screen feeling alive—tiles do peek animations to show more content. Let's see how such peek tile templates may be added through code:

```
XmlDocument wideTileXml =
TileUpdateManager.GetTemplateContent(TileTemplateType.TileWidePeekImageAndText01);
XmlDocument squareTileXml =
TileUpdateManager.GetTemplateContent(TileTemplateType.TileSquarePeekImageAndText04);

            XmlNodeList wideTileTextAttributes = wideTileXml.GetElementsByTagName("text");
            wideTileTextAttributes[0].InnerText = "Peek-A-Boo - Image + Text!";

            XmlNodeList wideTileImageAttributes = wideTileXml.GetElementsByTagName("image");
 ((XmlElement)wideTileImageAttributes[0]).SetAttribute("src", "ms-appx:///Assets/ApressBooth.png");
 ((XmlElement)wideTileImageAttributes[0]).SetAttribute("alt", "apress booth");

           var wideBindingElement = (XmlElement)wideTileXml.GetElementsByTagName("binding").Item(0);
           wideBindingElement.SetAttribute("branding", "none");

           XmlNodeList squareTileImageAttributes = squareTileXml.GetElementsByTagName("image");
 ((XmlElement)squareTileImageAttributes[0]).SetAttribute("src", "ms-appx:///Assets/HappyHolidays.png");
 ((XmlElement)squareTileImageAttributes[0]).SetAttribute("alt", "apress booth");

            XmlNodeList squareTileTextAttributes = squareTileXml.GetElementsByTagName("text");
            squareTileTextAttributes[0].InnerText = "Square Peeking Text";

            var squareBindingElement = (XmlElement)wideTileXml.GetElementsByTagName("binding").Item(0);
            squareBindingElement.SetAttribute("branding", "none");
```

You can see here that you are simply fetching peek tile templates and filling in image and text nodes; this time around, you turned off branding for both square and wide tiles. The results are shown in Figures 12-14 and 12-15. Static pictures really do not do justice here; run the code in your app to see the peeking animations in action!

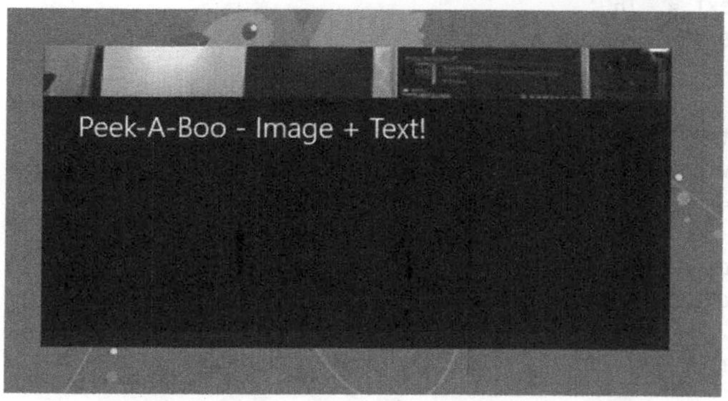

Figure 12-14. *Wide tile with peeking template*

***Figure 12-15.** Square tile with peeking template*

Scheduled Tile Updates

So far, all the examples of local tile updates that you have seen will go ahead and update the app tile immediately. What if you knew exactly the tile content for a future update, but did not want to update the app tile immediately? This can be useful if your app knew something that will happen in the future (like a birthday or calendar meeting, etc.) and your app wanted to schedule a tile update now for a specific time in the future. This is possible through a special API for scheduling tile updates. Here's some code:

```
XmlDocument wideTileXml = TileUpdateManager.GetTemplateContent(TileTemplateType.TileWideText09);
        XmlDocument squareTileXml =
TileUpdateManager.GetTemplateContent(TileTemplateType.TileSquareBlock);

          XmlNodeList wideTileTextAttributes = wideTileXml.GetElementsByTagName("text");
          wideTileTextAttributes[0].InnerText = "Morning!";
          wideTileTextAttributes[1].InnerText = "It's your Birthday!";

          var bindingElement = (XmlElement)wideTileXml.GetElementsByTagName("binding").Item(0);
          bindingElement.SetAttribute("branding", "none");

          XmlNodeList squareTileTextAttributes = squareTileXml.GetElementsByTagName("text");
          squareTileTextAttributes[0].InnerText = "16";
          squareTileTextAttributes[1].InnerText = "February";

         IXmlNode node =
wideTileXml.ImportNode(squareTileXml.GetElementsByTagName("binding").Item(0), true);
          wideTileXml.GetElementsByTagName("visual").Item(0).appendChild(node);
          TileNotification tileNotification = new TileNotification(wideTileXml);

          DateTime dueTime = DateTime.Now.AddSeconds(15);
          ScheduledTileNotification scheduledTile = new ScheduledTileNotification(wideTileXml,
dueTime);
          TileUpdateManager.CreateTileUpdaterForapplication().AddToSchedule(scheduledTile);
```

As you can see in the preceding code, the first parts of creating the XML templates for the tile updates is exactly the same. What changes is the fact that you are using the XML payload and a future date/time to schedule the tile update. The `ScheduledTileNotification` object holds the XML content and the timestamp of when it's due, and then you simply use the `CreateTileUpdaterForApplication().AddToSchedule()` method of the `TileUpdateManager` to add your tile update to a queue that Windows 8 OS maintains. When the due timestamp in the `ScheduledTileNotification` is current, Windows will pop this request from the queue and send out an immediate update to the app tile on the Start screen.

Tile Notification Queue

Windows 8 app tiles are capable of one last awesome trick to add to their liveliness and always-connected feel. So far, you have changed the app tile one update at a time. By default, local tile notifications do not expire until the next update arrives. Push, periodic, and scheduled notifications expire after three days, unless there is a specific expiry timestamp. But once a tile expires or is replaced by a new one, that particular app tile update is lost forever. Now, what if the last few updates to an app tile were important and relevant—even if there was a new app tile update? For example, a Windows 8 news app could send out multiple tile updates throughout the day about news headlines, and they are all relevant; in this case, the newest tile entirely replacing the old one isn't so great.

This is where Windows 8 has a unique solution to preserve app tile updates. Windows can maintain a notification queue of app tile updates and remember five of the last updates to cycle between them. When an app enables cycling on its tile updates, the system will automatically rotate through up to five current notifications on the tile. How does this rotation between tile updates work? Yes, with the same peek animations you saw earlier in the chapter. The overall impact of this notification queuing can be quite dramatic: up to five of the last tile updates can be cycled through one at a time. No wonder the Windows 8 Start screen feels alive to the user. Now, let's look at a little code:

```
XmlDocument wideTileXml = TileUpdateManager.GetTemplateContent(TileTemplateType.TileWideText09);
            XmlDocument squareTileXml =
TileUpdateManager.GetTemplateContent(TileTemplateType.TileSquareBlock);

            XmlNodeList wideTileTextAttributes = wideTileXml.GetElementsByTagName("text");
            wideTileTextAttributes[0].InnerText = "Good Morning!";
            wideTileTextAttributes[1].InnerText = "This is our first Tile update";

            var bindingElement = (XmlElement)wideTileXml.GetElementsByTagName("binding").Item(0);
            bindingElement.SetAttribute("branding", "none");

            XmlNodeList squareTileTextAttributes = squareTileXml.GetElementsByTagName("text");
            squareTileTextAttributes[0].InnerText = "12";
            squareTileTextAttributes[1].InnerText = "February";

IXmlNode node = wideTileXml.ImportNode(squareTileXml.GetElementsByTagName("binding").Item(0), true);
            wideTileXml.GetElementsByTagName("visual").Item(0).AppendChild(node);
            TileNotification tileNotification = new TileNotification(wideTileXml);
            tileNotification.Tag = "MorningWideTileUpdate";

TileUpdateManager.CreateTileUpdaterForApplication().EnableNotificationQueue(true);
            tileNotification.ExpirationTime = DateTimeOffset.UtcNow.AddDays(1);
            TileUpdateManager.CreateTileUpdaterForApplication().Update(tileNotification);
```

The creation of the square/wide tile updates is really no different. What's unique is the `EnableNotificationQueue(true)` API call on the `TileUpdateManager` object. This is what tells Windows 8 to start a notification queue and save the present update for cycling later on. This API call starts the notification queue, but it will not hurt if your app invokes this call every time a new tile update is being pushed out.

Now, there is one other thing to note: the notification queue is not infinite and can hold up to five of the last tile updates. This means that when the sixth tile update arrives, something would have to be popped off the queue and forgotten. The technique used here is FIFO (First In, First Out). This means that as the sixth tile update arrives, the very first one—the oldest—gets popped and replaced. This works most of the time, except when the developer may need more fine-grained control over the notification queue.

Envision this: you are writing a stock market app for Windows 8. The user is interested in five different stocks and you decide to enable tile update cycling for individual tiles, which each have information on a stock. The next time you have a stock update you send out as a tile, you do not want the very first stock update tile to be popped off the notification queue; what you really want is to only replace the tile for the stock that you have an update for. So, now you are talking handpicking tile updates to replace.

This, dear developer, is also possible. While a tile update is being pushed out, you can put some identifying information on the tile update by adding a custom `Tag`. Do you see the `tileNotification.Tag = "MorningWideTileUpdate"` in the preceding code? That is exactly what's being done. Now, on a subsequent tile update, if another update has the same tag information (the same stock name/number in your case), the matching older tile update will be replaced by the new update, regardless of the position of the update in the notification queue. Nifty, isn't it?

One last thing. What if you wanted to clear all tile updates and get back to the default app tile in one swoop? Sure, you ask and Windows delivers; simply add this one line of code:

```
TileUpdateManager.CreateTileUpdaterForApplication().Clear();
```

Secondary Tiles

All Windows 8 apps will have a primary app tile on the Start screen. This is the tile that you have been updating so far through local notifications. However, envision a weather app in which the user might actually want to follow multiple cities. Is it not possible to have multiple tiles on the Start screen? What if you had a news app and a certain user was really interested in the sports section? He or she should be able to customize the user experience by adding a tile to the Start screen that takes him or her directly to the sports section. Is this possible?

Absolutely. The technique of having separate sections of your app be pinnable to the Start screen is something that started with Windows Phone and is now a unique selling point of Windows 8 apps. If a user would benefit from diving directly to a certain section of your app, as the developer, you should absolutely offer the functionality to pin a separate tile on the Start screen. This is called the *secondary tile*. Secondary tiles are always associated with a single parent app. They are pinned to the Start screen to provide a user with a consistent and efficient way to launch directly into a frequently used area of the parent app. There is one caveat to keep in mind as your app offers pinning of secondary tiles: the action to add tiles on the Start screen can only be initiated by the user; you cannot do this programmatically.

Let's get back to your Apress demo app to see how you can make secondary tiles work. If you remember, you have a XAML page that shows the details about individual Apress books. This sounds like something that the user might want to pin to the Start screen. Do you like a particular book and want to get back to it directly the next time you are in the app? Yes, that is exactly what a secondary tile would achieve. Let's look at this scenario in a little more detail and see how you can enable the pinning of secondary tiles to the Start screen. Figure 12-16 shows the BookDetails page, now with a Pin To Start app bar icon.

Figure 12-16. *Page with Pin To Start icon*

The little bit of XAML markup that allows us to add the app bar icon is as follows:

```
<Page.BottomAppBar>
        <AppBar x:Name="bottomAppBar" Padding="10,0,10,0">
            <Grid>
                <StackPanel Orientation="Horizontal" HorizontalAlignment="Right">
                    <Button Style="{StaticResource PinAppBarButtonStyle}" x:Name="pinButton"
Click="pinButton_Click"/>
                </StackPanel>
            </Grid>
        </AppBar>
    </Page.BottomAppBar>
```

If the user is browsing through Apress books and wants to pin a secondary tile to the Start screen, here is what you would do to enable the action when the user hits the app bar icon:

```
private async void pinButton_Click(object sender, RoutedEventArgs e)
        {
            if (this.flipView.SelectedItem != null)
            {
                ApressBook selectedBook = (ApressBook)this.flipView.SelectedItem;

                this.BottomAppBar.IsSticky = true;
```

```
            string uniqueTileID = selectedBook.ApressBookISBN;
            string shortTileName = selectedBook.ApressBookName;
            string displayTileName = selectedBook.ApressBookTechnology;
            string tileActivationArguments = uniqueTileID;
            Uri logo = new Uri("ms-appx://" + selectedBook.ApressBookImageURI);

            SecondaryTile secondaryTile = new SecondaryTile(uniqueTileID, shortTileName,
displayTileName, tileActivationArguments, TileOptions.ShowNameOnLogo, logo);
            secondaryTile.ForegroundText = ForegroundText.Light;
            secondaryTile.SmallLogo = new Uri("ms-appx:///Assets/SmallLogo.png");

            FrameworkElement pinToStartButton = (FrameworkElement)pinButton;
            Windows.UI.Xaml.Media.GeneralTransform buttonTransform =
pinToStartButton.TransformToVisual(null);
            Windows.Foundation.Point point = buttonTransform.TransformPoint(new Point());
            Windows.Foundation.Rect rect = new Rect(point, new Size(pinToStartButton.
ActualWidth, pinToStartButton.ActualHeight));

            bool isPinned = await secondaryTile.RequestCreateForSelectionAsync(rect,
Windows.UI.Popups.Placement.Above);
            this.BottomAppBar.IsSticky = false;
        }
    }
```

Several things happened in the preceding code; let's break it down. First, to pin a secondary tile about a book on the Start screen, you need to make sure you have information about the book the user is looking at. If you remember, you used a `FlipView` control to allow the user to easily sift through books one at a time. So, your first job is to make sure that you have an `ApressBook` object from the `FlipView`'s currently selected item. Next, you start building up the `SecondaryTile` object that you will use to pin a secondary tile on the Start screen. Notice how you use the selected book's properties to build up your `SecondaryTile`. But, before you can pin a secondary tile, it is customary to confirm with the user that his action will end up creating an additional tile on the Start screen.

Accordingly, you figure out the location of the app bar icon on the screen and provide a little confirmation dialog that reassures the user about what is about to happen. You invoke `SecondaryTile.RequestCreateForSelectionAsync()` and pass in a rectangle with coordinates where this confirmation flyout needs to be shown. Windows takes care of the rest. Figure 12-17 shows how the user sees a confirmation dialog; notice that Windows throws in a preview of a secondary tile about to be created.

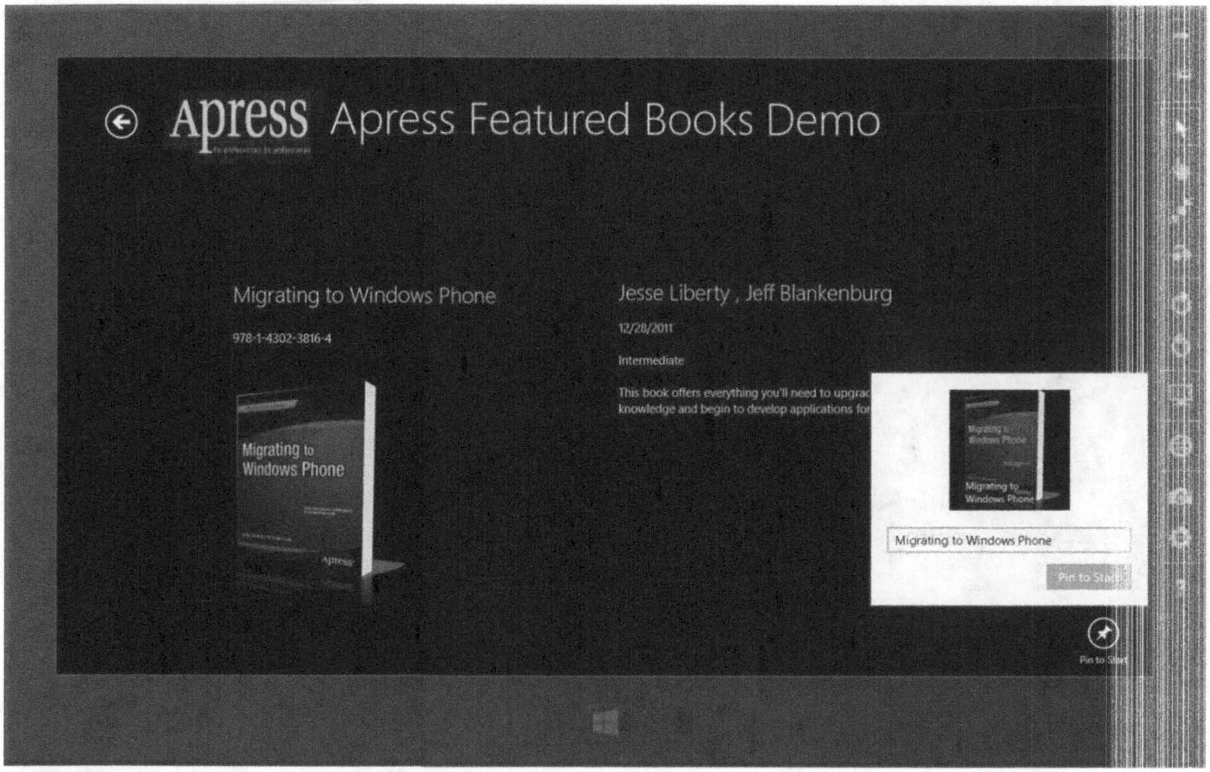

Figure 12-17. Secondary tile confirmation flyout

Did you notice the code where you made the bottom app bar sticky? This makes sure the app bar is not going to disappear if the user taps outside of it on the screen. Once he chooses to pin the secondary tile on the Start screen, you revert the stickiness of the app bar. Figure 12-18 shows how the pinned secondary tile looks on my Start screen. Remember, this is completely customizable to fit the needs of your app. Also, notice how the secondary tile can be unpinned from the Start screen, just like any other app tile.

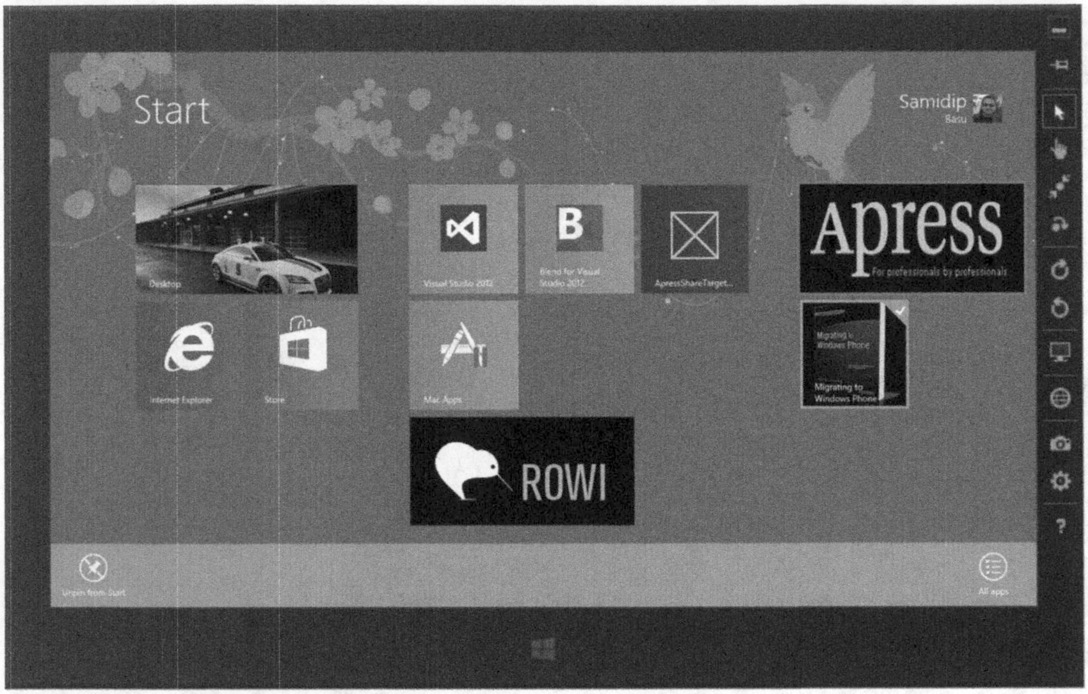

Figure 12-18. *Pinned secondary tile*

Now, please be aware that what you did here is only half the story around pinning a secondary tile to the Start screen. Ideally, your app should be aware of which secondary tiles are already pinned to the Start screen and toggle the Pin To Start button to Unpin From Start so that the user may unpin something from inside the app itself. Please see MSDN documentation at `http://msdn.microsoft.com/en-us/library/windows/apps/xaml/Hh868249(v=win.10).aspx` for details on pinning and unpinning secondary tiles.

Obviously when the user taps/clicks a secondary tile, like the specific book tile in your case, it would be a bad user experience to take the user to the generic app launch dashboard. There is a reason why the user pinned a secondary tile on the Start screen and gave your app precious real estate: the need to get back to something quickly. Developers need to honor that loyalty and provide the best user experience by taking the user to the specific part of the app that he or she desires. So, let's see how you can accomplish that.

First, you need a way to distinguish that the user tapped/clicked a secondary tile versus the primary app tile. This will help navigate the user to a different app launch experience; but you would still need to know which specific book was pinned. Sounds like some parameters need to be passed in on app launch so that you can identify where the user is coming from. That's exactly how Windows 8 wants you to do it. Notice the `tileActivationArguments` that you used to set up your secondary tile in the preceding code. That is a unique Apress book ISBN number that would help you figure out the fact that the user tapped on a secondary tile and which exact book he had pinned. This tile activation argument needs to be unique for every secondary tile, and will get passed back into the app as the user launches the app from the secondary tile.

Remember the `App.xaml.cs` had an `OnLaunched()` event handler where you wrote some of the first lines of code executed as your Windows 8 app launches. Once the user launches the app from the secondary tile, the `Onlaunched()` event handler will still be hit; but now you can inspect the `LaunchActivatedEventArgs` incoming parameters. The unique identifier of every secondary tile gets passed in back to the app inside `LaunchActivatedEventArgs`. So, the logic inside your app would be to inspect for any incoming parameters and accordingly take the user to the `BookDetails` page and load the book with a unique identifier; or if there is no parameter, launch the app normally. Make sense? Enable your app to support the pinning of secondary tiles wherever appropriate, and you will have a lot more intimacy with the user building loyalty with sections of your Windows 8 app.

Secondary Tile Updates

What is better than a secondary app tile? Why, of course, live secondary tiles. Every secondary tile that the user pins to the Start screen is uniquely identifiable through a tile ID; this was the `uniqueTileID` in your last example. This unique tile ID is assigned by the developer while creating the secondary tile; so the onus is on the developer to make sure this is unique.

If a secondary tile can be uniquely identified, there is no reason why it cannot be uniquely updateable. And all the techniques you learned about updating tiles holds true, except for the slightly different API call you make to update the actual secondary tile. You can push out updates for square/wide tiles and include any combination of text and images, as allowed by the tile template catalog. Here's some code:

```
private void UpdateSecondaryTile()
        {
            XmlDocument squareTileXml =
TileUpdateManager.GetTemplateContent(TileTemplateType.TileSquareBlock);

            XmlNodeList squareTileTextAttributes = squareTileXml.GetElementsByTagName("text");
            squareTileTextAttributes[0].InnerText = "14";
            squareTileTextAttributes[1].InnerText = "February";

            TileNotification tileNotification = new TileNotification(squareTileXml);
            tileNotification.ExpirationTime = DateTimeOffset.UtcNow.AddDays(1);
            TileUpdater secondaryTileUpdater =
TileUpdateManager.CreateTileUpdaterForSecondaryTile("978-1-4302-3816-4");
            secondaryTileUpdater.Update(tileNotification);
        }
```

As you can see, building up the tile is exactly the same as updating the main app tile. However, you use the `CreateTileUpdaterForSecondaryTile()` method off the `TileUpdateManager` to update a secondary tile. The parameter passed into the method is important: it is the same unique identifier that you use to distinguish one secondary tile from another. In this example, I'm simply hard-coding the ISBN of an Apress book that was pinned as a secondary tile on the Start screen. The result: the secondary tile gets updated just like the app tile, as seen in Figure 12-19.

***Figure 12-19.** Secondary tile updates*

Badges

In addition to all the information that tile templates can convey, Windows 8 supports another notification mechanism called badges. They appear on top of the live tiles and may often be confused as a part of the tile itself. Badges, however, stand on their own with matching templates and can be updated independent of the app tile. A *badge* is a form of notifications that conveys summary or status information concerning your Windows 8 Store app. Badges usually show up in the bottom-right corner of the tiles and are often the reason users tap/click a tile.

A badge can convey either a numeric value from 1 to 99 or a Windows-defined glyph. The numbers are often used to provide information that can be counted, such as the number of new e-mails. The glyphs are nonextensible and provide summary information like social media availability or media playback controls. Let's see badges in action through some sample code in your Apress demo app. Let's say that you are trying to convey the number of new books added to the Apress library, without the user having to open the app. A numeric badge seems appropriate on the app tile. Here's how:

```
private void UpdateBadge()
        {
            XmlDocument badgeXml = BadgeUpdateManager.GetTemplateContent(BadgeTemplateType.BadgeNumber);

            XmlElement badgeElement = (XmlElement)badgeXml.SelectSingleNode("/badge");
            badgeElement.SetAttribute("value", "99");

            BadgeNotification badgeUpdate = new BadgeNotification(badgeXml);
            BadgeUpdateManager.CreateBadgeUpdaterForapplication().Update(badgeUpdate);
        }
```

Let's run your app and see the effect on the app tile, as shown in Figure 12-20. As you can see, the technique used to update a badge is quite similar to updating a tile: fetch the template, manipulate XML DOM, and use an appropriate updater to push out content. The only difference is the use of the `CreateBadgeUpdaterForApplication().Update()` off the `BadgeUpdateManager` to push out badge updates.

***Figure 12-20.** Wide tile with numbered badge*

How about a badge with a glyph? This would be very similar, like so:

```
private void UpdateBadge()
        {
            XmlDocument badgeXml = BadgeUpdateManager.GetTemplateContent(BadgeTemplateType.BadgeGlyph);

            XmlElement badgeElement = (XmlElement)badgeXml.SelectSingleNode("/badge");
            badgeElement.SetAttribute("value", "attention");

            BadgeNotification badgeUpdate = new BadgeNotification(badgeXml);
            BadgeUpdateManager.CreateBadgeUpdaterForapplication().Update(badgeUpdate);
        }
```

And the result on the next app run is shown in Figure 12-21.

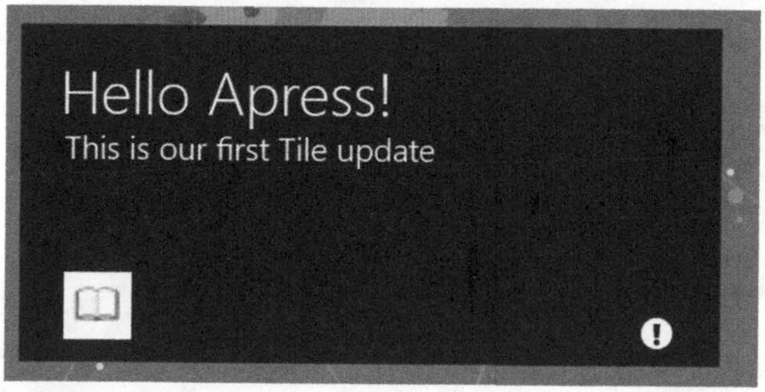

Figure 12-21. *Wide tile with glyph badge*

As expected, your badge changes to a glyph. The badge value was set to "attention" and you must be wondering what else you could use. Figure 12-22 shows the complete list of all possible Windows glyphs—along with their template values—that you can use in your badges.

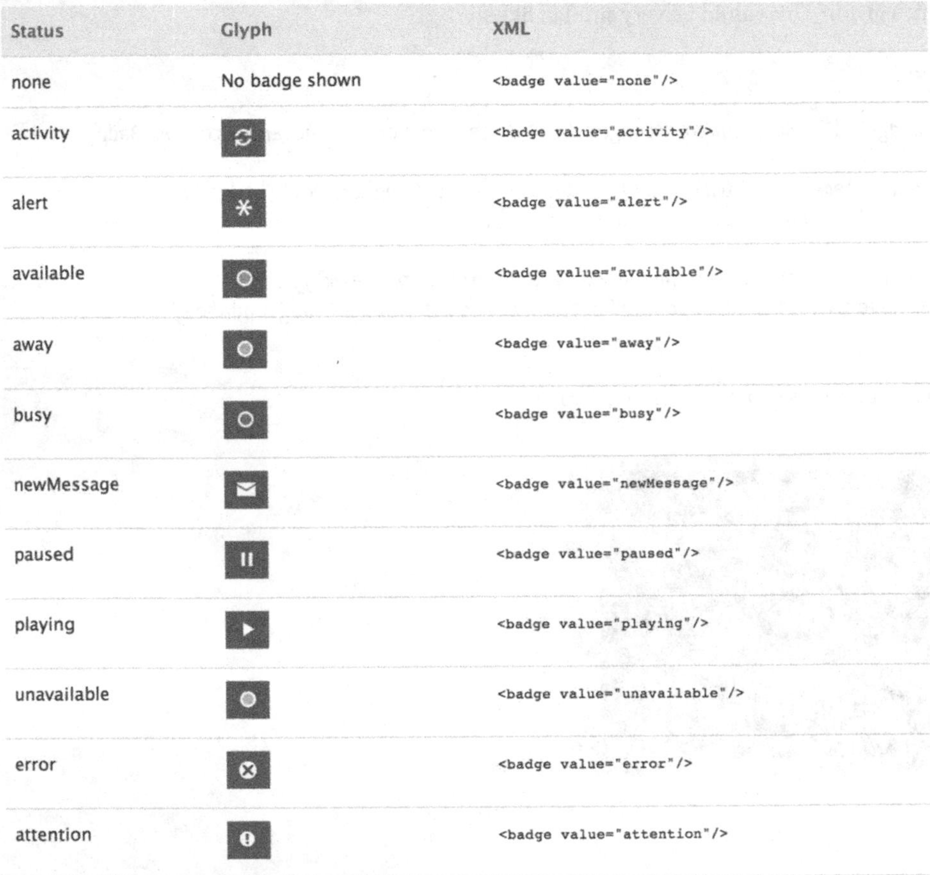

Status	Glyph	XML
none	No badge shown	<badge value="none"/>
activity		<badge value="activity"/>
alert		<badge value="alert"/>
available		<badge value="available"/>
away		<badge value="away"/>
busy		<badge value="busy"/>
newMessage		<badge value="newMessage"/>
paused		<badge value="paused"/>
playing		<badge value="playing"/>
unavailable		<badge value="unavailable"/>
error		<badge value="error"/>
attention		<badge value="attention"/>

Figure 12-22. *Badge glyph assortment*

Toasts

Just like tiles or badges, Windows 8 supports another convenient notification mechanism called toasts. A *toast notification* is a transient message that contains relevant, time-sensitive information for the user. It provides quick access to related content in the parent app. Unlike tiles or badges, which only show up in the user's Start screen, a toast notification shows up in the top-right corner (it could be the left, based on globalization settings) of the user's screen, and disappears after a few seconds. The user could be on the Windows 8 Start screen , or even in the desktop world in Windows 8. A transient toast notification always shows up regardless of what the user is up to. You can immediately see the power of such notifications; but with power comes responsibility.

Because toast notifications can show up anytime/anywhere, it is common practice to ask users to receive toasts from your app. Also, the user is in control and may turn off toast notifications (like during a presentation to prevent distractions); accordingly, toasts notifications should not be depended on for critical app functionality because the user may not always see a toast. Toast notifications, when turned on, should be used only for information of high interest to the user, something that might demand immediate action, and if the user taps/clicks a toast, he or she needs to be taken to the relevant part of the app that generated the toast in the first place.

Toast Anatomy

Wondering about the anatomy of a toast notification? Well, it is very similar to tiles, and simple Windows-defined XML templates control the toasts. A toast can be made up of any given combination of texts and/or images as allowed by the templates. Additionally, a toast can also play a system-defined sound when it displays. Figure 12-23 is a screen grab from MSDN that shows the anatomy of a sample toast notification.

ToastImageAndText01

An image and a single string wrapped across a maximum of three lines of text.

Example

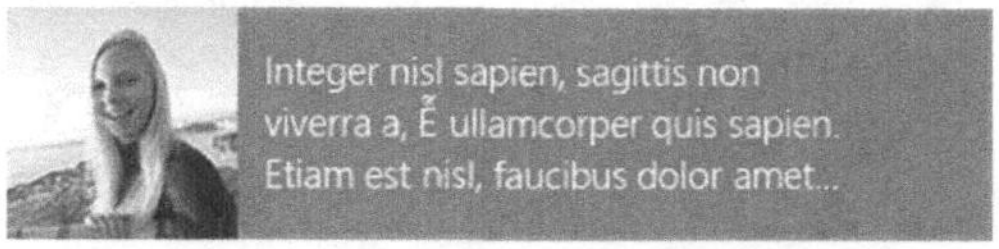

Integer nisl sapien, sagittis non
viverra a, Ě ullamcorper quis sapien.
Etiam est nisl, faucibus dolor amet...

Example XML

```
<toast>
    <visual>
        <binding template="ToastImageAndText01">
            <image id="1" src="image1" alt="image1"/>
            <text id="1">bodyText</text>
        </binding>
    </visual>
</toast>
```

Figure 12-23. *Anatomy of a toast*

Wondering what other combinations you can use for toasts? The MSDN toast template catalog has you covered, with details of every toast template and its accompanying XML. Find it at `http://msdn.microsoft.com/en-us/library/windows/apps/hh761494.aspx` and pick what you need for your Windows 8 Store app. Figure 12-24 shows a smattering of possible toast combinations.

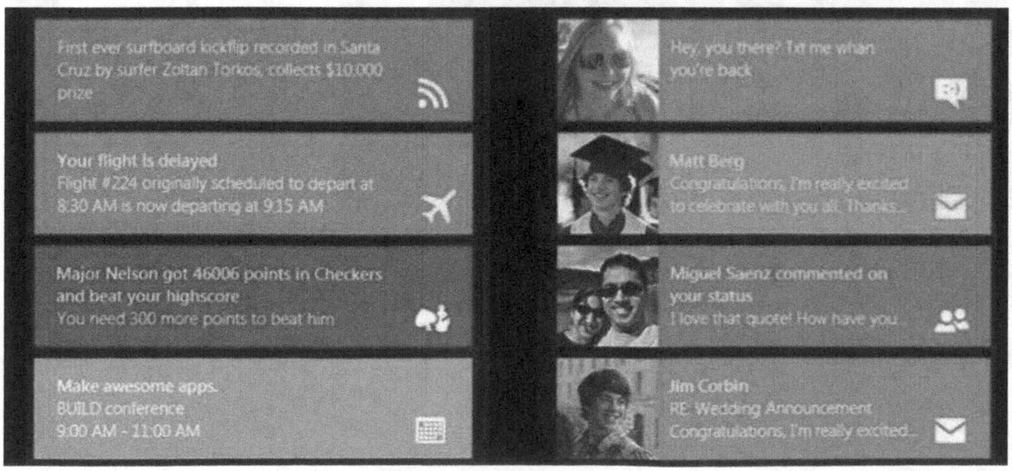

Figure 12-24. *Toast template assortment*

Now, before you start writing any code to support toasts, there is one important configuration setting. Every Windows 8 Store app needs to have explicit opt-in support before toasts can be delivered on its behalf. Pop open the `PackageAppxmanifest` file and make sure the toast capability drop-down is enabled (see Figure 12-25). Also, the user, at his or her discretion, can turn off notifications any time from the app's settings. Simply go into Charms ➤ Settings ➤ Permissions, and you will see the Notifications permission toggle (see Figure 12-26).

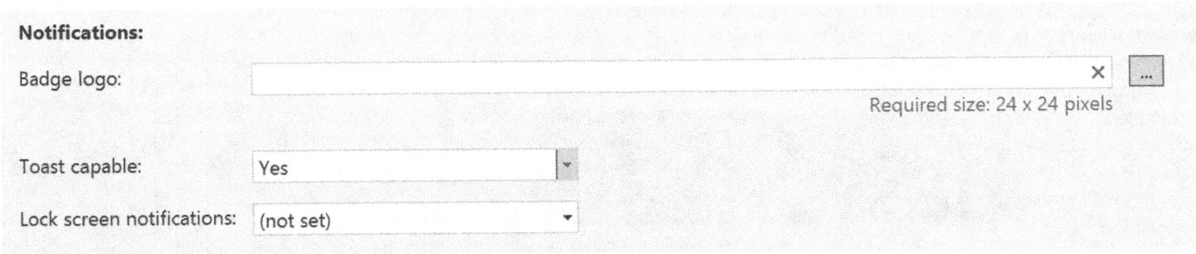

Figure 12-25. Toast capability

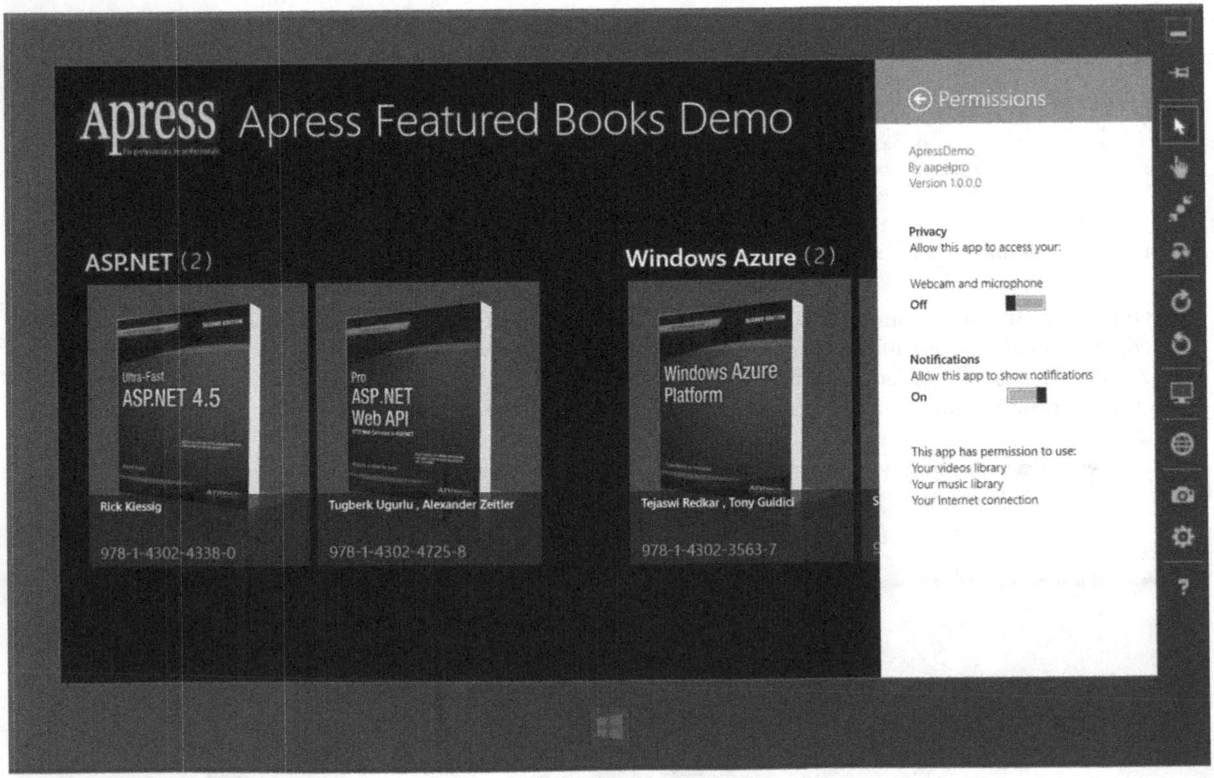

Figure 12-26. Notification permission

Toasts in Action

Now, with the caveats out of the way, do you want to see toasts in action? Let's write some code:

```
private void SendToasts()
        {
            XmlDocument toastXml =
ToastNotificationManager.GetTemplateContent(ToastTemplateType.ToastImageAndText01);

            XmlNodeList toastTextElement = toastXml.GetElementsByTagName("text");
            toastTextElement[0].AppendChild(toastXml.CreateTextNode("First Toast: Happy Holidays
from Apress!"));

            XmlNodeList toastImageAttribute = toastXml.GetElementsByTagName("image");
            ((XmlElement)toastImageAttribute[0]).SetAttribute("src",
"ms-appx:///Assets/HappyHolidays.png");
            ((XmlElement)toastImageAttribute[0]).SetAttribute("alt", "apress booth");

            IXmlNode toastNode = toastXml.SelectSingleNode("/toast");
            ((XmlElement)toastNode).SetAttribute("duration", "long");

            ((XmlElement)toastNode).SetAttribute("launch",
"{\"type\":\"toast\",\"BookISBN\":\"978-1-4302-3816-4\"}");

            ToastNotification toast = new ToastNotification(toastXml);
            ToastNotificationManager.CreateToastNotifier().Show(toast);
        }
```

A lot of this code should look familiar to what you did for tile updates. First, you use the `ToastNotificationManager` to grab the selected toast template, and then manipulate the XML DOM to format the toast the way you like. The rules for adding images remain the same; in this case, you are using an image from the app package using the `"ms-appx:///Assets/"` syntax. Two things are new to toasts, though: toast duration and `launch` attributes. Toasts come in two forms in terms of transience: *standard toasts* that stay on screen for 7 seconds and *long-duration toasts* that stay on screen for 25 seconds. Most toasts should normally use the standard format, except when a human may be waiting on another end, which dictates use of the long-duration format to attract more attention from the user. As you can see in the preceding code, you are using the long-duration toasts by setting the `"duration"` attribute.

Also, if the user does tap/click a toast notification, it is only polite to tend to the user's loyalty and not just launch your app normally; instead, you should take the user to the specific part of the app that piqued his attention. This is a similar scenario to what you encountered while handling secondary tile launches, and the solution is the same: have the toast pass in some parameters back into the app. These custom parameters are called toast `launch` attributes and are set as the `"launch"` attributes in the toast XML node. You can see in the preceding code how the toast launch attribute is set to the specific Apress book ISBN number that may have caused the toast message in the first place; this is, of course, for demo purposes. Now, enough talk—let's fire up your Apress demo app and see the toast pop up on the top corner of the screen, as seen in Figure 12-27.

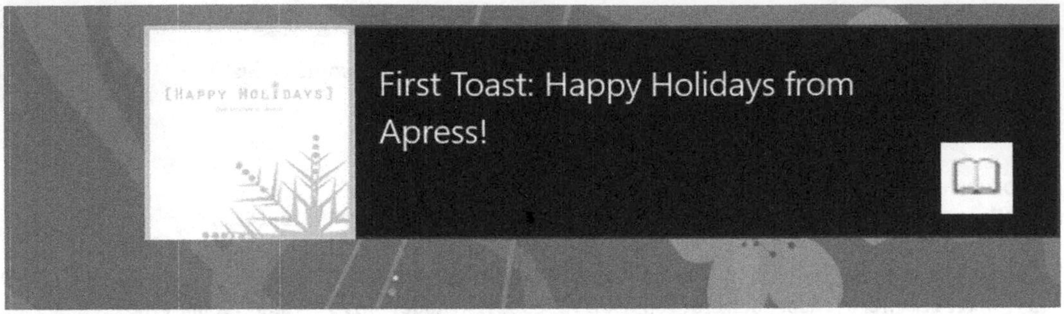

Figure 12-27. *Toast notification*

Lock Screen Apps

Just like most aspects of Windows 8, the OS lock screen is well thought-out and can have app interaction. Unlike bulky desktops/laptops, Windows 8 will now be used in superbly thin form factors like tablets or convertibles, and people do not need to sit down to use a PC anymore. So, it only makes sense that the Windows 8 lock screen also supports a mobile lifestyle—no need to unlock the device and run apps; one glance at the lock screen should provide the user with enough summary information to keep him or her posted as to what's going on inside the apps the user cares about. Imagine the possibilities: a lock screen glance would tell you if you have new e-mails or social media interactions, or what the weather is like outside. This potentially often dictates whether the user even wants to unlock his or her device; the lock screen may just be sufficient.

So, it is pretty clear that summary information on the lock screen is very useful. But how are you going to enable such summary information to bubble all the way up to the user's lock screen? Do you need a new type of app or notification? Thankfully, not; the simple tile/badge/toast notifications you have seen so far should suffice as lock screen information if you set up your app correctly.

There are three types of information from an app that can show up on the lock screen:

- Toasts normally show up in a top corner
- The app's current badge update (with numbers) shows up under the date/time
- The text part of the app's most recent tile update shows up next to the date/time

Up to seven Windows 8 Store apps can be set up to have a lock screen presence. Every one of such lock screen apps can show its latest badge and toast, but only one of those apps gets to show more details. This privileged app is also allowed to show the text of its latest tile notification.

Lock Screen App Configuration

So, let's see how you can make your Apress demo app support the lock screen—in short, make it lock-screen capable. Turns out, this is achieved through simple configuration changes. Pop open the `PackageAppxManifest` file and make sure your settings resemble what's in Figure 12-28.

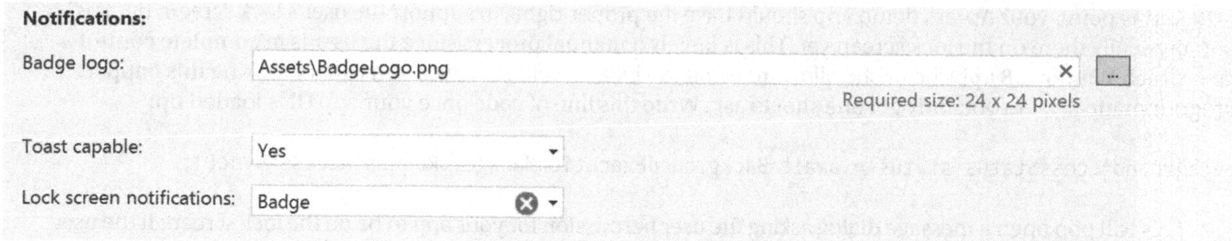

Figure 12-28. *Lock screen badge configuration*

As you can see, you are assigning a new badge logo of 24×24-pixel size. This is not to be confused with the actual app badge or the small logo used for branding. This is simply another opportunity to stamp your app's brand on the user's lock screen. You may choose to simply use a smaller version of your small logo here. Next, for the lock screen notifications, you are choosing to display only the badge. But what's going on with the red error symbol? Is some configuration incorrect?

This error is simply Windows 8 trying to help you out in setting up support for your Windows 8 app. If your app is signing up to be present on the lock screen, chances are that the app may not run for a long time, but yet be capable of pushing your tile/badge/toast updates. This can only be achieved through the use of background tasks running on defined system triggers, or external push notifications providing updates. Accordingly, hop over to the `PackageAppxManifest` Declarations tab and make sure you have a background task set up correctly (see Figure 12-29). You do not need to have a fully working background process to test lock screen apps; only the configuration needs to be there and the hope that your Windows 8 lock screen app will sometimes need to fall back to background processing.

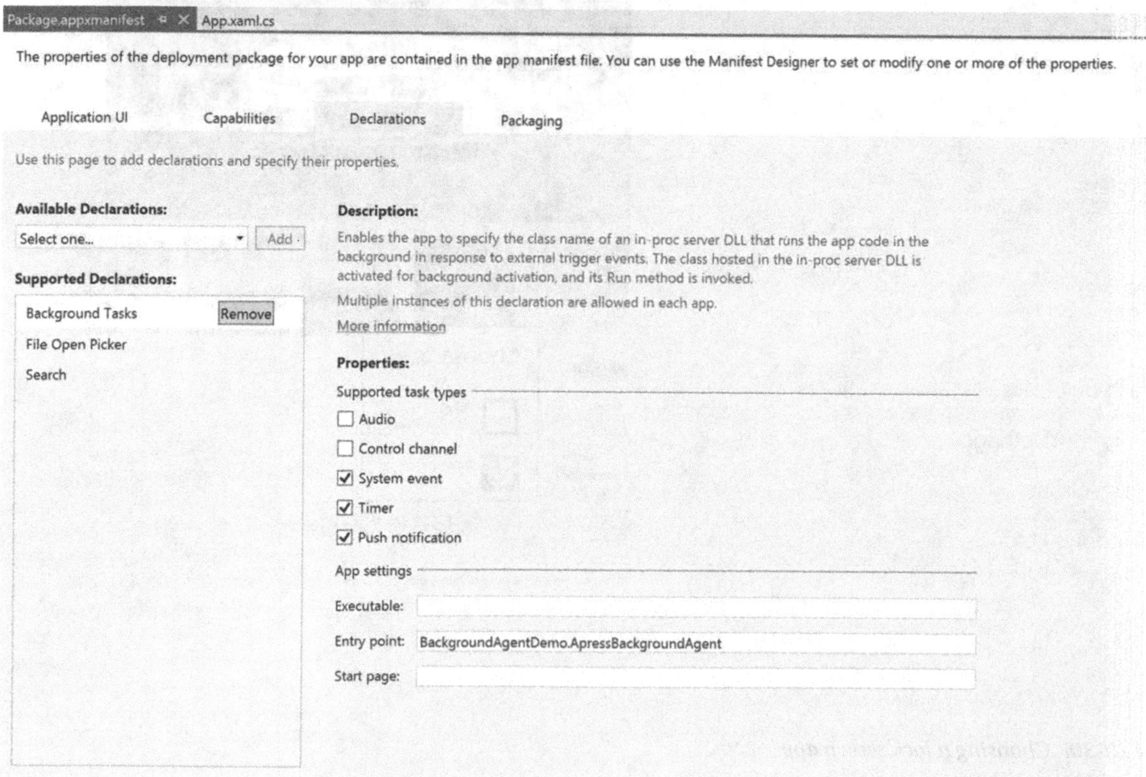

Figure 12-29. *Background task configuration*

At this point, your Apress demo app should have the proper rights to support the user's lock screen; but it is not physically there on the lock screen yet. This is largely a manual process since the user is in complete control over which Windows 8 apps he or she allows to be on the lock screen. However, you can try making this happen programmatically, but you only get one shot to ask. Write this line of code once your app UI is loaded up:

```
BackgroundAccessStatus status = await BackgroundExecutionManager.RequestAccessAsync();
```

This will pop open a message dialog asking the user permission for your app to be on the lock screen. If the user says yes, you're golden and your app is all set. If no, you will not have another opportunity to ask. Future invocations of the preceding code will simply be ignored in order to protect the user from zealous developers asking too many times.

So, how does the user choose which apps get to be on the lock screen? Tap the Windows account picture in the top corner of the Windows 8 Start screen and get into the Lock Screen section of PC Settings (see Figure 12-30). Do you see the placeholders for up to seven of the lock screen apps? If you have not chosen all seven yet, you can press the little "+" symbols or tap/click any of the existing ones to change the apps. The goal is to add a new one, as you are about to do for the Apress demo app. Once done, the app logo shows as a lock screen app, like in Figure 12-31.

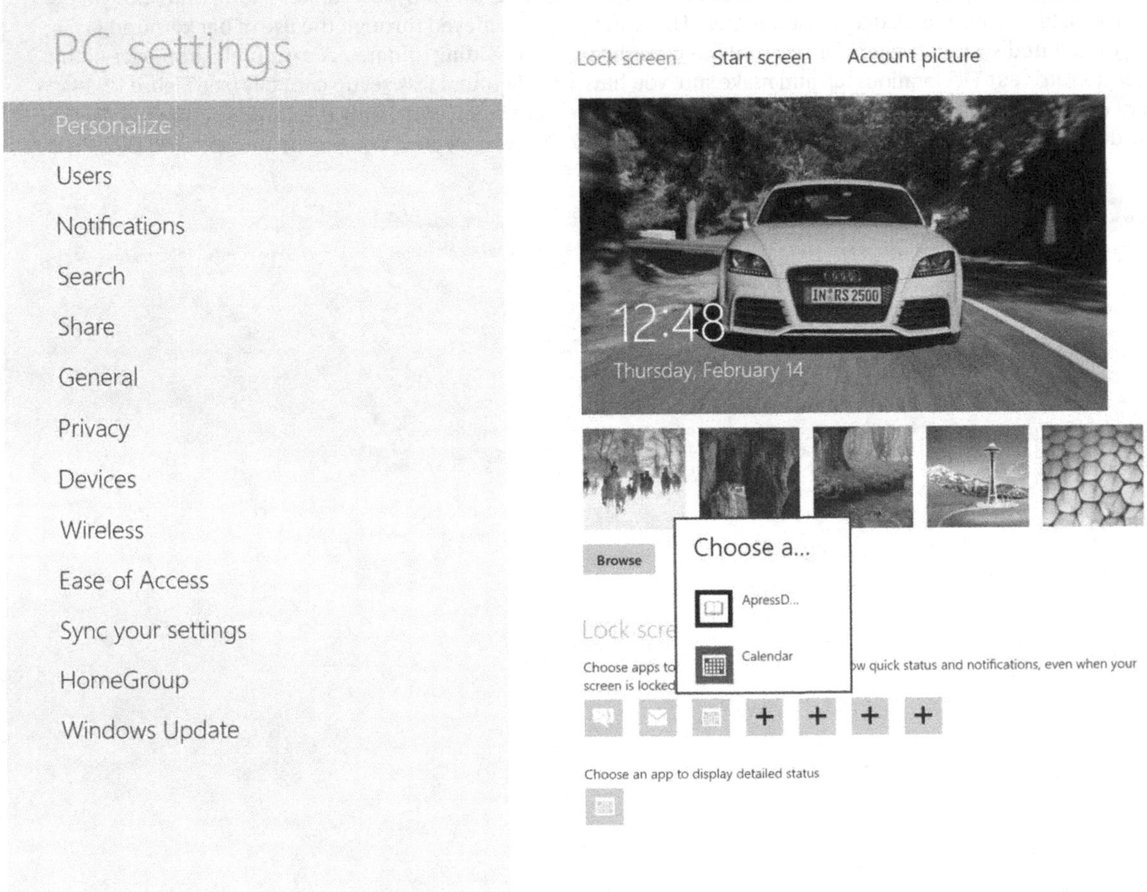

Figure 12-30. *Choosing a lock screen app*

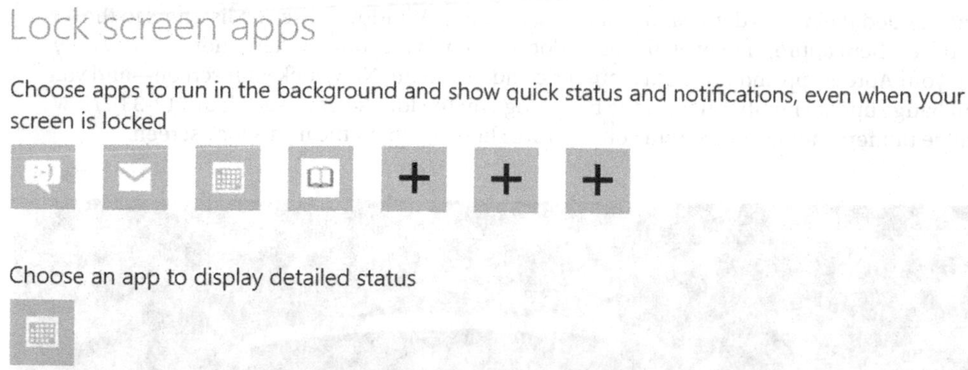

Lock screen apps
Choose apps to run in the background and show quick status and notifications, even when your screen is locked
Choose an app to display detailed status

Figure 12-31. Chosen lock screen apps

Your app is now among the privileged seven Windows 8 Store apps that are allowed to run under the lock screen. You have the user's attention—now go ahead and impress. Do not get too complacent though, since lock screen rights are entirely controlled by the user and he or she can change permissions any time. Care to see what the lock screen benefits do to your app permissions? Swipe to bring up the charms bar and navigate to app settings to expose the lock screen permissions (see Figure 12-32). As you can see, it is a flimsy toggle switch. Do everything so that the user sticks to his or her decision to have your app as a lock screen app.

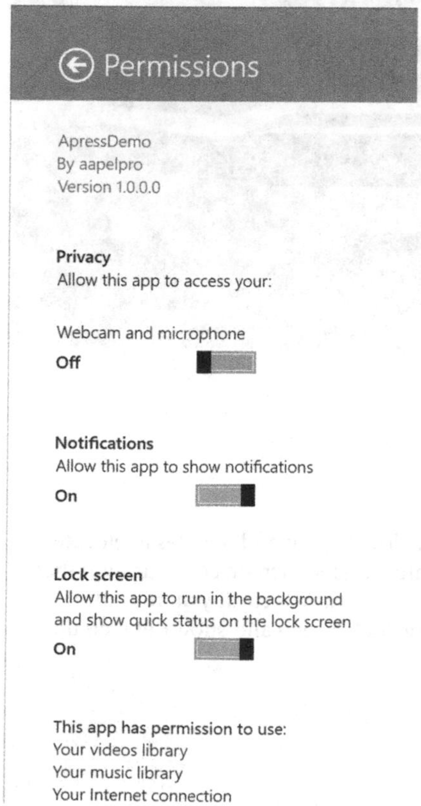

Figure 12-32. Lock screen permissions

Now, since you already added the Apress demo app as a lock screen app, Windows wires up listeners to the app's notifications and exposes them appropriately on the user's lock screen. With your configuration to show only the badge updates, fire up your Apress app and push out a numeric badge update. Now, lock your screen—and you should see the Apress app badge update number next to the badge logo on the lock screen (see Figure 12-33). How cool is that? The latest badge numeric notifications from your app are showing up on the user's lock screen.

Figure 12-33. *Lock screen badge update*

Lock Screen App Detailed Status

What if the user is happy with the badge notifications your app is sending to the lock screen and decides to elevate your app to show detailed notifications (text only) from the latest app tile update. The lock screen configuration that he or she ends up with is something similar to what's in Figure 12-34. Your Windows 8 app is royalty at this point: the single chosen Windows 8 Store app that the user has permitted to run on the lock screen and show detailed tile updates from the last notification.

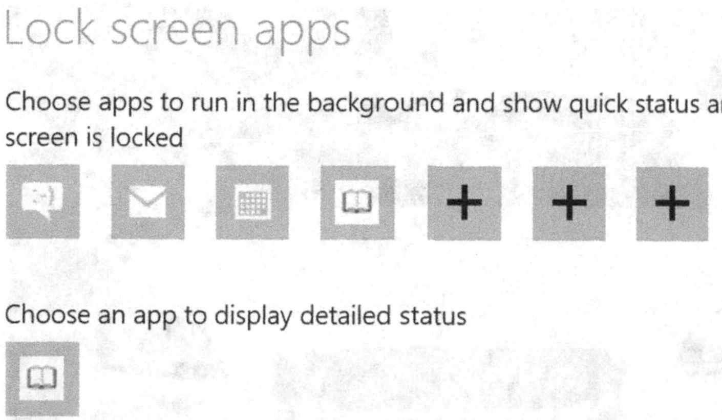

Lock screen apps
Choose apps to run in the background and show quick status and notifications, even when your screen is locked
Choose an app to display detailed status

***Figure 12-34.** Chosen lock screen app with detailed status*

But before you can leverage this privilege, a small configuration change needs to be done in your `PackageAppxManifest` file (see Figure 12-35): show both badge and tile text on the lock screen.

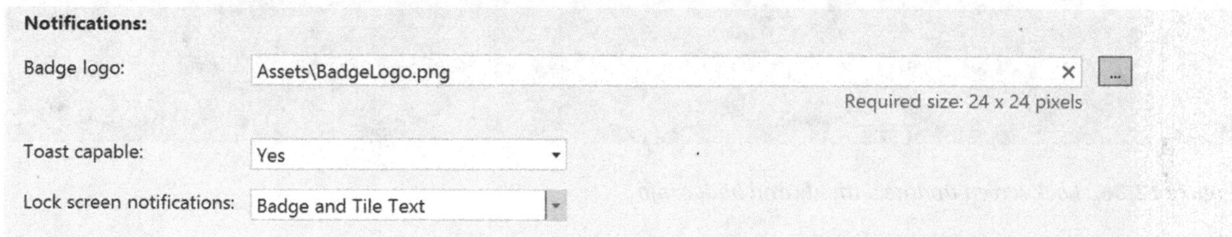

***Figure 12-35.** Lock screen badge and tile configuration*

With the lock screen permission to show detailed status for your Apress demo app, fire it up one more time and send out a fresh app tile update. Verify that the tile updated on the Start screen and then lock the screen. Whoa, detailed tile data in the form of text shows up right next to the system clock on the lock screen (see Figure 12-36). Fabulous, isn't it?

Figure 12-36. *Lock screen update with tile and badge info*

Once your app has all the needed permissions and is on the lock screen, there is no additional work required to route notifications to the lock screen. Windows faithfully bubbles up badge updates, tile updates, and toasts for normal appearance on the user's lock screen.

Details about lock screen apps and other considerations can be found in the MSDN documentation at `http://msdn.microsoft.com/en-us/library/windows/apps/hh779720.aspx`.

Summary

There you have it: app tiles, secondary tiles, badges, toasts, and lock screen apps. Very few operating systems will provide apps with so many ways to wow the user. Pick them all or pick the ones that are relevant to your Windows 8 Store app—and amaze the user. Consult the tile and toast template catalogs to change things up and use the badges to pique user interest. I hope that this chapter was your one-stop shop for learning about the various kinds of local app notifications and making the user's lock screen work in your favor. You do not always need to have external or cloud support to provide that alive-and-connected app user experience—turns out, the local update mechanisms pack a punch to keep the user engaged.

PART 5

Above and Beyond

So far, you have the core functionality working in your Windows 8 Store app. You have even added some bling to invite the user back into the app experience. But a lot of apps do so as well. How does your Windows 8 app stand out and go above and beyond? Functionality—just the hardcore enablement of app features using the latest technologies.

Offer the user choices in storage personalization, make authentication drop-dead easy, augment your app experience with cloud data/services, and amaze the user with push notifications. Oh, and what about real-time connectivity in your Windows 8 apps, all the while keeping your codebase sane and following best practices and patterns?

This is the last killer stretch. You will come out a winner!

CHAPTER 13

Cloud Augmentation

Turns out, there is gold behind the cloud glitter, because meaningfully leveraging the cloud means opening new user experiences for the users of your apps. This could not be truer for Windows 8 Store apps. Alive and connected, always on and inviting—if these are attributes that you want the user to use to describe your Windows 8 app, falling back on a cloud infrastructure can be a valuable tool.

This chapter starts with cloud and Azure basics, but quickly moves into useful techniques of leveraging cloud infrastructure for centralized data with SQL Azure and ubiquitous cross-platform services using OData. Next, you'll take a good look at Azure Mobile Services for enabling push notifications and taking of care of user authentications. There is so much more to talk about regarding cloud augmenting your Windows 8 Store apps, but this chapter will show you the tip of the iceberg and some must-implement techniques.

I realize this chapter turned out to be fairly long, but everything covered is an important fundamental that should not be skipped. A lot of the content is imagery, so fear not—this will be a quick read. Ready? Then off into the cloud you fly.

Cloud Computing

By popular definition, *cloud computing* "... is the use of computing resources (hardware and software) that are delivered as a service over a network (typically the Internet). The name comes from the use of a cloud-shaped symbol as an abstraction for the complex infrastructure it contains in system diagrams. Cloud computing entrusts remote services with a user's data, software, and computation." This is pretty accurate, but you must have also heard about the ubiquitous nature of cloud computing or that you have been using the cloud for years if you have a web-based mail account. So, let's break this down a little more, since public cloud computing seems to encompass a wide variety of technologies. The mainstream cloud-computing types are as follows:

- *Infrastructure as a Service (IaaS)*: This is the most basic type of cloud computing, where cloud providers simply offer the hardware infrastructure (servers/computers/virtual machines, etc.) for the user to install OS images or upload virtual machines to run application software. Although IaaS provides the most control, the user also has the most responsibility with maintainability. Windows Azure Virtual Machines, Amazon EC2, Rackspace Cloud, and so forth, are cloud providers in this space.
- *Platform as a Service (PaaS)*: In this model, the cloud infrastructure provider offers a computing platform in the form of web/storage servers; users are simply responsible for running their software applications within the infrastructure. The slightly less flexibility of PaaS is more than overcome by the convenience of a well-maintained guest OS and high reliability/scalability. Windows Azure Compute, Amazon's AWS, Heroku, Cloud Foundry, and so forth, are some of the cloud providers in this type of cloud computing space. You will see heavy usage of PaaS in this chapter.

- *Software as a Service (SaaS)*: This model of cloud computing has the least responsibility for the user, since the cloud infrastructure provider hosts the OS and software applications that run on it. All the user needs to leverage the cloud is to use a cloud client in the form of applications running on computers/tablets/smartphones or commonly through Internet browsers. Any Internet-based software application—like Gmail, Hotmail, and Outlook—or suites like Office 365 or Google Docs are major contenders in this space. Chapter 14 will demonstrate SaaS usage.

Although these categories are the most common types of cloud computing platforms, many more technologies can be offered up in a service model, like Security, Data, Desktop, API or even integrated development environments (IDEs) for developers. The primary benefit of cloud computing platforms lies in the sharing of resources to achieve user experience coherence and the economics of being charged per usage, like in the electricity grid. The fact that you only pay for what you need leads to on-demand services that have shown to reduce enterprise IT/individual software vendor spendings, along with lowering the barriers to entry. The other huge benefit of cloud computing is the elastic scalability, which offers the easy on-demand provisioning of resources to scale up or down as demanded. The reliability, capacity, and efficiency offered by cloud infrastructure providers through secure, highly available, and close-to-the-customer data centers make cloud computing a feasible choice for enterprises or individual software vendors.

The bigger point of cloud computing is delegation of responsibilities to better-capable systems and focus on what's most important for your consumer. If you are not ready to go all in, there are intermediate steps like a private cloud or hybrid solutions involving a public cloud, in addition to resources on-premise. The unique experiences possible through rock-solid cloud application architecture and engineering far outweigh the concerns around legality/privacy/compliance that will get worked out as laws and best practices catch up to the latest technologies. Bottom line: take a good hard look at your software/business workflows today to see if and how cloud computing can help.

Windows Azure

Now that you know cloud fundamentals, let's talk details. The last few years have seen a proliferation of successful cloud infrastructure providers, like Amazon, Oracle, Google, Heroku, Rackspace, and so forth. There are obviously strengths and weaknesses in every vendor offering, but it would be worthwhile to compare offerings from all providers before you begin your usage of cloud computing.

Windows Azure is Microsoft's extensive cloud computing infrastructure. Built from the ground up, Windows Azure offers an open, flexible, and highly reliable cloud infrastructure, enabling you to quickly build, deploy, and manage applications/servers/virtual machines/storage across a global network of Microsoft-managed data centers. The huge variety of supported operating systems and applications built with varied development languages and tools makes Windows Azure a rock-solid cloud solution offering.

Turns out, in this context, Windows Azure can be a perfect companion to your Windows Store app. With its unmatched variety in supported technologies, Windows Azure offers app developers flexibility in choosing back-end service/storage/authentication/push notifications to power their applications with cloud augmentation. Windows 8 apps may not always have the privilege of being run on the user's device; so any processing that can be off-loaded from the client app onto the cloud contributes immensely toward providing that continuous alive-and-connected user experience. Also, what if your app sees seasonally high traffic; you do not want to invest in a lot of hardware or miss out on business, right? And what if you wanted the same back-end services to power your mobile apps in other ecosystems, like Android or iOS? This is where Windows Azure comes in and can make life a whole lot easier. The rest of the chapter will be focused entirely on Windows Azure and what it can do to empower your apps. But I do want to urge you to take a good look at other cloud providers before you choose Azure for your production app. I can assure you that Azure will shine amid the ecosystem, especially in development tools integration and ease of use.

Want to get started with Windows Azure? Head over to `www.windowsazure.com` and learn all about Azure's offerings (see Figure 13-1). There is great, 90-day free trial to try out Azure (see the big buttons in Figure 13-1) without obligation; all you need is a credit card to prove that you are human. This card will never be charged unless you explicitly choose to go beyond your allotted free benefits or switch to a paid plan. Another great way to start leveraging

Windows Azure is to use a subscription plan, like the one that comes as a benefit of your (or your company's) MSDN subscription. There are substantial Azure benefits bundled with your MSDN plan that you should absolutely look to use (see Figure 13-2); further details are at `www.windowsazure.com/en-us/pricing/member-offers/msdn-benefits/`.

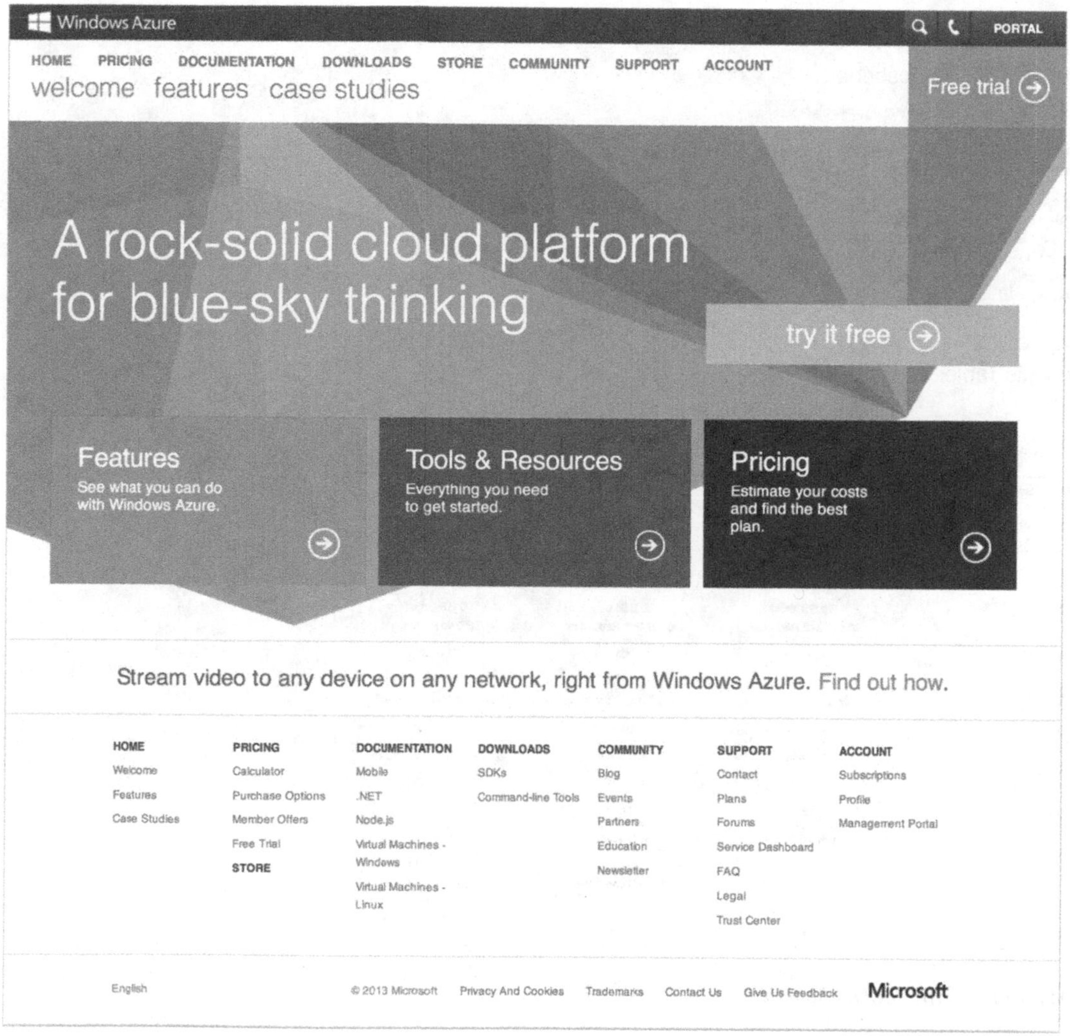

Figure 13-1. *Windows Azure*

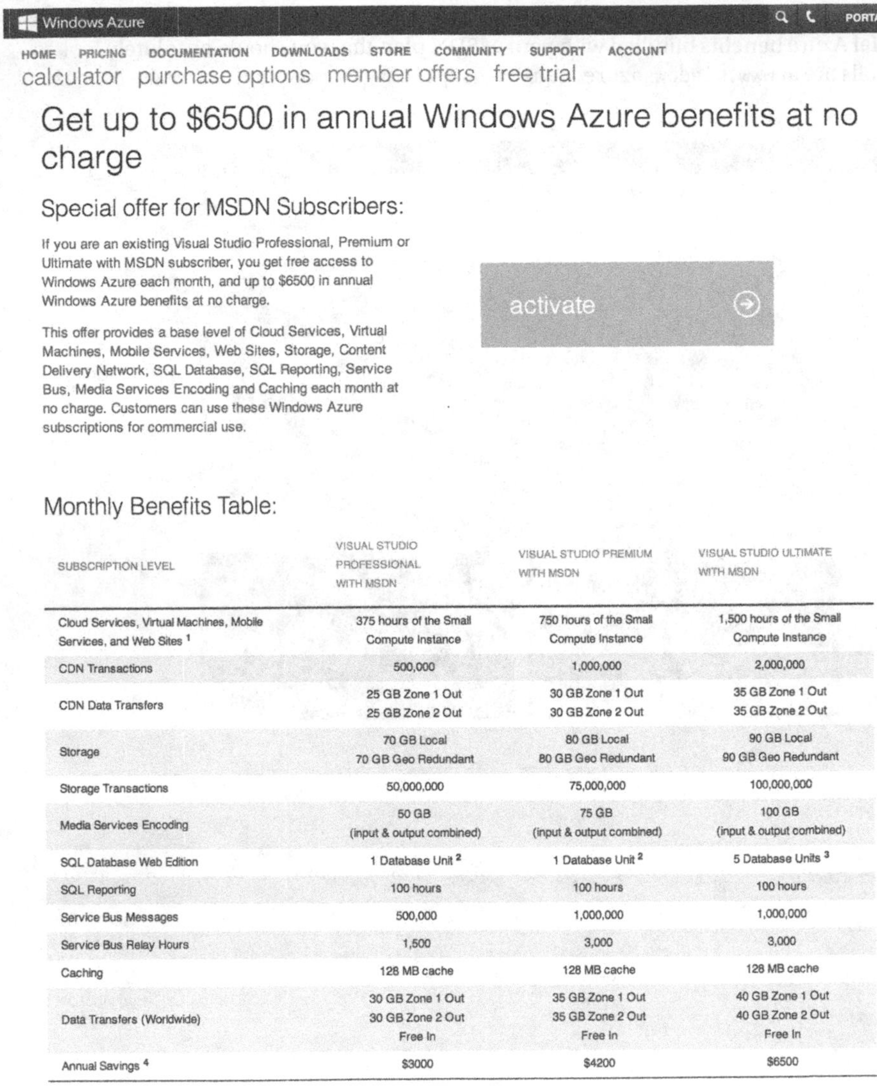

Figure 13-2. *Windows Azure MSDN benefits*

Handling Data

As you have seen in earlier chapters, data is king. Data is the crux of what most Windows 8 Store apps present to the user. And it pays to have a good strategy around data persistence, retrieval, and availability. Now, it is great to have data locally on Windows 8 devices or even use roaming storage to sync data between multiple devices for the user. But all this is very much tied to a single user. What if you wanted to handle bigger data in your app, something that is meant for all users (for example, leaderboards persisting game scores across users)? Or what if your app's data was to be pulled down for refreshes from a central repository to keep everything in sync?

You quickly realize that with these questions, your data persistence strategies start falling a little short. Enter the cloud—in particular, Windows Azure. Azure offers the wonderful SQL Azure service for relational data persistence. Think of it like any other SQL Server data storage, but running with huge amounts of orchestration on cloud infrastructure with high availability and data replication across continents. SQL Azure allows you to have a regular relational database running in the cloud and to have all your data in one central place for consumption by various services/applications across platforms. SQL Azure inspires confidence with 99.95% availability through an SLA (service-level agreement) and data replication across multiple data centers.

Data Persistence in Azure

So, let's get started. Say, while building your Apress demo Windows 8 app, you realized that it would be better to host all the data about Apress books in one central place for easy edits and consumption across platforms. SQL Azure can provide the perfect Azure support to host the relational database in the cloud. By now, you should have signed up for Azure (through the free trial or MSDN benefits) and have services activated. Head over to `https://manage.windowsazure.com/`—this is your Azure developer portal—after you sign in with the same Microsoft account that you subscribed to Azure with. The redesigned Azure management portal is all HTML5 and works on any device. It serves as your one-stop shop for managing all the things you have on Windows Azure, including services, data, and applications.

You want to first create a new SQL Azure database to host all of your Apress book information. So, head over to the SQL Databases section of the portal and go ahead with creating a new database through the link on the right or the big +New button at the bottom (see Figure 13-3).

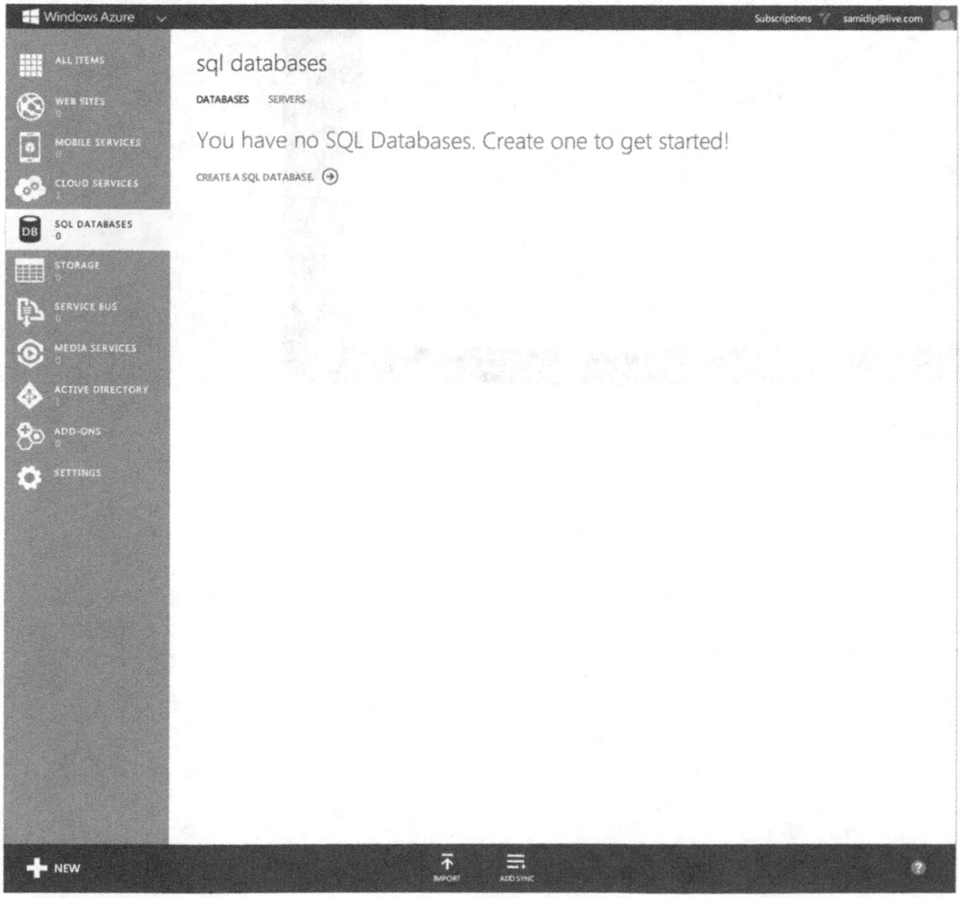

Figure 13-3. *SQL Azure database management*

Note how the new SQL Database creation wizard prompts you for an SQL server to host it on, the size of the database, an Azure subscription to use, admin authentication, and which data center region should spin up the server (see Figures 13-4 and 13-5). Your choice of region should be closest to your anticipated user base to reduce network latency. You can replicate the data among multiple servers and keep them in sync.

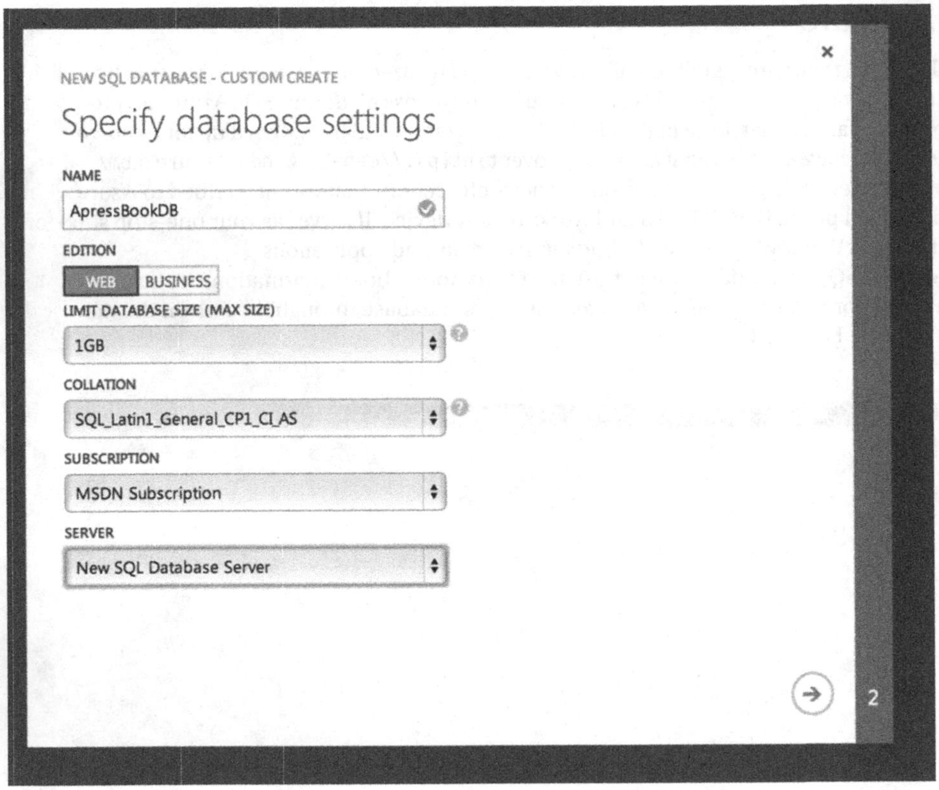

Figure 13-4. *New SQL Azure database*

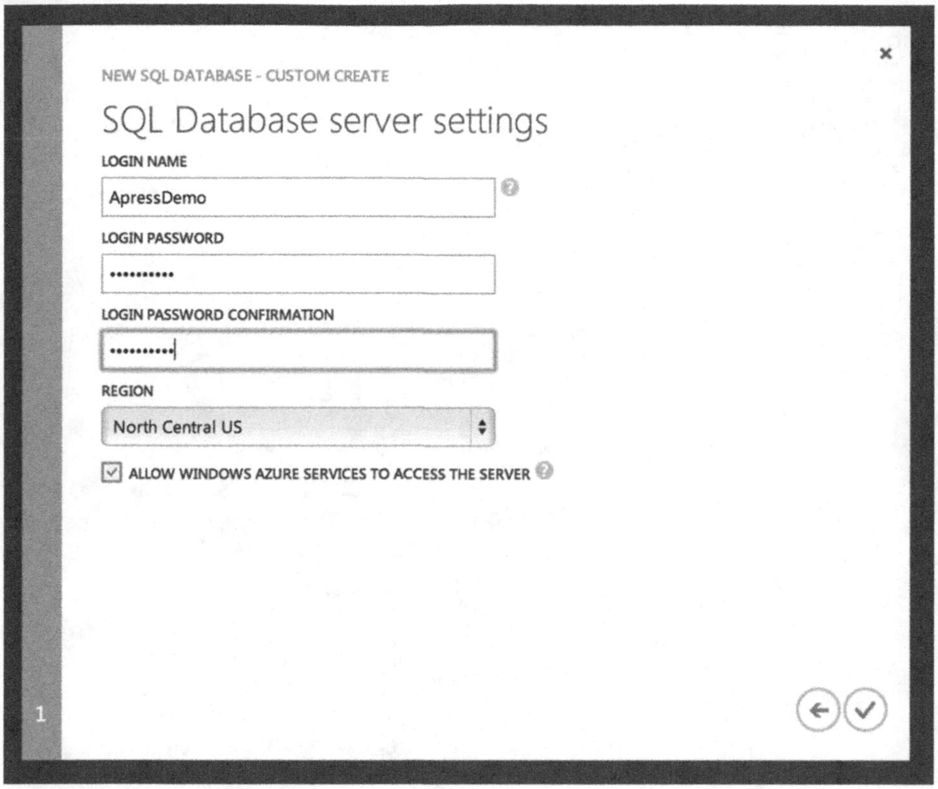

Figure 13-5. *New SQL Azure database setup*

Once the SQL Azure database is ready for use, you can see the online status in the Azure portal, as shown in Figure 13-6.

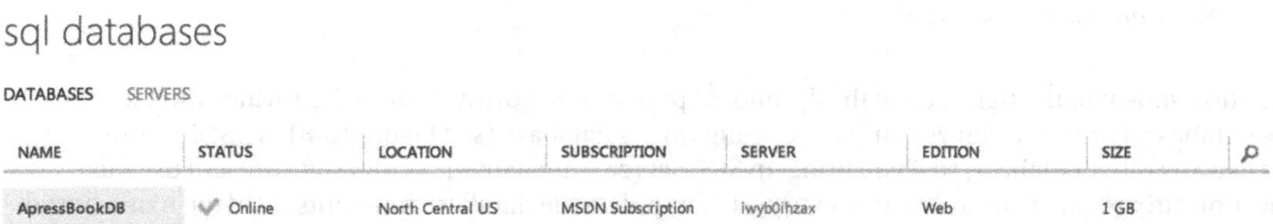

sql databases
DATABASES
SERVERS
NAME
STATUS
LOCATION
SUBSCRIPTION
SERVER
EDITION
SIZE
ApressBookDB
Online
North Central US
MSDN Subscription
lwyb0ihzax
Web
1 GB

Figure 13-6. *New SQL Azure database created*

Clicking the database name takes you into a dashboard mode, where you can see details about the SQL database and its health (see Figure 13-7).

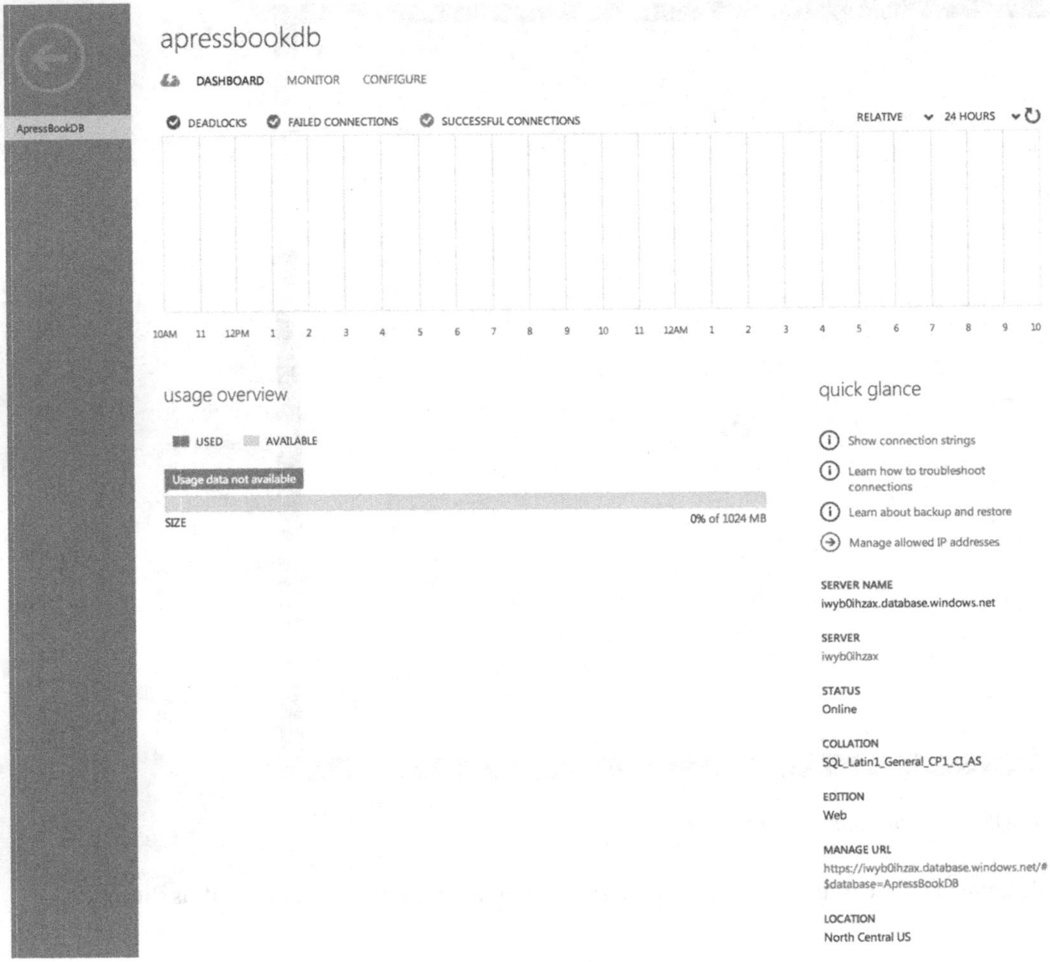

Figure 13-7. *SQL Azure database dashboard*

The information shown in the right side of the dashboard page is noteworthy because it provides ways to manipulate the database. For one, it shows connection strings to the database (see Figure 13-8). An SQL Azure database is just like any other database; so if you bring up SQL Server Management Studio software and use the provided connection strings, you can easily connect to and manipulate the database from outside of the Azure portal. Your Apress book database does not seem too complicated, so simply use the web-based database management portal. Once an SQL Azure database is ready, make note of the Manage URL on the dashboard—this is a direct link to the web-based interface.

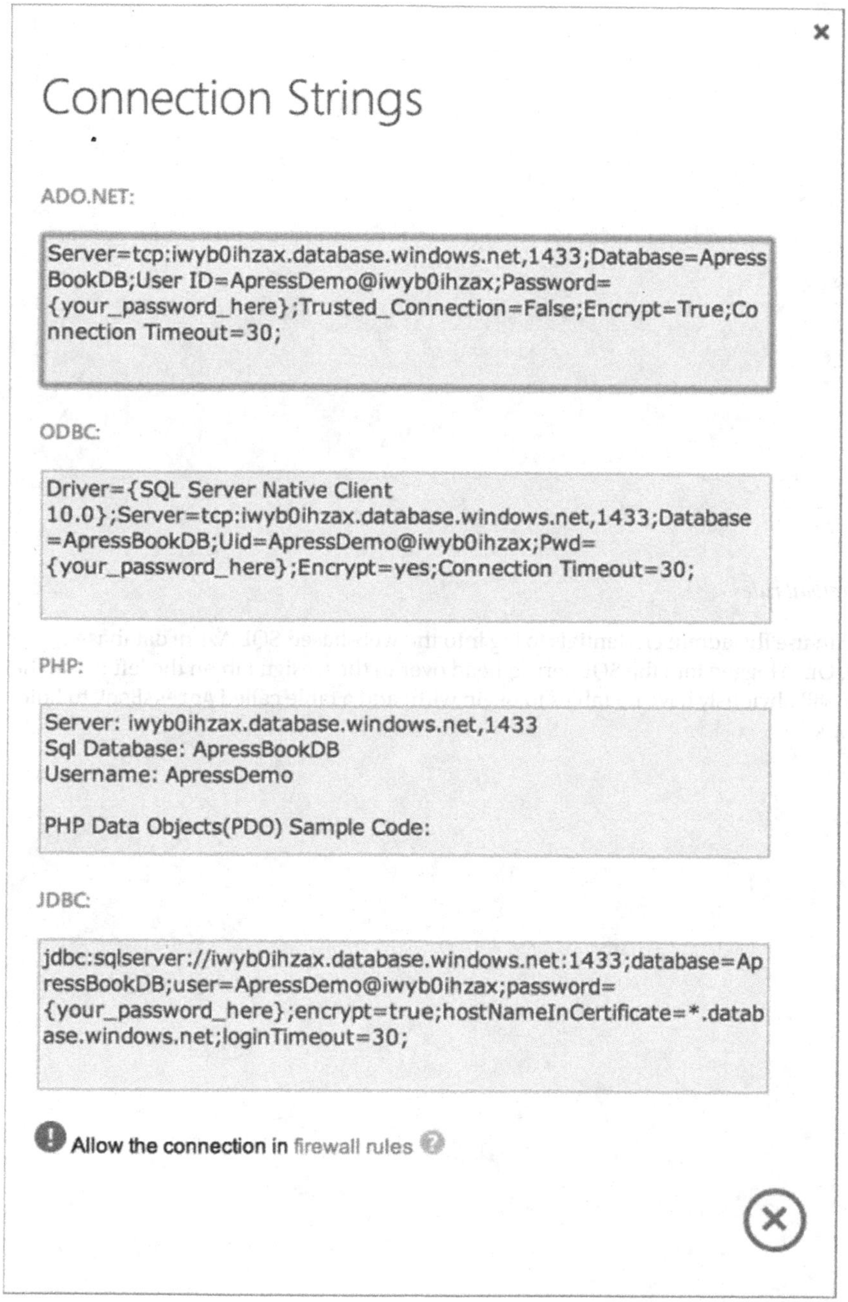

Figure 13-8. *SQL Azure database connection strings*

Now, there is one small step before you can web-edit the SQL Azure database. By nature, Azure wants to protect your SQL database and only declared IP (Internet Protocol) addresses or a range of them are allowed to connect to it. So, go ahead and provide your current network IP to Azure to allow connectivity (see Figure 13-9).

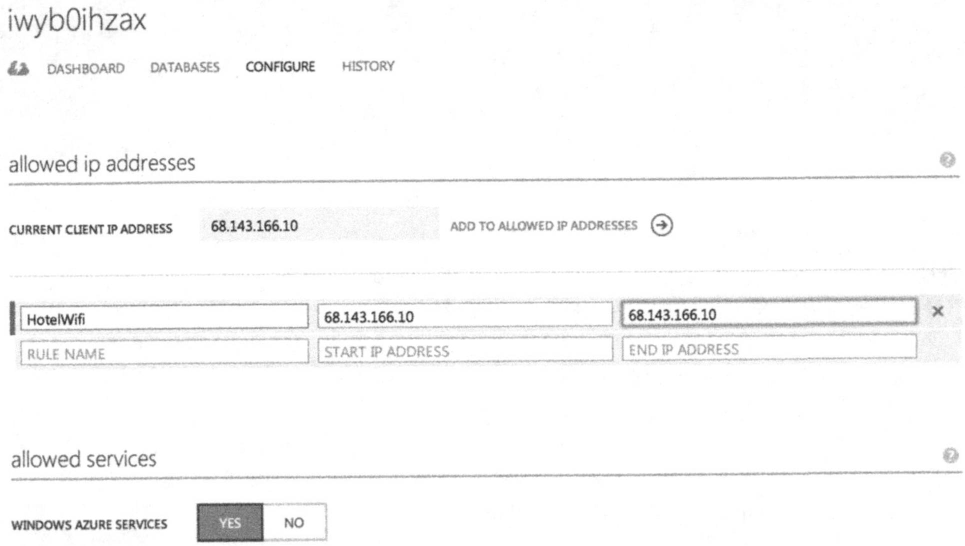

Figure 13-9. *SQL Azure database firewall rules*

Once everything is set up, you can use the admin credentials to log into the web-based SQL Azure database management site (see Figure 13-10). Once logged into the SQL server, head over to the Design tab on the left to see the database table details. The database will obviously have no tables to begin with; add a table called `ApressBook` to hold information about Apress publications.

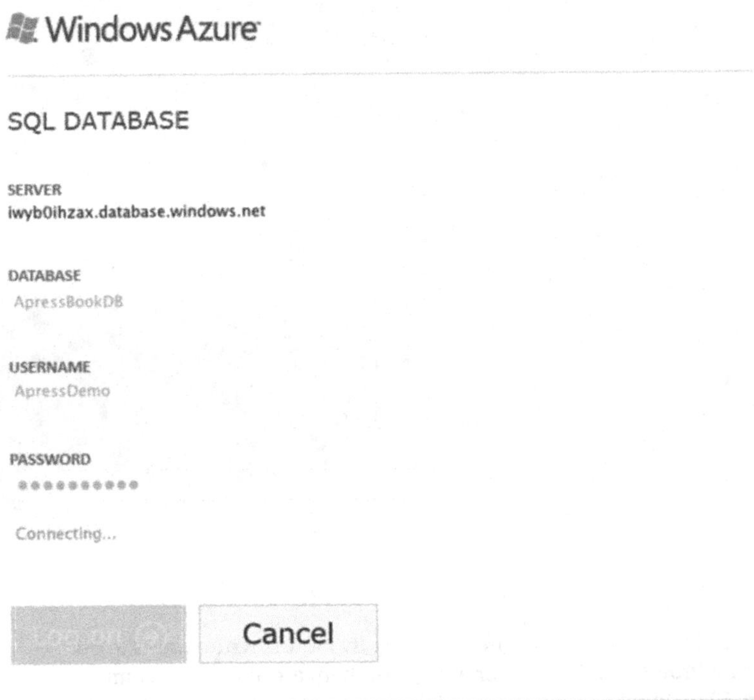

Figure 13-10. *SQL Azure database management portal*

The table schema (see Figure 13-11) reflects the normal data that you want to handle in columns for every Apress book, including an autoincrementing ID column that uniquely defines each book and acts as the primary key of the table.

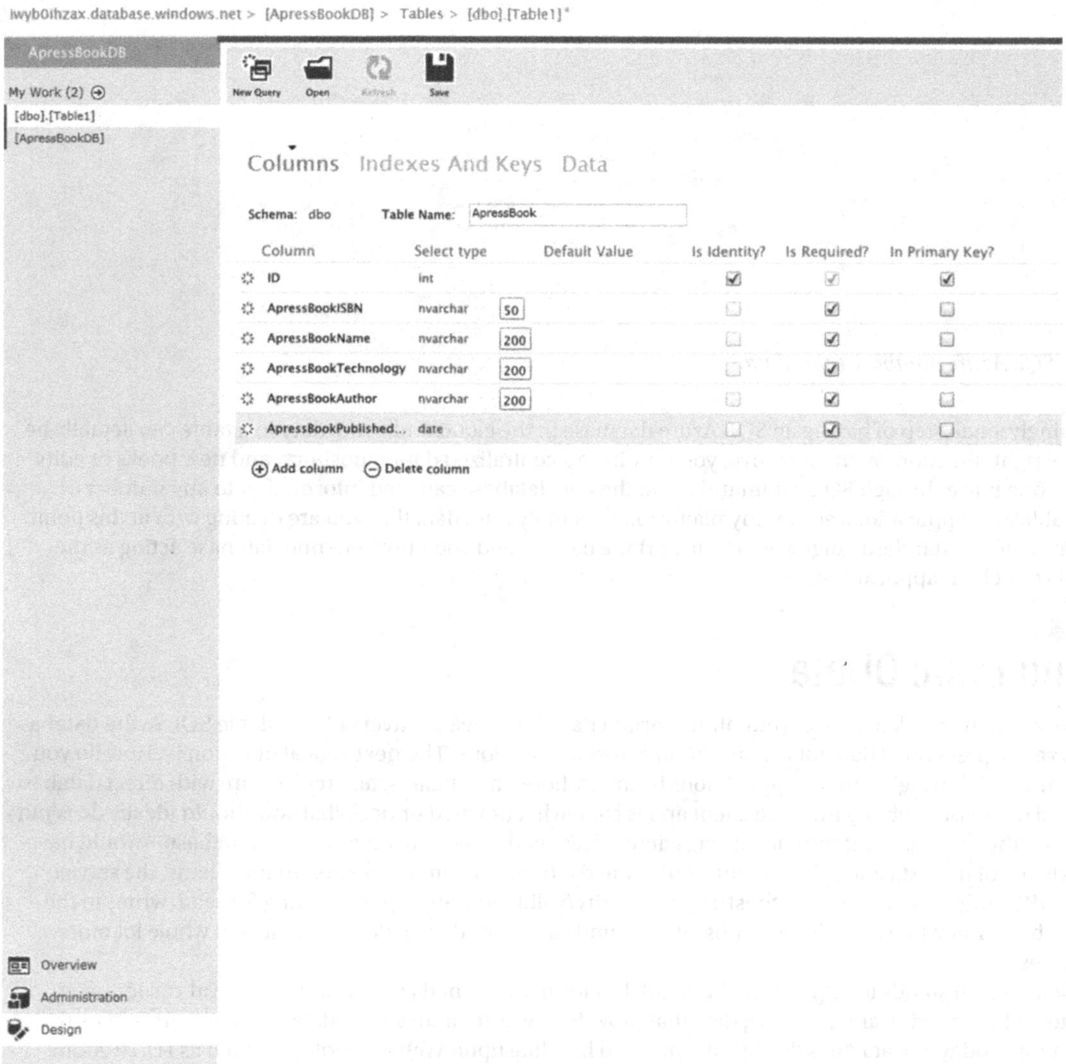

Figure 13-11. *SQL Azure database table schema*

Figure 13-12 shows some sample data inserted into your table.

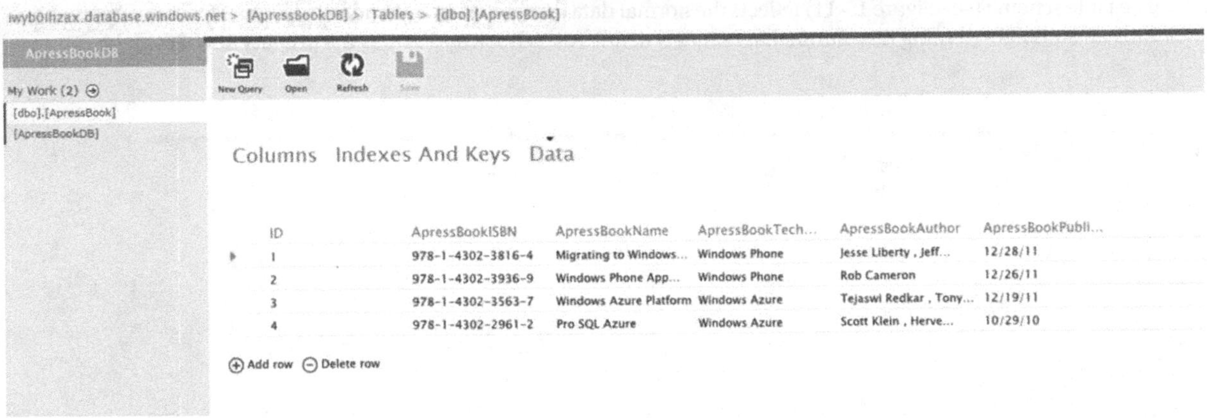

Figure 13-12. *SQL Azure database table data*

The seemingly small step of having an SQL Azure database in the cloud and some data in a table can actually be a big step in the right direction. With that move, you now have a centralized data repository, and new books or edits can be made in one place through SQL commands. And the one database can feed information to any number of smartphone/tablet/PC applications across any platform. It is simply pure data that you are dealing with at this point. Pick a platform-agnostic standard language to transport the data in, and you now have one database acting as the back end to all your client applications.

Accessing Data: OData

Now at this point, you have taken care of your all-important data. You have a universally available SQL Azure database that is hosting your Apress book data for consumption across applications. The next logical question is: How do you access this data? For lightweight mobile applications in smartphones and tablets, an architecture with direct database connectivity and database visibility from the client app is somewhat frowned upon. What you should ideally do is put a service between the database and the consuming clients. This service—sitting on top of the database—would have intimate knowledge of the data and schema, but would shield it from consuming clients. To the clients, the service is just another URL endpoint providing orchestration/security/validations on top of allowing for read/writes to the underlying database. But while a service to expose data sounds like a good idea, does that mean a whole lot more code and complexity?

Enter *OData*, which stands for Open Data Protocol. It is formally defined at `www.odata.org/introduction/` as "a Web protocol for querying and updating data that provides a way to unlock your data and free it from silos that exist in applications today. OData does this by applying and building upon Web technologies such as HTTP, Atom Publishing Protocol (AtomPub) and JSON to provide access to information from a variety of applications, services, and stores." So, in short, OData is promising to standardize information exchange by using well-established protocols. The request/response for data happens over HTTP, which is pretty much what today's Internet is based upon. The actual data being carried through is in the form of Atom (standardized form of XML) or JSON formats, both standards understood across application ecosystems. OData endpoints act like a RESTful (Representational State Transfer) service, making deep commitments to URIs for resource identification/manipulation, just like the Web. This is one of the primary reasons for OData's recent popularity for exposing data seamlessly and offering interoperability across multiple platforms through the use of standard information exchange formats. Also, OData does not simply expose data, but allows support for custom sorting and filtering of data from the database, and all this can be done through URI manipulations to slice up the underlying data. And if you thought OData is simply meant to produce read-only data from the database, you are in for a big surprise. OData, as one of its biggest strengths, supports full CRUD (create, read, update, delete) SQL operations against the data in the database. This means data can not only be read out of the database through the service by consuming clients, but it is also equally easy to use the same OData endpoints to insert/update/delete database records through the service.

For more information about OData, please visit `www.odata.org`. There you will find information about OData *producers*—software systems who expose their data through OData endpoints, and a list of *consumers*—those who use the OData feeds in building applications. The list of producers also includes several live OData feeds, which makes it easy for developers to play with hosted content before producing/consuming OData feeds.

Netflix has a prominent and a fun OData live feed. Head over to `http://odata.netflix.com/Catalog/` to see the Netflix OData catalog, a gigantic data repository of movies, genres, people, awards, and so forth, exposed in simple chunks through OData endpoints. As you can see, the Netflix OData root simply lists out several other URI endpoints (see Figure 13-13). Append the endpoint after the root catalog URI and you see details about the data entity. For example, `http://odata.netflix.com/Catalog/Titles` shows you information about Netflix movies in plain Atom (XML) format. Now, do you believe you are being given information about every single movie in the Netflix database? If you have not brought the Internet down, chances are there is a data cap showing a marked number of items. Hint: scroll all the way down to the end of the OData feed to discover a continuation token, to be used to fetch the next round of movies in the next request.

```
▼<service xmlns:atom="http://www.w3.org/2005/Atom" xmlns:app="http://www.w3.org/2007/app" xmlns="http://www.w3.org/2007/app" xml:base="http://odata.netflix.com/Catalog/">
 ▼<workspace>
    <atom:title>Default</atom:title>
   ▼<collection href="Genres">
      <atom:title>Genres</atom:title>
    </collection>
   ▼<collection href="Titles">
      <atom:title>Titles</atom:title>
    </collection>
   ▼<collection href="TitleAudioFormats">
      <atom:title>TitleAudioFormats</atom:title>
    </collection>
   ▼<collection href="TitleAwards">
      <atom:title>TitleAwards</atom:title>
    </collection>
   ▼<collection href="People">
      <atom:title>People</atom:title>
    </collection>
   ▼<collection href="TitleScreenFormats">
      <atom:title>TitleScreenFormats</atom:title>
    </collection>
   ▼<collection href="Languages">
      <atom:title>Languages</atom:title>
    </collection>
  </workspace>
</service>
```

Figure 13-13. *Netflix OData endpoint*

You may be wondering about the ubiquitous HTTP URI handling in an OData feed. One downside of the RESTful service magic is the need to support URI endpoints explicitly on the server and the handcrafting of complex custom requests from consuming client applications. To get developers around such pitfalls, there is a huge amount of help: simply head to `www.odata.org/libraries` (see Figure 13-14). What you see is a set of libraries, meant for developers working on OData, across several client and server technologies. These libraries do a terrific job abstracting low-level details of making/supporting HTTP requests around an OData endpoint; it's sort of acting like a wrapper and allowing the developer to not have to handcraft HTTP communication. So, pick your client/server technology and run with a library.

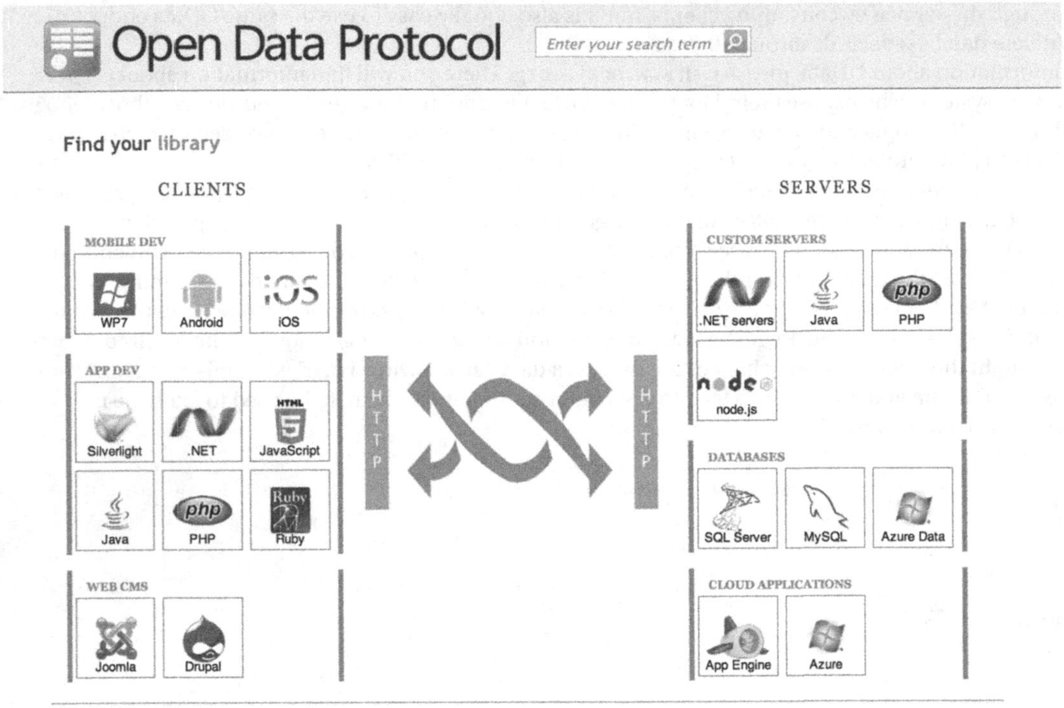

Figure 13-14. *A screenshot from* `www.odata.org/libraries` *shows the possibilities*

Setting Up the Service

So by now, you have seen that the promise offered by OData and Apress book data in the SQL Azure database is waiting to be exposed. Combine the two to produce an OData service endpoint that provides access to the underlying data in SQL Azure. Instead of using a cookie-cutter library, however, try to set up service by hand so that developer inquisitiveness is fulfilled by knowing what's happening under the covers.

Here is the goal: you will set up a simple WCF (Windows Communication Foundation) service on top of your SQL Azure database, and the service will expose an OData endpoint to provide data in Atom format. Now, compared to classic web services, you want to do this as lightweight as possible and with minimal coding. And once you have verified that the service is truly offering data access as promised, you will host the service in Windows Azure for a globally accessible URI endpoint.

Service Creation Process

First, for us to host any kind of service in Windows Azure, the software guts would need the Azure SDK for development purposes. So, head over to `www.windowsazure.com/en-us/downloads/` to download and install the .NET SDK for Visual Studio 2012 (see Figure 13-15). This provides Visual Studio templates for cloud-based solutions and all the wrappers and configuration that it takes to host an application in Windows Azure.

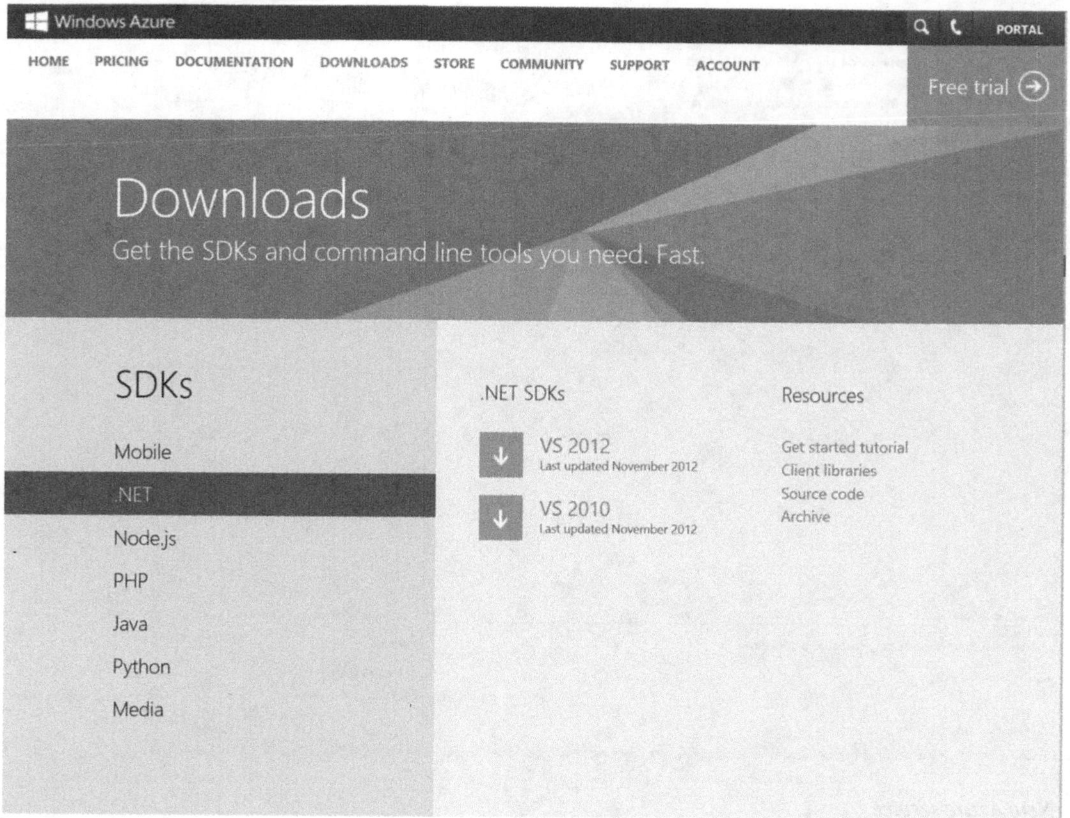

Figure 13-15. *Azure SDK download page*

Next, create a new cloud project using the fresh template (Windows Azure Cloud Service) available after your SDK installation (see Figure 13-16). This simply readies your Visual Studio solution for hosting the application in Azure by dropping appropriate Azure wrappers around packaging and configuration. Now, the Azure template is a placeholder; the very next step in the project creation wizard is choosing what kind of application you want to build and host in the cloud.

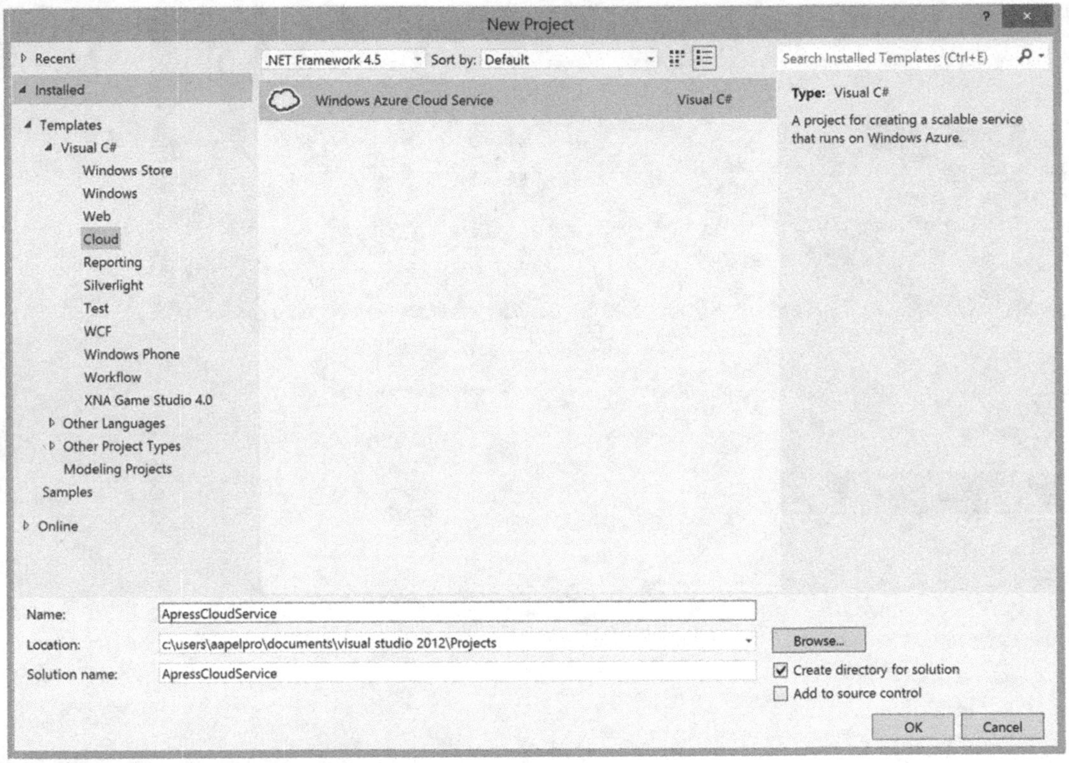

Figure 13-16. *New Azure service*

The *Azure Web Role* is the most basic form of application that can be hosted in Windows Azure. It is quite simply running a version of Windows Server OS with IIS (Internet Information Services) enabled and ready to host web applications and services. The web role option seems good enough for us; but instead of a web site/web application, choose a WCF service to be hosted inside the web role (see Figure 13-17). Give your service an appropriate name and off you start with a Visual Studio solution.

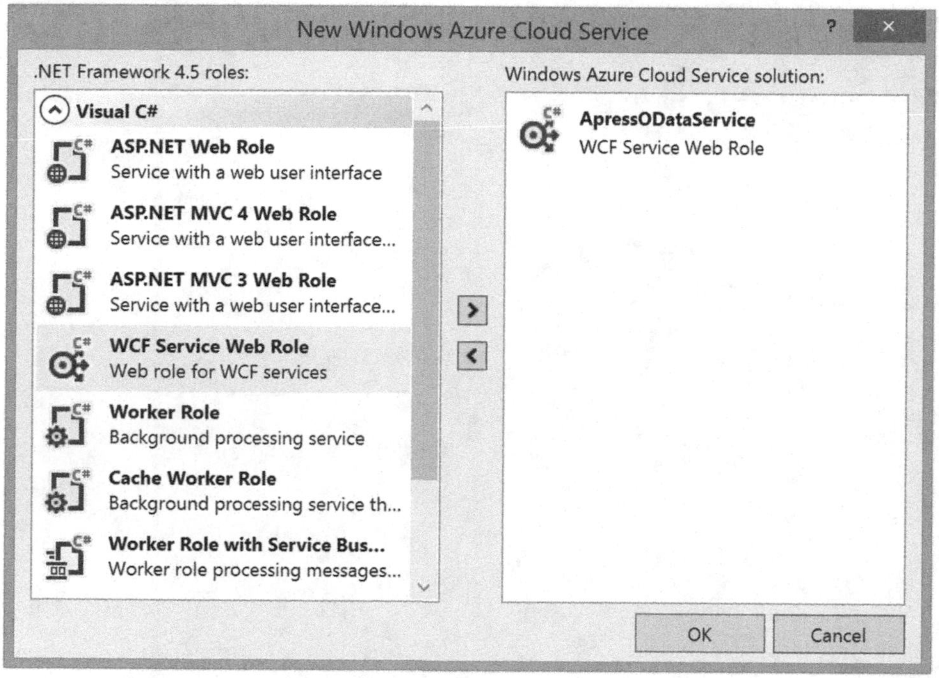

Figure 13-17. *WCF web role in Azure service*

Once your Visual Studio solution is ready, right-click the WCF Service project and add a new item of the type ADO.NET Entity Data Model (see Figure 13-18). This is a very interesting component since it provides the ORM (object-relational mapping) layer in your application. The goal of the ADO.NET Entity Data Model is to simply look at a database table and expose the table data as an object model in .NET, with every table column turned into an object property.

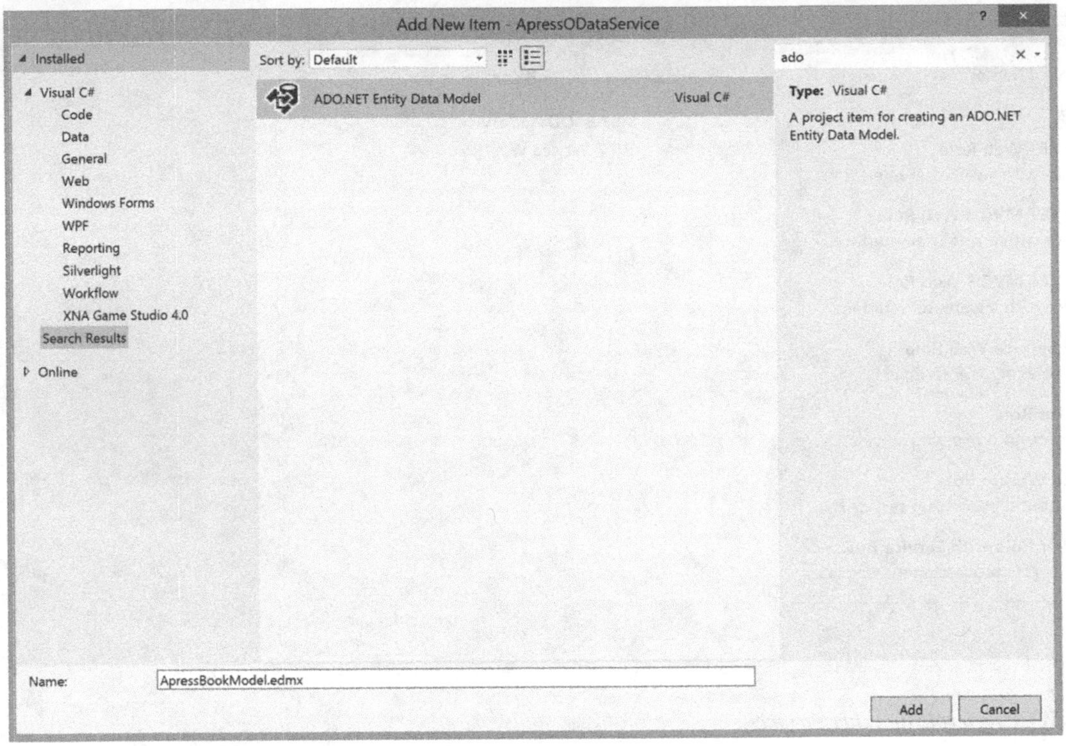

Figure 13-18. *ADO.NET Entity Data Model usage*

Now the ADO.NET Entity Data Model can create a fresh data model by creating a new database; but since you already have an existing SQL Azure database with a defined table schema, reuse that (see Figure 13-19). Generating the object model from an existing database means that you first have to connect to it so that table schema can be inspected.

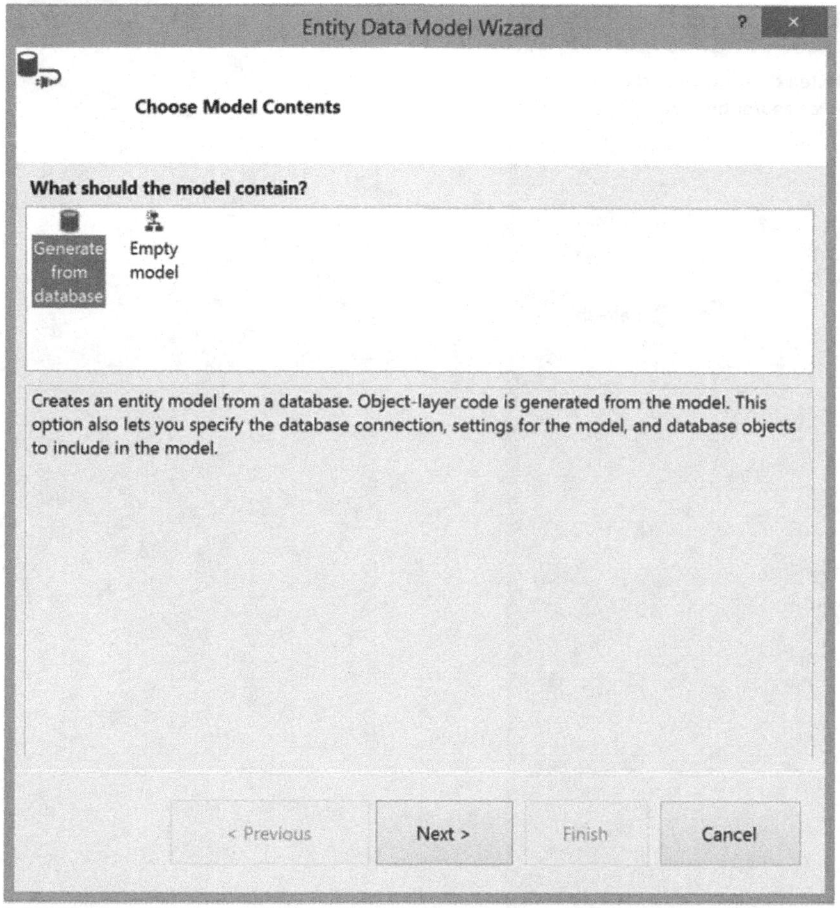

Figure 13-19. *ADO.NET Entity Data Model using existing database*

This obviously means that now you need to provide the database connections to the SQL Azure database for connectivity to the database to happen (see Figure 13-20). Notice how you select SQL Server as the data source type and specify the full Azure SQL Server name hosting your database, along with admin credentials to log in to the server. If everything is correct, the database selection drop-down lights up with choices based on what's running in the SQL Server. You simply pick the lone `ApressBookDB` that houses your Apress book data.

Figure 13-20. *ADO.NET Entity Data Model database connectivity*

Once everything is all set with the database connection, you save off the connection string in the WCF service `Web.Config` file (see Figure 13-21).

Figure 13-21. *ADO.NET Entity Data Model connection config*

Let's take note of one quick point before you move on. As you can see in the wizard shown in Figure 13-21, all that you are providing to your ADO.NET Entity Data Model is a connection string to reach a remote relational database. This has the brilliant advantage of interoperability. As long as your software system can reach a relational database with a supported client data source (like SQL Server, OLEDB, Oracle, etc.), the following steps will work exactly the same way. This is by design to allow flexibility—your database server could be on-premise, in the cloud, or under your desk. It all works the same way and you can easily create a service to expose the underlying data from the database.

Once your connection to the database has been established, the next step in the wizard is to select the tables that you want to include in your object model (see Figure 13-22). Again, you choose your lone `ApressBook` table to generate the corresponding data model. The check box to pluralize or singularize generated object names is a nice touch. In your case, the object model will be called `ApressBooks` to refer to the collection of Apress books from the table.

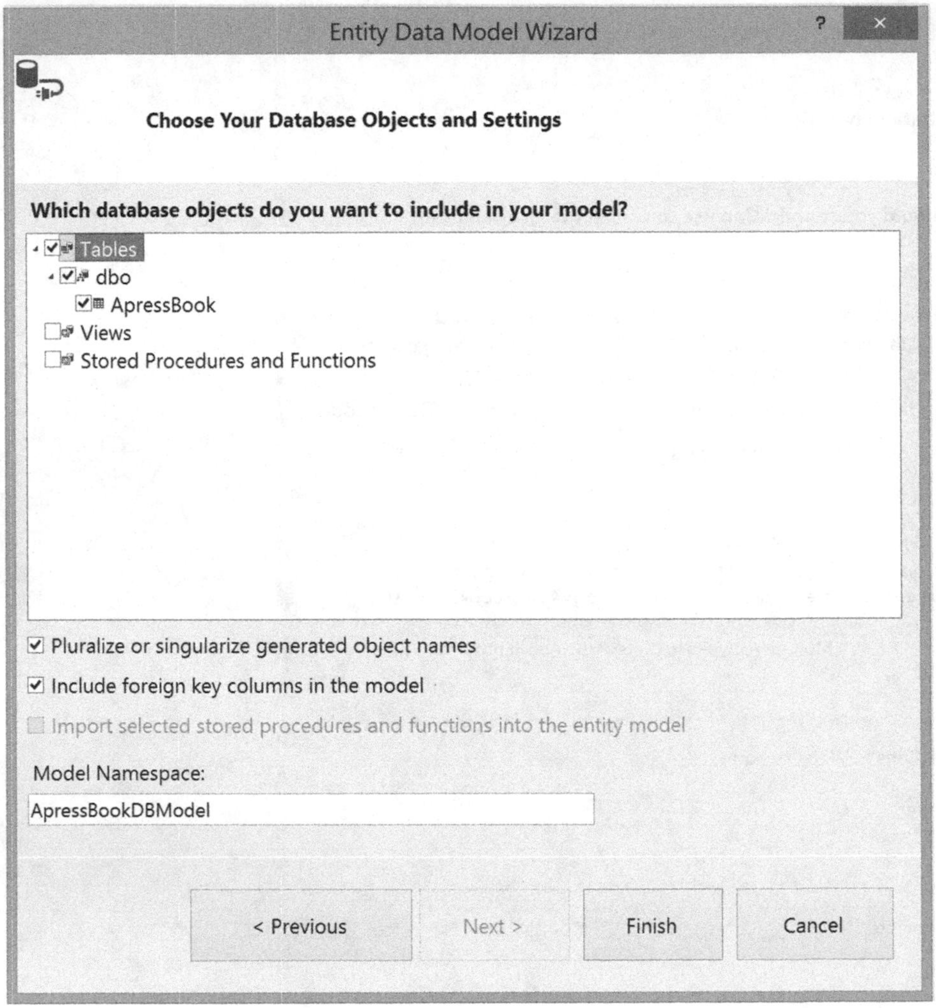

Figure 13-22. *ADO.NET Entity Data Model table selection*

Once all choices have been made in the ADO.NET Entity Data Model addition wizard, click Finish and wait for the magic to happen. Hopefully, the end result is an `.edmx` file, like the `ApressBookModel.edmx` file in your case (see Figure 13-23). This is the entity data model you were after. Look closely at the data model and you will notice an exact replica of the SQL Azure database table schema in the `EDMX` object model. So, you have essentially taken a database table and converted that to a .NET data object with matching properties. Tell me how this is not cool! Also, if you select multiple tables from the database with primary/foreign key relationships among them, the entity data model respects the relationships and re-creates them for the generated objects.

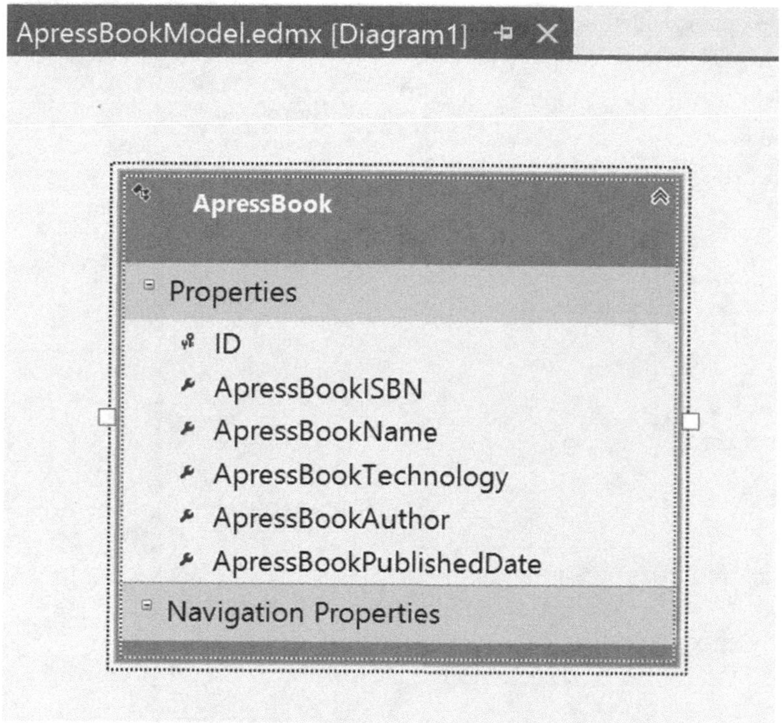

Figure 13-23. *ADO.NET Entity Data Model generated EDMX*

At this point, you have an object data model that reflects your table schema. The next obvious step is to expose this object model toward building that OData endpoint. Enter **WCF Data Services**. You are about to orchestrate the creation of a WCF service that will look at the entity data model objects and convert their data into a simple feed, accessible over a URI endpoint. So, right-click your WCF Service project in Visual Studio and add a new item of the type WCF Data Service (see Figure 13-24). Notice the file type is `.svc`. This would be your endpoint.

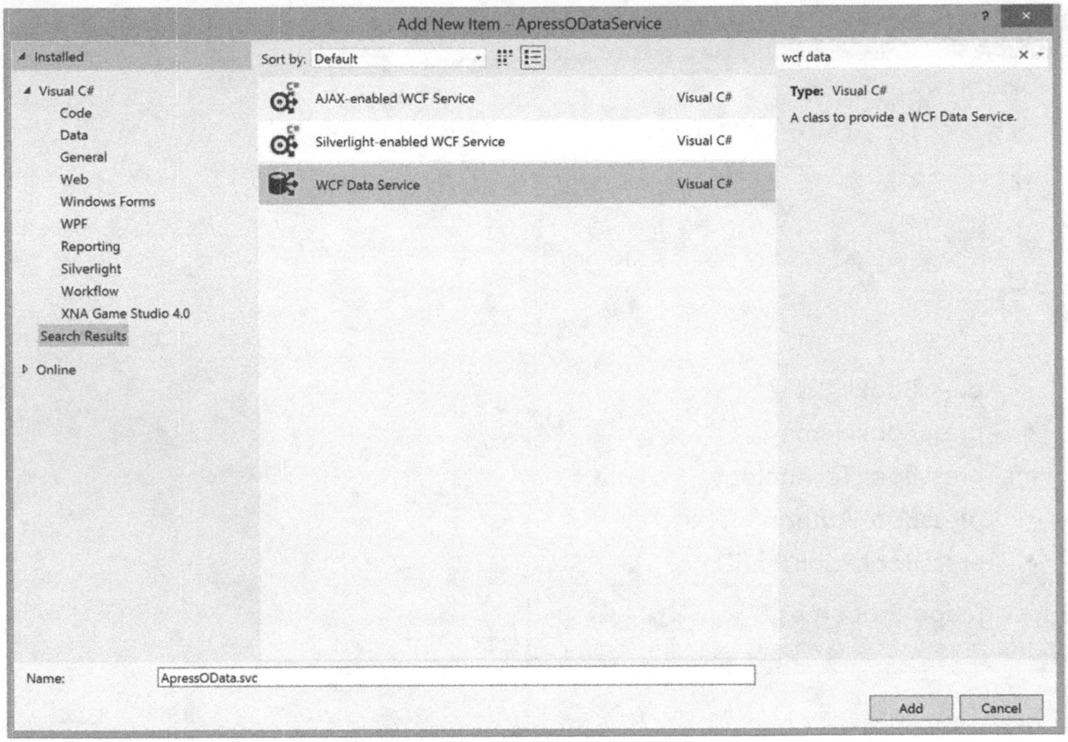

Figure 13-24. *WCF Data Services usage*

With the WCF Data Services addition, your project should now be all set with all that is needed to create a data feed out of the SQL Azure database through the entity data model. The Visual Studio solution looks Figure 13-25, with two projects: the `ApressODataService` (this is the WCF service that you configured) and the `ApressCloudService` (this is the Windows Azure wrapper to host the application in Azure). Within the WCF service, you have your `.edmx` file containing the mapped entity object model, and the `.svc` file, which acts as the URI endpoint for the WCF Data Services that you added.

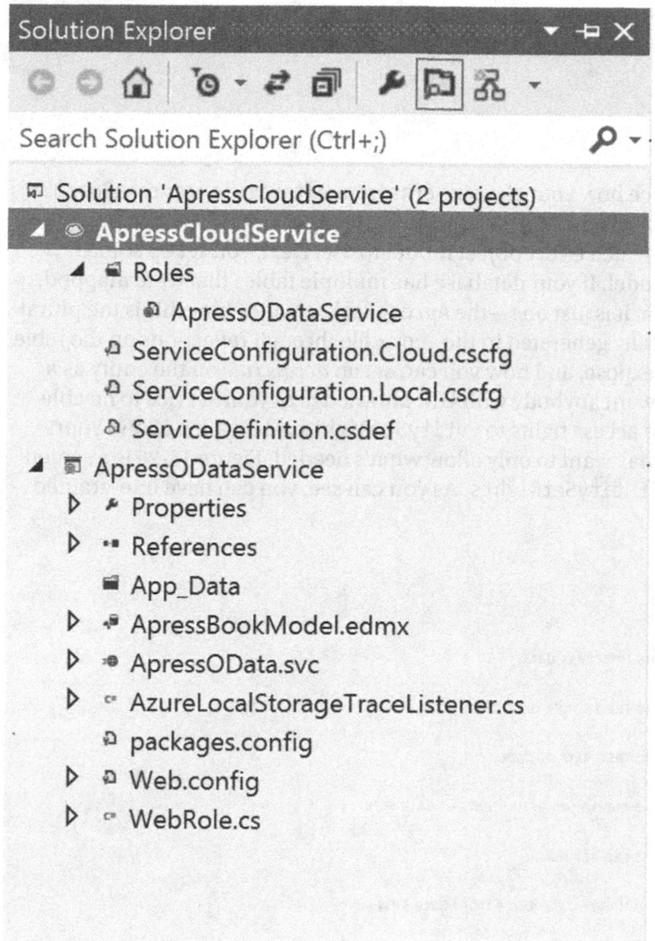

Figure 13-25. *Solution structure*

Service Setup Code

Did you notice that you haven't written any code yet? That's because the ADO.NET Data Entity Model mapped the database table to your entity object model purely through configuration and reflections on the database table schema. However, the WCF Data Services endpoint isn't doing anything yet because you have not made the association between the service and the object entities yet. Add some code to the `.svc` file code-behind, the `ApressOData.svc.cs` file in your case:

```
namespace ApressODataService
{
    public class ApressOData : DataService<ApressBookDBEntities>
    {
        public static void InitializeService(DataServiceConfiguration config)
        {
            // Set rules to indicate which entity sets and service operations are visible, updatable, etc.
```

```
            config.SetEntitySetAccessRule("ApressBooks", EntitySetRights.All);
            config.DataServiceBehavior.MaxProtocolVersion = DataServiceProtocolVersion.V3;
        }
    }
}
```

A couple of interesting things happened. First, notice how your class inherits from DataService<ApressBookDB Entities>. This is using the same database mapping objects that you set up while adding the ADO.NET Data Entity Model; so right here, you are telling WCF Data Services which entity object model to use. Next, you set up some configuration on every individual entity in the object model. If your database has multiple tables that were mapped, you will have to individually declare every entity; for you, it is just one—the ApressBooks. Notice how this is the plural form of your database table name, and it was automatically generated in the .edmx file through reflections on the table schema. So, ApressBooks is your collection of books to expose, and now you can set an *access rule* on the entity as a whole. Access control is important because you do not want anybody with URI knowledge of your service to be able to read/write data freely from your database. You set the access rights to EntitySetRights.All, which allows your service complete access to the database table, but you may want to only allow what's needed. Figure 13-26 is a screen grab from MSDN that shows the enumeration values of EntitySetRights. As you can see, you can have fine-grained control over data access.

	Member name	Description
	None	Denies all rights to access data.
	ReadSingle	Authorization to read single data items.
	ReadMultiple	Authorization to read sets of data.
	WriteAppend	Authorization to create new data items in data sets.
	WriteReplace	Authorization to replace data.
	WriteDelete	Authorization to delete data items from data sets.
	WriteMerge	Authorization to merge data.
	AllRead	Authorization to read data.
	AllWrite	Authorization to write data.
	All	Authorization to create, read, update, and delete data.

Figure 13-26. *EntitySetRights enum values*

Feeling lucky, and think the little code you added should be enough? Well, yes, you are right. That is literally all it takes to expose data from the database through a WCF Data Service. Let's test it out. After you build the solution, right-click the `.svc` file and choose the option of displaying in browser. Voilà, your local IIS server (Cassini) loads up the WCF service endpoint in the chosen browser (see Figure 13-27), and you see something that looks simple but effective. What you are looking at is the WCF service endpoint, which doubles up as the OData endpoint and displays a list of all supported URI data endpoints. This is purely in Atom format and easily human-readable. Do you see the similarities to the Netflix OData endpoint listing? Also, since you had exposed only one data entity, you see only one supported endpoint—`ApressBooks`. This is the same name as the data entity set you set up your WCF Data Services with.

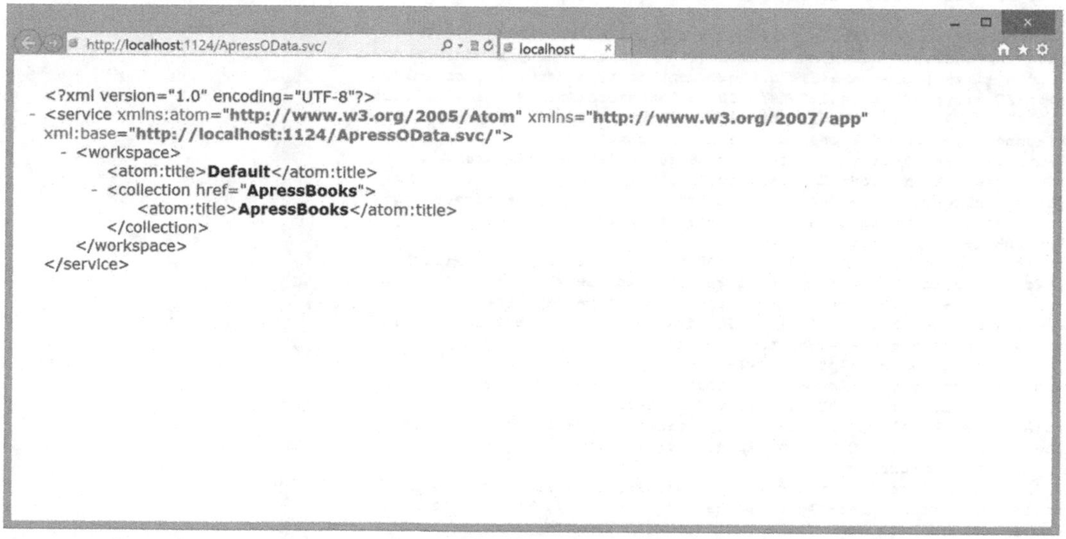

Figure 13-27. *Local OData endpoint*

Next, do the obvious test: try to navigate to the actual data entity URI endpoint by appending `/EntityName` at the end of the OData service endpoint. You can see the results in Figure 13-28. Voilà! You now have XML or Atom data. If you look closely or open the XML with better formatting software, you will notice a top-level `<Feed/>` node followed by any number of `<Entry/>` nodes. Since this data feed is out of the database, the `Feed` node corresponds to the table/data entity and each individual `Entry` node corresponds to individual records from the data table. So, there you have it: an SQL Azure database holds the table containing your book data and the WCF Data Services endpoint exposes the OData feed straight out of the database for every record in the table.

Figure 13-28. *Local OData entity*

And the best part about such OData feeds is that it can be accessed purely over HTTP and the data exchange format is Atom/JSON, which most standard application platforms would be able to understand. You have, in just a few simple steps, created a basic OData service that abstracts away database details and simply offers a URI endpoint to get access to the underlying data. When you make HTTP requests at supported endpoints, the service is turning around and running SQL commands on the database at the lowest level; all this is simply hidden from the consumer of the service.

A quick note before you move on. OData standards dictate that data entity feeds out of the underlying database should carry data in either Atom or JSON formats. So far, you have just seen Atom. So, how does a consuming client request data in JSON format? Simple: append the request with a format parameter. Something like `http://ODataEndpoint/Entity?format=JSon`. The service is supposed to honor the format request and serve up data in JSON.

However, if you create your OData endpoint through the WCF Data Services route, you'll notice that the service does accept the extra format parameter in the HTTP request, but still serves up data in Atom format. This is a little glitch in the WCF Data Services implementation and is easily fixable. If the clients of your OData service demand data in JSON, head over to `http://wcfdstoolkit.codeplex.com` to download the WCF Data Services Toolkit. After installation, simply reference the added DLL and have your WCF service inherit from `ODataService` instead of the vanilla `DataService`. The rest can all remain the same, but now you will notice your service honoring the format request and serve up data in JSON format.

Deploying to Windows Azure

At this point, your data service is ready and exposing data straight out of the database. But what good would a service be if it just ran locally on your machines? It's time to deploy the service to Windows Azure and make it globally available. Let's do it the old-school way so that you can see the steps, but the new way is even simpler.

This is where the `ApressCloudService` Azure wrapper in your Visual Studio solution comes into play. This project contains local and cloud configurations so that applications (in your case, the WCF service) can be hosted using the local Azure simulators or directly to the cloud. Go ahead and take a look at these configuration files. They primarily contain metadata about hardware needed to deploy the applications (such as how large an instance of a virtual machine is needed, the number of instances, etc.). You can tweak these for your production application as per your demand; but normally you want at least two instances so that any potential hardware/software failures in Azure servers do not interrupt the availability of your service or application.

Service Packaging

For your demo WCF service, the default configuration is fine. Right-click the `ApressCloudService` and select Package from the context menu (see Figure 13-29). What you are about to do is package up the entire container application or service, along with configuration data, and push it up to Azure for hosting. Choose between service/build configurations and fire up the packaging.

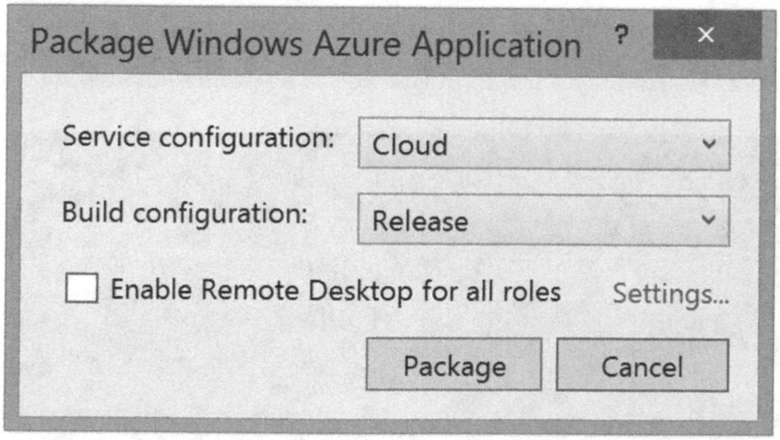

Figure 13-29. *Cloud packaging configuration*

If everything goes right, a Windows Explorer window pops up showing two generated files (see Figure 13-30) a service package (containing all the deployable artifacts) and a configuration file (containing all the deployment metadata). Mark the location where these files are created because you are going to need them in next step.

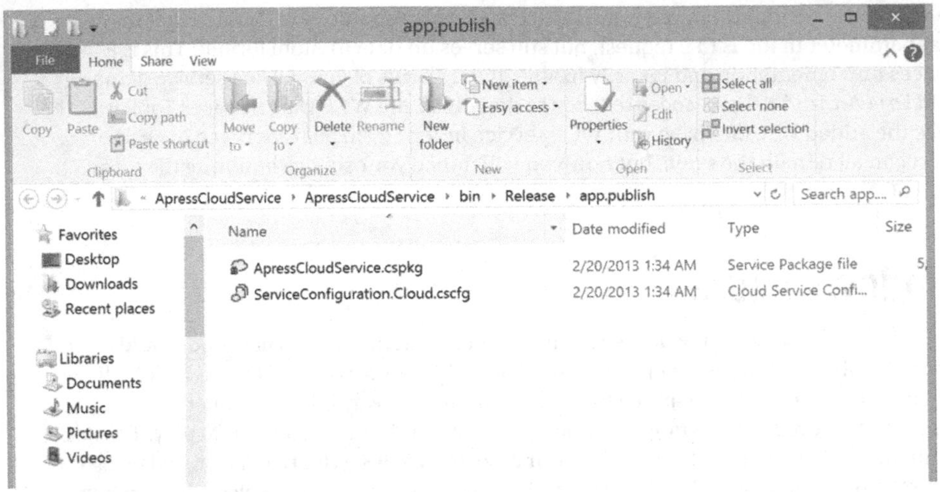

***Figure 13-30.** Cloud packaging artifacts*

Service Deployment

Now that you have the deployment artifacts ready, head back to the Azure management portal. Choose +New and select a new Cloud Service under Compute (see Figure 13-31).

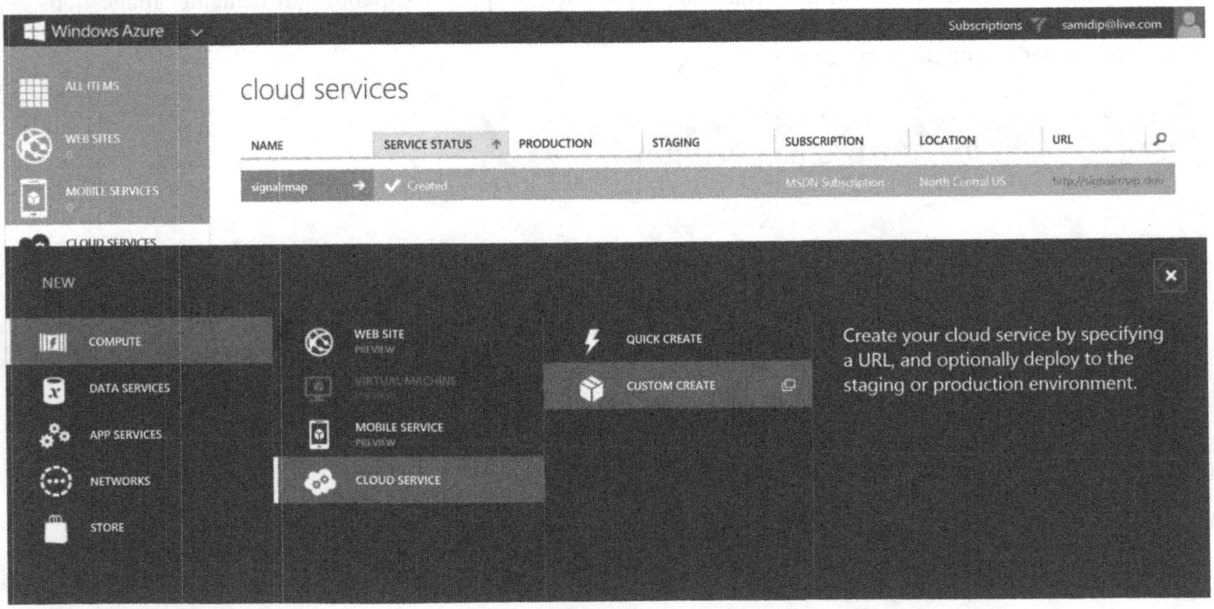

***Figure 13-31.** New Azure service*

The new service creation wizard will prompt you to name a URL endpoint for your application. Choose this well because this is the URI to reach your service/application. Next, pick the Azure subscription to create it and the physical datacenter region where you prefer the deployment to happen (see Figure 13-32).

Figure 13-32. *Azure service setup*

Next step, give your deployment a name and click the From Local button to point Azure to the service package/configuration files you just created locally from Visual Studio (see Figure 13-33). You can deploy your service or application to a staging environment to make sure everything is working fine, and then flip the switch to make it go live. For your demo, you will live on the edge and go straight to production. That's it—you have now provided Windows Azure with all that is needed to host your service or application. Press the last button (it looks like a tick mark) and wait for the behind-the-scenes magic. Azure will spin up the server needed and let you know (through a green check mark) that everything is online and live.

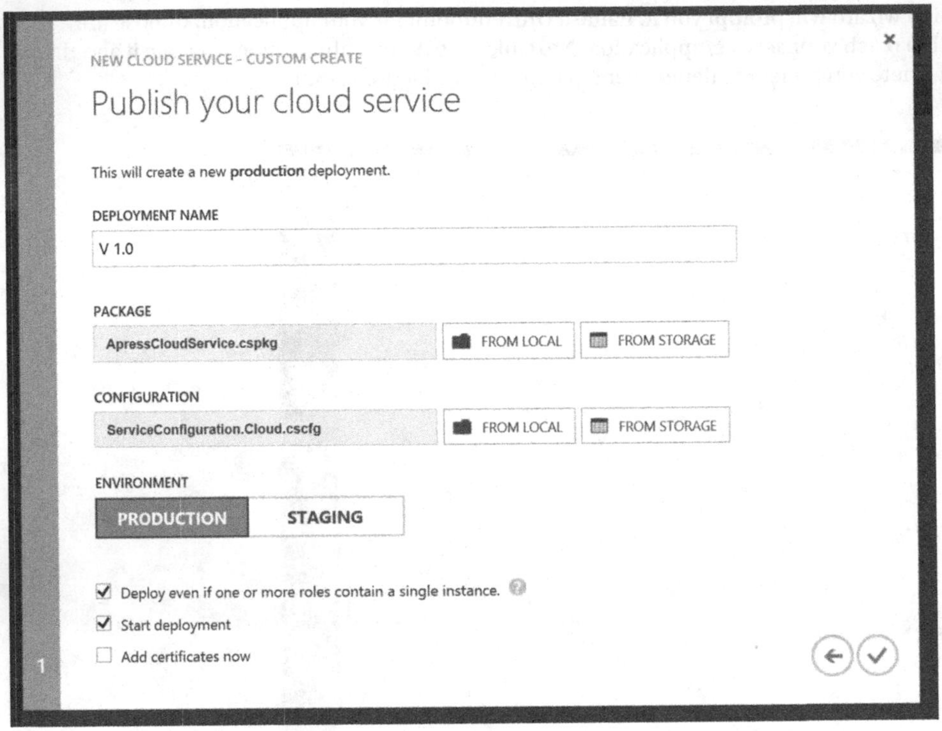

Figure 13-33. *Azure service publication*

Let's go ahead and pull up the WCF service SVC endpoint in a browser, this time with the Azure-hosted URL (see Figure 13-34). If all goes well, bingo—you now have your service live in Azure and globally accessible through URI endpoints.

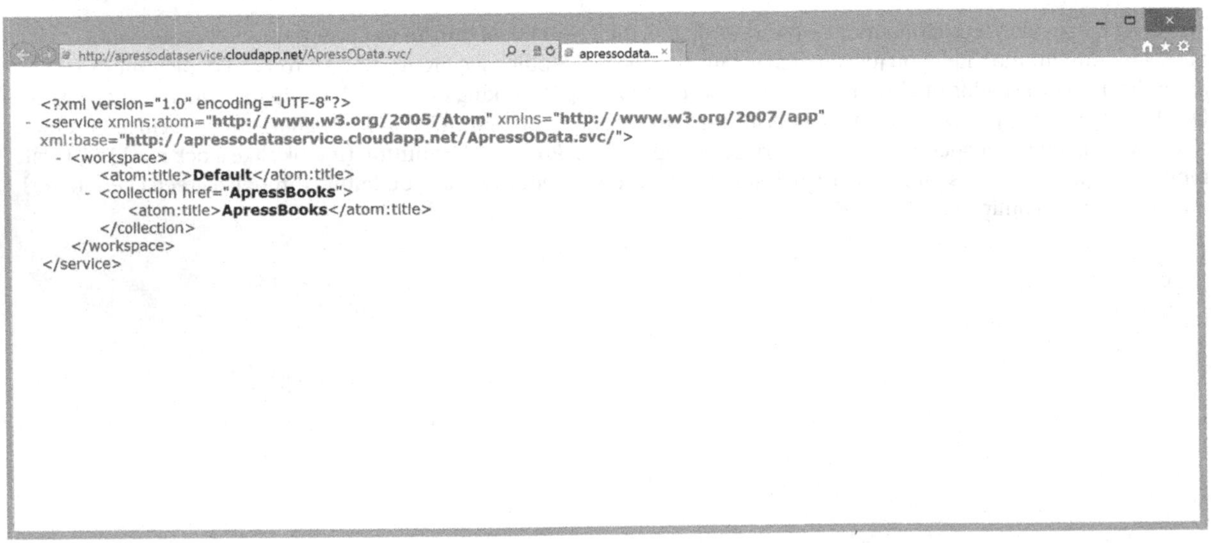

Figure 13-34. *Azure OData endpoint*

Before you move on, the latest Windows Azure SDK provides a more streamlined process where you can publish applications/services to Azure from inside Visual Studio itself. For more details, check out the details at `www.windowsazure.com/en-us/develop/net/tutorials/cloud-service-with-sql-database/`.

For sanity, try the `/EntityName` URL to see if you can fetch data out of the named database entity (see Figure 13-35). As you can see, you do bring back data in Atom format and it also has the same `Feed/Entry` node XML tree (see Figure 13-36) to consume the data easily. This, has to be empowering. With this Azure hosted service, you have deployed an OData feed that talks directly to your SQL Azure database while keeping the details hidden from consumers.

Figure 13-35. *Azure OData entity*

```
<?xml version="1.0" encoding="iso-8859-1" ?>
- <feed xml:base="http://apressodataservice.cloudapp.net/ApressOData.svc/" xmlns="http://www.w3.org/2005/Atom"
   xmlns:d="http://schemas.microsoft.com/ado/2007/08/dataservices" xmlns:m="http://schemas.microsoft.com/ado/2007/08/dataservices/metadata">
   <id>http://apressodataservice.cloudapp.net/ApressOData.svc/ApressBooks</id>
   <title type="text">ApressBooks</title>
   <updated>2013-02-20T19:03:23Z</updated>
   <link rel="self" title="ApressBooks" href="ApressBooks" />
 - <entry>
     <id>http://apressodataservice.cloudapp.net/ApressOData.svc/ApressBooks(1)</id>
     <category term="ApressBookDBModel.ApressBook" scheme="http://schemas.microsoft.com/ado/2007/08/dataservices/scheme" />
     <link rel="edit" title="ApressBook" href="ApressBooks(1)" />
     <title />
     <updated>2013-02-20T19:03:23Z</updated>
   - <author>
       <name />
     </author>
   - <content type="application/xml">
     - <m:properties>
         <d:ID m:type="Edm.Int32">1</d:ID>
         <d:ApressBookISBN>978-1-4302-3816-4</d:ApressBookISBN>
         <d:ApressBookName>Migrating to Windows Phone</d:ApressBookName>
         <d:ApressBookTechnology>Windows Phone</d:ApressBookTechnology>
         <d:ApressBookAuthor>Jesse Liberty , Jeff Blankenburg</d:ApressBookAuthor>
         <d:ApressBookPublishedDate m:type="Edm.DateTime">2011-12-28T00:00:00</d:ApressBookPublishedDate>
       </m:properties>
     </content>
   </entry>
 + <entry>
 + <entry>
 + <entry>
 </feed>
```


Figure 13-36. *Azure OData entity nodetree*

OData Service Integration

Now that data from your SQL Azure database is easily accessible through the Azure-hosted WCF service and via the OData endpoint, turn your attention toward consuming the data feed in your Windows 8 Store apps—and yes, that means going back to the Apress demo app.

There are a couple of ways in which to integrate the WCF service in your Windows 8 app, but the bottom line is that you want a tight integration so that the client knows about data entities exposed by the service for easy consumption. Also, since the OData endpoint is RESTful, this means that your client has to accommodate plenty of HTTP communication to specific URIs while going after given data entities. You developers would not want to hand-code HTTP communication. So, it looks like you need a tool that makes it easy to consume the OData service and provides .NET wrappers over the most common communication through the service.

The answer is a brilliant toolkit called WCF Data Services Tools for Windows Store apps. It is not included as a part of the Windows app SDK; so head over to `www.microsoft.com/en-us/download/details.aspx?id=30714` to download and install the toolkit (see Figure 13-37).

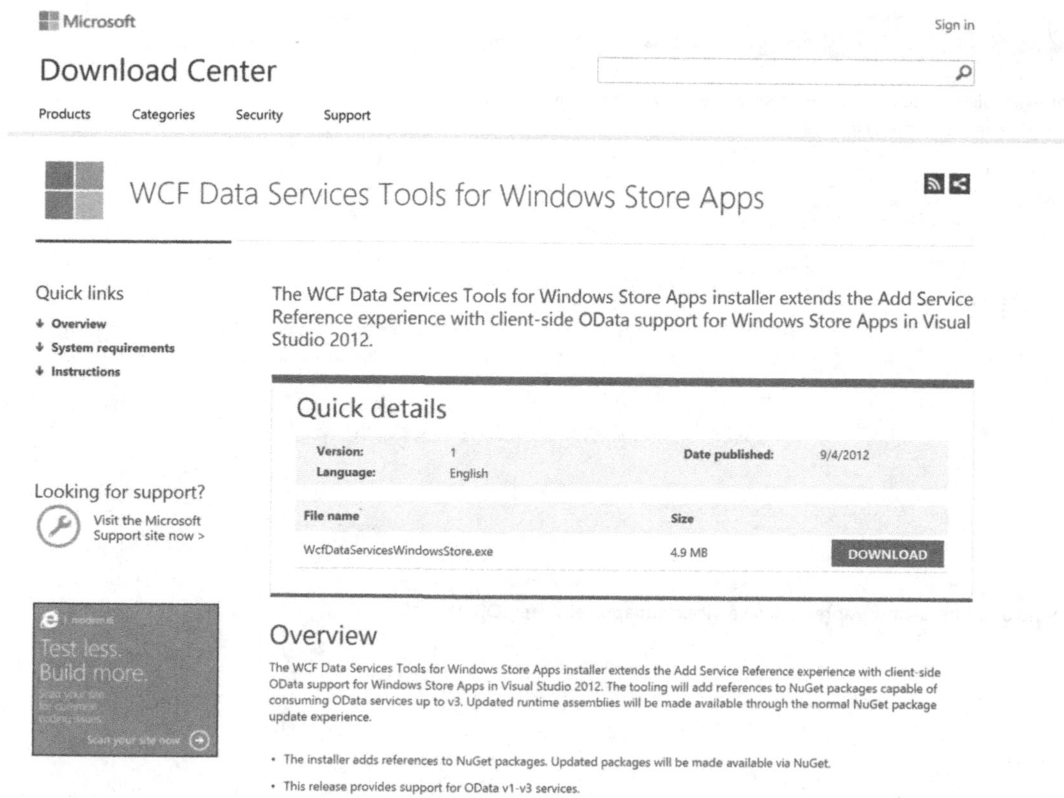

Figure 13-37. *WCF Data Services Tools download*

Among the best things that this toolkit does is the way you integrate with an OData/WCF service. Right-click in your Windows 8 Store app Visual Studio solution, and select Add New Service Reference (see Figure 13-38). Provide the wizard with the base WCF/OData service `.svc` endpoint and the WCF Data Services Tools for Windows Store apps will discover the data entities exposed by the service. Give the service reference a name, and you're done (see Figure 13-39)! Behind the scenes, the toolkit reflected on the WCF service and built local proxies to the data entities exposed. Suddenly, your client app has intimate knowledge of data structures used by the service, and you, the developer, are free to use this tight integration to read and manipulate data off the service. You can see the results of adding an OData/WCF service reference in your Visual Studio solution for the Apress demo app.

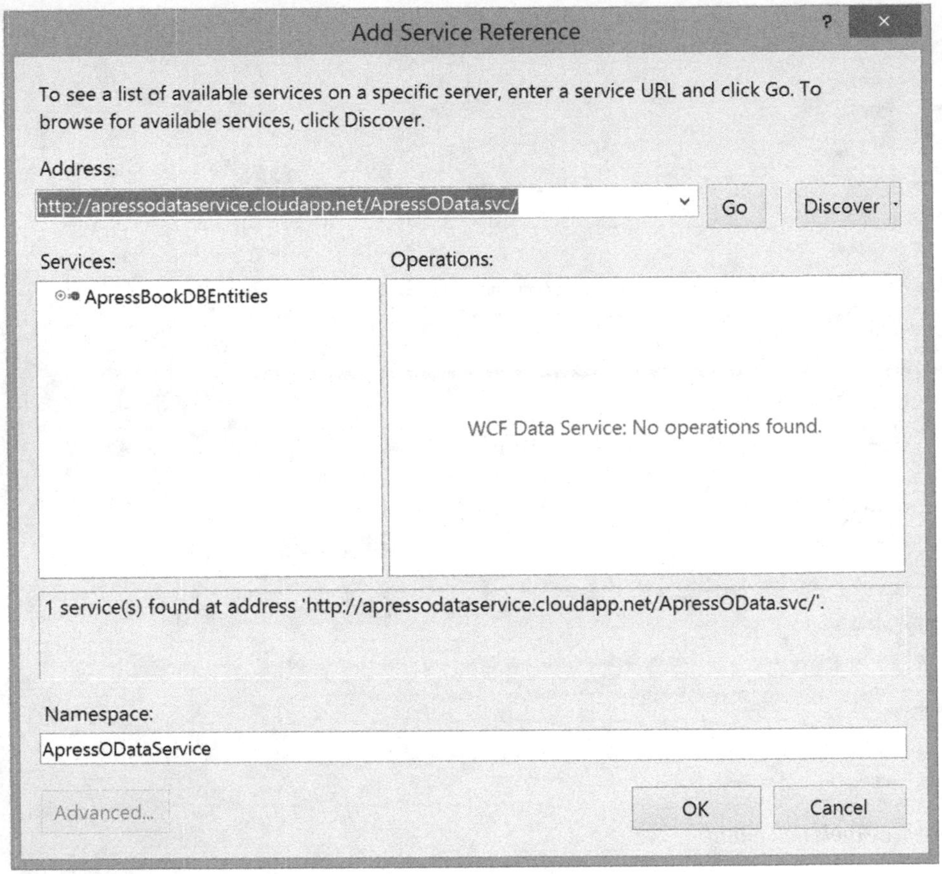

Figure 13-38. *Adding an OData service reference*

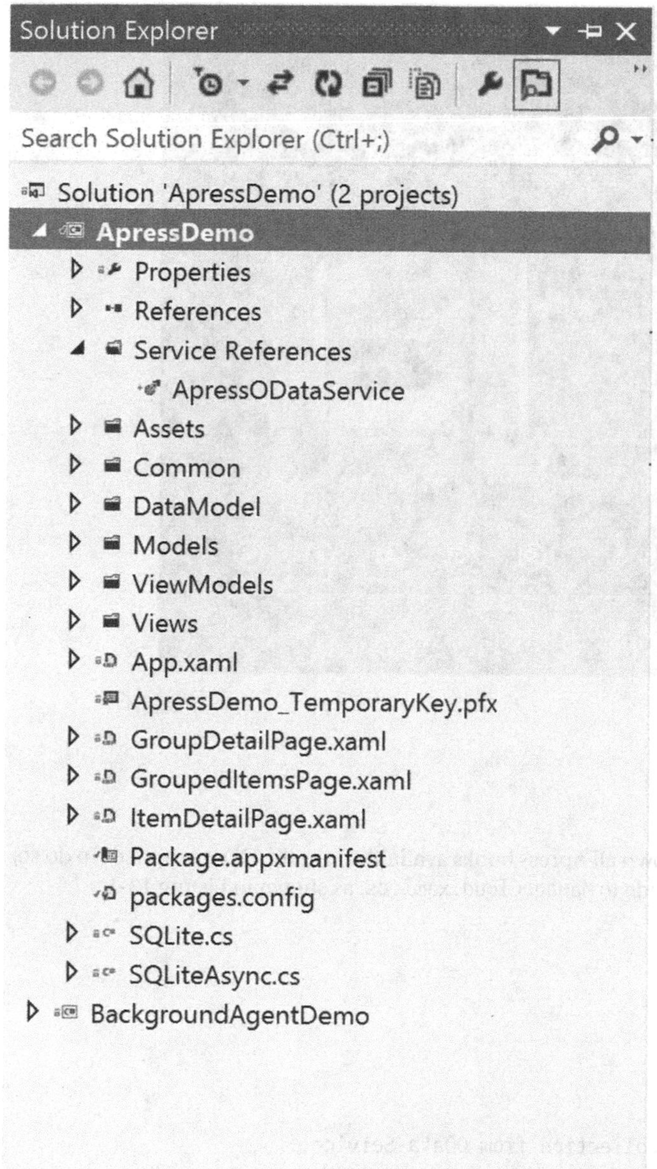

Figure 13-39. *The added OData service reference*

Now, back in your Apress demo app, differentiate between the book data you were showing for so long and the fresh data you are about to pull down from the crowd. Accordingly, I added a new app bar icon to take the user to a new XAML page called `ManageCloud.xaml`, dedicated to handling data from your WCF service (see Figure 13-40).

Figure 13-40. *Additional app bar icon*

Consumption

Let's prepare your dedicated XAML page to first pull down all Apress books available from the OData service. To do so, you shall utilize some special classes. Let's add some code to `ManageCloud.xaml.cs`, as shown in Listing 13-1.

Listing 13-1. OData Consumption

```
using System.Data.Services.Client;
using ApressDemo.ApressODataService;

       #region "Members"

        // Reference to Data Context & Object Collection from OData Service.
        DataServiceContext oDataContext;
        DataServiceCollection<ApressODataService.ApressBook> bookListFromService;

        #endregion

protected override void LoadState(Object navigationParameter, Dictionary<String, Object> pageState)
        {
            // Initialize.
            oDataContext = new DataServiceContext(new
Uri("http://apressodataservice.cloudapp.net/ApressOData.svc"));
            bookListFromService = new
DataServiceCollection<ApressODataService.ApressBook>(oDataContext);
```

```
            // Fetch all the entities.
            Uri query = new Uri("/ApressBooks", UriKind.Relative);

            // Asynchronously load the fresh data from Service.
            bookListFromService.LoadAsync(query);

            // Completion event handler.
            bookListFromService.LoadCompleted += (sender, args) =>
            {
                if (args.Error != null)
                {
                    // Do appropriate error handling.
                }
                else
                {
                    // Success. Bind to UI.
                    this.odataBookListView.ItemsSource = bookListFromService;
                }
            };
        }
```

There were few interesting bits in this code. First, notice your use of `DataServiceContext` and `DataServiceCollection` classes. These are special objects dedicated to handling reference to data services like yours. The `DataServiceContext` provides a direct reference to your OData service; take note on how you initialized it with the SVC endpoint. The `DataServiceCollection` is another super-helpful class. It is meant to represent a dynamic data entity collection from the service source that provides notifications when items get added, removed, or when the list is refreshed. And you know what this means, right? Yes, INPC—as in `INotifyPropertyChanged` interface implementation. This makes `DataServiceCollections` very friendly toward XAML UI data binding, as well as maintaining a collection that can be used to respond to changes on the client or server. More information about `DataServiceContext` and `DataServiceCollection` can be found at the following web sites: `http://msdn.microsoft.com/en-us/library/system.data.services.client.dataservicecontext.aspx` and `http://msdn.microsoft.com/en-us/library/ee474331.aspx`, respectively.

So, now it becomes a little clearer what you are doing with the code in Listing 13-1. Create a reference to the OData service and a local collection of Apress books, which you are going to asynchronously fill with data. Notice that the URI object uses the simple `/EntityName` convention to try pull down all data that is offered from the service. The `DataServiceCollection`'s `LoadAsync()` method fires off the request to the OData service. There is definitely HTTP communication happening under the covers, just not in this code, thanks to the WCF Data Services Tools. And once you get data back, you simply bind it to whatever UI your app needs. Listing 13-2 shows the little XAML I'm using for the Apress demo app's `ManageCloud` page to bind to the results of the OData query.

Listing 13-2. OData UI Binding

```
<ListView x:Name="odataBookListView" Grid.Row="1">
            <ListView.ItemTemplate>
                <DataTemplate>
                    <StackPanel Orientation="Vertical">
                        <TextBlock Text="Apress Book Details:" Style="{StaticResource
SubheaderTextStyle}" Margin="150,10,0,0"/>
                        <StackPanel Orientation="Horizontal" Margin="200,10,40,15"
HorizontalAlignment="Left">
                            <TextBlock Text="ISBN:" Style="{StaticResource ItemTextStyle}" />
                            <TextBlock Text="{Binding ApressBookISBN}" Style="{StaticResource
ItemTextStyle}" Width="250" Margin="10,0,0,0"/>
```

```
                            <TextBlock Text="Book Name:" Style="{StaticResource
ItemTextStyle}" Margin="90,0,0,0"/>
                            <TextBlock Text="{Binding ApressBookName}" Style="{StaticResource
ItemTextStyle}" Width="250" Margin="10,0,0,0"/>
                        </StackPanel>
                        <StackPanel Orientation="Horizontal" Margin="200,0,0,15" HorizontalAlignment="Left">
                            <TextBlock Text="Book Author:" Style="{StaticResource ItemTextStyle}"/>
                            <TextBlock Text="{Binding ApressBookAuthor}" Style="{StaticResource
ItemTextStyle}" Width="250" Margin="10,0,0,0"/>
                            <TextBlock Text="Book Technology:" Style="{StaticResource
ItemTextStyle}" Margin="40,0,0,0"/>
                            <TextBlock Text="{Binding ApressBookTechnology}"
Style="{StaticResource ItemTextStyle}" Width="250" Margin="10,0,0,0"/>
                        </StackPanel>
                    </StackPanel>
                </DataTemplate>
            </ListView.ItemTemplate>
        </ListView>
```

Fire up the Apress demo app and you should see data populated in your UI, as in Figure 13-41. There you have it—data straight out of your SQL Azure database table consumed in a Windows 8 Store app through an Azure-hosted OData service. Are you starting to see the benefits here?

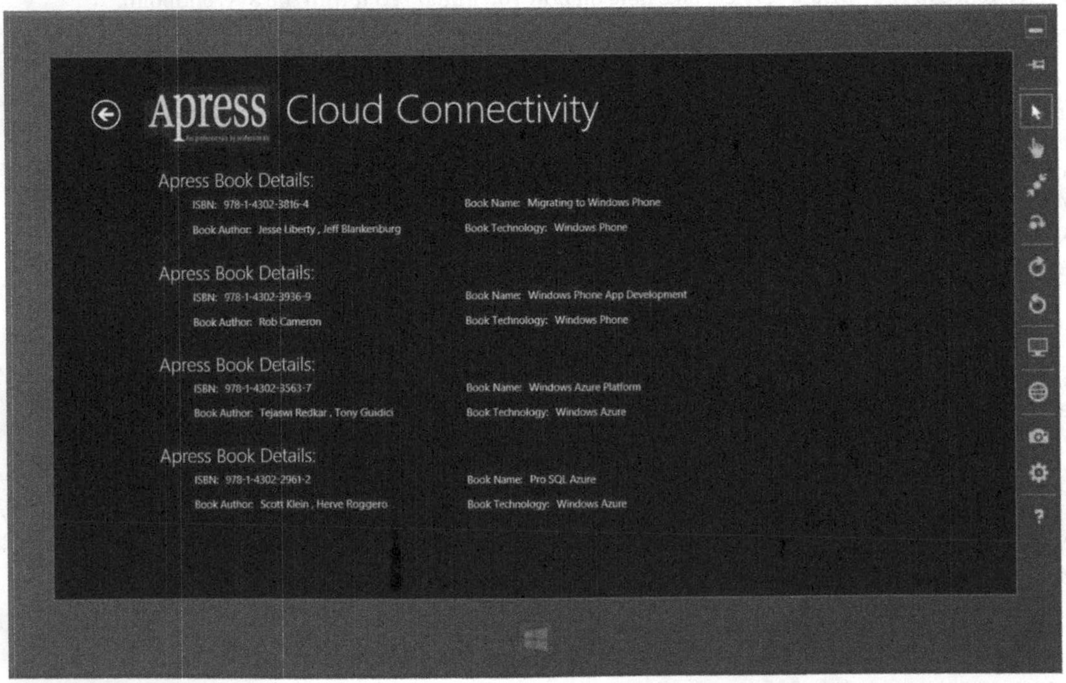

Figure 13-41. *Fetching entities through OData*

OData CRUD

Now, you can easily consume an OData feed from a database, as you just saw, but would you dare write anything back to the database? Well, sure. Remember that your access control at the data entity level for the WCF service allowed all reads/writes. Let's see how the WCF/OData service will handle database CRUD operations from the consuming client.

For the sake of demonstration, I've added a simple Save button in the page's app bar. The idea is that the user gets to select a record and edit it (see Figure 13-42). Your app would have to turn around and write the changes back to the SQL Azure database through the service.

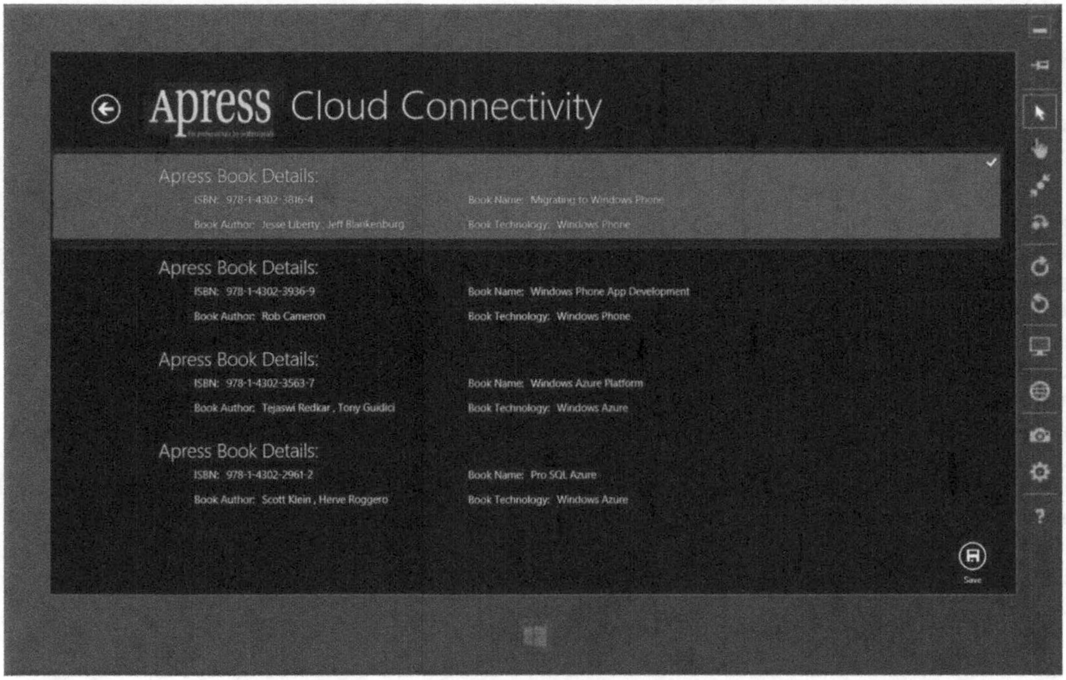

Figure 13-42. *OData CRUD*

For brevity, I do not actually have any UI to make changes to the selected Apress book. You can envision some text boxes that allow edits to the book's properties. You will simply pick a book from your `DataServiceCollection`, and then hard-code some edits and try writing it back to the database through the service. You will get the point, I promise. Listing 13-3 presents some code added to handle the Save button click.

Listing 13-3. OData CRUD

```
private void saveButton_Click(object sender, RoutedEventArgs e)
        {
            // Find the object to update from local list.
            ApressODataService.ApressBook selectedBook = bookListFromService.First(Book =>
Book.ApressBookISBN == "978-1-4302-3816-4");

            // Make local changes.
            selectedBook.ApressBookAuthor = "Samidip Basu";
```

```
        // Mark the object dirty & ready for update to DB.
        oDataContext.UpdateObject(selectedBook);

        // Commit all at once.
        oDataContext.BeginSaveChanges(new AsyncCallback(SaveDoneCallBack), null);
    }

    private void SaveDoneCallBack(IAsyncResult asynchronousResult)
    {
        // Possibly on a different thread here!
        if (asynchronousResult.IsCompleted)
        {
            // Indicate completion.
            // Bubble event up to any listeners or update UI.
        }
    }
```

So, you are iterating through your local `DataServiceCollection` to find the book the user has selected. Once you have the selected book object, I am going to pretend I wrote it (just for kicks) by changing the author's name. Once local changes are ready for commit, you utilize the `UpdateObject()` and `BeginSaveChanges()` methods off the `DataServiceContext` to mark your object for updates and start pushing out the data changes back to the database through the service. Notice the use of the `AsyncCallBack` event handler that allows for error handling or successful depiction once the update operation completes. What's happening here is complex: an HTTP Post message gets generated with appropriate object changes marked, and then gets posted at the OData service endpoint. The service then turns around and runs the appropriate SQL commands to update the database and returns a response back to the caller. All the while, your code looks incredibly simple—plain C# without a hint of HTTP communication. This is the power of the WCF Data Services Tools. Its inserts and deletes to the database follow the exact same pattern.

Do you have doubts as to whether your code really did go back to update the SQL Azure database? Let's check it out by going to the SQL Azure management portal and inspecting the database table for Apress books (see Figure 13-43). Sure enough, I am now denoted as the author of an awesome book that I did not write!

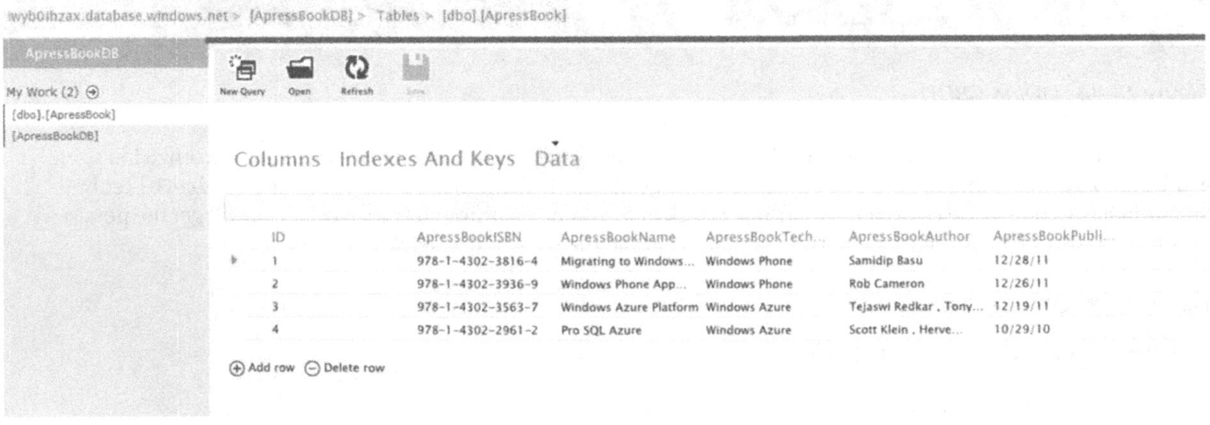

***Figure 13-43.** OData CRUD updates in database*

As an added advantage of using a `DataServiceCollection` to bind your UI to, you get notified immediately in case anything changes in the collection. For example, as a part of the last update that marked the book as dirty before committing to the database through the service, the `DataServiceCollection` picks up the change and raises the event for seamless UI updates without your having to do anything (see Figure 13-44). Neat, isn't it?

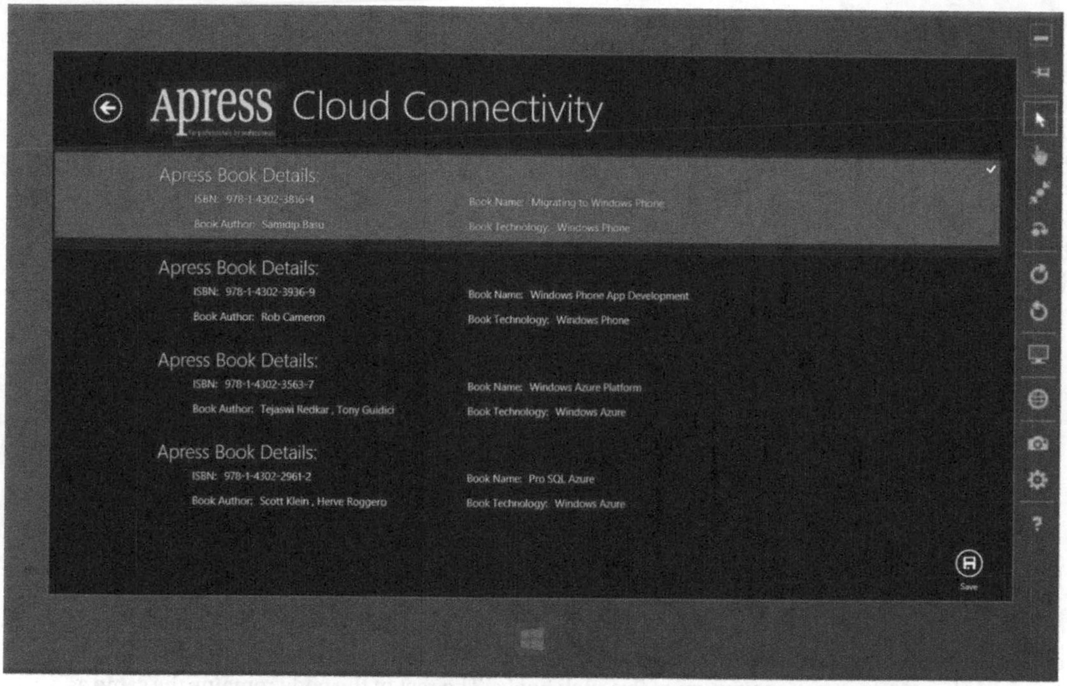

Figure 13-44. *OData CRUD updates in XAML page*

Other OData Tricks

Let's look at two other quick benefits of using a WCF/OData service endpoint for data consumption in your Windows 8 Store apps. First is filtering. Surely, you can use the /EntityName convention to pull down all data offered by a data entity. But often this might be too much data and not required by the client app. How do you filter down the results so that there is less data brought back across the wire? The answer is LINQ.

You write LINQ statements against the DataServiceCollection to denote the filtered request you want to make off the OData service. The WCF Data Services Tools then converts the request into appropriate HTTP communication and only brings back matching records through the OData service. Let's look at the example in Listing 13-4. Let's say you were only interested in Apress books about Windows Phone.

Listing 13-4. Custom OData Queries

```
protected override void LoadState(Object navigationParameter, Dictionary<String, Object> pageState)
        {
            // Initialize.
            oDataContext = new DataServiceContext(new
Uri("http://apressodataservice.cloudapp.net/ApressOData.svc"));
            bookListFromService = new DataServiceCollection<ApressODataService.ApressBook>(oDataContext);

            // Custom queries.
            var bookCatalog = new ApressBookDBEntities(new
Uri("http://apressodataservice.cloudapp.net/ApressOData.svc"));
```

```
        var customQuery = (from Book in bookCatalog.ApressBooks
                           where Book.ApressBookTechnology == "Windows Phone"
                           select Book).Take(5);

        // Asynchronously load the fresh data from Service.
        bookListFromService.LoadAsync(customQuery);

        // Completion event handler.
        bookListFromService.LoadCompleted += (sender, args) =>
        {
            if (args.Error != null)
            {
                // Do appropriate error handling.
            }
            else
            {
                // Success. Bind to UI.
                this.odataBookListView.ItemsSource = bookListFromService;
            }
        };
    }
```

As you can see, you wrote a custom LINQ query this time and only requested the service to provide books that belong to a given technology and return a maximum of five such books. The rest of the code remains the same as before. That's all that is needed for filtering. Fire up the app, and now you should only see the Apress books about Windows Phone (see Figure 13-45).

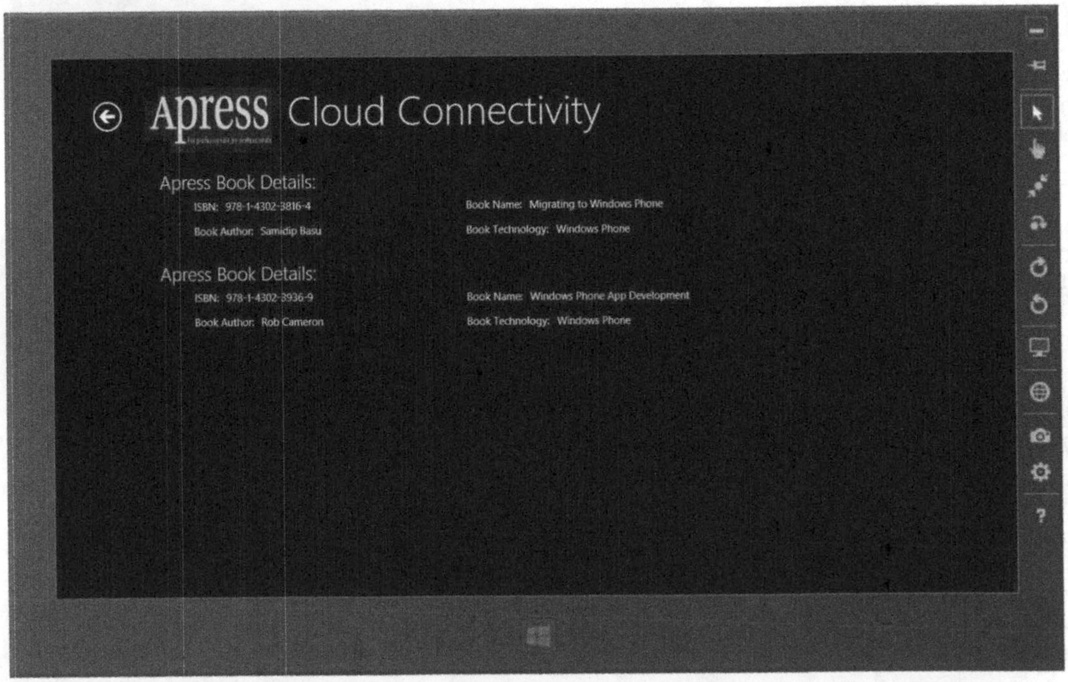

Figure 13-45. *Filtered OData feed*

OData Paging

What if you were building a Netflix movie browser in your Windows Store app, or something else that offered a large quantity of data? Every OData service hit for a given data entity would bring back a fixed number of records, with a continuation token at the end of the response XML. If you do not see the raw Atom/XML in your .NET code, how would you support paging through a given number of Netflix movies at a time? Simple, the WCF Data Services Tools offers a solution. Here's some code for your Apress books collection:

```
if (bookListFromService.Continuation != null)
{
    bookListFromService.LoadNextPartialSetAsync();
}
```

As you can see, you simply check for the presence of a continuation token in the response through the `DataServiceCollection`'s `Continuation` property. If so and when appropriate based on user interaction, you can easily request the next set off the OData service.

By now, you should see the incredible benefits of a structured and standards-compliant data service, like OData, that sits on top of your relational database. What you get is a ubiquitous service presence for consumption across application platforms, and easy, fine-grained control over data security. You have to love this as a developer.

Push Notifications

One of the areas where cloud augmentation of Windows 8 Store apps really shines is in its push notifications. It is an incredibly inviting user experience when the user of a Windows 8 app does not even need to interact with the app, yet he or she gets a toast, tile, or badge update from the cloud. A picture is worth a thousand words, so let's start the discussion on push notifications with the most complete depiction of the whole process through the MSDN diagram shown in Figure 13-46.

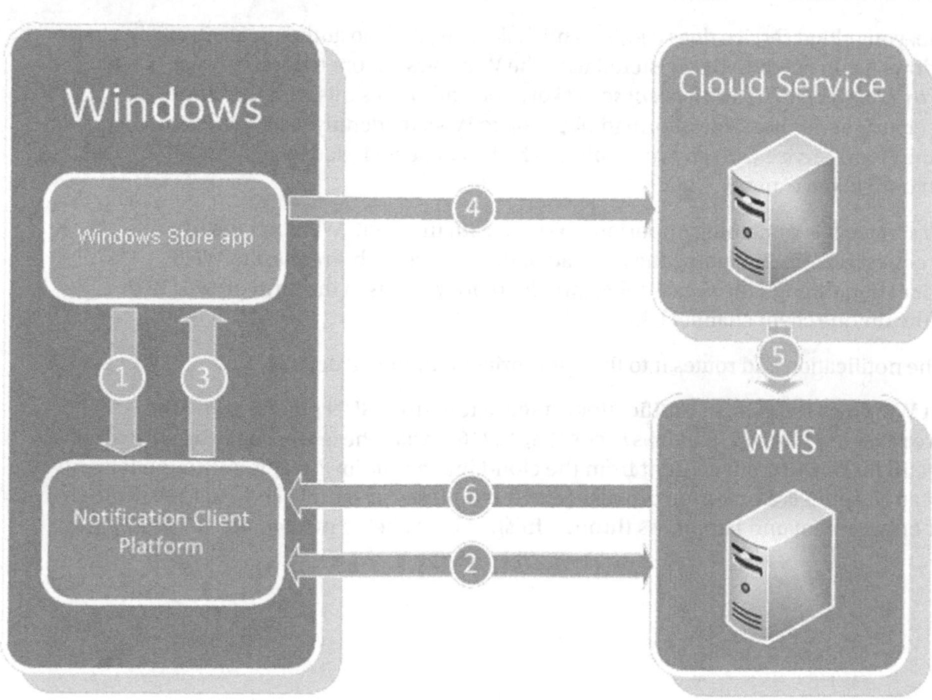

Figure 13-46. *Push notification framework*

As you start looking into the players and their roles in push notifications, I'm reminded of an excellent story that my friend Jeff Blankenburg, MSFT Evangelist, uses to describe push notifications. Let me narrate.

Let's say you got a new house. What's the first thing you do? You head over to the post office to change your address. Next, you immediately inform your family and friends of your new home address—maybe you even ask for housewarming gifts. Your family and friends want to send you packages, but they do not swing by your house in person. Instead, they take the packages to the post office, which in turn, sends out postal workers to deliver the packages. This real-world scenario is very similar to what goes on to empower the Windows 8 app ecosystem with push notifications from the cloud. Here are the complete steps to get push notifications set up:

- First, your Windows 8 Store app needs to get a unique address for the device it is running on, similar to the home address.
- The Windows 8 app requests for a unique identifier from the Windows 8 *Notification Client Platform*, which conveys the message to Windows Notification Service asking for a *notification channel.*
- The *Windows Notification Service* (commonly called the WNS) is the post office in this story. Upon request, the WNS generates a unique URI as the notification channel that identifies the given Windows 8 app on the user's given device and returns the URI to the caller. This URI makes it back to the Windows 8 Store app through the Notification Client Platform.
- Next, a *cloud service* comes into the play, taking the role of family/friends; this, in other words, is the back-end companion to your Windows 8 app. While I would suggest using Windows Azure to host this service, in reality, this cloud service can be deployed to any Internet-facing server you desire. In fact, it does not even strictly have to be a cloud service; anything that can host a service and connects over the Internet should suffice.
- Once the Windows 8 app knows the notification channel URI, it sends it to the companion cloud service through secured web standards. The cloud service, in most cases, holds on to the URI sent up as a collection of subscribers.
- In the meantime, your cloud service does a little handshake with WNS to authenticate itself. First, your Windows 8 app needs to be registered with the Windows 8 Store to receive a *Package security identifier* (*SID*) and a *client secret* key. The app shares this with the cloud service and the cloud service uses this information to talk to WNS to identify itself. In return, WNS provides the cloud service with an *access token*, which is to be included in all future communication until token expiry.
- When the cloud service has something important to share with the client Windows 8 Store app, it sends a request to WNS, including the payload of the message. This request to WNS requires authentication through the access token provided prior and is in the form of an HTTP Post request at the unique client channel URI.
- WNS receives the notification and routes it to the appropriate Windows 8 device.

For more details about Windows 8 app push notifications, please refer to MSDN guidance over at `http://msdn.microsoft.com/en-us/library/windows/apps/hh913756.aspx`. These steps are the sure-shot way to get push notifications set up for pushing out content from the cloud into a Windows 8 app. Although it involves a few steps, the push notification setup is a one-time process (and it has plenty of sample code to look through in MSDN), but it enables user engagement and happiness through fresh content being pushed out to the app from outside the device.

You may also be wondering what kind of messages can be included as a part of push notifications. Turns out, all kinds of tiles, toasts, or badges are supported. Remember the tile/toast/badge catalogs that detailed predefined styles with corresponding XML payloads? That is exactly what you would do for push notifications as well. The cloud service simply creates the XML payload and sends it over to WNS as an HTTP Post at the app channel URI. Also, if your Windows 8 app is running on the user's device, you have the option of sending out raw communication from the cloud down to the device to be processed by the application's own code, not requiring your push notifications to adhere to predefined payloads.

However, there is now a new kid on the block that makes push notifications setup for Windows 8 apps quite a snap. Yes, enter Azure Mobile Services!

Azure Mobile Services

One of the small complaints against the use of Azure to power your back-end services or set up push notifications for your Windows 8 apps was the initial barrier to entry. The developer would have to know the intricacies of how to set up an SQL Azure database (if hosting relational data in the cloud), or know how to deploy services. In getting push notifications to work, the developer would need a little OAuth knowledge (although MSFT provides very easy sample code to follow) to make sure his/her cloud service for push notifications could do the handshake with WNS. Since you are putting in the effort to host a back-end service in Windows Azure, would it not be nice if it could serve mobile applications in other platforms? Microsoft heard the feedback.

Enter Azure Mobile Services, a new offering for developers looking to leverage Windows Azure as their cloud back-end. This was the secret Microsoft project ZuMo for a while (Zu from Azure and Mo from mobile to make up the acronym). Think of it as a thin veneer over existing Azure services, that makes life a whole lot easier. Everything that you could do with data/services in Azure is still there. The Azure Mobile Services interface just makes the process much easier. Also, Azure Mobile Services has extra tricks up its sleeve to assist with data validation/paging during persistence in the cloud, authenticating users or sending out push notifications to multiple mobile platforms.

As of now, Azure Mobile Services is in preview mode, but everything is functional. In fact, you can host up to ten mobile services for free during the trial. Your starting point for Azure Mobile Services should definitely be the developer portal at `www.windowsazure.com/en-us/develop/mobile/` (see Figure 13-47). Every Azure Mobile Services feature is explained with code samples, along with plenty of learning resources. Let's invest some time to figure out two features where Azure Mobile Services really shine: sending push notifications to Windows 8 Store apps and authenticating users in apps.

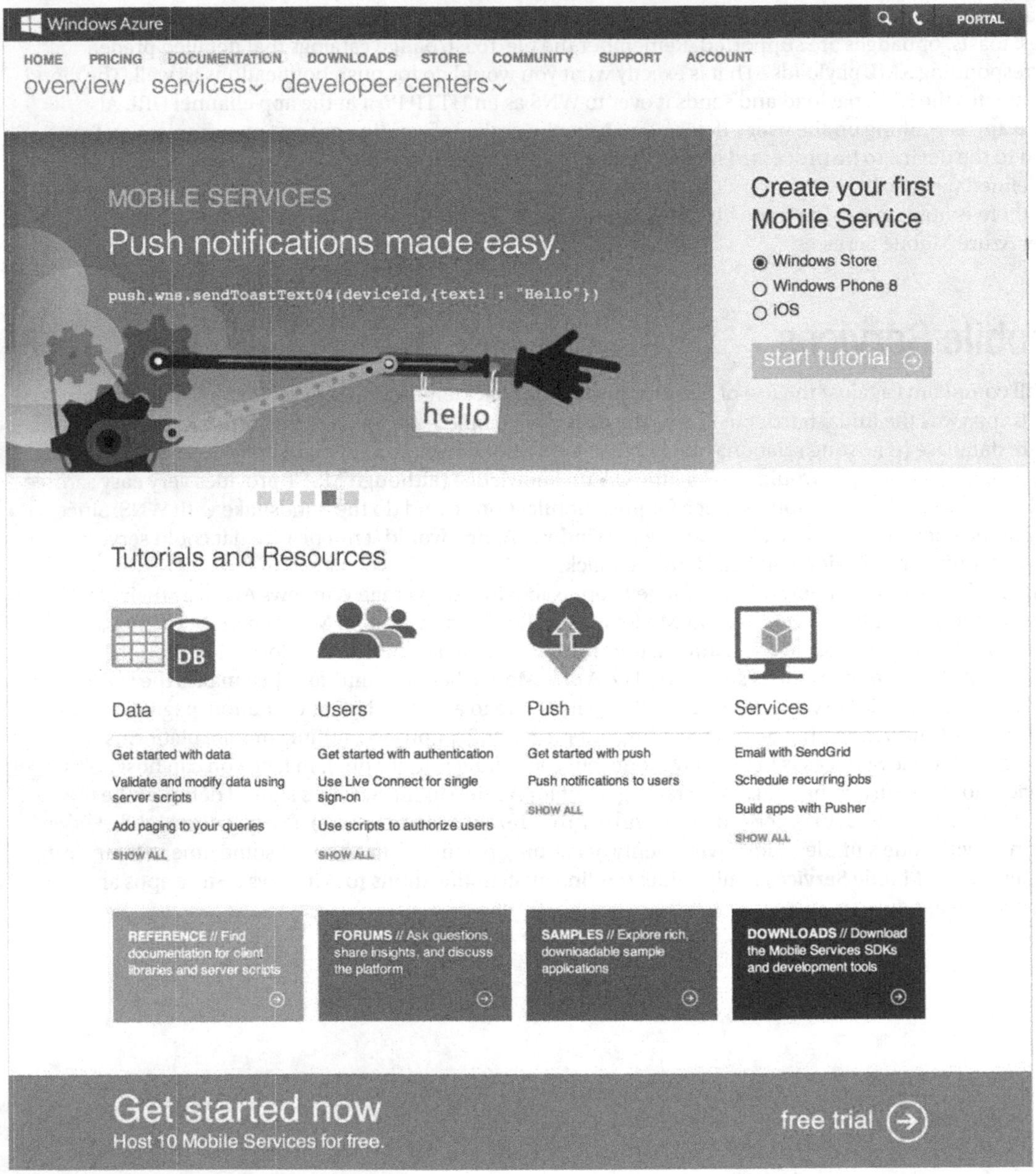

Figure 13-47. *Azure Mobile Services portal*

If you log on to your Azure subscription management portal and see nothing about mobile services on the left pane, it may be because you have not signed up to use Azure Mobile Services in preview mode. Head over to `https://account.windowsazure.com/PreviewFeatures` and sign up to try Azure Mobile Services (see Figure 13-48).

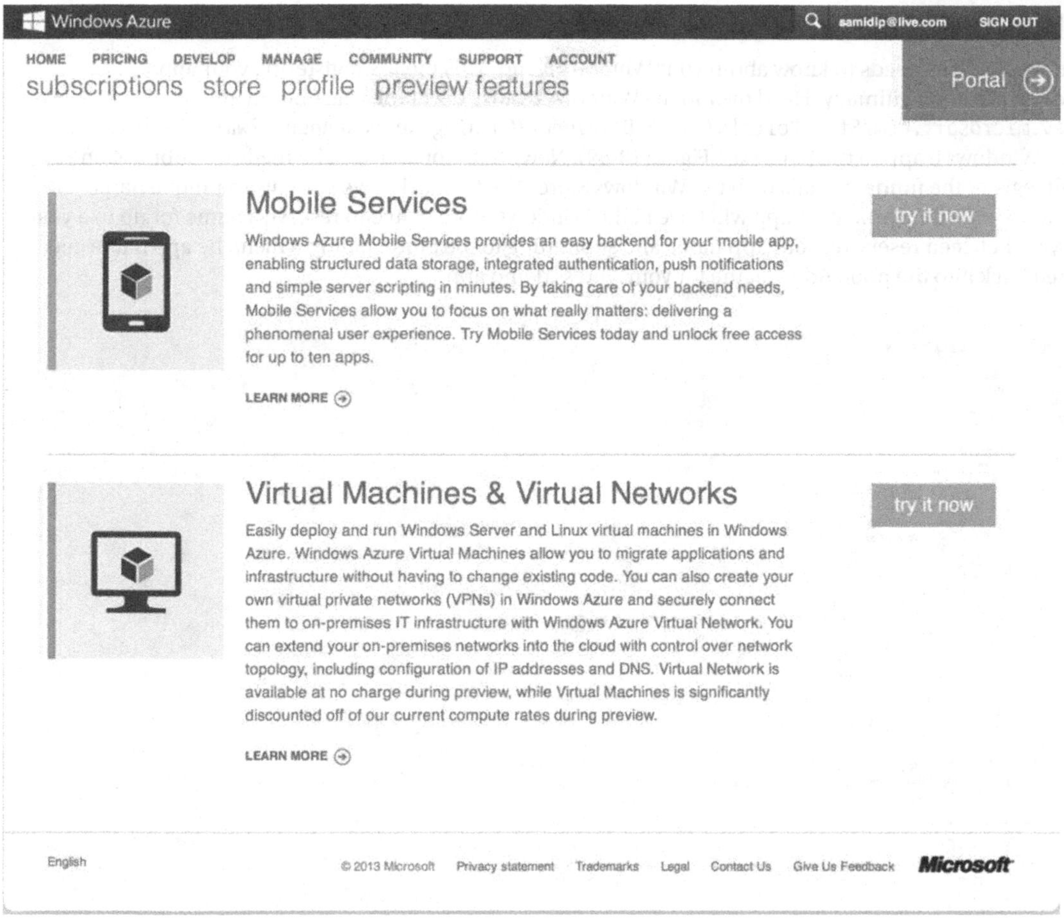

Figure 13-48. *Azure Mobile Services in preview*

Push Notifications Through Mobile Services

Let's see how the Mobile Services can help in automating setting up push notifications to Windows 8 Store apps. Normally, your cloud service will only send out a notification to subscribing Windows 8 apps if something interesting happens in the back end that the client does not have knowledge of yet. Often the trigger to know if something has changed may be in the back-end database—maybe somebody did a CRUD operation on the database table that every subscribing Windows 8 app user should know.

This is the kind of setup where mobile services shine. Once a mobile service knows about a Windows 8 app and its underlying SQL Azure database, it can watch the database tables (through JavaScript scripting) for CRUD operations. A mobile service can also be handed notification channel URIs from clients, along with Windows Store app credentials. This allows the mobile service to perform the OAuth2 WNS handshake and keep an access token handy along with persisting the client channel URIs. Once a database trigger is hit, a push notification to subscribing Windows 8 apps is an HTTP POSTaway, which is all handled behind the scenes by the mobile service. Let's try your hand at setting up the preceding scenario.

App Setup

First, Azure Mobile Services needs to know about your Windows 8 app. This means registering your app with the Windows Store for legitimacy. Head over to the Windows 8 Store developer dashboard at `https://appdev.microsoft.com/StorePortals/en-US/Developer/Catalog/ReleaseAnchor?wa=wsignin1.0` for submitting your Windows 8 app to the Store (see Figure 13-49). Now, your app may not be ready for submission yet, but you can still register the fundamentals with the Windows Store. The first task: give your app a unique name (see Figure 13-50). This is the name your app will have in the Windows Store. You can reserve a name for up to a year. So, you have a year between reserving your app name and submitting to the Store, failing which, the app name gets decommissioned back into the pool. Add a name for your Apress demo app.

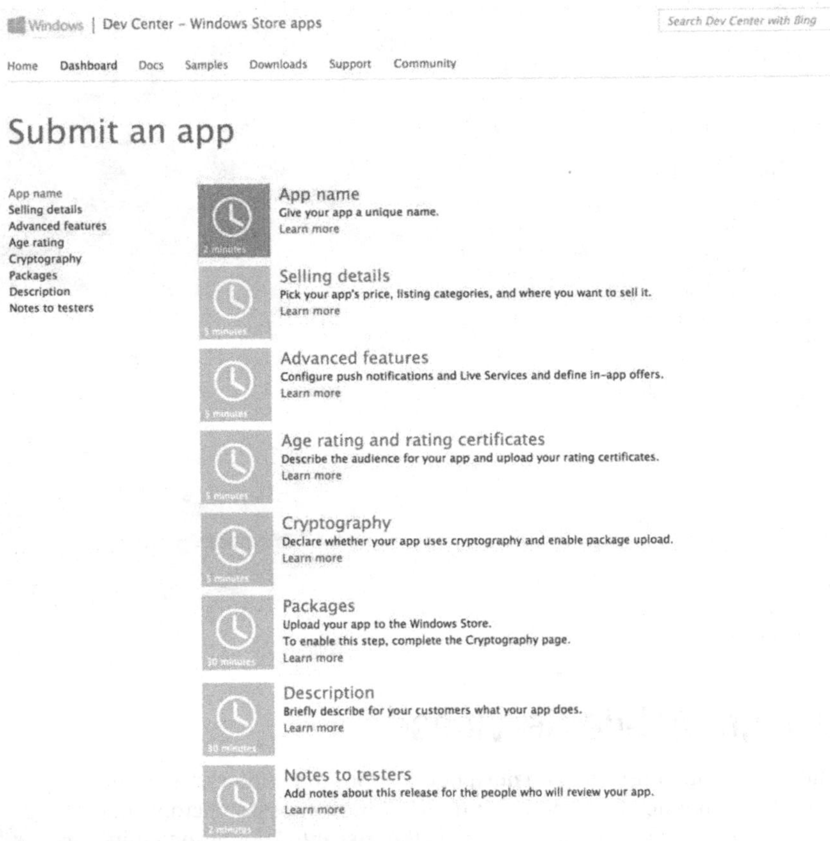

***Figure 13-49.** Windows Store dashboard*

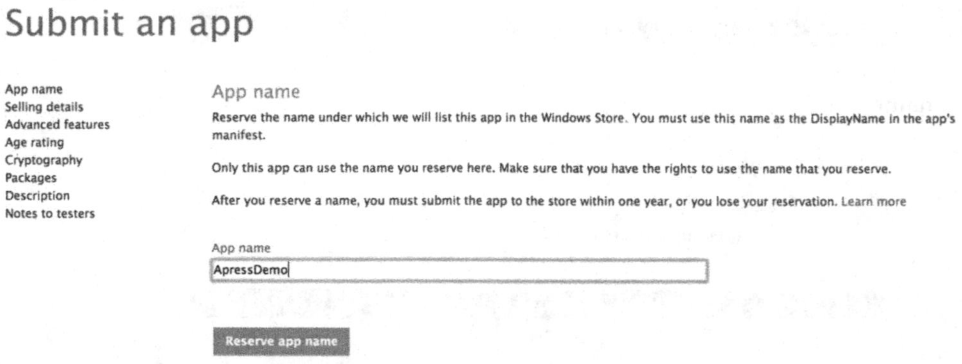

Submit an app
App name
Selling details
Advanced features
Age rating
Cryptography
Packages
Description
Notes to testers
App name
Reserve the name under which we will list this app in the Windows Store. You must use this name as the DisplayName in the app's manifest.
Only this app can use the name you reserve here. Make sure that you have the rights to use the name that you reserve.
After you reserve a name, you must submit the app to the store within one year, or you lose your reservation. Learn more
App name
ApressDemo
Reserve app name

Figure 13-50. *Store app name*

Once you have your app name reserved, come back to the Visual Studio project and associate the app you have been working on with the Store name, as you do for your Apress app (see Figure 13-51). You'll notice that the wizard automatically pulls up the list of all Store app names you have registered so far (see Figure 13-52) and you have to pick one.

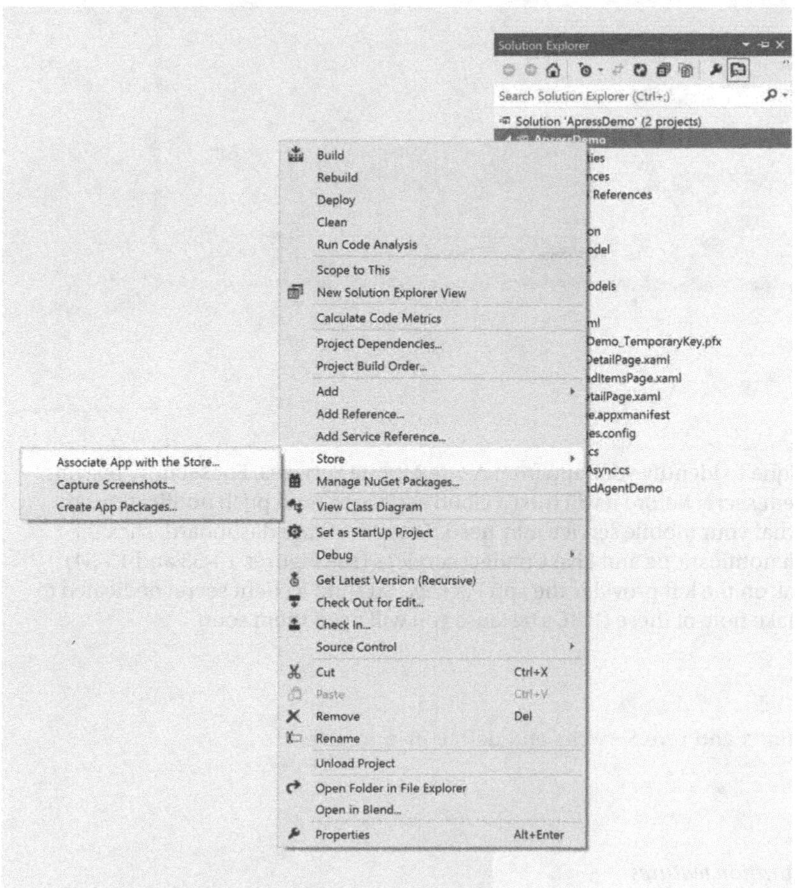

Figure 13-51. *Store association*

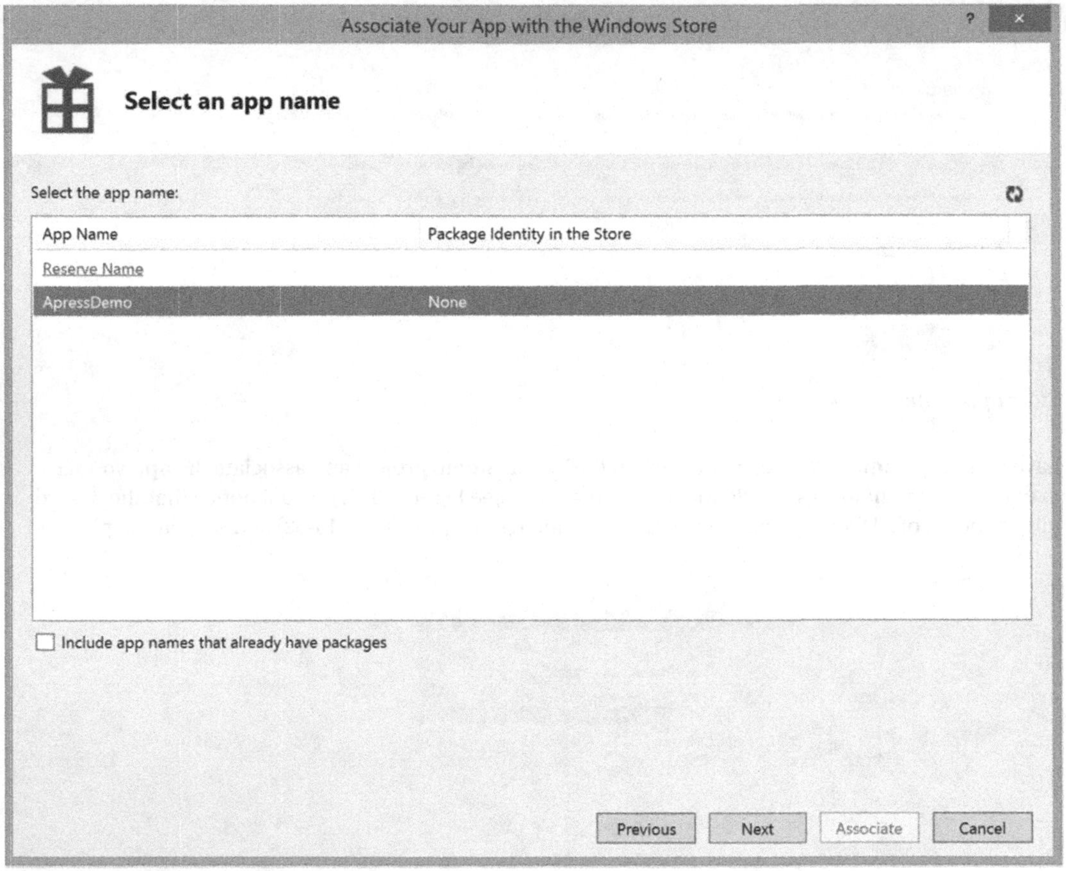

Figure 13-52. *Store app name selection*

App Identification

The next step is to provide something unique to identify your app from Azure Mobile Services. For security reasons, WNS needs an app Package SID and a client secret before it will trust a cloud service to send push notifications to client Windows 8 apps. So, let's find out what your mobile service may need. From the Store dashboard, click the Advanced Features link to configure push notifications and Live Connect services (see Figures 13-53 and 13-54). Once in, the Authenticate Your Service link on the left provides the app Package SID and a client secret dedicated to your app's name in the Windows Store. Make note of these GUIDs because you will need them soon.

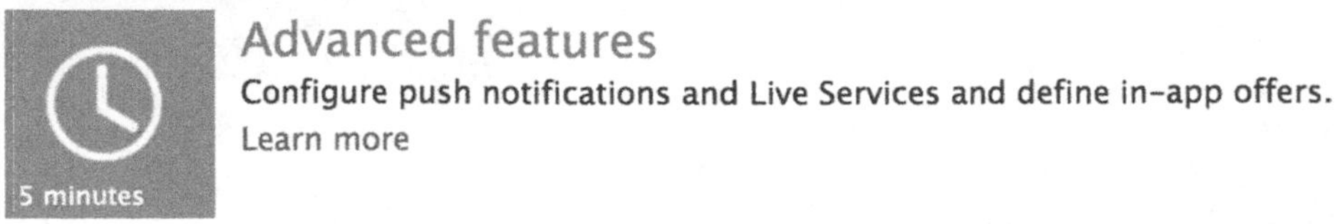

Advanced features
Configure push notifications and Live Services and define in-app offers.
Learn more
5 minutes

Figure 13-53. *Store advanced app configuration features*

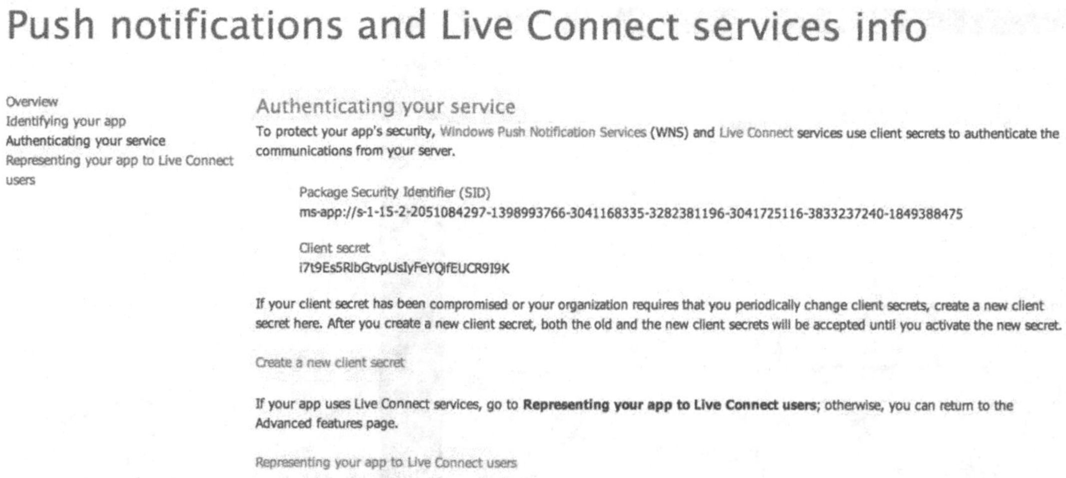

Push notifications and Live Connect services info
Overview
Identifying your app
Authenticating your service
Representing your app to Live Connect users
Authenticating your service
To protect your app's security, Windows Push Notification Services (WNS) and Live Connect services use client secrets to authenticate the communications from your server.
Package Security Identifier (SID)
ms-app://s-1-15-2-2051084297-1398993766-3041168335-3282381196-3041725116-3833237240-1849388475
Client secret
i7t9Es5RlbGtvpUslyFeYQifEUCR9I9K
If your client secret has been compromised or your organization requires that you periodically change client secrets, create a new client secret here. After you create a new client secret, both the old and the new client secrets will be accepted until you activate the new secret.
Create a new client secret
If your app uses Live Connect services, go to Representing your app to Live Connect users; otherwise, you can return to the Advanced features page.
Representing your app to Live Connect users

Figure 13-54. *Store authentication credentials*

Service Setup

Now, set up your custom mobile service. Head back to the Azure management portal and you should see Mobile Services show up in the left pane. Start there or click the +New button to create a new service (see Figure 13-55).

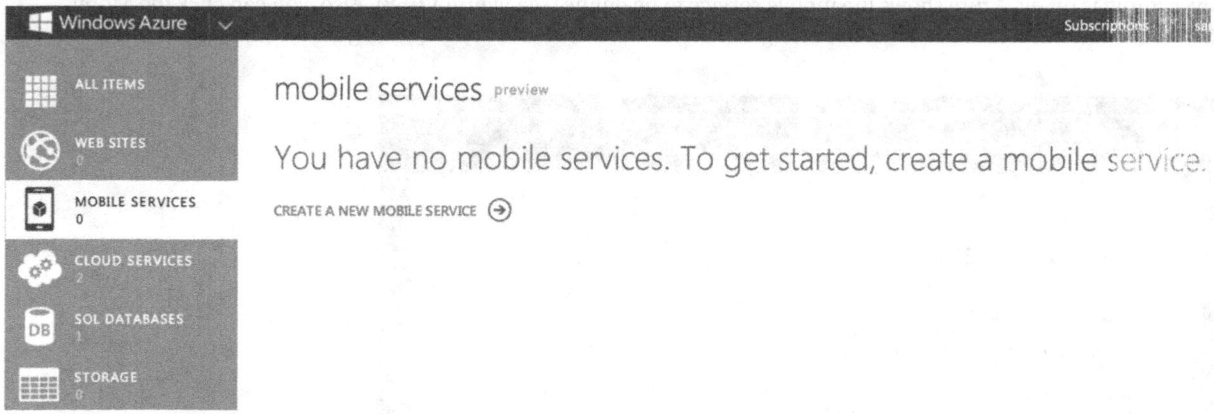

Figure 13-55. *New Azure Mobile Services*

Give your service a unique name and choose to create a new SQL Azure database or use an existing one (see Figure 13-56). This is an underlying SQL database that you will be able to write scripts for to watch for CRUD operations on data. You choose to reuse the same SQL Azure database you created earlier. A small caveat if you are reusing databases: your mobile service and the SQL Azure server should ideally be in the same geographic region to reduce network latency and bandwidth costs.

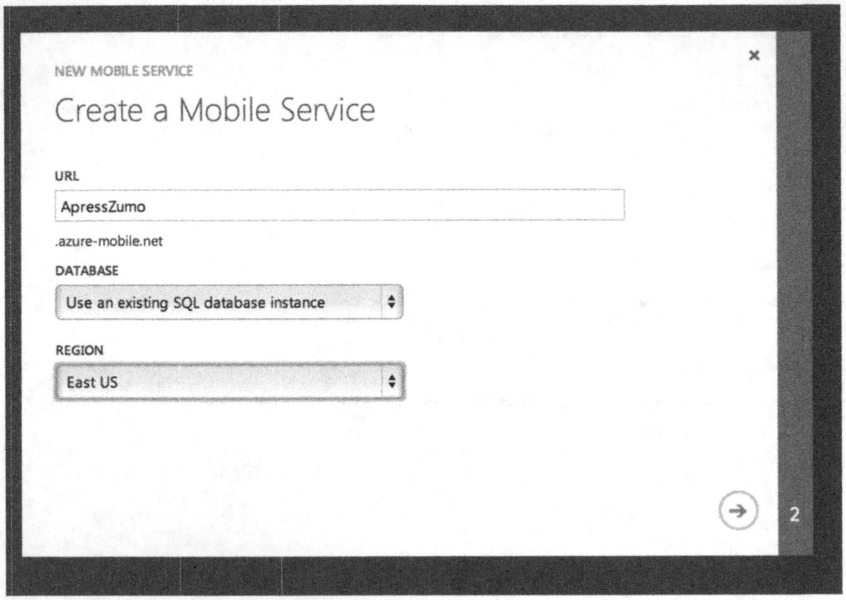

Figure 13-56. *New Azure Mobile Services database configuration*

You can see that mine are not, and accordingly, Azure shows a little warning, as shown in Figure 13-57. Once everything is ready, Azure shows the mobile service to be online (see Figure 13-58). Also, you can click the Mobile Service link to see a dashboard on the configuration and health of the service (see Figure 13-59).

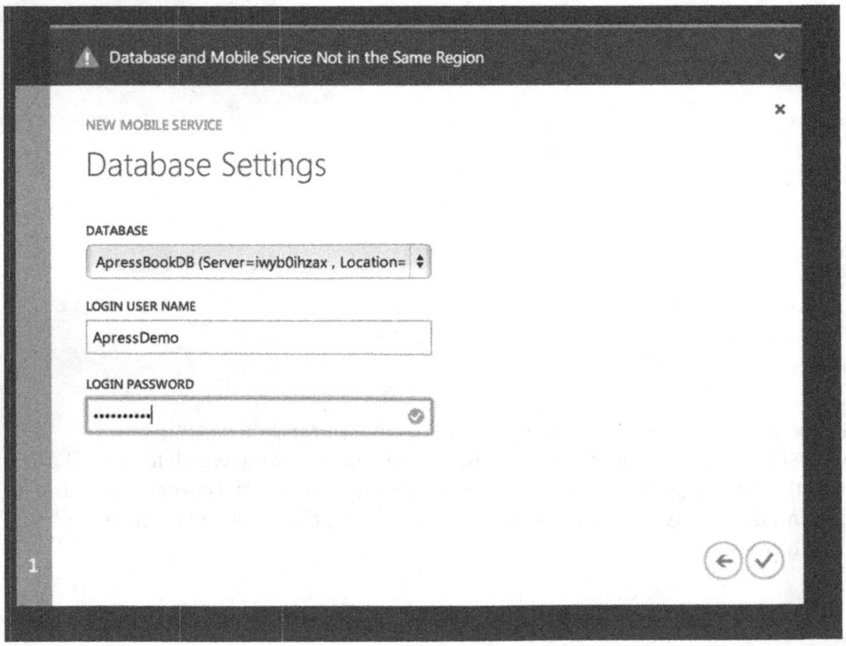

Figure 13-57. *New Azure Mobile Services database settings*

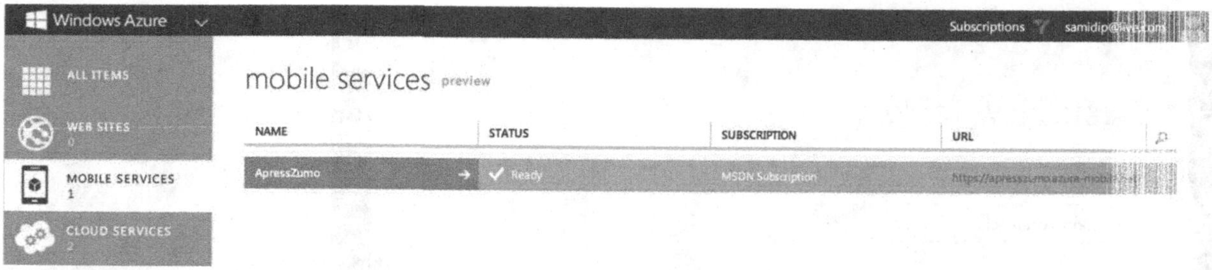

Figure 13-58. *New Azure Mobile Services are ready*

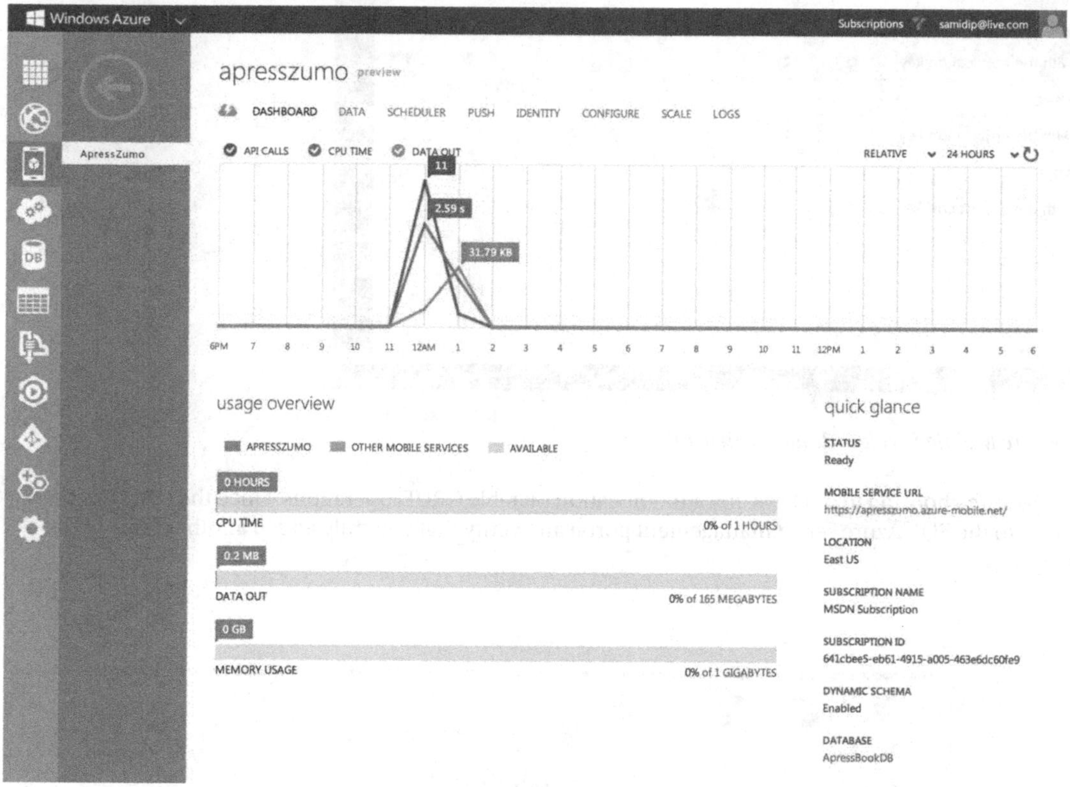

Figure 13-59. *New Azure Mobile Services dashboard*

Within the existing SQL Azure database, however, create a fresh table so that you get see a dynamic table schema in action. Head over to the Data tab on the dashboard to do so (see Figure 13-60).

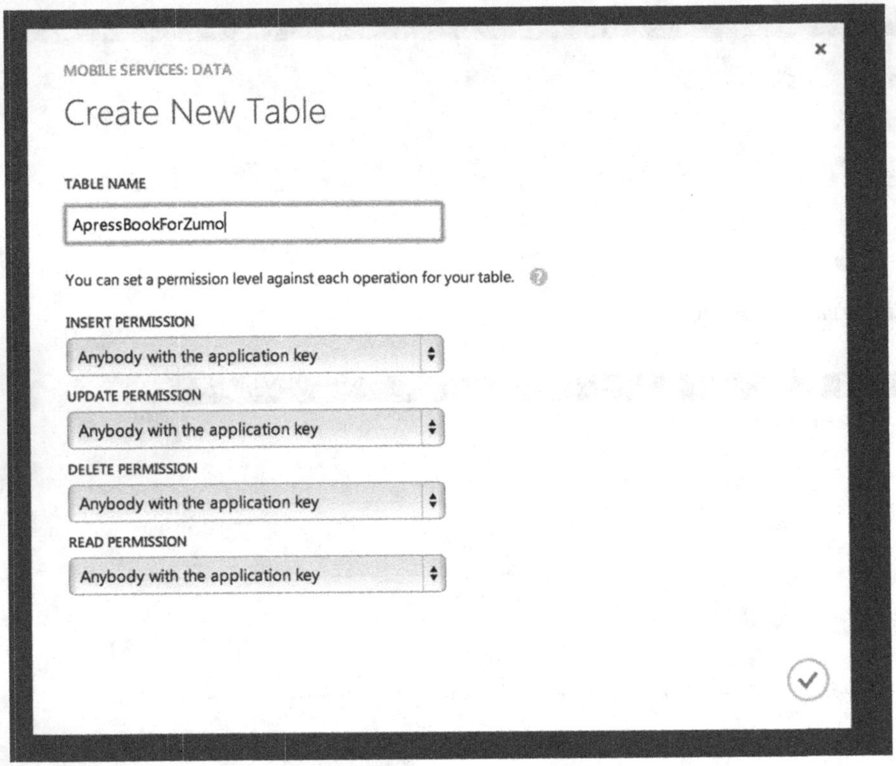

Figure 13-60. *Azure Mobile Services database new table*

Notice how you are choosing to not have any authentication on table CRUD operations. Once the table has been created, head back to the SQL Azure server management portal and verify that you truly added another table in the mix (see Figure 13-61).

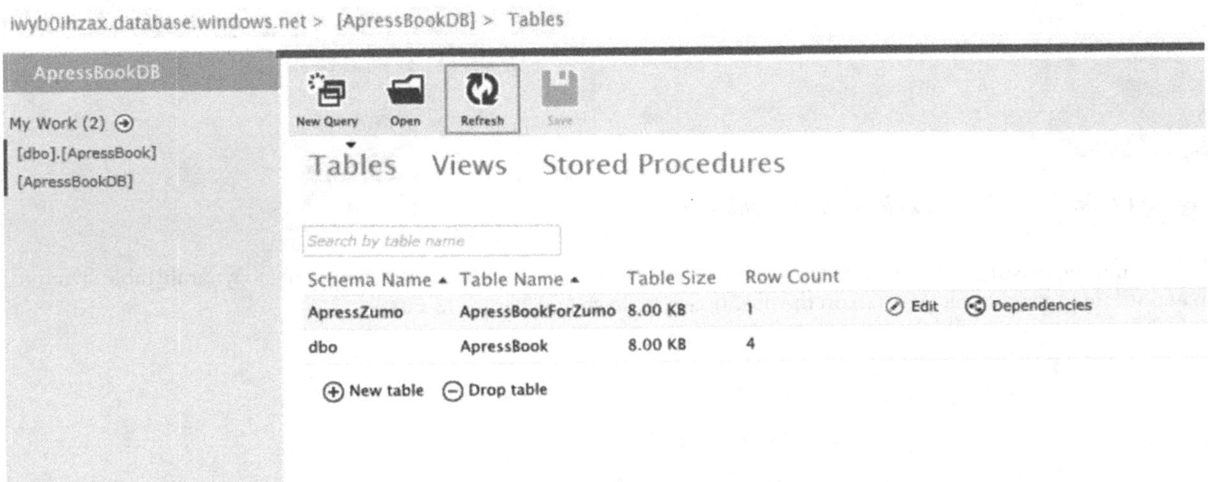

Figure 13-61. *Azure Mobile Services new table created in database*

Once the table has been created, click its link in the Azure Mobile Services dashboard to view the table schema (see Figure 13-62). As you can see, it has only one column called `id`, which is numeric and acts as the primary key for the table. This is the default behavior, but the table schema will change as you try manipulating content into the table.

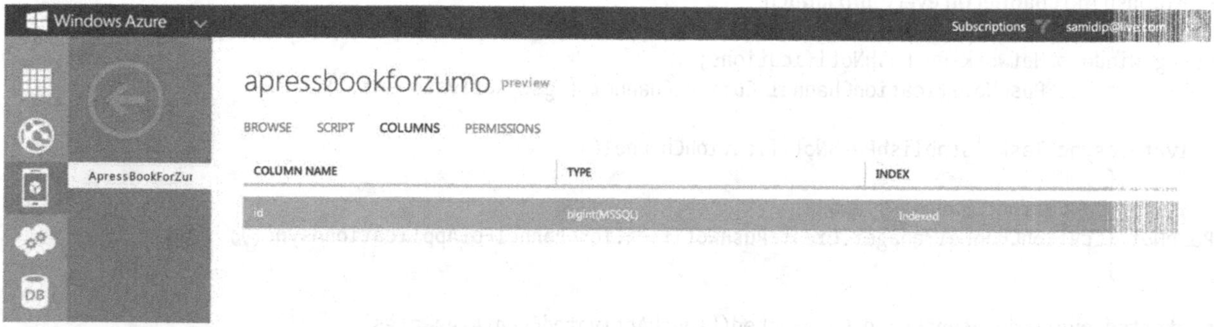

Figure 13-62. *Azure Mobile Services database new table schema*

Service-App Handshake

Do you remember the app's Package SID and client secret that you took note of for your Windows 8 app? Now is the time to use it. On the dashboard of the newly created Azure Mobile Service, go to the Push tab for setting up push notifications. The cloud service will need to authenticate itself with WNS and the client details are needed to do the handshake. So, go ahead and enter the app's Package SID and the client secret for setting up the service (see Figure 13-63). Don't forget to click the Save button at the bottom of the page.

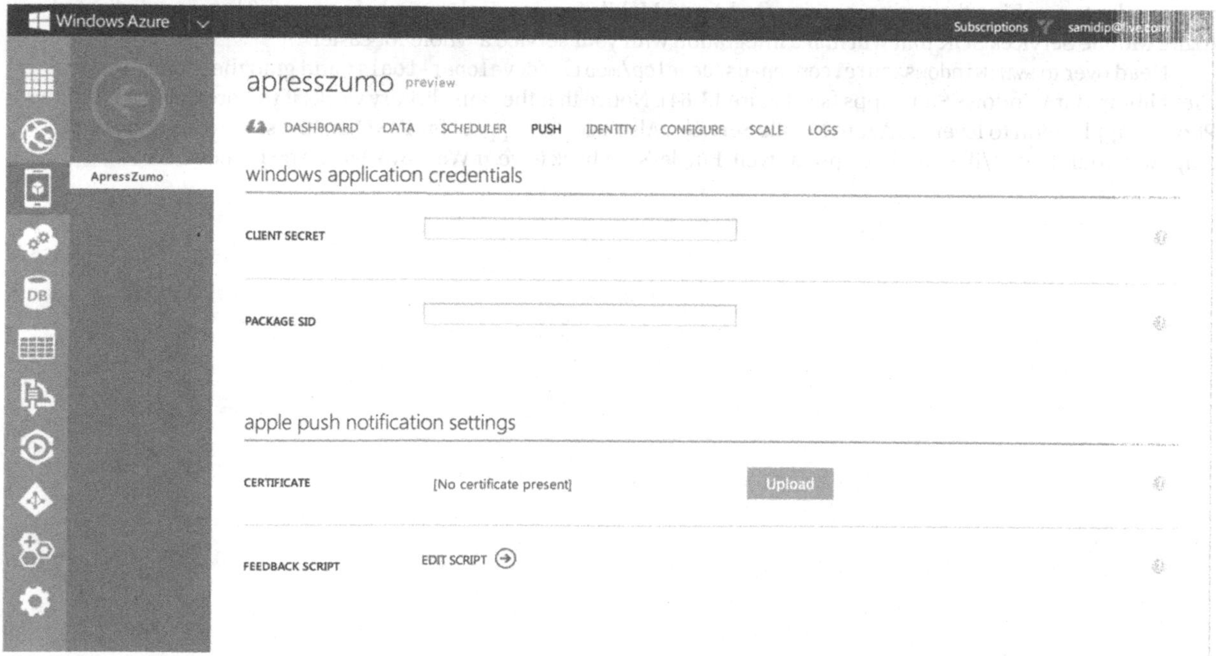

Figure 13-63. *Azure Mobile Services push notification configuration*

Your mobile service now has everything it needs to send a push notification, except where to send the notification. This is the notification channel URI that your Windows 8 app is supposed to create and then pass up to the cloud service. So, let's get that part done. Here's some code in the Apress demo app's `App.xaml.cs` file to create a push notification channel. Notice how you persist the channel URI through an app-wide static container and reestablish the channel on every app launch.

```
using Windows.Networking.PushNotifications;
public static PushNotificationChannel CurrentChannel { get; private set; }

private async Task EstablishPushNotificationChannel()
        {
            CurrentChannel = await
PushNotificationChannelManager.CreatePushNotificationChannelForApplicationAsync();
        }

protected override async void OnLaunched(LaunchActivatedEventArgs args)
        {
            EstablishPushNotificationChannel();
            ...
            ...
        }
```

Mobile Service SDK

So, your Windows 8 app has to accomplish two things now: sending the push notification channel URI to Azure Mobile Services and firing off a CRUD operation on the newly created table in the SQL Azure database. The easiest way may be to combine the two operations, and Azure Mobile Services is there to help as well. There is a dedicated Azure Mobile Services SDK that will make integration with your service a whole lot easier.

Head over to `www.windowsazure.com/en-us/develop/mobile/developer-tools/` and grab the Mobile Services client library for Windows Store apps (see Figure 13-64). Notice that the same library works if you are doing a Windows Phone 8 application to leverage Azure Mobile Services. Also, see the support for iOS? Yep, the same techniques can empower your iPhone/iPad mobile apps as well. But, let's get back to your Windows Store app for now.

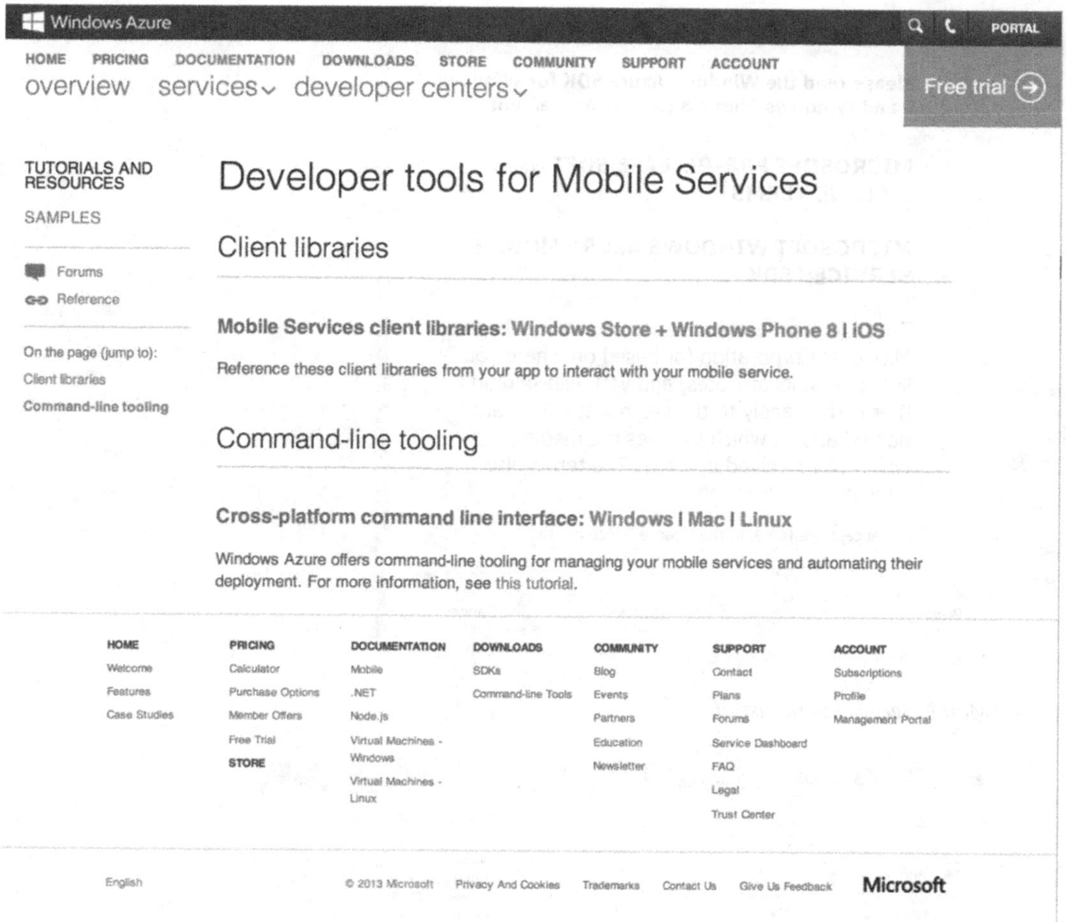

Figure 13-64. *Azure Mobile Services client SDK*

Go ahead and install the SDK, and then add a reference to the mobile service client DLL in your Visual Studio solution containing the Windows 8 app code, as you do for your Apress demo app (see Figures 13-65 and 13-66).

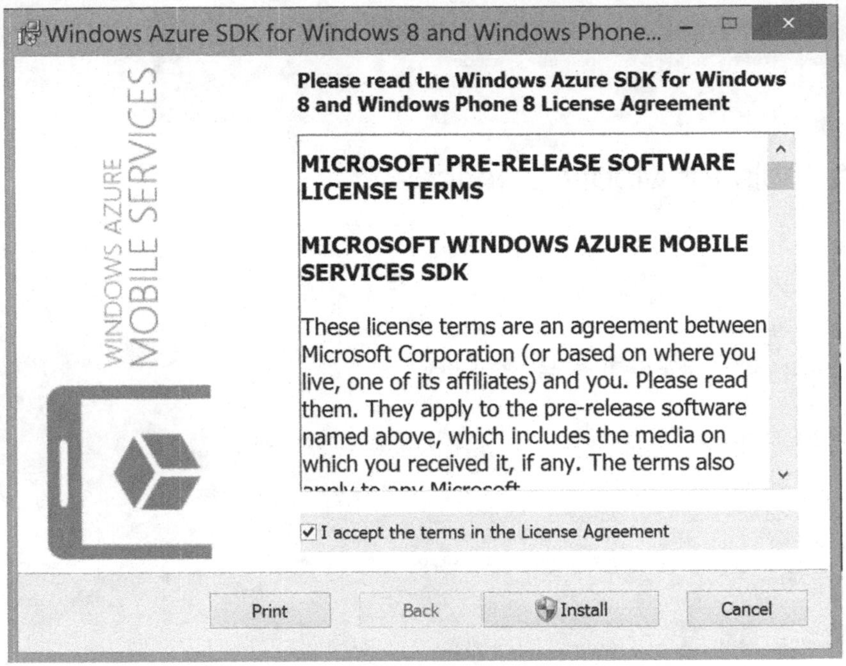

Figure 13-65. Azure Mobile Services SDK install

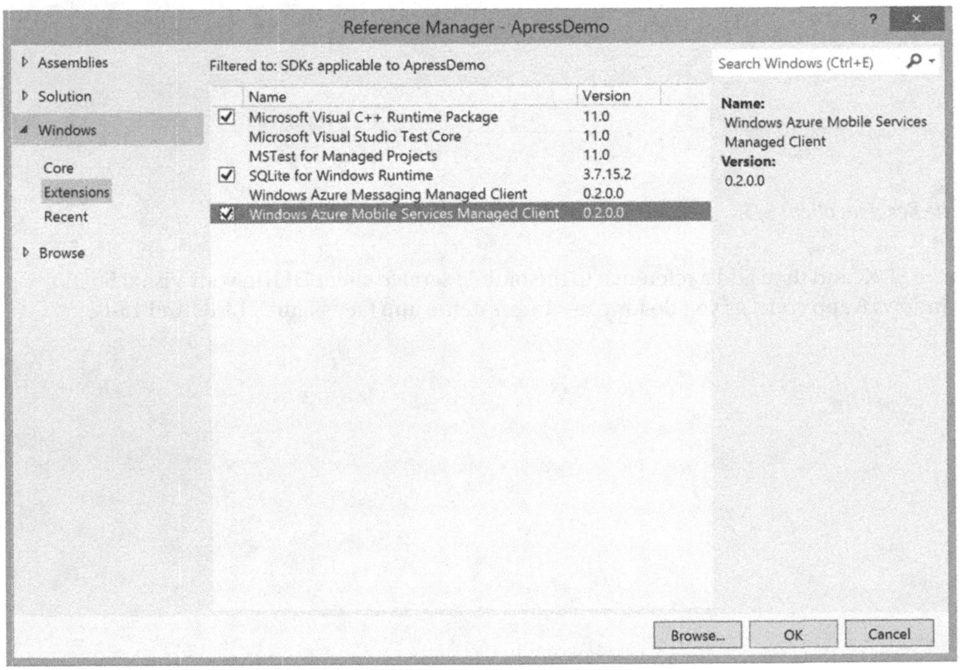

Figure 13-66. Azure Mobile Services client DLL reference

Service Operations from Client

Now, you want your client-side code to have a reference to the mobile service you created so that you can invoke operations on it. So, back on the Azure Mobile Services dashboard, grab service URL and management access keys from the link at the bottom (see Figure 13-67). This simply confirms that you are using a service that belongs to us. Yes, I am showing you part of my secret keys; but it is a demo Apress app.

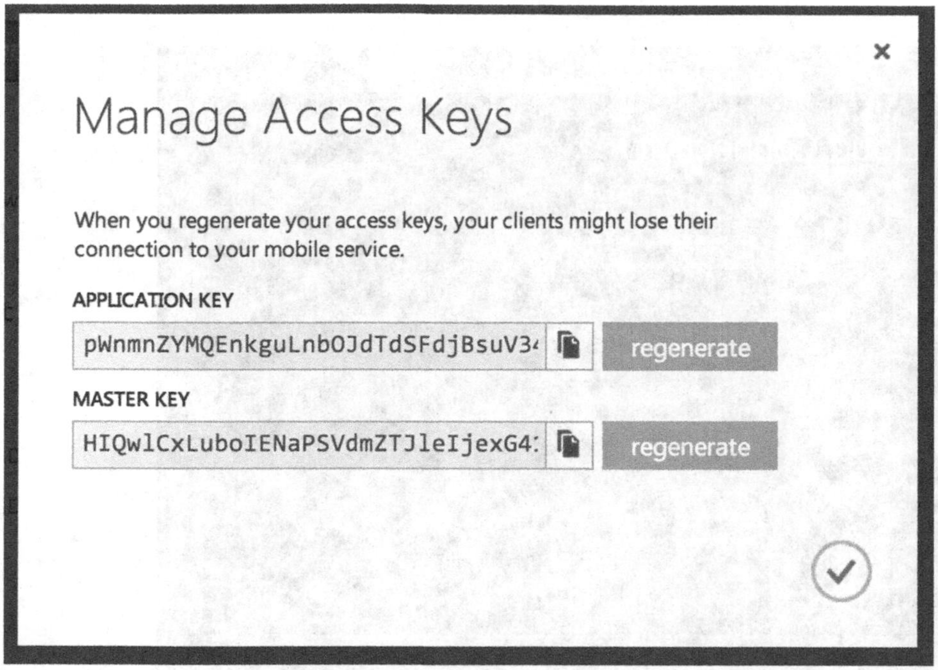

Figure 13-67. *Azure Mobile Services management keys*

Once all references are in place, you can now create an instance handler of your mobile service in the code inside your Windows 8 app, and also in the `App.xaml.cs` file of your Apress demo app. Note the use of a specific mobile service URL and the use of access keys.

```
public static MobileServiceClient ZumoClient = new
MobileServiceClient("https://apresszumo.azure-mobile.net/", "pWnmnZYMQEnkguLnbOJdTdSFdjBsuV34");
```

Next step, decide what you want to store in your new database table. Why, of course, the Apress book information since you already have classes built for that purpose. However, extend the `ApressBook` class to include the app's notification channel URI so that you can achieve the data table insert and also pass along the channel URI to the service in one sweep. This extension of the `ApressBook` class, already exposed by your OData service, makes for the easy addition of a partial class.

```
public partial class ApressBookForZumo : ApressODataService.ApressBook
    {
        #region "Properties"

        [DataMember(Name = "channel")]
```

```
        public string Channel { get; set; }

        #endregion
    }
```

So, to add a new Apress book to the new data table in the SQL Azure database, add an extra app bar button icon to the `ManageCloud.xaml` page to facilitate the user action (see Figure 13-68).

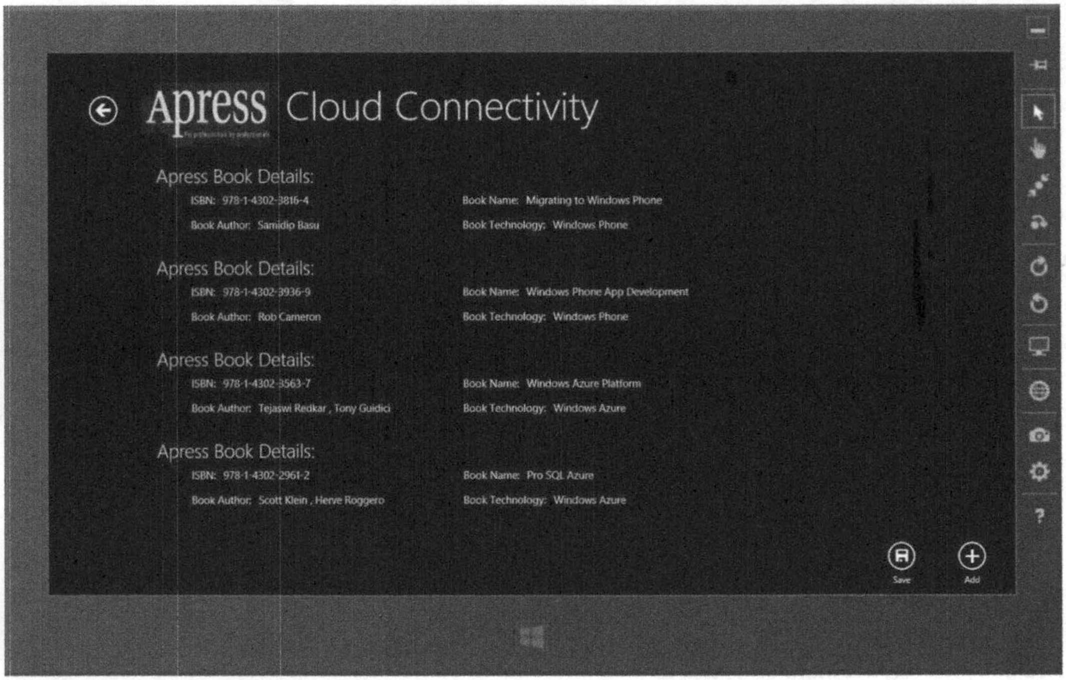

***Figure 13-68.** Azure Mobile Services data update icon on the app bar*

Now, you are ready for action. Here's some code where you create a new sample Apress book using the custom class and try saving off the data in the database table through the Azure Mobile Services client reference. This code is simply wired up to the button-click event handler of the new app bar icon.

```
private async void addButton_Click(object sender, RoutedEventArgs e)
        {
            ApressBookForZumo bookToInsert = new ApressBookForZumo();
            bookToInsert.ApressBookISBN = "978-1-4302-4338-0";
            bookToInsert.ApressBookName = "Ultra-Fast ASP.NET 4.5";
            bookToInsert.ApressBookTechnology = "ASP.NET";
            bookToInsert.ApressBookAuthor = "Rick Kiessig";
            bookToInsert.ApressBookPublishedDate = new DateTime(2012, 7, 25);

            bookToInsert.Channel = App.CurrentChannel.Uri;

            await App.ZumoClient.GetTable<ApressBookForZumo>().InsertAsync(bookToInsert);
        }
```

Notice how you leverage the app-level notification channel and the reference to your custom mobile service, both created in the `App.xaml.cs` file. This code is meant to insert the built-up Apress book object as a record in the new table through the mobile service. If everything went right, you should not be seeing any errors. Let's head back to the Azure Mobile Services dashboard to see the effects of your code.

First, the new table schema has been altered to match the customized `ApressBook` class, and now includes a column for the channel URI (see Figure 13-69). Also, head over to the Browse tab and you will see that your code did actually insert a record in the table, including a channel URI (see Figure 13-70).

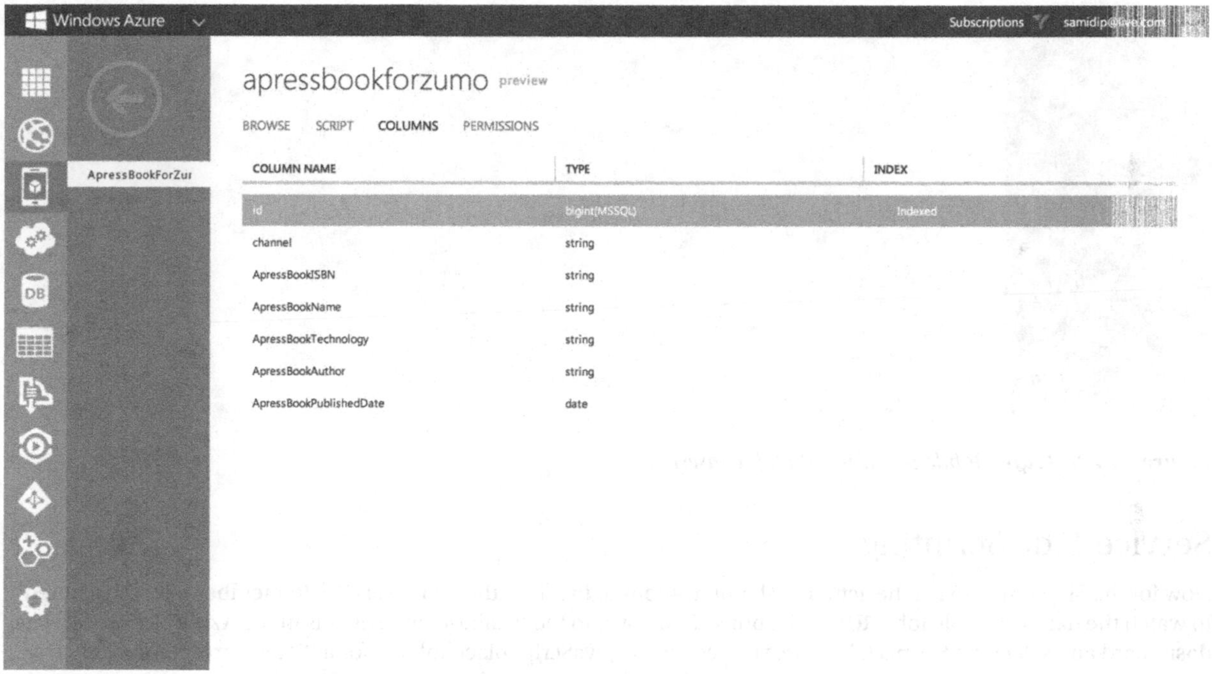

Figure 13-69. *Azure Mobile Services data table dynamic schema*

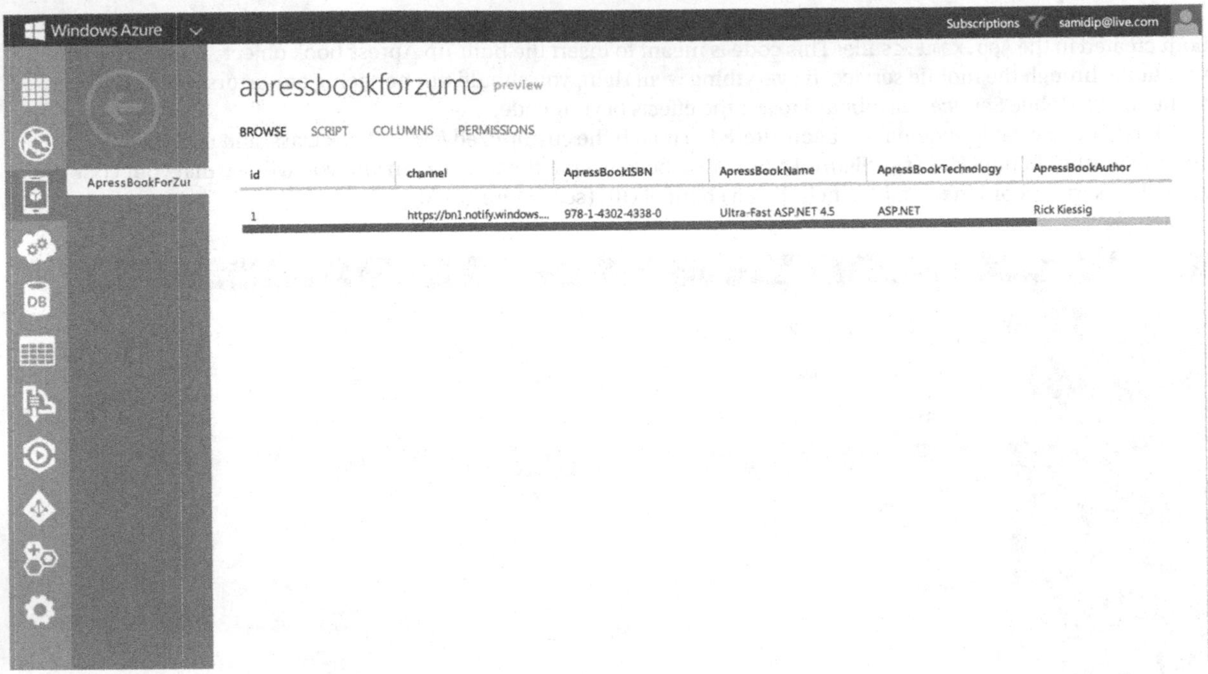

Figure 13-70. *Azure Mobile Services data table insert*

Service-Side Scripting

Now for the last stretch to get the actual push notifications to fire from the Azure service. Remember how you wanted to watch the database table for CRUD operations? Head over to the database table details in the Azure Mobile Services dashboard and select the Scripts tab. Here, you see several JavaScript placeholders for actions corresponding to CRUD operations against the table (see Figure 13-71). Right now, everything is blank. But this is your opportunity to watch for operations happening on the data table and to take appropriate action. Let's manipulate the insert script to something of your own, like in Figure 13-72.

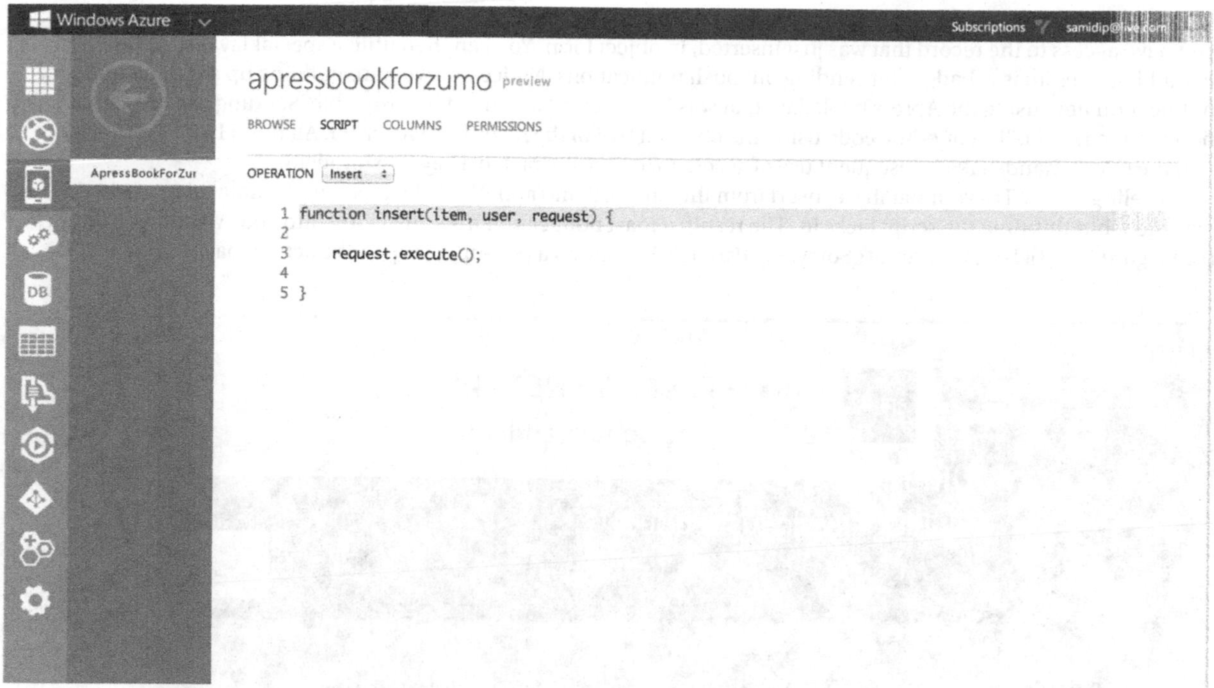

Figure 13-71. Azure Mobile Services data table scripting

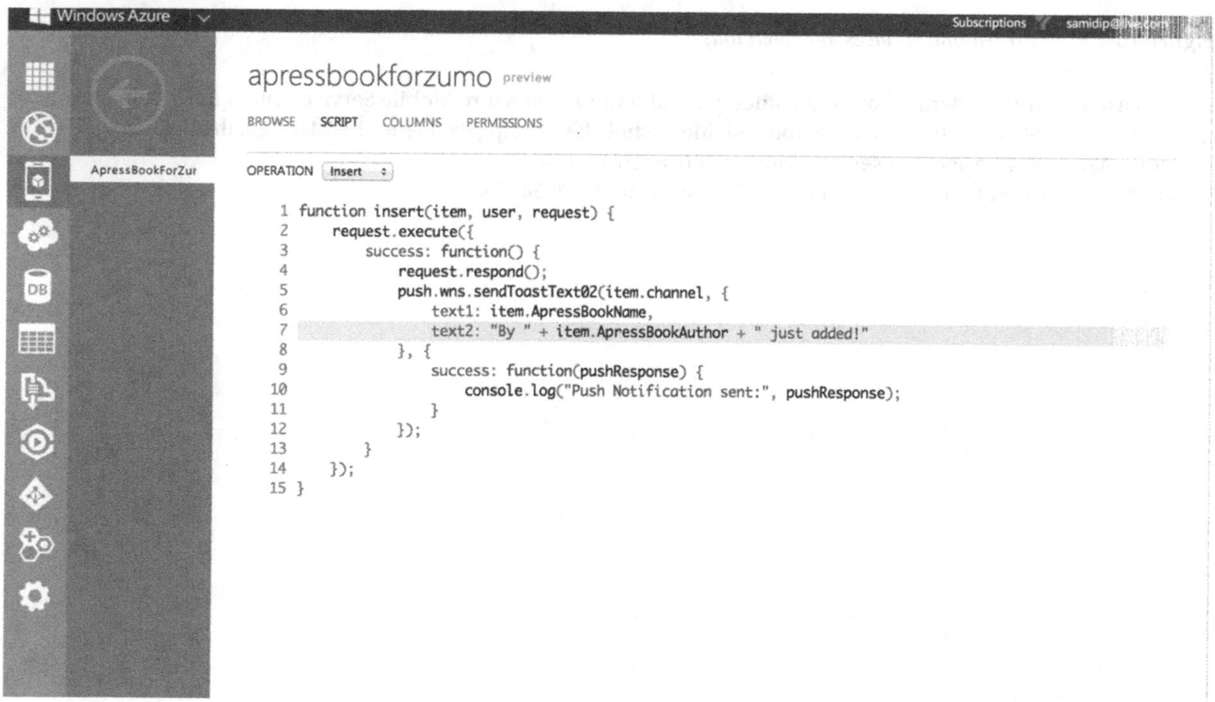

Figure 13-72. Azure Mobile Services data table custom scripting

As you can see, you are first making sure that the database insert record worked on the underlying table. If so, you have access to the record that was just inserted, in object form. You can then utilize special JavaScript functions to build up tiles/toasts/badges for sending out push notifications. Notice how you are building up a named toast notification here using the Apress book data that was just inserted into the database table. Sending out the actual push notification is actually a one-line code using the channel URI of the record just inserted. All the HTTP POST details and the OAuth handshake/subsequent use of access tokens is abstracted away for simplicity.

Feeling lucky? Try your database insert from the Apress demo app. Now, the insert to the data table works as expected, but this time the script kicks in. The result: a toast notification from the cloud into your Windows 8 device (see Figure 13-73)! Isn't that sweet? Sorry, my Parallels VM shows a pop-up on top of the actual toast.

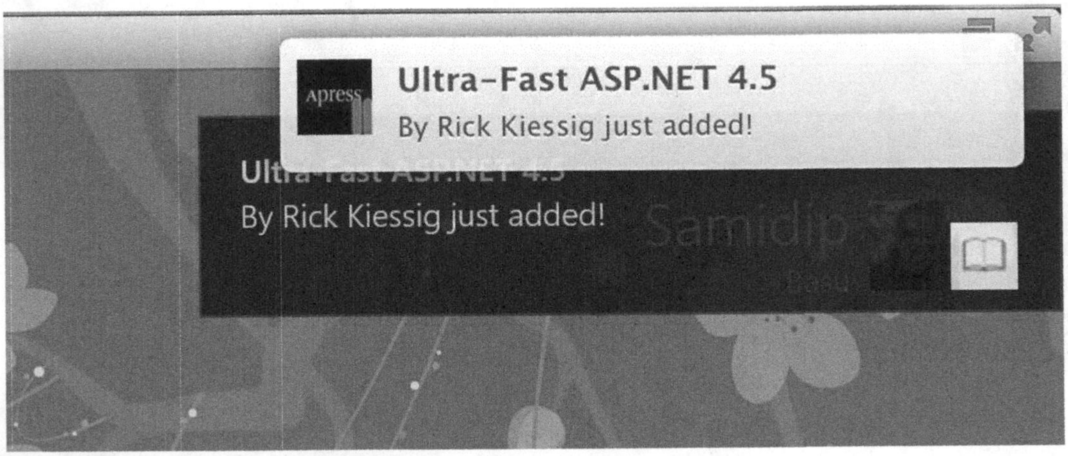

Figure 13-73. *Azure Mobile Services–powered toast*

In case you are wondering how to do other types of scripting on Azure Mobile Services, press the ? Help button while on the Script tab of the data table. You will find a whole lot of help (see Figure 13-74). Also, the detailed Windows Azure Mobile Services server script reference is over at `http://msdn.microsoft.com/en-US/library/windowsazure/jj554226`.

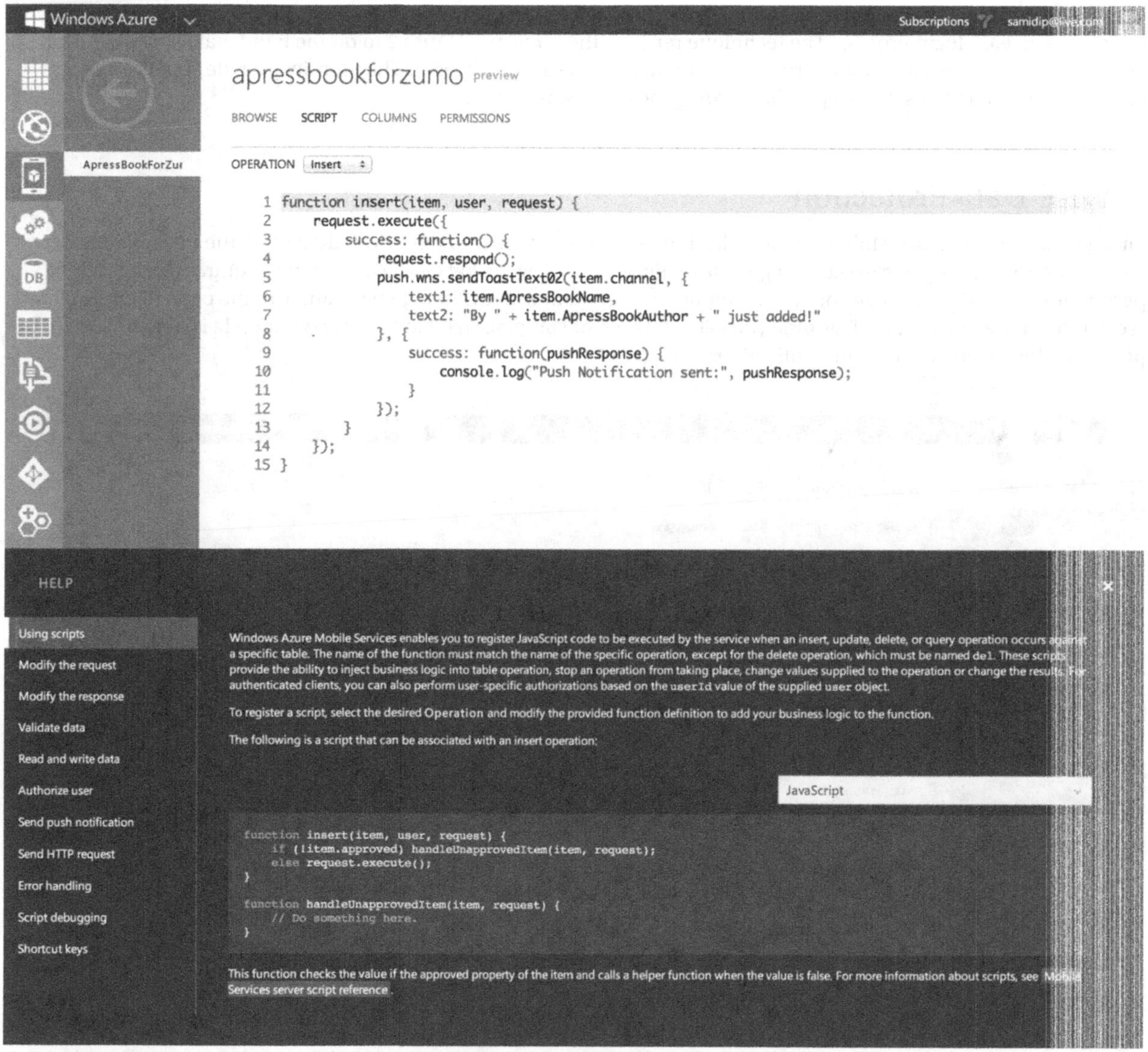

Figure 13-74. *Azure Mobile Services scripting help*

User Authentication

One other area that Azure Mobile Services can be very useful is authenticating users. I will talk about authentication in more detail in Chapter 14, but simply know that it's better if your Windows 8 app does not do custom forms-based authentication unless absolutely required. Your user is already burdened with ID/password collections; this would be one more thing to remember. Instead, if your app falls back to leverage well-known identity providers, you are simply allowing the user to log in to your app more easily.

Azure Mobile Services can help in authenticating your users, if needed for restricted functionality, using established and supported identity providers. As of now, Azure Mobile Services support authentication using

Microsoft Account, Facebook, Twitter, and Google. Between these four major providers, you are providing most of your users an easy login process. The technique remains the same: use OAuth 2 to do the handshake and share app credentials. The user is asked for permission once and upon successful login. The identity provider offers an access token for repeated logins. Let's try authenticating the user using Twitter logins.

Service Data Protection

First, go back to the Azure Mobile Services dashboard and select the data table link; then on to the Permissions tab (see Figure 13-75). As you can see, you get fine-grained control over what CRUD operations require which levels of permissions. Flip the Insert permission to require user authentication. Now, go back and run the code to insert table records from the last section. This time you get a nasty error complaining that the user/your code is not allowed to perform table inserts without authentication.

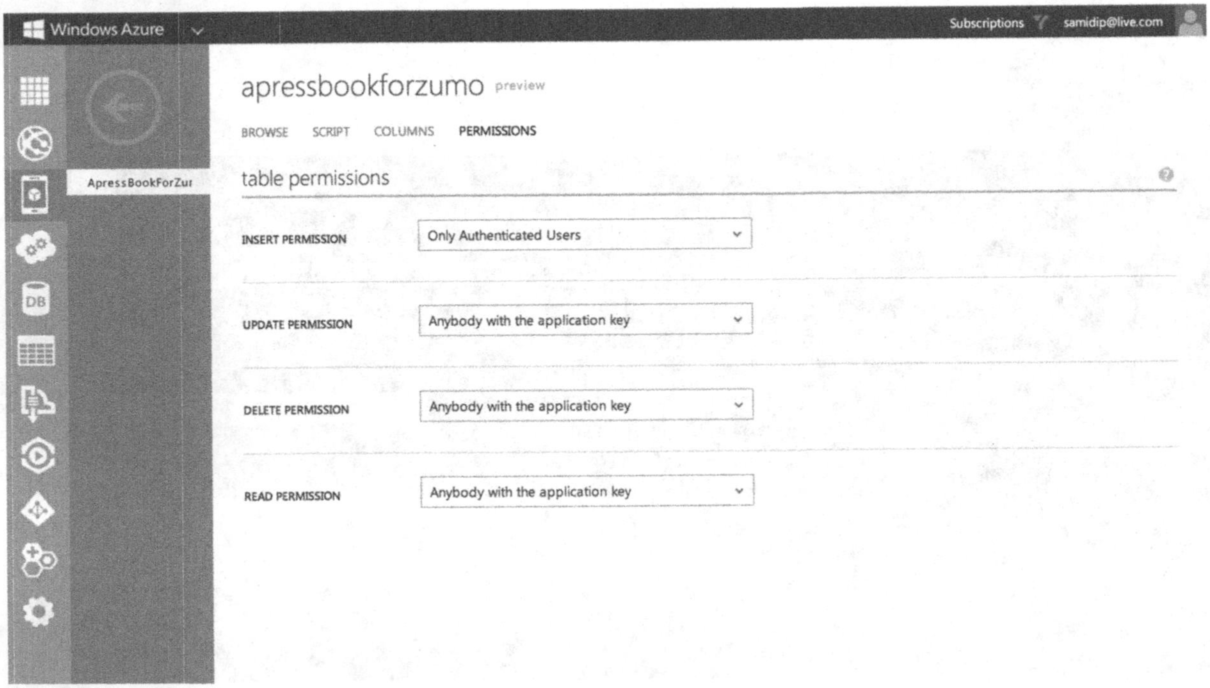

Figure 13-75. *Azure Mobile Services data table increased security*

Let's see how you may enable user authentication now needed for the table inserts. First, go back to the Azure Mobile Services dashboard and take note of the service URL, as shown in Figure 13-76.

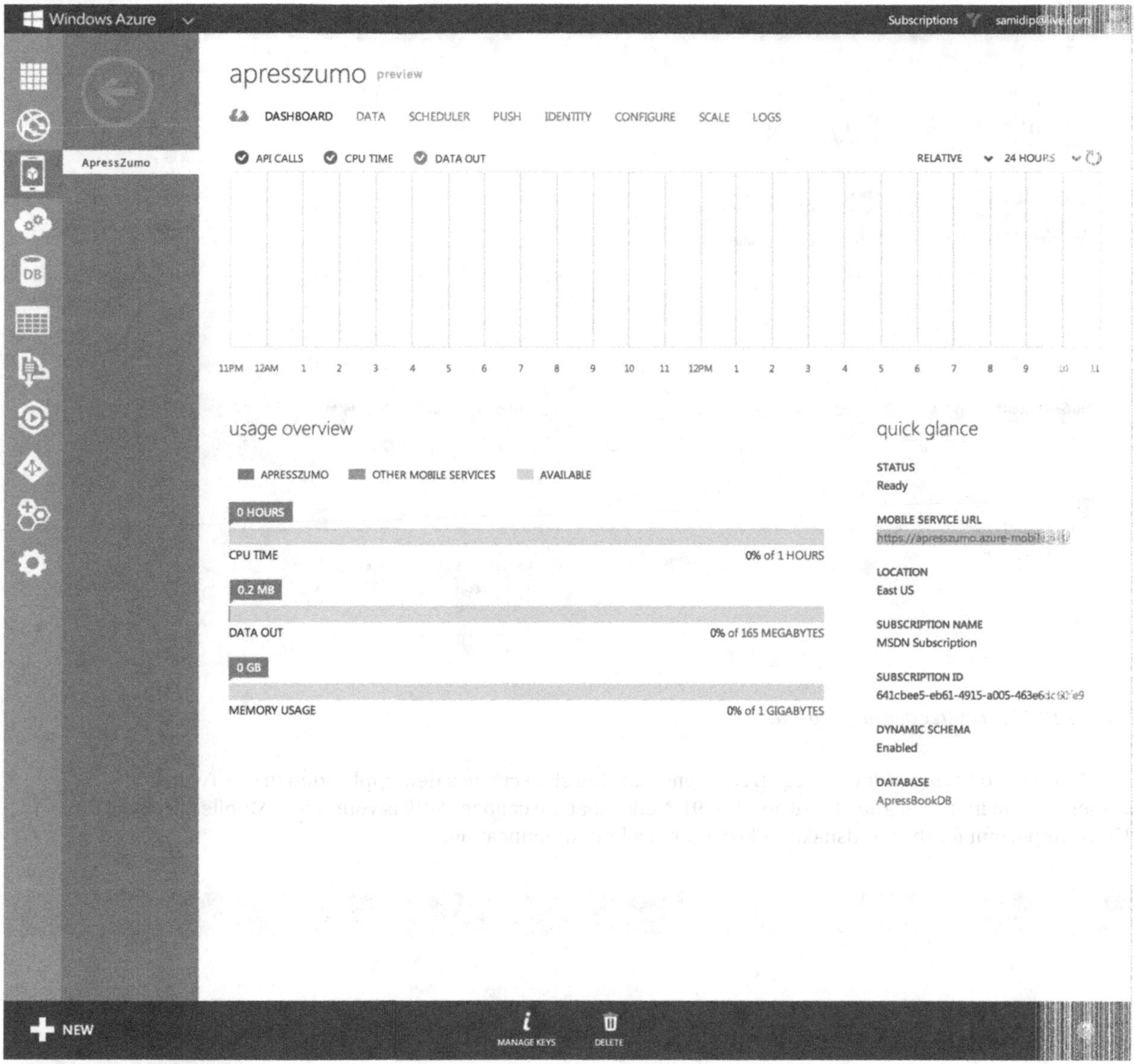

Figure 13-76. *Azure Mobile Services dashboard*

Enabling Twitter Authentication

Next, let's head over to the Twitter developer portal at `https://dev.twitter.com` (see Figure 13-77). Sign in with your Twitter account, and you will see several options light up. You can read up all about Twitter's API for developers at this site.

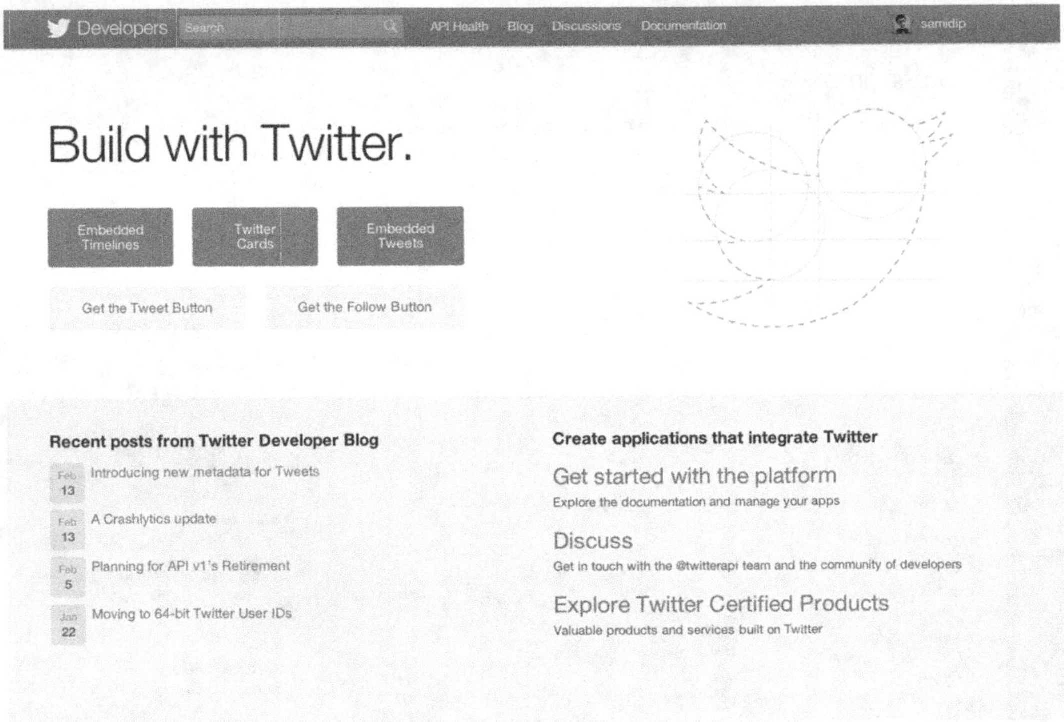

Figure 13-77. *Twitter developer portal*

Navigate to `https://dev.twitter.com/apps`, and you shall create a new application to use Twitter authentication in (see Figures 13-78 and 13-79). Notice that the callback URL is your Azure Mobile Services URL. This is important for the handshake with Twitter to allow authentication.

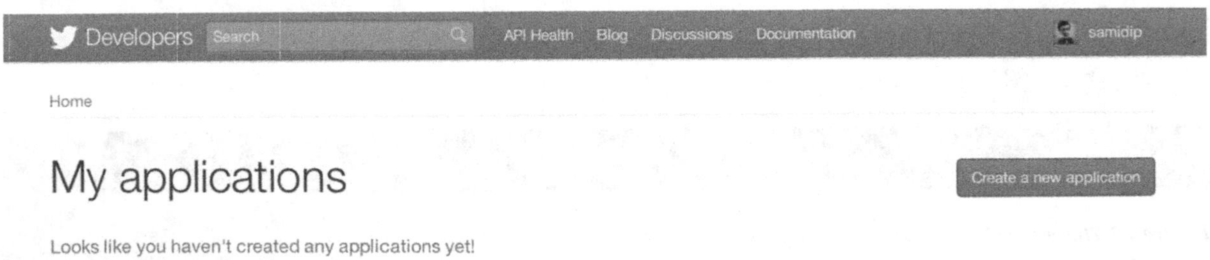

Figure 13-78. *Twitter New Application*

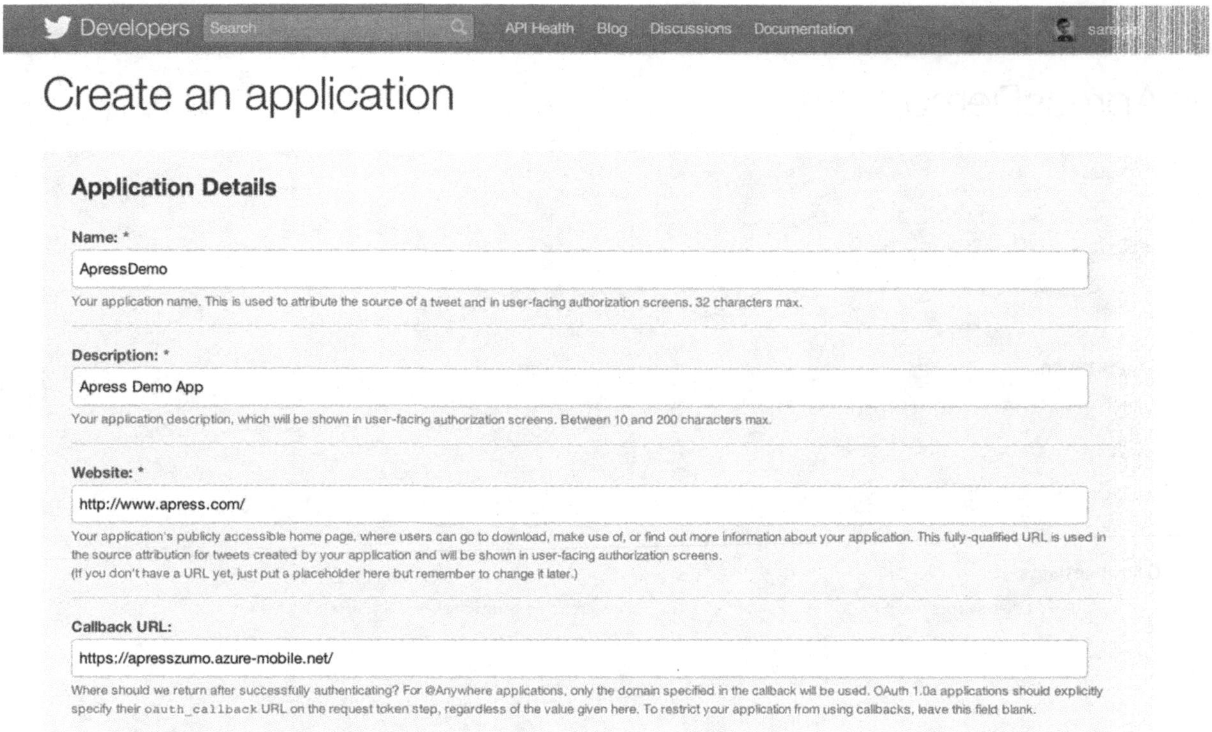

Developers
Search
API Health
Blog
Discussions
Documentation
Create an application
Application Details
Name: *
ApressDemo
Your application name. This is used to attribute the source of a tweet and in user-facing authorization screens. 32 characters max.
Description: *
Apress Demo App
Your application description, which will be shown in user-facing authorization screens. Between 10 and 200 characters max.
Website: *
http://www.apress.com/
Your application's publicly accessible home page, where users can go to download, make use of, or find out more information about your application. This fully-qualified URL is used in the source attribution for tweets created by your application and will be shown in user-facing authorization screens.
(If you don't have a URL yet, just put a placeholder here but remember to change it later.)
Callback URL:
https://apresszumo.azure-mobile.net/
Where should we return after successfully authenticating? For @Anywhere applications, only the domain specified in the callback will be used. OAuth 1.0a applications should explicitly specify their oauth_callback URL on the request token step, regardless of the value given here. To restrict your application from using callbacks, leave this field blank.

Figure 13-79. *Twitter new application configuration*

Once you accept the terms and create the application, Twitter shows you details of the application you just created (see Figure 13-80). Take note of two key pieces for identifying information for your new application: the consumer key and consumer secret.

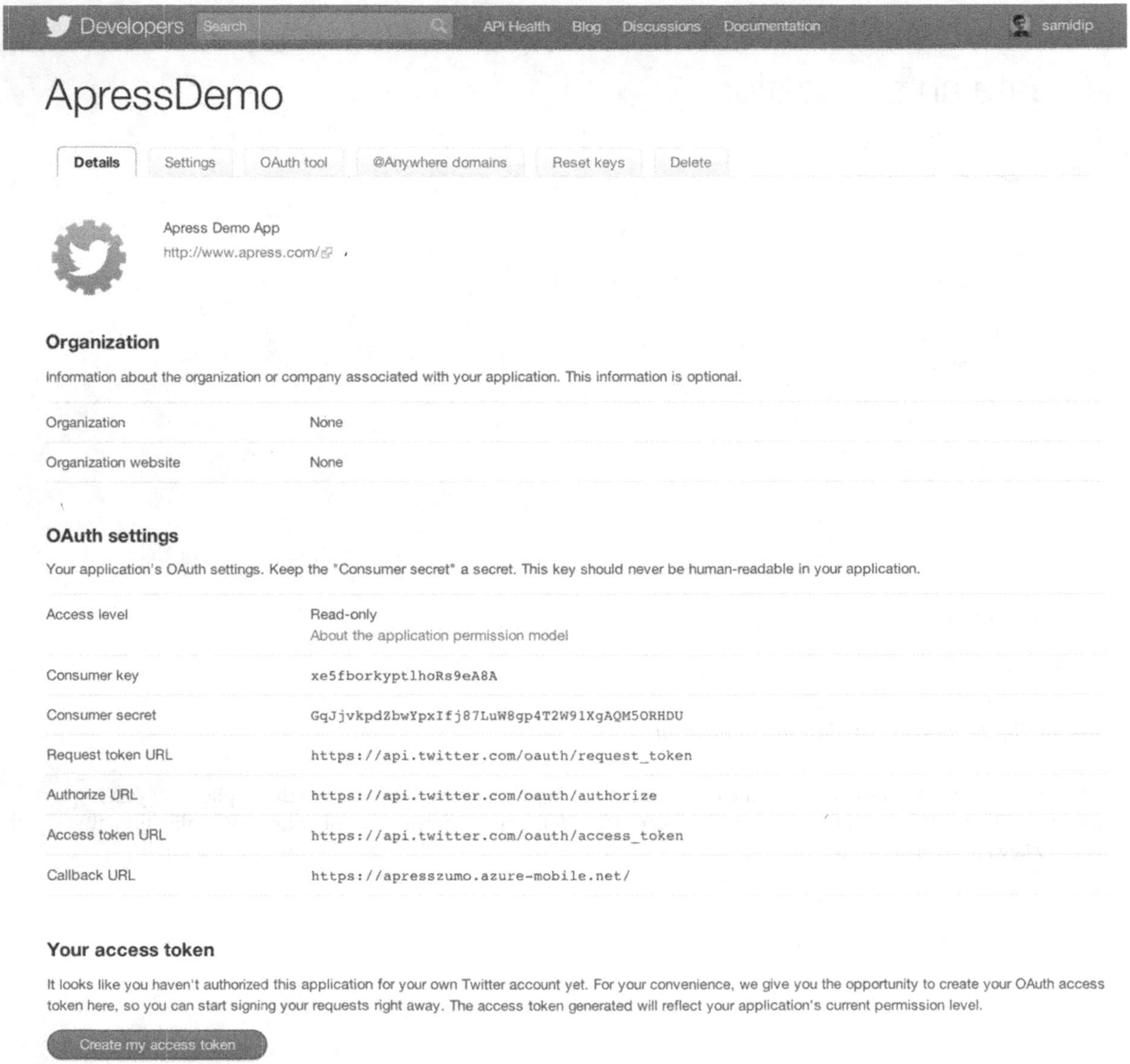

Figure 13-80. *Twitter new application details*

Once done, let's head back to the Azure Mobile Services dashboard and to the Identity tab. Punch in the consumer key and consumer secret you got from Twitter in the Twitter Settings of the Identity tab, (see Figure 13-81). That's it—this completes the handshake between Twitter and your mobile service. The authentication magic happens behind the scenes.

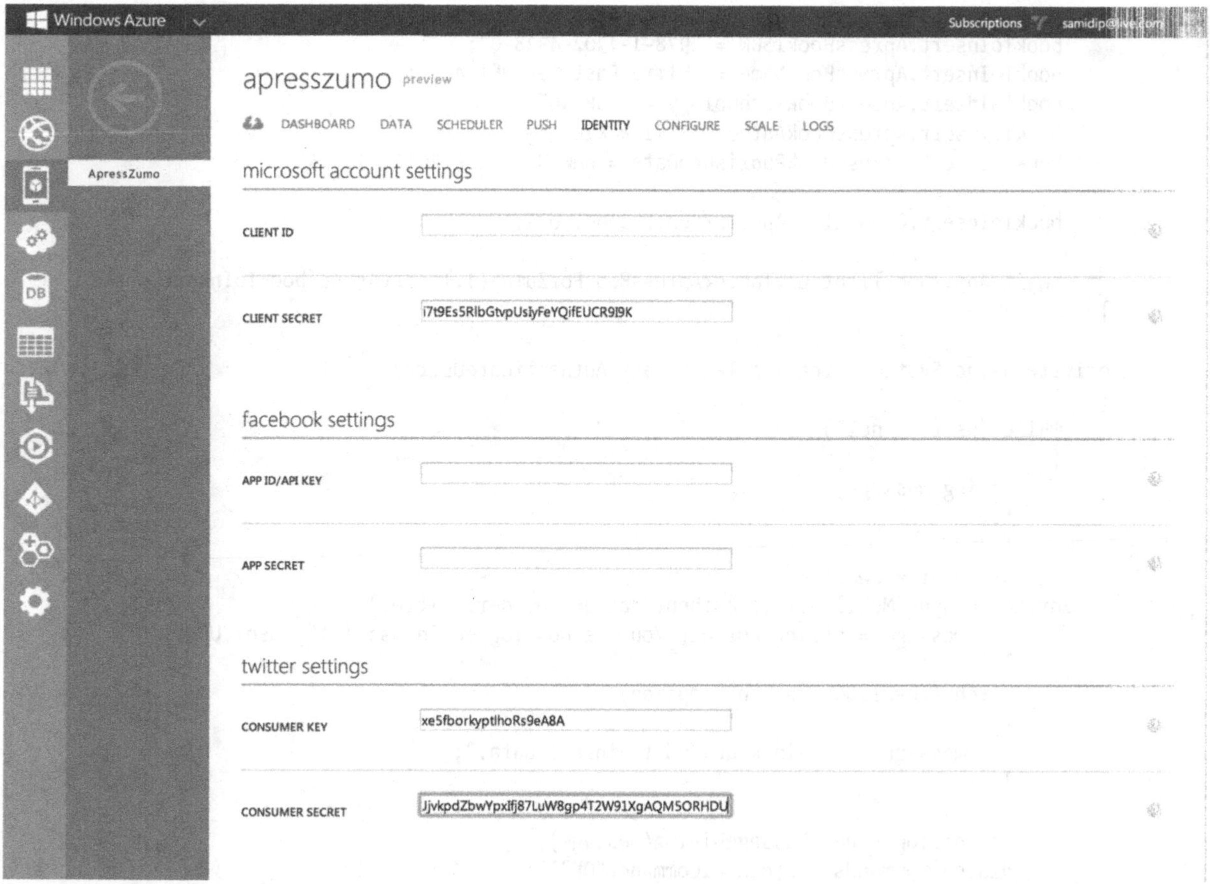

Figure 13-81. *Twitter credentials in Azure Mobile Services*

Custom Authentications in Code

Let's head back to the `ManageCloud.xaml.cs` page and allow the user a way to authenticate him or herself before trying to insert table records. Listing 13-5 shows some code.

Listing 13-5. Custom User Authentication

```
using Windows.UI.Popups;
using Microsoft.WindowsAzure.MobileServices;

private MobileServiceUser user;

private async void addButton_Click(object sender, RoutedEventArgs e)
        {
            await AuthenticateUser();
```

```
            ApressBookForZumo bookToInsert = new ApressBookForZumo();
            bookToInsert.ApressBookISBN = "978-1-4302-4338-0";
            bookToInsert.ApressBookName = "Ultra-Fast ASP.NET 4.5";
            bookToInsert.ApressBookTechnology = "ASP.NET";
            bookToInsert.ApressBookAuthor = "Rick Kiessig";
            bookToInsert.ApressBookPublishedDate = new DateTime(2012, 7, 25);

            bookToInsert.Channel = App.CurrentChannel.Uri;

            await App.ZumoClient.GetTable<ApressBookForZumo>().InsertAsync(bookToInsert);
        }

        private async System.Threading.Tasks.Task AuthenticateUser()
        {
            while (user == null)
            {
                string message;
                try
                {
                    user = await
App.ZumoClient.LoginAsync(MobileServiceAuthenticationProvider.Twitter);
                    message = string.Format("You are now logged in as: {0}", user.UserId);
                }
                catch (InvalidOperationException)
                {
                    message = "Login Required to insert data.";
                }

                var dialog = new MessageDialog(message);
                dialog.Commands.Add(new UICommand("OK"));
                await dialog.ShowAsync();
            }
        }
```

As you can see, the code to insert a new Apress book into the table remains the same, except you add a method call to try authenticating the user. For authentication, you fall back to the `LoginAsync()` method exposed by the reference to the mobile service and indicate the chosen identity provider, in this case, Twitter. The whole interaction is simply shown in a message dialog, which asks for user permission to use the Twitter application that you set up (see Figure 13-82). This is UI shown from Twitter inside your Windows 8 app and is standard practice while using identity providers.

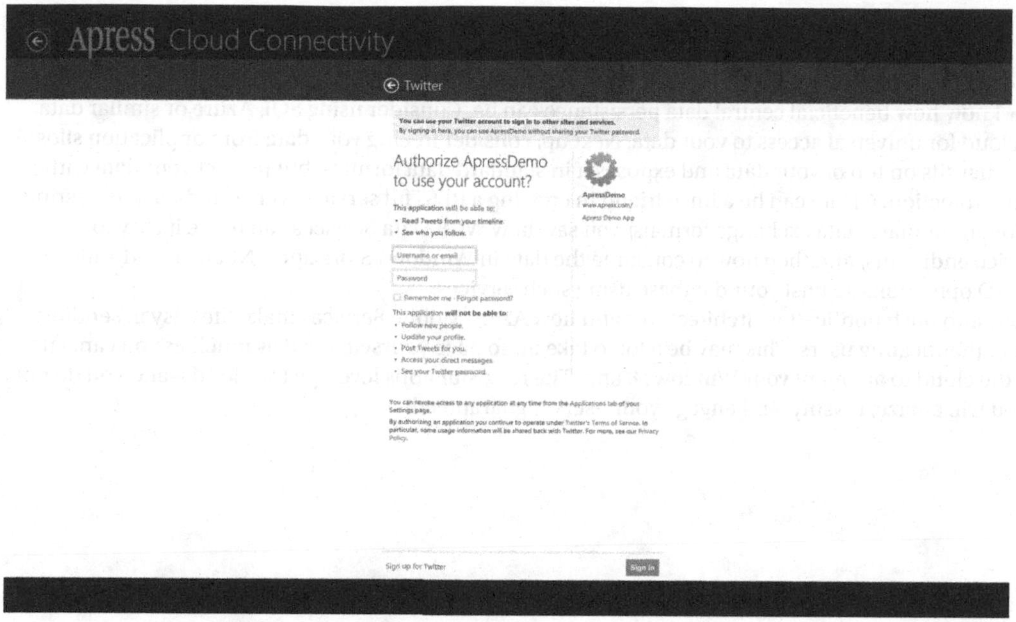

Figure 13-82. Authentication through Twitter

Once the user logs in using his or her Twitter credentials, Twitter turns around to pass the user details on to the callback URL, which was the Azure Mobile Services URL. Your service now has the `user` object filled in and you have authenticated the user (see Figure 13-83), resulting in your service getting access to a unique user ID that Twitter uses to know the user internally. Beyond this, the table inserts and the toast notification shown in Figure 13-83 happens as usual.

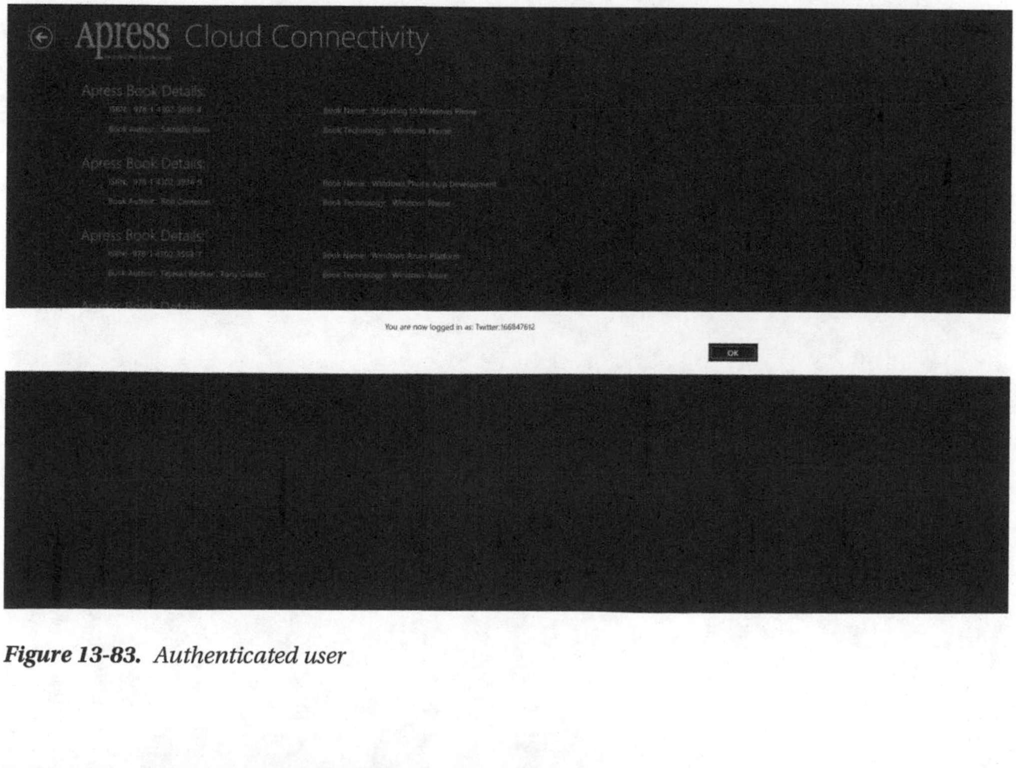

Figure 13-83. Authenticated user

Summary

Agreed, this was a long chapter. But discussion about cloud augmentation of your Windows 8 apps needs to hit several key points. You now know how beneficial central data persistence can be. Consider using SQL Azure or similar data repositories in the cloud for universal access to your data. Next up, consider freeing your data from application silos. Create a service API that sits on top of your data and exposes it in standard data formats, but protect your data with appropriate levels of protection. OData can be a huge friend in creating a RESTful service over your data and offering interoperability through standard data exchange formats. You saw how WCF Data Services can make it easy to produce OData service endpoints, and then how to consume the data in Windows Store apps. Not just read-only, you can support full CRUD operations against your database using such services.

Next, you looked into push notification architectures and how Azure Mobile Services make life easy in sending out notifications or authenticating users. This may be a lot to take in, so pace yourself. Read as much as you can, and then truly leverage the cloud to augment your Windows 8 app. The rock-star apps leverage the cloud—and you do not want to miss out. You will amaze, mystify, and engage your users— guaranteed!

CHAPTER 14

Live Services Integration

After the cloud augmentation discussion in the last chapter, hopefully you see the clear benefits it brings to Windows 8 Store apps, providing the alive-and-connected feel and centralized data/services for the developer to manage. But are you a little suspect of feasibility and concerned about the user base and costs as you maintain databases/services in the cloud? Sounds like you need a cloud-in-a-box delivered for your developer usage at no cost to you. Enter Microsoft's Live Services, a suite of services empowering users with open APIs for developer consumption. This chapter will walk you through integrating Live Services in Windows 8 Store apps. You get to leverage the cloud as a service, and users gets to reuse what's already well known. Sounds like a win-win situation, right? Let's get started.

Live Services

Live Services is a family of services offered by Microsoft to users of its popular web-based products. If you have ever used `Hotmail/Live/Outlook.com` e-mail services, Windows Live Messenger chat, SkyDrive cloud storage/sync, or signed in to any application using your Microsoft account, you have unknowingly consumed Live Services. It is the suite of software services that powers the ubiquitous Microsoft products, and it is hosted entirely by Microsoft. Live Services are without doubt popular because the user base of these combined services surpasses 500 million users worldwide.

Do you remember the discussion of cloud computing in the last chapter? Live Services fall under the category of SaaS (Software as a Service)-type cloud computing. When you, as a user, access your Hotmail/Live/Outlook e-mail or your files/folders stored in SkyDrive, you simply open your Internet browser and the content is accessed through a URL. There is no other software that you need to install or run in your local device; you simply access the information over the Internet. This is because of the SaaS setup powering these applications, where Microsoft is already hosting the needed hardware/servers along with the host operating systems. Microsoft is also running applications on those servers, which you get to access simply through data connections over the Web. Users are not supposed to know anything about the servers that run such applications or maintain the OS/applications themselves; they simply use them.

With such a broad user base and ubiquity/ease of use of applications, no wonder Microsoft applications powered by Live Services have gained popularity. With the explosion of mobile computing, you have now taken the usage of Microsoft-hosted e-mail, storage, and other applications down to your smartphones or tablets. This flexibility is, again, courtesy of SaaS. There is no need to install or run any software, just simply consume. There have been client applications (like e-mail client or SkyDrive apps for mobile, etc.) built to consume content from these applications, and many of them run on disparate ecosystems, like iOS or Android. This is possible due to ubiquitous services that Microsoft has built on top of the application data, which offer up content in industry-standard data exchange formats.

Now, with so many goodies in Live Services, you must be wondering if it is possible to incorporate some of it in your third-party applications. Surely, Windows 8 Store apps could benefit from integration with Live Services. This has the obvious advantage of user familiarity with the content—it's something they already use. However, integration with Live Services would need open APIs for developers to utilize—and thankfully, Microsoft agrees!

Live Connect

Live Services have been around for a while and they are awesome. But when your mobile apps integrate with these Live Services, you are providing users with new ways to engage with familiar content; and this familiarity breeds increased app usage. To help developers create this value and build successful apps across platforms, Microsoft offers *Live Connect*—a collection of APIs on top of Live Services that help in quick app integration and compatibility with services like SkyDrive, Hotmail, Live, Outlook, and Windows Messenger (which will be replaced by Skype).

MSDN states: "The Live Connect APIs use industry standard protocols such as OAuth 2.0, JavaScript Object Notation (JSON), and Extensible Messaging and Presence Protocol (XMPP). To call the APIs, you primarily use Representational State Transfer (REST) requests that return information formatted in JSON. This architecture enables us to support a variety of platforms, including those for web, desktop, and mobile apps . . ." (`http://msdn.microsoft.com/en-us/library/live/hh243641.aspx`). As a developer, you can quickly see where Microsoft is going with this: a thin platform-independent veneer over the existing Live Services content, designed for consumption across various types of apps and ecosystems.

The focus of the Live Connect APIs is clearly service over platform. The choice of standard protocols shows the zeal to encourage usage of Live Services across device form factors and ecosystem boundaries. With REST service endpoints, all communication is over HTTP and response is in JSON format. This means that no special software is needed to consume these services; only a browser address bar is sufficient to interact with the endpoints. Flexibility through standard adherence offers up Live Services consumption from a variety of mobile platforms and competing ecosystems. However, the deal is sweeter in the Windows ecosystem—if you need to leverage Live Services from Windows 8 or Windows Phone or most .NET clients. There is a dedicated Live SDK that make life a whole lot easier. No longer do you have to hand-code HTTP communication; easy C# wrappers do the job for you. I will get back to this in just a bit.

Live Services Benefits and Considerations

Now, what's in it for you, as a Windows 8 Store app developer, to look at integrating Live Services? Well several things, as listed:

- *Cloud service as SaaS*: Not only does the user get to use Live Services as SaaS, but as a developer, you also get to integrate with these services for your apps. The result: you no longer have to host databases/services on your own—you simply use what Microsoft has already hosted. As a consequence, the cost to you is zilch!
- *User familiarity*: The user is already comfortable using Hotmail/Live/Outlook e-mail services, knows his or her contacts and calendar intimately, and uses SkyDrive to store documents with multiple-device sync. When your Windows 8 app leverages Live Connect APIs to reuse the same contacts and calendars, the experience is immediately familiar to the user. If you read/edit/move files and folders in the user's SkyDrive, the changes are visible to the user, not only through the Web (`http://skydrive.com`) but also any other device that he or she is using in SkyDrive.
- *Availability*: Since Live Services are used by millions of users worldwide, extremely high availability is required, and it is managed by Microsoft's hosting. And because services are operating 24/7 throughout the year, so are the Live Connect APIs for your app consumption. No longer do you have to set up your own service and lose sleep over supporting SLAs (service-level agreements) for availability.
- *Scalability*: Along the same lines of the ubiquitous availability of Live Services comes scalability of services. If 500 million more users start using applications powered by Live Services tomorrow—no worries. Microsoft will adjust the scale of services as needed. You also get scaling for free. If your Windows 8 app suddenly becomes insanely popular, you can rest assured that all of your Live Connect API calls will work just as they should.

- *Security and maintenance*: Live Services often deal with sensitive user data—e-mails, authentications, SkyDrive storage, and so forth—all of which can be very personal, and a security breach could be devastating. So Microsoft does not take lightly the security and maintenance of Live Services and its supported applications. You, on the other hand, get all of that for free.

The only thing Microsoft asks in return for so many favors with Live Services is *responsibility*. For years, users of Microsoft accounts and products have built up a trusting relationship with Live Services, which is even truer now with a cloud-ready OS like Windows 8. Users entrust Microsoft with a lot of sensitive information, including their e-mails, calendars, and documents, and they expect ubiquitous availability. When your Windows 8 apps leverage Live Connect APIs, some of this responsibility falls back to you, the developer. Do not do anything that undermines the user's trust in Live Services. Use user data responsibly, have a privacy statement regarding what you intend to do with user data, and then have your app do what you have promised. This is critically important.

Live Connect APIs

Now, let's get to know Live Connect APIs a little better by inspecting the kind of services offered.

- *Access control*: If you have a Hotmail/Live/Outlook e-mail account, you already have what's been touted as a Microsoft account. You have one set of credentials or one identity that identifies you on the entire Microsoft ecosystem, like web sites and applications. In fact, Microsoft Live is one of the well-established identity providers (IPs). Wouldn't it be nice to not have the responsibility to authenticate users in your application? For one, the user would have one less ID/password to remember, and you need not handle all the security yourself. Live Connect APIs offer access control services by allowing user authentication through the Microsoft account. It does the handshaking with Microsoft security to identify the user, and then returns an innocuous access token for use in your application. Furthermore, Live Connect provides ways to access the user's profile information so that applications can customize the intimate user experience with personally identifiable data.

- *Hotmail*: This is a wrapper service that combines content from interchangeable e-mail services like Hotmail, Live, or `Outlook.com`. With any modern e-mail service, users get to have a list of contacts and an events calendar. Live Connect provides APIs to read/manipulate the signed-in user's contacts and calendars.

- *SkyDrive*: SkyDrive is like the user's personal storage in the cloud, and anybody with a Microsoft account gets 7GB free (upgradeable to more). SkyDrive is immensely popular for hosting documents and media, as well as for its ubiquitous presence and syncing across multiple user devices. Live Connect APIs give the developer complete access to a signed-in user's SkyDrive to read/write/manipulate information about files, folders, photos, music, and so forth.

- *Messaging*: Live Connect APIs allow the developer to provide instant messaging capabilities through the use of XMPP protocol. This can be done with a signed-in user's Windows Messenger buddies, as well as by communicating the current presence and status message. Although, with Microsoft's acquisition of Skype, Windows Messenger is being phased out; so developers are encouraged to look at Skype APIs over XMPP for instant communication.

Getting Started with Live Connect

Do you want to get started with Live Connect APIs? Head over to `http://msdn.microsoft.com/en-US/live/ff519582` and bookmark it. This is the Live Connect Developer Center (see Figure 14-1) and everything that you need to know is there. One of the really nice things about the Live Connect documentation is the fact that the code samples are meant for flexibility. The documentation shows you how to do the same thing in various programming languages and application ecosystems, notably JavaScript/C# for Windows 8 apps, Objective C for iOS, Java for Android, and even plain REST invocations. It's simply awesome for polyglot developers!

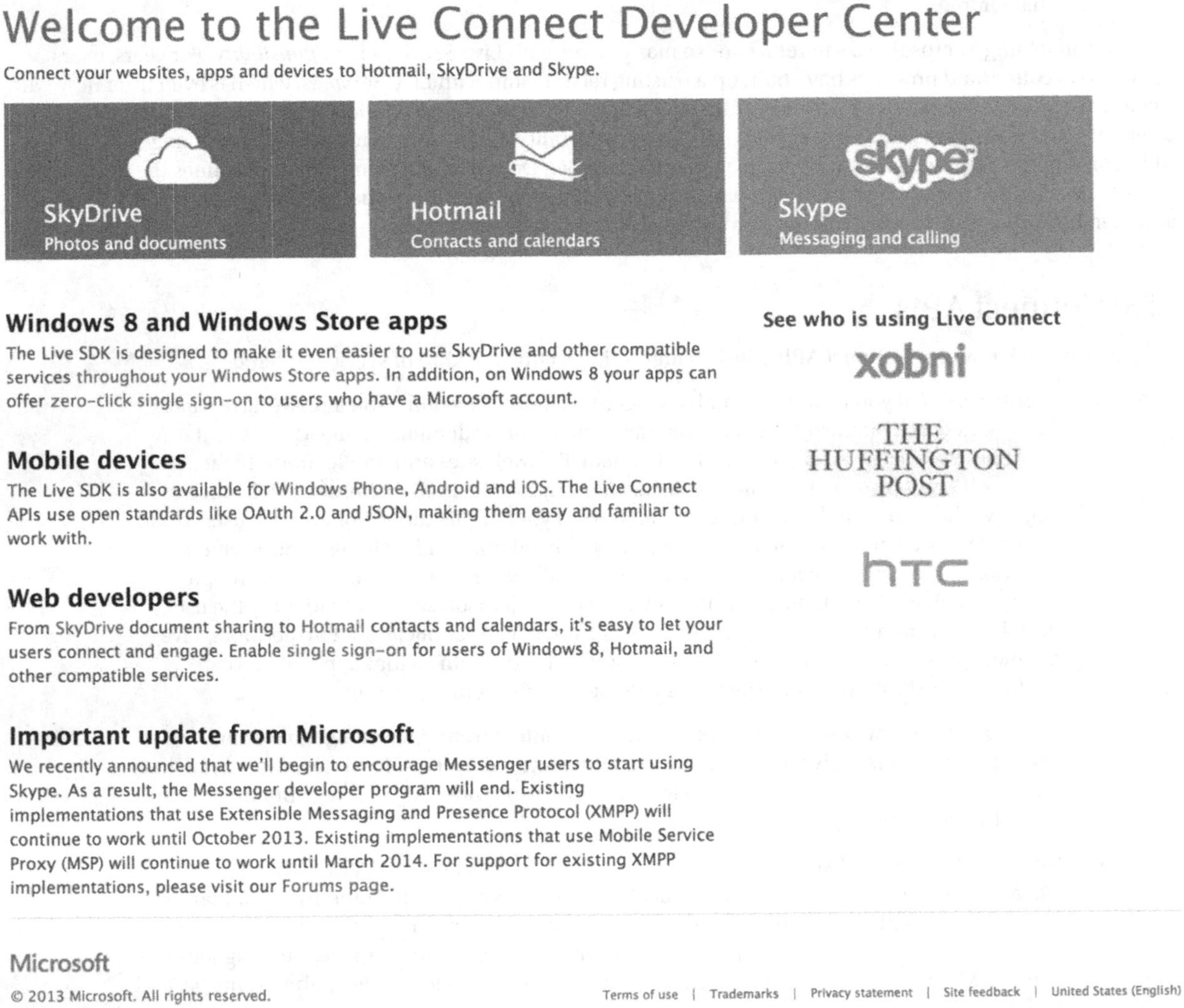

Welcome to the Live Connect Developer Center
Connect your websites, apps and devices to Hotmail, SkyDrive and Skype.
SkyDrive
Photos and documents
Hotmail
Contacts and calendars
skype
Skype
Messaging and calling
Windows 8 and Windows Store apps
The Live SDK is designed to make it even easier to use SkyDrive and other compatible services throughout your Windows Store apps. In addition, on Windows 8 your apps can offer zero-click single sign-on to users who have a Microsoft account.
Mobile devices
The Live SDK is also available for Windows Phone, Android and iOS. The Live Connect APIs use open standards like OAuth 2.0 and JSON, making them easy and familiar to work with.
Web developers
From SkyDrive document sharing to Hotmail contacts and calendars, it's easy to let your users connect and engage. Enable single sign-on for users of Windows 8, Hotmail, and other compatible services.
Important update from Microsoft
We recently announced that we'll begin to encourage Messenger users to start using Skype. As a result, the Messenger developer program will end. Existing implementations that use Extensible Messaging and Presence Protocol (XMPP) will continue to work until October 2013. Existing implementations that use Mobile Service Proxy (MSP) will continue to work until March 2014. For support for existing XMPP implementations, please visit our Forums page.
See who is using Live Connect
xobni
THE HUFFINGTON POST
htc
Microsoft
© 2013 Microsoft. All rights reserved.
Terms of use | Trademarks | Privacy statement | Site feedback | United States (English)

Figure 14-1. *Live Connect developer portal*

SDK and Reference

While you are in the Live Connect Developer Center, you might as well get the Live Connect SDK that you will soon need. It gets you wrappers on HTTP communication and makes your life a whole lot easier when building Windows 8, Windows Phone, and .NET apps. So, head over to the Downloads section in the developer portal and install the Live Connect SDK (see Figure 14-2).

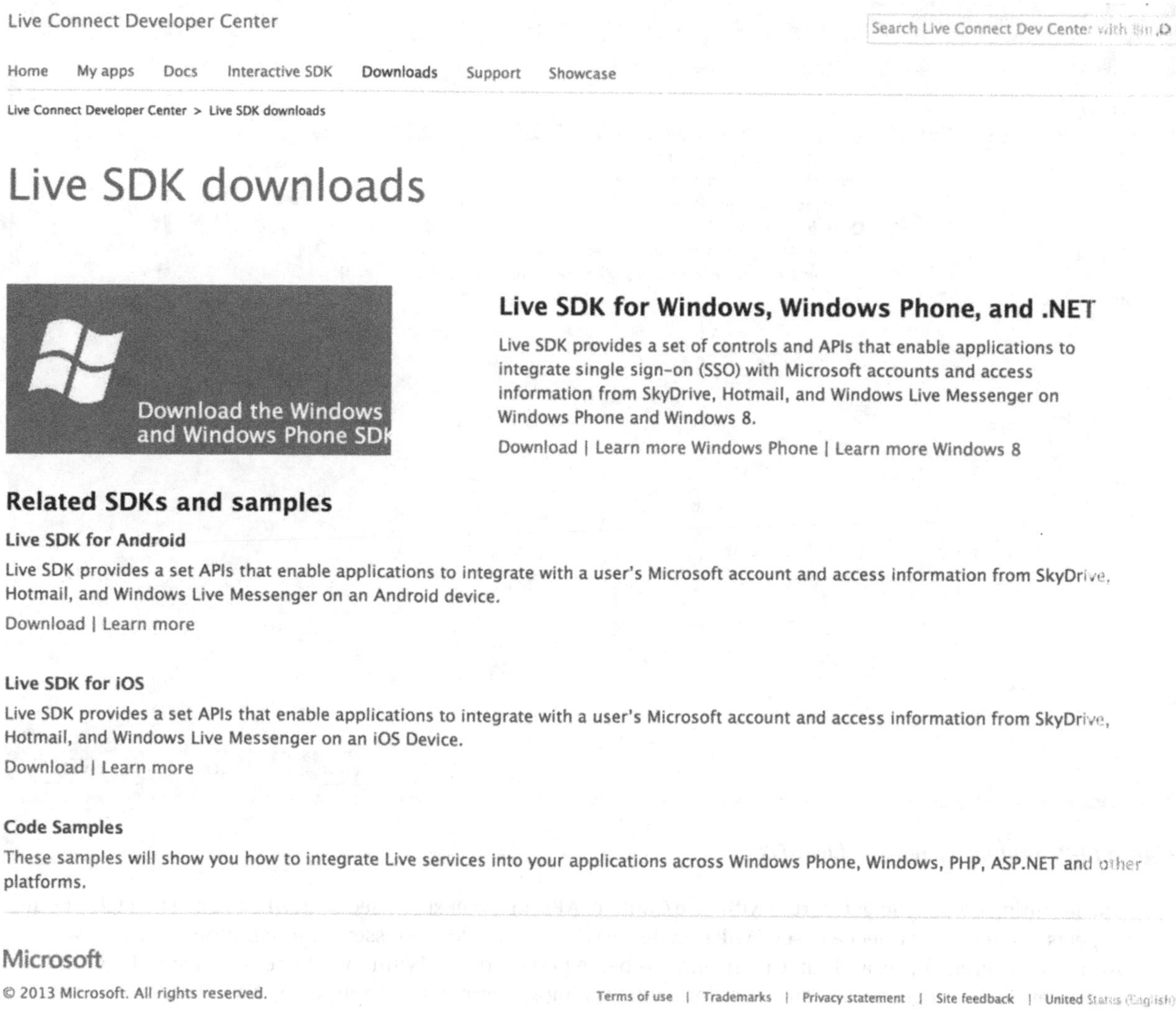

Live Connect Developer Center
Search Live Connect Dev Center with Bing
Home My apps Docs Interactive SDK Downloads Support Showcase
Live Connect Developer Center > Live SDK downloads
Live SDK downloads
Download the Windows and Windows Phone SDK
Live SDK for Windows, Windows Phone, and .NET
Live SDK provides a set of controls and APIs that enable applications to integrate single sign-on (SSO) with Microsoft accounts and access information from SkyDrive, Hotmail, and Windows Live Messenger on Windows Phone and Windows 8.
Download | Learn more Windows Phone | Learn more Windows 8
Related SDKs and samples
Live SDK for Android
Live SDK provides a set APIs that enable applications to integrate with a user's Microsoft account and access information from SkyDrive, Hotmail, and Windows Live Messenger on an Android device.
Download | Learn more
Live SDK for iOS
Live SDK provides a set APIs that enable applications to integrate with a user's Microsoft account and access information from SkyDrive, Hotmail, and Windows Live Messenger on an iOS Device.
Download | Learn more
Code Samples
These samples will show you how to integrate Live services into your applications across Windows Phone, Windows, PHP, ASP.NET and other platforms.
Microsoft
© 2013 Microsoft. All rights reserved.
Terms of use | Trademarks | Privacy statement | Site feedback | United States (English)

***Figure 14-2.** Live SDK download*

Next, you want to add a reference to the Live SDK inside the Visual Studio projects that you are using to build apps. This gives you access to the Live SDK DLL that has much of the HTTP communication functionality wrapped in easy method calls. Go back to your Apress Featured Books Demo app and add reference in your project to the Live SDK, after its installation (see Figure 14-3). Now you are all set to dig into functionality.

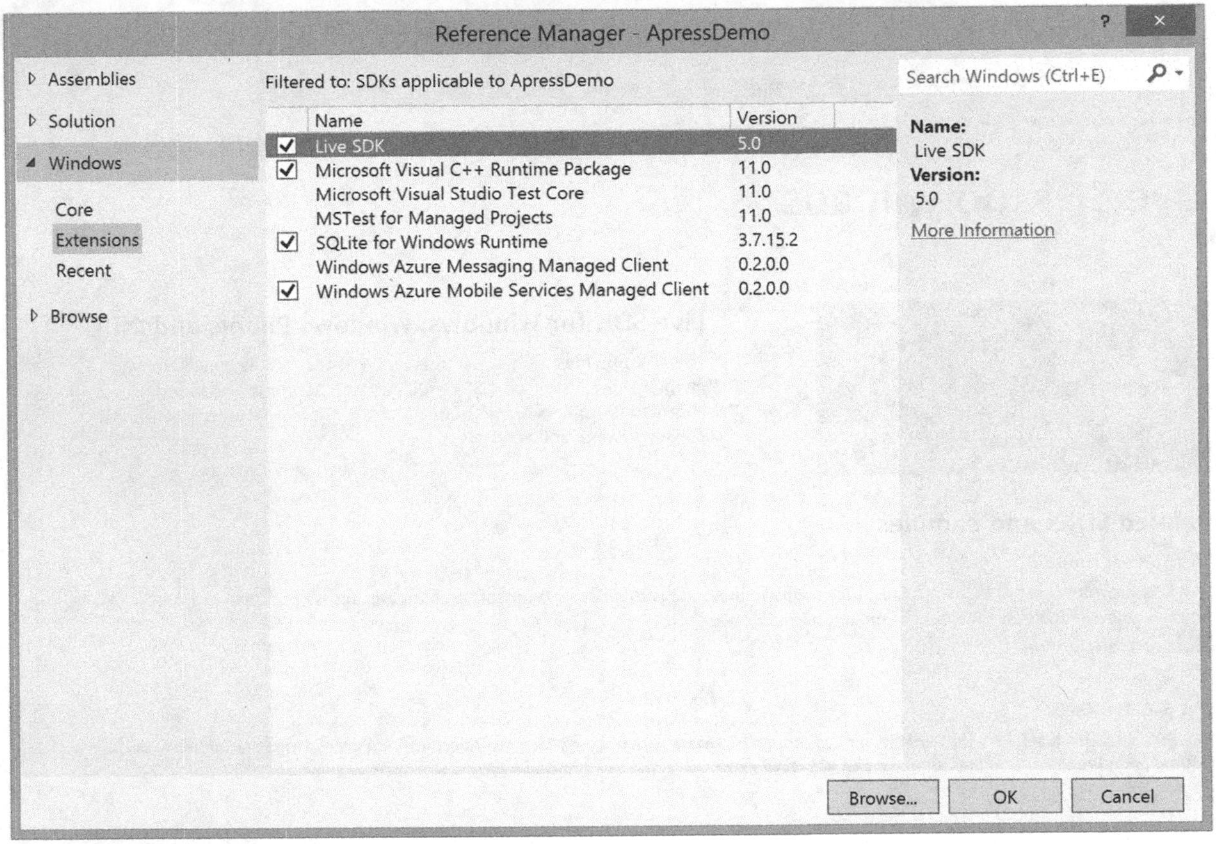

Figure 14-3. *Adding reference to Live SDK*

One last thing before you get started with Live Connect APIs in the next few sections. Although I shall talk about most aspects of the Live Connect API set, I will skip discussions on Windows Messenger integration through XMPP. Microsoft has acquired Skype, and since then, Skype is being preferred over Windows Messenger. Accordingly, the Messenger developer program will come to a slow end. Existing app implementations using XMPP will work until October 2013, so new development with it is not recommended. Instead, developers are encouraged to look at Skype APIs for providing real-time multiuser connectivity in applications.

Skype Integration

Do you have a genuine need to build real-time chat in the form of text, audio, or video? Do you need a real-time online presence status from users of your Windows 8 Store app? Then you need to look at what Skype offers for developers. Head over to `http://dev.skype.com` for more information (see Figure 14-4). You will find all sorts of information for leveraging Skype across multiple application platforms.

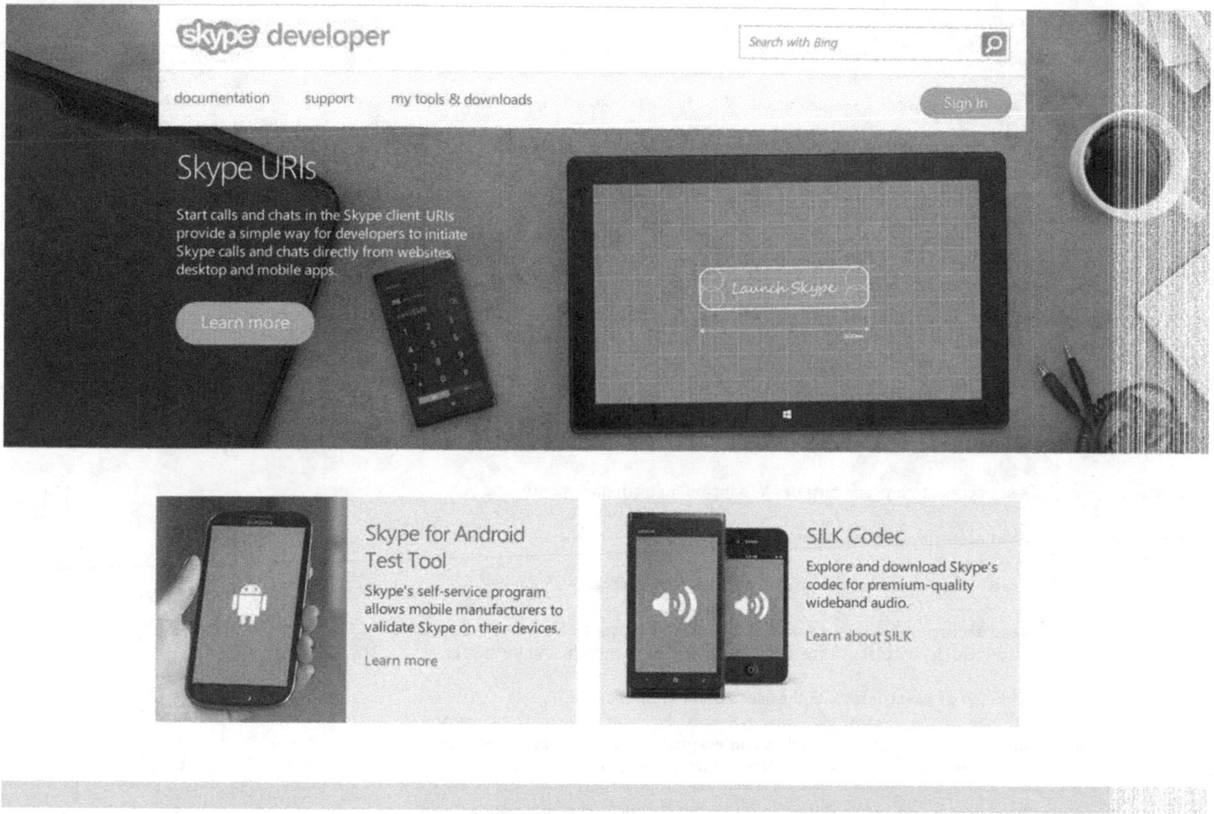

Figure 14-4. *The Skype dev center*

Now, let's get to the meat of the Live Services integration and get started consuming the Live Connect APIs.

Scopes

As your Windows 8 app starts consuming Live Connect APIs to work with Live Services information, you will immediately run into a permissions issue—so let's get that out of the way first. Since you may be dealing with very sensitive user data, information is segregated into disparate buckets based on functionality, like contacts, calendars, SkyDrive, and so forth. And as a developer, you need to ask the user for permission before you have access to an information bucket. In the Live Connect APIs, this permission is called a *scope*. Each scope grants a different permission level. Continuing the trust proposition while using Live Services, you should only ask for scopes that your app absolutely needs, and no more.

Scopes are of two types: core and extended. The *core scopes* are pivotal in Live Connect to authenticate the user and work with his or her profile information. The *extended scopes* allow the developer to work with a signed-in user's extended profile around contacts, calendars, and SkyDrive. And there may be different scopes allowing reads versus writes on the same information. So, head over to `http://msdn.microsoft.com/en-us/library/live/hh243646.aspx` and read well. A smattering of available scopes is shown in Figure 14-5.

Core scopes

Scope	Enables
wl.basic	Read access to a user's basic profile info. Also enables read access to a user's list of contacts.
wl.offline_access	The ability of an app to read and update a user's info at any time. Without this scope, an app can access the user's info only while the user is signed in to Live Connect and is using your app.
wl.signin	Single sign-in behavior. With *single sign-in*, users who are already signed in to Live Connect are also signed in to your website.

Top

Extended scopes

Scope	Enables
wl.birthday	Read access to a user's birthday info including birth day, month, and year.
wl.calendars	Read access to a user's calendars and events.
wl.calendars_update	Read and write access to a user's calendars and events.
wl.contacts_birthday	Read access to the birth day and birth month of a user's contacts. Note that this also gives read access to the user's birth day, birth month, and birth year.
wl.contacts_create	Creation of new contacts in the user's address book.
wl.contacts_calendars	Read access to a user's calendars and events. Also enables read access to any calendars and events that other users have shared with the user.
wl.contacts_photos	Read access to a user's albums, photos, videos, and audio, and their associated comments and tags. Also enables read access to any albums, photos, videos, and audio that other users have shared with the user.
wl.contacts_skydrive	Read access to Microsoft SkyDrive files that other users have shared with the user. Note that this also gives read access to the user's files stored in SkyDrive.
wl.emails	Read access to a user's personal, preferred, and business email addresses.
wl.events_create	Creation of events on the user's default calendar.
wl.phone_numbers	Read access to a user's personal, business, and mobile phone numbers.
wl.photos	Read access to a user's photos, videos, audio, and albums.
wl.postal_addresses	Read access to a user's postal addresses.
wl.share	Enables updating a user's status message.
wl.skydrive	Read access to a user's files stored in SkyDrive.
wl.skydrive_update	Read and write access to a user's files stored in SkyDrive.
wl.work_profile	Read access to a user's employer and work position information.

Figure 14-5. *Live Connect scopes*

As you use these Live Connect scopes, keep in mind that you need user permission every time you access a new type of information tied to the signed-in user. In your Windows 8 app, and based on functionality, you will have prior knowledge of the exact scopes you need. However, be a little wary of asking for all the necessary scopes from the start—this may make the user nervous about data security. This is where a privacy statement helps in detailing your intentions with the user's information. Asking for permission as users go along may not be a bad thing.

The scopes are pivotal in understanding how to leverage Live Services in your apps and making sure that you have the permission needed for service interaction. Now, let's talk about user authentication— the all-important mechanism to identify users of your apps.

Authentication

Count the number of IDs and passwords that you have to remember for all the web sites/applications that you interact with combined. Yeah, your users don't like remembering all their IDs and passwords either. Unless explicitly needed for an enterprise application or when the user profile is very important for your application (as with paid subscriptions, etc.), developers need to get out of the business of authenticating users, and this stands very true for Windows 8 apps. Instead, you should allow the user to sign in to your app using the myriad, trusted identity providers that will authenticate a user for you and return a token instead. Trust the tokens and get to know who the user is, rather than having to validate whether the user is truly who he/she says. This means less security for your app to handle and one less ID/password that the user has to remember. In fact, ease in signing in means that the user is more likely to use the app, and the developer gets to personalize the user experience by only knowing what is required.

A key benefit of using the Live SDK is to leverage easy authentication through the underlying Live Services. In fact, what you want to enable in your Windows 8 app is called a single sign-on (SSO) with a Microsoft account, which subsequently empowers the user to have a zero-click sign-in experience. Remember that many Windows 8 users actually sign in to their device using their Microsoft accounts. By trusting the Microsoft account to be the identity provider, the user is already one step closer because Windows 8 knows who the user is. Even if the user does not sign in with a Microsoft account, he or she can be presented with a login screen the first time around. Beyond that point, the user has to provide permission for your app to have access to specific information via Live Services through a one-time process. That's it. If done right, the user never again has to sign in to your app, and your app gets to reuse any permitted information through Live Connect APIs.

What's happening with single sign-on is simple to understand. With your Windows 8 app using Live Connect to sign the user in with a Microsoft account, your app never sees the user's access credentials. The Microsoft account acts as a broker and authenticates the user, who then allows your app specific permissions. Live Connect combines the user's identity and all of the allowed access rights into one access token, which gets returned to your app. In any subsequent interaction with Live Services, simply provide the access token, and your app provides no-questions-asked service. Every Windows 8 app that uses such authentication mechanisms is supposed to cache the access tokens and reuse until expiry. An automatic access token renewal is also possible.

One key benefit of using a trusted identity provider like the Microsoft account is enabling the single-sign-on paradigm across applications. Suppose your Windows 8 app has a companion web site or you offer supporting iOS or Android mobile apps. All of these could use a single authentication mechanism and cache access tokens centrally. This means the user could sign in once through the web site or one of the apps, and the next time around, the other platforms' apps will immediately know who the user is and provide a zero-click customized sign-in experience. You can see how lucrative this idea is—where you let an identity provider like a Microsoft account do the user authentication on your behalf. You do not have to deal with user credential security; instead, you can focus on providing a personal user experience across multiple application platforms.

Providing choice is another thing to keep in mind when using Live Connect to enable user sign-on. If you are only going to use the Microsoft account as an identity provider, then Live Connect is perfect. If, however, you want to increase flexibility for the user and provide options to sign on with other standard identity providers, such as Twitter, Facebook, Google, or Active Directory Federation Services (ADFS), you need to look outside of Live Connect. For orchestrating such authentications, your options could be the excellent Azure Access Control Service (`http://msdn.microsoft.com/en-us/library/hh147631.aspx`) or Azure Mobile Services (`www.windowsazure.com/en-us/develop/mobile/resources/#header-2`), which was discussed in Chapter 13.

Integrating Authentication

Ready to see some code? OK, let's start with adding a new app bar icon to the dashboard of your Apress demo app so that you have a fresh XAML page to play with, as shown in Figure 14-6. The app bar is possibly becoming too busy, but you will let that slide for the purpose of the demo.

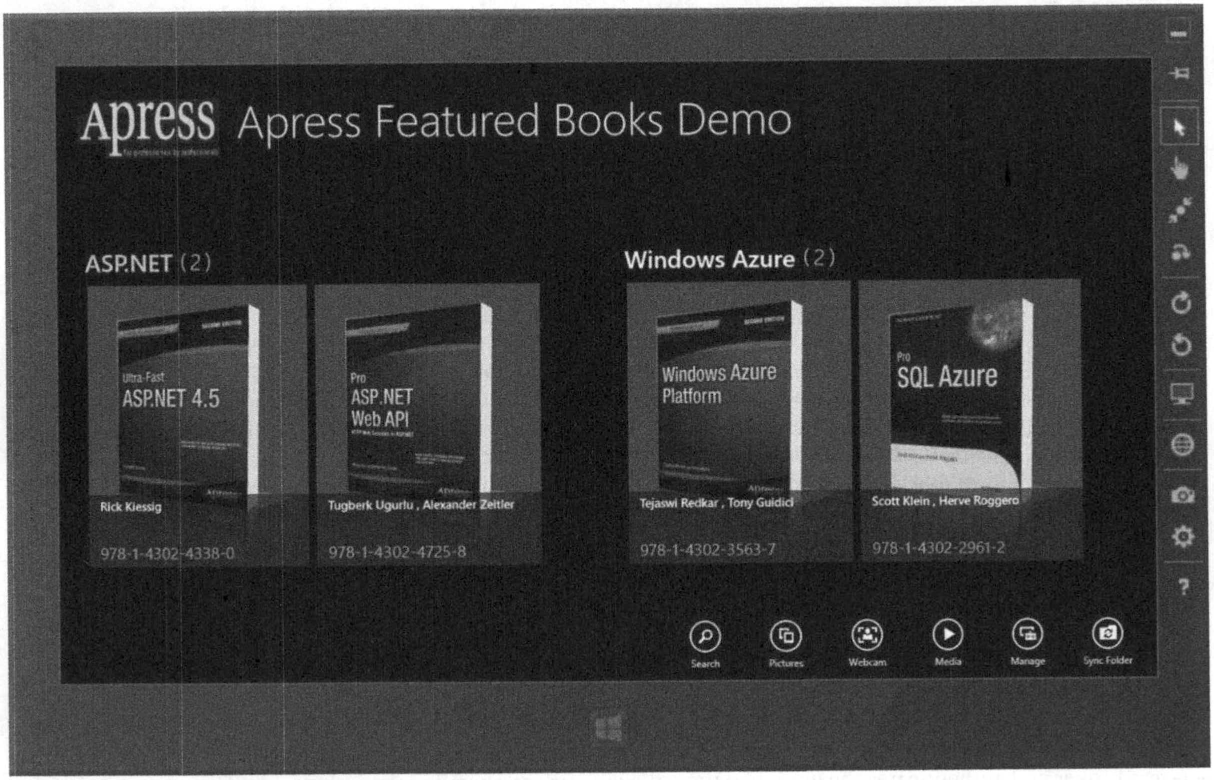

Figure 14-6. *New app bar icon*

Listing 14-1 shows the XAML markup. When the user clicks the Sync/Live button, you simply take him to the new XAML page.

Listing 14-1. Customized App Bar

```
<Page.BottomAppBar>
        <AppBar x:Name="bottomAppBar" Padding="10,0,10,0">
            <Grid>
                <StackPanel Orientation="Horizontal" HorizontalAlignment="Right">
                    <Button Style="{StaticResource SearchAppBarButtonStyle}"
x:Name="searchButton" Click="searchButton_Click"/>
                    <Button Style="{StaticResource PicturesAppBarButtonStyle}"
x:Name="loadButton" Click="loadButton_Click"/>
                    <Button Style="{StaticResource WebcamAppBarButtonStyle}"
x:Name="accountButton" Click="accountButton_Click"/>
```

```
                    <Button Style="{StaticResource PlayAppBarButtonStyle}"
x:Name="mediaButton" Click="mediaButton_Click"/>
                    <Button Style="{StaticResource ManageAppBarButtonStyle}"
x:Name="manageButton" Click="manageButton_Click"/>
                    <Button Style="{StaticResource SyncFolderAppBarButtonStyle}"
x:Name="liveButton" Click="liveButton_Click"/>
                </StackPanel>
            </Grid>
        </AppBar>
    </Page.BottomAppBar>
```

On the new XAML page, you intend to have functionality that will leverage Live Connect APIs, and as such, requires users to log in with their Microsoft accounts. For consistency, the new Microsoft guidelines state that such authentication mechanisms be presented to the user through the Settings pane, along with a privacy policy on sensitive data usage. Accordingly, two Settings pane options are mandatory: Account and Privacy Statement. Figure 14-7 shows the kind of UI that you are shooting for in the Apress demo app.

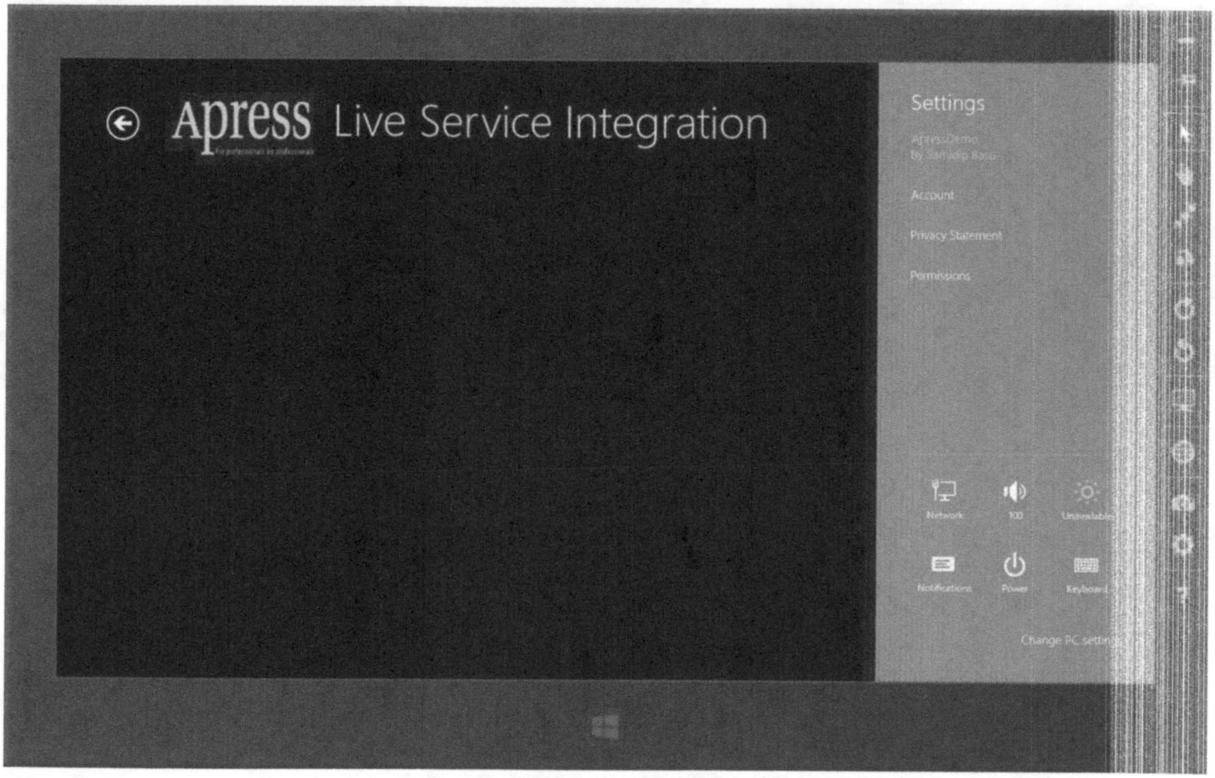

Figure 14-7. *Required settings*

So, the Settings pane integration is a must on pages that need the user to sign in to their Microsoft account, but you may also choose to do this throughout your Windows 8 app if user privileges carry throughout. As you have seen with Settings pane integration in past chapters, the steps are simple:

1. Define custom user controls to host your content.
2. Use the Windows pop-up control to show the Settings flyout.
3. Position the flyout exactly where Settings should be on the charms menu.
4. Match OS animations and support light dismiss of the pop-up.

Settings Pane Integration

So, let's get to work. First, you define two custom user controls: `AccountSettingsFlyout.xaml` (see Figure 14-8) and `PrivacyStatementSettingsFlyout.xaml`. These file names easily tell you that they are meant to support the two new Settings menu options that you are about to add.

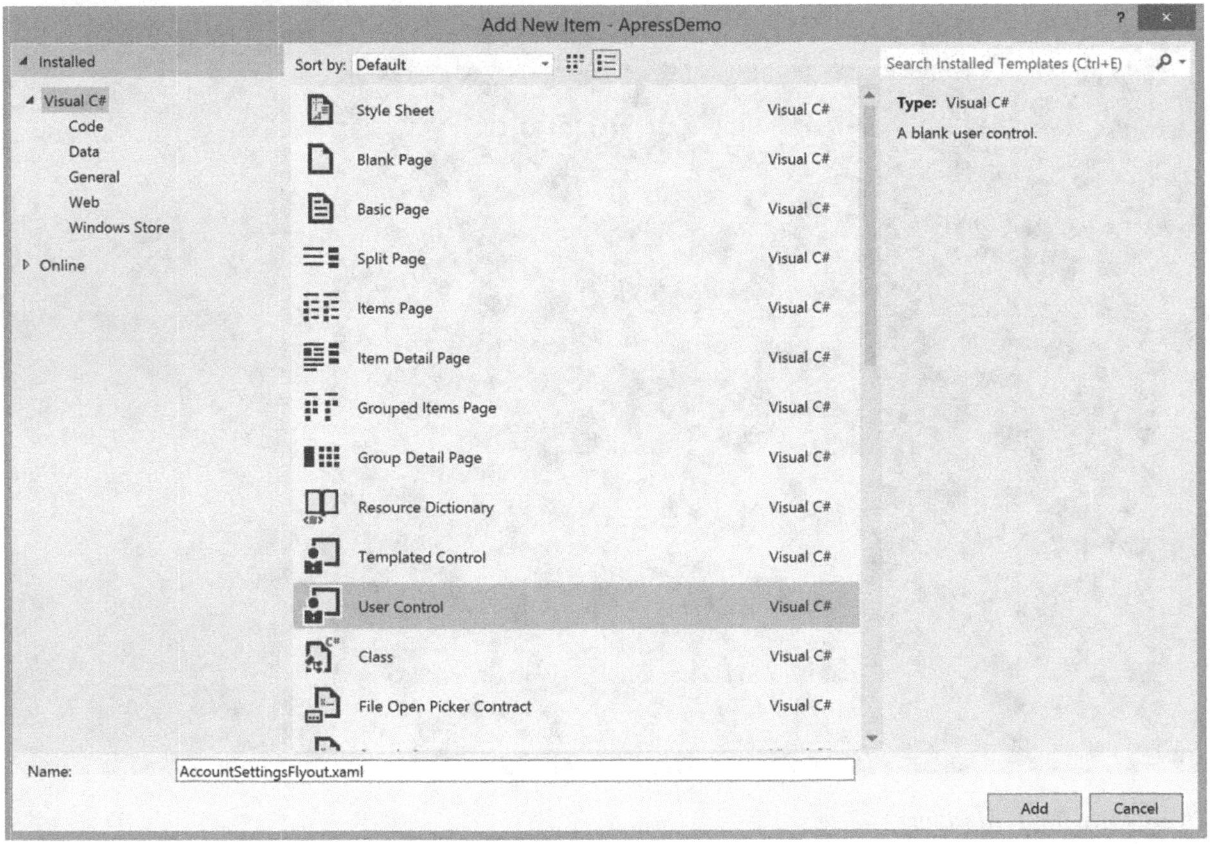

Figure 14-8. *New user control for Settings*

Next, wire up the new XAML page to expect the user popping open the Settings menu, so that you may add your custom options (see Listing 14-2).

Listing 14-2. Wiring a Custom User Control As a Pop-up

```
#region "Members"

    // A popup control to display the special Settings Flyouts.
    private Popup settingsPopup;

    // Used to determine the correct height to ensure your custom UI fills the screen.
    private Rect windowBounds;

    // Desired width for the settings UI. UI guidelines specify this should be 346 or 646 depending
on your needs.
    private double settingsWidth = 346;

    #endregion

    protected override void OnNavigatedTo(NavigationEventArgs e)
    {
        base.OnNavigatedTo(e);
        windowBounds = Window.Current.Bounds;

        // Listen to Settings Pane events.
        SettingsPane.GetForCurrentView().CommandsRequested += Settings_CommandsRequested;
    }

    protected override void OnNavigatedFrom(NavigationEventArgs e)
    {
        base.OnNavigatedFrom(e);

        SettingsPane.GetForCurrentView().CommandsRequested -= Settings_CommandsRequested;
    }

private void Settings_CommandsRequested(SettingsPane sender, SettingsPaneCommandsRequestedEventArgs args)
    {
        UICommandInvokedHandler accountSettingshandler = new
UICommandInvokedHandler(onAccountSettingsCommand);
        SettingsCommand accountSettingsCommand = new
SettingsCommand("ApressAccountSettings", "Account", accountSettingshandler);
        args.Request.ApplicationCommands.Add(accountSettingsCommand);

        UICommandInvokedHandler privacySettingshandler =
new UICommandInvokedHandler(onPrivacySettingsCommand);
        SettingsCommand privacySettingsCommand = new
SettingsCommand("ApressPrivacySettings", "Privacy Statement", privacySettingshandler);
        args.Request.ApplicationCommands.Add(privacySettingsCommand);
    }
```

So far, you have wired/unwired an event handler to the Settings charm being invoked by the user. You have two custom `UICommandInvokedHandlers` that would add your custom Settings options to the Settings pane. Now you also have a pop-up control ready, and you know the bounds of the app window. So, what happens when the user clicks one of the Settings options? You wire the pop-up to open with matching animation, and host the appropriate user control inside the pop-up. Listing 14-3 shows how to do this for the Account Settings flyout:

Listing 14-3. Settings Flyout Implementation

```
void onAccountSettingsCommand(IUICommand command)
        {
            // Create a Popup window which will contain your flyout.
            settingsPopup = new Popup();
            settingsPopup.Closed += OnPopupClosed;
            Window.Current.Activated += OnWindowActivated;
            settingsPopup.IsLightDismissEnabled = true;
            settingsPopup.Width = settingsWidth;
            settingsPopup.Height = windowBounds.Height;

            // Add the proper animation for the panel.
            settingsPopup.ChildTransitions = new TransitionCollection();
            settingsPopup.ChildTransitions.Add(new PaneThemeTransition()
            {
                Edge = (SettingsPane.Edge == SettingsEdgeLocation.Right) ?
                        EdgeTransitionLocation.Right :
                        EdgeTransitionLocation.Left
            });

            // Create an Account Settings Flyout the same dimensions as the Popup.
            AccountSettingsFlyout mypane = new AccountSettingsFlyout();
            mypane.Width = settingsWidth;
            mypane.Height = windowBounds.Height;

            // Place the SettingsFlyout inside your Popup window.
            settingsPopup.Child = mypane;

            // Let's define the location of your Popup.
            settingsPopup.SetValue(Canvas.LeftProperty, SettingsPane.Edge ==
SettingsEdgeLocation.Right ? (windowBounds.Width - settingsWidth) : 0);
            settingsPopup.SetValue(Canvas.TopProperty, 0);
            settingsPopup.IsOpen = true;
        }

        void OnPopupClosed(object sender, object e)
        {
            Window.Current.Activated -= OnWindowActivated;
        }
```

```
        private void OnWindowActivated(object sender, Windows.UI.Core.WindowActivatedEventArgs e)
        {
            if (e.WindowActivationState == Windows.UI.Core.CoreWindowActivationState.Deactivated)
            {
                settingsPopup.IsOpen = false;
            }
        }
```

Did you notice that you opened your pop-up exactly where required following the Settings pane, and that you also wired up its dismissal when the main app window is activated? The Privacy Statement user control launching follows the exact same trend.

Now, as for the contents of the Settings user controls, let's start with the easier Privacy Statement pane. You dummy up the privacy statement (see Figure 14-9), but this is where you need to declare exactly how your Windows 8 app intends to use sensitive user data, available only when the user signs in. Did you notice the Back button at the top of the user control? You need to support this so that the user can get back to app Settings as if from the charms menu. Here's how:

```
private void MySettingsBackClicked(object sender, RoutedEventArgs e)
        {
            // First close your Flyout.
            Popup parent = this.Parent as Popup;
            if (parent != null)
            {
                parent.IsOpen = false;
            }

            // If the app is not snapped, then the back button shows the Settings pane again.
            if (Windows.UI.ViewManagement.ApplicationView.Value != Windows.UI.ViewManagement.
ApplicationViewState.Snapped)
            {
                SettingsPane.Show();
            }
        }
```

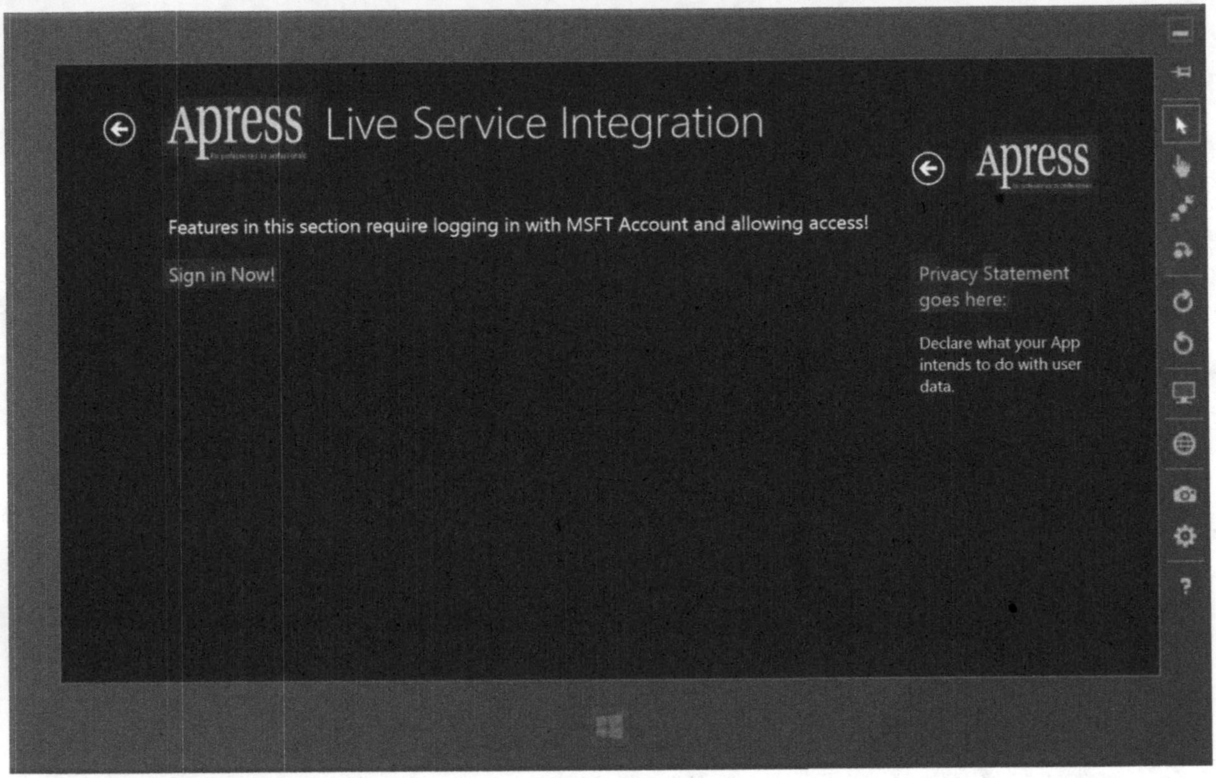

Figure 14-9. Privacy Statement settings

Since you need the user to sign in to access specific Live Services features, one major requirement needs to be satisfied: there needs to be explicit ways through which the user can sign in and sign out. The Settings pane is supposed to be the defacto place where the user manages his or her state with the Microsoft account. But the app UI should also include indications that show whether the user is signed in or out. This is just a security feature so that the user knows, in one glance, whether he or she is in secured or unsecured mode, and is thus more conscious when the Windows 8 app is handling his or her sensitive data. Accordingly, as the user has not signed in before first use, your XAML page clearly hints that the user needs to sign in to access functionality on this page. Later on, after the user does sign in, you will toggle the status.

Even if you are showing the user's status onscreen, the actual handling of the user authentication through Live Connect still needs to happen from the Settings pane. So perhaps if the user needs to sign in or out, you can nudge him or her in the right direction by programmatically opening the Settings pane (see Figure 14-10), and through the following code. The `actionText` mentioned is the Sign In/Out text in app UI.

```
private void actionText_Tapped(object sender, TappedRoutedEventArgs e)
        {
            if (Windows.UI.ViewManagement.ApplicationView.Value !=
Windows.UI.ViewManagement.ApplicationViewState.Snapped)
            {
                SettingsPane.Show();
            }
        }
```

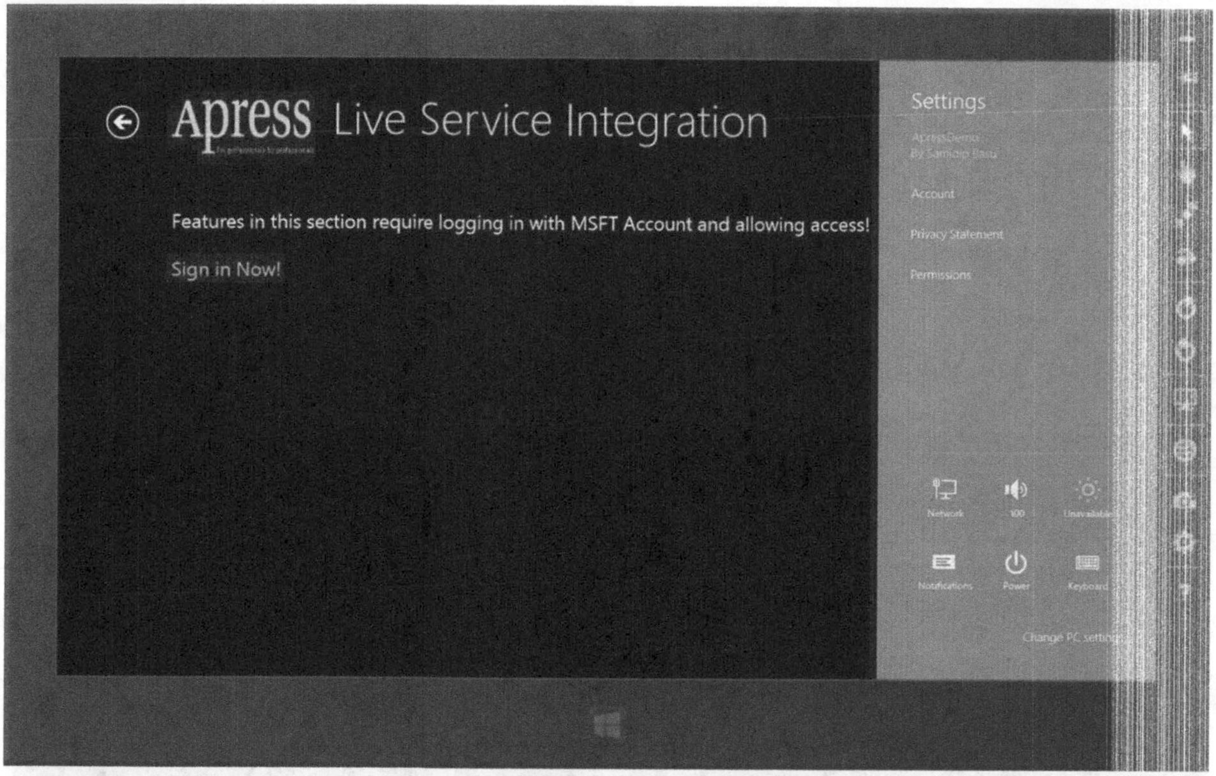

***Figure 14-10.** In-app authentication status*

Account Settings

Now let's look at the all-important Account Settings flyout. The goal here is two fold: allow the user to sign in/out and indicate current status. You can choose to go as fancy as you want in your app. Here's the XAML markup to show the bare bones needed in the `AccountSettingsFlyout.xaml` user control:

```
<Grid Style="{StaticResource LayoutRootStyle}" Background="Black">
        <Grid.RowDefinitions>
            <RowDefinition Height="160"/>
            <RowDefinition Height="*"/>
        </Grid.RowDefinitions>

        <!-- Logo Area -->
        <Grid Grid.Row="0">
            <StackPanel Orientation="Horizontal">
                <Button x:Name="backButton" Click="MySettingsBackClicked" Style="{StaticResource
BackButtonStyle}" Margin="40, 0, 25, 0"/>
                <Image x:Name="Logo" Source="/Assets/ApressLogo.png" Width="180" Height="80"
Margin="2, 80, 40, -30" VerticalAlignment="Center" HorizontalAlignment="Left"/>
            </StackPanel>
        </Grid>
```

```
        <!-- App Settings -->
        <Grid x:Name="settingsContent" Grid.Row="1" Margin="50">
            <StackPanel Margin="0, 30, 0, 0" Orientation="Vertical">
                <TextBlock Text="Account Settings go here:" TextWrapping="Wrap"
Style="{StaticResource BasicTextStyle}" HorizontalAlignment="Left" FontSize="20"
Foreground="Orange"/>
                <TextBlock x:Name="statusText" FontSize="16" Margin="5,20,0,0"/>
                <Button x:Name="actionButton" Click="actionButton_Click" Margin="5,10,0,0"/>
            </StackPanel>
        </Grid>
    </Grid>
```

Figure 14-11 shows the UI that it produces.

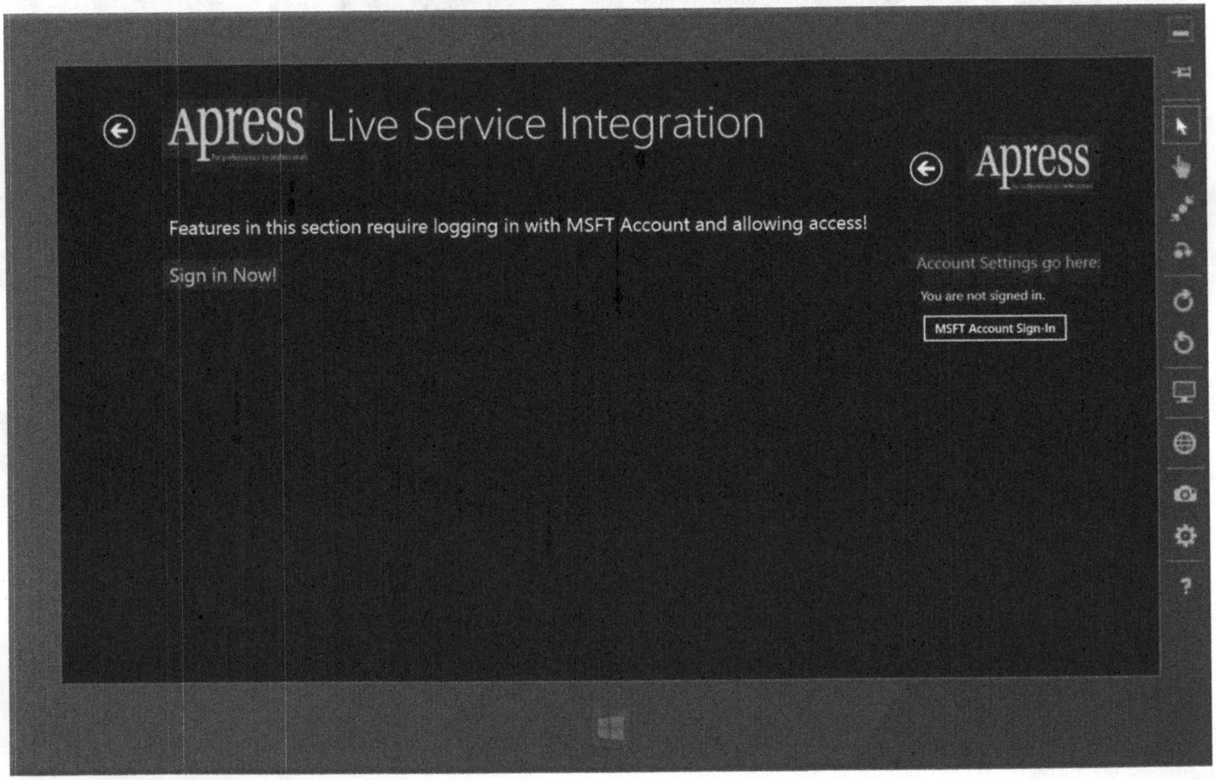

Figure 14-11. *Account Settings*

User Sign-In

Now let's add some code so that the user might actually be able to sign in. You can choose to have this code anywhere you like, but `App.xaml.cs` is usually a good idea since it makes the code globally accessible so that any page of your app can sign the user in. Here's some code:

```
using Microsoft.Live;
private LiveConnectSession _session = null;

public LiveConnectSession LiveSession
        {
            get { return _session; }
            set {_session = value; }
        }

public async Task AuthenticateUserThroughLive()
        {
            try
            {
                // Use Live Connect SDK client to authenticate user.
                LiveAuthClient LCAuth = new LiveAuthClient();
                LiveLoginResult LCLoginResult = await LCAuth.InitializeAsync();

                try
                {
                    LiveLoginResult loginResult = null;
                    loginResult = await LCAuth.LoginAsync(new string[] { "wl.signin", "wl.basic",
"wl.skydrive", "wl.skydrive_update" });

                    if (loginResult.Status == LiveConnectSessionStatus.Connected)
                    {
                        this.LiveSession = loginResult.Session;
                    }
                }
                catch (LiveAuthException)
                {
                    // Handle exceptions.
                }
            }
            catch (LiveAuthException)
            {
                // Handle exceptions.
            }
        }
```

Let's inspect what you did here. First, you defined a global variable of the type LiveConnectSession. This is critical because once the user signs in, the LiveConnectSession contains the Live Services access token, which is required for all communication. You will reuse this LiveConnectSession, throughout your app, whenever you talk to Live Connect APIs, and this means you need to cache the LiveConnectSession object carefully in app storage. Also, as a natural consequence, any time the user signs in/out or adds fresh permissions to your app, this LiveConnectSession placeholder needs to be updated so that it always reflects the latest access token and the user's status.

Beyond this, you leveraged the LiveAuthClient wrapper and invoked the LoginAsync() method on it to actually sign the user in. Did you notice the parameters you are passing in to the LoginAsync() method? Yes, you guessed it right, those are the permission scopes your app is declaring. Essentially, you are trying to sign the user in, but in one swoop, also declare the scopes your app is going to need so that the user can provide permissions. Once everything goes as planned and the user is able to sign in, the LiveConnectSessionStatus changes to Connected and you save from the resulting LiveConnectSession object for reuse. There are HTTP calls being made to RESTful Live Services endpoints during this process. The Live SDK simply hides such details so that the developer gets to write plain C# code. Isn't that nice?

User Sign-Out

While you are at it, also declare a way for the user to sign out once ready. You do this in the App.xaml.cs as well. The code follows. As you can see, no surprises here since you call the LogOut() method and clear out your LiveConnectSession object.

```
public async Task UnAuthenticateUserThroughLive()
        {
            try
            {
                LiveAuthClient LCAuth = new LiveAuthClient();
                LiveLoginResult LCLoginResult = await LCAuth.InitializeAsync();

                LCAuth.Logout();
                LiveSession = null;
            }
            catch (LiveAuthException)
            {
                // Handle exceptions.
            }
        }
```

Back in your AccountSettingsFlyout.xaml.cs user control code-behind, wire up the user authentication to the button click, like so:

```
private async void actionButton_Click(object sender, RoutedEventArgs e)
        {
            if (((App)Application.Current).LiveSession == null)
            {
                await ((App)Application.Current).AuthenticateUserThroughLive();
            }
            else
            {
                await ((App)Application.Current).UnAuthenticateUserThroughLive();
            }

            Popup parent = this.Parent as Popup;
            if (parent != null)
            {
                parent.IsOpen = false;
            }
        }
```

You'll notice how you utilize the global LiveConnectSession object to figure out if the user is signed in or not. Accordingly, you turn around and invoke the AuthenticateUserThroughLive() or UnAuthenticateUserThroughLive() methods defined in the App.xaml.cs, and also proceed to close the Account Settings flyout pop-up.

Check Implementation

Feeling lucky? Let's fire up your Apress demo app and click the MSFT Account Sign-In button in the Account Settings pane. You should see a UI like the one shown in Figure 14-12. That is definitely not a UI that you built. True, this is the Live Services permissions UI being overlaid on top of your app UI so that the user can allow/reject permitting your app to utilize the scopes declared. Do you remember the scopes you passed in as the user was trying to authenticate? This permissions UI reflects all of those declared scopes—only with user-friendly descriptions so that the user can say yay or nay. This permissions UI utilizes the user's selected theme color and shows up as a modal message on top of whatever the app UI may be.

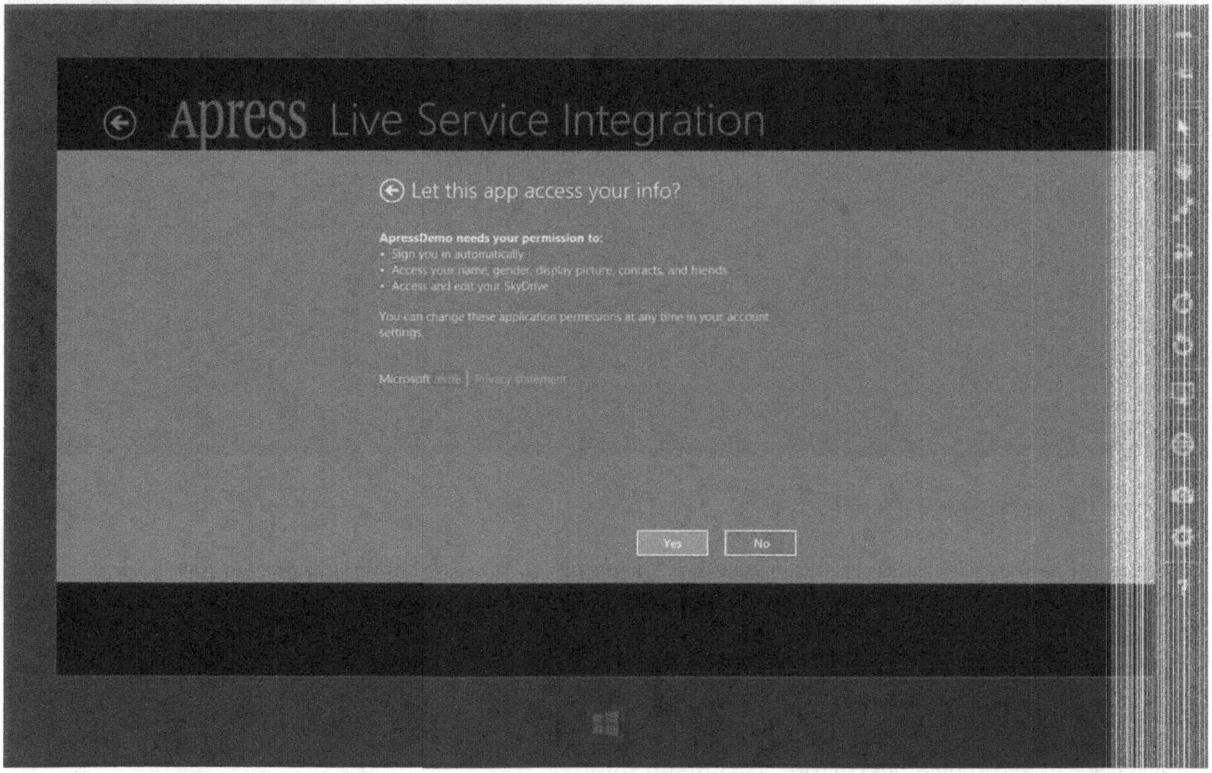

Figure 14-12. *App permissions*

Did you notice something strange? You wanted the user to sign in to his or her Microsoft account, but the user was never prompted to do so. Instead, the user was taken directly to the app permissions UI, as if the user is already authenticated. Turns out that this is true. Your attempt to sign the user in meant handshaking with the Live Connect API. And this being a Windows 8 app, the user is already signed in with his or her Microsoft account, which can be reused. The `LiveAuthClient` realizes this and passes on the logged-in user's information to Live Services, which does the handshake with the Microsoft account to verify that the user is, in fact, signed in, and then proceeds to app permissions. If the user was not signed in with a Microsoft account, he will, in fact, see the step of signing into his Microsoft account, as the stock image from MSDN shows in Figure 14-13. Once signed in, the user can then proceed to app permissions. Did you notice that even if the user was signed in to his Windows 8 device with a Microsoft account, your Windows 8 app did not automatically have permission to access the user's information without permission. This is an example of the subtle ways that Windows 8 tries to protect the user's sensitive information.

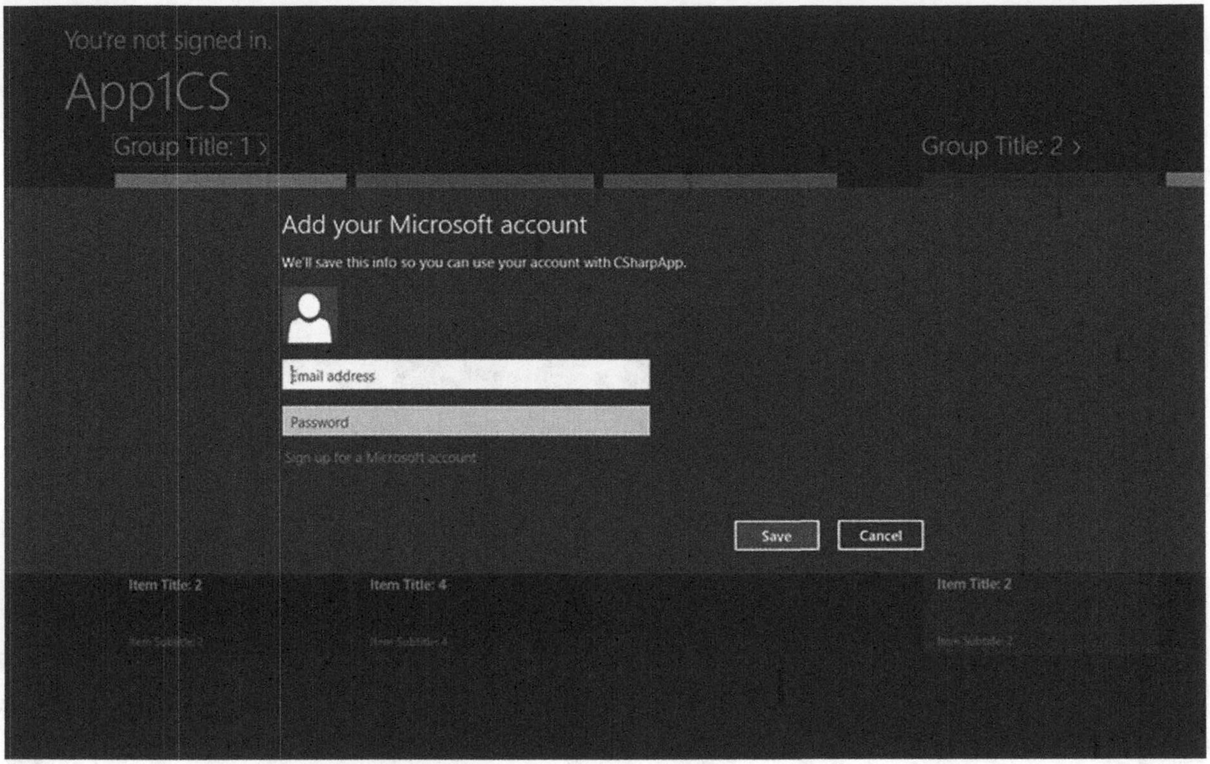

Figure 14-13. *Microsoft account sign-in*

Once the user provides permissions to your app, you are all set. Your app should feel privileged to be given access to sensitive user data. Accordingly, you need to welcome the user with personalization so that he or she feels that the app permissions were worth it. In your Apress demo app, welcome the user with a personalized greeting, and pull down their profile image to increase intimacy with your app. Listing 14-4 shows the code.

Listing 14-4. Greeting the User

```
<StackPanel Orientation="Horizontal" Margin="0,5,0,0">
            <TextBlock x:Name="userInfoText" FontSize="24" VerticalAlignment="Center" />
            <Image x:Name="profilePicture" Width="100" Height="100" Margin="30,0,0,0"
VerticalAlignment="Bottom"/>
        </StackPanel>

private async Task GreetUserByName()
        {
            if (((App)Application.Current).LiveSession != null)
            {
                try
                {
                    LiveConnectClient liveClient = new
LiveConnectClient(((App)Application.Current).LiveSession);
```

```
                LiveOperationResult operationResult = await liveClient.GetAsync("me");
                dynamic result = operationResult.Result;
                if (result != null)
                {
                    this.userInfoText.Text = "Hello " + result.name + "!";
                    this.actionText.Text = "Sign out Now!";
                }
            }
            catch (LiveConnectException)
            {
                // Handle exceptions.
            }
        }
        else
        {
            this.userInfoText.Text = string.Empty;
            this.actionText.Text = "Sign in Now!";
            this.profilePicture.Visibility = Windows.UI.Xaml.Visibility.Collapsed;
        }
    }

private async Task FetchUserProfilePicture()
    {
        try
        {
            LiveConnectClient liveClient = new
LiveConnectClient(((App)Application.Current).LiveSession);
            LiveOperationResult operationResult = await liveClient.GetAsync("me/picture");
            dynamic result = operationResult.Result;

            BitmapImage image = new BitmapImage(new Uri(result.location, UriKind.Absolute));
            this.profilePicture.Source = image;
        }
        catch (LiveConnectException)
        {
            // Handle exceptions.
        }
    }
```

As you can see, you defined a couple of placeholders in XAML to show the user's name and profile picture. Next, you created the `LiveConnectClient` object using the `LiveConnectSession` object that was already cached from `App.xaml.cs`, where you first authenticated the user. This makes sure that subsequent calls to Live Connect endpoints do not need the user to reauthenticate, and that the access token passed in already has the permissions needed to access the information requested. In this case, you are asking for the signed-in user's profile data in the form of his or her name and image.

Fetching User Data

Next, you make the asynchronous `GetAsync()` call using the `LiveConnectClient` and send in a special parameter called "`me`". This simply stands for the signed-in user and his or her data. It's just another way that Live SDK makes life easier for developers. The `GetAsync()` call fires up an HTTP GET request to Live Services endpoints. You can see these requests if you watch network traffic out of your development machine. That's it. Once results come back successfully, you update the UI. With the Apress demo app, I'm already logged in to the Windows 8 device using my Microsoft account, as shown in Figure 14-14, so you see my profile data. Yes, no escaping it now—that is how I look! Also, you'll notice that the Sign In/Out text is toggled to reflect the user's status.

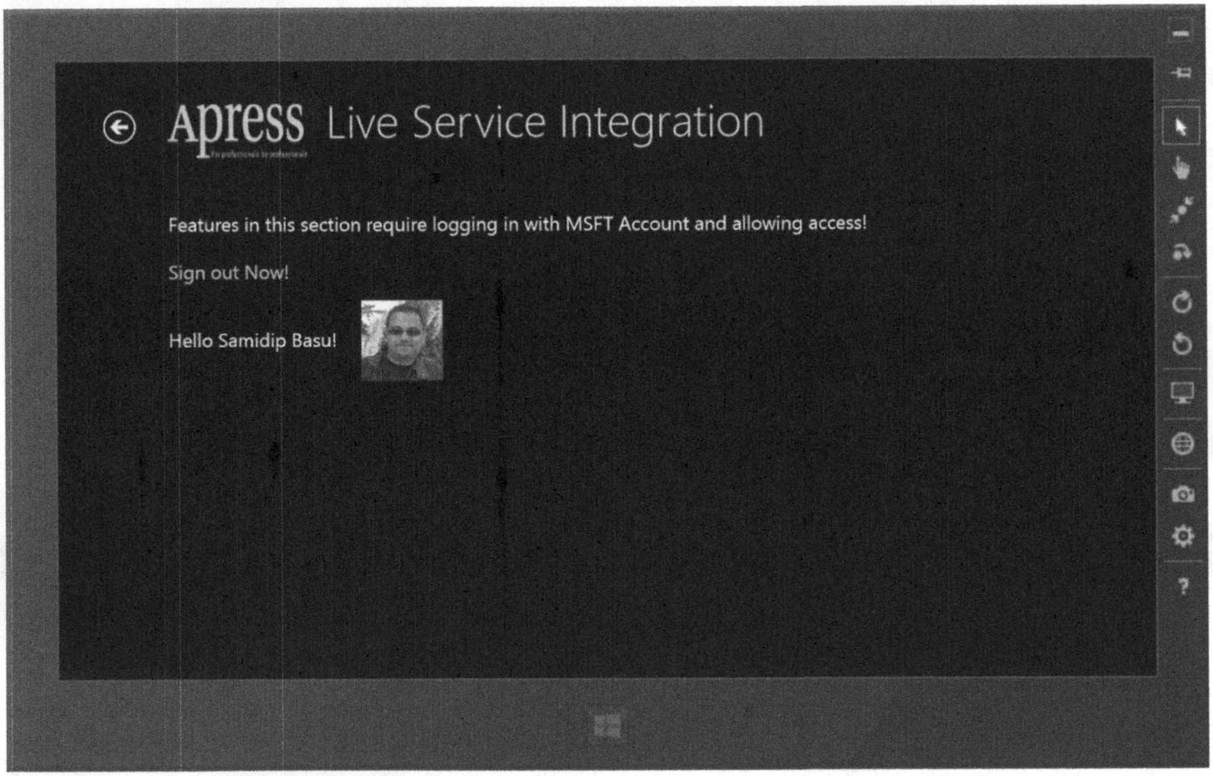

Figure 14-14. *Welcome user after sign-in*

Also, once the user successfully signs in, you need to toggle the contents of the Account Settings flyout to allow for signing out (see Figure 14-15). This is easily done by checking your global `LiveConnectSession` indicator. Add some code to the user control's initialization to make this toggle happen, as follows. The results are shown next.

```
public AccountSettingsFlyout()
        {
            this.InitializeComponent();

            if (((App)Application.Current).LiveSession == null)
            {
                this.actionButton.Content = "MSFT Account Sign-In";
                this.statusText.Text = "You are not signed in.";
            }
```

```
        else
        {
            this.actionButton.Content = "MSFT Account Sign-Out";
            this.statusText.Text = "You are signed in";
        }
    }
```

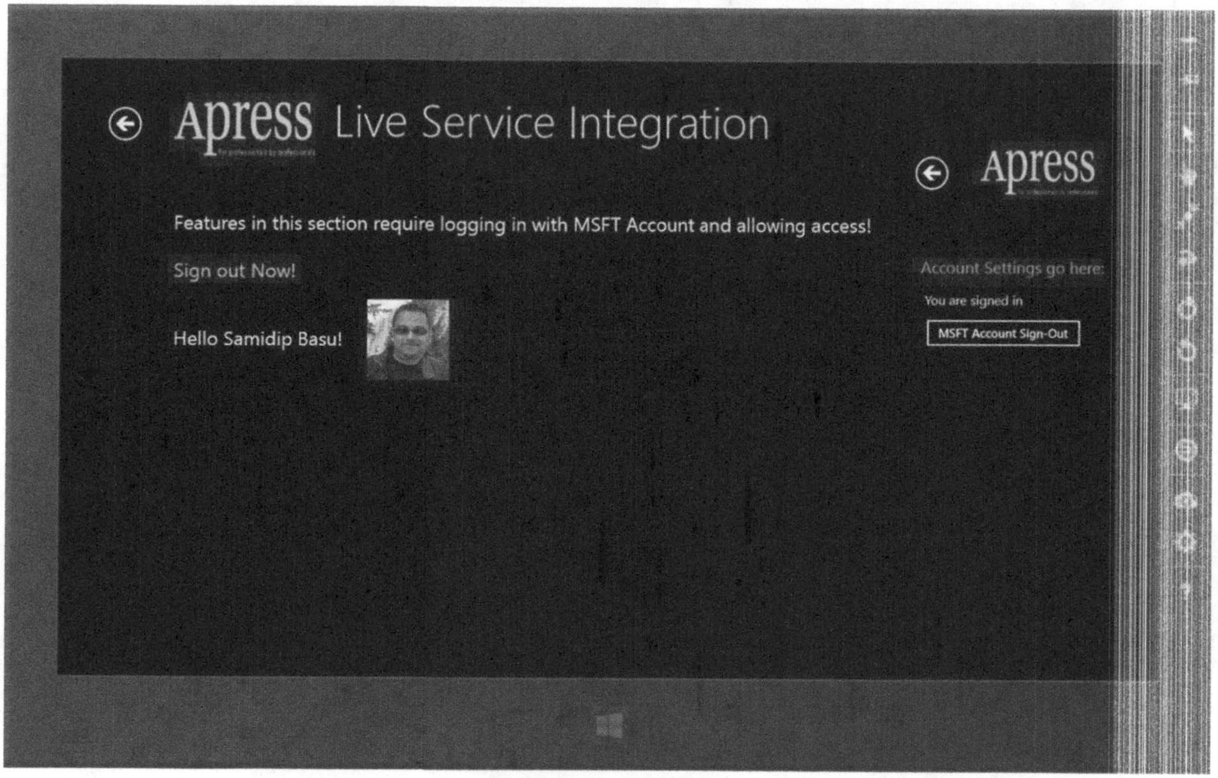

Figure 14-15. *Toggle account settings*

Live Services Microsoft account authentication is starting to make sense, hopefully, and you can see how easy it is. You do not handle any security or user credentials; simply trust Live Services to give an access token containing app permissions from an authenticated user so that you can customize the user experience. For more information about the user's identity while using Live Connect, please see MSDN documentation at `http://msdn.microsoft.com/en-us/library/live/hh826537.aspx`.

Contacts

Now that your app has the user's attention and permission to use some sensitive profile information, wow the user by adding more customizations. What about reading all of the user's friends or contacts? Perhaps your app wants to offer sending out e-mails to all of the user's friends. Let's write some code, as shown in Listing 14-5.

Listing 14-5. Fetching User Contacts

```
<StackPanel Orientation="Vertical" x:Name="contactsSection" Visibility="Collapsed"
Margin="0,10,0,0">
                    <TextBlock Text="Contacts List:" FontSize="20" />
                    <ScrollViewer>
                    <ListBox x:Name="contactsList" Height="300" Margin="0,5,0,0">
                            <ListBox.ItemTemplate>
                                <DataTemplate>
                                    <TextBlock Text="{Binding name}" FontSize="10" />
                                </DataTemplate>
                            </ListBox.ItemTemplate>
                        </ListBox>
                    </ScrollViewer>
                </StackPanel>

private async Task FetchContacts()
        {
            if (((App)Application.Current).LiveSession != null)
            {
                try
                {
                    LiveConnectClient liveClient = new
LiveConnectClient(((App)Application.Current).LiveSession);
                    LiveOperationResult operationResult = await liveClient.GetAsync("me/contacts");

                    dynamic contactsResult = operationResult.Result;
                    List<dynamic> contactsList = contactsResult.data;

                    this.contactsList.ItemsSource = contactsList;
                    this.contactsSection.Visibility = Windows.UI.Xaml.Visibility.Visible;
                }
                catch (LiveConnectException)
                {
                    // Handle exceptions.
                }
            }
            else
            {
                this.contactsSection.Visibility = Windows.UI.Xaml.Visibility.Collapsed;
            }
        }
```

As you can see, you first add a little XAML placeholder to your page to show a list of contacts in a `Listbox` control. Notice the `DataTemplate TextBlock` binding to data elements, which will hopefully have a property called "`name`". Turns out, every entity in the signed-in user's Contacts list does have a name. You simply fire up a `GetAsync()` asynchronous call off the `LiveConnectClient`, and this time, send in a parameter of "`me/contacts`". This translates to providing you all the Contacts in the signed-in user's friends list through the invisible HTTP GET request. Live Services obliges and sends back a list of data entities (dynamic) containing contact information, which you can bind your UI collections to (see Figure 14-16).

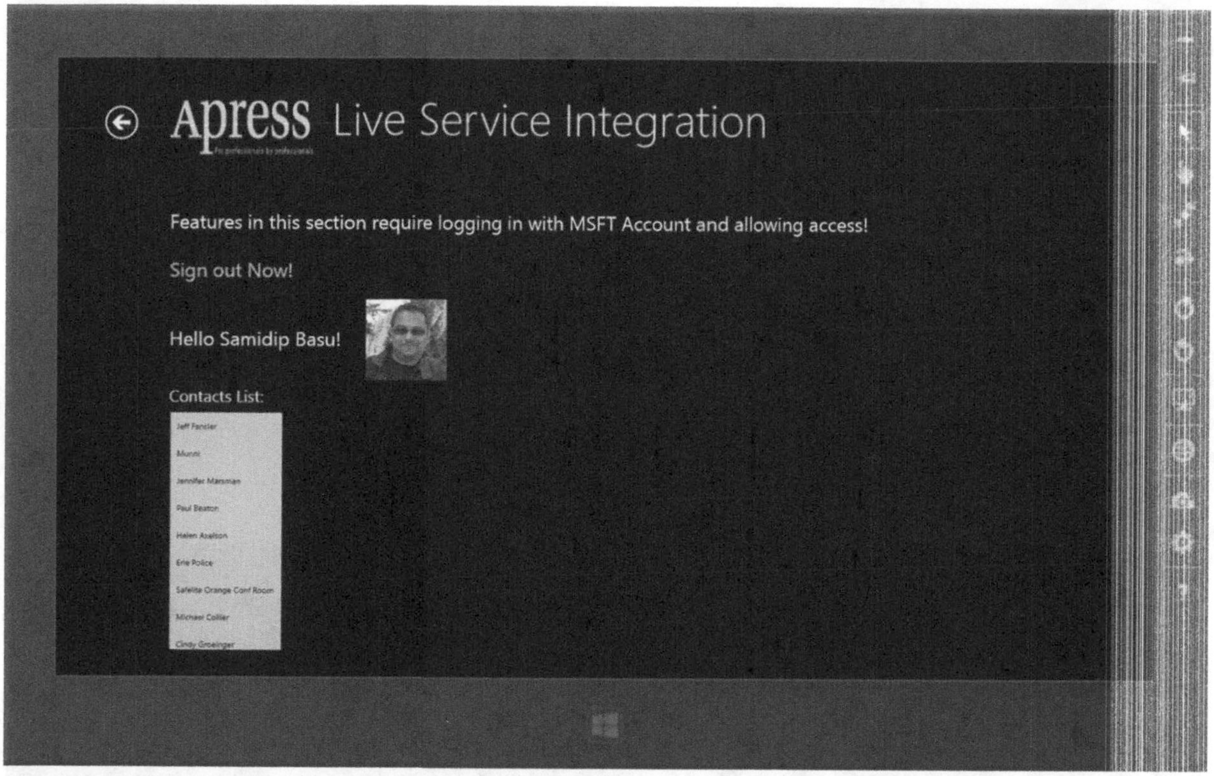

Figure 14-16. *Contacts list*

Did I mention that you could programmatically add contacts for the signed-in user? Yes, very cool to have this kind of control through APIs. For more details, check out MSDN documentation at `http://msdn.microsoft.com/en-us/library/live/hh826527.aspx`.

Calendars

What is the one thing that keeps our lives organized and helps us remember work and personal appointments? Yep, calendars. And every user with a Microsoft account has at least one calendar, often accessible through e-mail services like Live, Hotmail, and `Outlook.com`. Do you want to integrate your Windows 8 Store app with the signed-in user's calendar? You asked—and Live Connect delivers. The available APIs can be used to create, read, update, and delete the signed-in user's calendar and the events on it. In addition, you can have your app subscribe the user to public calendars (like US holidays, etc.) so that such events show up in his or her timeline of calendar events.

Let's write some code in your Apress demo app to try reading the signed-in user's calendar events. If you remember the first time you tried signing the user in, you passed in some scopes to declare what your app wanted to access. These scopes did not have anything about the user's calendar, and this is a problem because Live Services will simply refuse your app access to undeclared information from the user's sensitive Live Services profile. So, first try to sign the user in again, this time with the added scope for calendar access. This will trigger another round-trip to Live Services endpoints; but since the user is already signed in, it will be quick. Update the sign-in logic with the following:

```
try
            {
                LiveLoginResult loginResult = null;
                loginResult = await LCAuth.LoginAsync(new string[] { "wl.signin", "wl.basic",
"wl.calendars", "wl.skydrive", "wl.skydrive_update" });

                if (loginResult.Status == LiveConnectSessionStatus.Connected)
                {
                    this.LiveSession = loginResult.Session;
                }
            }
```

Figure 14-17 shows what the user sees on the next app run.

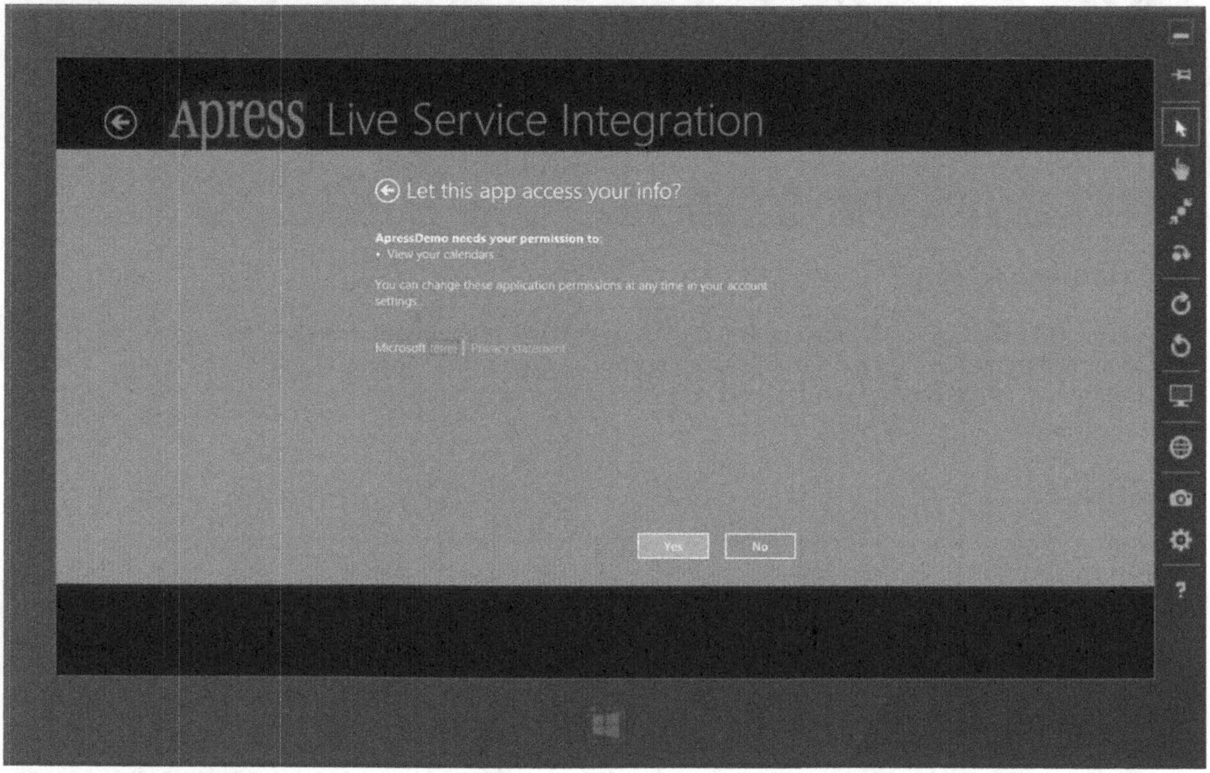

Figure 14-17. *Extra permission required*

You'll notice a couple of things. First, since the user is already signed-in, no authentication is required. Live Services, however, do pick up the fact that you slipped in an extra scope for the user's calendar. Accordingly, the user gets to see another permissions UI, this time asking for the app's permission to access the new scope. Once the user obliges, a new access token is generated and sent back to the app, this one containing the permission to use all of the contained scopes, including the new one that the user just agreed to. Cache this access token, and you are set.

Now that you have access to the user's calendar, let's try writing some code to read events off of it. Listing 14-6 is a sample.

Listing 14-6. Reading the User's Calendar

```
<StackPanel Orientation="Vertical" x:Name="calendarSection" Visibility="Collapsed"
Margin="40,10,0,0">
                    <TextBlock Text="Live Calendar Events:" FontSize="20" />
                    <ScrollViewer>
                        <ListBox x:Name="eventsList" Height="300" Width="230" Margin="0,5,0,0">
                            <ListBox.ItemTemplate>
                                <DataTemplate>
                                    <StackPanel Orientation="Horizontal">
                                        <TextBlock Text="{Binding name}" FontSize="10" />
                                        <TextBlock Text=" @ " FontSize="10" />
                                        <TextBlock Text="{Binding start_time}" FontSize="10" />
                                    </StackPanel>
                                </DataTemplate>
                            </ListBox.ItemTemplate>
                        </ListBox>
                    </ScrollViewer>
                </StackPanel>

private async Task FetchCalendarEvents()
        {
            if (((App)Application.Current).LiveSession != null)
            {
                try
                {
                    LiveConnectClient liveClient = new
LiveConnectClient(((App)Application.Current).LiveSession);
                    LiveOperationResult operationResult = await liveClient.GetAsync("me/events");

                    dynamic calendarEventsResult = operationResult.Result;
                    List<dynamic> eventsList = calendarEventsResult.data;

                    this.eventsList.ItemsSource = eventsList;
                    this.calendarSection.Visibility = Windows.UI.Xaml.Visibility.Visible;
                }
                catch (LiveConnectException)
                {
                    // Handle exceptions.
                }
            }
            else
            {
                this.calendarSection.Visibility = Windows.UI.Xaml.Visibility.Collapsed;
            }
        }
```

First, you wrote a little XAML markup to show events from the user's calendar in a `Listbox` control. Note the `DataTemplate` used in the `ItemTemplate` that defines how data binding should display each item in the collection that the UI is bound to. You are expecting every data entity to have a `name` and a `start_time` property, which all events on a calendar should have. Next, you use the `LiveConnectClient` and fire off a `GetAsync()` call with the parameter `"me/events"`, which translates to an HTTP GET request to Live Services asking for events on the signed-in user's default Live/Hotmail/Outlook calendar. Figure 14-18 shows the result.

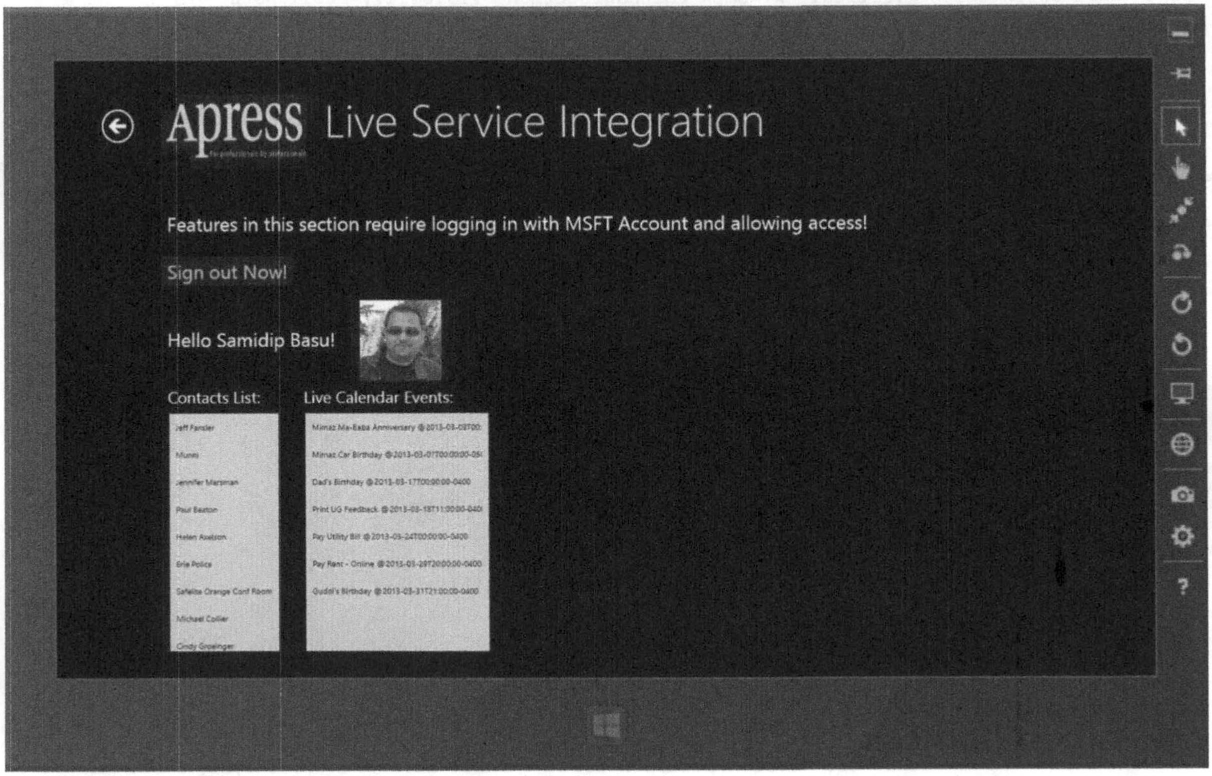

Figure 14-18. *Calendar events list*

As you can see, the UI shows events from the signed-in user's calendar, that being me in the demo. Let's take note of a few tricks when interacting with Live Services–provided user calendar data; such techniques are actually good for most Live data entities. Every one of the user's calendars has a unique ID, and so does every calendar event. A request to `"me/calendars"` returns information about all the signed-in user's calendars, including the IDs of the calendars. Beyond that, you can reference individual calendars with requests like "`calendar.<calendarID>`". In your case, where you requested for `"me/events"`, all of the signed-in user's calendars are looked at from today to 30 days in future. If you envision any data entity lookup to return too much data, you may limit the scope by counts, like `"me/events?limit=10"`, or provide start/end time ranges to look for matching events in the user's calendar.

Not only can you read the user's calendar/events, you are also free to provide updates from your Windows 8 app. You can update calendar properties or completely delete calendars, although you need to pay close attention to deletions and double-confirm with the user before firing off actions that cannot be undone. Did I mention that you could also read, create, update, or delete individual events from the user's calendar? So, go ahead and integrate your Windows 8 app with the user's life—you are bound to get more usage. For more information about interacting with the user's calendar through Live Connect APIs, please see MSDN documentation at `http://msdn.microsoft.com/en-us/library/live/hh826523.aspx#cal_cs`.

SkyDrive

Every user with a Microsoft account also has access to a personal cloud storage called SkyDrive. Up to 7GB is free for any kind of storage, and it is upgradeable for higher capacities. The lure of SkyDrive isn't just through a huge free-storage offer in the cloud; it comes from the ubiquitous nature of SkyDrive and the way it integrates into products in the Microsoft ecosystem. You have access to SkyDrive as the go-to cloud storage from Windows 8 and Windows Phone devices, computers (both PCs and Macs), mobile devices on platforms like iOS and Android, the Web, Office products, gaming consoles, and so forth. And the best part: SkyDrive knows how to keep content in sync between the user's devices and the cloud. Change a document in one device and save it, and it immediately syncs up to the cloud and down to other devices.

SkyDrive is popular no doubt, and integration with SkyDrive from your Windows 8 app definitely earns cookie points. If your app provides read/write/copy functionality to SkyDrive, you are providing the user with another choice in managing his or her content—and you know, choice is a good thing. Also, any documents, files, photos, or media that your app deals with can be uploaded to the user's SkyDrive. To you the developer, the deal does not get better. You no longer have to host a cloud storage solution on your own dime—you simply leverage the huge Microsoft-hosted storage in the cloud that the user is already comfortable using. To the user, uploading his or her content to SkyDrive is plain convenient. The content will be there the next time the user checks the Web and will sync down to every connected device where SkyDrive is in use. Also, there are things SkyDrive is plain good at. It provides high-quality document viewing and editing, and easy management/viewing/sharing of photo albums and multimedia. If possible, you should have your Windows 8 apps take advantage of these features, so that SkyDrive shines more for the user.

So, good stories all around on SkyDrive integration in your Windows 8 Store apps. Let's try to code something for your Apress demo app (see Listing 14-7).

Listing 14-7. SkyDrive Access

```
<StackPanel Orientation="Vertical" x:Name="skyDriveSection" Visibility="Collapsed"
Margin="40,10,0,0">
                    <TextBlock Text="SkyDrive Content:" FontSize="20" />
                    <ScrollViewer>
                        <ListBox x:Name="skyDriveList" Height="300" Margin="0,5,0,0">
                            <ListBox.ItemTemplate>
                                <DataTemplate>
                                    <StackPanel Orientation="Horizontal">
                                        <TextBlock Text="{Binding name}" FontSize="10" />
                                    </StackPanel>
                                </DataTemplate>
                            </ListBox.ItemTemplate>
                        </ListBox>
                    </ScrollViewer>
                </StackPanel>

private async Task FetchSkyDriveInfo()
        {
            if (((App)Application.Current).LiveSession != null)
            {
                try
                {
                    LiveConnectClient liveClient = new
LiveConnectClient(((App)Application.Current).LiveSession);
```

```
                LiveOperationResult operationResult = await
liveClient.GetAsync("me/skydrive/files");

                dynamic skydriveContentResult = operationResult.Result;
                List<dynamic> skydriveContentsList = skydriveContentResult.data;

                this.skyDriveList.ItemsSource = skydriveContentsList;
                this.skyDriveSection.Visibility = Windows.UI.Xaml.Visibility.Visible;
            }
            catch (LiveConnectException)
            {
                // Handle exceptions.
            }
        }
        else
        {
            this.skyDriveSection.Visibility = Windows.UI.Xaml.Visibility.Collapsed;
        }
    }
```

As you can see, you marked up a little XAML with placeholders to show SkyDrive content for the signed-in user. Notice how you expect a `TextBlock` data binding to data entities with a `name` property. This seems like a good plan since all SkyDrive content usually has a `name` attribute. Next, you fire up the `GetAsync()` call off the `LiveConnectClient` and pass in the parameter `"me/skydrive/files"`. This translates to HTTP GET requests to Live Services endpoints asking for a complete listing of the content, including files/folders from the signed-in user's SkyDrive root directory.

Fire up the Apress demo app, and after the user signs in, you are greeted with a SkyDrive content listing, as shown in Figure 14-19. Since I am the one logged on with the Microsoft account on my developer machine, what you see are files/folders directly under the root directory of my SkyDrive. You don't believe me? Let me open `http://skydrive.com` and sign in with the same Microsoft account. What you see in Figure 14-20 is a slice of my SkyDrive content. Do you see the exact match in file/folder hierarchy?

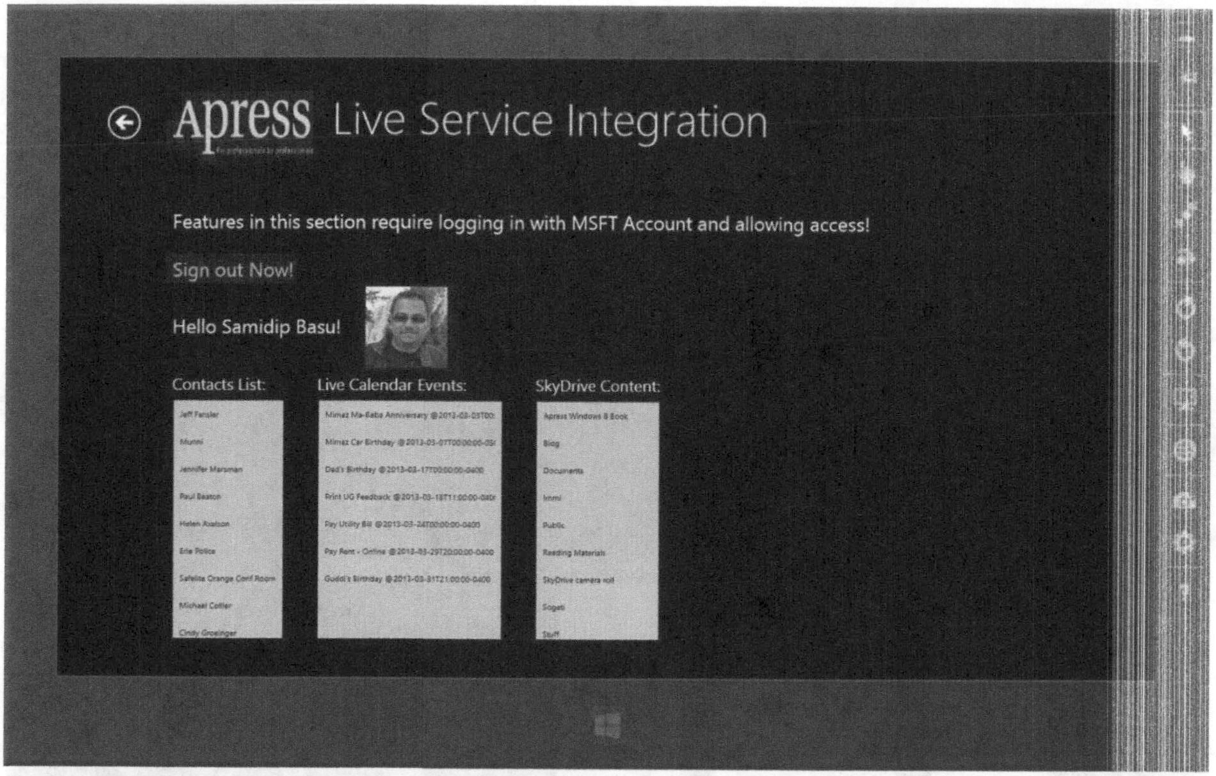

Figure 14-19. *SkyDrive contents list*

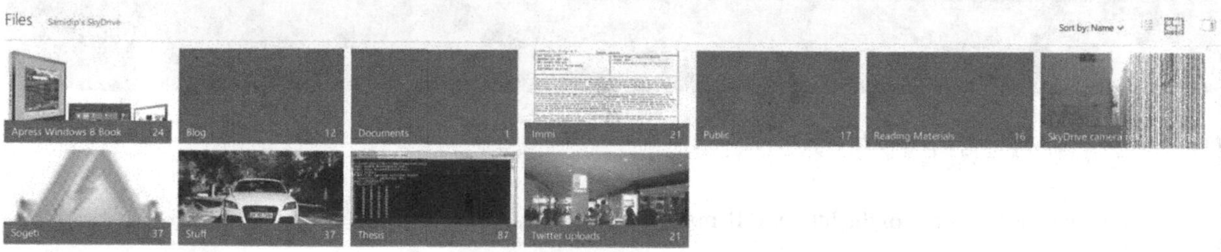

Figure 14-20. *Actual SkyDrive contents*

So, now you have established that you can see all the content in the signed-in user's SkyDrive cloud storage. From this point forward, your app can freely traverse up and down the content tree/directory in the user's SkyDrive. Every folder/file has a unique ID that you could use to jump to it. Many common SkyDrive folders (like Documents, Pictures, Public, etc.) have friendly names that you can refer them to instead of IDs. You can also get a list of objects that are shared with the user, or a list of the most recently used documents, or information about the user's used/remaining SkyDrive quota. In short, a ton of information about the user's SkyDrive is at your fingertips as a developer.

SkyDrive Updates

So far, however, you have only done reads off the user's SkyDrive. Wouldn't it be cool if you could write something back? Next up, try adding code to have the user upload a picture from his/her device running the Apress Demo app onto their SkyDrive. You add a little UI to do so, as shown in Figure 14-21.

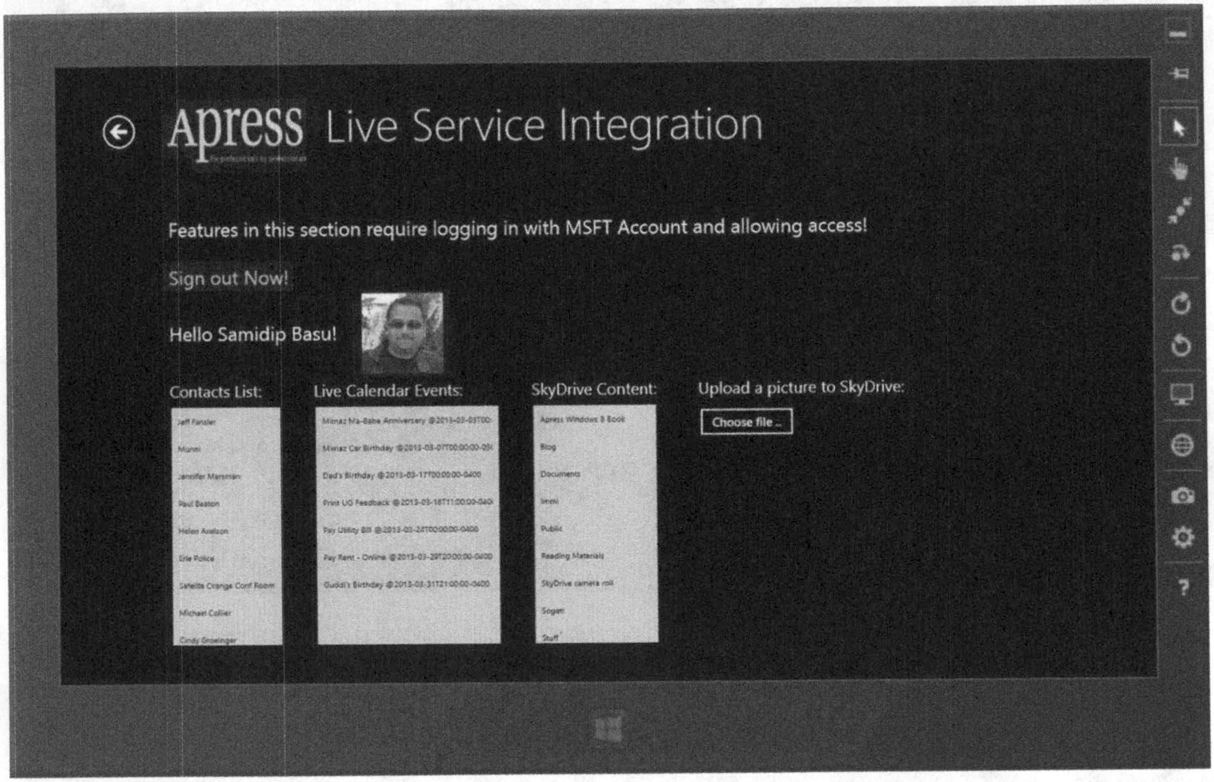

***Figure 14-21.** Uploading a photo to SkyDrive*

The following is the result of the little XAML markup:

```
<StackPanel Orientation="Vertical" x:Name="uploadSection" Visibility="Collapsed" Margin="50,10,0,0">
                    <TextBlock Text="Upload a picture to SkyDrive:" FontSize="20" />
                    <Button x:Name="fileUpload" Content="Choose file .." Margin="0,10,0,0"
Click="fileUpload_Click"/>
                </StackPanel>
```

Now, write some code to try responding to the button click. The point is that you will ask the user to pick a photo from his or her device, starting from the Picture Library, and then you will grab the file and upload it to the root directory of the user's SkyDrive. Here's some code:

```
private async void fileUpload_Click(object sender, RoutedEventArgs e)
        {
            try
            {
                var picker = new Windows.Storage.Pickers.FileOpenPicker();
                picker.ViewMode = Windows.Storage.Pickers.PickerViewMode.Thumbnail;
                picker.SuggestedStartLocation =
Windows.Storage.Pickers.PickerLocationId.PicturesLibrary;
                picker.FileTypeFilter.Add(".png");
                Windows.Storage.StorageFile file = await picker.PickSingleFileAsync();

               if (file != null)
               {
                   LiveConnectClient liveClient = new
LiveConnectClient(((App)Application.Current).LiveSession);
                   await liveClient.BackgroundUploadAsync("me/skydrive",
"MyUploadedPicture.pnsg", file, OverwriteOption.Overwrite);
               }
           }
           catch (LiveConnectException)
           {
               // Handle exceptions.
           }
        }
```

You will notice how you use the `FilePicker` to allow the user to pick a photo from his or her Pictures Library. The `SuggestedStartLocation` points to the Picture Library, but the user is free to pick from other locations; and you limit the file type to being PNGs. Figure 14-22 shows a quick view of what the `FilePicker` UI looks like. Once the user picks a photo out of the modal dialog mode, your app gets returned a handle to a `StorageFile` that stands for the user-selected photo. Next, you use the `LiveConnectClient` and the `UploadAsync()` method off of it to try uploading the file to the user's SkyDrive. This results in a HTTP POST at the Live Services endpoints, instead of the usual GETs you have been using to read information. Give your photo an explicit name and allow for overwrites on existing content. Notice how you passed in `"me/skydrive"` as a parameter. This signifies the root directory of the user's SkyDrive. You are also free to create new folders or reuse existing folders by their IDs. So, let's fire up the Apress demo app and see if this works when I select a photo for upload. I do not have any explicit success/failure messages for the user; you may want to communicate this in your app. Once all is done, I simply head over to the SkyDrive content through the browser (see Figure 14-23)—and there is the newly updated photo file, sitting at the root of my SkyDrive.

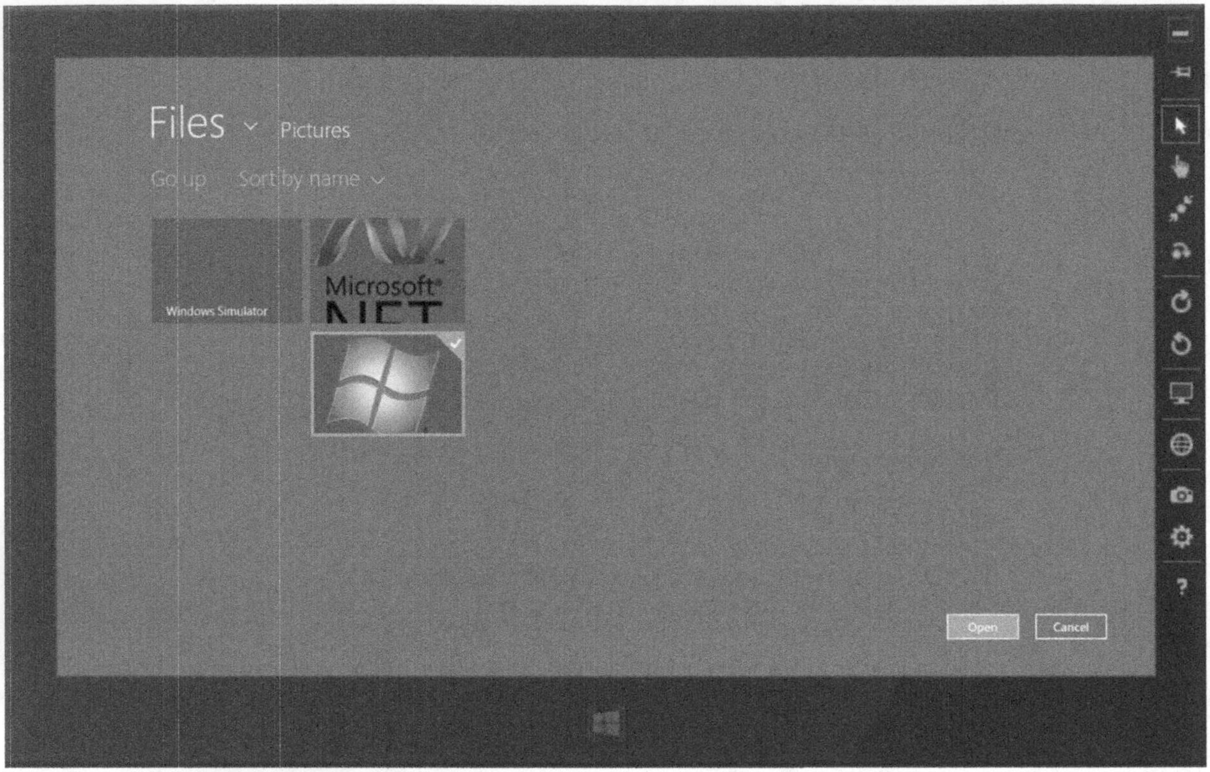

Figure 14-22. *FilePicker in action*

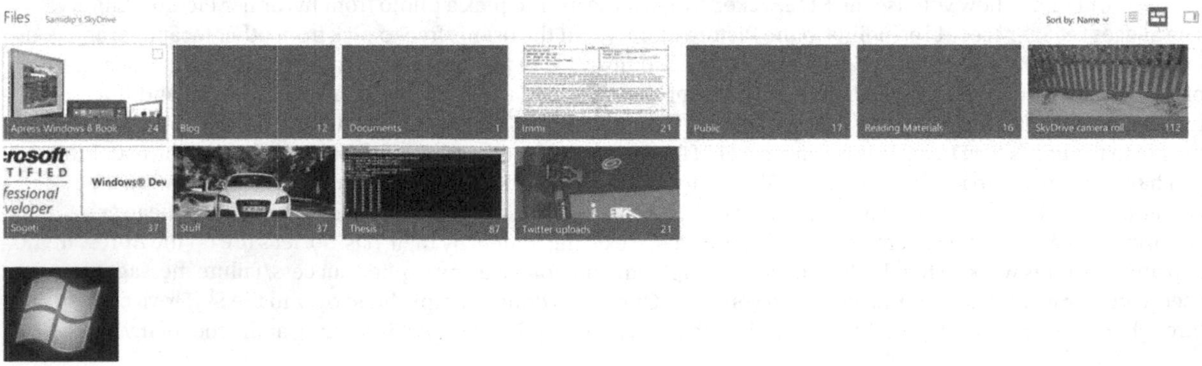

Figure 14-23. *Uploaded photo in SkyDrive*

So, the bottom line is that SkyDrive APIs in Live Connect are very powerful, and you should take advantage of them in your Windows 8 Store app. You can traverse up and down the user's content tree, create/update/delete folders, upload/download/read/change files, get links to files/folders for sharing, and also move content around within the user's SkyDrive. For more information on SkyDrive APIs, please see MSDN documentation at `http://msdn.microsoft.com/en-us/library/live/hh826521.aspx`.

App Management

Let's talk about one last point as we wrap up the discussion on Live Services. No matter what you do as a developer, the user is always in control. Do you wonder how the user can affect app permissions? Sign in to your `HotMail/Live/Outlook.com` e-mail or SkyDrive site and navigate to Edit Profile/Manage Apps. Figure 14-24 is a screenshot from my account. Notice how the Apress demo app is listed as one of the apps using Live Services under my Microsoft account. This is the result of leveraging the Live Connect APIs so far.

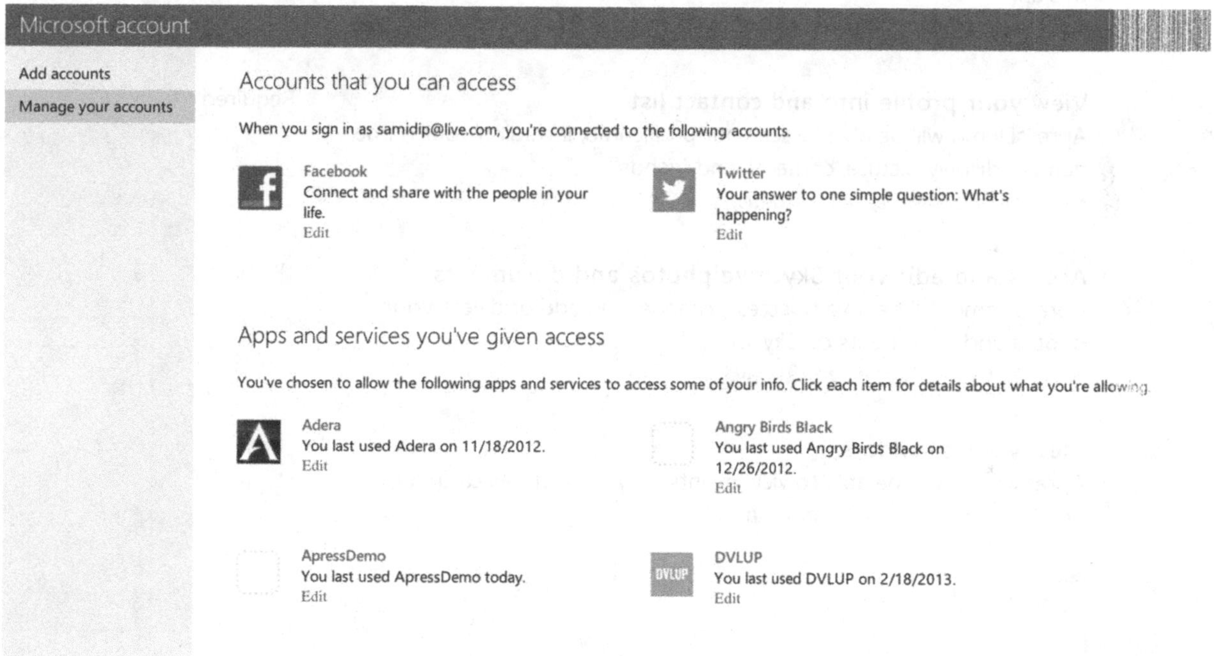

Figure 14-24. *App list tied to Live Services usage*

Let's click the Edit link next to the Apress demo app. Now you are taken to customized app permissions page showing all the permissions the app has (see Figure 14-25). This is driven entirely off the scopes your app has submitted while signing the user in, and all the ones that the user has given access to. Notice how the user has the choice to remove individual scope permissions or the entire app altogether. In your code to talk to Live Connect APIs, you must handle exceptions so that you know when Live Services denies your request access to previously allowed information. This may happen if the user has explicitly denied your app access to something. In this case, instead of failing flatly, your app code needs to recognize this access-denied situation and gently ask for user permission through the scope declarations, and then ask for a fresh access token from Live Services—like a law-abiding citizen.

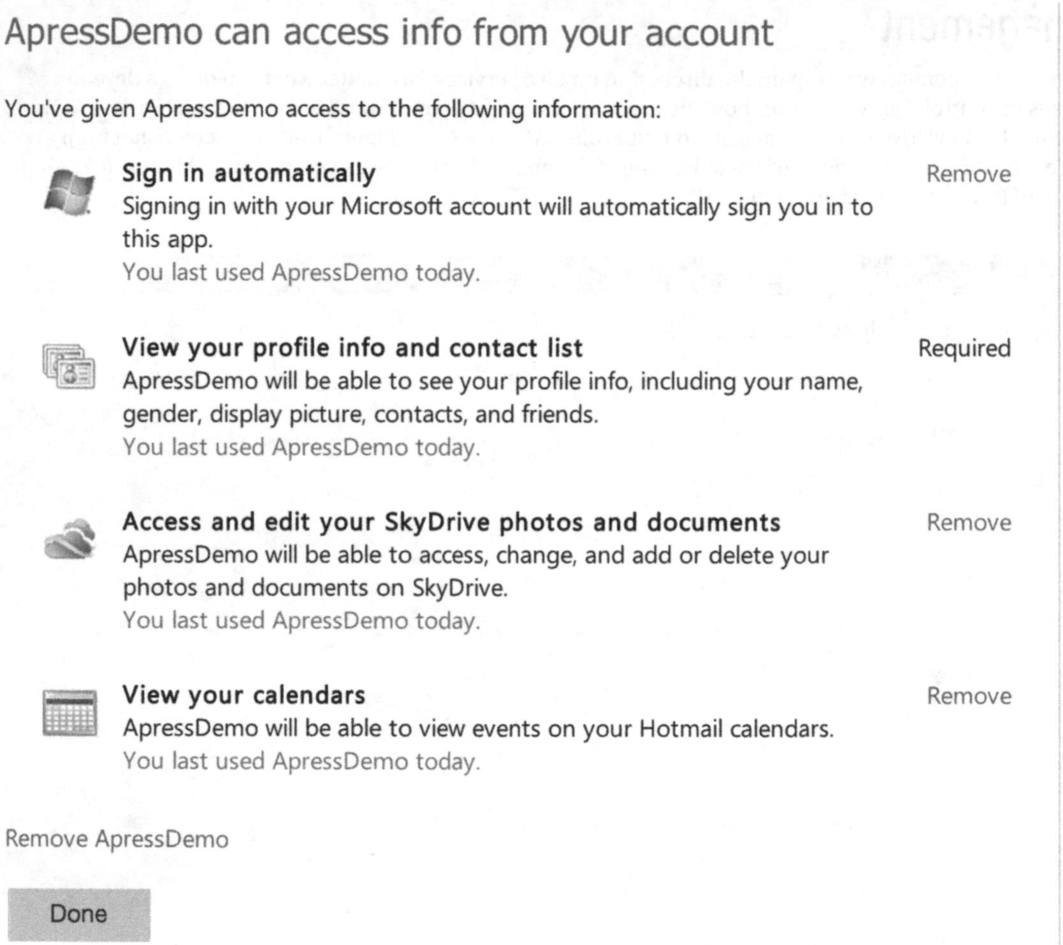

ApressDemo can access info from your account
You've given ApressDemo access to the following information:
Sign in automatically
Remove
Signing in with your Microsoft account will automatically sign you in to this app.
You last used ApressDemo today.
View your profile info and contact list
Required
ApressDemo will be able to see your profile info, including your name, gender, display picture, contacts, and friends.
You last used ApressDemo today.
Access and edit your SkyDrive photos and documents
Remove
ApressDemo will be able to access, change, and add or delete your photos and documents on SkyDrive.
You last used ApressDemo today.
View your calendars
Remove
ApressDemo will be able to view events on your Hotmail calendars.
You last used ApressDemo today.
Remove ApressDemo
Done

Figure 14-25. *App permissions for user*

Summary

This chapter hopefully did enough to pique your interest in Live Services integration for Windows 8 apps. With powerful Live Connect APIs allowing your app access to sensitive information from the signed-in user's profile, contacts, calendars, and SkyDrive, you have a lot of power to impress the user through a personalized UI. Remember, however, that with power comes responsibility, and Live Services access is a privilege for your app to have. So, declare your app's intentions and follow them up. The user is going to absolutely love your app because you used something that they already know, and therefore you are adding to their convenience. A little due diligence from you—and your Windows 8 app comes out a winner!

CHAPTER 15

Real-World Techniques

You are close, very close to wrapping up your first Windows 8 Store app. You have all the functionality working to wow the user, and you even have cloud support in your app. Now, before you try submitting your app to the Windows Store, here are a few, quick, real-world techniques to add to your arsenal. These techniques are some that I have used, and are certainly not exhaustive, but should give you a feel for what's outside the realm of just getting your Windows 8 app functional. I will talk about building real-time Windows 8 apps to amaze the user, with a full server back-end support and extendibility to other mobile platforms. Then, you will look at a few techniques to keep the developer and designer in you feeling sane as your code base and functionality grows over time. Ready for the last stretch of development?

Building Real-Time Applications

Do you envision your Windows 8 Store app displaying real-time data to the user, or supporting real-time communication between two or more parties? If yes, this section is for you. There is, of course, a genuine need for real-time applications in today's world. Chat applications, document collaboration, stock tickers, live auctions, game score applications, and shooter games are all examples of scenarios where you take real-time communication for granted. But no matter what your application or programming platform of choice, building real-time applications isn't very easy.

Part of the challenge is that when you exchange information over the Internet, the transport mechanism is most often HyperText Transfer Protocol (HTTP), the backbone of what the Web, as you know it, is built upon. HTTP is great, but it is primarily a request-response protocol. This means a web server needs a client to make a request before it can respond. The after-effect of this is that the server may have all the latest information that a consuming application may need, but the server cannot push information over the Internet unless the clients asks for it first. This is potentially a problem since there is no open channel where the client and server can have a full-duplex bidirectional communication with each other.

But you have been using the Web for a long time now, and you have obviously learned some tricks. You have learned that your web pages do not always need to reload entirely to bring back fresh content from the server. You have learned that there can be low-level communication implementations where the client and server do not always need to talk over HTTP. Here are few commonly used techniques for writing near real-time applications:

- *Periodic/Ajax polling*: This technique requires setting up a polling interval at the end of which the client requests information from the server and the whole process repeats itself. While this is widely used, this type of polling suffers from two drawbacks. One, until the next polling interval is due, the client will not know about anything interesting happening on the server. And two, the client could be making a lot of back-and-forth trips to the server without the assurance of fresh content, thus wasting bandwidth.
- *Long polling*: This is a technique where the server, once it gets a request from the client, simply sits on the request until it has something interesting to say. If done right, with time-out handling and managing thread scalability issues on the server, it can really provide an always-connected feeling to consumers on the client side.

- *Plug-ins*: Over time, device browsers have become smarter, and technologies like Adobe Flash or Microsoft Silverlight run applications as a plug-in inside the browser. Both of these popular technologies support low-level and managed implementation of network *sockets*, which allow bidirectional communication over protocols like TCP (Transmission Control Protocol) and UDP (User Datagram Protocol). These sockets, implemented through the plug-ins, can actually help you build real-time applications by keeping full-duplex open communication channels between the client and the server. The downside is that support can be flaky. Apple products do not run Flash, and the industry as a whole is moving away from plug-ins. Your application would have to depend on the user's browser.

- *Forever Frame*: The Forever Frame technique uses HTTP 1.1 chunked encoding to establish a single, long-lived HTTP connection in a hidden `iFrame`. Data is pushed incrementally from the server to the client over this connection, and rendered incrementally by the client web browser (it works especially well in Internet Explorer).

- *Server-sent events*: When communicating using server-sent events (SSE), a web server can push data to client applications whenever it wants, without the need for clients to make an initial request to the server. In other words, updates can be streamed from server to client as they happen. SSEs open a single unidirectional channel between server and client to facilitate communication. This technique can be very useful for media-streaming web sites.

- *WebSockets*: This technique is really the holy grail of real-time connectivity, allowing the client web browser and the server to natively maintain a full-duplex communication channel over a single TCP connection. Being standardized by the W3C (Worldwide Web Consortium), WebSockets allow interaction between a browser and a web site at the lowest port level, facilitating live content being sent in either direction. This is made possible by providing a standardized way for the server to send content to the browser without being solicited by the client, and allowing for messages to be passed back and forth while keeping the connection open. As good as WebSockets sounds, there are conditions that need to be true for WebSockets to work seamlessly. It calls for modern web browsers and a supporting web server environment; for applications running on Microsoft's IIS (Internet Information Services), the minimum requirement is IIS 8.

So by now, you should start seeing light at the end of the tunnel. Making real-time applications isn't a new challenge, and over time, software development has used any of these techniques to meet goals. There is no one good answer; you need to pick the technology that works for your given application demands. But wouldn't it be nice if someone could abstract away the transport layer as you build your real-time application? Maybe someone could have a fallback mechanism to pick the best technique to keep a consistent open communication channel between client and server, so that you, the developer, could focus on the functionality of your real-time application. Enter SignalR.

SignalR

SignalR is an asynchronous persistent connection/signaling library for .NET-based web applications. The primary goal of SignalR is to make the developer's life easy. This is done by abstracting the transport mechanism used to persist the communication channel between the client and the server. You tell SignalR that your real-time application needs a continuous connection to the web server, and SignalR takes care of the rest by figuring out the best transport mechanism for the given client-server pair, and even has fallback plans to keep the connection alive. Any combination of the techniques I discussed can be used, just choose whichever works best given the client and the web server. The obvious first choice is to use WebSockets, but if that cannot be supported, SignalR falls back to use any combination of SSEs, Forever Frames, or polling mechanisms. The result: it gets very easy for developers to build real-time multiuser connected applications.

SignalR was started by two very talented members of the Microsoft ASP.NET team: Damian Edwards and David Fowler. The source code for SignalR is open source and available at `https://github.com/SignalR/SignalR`. However, SignalR as a technology has come a long way and is stable enough in the RTW (Release to Web) 1.0 release to now be included as a part of the official Microsoft ASP.NET stack. This inclusion also means Microsoft support for enterprise customers, so you can use SignalR with complete peace of mind.

What can you build with SignalR? Well, real-time applications of all kinds. The only requirement is to build an ASP.NET-based back-end web application, which could be web forms or any flavor of Model-View-Controller-based application. As long as IIS can run the web application, you are good to go. With the SignalR-powered web application hosted, you can now turn it into a back-end server for building client real-time applications. And your choice of client applications is wide open: web, desktop, Windows Phone, Windows 8, iOS, Android, and so forth. Since the implementation of SignalR works over HTTP connections between client and server, you have lot of flexibility to build real-time applications that talk to your scalable web back-end server. With connections established over the best possible transport, the client and server can talk to each other seamlessly, with built-in retry logic if transport fails. For more information on SignalR, start at `www.asp.net/signalr`.

Building a SignalR Back End

Now that you know the basics of SignalR, build something fun using this new technology to make real-time communication possible through a Windows 8 Store app. But first, you need to build a web application that is powered by SignalR and acts as the back-end server for your client Windows 8 app. Let's try building a simple quintessential chat application. You will empower client-server real-time chatting using SignalR and hopefully get a glimpse of everything else that is possible.

My apologies for the upcoming detour through some web development stuff. No need to pinch yourself; you are still reading a book on Windows 8 app development and you shall get right back to it. I just did not want to give you a black box with no transparency into how you built the SignalR back-end server. Hopefully, this will be interesting. SignalR, in my opinion, is one of most exciting things coming from the One ASP.NET stack.

So, let's get started. You are going to create a separate web application project before tying it to your Apress demo Windows 8 app. Fire up Visual Studio and select a web project template to start (see Figure 15-1). I went with an MVC 3 template, but it could really be anything you choose. Once the Visual Studio template fires up a solution, you should see the usual web project setup, complete with folders to hold your models, controllers, views, and scripts, and so forth.

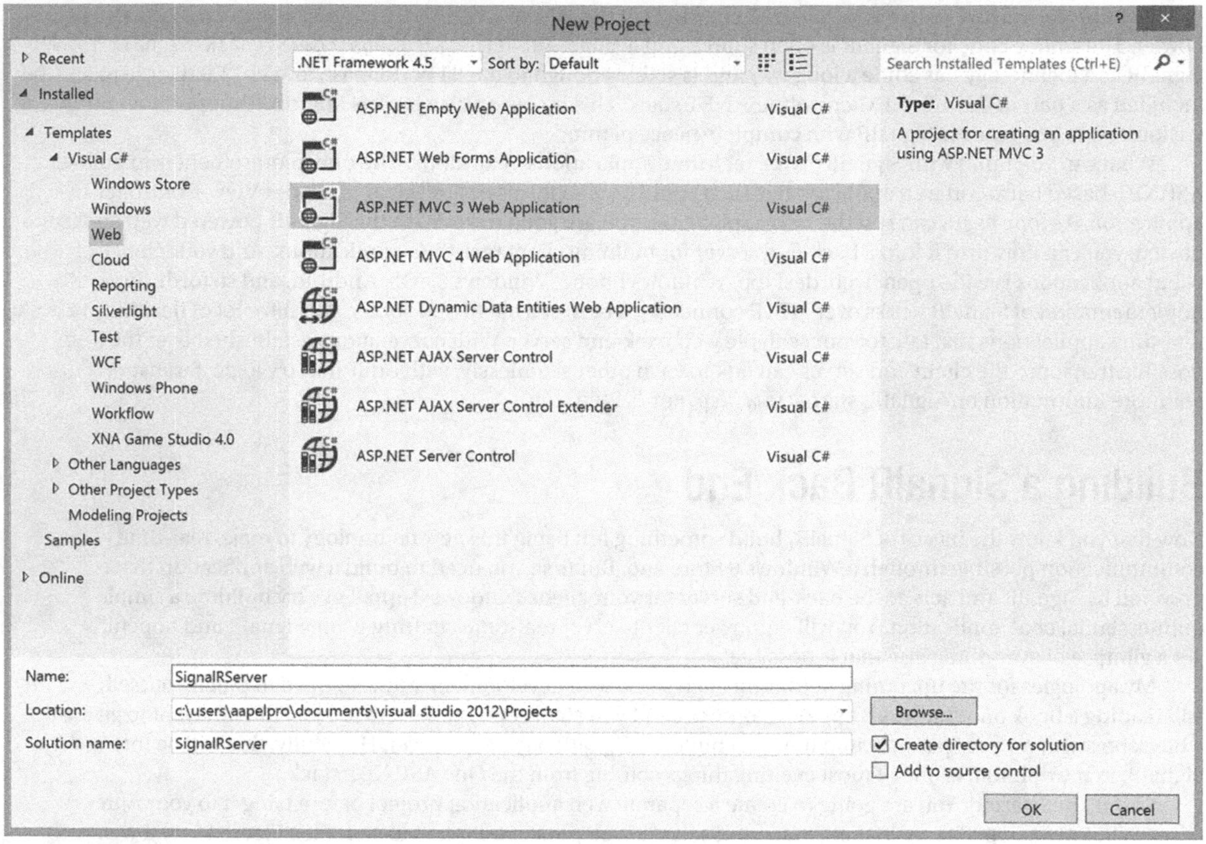

Figure 15-1. *MVC 3 web application template*

Next, you are going to start integrating SignalR right into your web project. If you have the latest Visual Studio 2012 updates, a SignalR Hub template shows up as one of the options under the web category. Even if you don't, it is pretty easy to incorporate SignalR into your project through NuGet.

Right-click your project, click Manage NuGet Extensions, and search online for SignalR NuGet (see Figure 15-2). SignalR is broken up into several components: specific to server, JavaScript, and the client libraries. But you could just grab one that should suffice for your web back end: the Microsoft ASP.NET SignalR NuGet package. With the NuGet addition, you will see several new files light up your solution. Take a moment to notice the changes in your `Reference` and `Script` folders.

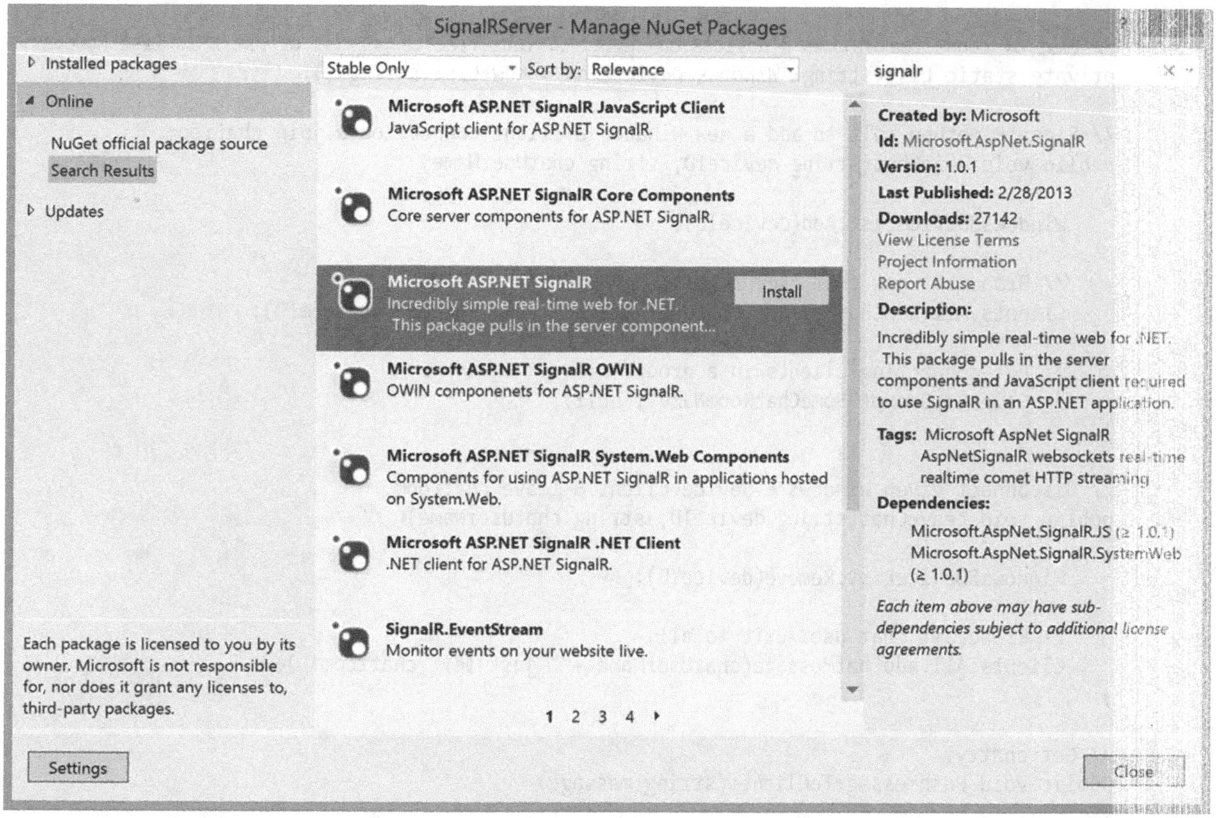

Figure 15-2. *ASP.NET SignalR NuGet*

SignalR Hub

With the needed reference to SignalR libraries in place, let's write some code. A SignalR Hub is a new and unique concept. It is an abstraction over clients that are connected to a given server at a particular time, as well as associated actions that the server may take on the connections. A Hub keeps track of clients as they connect to the server by assigning each a unique connection ID. It maintains a list of connected clients in the application session memory, which can, of course, be persisted in a data repository. You can inherit from the Hub base class to get all of the SignalR heavy lifting for free, but add your methods to it (see Listing 15-1).

Listing 15-1. SignalR ChatHub

```
using System;
using System.Collections.Generic;
using System.Linq;
using System.Web;

using Microsoft.AspNet.SignalR;

namespace SignalRServer
{
    public class ChatHub : Hub
```

```
    {
        // List of connected Windows 8 devices on server .. feel free to persist or use this list however.
        private static List<string> Windows8DeviceList = new List<string>();

        // SignalR method call to add a new Windows 8 client connection & join chatroom.
        public void JoinChat(string deviceID, string chatUserName)
        {
            Windows8DeviceList.Add(deviceID);

            // Broadcast new chat user to all.
            Clients.All.addChatMessage(chatUserName + " just joined chatroom!");

            // Put connecting clients in a group.
            // Clients.Group("SomeChatRoomName", null);
        }

        // Disconnect given Windows 8 device client & leave chatroom.
        public void LeaveChat(string deviceID, string chatUserName)
        {
            Windows8DeviceList.Remove(deviceID);

            // Broadcast chat user exit to all.
            Clients.All.addChatMessage(chatUserName + " just left chatroom!");
        }

        // Get chatty.
        public void PushMessageToClients(string message)
        {
            // Push to all connected clients.
            Clients.All.addChatMessage(message);

            // Guess what the next few lines do ...

            // Invoke a method on the calling client only.
            // Clients.Caller.addChatMessage(message)

            // Communicate to a Group.
            // Clients.OthersInGroup("SomeChatRoomName").addChatMessage(message);
        }
    }
}
```

In Listing 15-1, you wrote a little `ChatHub` meant to serve as a chatroom on the server. And you wrote three methods in it: `JoinChat()`, `LeaveChat()`, and `PushMessageToClients()`. The first two are meant to handle users connecting to and leaving the chatroom, whereas the last one broadcasts messages to connected clients during a chat session. See the keyword `Clients`? That is the `ChatHub`'s in-memory list of clients who have connected to the Hub. All the clients can be referred to as `Clients.All`; while incoming clients can also be put in groups, and messages broadcast just to the group through `Clients.Group("`*GroupName*`")`.

Do you see the `addChatMessage()` call that you are invoking in every method? Mouse-hover over it and you will notice that it is a *dynamic* type, meaning that the actual method call will be figured out at runtime. Where do you think this is defined? It is certainly not defined on the server side or in the `ChatHub`. This is where the SignalR magic begins.

It is something you will define on the client side in JavaScript. The server will invoke it seamlessly with the persistent open connection that SignalR will maintain.

Now, before you go any further, you need to make sure that a SignalR handshake between the client and the server, as well as subsequent communications, can happen seamlessly at a predefined route URL. So, get to your `Global.asax.cs` configuration file and add this bit of code as your web application starts up:

```
using System.Web.Routing;
using Microsoft.AspNet.SignalR;

protected void Application_Start()
        {
            AreaRegistration.RegisterAllAreas();

            // Register the default hubs route: ~/signalr
            RouteTable.Routes.MapHubs();

            // Use LocalDB for Entity Framework by default
            Database.DefaultConnectionFactory = new SqlConnectionFactory(@"Data Source=(localdb)\v11.0;
            Integrated Security=True; MultipleActiveResultSets=True");

            RegisterGlobalFilters(GlobalFilters.Filters);
            RegisterRoutes(RouteTable.Routes);
        }
```

Although the rest of the code is boilerplate, the only thing you are adding is `RouteTable.Routes.MapHubs()` to make sure SignalR communication can happen with a dedicated `HTTPHandler` on the server that works with the predefined route.

With that set, let's build the UI for your chatroom on the server. First, replace the generic MVC template look with your own style sheet. I've added a `ModernUI.css` style sheet with the following content:

```
body
{
    background-color: White;
    font-family: Segoe UI;
    font-size: medium;
    width: 50%;
    margin-left: auto;
    margin-right: auto;
    margin-top: 10px;
}

#chat
{
        width: 80%;
        font-family: Segoe UI;
        font-size: medium;
        margin-left: auto;
        margin-right: auto;
        padding: 20px;
        border-width: 1px;
        border-style: outset;
}
```

```
#broadcast
{
        height: 30px;
        background-color: #3C5A76;
        color: #EEEEEE;
        font-weight: bold;
}

#clear
{
        height: 30px;
        background-color: #3C5A76;
        color: #EEEEEE;
        font-weight: bold;
}

#message
{
        height: 25px;
        width: 300px;
}
```

And a `Layout.cshtml` base razor view for all other views in your web site has been updated to pick up the new minimalist styling, like so:

```
<!DOCTYPE html>
<html>
<head>
    <title>@ViewBag.Title</title>
    <link href="@Url.Content("~/Content/ModernUI.css")" rel="stylesheet" type="text/css" />
    <script src="@Url.Content("~/Scripts/jquery-1.7.1.min.js")" type="text/javascript"></script>
</head>
<body>
    <div>
        @RenderBody()
    </div>
</body>
</html>
```

SignalR Application Front End

The web MVC templates offer convention over configuration. So, at this point, if you fire up your web application, the default routing is going to use the `Index ActionResult` off the `Home Controller`, and eventually look for an `Index.cshtml` razor view in the `Home` folder under `Views`, which is already present but empty. Let's press F5 to run your web application, just for sanity. You should see the application showing the base `Index.csthml` view with the default `Home` controller (see Figure 15-3). Notice that you have changed a little text to help the user navigate to what's coming next.

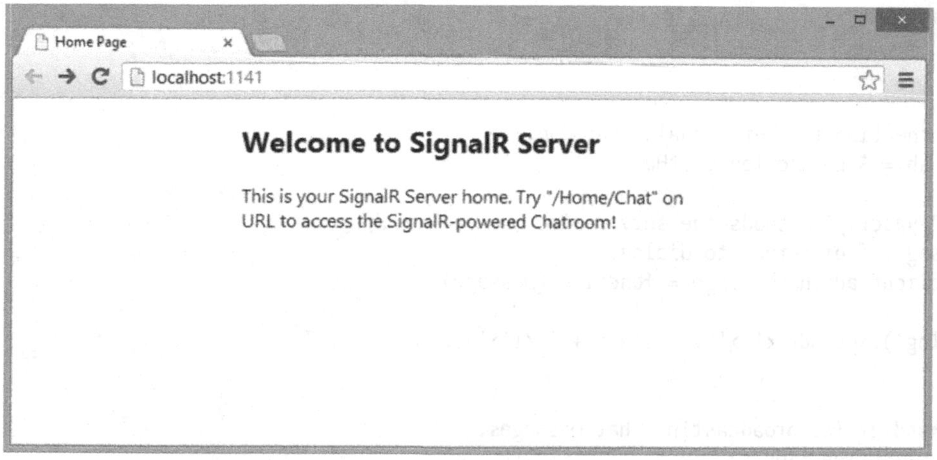

Figure 15-3. *SignalR server home*

For the sake of simplicity, add your chatroom UI as another view under the `Home` folder so that it is easy to get to. The `Home` controller is updated to reflect the newly supported `ActionResult` with the corresponding view to render, like so:

```
public ActionResult Chat()
{
    return View("Chat");
}
```

Now you get to the best part. Add a `Chat.cshtml` razor view under the `Home` folder within Views. This will be your chatroom UI. And you add the code in Listing 15-2 on the view.

Listing 15-2. SignalR Chatroom UI

```
<script src="@Url.Content("~/Scripts/jquery-1.7.1.min.js")" type="text/javascript"></script>
<script src="@Url.Content("~/Scripts/jquery.signalR-1.0.1.min.js")" type="text/javascript"></script>
<script type="text/javascript" src="@Url.Content("~/signalr/hubs")"></script>

<div id='container'>
   <div id='chat'>
       <b>Chatroom:</b>
       <br /><br />
       <input type="text" id="message" maxlength="100" />
       <br /><br />
       <input type="button" id="broadcast" value="Broadcast" />
       <input type="button" id="clear" value="Clear" />
       <br /><br />
       <ul id="chatdialog"></ul>
   </div>
</div>
```

```
<script type="text/javascript">

   $(function ()
   {
       // Create the connection to your SignalR Chat Hub.
       var signalRChatHub = $.connection.chatHub;

       // Define some Javascript methods the server-side Hub can invoke.
       // Add chat messages from server to dialog.
       signalRChatHub.client.addChatMessage = function (message)
       {
           $('#chatdialog').append('<li>' + message + '</li>');
       };

       // Click event-handler for broadcasting chat messages.
       $('#broadcast').click(function ()
       {
           // Call Server method.
           signalRChatHub.server.pushMessageToClients($('#message').val());

           $('#message').val("");
       });
// Click event-handler for clearing chat messages.
       $('#clear').click(function ()
       {
           $('ul li').remove();
       });

       // Start the SignalR Hub.
       $.connection.hub.start(function ()
       {
           // Do stuff here, if needed.
       });
   });

</script>
```

There is a lot to chew on in Listing 15-2, so let's get started. First, you start by adding a few script references. The first two are jQuery script files, one generic and the other specific with SignalR functionality that the NuGet dropped in your project. Next, did you notice the third script reference addition—the one with the `"~/signalr/hubs"` reference? You might look for this file in your `Scripts` folder, but you would not find it. So, what's going on here? This is a bit of the under-the-covers magic. There is JavaScript generated dynamically on the server based on the Hubs you defined, and it is pushed down to the clients at the URL `"~/signalr/hubs"`. Append that after the URL address of your view, and you can actually see the JavaScript that is generated from the server and sent down, containing information on the SignalR `Hubs` and the methods they support.

Next, you see a few `<div/>` tags that actually define your simplistic UI for the chatroom. You have a text box for the user to type, a couple of buttons, and a text area that shows the full chat dialogue as it happens. Following the UI tags is some simple JavaScript, and you'll see that a lot of the magic happens here.

Did you notice these lines of code?

```
// Create the connection to our SignalR Chat Hub.
var signalRChatHub = $.connection.chatHub;

// Start the SignalR Hub.
        $.connection.hub.start(function ()
        {
            // Do stuff here, if needed.
        });
```

This is how you reference the SignalR Hub back on the server and start communicating. The `start()` call is all that it takes for the client and the server to have the SignalR handshake, figure out the best transport mechanism for an open bidirectional channel, and start communicating freely.

Now inspect the next piece of code:

```
// Add chat messages from server to dialog.
   signalRChatHub.client.addChatMessage = function (message)
   {
       $('#chatdialog').append('<li>' + message + '</li>');
   };
```

This is a simple JavaScript method that responds to a chat message coming in and appends it to the chat dialogue. Remember that the server `ChatHub` had this line of code: `Clients.All.addChatMessage(message);`. The `addChatMessage()` method call actually refers to this JavaScript method, defined on the client. Because the server and the client can freely talk to each other over the SignalR-powered open channel, the server is able to reach into the JavaScript running on client browsers, and invoke this method that updates the client with the latest chat message from the server. If you come from a web development background, this should blow your mind. Yes, server-side code is invoking JavaScript on the client browser!

The next piece of JavaScript code is easier to understand:

```
// Click event-handler for broadcasting chat messages.
        $('#broadcast').click(function ()
        {
            // Call Server method.
            signalRChatHub.server.pushMessageToClients($('#message').val());

            $('#message').val("");
        });
```

You are simply waiting for the user to type something in the chat text box and click the Broadcast button to send it. At this point, your JavaScript uses the `Hub` reference to call the `PushMessageToClients()` method on the server, and that, in turn, invokes the `addChatMessage()` method on every subscribing client, thus broadcasting the chat message. Let's fire up your web application and see the results of what you've done so far (see Figure 15-4).

Figure 15-4. *SignalR server chatroom*

Try typing some chat messages and see the broadcasting in action, with your browser acting as a connected client. Your SignalR-powered server back end is now ready!

SignalR-Powered Windows 8 App

Now, with a SignalR-powered chatroom ready and waiting, try building a Windows 8 app client that can talk to it. And, of course, you will go back to your Apress demo app and extend more functionality to showcase the SignalR server connectivity. Accordingly, I've added a couple more app bar icons to the dashboard so that you can get to fresh XAML pages (see Figure 15-5). The Video Chat button is what you will use to take the user to a fresh chat page, although you are technically only using text chat. Again, the caveat here is to not get inspired and add so many app bar icons unless they are really needed. This is for demonstration only.

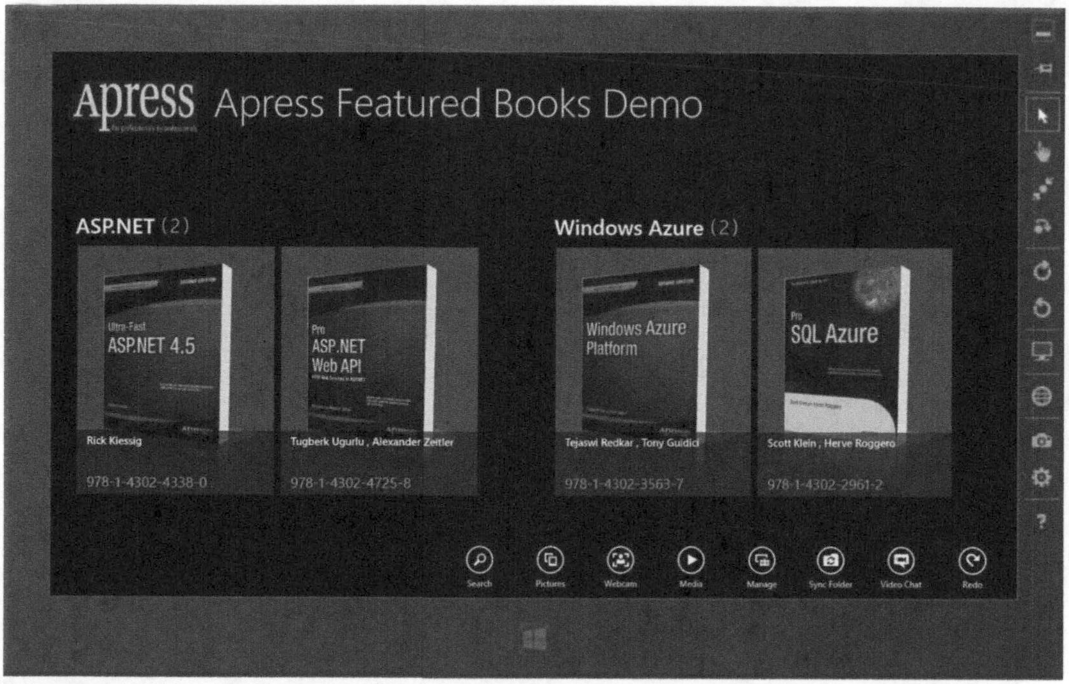

Figure 15-5. *Apress demo app dashboard with added app bar buttons*

For your Windows 8 Store app to communicate with a SignalR-powered back-end server, your app would definitely have to communicate over HTTP. There would need to be some handshaking to figure out the best transport mechanism, before the real-time communication starts happening. Would you end up hand-coding these interactions? Thankfully, the answer is no. There is a NuGet wrapper (SignalR .NET Client) to handle all of that for you. So, the first step in your Apress demo app is to add this NuGet to your project (see Figure 15-6).

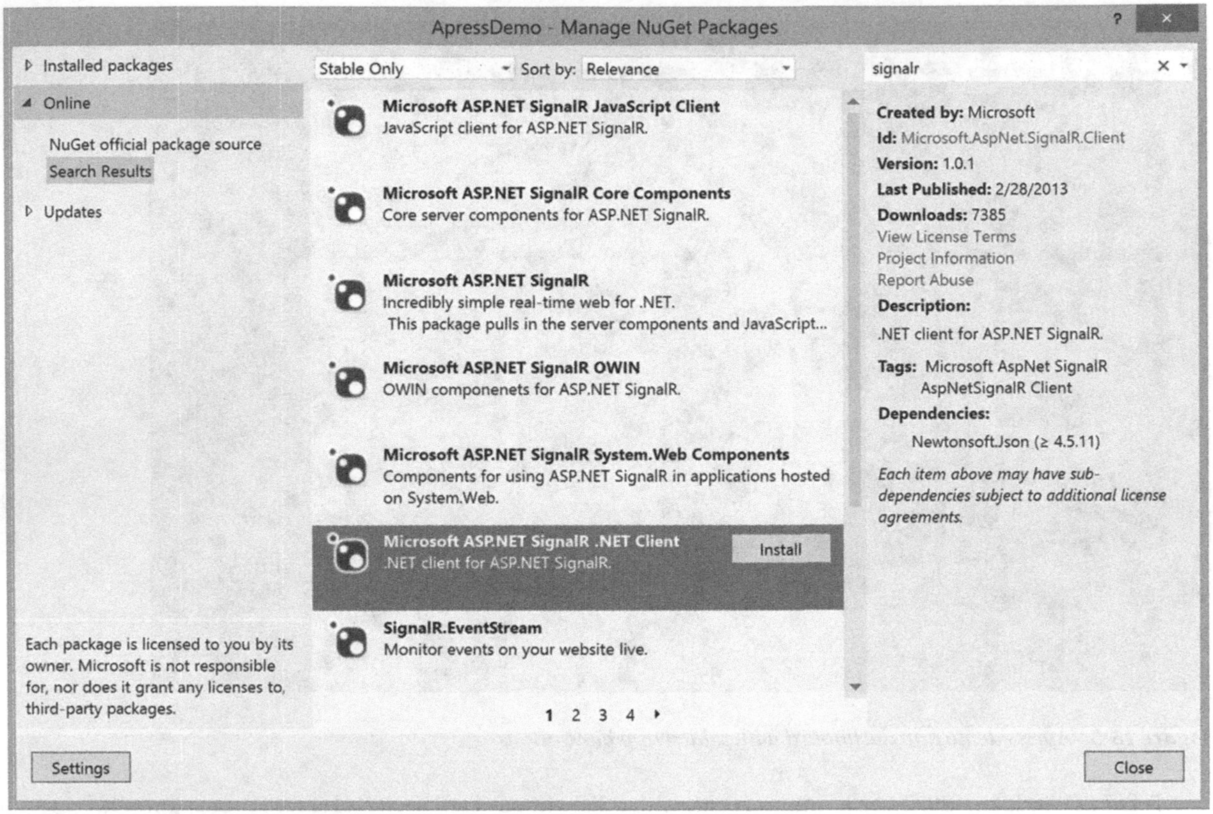

Figure 15-6. *SignalR .NET Client NuGet*

SignalR Integration in Windows 8 Apps

With the reference in place, look to integrate the SignalR-powered chat functionality in your Windows 8 Apress demo app. The goal is similar to the web interface: a simple text box to type chat messages and a button to send it, followed by a text area where chat dialogues will show up. Accordingly, I've added a simple `SignalRChat.xaml` page and the following XAML markup in it:

```
<!-- Page Content -->
        <StackPanel Grid.Row="1" Orientation="Vertical" Margin="150,60,0,0">
            <StackPanel Orientation="Horizontal">
                <TextBox x:Name="chatMessage" Width="400" FontSize="20"/>
                <Button x:Name="postChatMessage" Content="Chat!" Click="postChatMessage_Click"
                Margin="30,0,0,0"/>
            </StackPanel>
            <TextBlock x:Name="chatDialogue" FontSize="20" Margin="0,30,0,0"/>
        </StackPanel>
```

Before you can start your chat session with the SignalR-powered chatroom, however, some handshaking is due so that you know the server you are talking to and allow SignalR to figure out the transport mechanism. Here's some code in the SignalRChat.xaml.cs file:

```
using Microsoft.AspNet.SignalR.Client.Hubs;

// Reference to the SignalR Server.
    IHubProxy SignalRChatHub;

    protected async override void OnNavigatedTo(NavigationEventArgs e)
    {
        base.OnNavigatedTo(e);

        HubConnection chatConnection = new HubConnection("http://localhost:1141/");
        SignalRChatHub = chatConnection.CreateHubProxy("ChatHub");

        // Start connection back to Hub.
        try
        {
            await chatConnection.Start();

            if (chatConnection.State == Microsoft.AspNet.SignalR.Client.ConnectionState.Connected)
            {
                // Join the ChatRoom.
                await SignalRChatHub.Invoke("JoinChat", "DeviceID123", "ChatUserSam");
            }
        }
        catch (Exception)
        {
            // Do some error handling.
        }
    }
```

Let's break down what you just did. First, you used a HubConnection object to create a reference back to your SignalR server. Notice that in this case, you used the hard-coded LocalHost base address for the SignalR web application you just built. This is something you would have to update if you host your application somewhere other than your local machine; you may even to choose to have the server URL be configurable. Next, you created an IHubProxy using the connection to the server and created it squarely pointed at the ChatHub interface in the SignalR chatroom. This is key since it serves as the proxy to all your communication with the SignalR server.

Once all is set, you fire up the Start() method off the connection object, hoping to establish connection with the SignalR server and do the handshake to figure out the best transport mechanism. If everything goes according to plan, the connection's State changes to being Connected and you are all set. You now have an open, bidirectional communication channel between your Windows 8 app and a SignalR back-end server. How cool is that?

You'll notice that after the connection to the SignalR chatroom succeeds, you send out an automated message by invoking the JoinChat() method on the ChatHub server. This method takes in the name of the user joining the chat and a unique device ID, in case the server wants to persist or identify devices connected to the chatroom. What you want to send over is completely up to your app's needs. Also, notice how you invoked the JoinChat() method. You certainly did not have IntelliSense support and you are hoping that the server has a matching method with a matching signature. This, you may say, is one downside to an otherwise awesome SignalR client library for .NET. What's happening behind the scenes of the handshaking and communication exchange with the SignalR server over HTTP? All of that is hidden from your app's implementation.

Testing Your Chatroom Implementation

Feeling lucky? Let's fire up your Windows 8 Apress demo app and also the SignalR chatroom through the web client, side by side, as shown in Figure 15-7.

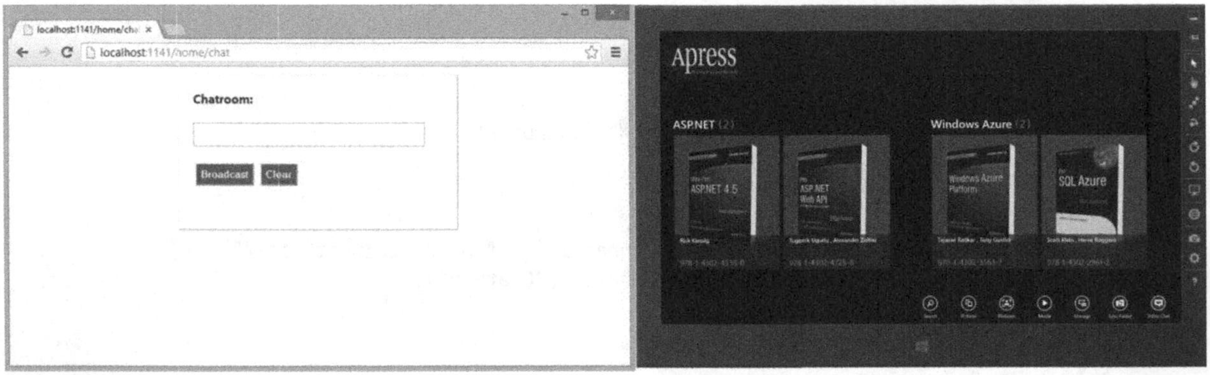

Figure 15-7. *SignalR chat demo*

As you can see, you start out as usual with the server chatroom and your Apress Windows 8 app looking as they should without any hint of communication. Now, the moment the app bar icon is tapped to navigate to the new SignalR chat page in the Windows 8 app, the code that you wrote on the `OnNavigatedTo()` event should fire. This will fire up a connection to the SignalR chatroom, establish the best transport mechanism, and post your joining message to the chatroom. Bingo! That's exactly what happens, as shown in Figure 15-8. The web client gets the chat message about the Windows 8 user joining. Note that the SignalR `ChatHub` now has two clients connected to it: the web client through the browser and the Windows 8 app.

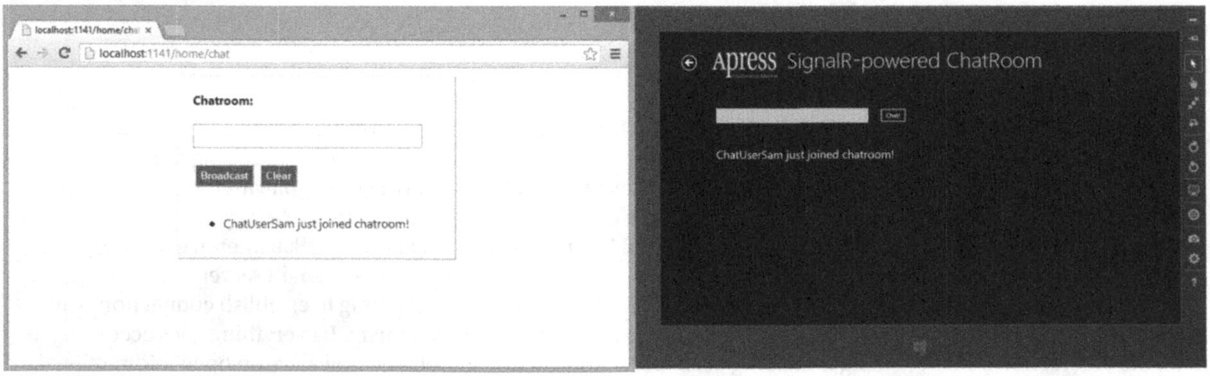

Figure 15-8. *SignalR chat demo: a Windows 8 user has joined*

From Windows 8 to Server

Now, on to the next part. Allow the user to type a chat message in the Windows 8 app text box and broadcast it to everyone in the chatroom. This should be elementary with your previously established SignalR connection and proxy. Here's the code:

```
private async void postChatMessage_Click(object sender, RoutedEventArgs e)
        {
            if (!string.IsNullOrWhiteSpace(this.chatMessage.Text))
            {
                // Broadcast message to ChatRoom
                await SignalRChatHub.Invoke("PushMessageToClients", this.chatMessage.Text.Trim());

                this.chatMessage.Text = string.Empty;
            }
        }
```

Quite naturally, you now invoke the `PushMessageToClients()` method of the SignalR `ChatHub` and hand it the message the user has typed in. The result: text typed on the Windows 8 app shows up instantaneously on the web client, as shown in Figures 15-9 and 15-10.

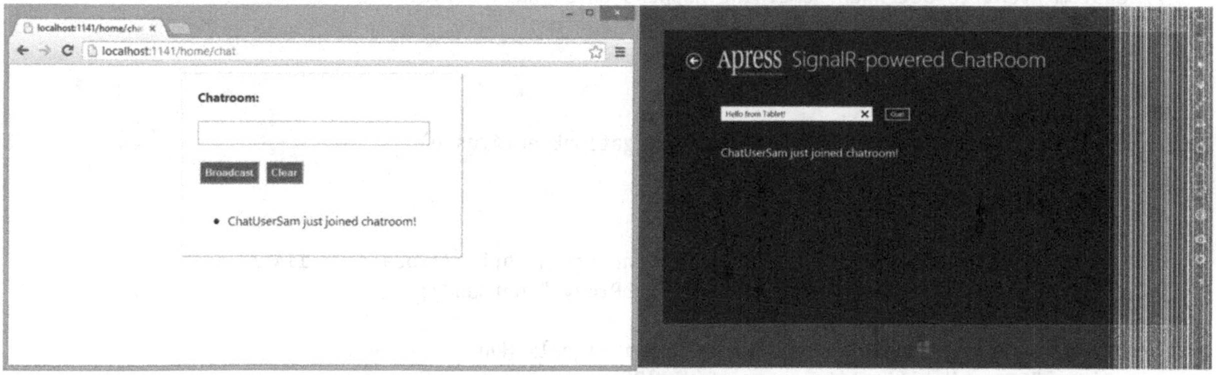

Figure 15-9. *SignalR chat demo: a Windows 8 user is typing*

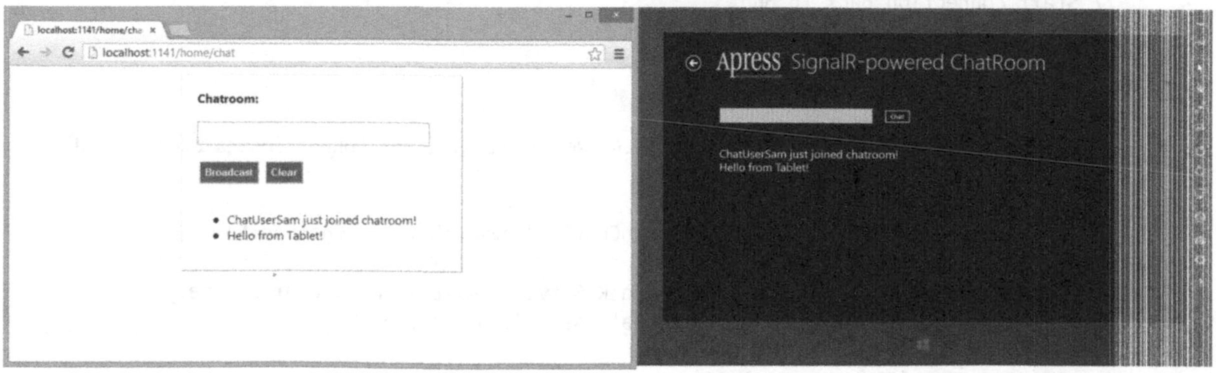

Figure 15-10. *SignalR chat demo: a Windows 8 user types a chat message*

From Server to Windows 8

Chat messages from Windows 8 showing up through the Hub in the web client is good, but it is still half the story. You also want chat messages from the Web or any other connected client to show up in the Windows 8 app. Now, as compared to the web clients where the SignalR Hub could call back into the JavaScript directly, the .NET implementation would be a little different. For security reasons, you possibly do not want an outside program to reach inside your .NET DLL and invoke methods, right? So, what's the solution?

You fall back to an event-based approach. You can listen to events happening on the SignalR server and take action appropriately. This also means that as the SignalR server is taking action by invoking methods off its JavaScript clients, you get to listen in. Listing 15-3 demonstrates how to do it.

Listing 15-3. Listening to Events on SignalR Back End

```
#region "Members"

    // Reference to the SignalR Server.
    IHubProxy SignalRChatHub;

    // Custom delegate.
    public delegate void SignalRServerHandler(object sender, SignalREventArgs e);

    // Custom event to act when something happens on SignalR Server.
    event SignalRServerHandler SignalRServerNotification;

    #endregion

protected async override void OnNavigatedTo(NavigationEventArgs e)
    {
        base.OnNavigatedTo(e);

        HubConnection chatConnection = new HubConnection("http://localhost:1141/");
        SignalRChatHub = chatConnection.CreateHubProxy("ChatHub");

        // Wire-up to listen to custom event from SignalR Hub.
        SignalRServerNotification += new SignalRServerHandler
        (SignalRHub_SignalRServerNotification);

        // Start connection back to Hub.
        try
        {
            await chatConnection.Start();

            if (chatConnection.State == Microsoft.AspNet.SignalR.Client.ConnectionState.Connected)
            {
                // Join the ChatRoom.
                await SignalRChatHub.Invoke("JoinChat", "DeviceID123", "ChatUserSam");

                // Listen to chat events on SignalR Server & wire them up appropriately.
                SignalRChatHub.On<string>("addChatMessage", message =>
                {
                    SignalREventArgs chatArgs = new SignalREventArgs();
                    chatArgs.ChatMessageFromServer = message;
```

```
                // Raise custom event & let it bubble up.
                SignalRServerNotification(this, chatArgs);
            });

        }
    }
    catch (Exception)
    {
        // Do some error handling.
    }
}

public class SignalREventArgs : EventArgs
{
    // Custom args.
    public string ChatMessageFromServer { get; set; }
}
```

First, since you are about to do event handling, I defined a custom event called `SignalRServerNotification`, complete with custom event arguments in `SignalREventArgs`, and the event delegate in `SignalRServerHandler`. Note how you wire up the event being raised to a custom event handler.

Now, when do you raise your event? You listen to an extension off the proxy called `On` and wait for an event to happen on the SignalR `ChatHub`. `SignalRChatHub.On<string>("addChatMessage", message =>..);` is your code to latch onto the `On` extension and wait for the `addchatMessage()` method to be invoked on the SignalR `ChatHub`. This is intentional because on the `ChatHub`, you call this method any time you need to broadcast chat messages from any client back out to all connected clients. So, you essentially have listeners on the client side any time the `ChatHub` wants to broadcast messages. Perfect. Once this happens, you raise your custom event, passing along the string chat message you get from the server.

Once this custom event is raised, it is up to you to have a custom event handler to update your UI with chat messages from the server. A word of caution: because this event bubble up can happen any time, you are not guaranteed to be on the UI thread, so a little marshaling is required for you to have access to UI components. Here's the event handler:

```
private async void SignalRHub_SignalRServerNotification(object sender, SignalREventArgs e)
        {
            await Dispatcher.RunAsync(CoreDispatcherPriority.Normal, () =>
            {
                // Add to local ChatRoom.
                this.chatDialogue.Text += "\r\n" + e.ChatMessageFromServer;
            });
        }
```

The Final Test and Wrap Up

Let's try out your code. Fire up both applications again. This time, type something on the web chat client, and sure enough, it shows up instantaneously on the Windows 8 app, as shown in Figures 15-11 and 15-12. Voilà!

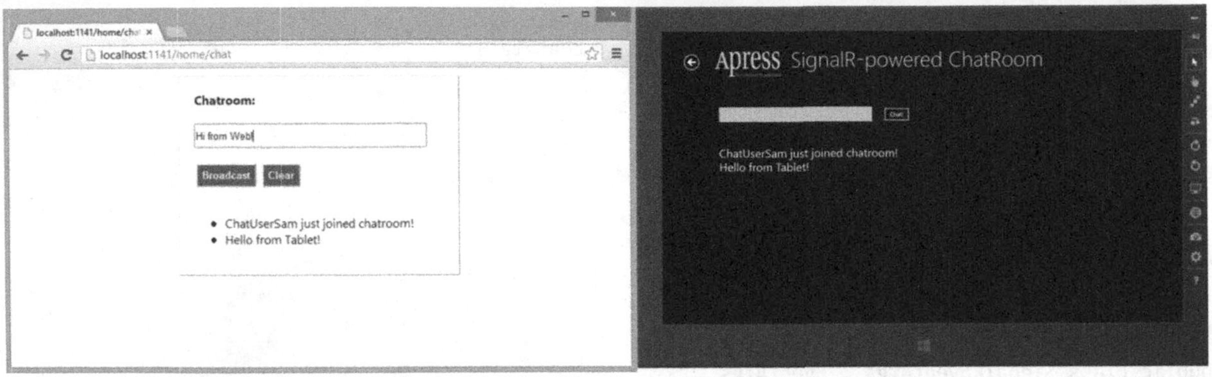

Figure 15-11. SignalR chat demo: web user typing

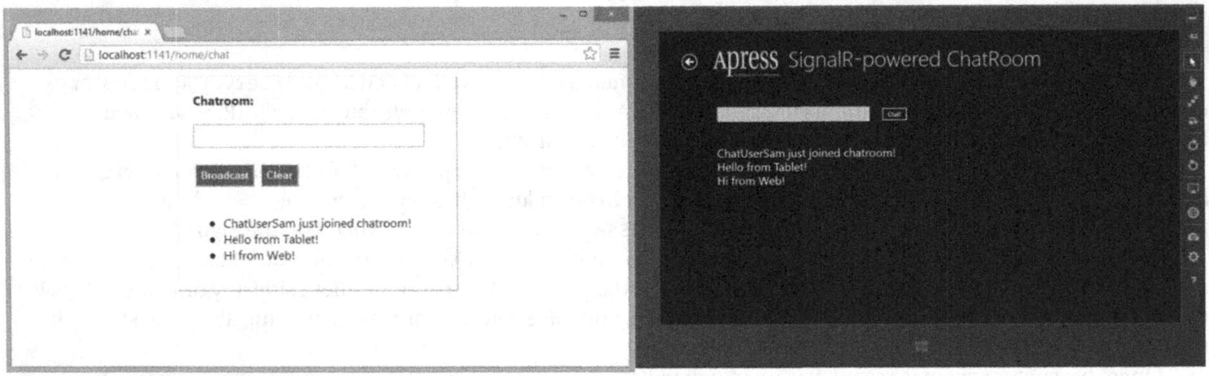

Figure 15-12. SignalR chat demo: web user types chat message

Now, at this point, you have a live chatroom between the Web and the Windows 8 app. Type anything on either end—and it instantly shows up in both places. You did, however, subscribe to a custom event with your event handler, so best practice dictates that you unwire the event handler when no longer needed. Also, if the user of your Windows 8 app steps away from the chat XAML page, you should let the chatroom know that the user left. Let's accomplish both in one strike:

```
protected async override void OnNavigatedFrom(NavigationEventArgs e)
        {
            base.OnNavigatedFrom(e);

            // Tell Chatrrom you are leaving.
            await SignalRChatHub.Invoke("LeaveChat", "DeviceID123", "ChatUserSam");

            // Unwire event handler.
            SignalRServerNotification -= new SignalRServerHandler
            (SignalRHub_SignalRServerNotification);
        }
```

Return to the XAML chat page and you will see a user-sent notification pop-up in the web chatroom (see Figure 15-13). Navigate to the chat page again in the Windows 8 app, and a new connection to the SignalR `ChatHub` gets established and you proceed as before.

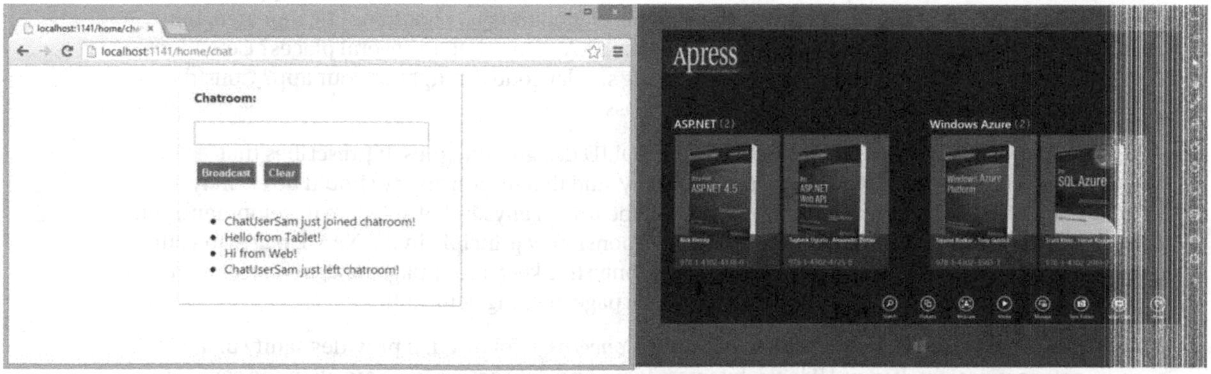

Figure 15-13. *SignalR chat demo: the Windows 8 user has left the chatroom*

So, now you have a fully functional real-time chatroom powered by a SignalR back-end web application. All you need to host such a back end is any web server that hosts IIS. It's even supported on web server farms. And you can connect to the SignalR chatroom in real-time from a variety of clients, like the Web, desktop, Windows 8, and a host of other mobile platforms. Hopefully, you see the promise of real-time Windows 8 apps. You can empower a plethora of functionality, like real-time mapping of user locations, game scores, tech support, object sync, document collaboration, and so forth. For more ideas on what a SignalR-powered back end can do for mobile applications, such as on a Windows Phone, please check out one of my open-source libraries, the Windows Phone SignalR Helper, at `http://wp7signalrhelper.codeplex.com`. All of the Windows Phone app possibilities that the Helper library talks about are perfectly possible in Windows 8 Store apps as well. In fact, I will soon update the library to support Windows 8 apps, so you can download the `Helper` classes and be on your way. For now, replicating the Windows Phone code in your Windows 8 apps should not be difficult. With your real-time-enabled Windows 8 Store app and a SignalR back end—the sky is the limit.

Programming Patterns

You are now that much closer to finishing your Windows 8 Store app and pushing it out to the Windows Store. But did the first iteration of your app accomplish all the features that you had planned? If you are like most developers, your first Windows 8 app probably does not do everything under the sun. And that's not a bad thing. You can strike gold early with selected features done well. Grab a steady user base and keep building features in upcoming releases and iterations. Even if you are not building features, you will surely want to support your Windows 8 app after it goes live in the Store. Perhaps users will report issues, or your testing will discover crashes—either of these means that you will return to the code base that makes up your Windows 8 app. So, the code you write isn't a one-time thing. You are going to have to go back into it, care for it, and nurture it to maintain a healthy life cycle.

Enter programming patterns. In software engineering, a design pattern is a general, reusable solution to a commonly occurring problem within a given context in software design. Patterns have been around for a long time and are there for a reason: to provide guidelines and best practices on how to solve a problem through the science of software development. As your Windows 8 Store app grows in functionality, you will notice a proportional increase in the size and complexity of your code base. This is when knowing software design patterns really helps. Following best practices helps keep you sane. Here are some patterns that will help the code base of your Windows 8 Store app:

- *DRY*: This acronym stands for Don't Repeat Yourself. The DRY design principle applies to a wide variety of genres, particularly in software engineering, and it is definitely applicable to your Windows 8 app code base. Critical pieces of functionality should not be repeated, but abstracted out for reuse. Are you using the same XAML markup in several places? Consider making a reusable user control. Are you using similar code throughout your app? Consider making a reusable library or utility/helper classes.

- *Single Responsibility*: This is the first of the SOLID design principles. It prescribes that every class should have a single responsibility, and that responsibility should be entirely encapsulated by the class. While this should be true in any kind of software development, you can also take inspiration from the Single Responsibility principle in the XAML pages in your Windows 8 app. Let each page do one thing only; this keeps your page navigation clean and allows your content to breathe in each XAML page, helping in usability.

- *SoC*: This acronym stands for *Separation of Concerns*. If followed, it provides sanity in a software project. If your UI logic, business logic, and data access logic are all in the same code file, you are looking at a spaghetti architecture, and any entanglements are going to be hard to straighten out. On the other hand, if the components of a Windows 8 Store app code base are split into discrete entities with marked roles, the separation aids in testability of individual pieces. You should not need the UI to function in order to test your data persistence logic, and vice versa. The value of SoC is in simplifying development and maintenance of your Windows 8 app code base. Components should be loosely coupled to each other and talk through interface/abstractions, so that you may test/modify one component without depending on changes in another.

- *Repository*: This is a commonly used design pattern that is especially useful in Windows 8 apps. The way you fetch and persist data should be independent of the rest of the business logic, and the UI for that matter. A repository pattern helps separate the logic that retrieves/updates the data and provides an easy mapping to the entity model that the business logic acts on. The point is plug and play. You should be able to swap out your data source between a database and a web service, without affecting app functionality.

- *MVVM*: This acronym stands for Model-View-ViewModel. Starting from roots in the Model-View-Controller (MVC) pattern, MVVM has gained enormous popularity for software with a XAML-based UI layer. This is because MVVM draws much of its strengths from the XAML fundamentals of data binding, data context, and commanding. In fact, MVVM—if done right in a Windows 8 app project—can take care of several of the design principles in one sweep. MVVM became popular with WPF (Windows Presentation Foundation), Silverlight, and Windows Phone development, and has now made its way to Windows 8 development because of the similarity in development paradigms. In fact, you will spend the entire next section taking a close look at using MVVM for Windows 8 apps.

You may be wondering why I am talking about programming patterns at the very end of the book. Are you expected to make huge changes to your Windows 8 app code base to follow a design pattern now that you are so close to completion? Absolutely not! The discussion of patterns has been saved for last because of a programming antipattern: overengineering.

A design pattern is not an absolute requirement. It is a set of best practices that keeps your code base clean. You should not be blindly following a pattern just because it is cool and everyone else is doing so. Worse, you should not be sacrificing app features for the sake of following a pattern to death. Remember, your code base may follow every guideline to a T, but to the users of your app, the UI still looks the same. So, prioritize your app functionality first, and then as you see your code base growing in complexity, refactor your code to slowly adhere to principles. Do not overengineer your Windows 8 app code base to anticipate future needs and add complexity just for kicks.

It is true that some patterns, like MVVM, would end up changing how you manage your views and data, but that should not be a precursor to getting your Windows 8 app ready first, in a way that you feel comfortable. If you feel you have a good grasp of patterns, go ahead and do it from the get-go. Otherwise, focus on functionality first. There is nothing that you cannot refactor to apply a pattern correctly at a later point. You want to avoid premature optimization. Do what makes sense and what you are comfortable with.

Model-View-ViewModel

After the legitimate caveats about overengineering, let's step into arguably the most important of all patterns on the XAML technology stack. If you have proper grasp of MVVM concepts and utilize the right toolsets, this pattern has the power to transform your Windows 8 app code base into a more manageable, testable, and cleaner endeavor. If MVVM is done right, you will achieve SoC (Separation of Concerns), IoC (Inversion of Control), and Locator patterns, and unit testability—all in one sweep. Let's dig in.

One challenge in the traditional way of writing code for a Windows 8 Store app is the XAML code-behind file. This is tied to the XAML view and interacts with it through event handling. And what do you commonly do in event handlers in the code-behind? Yep, business logic and data manipulation. You can now take a step back, and right away you will see the problems with having hefty code in the XAML code-behind files. SoC flies out of the window—the code-behind is one giant entity with everything mixed in, which is obviously not good for unit testing. MVVM advocates that you not write all of your code in the code-behind, and it accomplishes SoC by breaking up the Windows 8 app code into components with unique responsibilities (see Figure 15-14 as in MSDN documentation found at `http://msdn.microsoft.com/en-us/library/hh848246.aspx`).

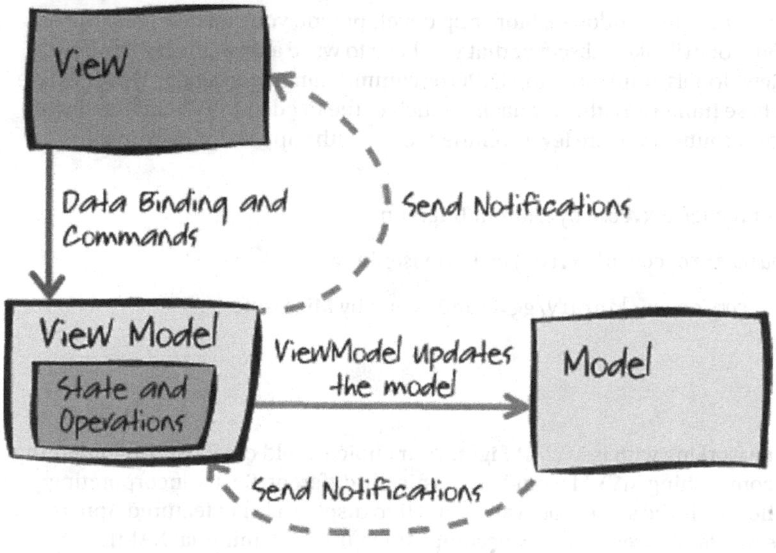

Figure 15-14. *MVVM design pattern*

Here are the three components in MVVM, along with their intended responsibilities:

- *Model*: This layer is meant to house your business entities and their data access logic, complete with service references and validation logic.
- *View*: This is meant to serve as the UI that finally gets displayed to the user and mostly contains XAML markup. Code-behind in the XAML pages/user controls is meant to be nonexistent or minimal to achieve visual adornments.

- *ViewModel*: This layer is the key player in MVVM and serves as the orchestrator between the View and the Model. A ViewModel is supposed to bring data to the View and allow for operations on the data, based on user interactions on the View through the use of commanding. The ViewModel is a representation of what's being displayed in the View and often implements the `INotifyPropertyChanged` (INPC) pattern to aid in data entity updates being pushed to the UI through XAML data binding.

The glue between the View and the ViewModel is an important one, managing much of the interaction between the UI layer and state changes or updates to the underlying object model. A lot of this magic happens through the power of XAML data binding. The View is given an object collection and proceeds to build its XAML visual tree by building on declared data bindings in the UI. A View could statically create a ViewModel and set its own `DataContext`, or the link could be dynamic where the View selects its ViewModel at runtime and binds to it. This dynamic View allocation is often courtesy of the Locator pattern, where the View simply asks for a ViewModel and an instance is returned at runtime for data binding, requiring almost no code in the code-behind.

Much of the magic in responding to user interactions on the View, but running code in the ViewModel instead of the code-behind, is courtesy of XAML `Commands`. This approach requires implementing an interface (`ICommand`) that maps UI control events into methods to be invoked on the ViewModel. However, you will soon realize that not all UI controls support *commanding*. This is where XAML behaviors or variants of it come into play, providing another layer of abstraction and mapping unsupported UI events into methods inside the ViewModel, through attaching a block of code to most XAML elements. Behaviors are not yet supported in Windows 8 XAML apps, but there are workarounds, as you will see in a bit. Also, ViewModels may need to communicate between each other to share information about UI state—enter *messaging*. This messaging between ViewModels is achieved through a simple pub-sub model: one ViewModel publishes a message to a message aggregator and the other interested ViewModels can choose to listen to the messages through subscriptions.

If you have decided to go the MVVM route in your Windows 8 Store app development, you can definitely roll on your own with the fundamental concepts. But you will likely discover that you have to write a lot of the boilerplate to handle interactions between your Views/ViewModels, implementing INPC or commanding/messaging. This is where MVVM toolkits come into play, providing a base framework that managing much of the needed MVVM interactions for you. While there are lots of MVVM toolkits around, here are few prominent ones with support for building Windows 8 apps:

- *MVVM Light* (`http://mvvmlight.codeplex.com`) by Laurent Bugnion.
- *Caliburn.Micro* (`http://caliburnmicro.codeplex.com`) by Rob Eisenberg.
- *Prism* (`http://msdn.microsoft.com/en-us/library/gg406140.aspx`) by Microsoft.

MVVM Light Toolkit

Among the MVVM toolkits, the one that I like working with is MVVM Light. Your choice could obviously be something else, but I doubt if the general pattern of accomplishing MVVM would be drastically different. So, try incorporating MVVM Light into your Apress demo app. The goal is the same: you want your UI to display a list of featured Apress books. This time, though, you will use some MVVM concepts and try accomplishing this with minimal XAML code-behind logic.

The first task is to open the Visual Studio solution for your Apress demo app, right-click the project, and go into Manage NuGet packages. Once the NuGet manager pops up, search online for MVVM Light. Once you find the toolkit, select and install it (see Figure 15-15). This installation will drop some files in your solution, along with some plumbing. You can clean up what you don't like, but only after figuring out what the dropped components do individually.

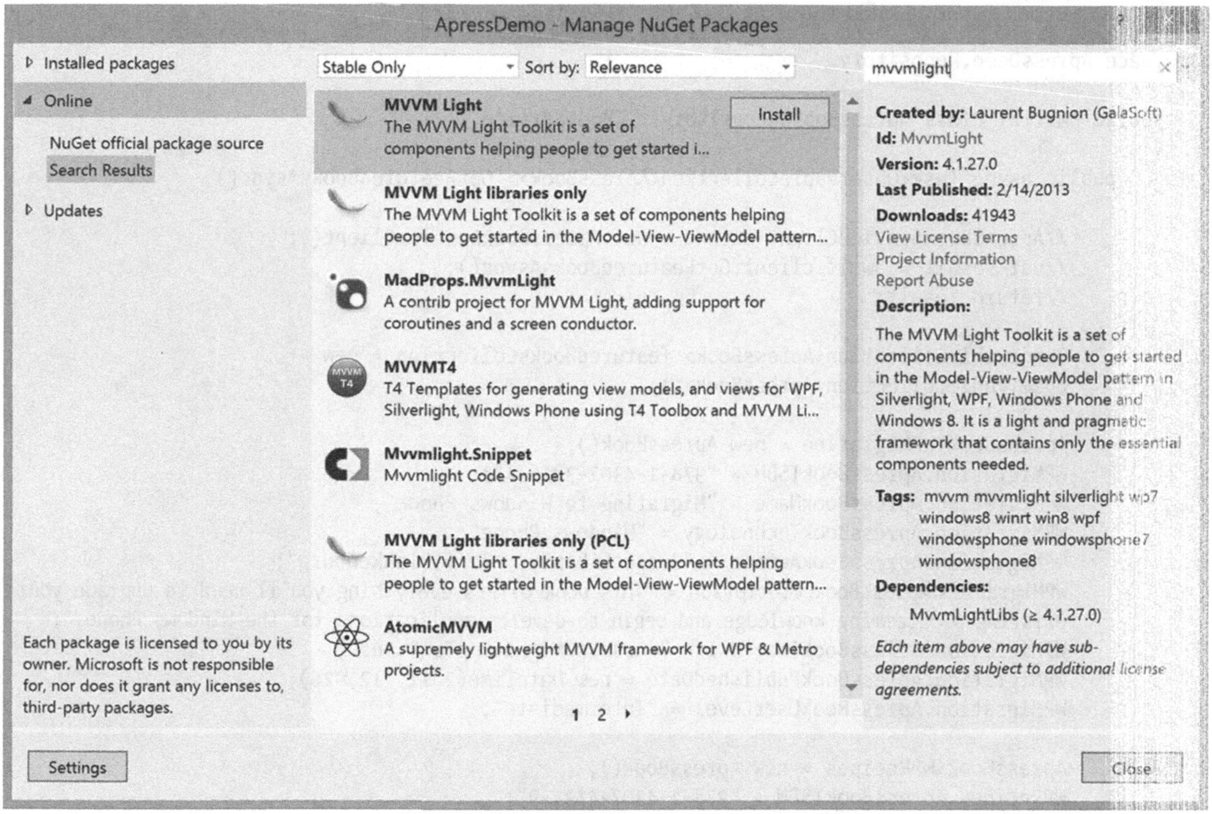

Figure 15-15. *MVVM Light NuGet*

The Repository

Let's get started. First, you will implement a repository pattern so that fetching data can be abstracted away from the ViewModels. Add a `Repository` folder in your solution and build a simple interface called `IBookService,` like so:

```
namespace ApressDemo.Repository
{
    public interface IBookService
    {
        Task<ObservableCollection<ApressBook>> GetFeaturedBooksAsync();
    }
}
```

As you can see, the interface has just one job: return a list of featured Apress books through an awaitable `Task`. If you need to persist data, add more operations to the interface and implement them accordingly. Your `ApressBookRepository` class implements the IBookService interface and actually does the job of fetching featured Apress books (see Listing 15-4).

Listing 15-4. Repository Implementation

```
namespace ApressDemo.Repository
{
    public partial class ApressBooksRepository : IBookService
    {
        public async Task<ObservableCollection<ApressBook>> GetFeaturedBooksAsync()
        {
            //ApressBookServiceClient client = new ApressBookServiceClient();
            //var result = await client.GetFeaturedBooksAsync();
            //return result;

            ObservableCollection<ApressBook> featuredBooksCollection = new
            ObservableCollection<ApressBook>();

            ApressBook WPMigration = new ApressBook();
            WPMigration.ApressBookISBN = "978-1-4302-3816-4";
            WPMigration.ApressBookName = "Migrating to Windows Phone";
            WPMigration.ApressBookTechnology = "Windows Phone";
            WPMigration.ApressBookAuthor = "Jesse Liberty , Jeff Blankenburg";
            WPMigration.ApressBookDescription = "This book offers everything you'll need to upgrade your
            existing programming knowledge and begin to develop applications for the Windows Phone.";
            WPMigration.ApressBookImageURI = "/Assets/MigratingToWP.png";
            WPMigration.ApressBookPublishedDate = new DateTime(2011, 12, 28);
            WPMigration.ApressBookUserLevel = "Intermediate";

            ApressBook WPRecipes = new ApressBook();
            WPRecipes.ApressBookISBN = "978-1-4302-4137-9";
            WPRecipes.ApressBookName = "Windows Phone Recipes";
            WPRecipes.ApressBookTechnology = "Windows Phone";
            WPRecipes.ApressBookAuthor = "Fabio Claudio Ferracchiati , Emanuele Garofalo";
            WPRecipes.ApressBookDescription = "Are you interested in smartphone development?
            Windows Phone 7.5 (code-named Mango) is packed with new features and functionality
            that make it a .NET developer's dream. This book contains extensive code samples and
            detailed walkthroughs that will have you writing sophisticated apps in no time!";
            WPRecipes.ApressBookImageURI = "/Assets/WPRecipes.png";
            WPRecipes.ApressBookPublishedDate = new DateTime(2011, 12, 14);
            WPRecipes.ApressBookUserLevel = "Beginner to Intermediate";

            featuredBooksCollection.Add(WPMigration);
            featuredBooksCollection.Add(WPRecipes);

            return featuredBooksCollection;
        }
    }
}
```

The first few lines of commented code in the `GetFeaturedBooks()` method fake the code you would have to write if the featured books were truly being fetched from a data/web service over the Internet. You would add a service reference to such a service, create a proxy client, and pull down the featured books asynchronously. But in this demo, you don't have such a service, so I am simply creating a couple of `ApressBook` objects as featured books and returning them from the method.

The ViewModel

With the repository pattern in place, proceed to declare your all-important ViewModel to handle displaying featured Apress books in a View. Let's call it `MVVMFeaturedBookListViewModel` and drop it in the `ViewModels` folder. Listing 15-5 provides the code.

Listing 15-5. Custom ViewModel

```
using GalaSoft.MvvmLight;
using System.Collections.ObjectModel;
using ApressDemo.Models;
using ApressDemo.Repository;
using GalaSoft.MvvmLight.Ioc;
using GalaSoft.MvvmLight.Command;

namespace ApressDemo.ViewModels
{
    public partial class MVVMFeaturedBookListViewModel :ViewModelBase
    {
        #region "Members"

        private ObservableCollection<ApressBook> featuredApressBooks;
        private ApressBook selectedBook;

        private IBookService apressBookService;

        #endregion

        #region "Properties"

        public ObservableCollection<ApressBook> MVVMFeaturedApressBooks
        {
            get
            {
                return featuredApressBooks;
            }
            set
            {
                featuredApressBooks = value;
                RaisePropertyChanged("MVVMFeaturedApressBooks");
            }
        }

        public ApressBook SelectedBook
        {
            get
            {
                return selectedBook;
            }
            set
            {
                selectedBook = value;
```

```
                RaisePropertyChanged("SelectedBook");
            }
        }

        #endregion

        #region "Constructor"

        public MVVMFeaturedBookListViewModel()
        {
            apressBookService = SimpleIoc.Default.GetInstance<IBookService>();

            LoadFeaturedBooks();
        }

        #endregion

        #region "Methods"

        private async void LoadFeaturedBooks()
        {
            MVVMFeaturedApressBooks = await apressBookService.GetFeaturedBooks();
        }
    }
}
```

As you can see in the code, your ViewModel inherited from the `ViewModelBase`, which is defined inside MVVM Light and gets you a few freebies. For one, notice how you are implementing the INPC pattern in your class properties—a simple method called `RaisePropertyChanged()` suffices. You have an `ObservableCollection` of `ApressBooks`, which will be the primary collection to bind your UI to. You also define a single `ApressBook` as the selected Apress book. You will see the usefulness of this later; it is meant to automatically know which book the user has selected from the displayed list.

Notice how the ViewModel `Constructor` gets a reference to an IBookService implementation and fills up the `ObservableCollection` of featured Apress books. You are using the `SimpleIoC` class from the MVVM Light toolkit. It offers an IoC pattern so that the appropriate instance of the IBookService interface can be supplied at runtime and able to be swapped out. In this case, your only implementation of IBookService is the `ApressBookRepository` you wrote before, so the code does not look all that exciting. But envision that if tomorrow you need to fetch the featured Apress books from a database instead of a web service, the IoC pattern can be used to swap out the repository so that your code in the ViewModel does not need to change.

ViewModelLocator

Next up, you are going to define a `ViewModelLocator`, which will serve your purpose of decoupling and locating a ViewModel on demand from the View, using the Locator pattern. Here's some code:

```
using GalaSoft.MvvmLight;
using GalaSoft.MvvmLight.Ioc;
using Microsoft.Practices.ServiceLocation;
using ApressDemo.Repository;
```

```
namespace ApressDemo.ViewModels
{
    public class ViewModelLocator
    {
        public ViewModelLocator()
        {
            ServiceLocator.SetLocatorProvider(() => SimpleIoc.Default);

            SimpleIoc.Default.Register<MVVMFeaturedBookListViewModel>();
            SimpleIoc.Default.Register<IBookService, ApressBooksRepository>();
        }

        public MVVMFeaturedBookListViewModel MVVMFeaturedBookListViewModel
        {
            get
            {
                return ServiceLocator.Current.GetInstance<MVVMFeaturedBookListViewModel>();
            }
        }
    }
}
```

As you can see, you use a `ServiceLocator` and hand it the `SimpleIoC` that comes with MVVM Light to act as the Locator provider. Next up, register your ViewModel and the IBookService with the IoC container so that it knows how to instantiate these classes. Notice how the IBookService registry also mentions a default implementing class: the `ApressBooksRepository`. Then, the public `MVVMFeaturedBookListViewModel` property simply says that if someone asks for a ViewModel of the type `MVVMFeaturedBookListViewModel`, return an instance of the specific class. You do not need to do the same for the IBookService implementation because there is only one concrete class, and you provided a reference to `ApressBooksRepository` during registration.

That's it. Your Locator pattern is set. The last step is to go inside the `App.xaml` file and add a global reference to the `ViewModelLocator` that you just defined, like so:

```
<?xml version="1.0" encoding="utf-8"?>
<Application x:Class="ApressDemo.App" xmlns="http://schemas.microsoft.com/winfx/2006/xaml/presentation"
             xmlns:x="http://schemas.microsoft.com/winfx/2006/xaml"
             xmlns:vm="using:ApressDemo.ViewModels"
             xmlns:local="using:ApressDemo" xmlns:localData="using:ApressDemo.Data"
             xmlns:d="http://schemas.microsoft.com/expression/blend/2008"
             xmlns:mc="http://schemas.openxmlformats.org/markup-compatibility/2006"
             mc:Ignorable="d">

  <Application.Resources>

    <ResourceDictionary>
      <ResourceDictionary.MergedDictionaries>
        <ResourceDictionary Source="Common/StandardStyles.xaml" />
      </ResourceDictionary.MergedDictionaries>
          <x:String x:Key="AppName">Apress Featured Books Demo</x:String>
          <vm:ViewModelLocator x:Key="Locator" />
      </ResourceDictionary>

    </Application.Resources>
</Application>
```

Throughout your app code, you can always use the `ViewModelLocator`, and it will give back an instantiated reference to the ViewModel. Back in your Apress demo app dashboard, wire up the Redo app bar icon to navigate the user to a fresh XAML page so that you can see MVVM in action. Accordingly, an `MVVMFeaturedBookList.xaml` page has been added. Listing 15-6 shows the selective XAML markup in it, followed by the one-line code-behind code.

Listing 15-6. XAML Markup in MVVM-Powered View

```
<common:LayoutAwarePage
    x:Name="pageRoot"
    x:Class="ApressDemo.Views.MVVMFeaturedBookList"
    xmlns="http://schemas.microsoft.com/winfx/2006/xaml/presentation"
    xmlns:x="http://schemas.microsoft.com/winfx/2006/xaml"
    xmlns:local="using:ApressDemo.Views"
    xmlns:common="using:ApressDemo.Common"
    xmlns:d="http://schemas.microsoft.com/expression/blend/2008"
    xmlns:mc="http://schemas.openxmlformats.org/markup-compatibility/2006"
    mc:Ignorable="d"
    DataContext="{Binding Source={StaticResource Locator}, Path=MVVMFeaturedBookListViewModel}">
<Grid Style="{StaticResource LayoutRootStyle}" Background="Black">
        <Grid.RowDefinitions>
            <RowDefinition Height="140"/>
            <RowDefinition Height="*"/>
        </Grid.RowDefinitions>

        <!-- Page title -->
        <Grid Grid.Row="0">
            <StackPanel Orientation="Horizontal" Margin="20,10,0,0">
                <Button x:Name="backButton" Click="GoBack" IsEnabled="{Binding Frame.CanGoBack,
                ElementName=pageRoot}" Style="{StaticResource BackButtonStyle}"/>
                <Image Source="/Assets/ApressLogo.png" Width="200" Height="100"
                VerticalAlignment="Center" Margin="-10,20,0,0"/>
                <TextBlock x:Name="pageTitle" Text="MVVM-powered Featured Books" Style="{StaticResource
                PageHeaderTextStyle}" VerticalAlignment="Center" Margin="10,10,0,10"/>
            </StackPanel>
        </Grid>

        <!-- Page Content -->
        <ListView x:Name="featuredBookListView" Grid.Row="1" Margin="150,50,100,0"
        SelectedItem="{Binding SelectedBook, Mode=TwoWay}" >
            <ListView.ItemTemplate>
                <DataTemplate>
                    <StackPanel Orientation="Horizontal">
                        <Image Source="{Binding ApressBookImageURI}" Stretch="UniformToFill"
                        Width="150" Height="200" />
                        <StackPanel Orientation="Vertical">
                            <StackPanel Orientation="Horizontal" Margin="40,10,40,15"
                            HorizontalAlignment="Left">
                                <TextBlock Text="ISBN:" Style="{StaticResource ItemTextStyle}" />
                                <TextBlock Text="{Binding ApressBookISBN}" Style="{StaticResource
                                ItemTextStyle}" Width="250" Margin="10,0,0,0"/>
                                <TextBlock Text="Book Name:" Style="{StaticResource ItemTextStyle}"
                                Margin="90,0,0,0"/>
```

```
                        <TextBlock Text="{Binding ApressBookName}" Style="{StaticResource
                        ItemTextStyle}" Width="250" Margin="10,0,0,0"/>
                    </StackPanel>
                    <StackPanel Orientation="Horizontal" Margin="40,0,0,15"
                    HorizontalAlignment="Left">
                        <TextBlock Text="Book Author:" Style="{StaticResource
                        ItemTextStyle}"/>
                        <TextBlock Text="{Binding ApressBookAuthor}" Style="{StaticResource
                        ItemTextStyle}" Width="250" Margin="10,0,0,0"/>
                        <TextBlock Text="Book Technology:" Style="{StaticResource
                        ItemTextStyle}" Margin="40,0,0,0"/>
                        <TextBlock Text="{Binding ApressBookTechnology}"
                        Style="{StaticResource ItemTextStyle}" Width="250" Margin="10,0,0,0"/>
                    </StackPanel>
                </StackPanel>
            </StackPanel>

        </DataTemplate>
    </ListView.ItemTemplate>
</ListView>

public MVVMFeaturedBookList()
{
    this.InitializeComponent();

    this.featuredBookListView.ItemsSource = (this.DataContext as
    MVVMFeaturedBookListViewModel).MVVMFeaturedApressBooks;
}
```

The XAML markup isn't doing anything spectacular. There is the generic Page title section and a Page contents section, which only consists of a simple `ListView` to display the list of featured Apress books. Note this one line of code in the page declaration, though:

```
DataContext="{Binding Source={StaticResource Locator}, Path=MVVMFeaturedBookListViewModel}"
```

Can you guess what it is trying to do? You are using the `ViewModelLocator` defined globally in the `App.xaml` file and asking for the `MVVMFeaturedBookListViewModel` ViewModel. You need to look further than your `ViewModelLocator` definition to know that this would return a fresh instance of the required ViewModel. And the entire ViewModel becomes the `DataContext` in your XAML page, ready for data binding to UI elements. Pretty slick, huh? Next, you simply set the `ItemSource` of the `ListView` to point to your `ObservableCollection` of ApressBooks from the ViewModel, which can be done either in the code-behind or in the XAML markup. That's it. Your View and ViewModel are linked up. Let's run the Apress demo app and navigate to the new XAML page (see Figure 15-16). You should see the results of seamless data binding displaying the ViewModel's collection of featured Apress books in the UI.

Figure 15-16. *MVVM-powered Apress Featured Books Demo*

Commands

Now that you are able to use MVVM for seamless binding of data in the View, let's take the next obvious step of handling user interaction. What if the user selects a book from the list, and the app needed to take some action—like showing the details of the selected book? You have access to the `ListView` and its `SelectedItem` or other properties in the XAML code-behind, but that is not where you would like to have your event handler. Remember, you are aiming for SoC, and business logic in the UI event handlers is something to avoid.

Try handling this selection user interaction through commanding in XAML. But first, go back to your ViewModel and add some support to handle the user selection, such as the following code:

```
using GalaSoft.MvvmLight.Command;
public RelayCommand<ApressBook> BookSelectedCommand { get; set; }

public MVVMFeaturedBookListViewModel()
        {
            apressBookService = SimpleIoc.Default.GetInstance<IBookService>();

            LoadFeaturedBooks();
            RespondToCommands();
        }

private void RespondToCommands()
        {
            BookSelectedCommand = new RelayCommand<ApressBook>((book) =>
                {
                    // Take some action with the user-selected book.
```

```
                string chosenBookID = SelectedBook.ApressBookISBN;
                string chosenBookName = selectedBook.ApressBookName;
            });
    }
```

As you can see, you declared a RelayCommand (MVVM light encapsulation of the ICommand interface) in your ViewModel that will handle the user's selection of an Apress book. You initialize it in the ViewModel Constructor and provide a delegate to execute some code in response to the command. You'll notice that you do not actually do anything constructive in the command handler. Your only goal is to establish that the ViewModel can get a book selection triggered in the UI by the user.

Back in your View's XAML markup, add a bottom app bar with an Edit button to respond to the user selecting a book. The user taps a book for selection and then taps the app bar icon to take some action (see Figure 15-17). See if you can wire something up for this app bar button so that the ViewModel, even though completely separated from the View, can get notified that the user tapped/clicked the button. And not only do you need to know when the user initiated the action in the UI, you also need to grab his or her book selection. This is possible through a little XAML magic. Here's the markup of the app bar button:

```
<Page.BottomAppBar>
    <AppBar x:Name="bottomAppBar" Padding="10,0,10,0">
        <Grid>
            <StackPanel Orientation="Horizontal" HorizontalAlignment="Right">
                <Button Style="{StaticResource ApressEditAppBarButtonStyle}" x:Name="editButton"
                Command="{Binding Path=BookSelectedCommand}" />
            </StackPanel>
        </Grid>
    </AppBar>
</Page.BottomAppBar>
```

Figure 15-17. *MVVM demo: select an Apress book to act on*

As you saw in the XAML markup of the app bar button, instead of the button's usual click event handler, you instead gave it a `Command` binding. Did you notice the Command name? Yes, it's the same as the `RelayCommand` you set up in your ViewModel. That's all the mapping that is required. The View's `DataContext` mapping takes care of the rest and translates the button's click to mean invocation of the bound `Command`.

Command Binding

So at this point, any time the user taps the app bar button, you have the `RelayCommand` delegate fire in the ViewModel, which can handle the user interaction. But how does the ViewModel know which book the user selected? Well, that comes free and is another example of a little XAML magic. Remember, you defined a single `ApressBook` object in the ViewModel to hold the selected book. Now, let's revisit this single line of XAML markup on the `ListView`:

```
<ListView x:Name="featuredBookListView" SelectedItem="{Binding SelectedBook, Mode=TwoWay}" >
```

The View already has access to the entire ViewModel as a `DataContext`. And now, you are binding the `ListView's SelectedItem` property to the ViewModel's `SelectedBook` property, and making that a two-way binding. This means that if the ViewModel sets its `SelectedBook` property to a specific book, it gets set as the `ListView's SelectedItem` property. More importantly, as the user makes a book selection from the list, the `SelectedItem` property of the `ListView` gets set appropriately, thus also updating the `SelectedBook` property in the ViewModel. So, by the time the ViewModel's `RelayCommand` gets to act on the user's button click, the ViewModel already knows the book that the user selected from the `SelectedBook` property. Isn't that nifty?

Behaviors

Now, as handy as your Command and two-way binding have been, you may sometimes run up against limitations while trying such commanding in your Windows 8 app. What if your app wanted to take action the moment the user taps/clicks to select an Apress book from the list, instead of waiting on the secondary step of clicking an app bar button. The challenge that you will run up against is that not all XAML controls support commanding. For example, the `ListView` exposes a `SelectionChanged` event, but you could not assign a Command to it. The solution is *behaviors*—little chunks of code that can be attached for execution on most XAML elements. But the big problem is that the Windows 8 XAML framework does not support behaviors!

Thankfully, the developer community has stepped up with a solution: WinRTBehaviors. Developed by Joost van Schaik and others, WinRTBehaviors provides a solution for the lack of behavior support in Windows 8 apps. It is available as an open-source NuGet. The idea is to use the `EventToBoundCommandBehavior` to attach a behavior to non-Command-supporting XAML elements so that you can still map their events to `Commands`. But first, right-click your project, fire up the NuGet manager, and install the WinRTBehaviors NuGet in your Apress demo app Visual Studio solution (see Figure 15-18).

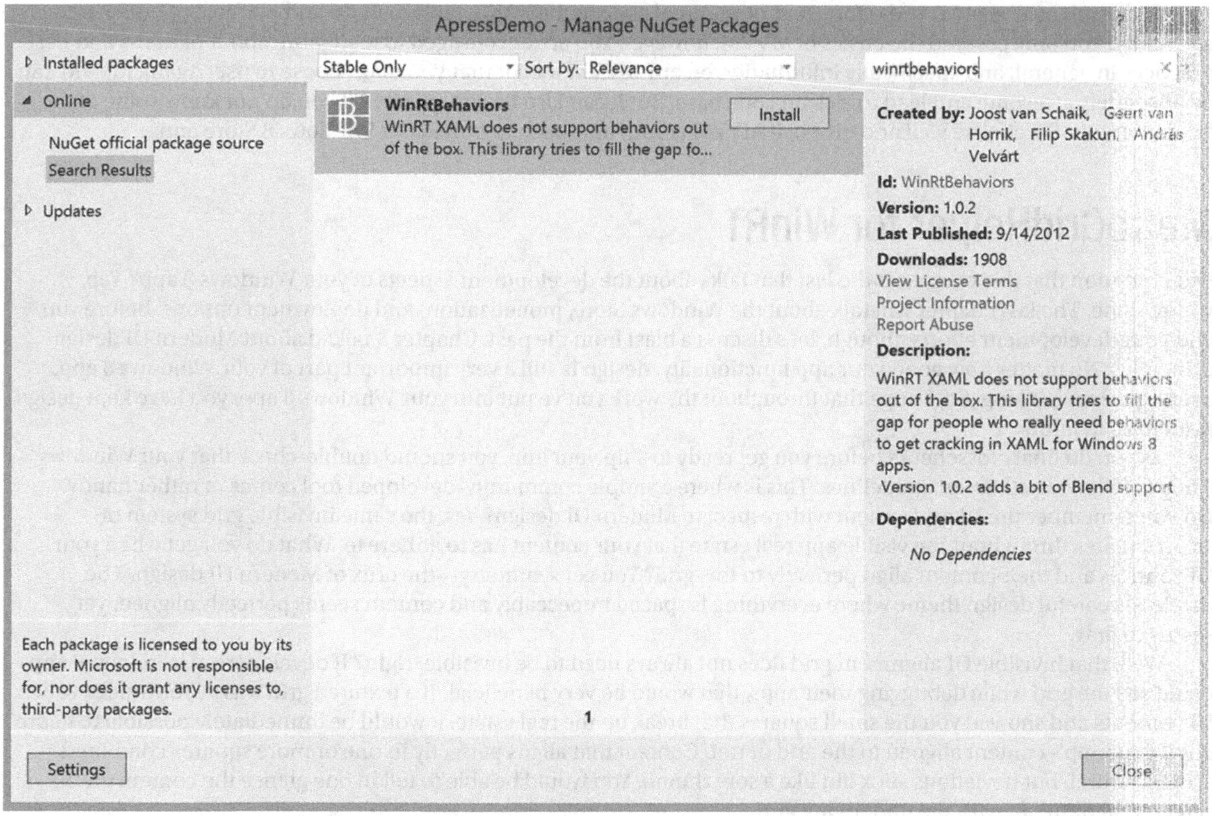

Figure 15-18. *WinRTBehaviors NuGet*

Once the WinRTBehaviors NuGet has been installed, come back to your existing XAML to display the featured Apress books through a `ListView`, and add some XAML markup, like so:

```
xmlns:Win8nl_Behaviors="using:Win8nl.Behaviors"
xmlns:WinRtBehaviors="using:WinRtBehaviors"

<ListView ...>
<WinRtBehaviors:Interaction.Behaviors>
        <Behaviors:EventToBoundCommandBehavior Event="SelectionChanged"
                   Command="{Binding BookSelectedCommand }"
                   CommandParameter="{Binding SelectedBook,  Mode=TwoWay}"/>
</WinRtBehaviors:Interaction.Behaviors> ...
</ ListView >
```

As you see in this code, you attach a new WinRTBehavior to your vanilla XAML `ListView`, and this behavior is responsible for mapping the `ListView`'s `SelectionChanged` event to the `RelayCommand` defined in the ViewModel. The Command invocation and the two-way binding to the ViewModel's `SelectedBook` property happens as before. So, with a little XAML markup, you are able to transform a non-Command-supporting XAML element's event to a Command that can be acted upon in the ViewModel, with proper context.

The result of all this MVVM effort: zero or minimal code in the XAML code-behind and perfect SoC, offering easy testability. You only covered the basics of MVVM, however. You are encouraged to read more about patterns and best practices in general, and specifically information on any MVVM toolkit that you may choose to use. Again, MVVM can be absolutely awesome and lead to a clean code base. But it can also be complicated if you do not know some of the fundamentals. So, choose well and dive in if MVVM is your approach to build your Windows 8 Store app.

MetroGridHelper for WinRT

Did I mention that this chapter is the last that talks about the development aspects of your Windows 8 app? Yep, you're done. The last chapter will talk about the Windows Store, monetization, and deployment options. Before you end your development efforts, though, let's discuss a blast from the past. Chapter 3 talked about Modern UI design principles. No matter how good your app functionality, design is still a very important part of your Windows 8 app; user experience is king. So, I hope that throughout the work you've put into your Windows 8 app, you have kept design principles in mind.

As you do final crosschecks before you get ready to ship your app, you should double-check that your Windows 8 app is following all design guidelines. This is where a simple community-developed tool comes in rather handy. Do you remember the UI grid system with respect to Modern UI design? Yes, the same invisible grid system of small squares throughout the visible app real estate that your content has to adhere to. What do you get when your UI controls and their content align perfectly to this grid? You get symmetry—the crux of Modern UI design. The carelessly careful design theme where everything is spaced impeccably and content seems perfectly aligned, yet seems to flow.

Well, that invisible UI alignment grid does not always need to be invisible, right? If developers of Windows 8 apps could see the grid while debugging their apps, that would be very beneficial. If a textured grid was visible under your UI contents and showed you the small squares that break up the real estate, it would be immediately possible to figure out if your app's content aligned to the grid or not. Content that aligns perfectly in one or more squares combined seems natural, but deviations stick out like a sore thumb. You would be able to tell in one glance the content on the screen that didn't fit with the underlying grid.

Turns out, you are not the first to see the potential of this brilliantly simple idea. Jeff Wilcox of Microsoft released a MetroGridHelper toolkit for Windows Phone developers. This toolkit did exactly what I talked about; if developers ran a Windows Phone app in debug mode, the toolkit would grab the underlying app frame and paint little square tiles (of chosen color) underneath the app's content. This simple approach immediately showed Windows Phone developers what in their apps was off the grid. More information about the MetroGridHelper and its NuGet can be found at `http://nuget.org/packages/MetroGridHelper`.

Thanks to community developer folks like Mark Monster, the MetroGridHelper has been extended to work with Windows 8 app development. The MetroGridHelper for Windows 8 functions similarly to its Windows Phone counterpart—underlaying UI content with a visible grid of small squares. And this works for filled, snapped, and full-screen Windows 8 app modes, in addition to supporting orientation changes. More information about the MetroGridHelper for WinRT can be found at `https://nuget.org/packages/WinRT.MetroGridHelper`. To play with it a little, I'll install the NuGet in the Apress demo app Visual Studio project (see Figure 15-19).

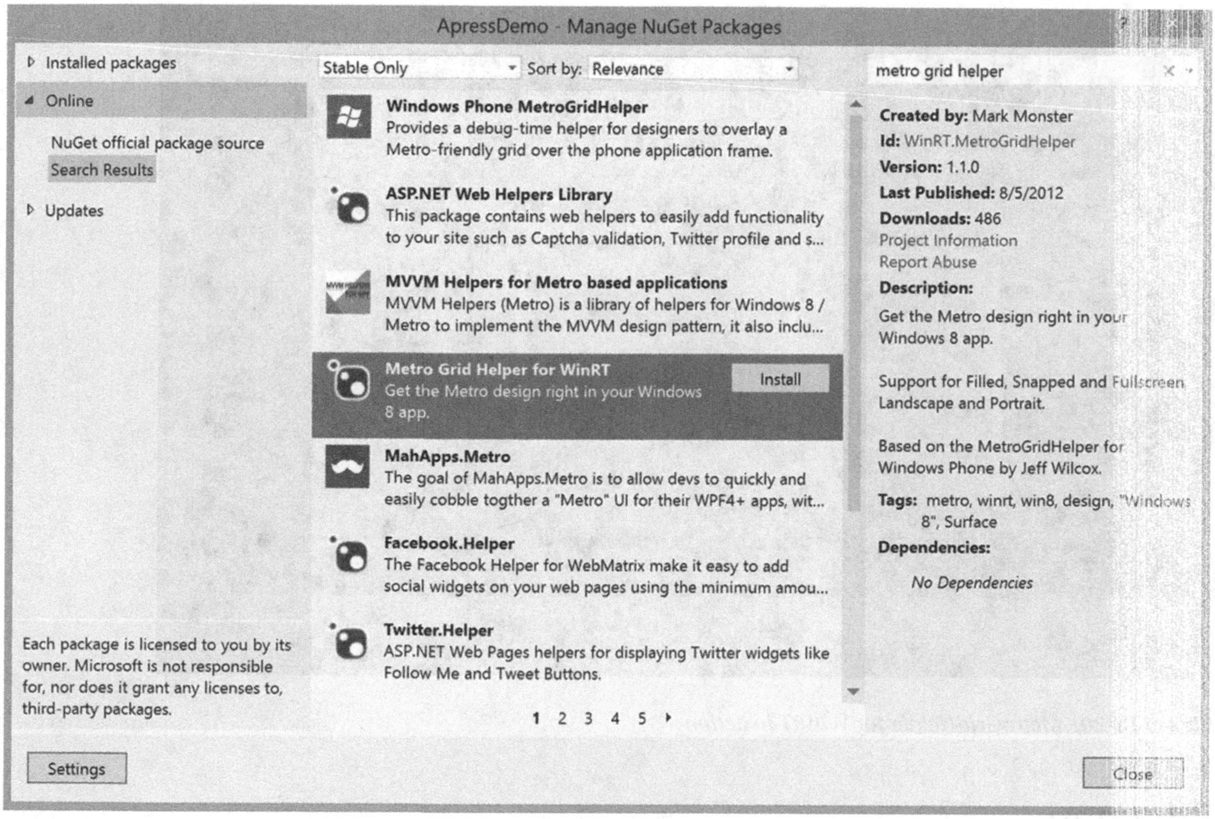

Figure 15-19. *MetroGridHelper for WinRT NuGet*

Once the MetroGridHelper for WinRT NuGet has been added to your Apress demo app project, simply go into the `OnLaunched()` event handler in the `App.xaml.cs` file and add a one-line code, like so:

```
MetroGridHelper.IsVisible = true;
```

That's all it takes to get the MetroGridHelper for WinRT into action. Let's fire up your Apress demo app again, and this time you should see a grid of small colored squares underlying the UI content of your app (see Figure 15-20). You can change the visual state or the orientation of the app, and the underlying grid follows. And with the invisible design grid now visible, you can immediately see that a few content pieces are not perfectly aligned. Do you see the benefit of this little NuGet?

Figure 15-20. *MetroGridHelper for WinRT in action*

Summary

Throughout this chapter, I wanted to introduce you to some real-world techniques that should commonly be used by Windows 8 app developers. While not an exhaustive list in any way, I hope it gave you a smattering of what's available out there in terms of extending your Windows 8 app's functionality, or gaining code base sanity through third-party extensions and toolkits. You saw how cool real-time Windows 8 apps can get and that you can build it all easily using a SignalR back end. Choose a MVVM technique and any of the available toolkits. You gain adherence to tried and tested software design patterns and a cleaner code base. Did I mention that the sky is the limit for your Windows 8 app?

CHAPTER 16

Deployment

Congratulations! This is long overdue. You have worked hard on your dream Windows 8 Store app and after reading and coding along through 15 chapters of this book, your app is ready for primetime. A pat on the back is due—but this isn't a time to let off the gas. While the hard work may be behind you, the most important step is ahead: deployment of your Windows 8 app! How do you get the Windows 8 app in the hands of your users, and what are the considerations as you get ready to pull the trigger? Will you go for the Windows Store, or opt for sideloading your Windows 8 app on eligible devices? How do you make sure that you are meeting the certification requirements for your app? And after all the hard work you put into your Windows 8 app, a little green never hurt anybody.

This chapter will be your final checklist and it includes all the things to keep in mind as you deploy your Windows 8 app. And after hectic coding in all of your previous chapters, this chapter will be lean—no code, only pointers to well-documented resources to keep in mind as you take your Windows 8 app to glory.

Deployment Options

Once you are ready to ship your Windows 8 app, the next question is: How do you get it in the hands of your users? Turns out, you have the following options:

- *Windows Store*: You can release your Windows 8 app to the Windows Store for public consumption. This gives your app the widest possible audience and visibility on any Windows 8 machine. I will talk about the Store option in detail in just a bit.
- *Windows Store, but with caveats*: If your Windows 8 app caters to a wide audience, but has some functionality available to selected users, you can still leverage the Windows Store for hosting your app for user downloads. Upon installation, the app should work normally for the general public, but certain app functionalities may be available to only those users who clear some kind of authentication.
- *Enterprise line of business (LOB)*: You may be writing a Windows 8 app that is meant to convert a business workflow to an easy-to-use Windows 8 app workflow for an enterprise/business, transforming a rudimentary system to a digital representation—much to the delight of end users. If your Windows 8 app is truly an enterprise LOB app, it does not need to be released to the Windows Store. Instead, you can have it distributed locally to a controlled group of enterprise users. This process is called *sideloading* a Windows 8 app.

Let's first review the LOB Windows 8 deployment option in detail, and then the Windows Store.

Enterprise Line of Business

If you choose the sideloading Windows 8 option for deployment, your LOB Windows 8 app certainly does not need to be certified or released through the Windows Store. This does not, however, mean that all bets are off and your Windows 8 app can bypass all guidelines. The enterprise users of your LOB Windows 8 app are still going to have access to other apps offering a unique and fluid user experience; you do not want your LOB app to stick out like a sore thumb.

In fact, you can argue that it is more important for LOB apps to integrate closely with the Windows 8 OS features to streamline usage of LOB Windows 8 apps in various orientations or visual states as available on the user's device. Envision a technician on the field using a Windows 8 tablet device running your touch-enabled LOB app, or a C-level executive glancing over summary data presented with semantic zooming. Enterprises will also be drawn to hybrid devices that offer touch-interactivity on the go, but transform into a fully powered work PC when back in office. The business possibilities for LOB Windows 8 apps are endless; if you are not talking to your enterprise clients about Windows 8 opportunities, trust me, someone else will.

Now, LOB apps that aren't signed by the Windows Store can only be installed on sideloading-enabled devices and they must be signed with a certificate chained to a trusted root certificate. This device enablement to support sideloading can happen in three ways: domain joining a Windows 8 Pro device, using a sideloading key for RT devices, or using the developer license on individual devices. LOB Windows 8 apps can be scripted through PowerShell commands for installation, or IT administrators may include the LOB app in the Windows image on a per-user basis. For more information on sideloading LOB Windows 8 apps, please refer to MSDN documentation at `http://technet.microsoft.com/en-us/library/hh852635.aspx#SideloadingRequirements`.

The Windows Store

Windows 8 as an OS, as well as the overall platform ecosystem, comes with heavy investments from Microsoft. Nothing, however, compares to the importance of the Windows Store. For the first time in the Windows OS space, you now have a ubiquitous Microsoft-hosted store to hold all kinds of Windows 8 apps. The Windows Store serves as the one-stop-shop for Windows 8 users to browse and download apps. I have talked about the massive reach Windows 8 OS has worldwide, and the audience base is only going to get wider with time. Here's the kicker: no matter what type of desktop/laptop/tablet/hybrid Windows 8 device that the user buys, the Windows Store is always present. Herein lies your majestic developer opportunity with millions as an audience. Windows Store is your platform to ship awesome code in the form of Windows 8 apps.

The Windows Store offers broad reach, flexibility, and transparency for developers. It's also designed to ensure the visibility and discoverability of Windows 8 apps. Discoverability mechanisms like search integration through the charms, app categorization, app rankings, and editorial curating help Windows 8 users find apps quickly. In addition to being available on all Windows 8 devices as an app, the Windows Store is accessible through Internet search engines, offering indexed app listings that are driven by the same content that is in the Windows Store app on Windows 8. The Windows Store reaches consumer markets in over 200 countries, and it makes your Windows 8 apps available in selected locales, if supported. Windows Store also identifies the user's consumer market and presents market-specific catalogs for each country, in accordance with local laws, so that Microsoft and the Windows 8 app developers are legally protected.

Windows Store also offers developers a personalized app dashboard. MSDN states at `http://msdn.microsoft.com/en-us/library/windows/apps/br230836.aspx`: "The Windows Dev Center provides a dashboard that includes many ways to improve your apps by monitoring their success. View reports on downloads, revenue, aggregate usage, in-app transactions, customer ratings, market trends, and crash and hang data."

So, how do you get your Windows 8 app in the Windows Store and beyond? Here are the steps:

1. Head over to the Windows Store portal (`http://build.windowsstore.com`) and register yourself as a Windows Store developer. This sets up your account and gives you access to the Windows developer dashboard. Annual registration is $49 for individual developers and $99 for company accounts.

2. Next, head over to the Windows developer portal (`http://msdn.microsoft.com/en-us/windows/apps`)and look up any necessary documentation/samples to build your dream Windows 8 app. Follow the chapters of this book and revisit the developer portal often to make sure that you are developing features correctly.

3. Reserve a name for your app in the Windows Store. This was covered in Chapter 13. Essentially, you do not need to have your Windows 8 app ready for submission to register your app name; you can do this anytime, preferably sooner. Once an app name has been reserved, you have *one year* to submit your app to the Store, beyond which the app name goes back into the pool. So, there is an incentive for you to reserve app names and have a time frame in which you need to have your app ready for submission.

4. Once functionality is complete, test your Windows 8 app thoroughly, particularly looking out for edge conditions that might be error traps. If you have access to a Windows 8 touch-based device, it is imperative to test your app on it to iron out user-experience quirks. Hand your app to nontechie family and friends and have them provide feedback on user interactivity. Listen, fix, and repeat.

5. When you are ready to submit your Windows 8 app to the Store, your app will go through a *certification process*, where automated and manual testing is performed on the app. This validation is a critical aspect to the trust factor in the Windows Store—when consumers download Windows 8 apps from the Store, they are assured quality apps that meet certain criteria and will not negatively impact their device in any way.

6. Thoroughly read the app certification requirements found at `http://msdn.microsoft.com/en-us/library/windows/apps/hh694083.aspx`. The good news is that it is a very objective set of requirements. Do all the right things and you will fly through the certification process. Pay particular attention to user privacy and content policies to avoid certification hiccups.

7. Do not get flustered if your Windows 8 app fails certification once—or even twice. It is only to your app's benefit if you fix the issues being pointed out; every certification failure will provide a detailed report as to which certification requirements are not being met.

8. To increase your confidence to clear Windows 8 app certification before you submit your Windows 8 app to the Store, there is the *Windows App Certification Kit* (*WACK*). This tool runs many of the automated tests that the Windows Store certification process would run, locally on your development machine. So use the WACK tool to fix any failing issues upfront and to go into your app submission with much more confidence. I'll talk about WACK a little more in a bit. Do not forget to submit all the app metadata and a few extra imagery that the Windows Store needs for your Windows 8 app. The Store submission wizard will guide you through the process to collect everything that is needed.

9. Once your Windows 8 app clears certification, it will be live in the Windows Store for millions to consume. This calls for celebration since it marks the culmination of your development efforts.

10. But even after your Windows 8 app is live in the Store, your work isn't completely over yet. Now comes the *marketing*—spread the word about your app any way that you can. Cater to social media channels, build a web presence for your app, ask for app reviews, and so forth. In short, market your Windows 8 app to give it all the visibility it deserves.

11. Take care of your Windows 8 app after it is live in the Store. If you are an individual developer, Microsoft calls you an *ISV* or *independent software vendor*. Note the word *vendor*. You need to develop the attitude of supporting your Windows 8 app like a vendor providing services. Fix reported app errors and improve functionality through app updates pushed out to the Windows Store using the same steps I just described. In short, be answerable to your users. It will pay huge dividends.

Packaging for LOB and Windows Store

So, once you have your Windows 8 app ready to ship, how do you start building the app artifacts that need to be uploaded to the Windows Store portal? Turns out, from within Visual Studio through a technique called *packaging* that bundles all the app artifacts into a single package file (see Figure 16-1).

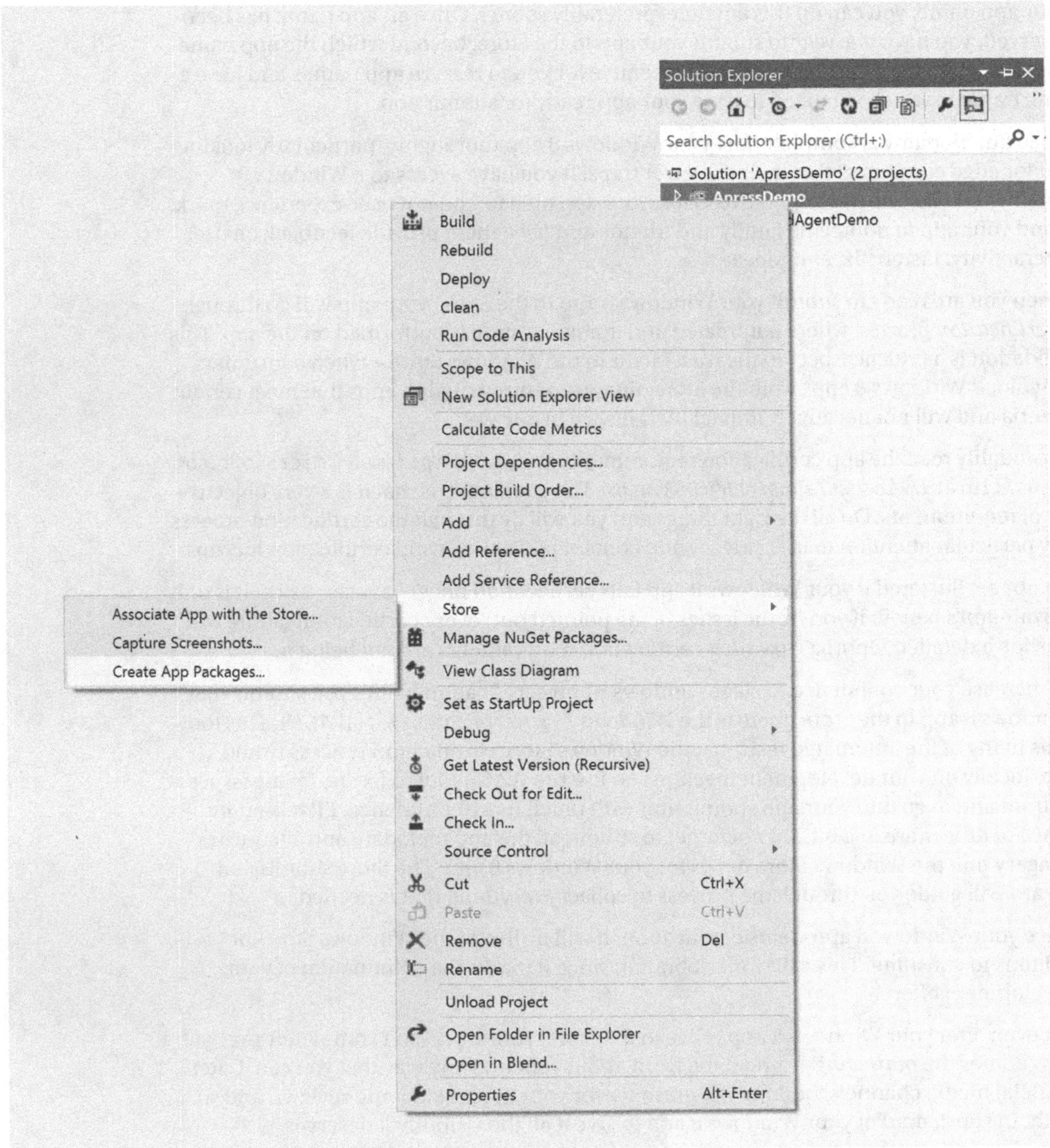

Figure 16-1. *Creating an app package from Visual Studio*

Once you start the packaging process, you'll notice that the wizard immediately asks whether you are packaging for the purpose of releasing your Windows 8 app to the Store or whether it is meant for LOB enterprise app distribution (see Figures 16-2 and 16-3). The end result is the same app package; the intermediate steps are a little different.

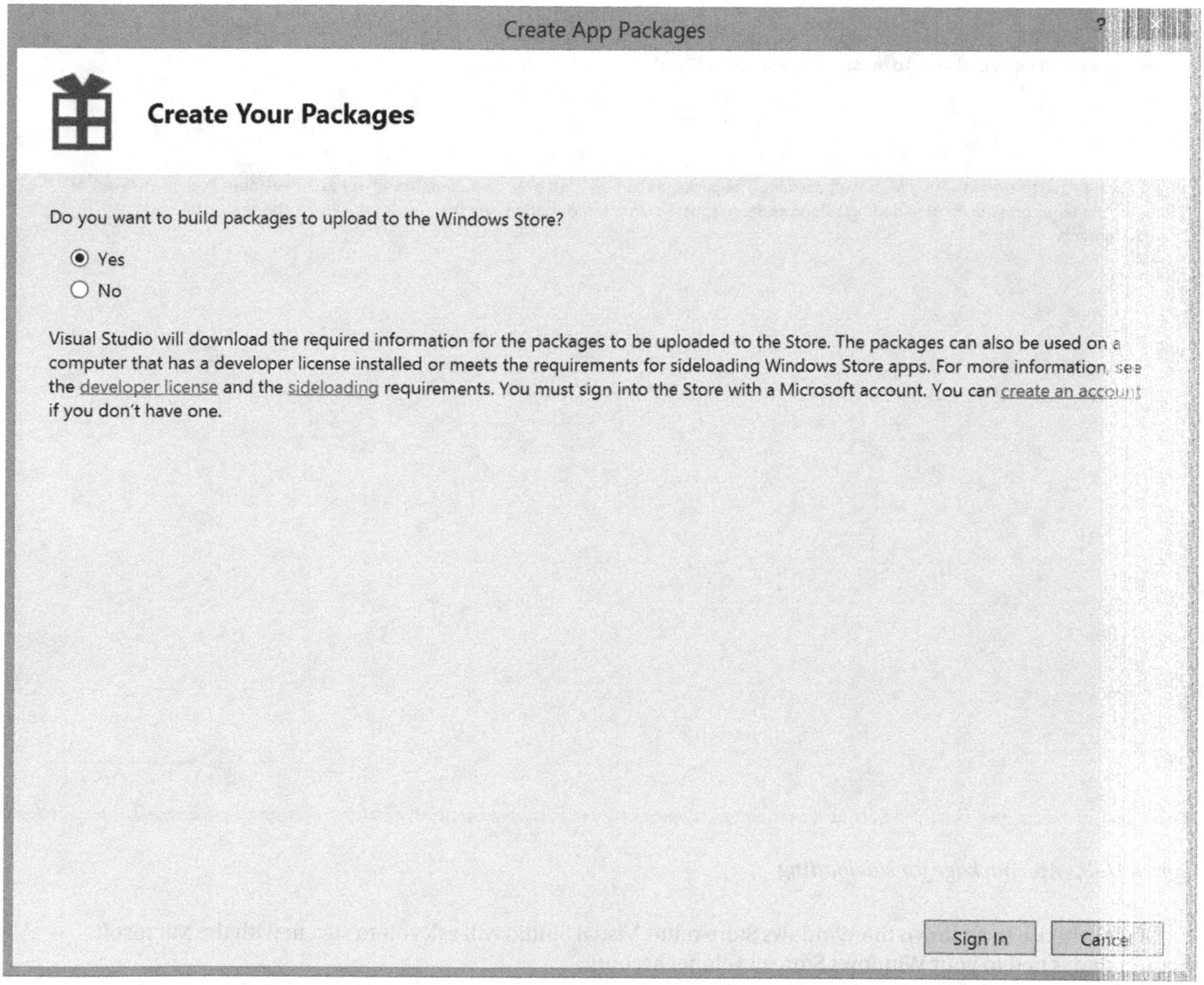

Figure 16-2. *App package for Windows Store*

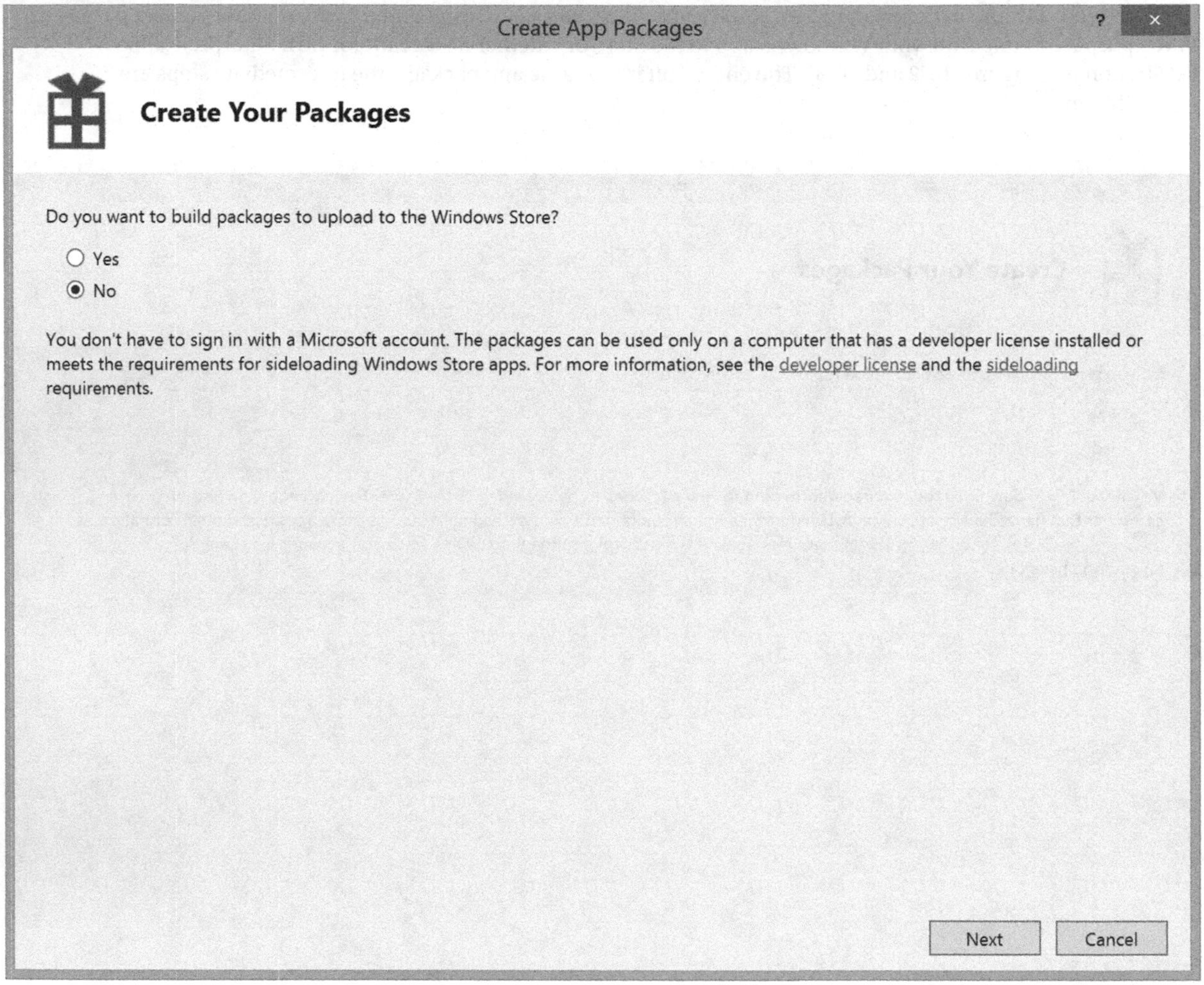

Figure 16-3. *App package for sideloading*

If you choose to go down the Windows Store route, Visual Studio will ask you to sign in with the Microsoft account that is tied to your Windows Store developer account.

The next step is to associate the submitted app to the app name that you (hopefully) already reserved (see Figure 16-4). The preceding steps make certain that your Windows 8 app is properly signed with a certificate, through a Windows Store handshake. This signing ensures that your app can be safely released to the Windows Store and is available for safe download on any Windows 8 device. If going the LOB enterprise sideloading route, your Windows 8 app gets signed with a certificate tied to your developer account.

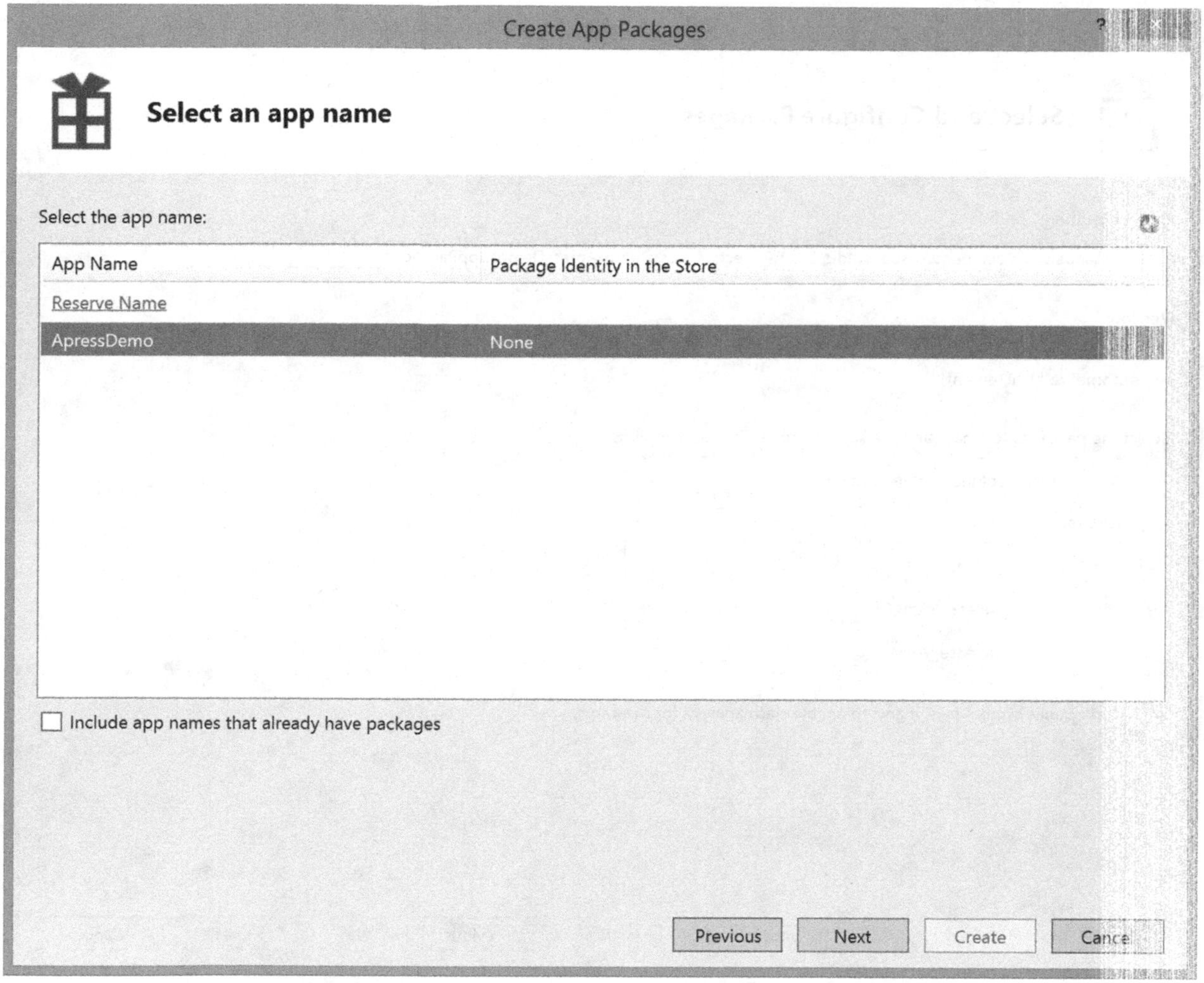

Figure 16-4. *Selecting the app name*

The next step in the packaging process is to select the platform architecture support so that your Windows 8 app package is configured correctly (see Figure 16-5). The options are Neutral (for any CPU), x86 (for 32-bit PCs), x64 (for 64-bit PCs), and ARM (for ARM processor-based PCs). This is an important step because you do not want app incompatibility on user devices. Normally, you want your app to have the widest possible audience, unless you are using libraries that restrict your app's platform support to specific architectures.

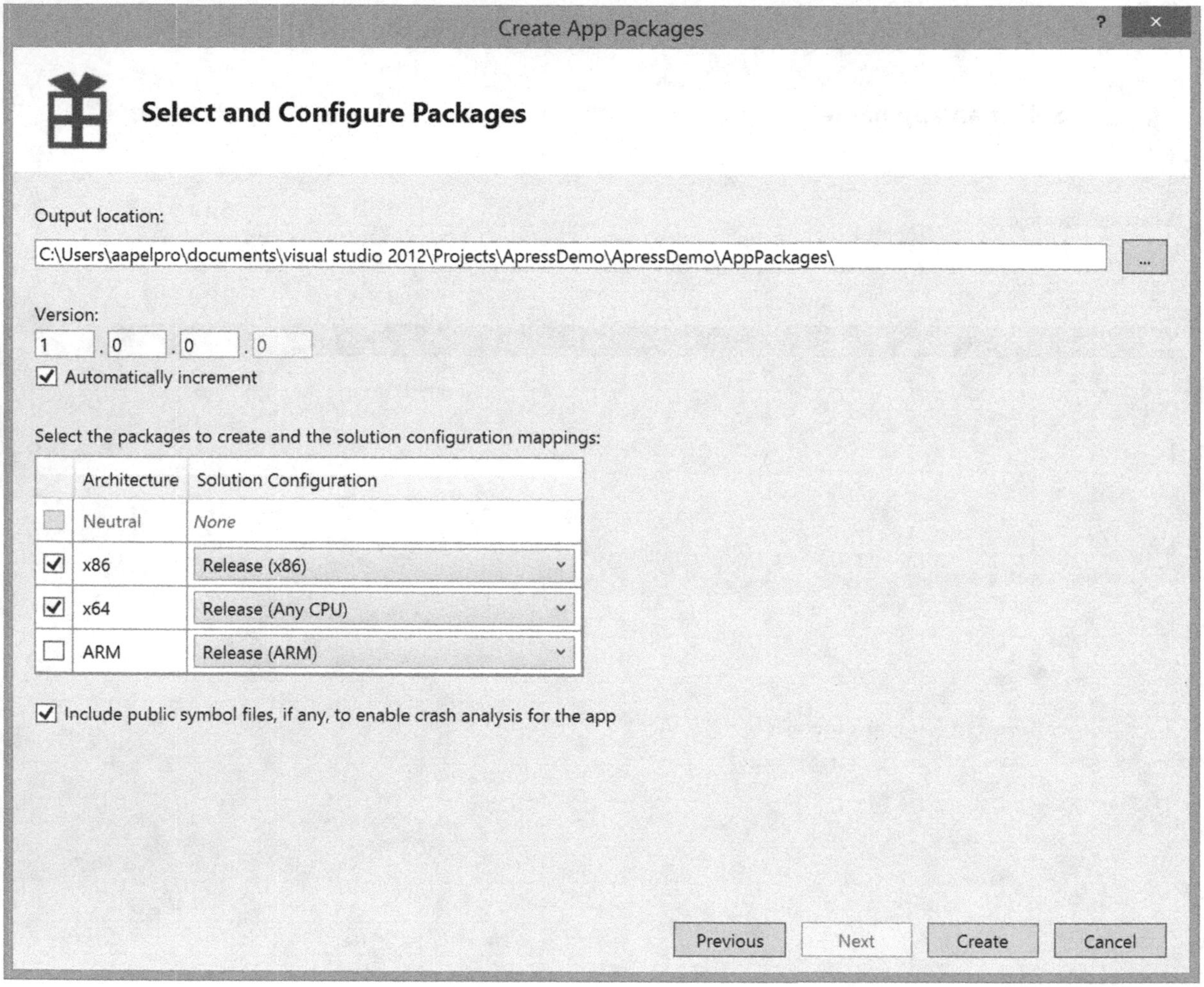

Figure 16-5. *App package architecture configuration*

Once all that is done, the end result is a set of packages (marked per their platform architecture configuration) in your specific app directory (see Figure 16-6). The `.appxupload` file is the all-important artifact that you upload to the Windows Store.

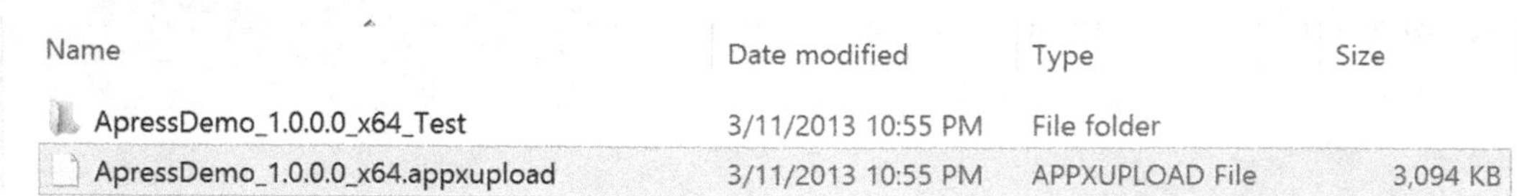

Name
Date modified
Type
Size
ApressDemo_1.0.0.0_x64_Test
3/11/2013 10:55 PM
File folder
ApressDemo_1.0.0.0_x64.appxupload
3/11/2013 10:55 PM
APPXUPLOAD File
3,094 KB

Figure 16-6. *Created app packages*

If you chose the Windows Store option while creating packages, upon creation you are encouraged to the run the WACK validations (see Figure 16-7).

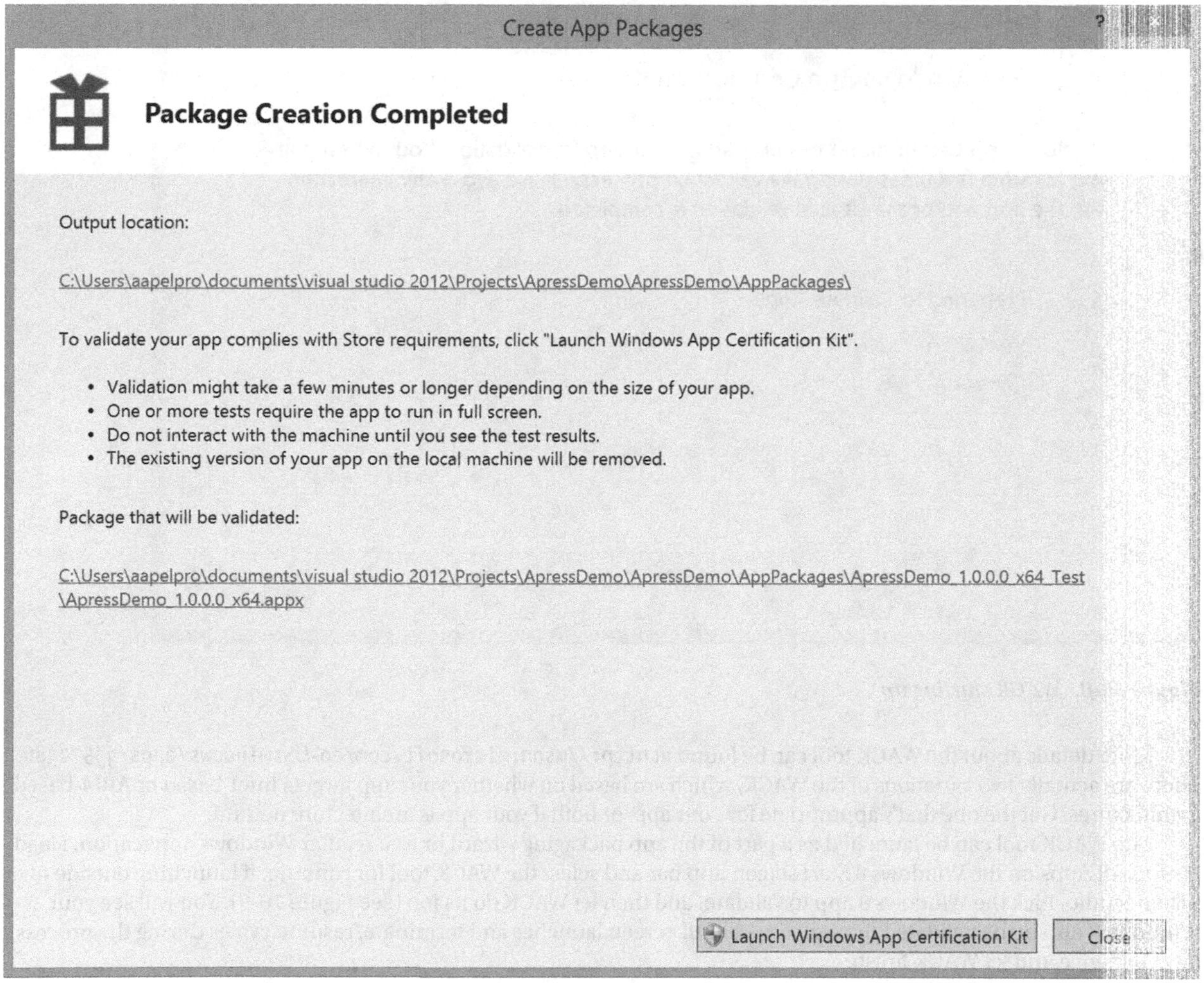

***Figure 16-7.** App package wizard completion*

WACK Validations

Let's talk a little bit more about the Windows App Certification Kit. As you are submitting your Windows 8 app to the Store, the last step of the packaging process points you to run the WACK validation tool. Go ahead and run the WACK validations, as seen in Figure 16-8. This is a very important step that gives you an upfront indication if anything in your app package needs fixing. It checks artwork, app launch/termination/resume, app manifest, performance counters, and so forth. The WACK tool gives you confidence that your Windows 8 app will at least clear the automated testing that Windows Store will throw its way. In fact, enterprise LOB apps, which do not go through the Store certification, will also benefit from WACK validations, and IT administrators are encouraged to enforce developers to use the WACK validations before LOP app distribution.

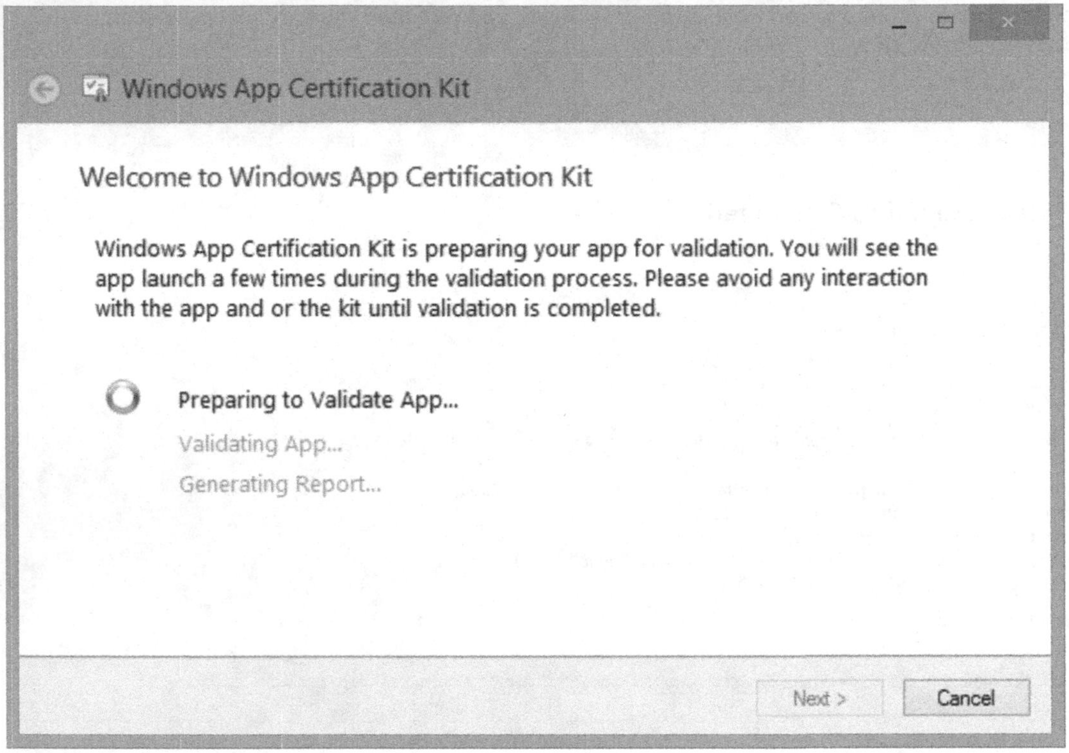

Figure 16-8. *WACK starting up*

More details about the WACK tool can be found at `http://msdn.microsoft.com/en-US/windows/apps/jj572486`. There are actually two variations of the WACK, which are based on whether your app targets Intel-based or ARM-based architectures. Get the one that's appropriate for your app, or both if your app is architecture neutral.

The WACK tool can be launched as a part of the app packaging wizard or as a regular Windows application. Head over to All Apps on the Windows 8 Start screen app bar and select the WACK tool for running, if launching outside of Visual Studio. Pick the Windows 8 app to validate, and then let WACK do its job (see Figure 16-9). You will see your Windows 8 app being validated through several full-screen launches and terminate/resume cycles during the process; have patience and let WACK finish.

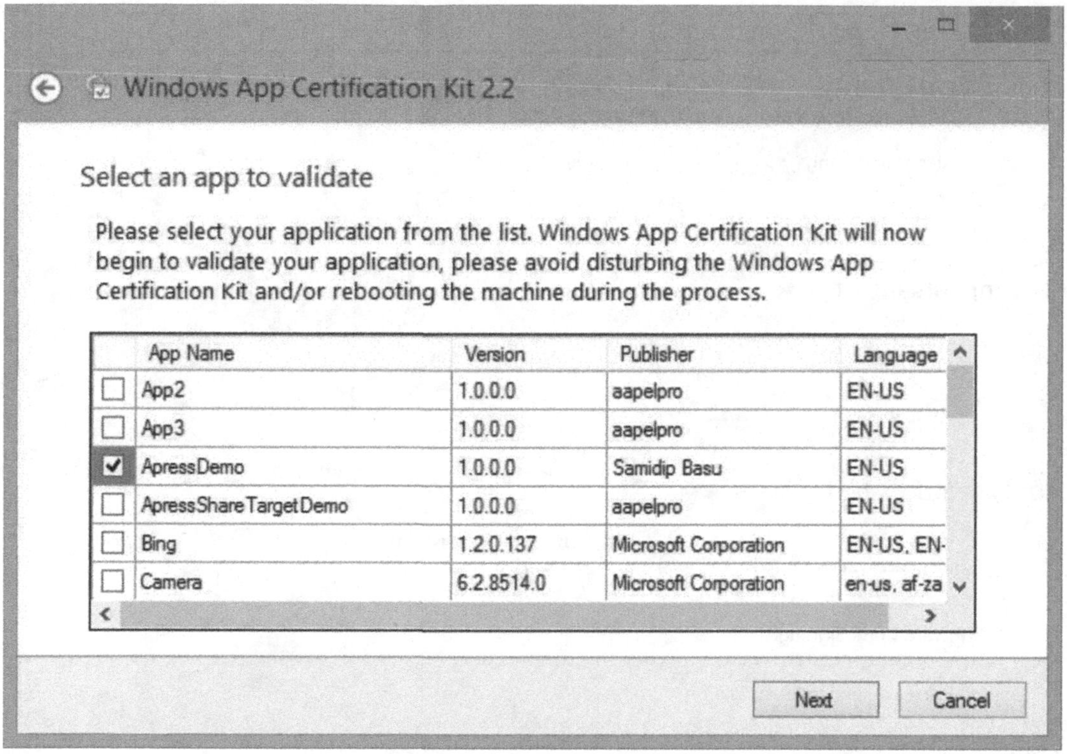

Figure 16-9. *Choosing app for WACK validations*

The end result is a detailed report about the validations that worked and the ones that failed, and for what reasons. Save the file and load it on any browser to display the results. As usual, green is good and red is bad (see Figures 16-10 and 16-11). Fix what's broken and repeat until you have perfection. While you are still not guaranteed to pass the manual Windows Store certification checks, you do have much more confidence and a better shot at clearing the Store certifications on the first attempt.

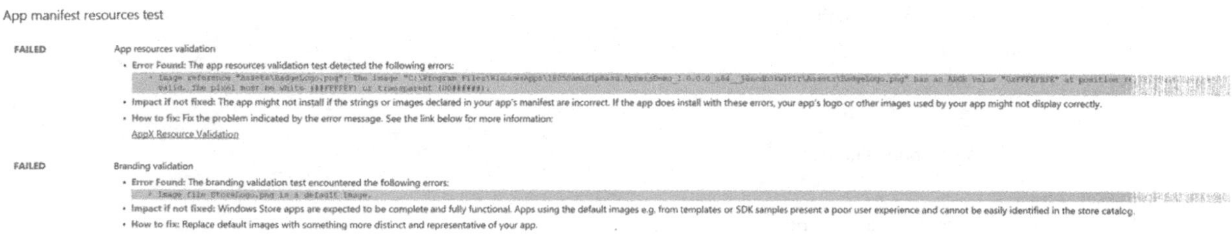

Figure 16-10. *WACK validation failures*

Crashes and hangs test

PASSED	App launch tests
PASSED	Crashes and hangs

App manifest compliance test

PASSED	App manifest

Windows security features test

PASSED	Binary analyzer
PASSED	Private Code Signing

Supported API test

PASSED	Supported APIs

Performance test

PASSED	Bytecode generation
PASSED	Optimized Binding References
PASSED	Performance launch
PASSED	Performance suspend

Figure 16-11. *WACK validation successes*

Show Me the Money

You put in a lot of effort building your dream Windows 8 app, and you even published it successfully to the Windows Store. Isn't it time you got a little something back? Turns out, it does not have to be little—you have much to gain. Monetization of developer efforts is now a critical piece to any app platform ecosystem, and the opportunities are magnified in Windows 8. Let's dig in a little as to how you can reap some monetary benefits from your Windows 8 apps.

I am exclusively talking about apps that are in the Windows Store, though; if you are deploying enterprise LOB Windows 8 apps, I would hope that you have compensation through the company whose business workflows are being transformed by your Windows 8 app.

We developers have a tendency to underestimate our work and to believe that a product is not very valuable to the user. Well, you are not the user and should stop guessing. Let the users be the judge of your work and decide how much it is worth. If you have put in appreciable effort in building a great Windows 8 app, you absolutely do not have to give away your work for free. Look at the value provided by other similar apps in the Windows Store, and make a sound decision as to how much your work is worth.

Microsoft has always been a developer-friendly company and the Windows Store ecosystem is their biggest invitation to you, the developer. The Store is designed for best-in-class economics for the developers who participate with Windows 8 apps. MSDN states at `http://msdn.microsoft.com/en-us/windows/apps/hh852650.aspx`: "Windows 8 represents the single biggest platform opportunity available, and business terms of the Windows Store represent a developer-first point of view. The revenue share is 70%, but when an app achieves $25,000 USD in revenue aggregated across all sales in every market, that changes to 80% revenue share for the rest of the lifetime of the app."

The Windows Store hosts all Windows 8 Store apps and is doing a huge amount of orchestration to be available 24/7 across 200 countries. In addition to the Store's availability, Microsoft also has to support the Store's e-commerce, as well as accurate developer dashboards and thorough testing of Windows 8 apps before inclusion/updates hit the Store. So, for hosting your Windows 8 apps, it is obvious that Microsoft deserves some portion of the benefits. For the first $25,000 that your app makes, Microsoft will charge you a 30% fee; but after your app crosses the $25,000 mark, that fee drops to 20% and continues through the app's lifetime in the Store. These numbers are industry leading.

Now, how do you, as a Windows 8 app developer, capitalize on this huge monetization opportunity? Well, there are several avenues.

- *App price*: If you make a rock-solid Windows 8 app and clearly see the value that you are offering your users, there is absolutely nothing wrong in charging a price to download your app from the Windows Store. Price tiers start at $1.49, and go up in increments of $0.50. Also, each price tier has a corresponding value in each of the more than 60 currencies offered by the Store.

- *Trials*: While charging for an app upfront isn't a bad idea, a lot of folks may be willing to shell out the money after seeing the value you offer in your Windows 8 app, much like test-driving a car. So, another option is to allow your users to test-drive your app through carefully crafted trials. These trials can be feature-limited (offer a subset of the app's functionality) or time-limited (the app stops working after a predetermined time), each designed to give the user a taste of what the full-blown app can do, with the ultimate goal being to entice a purchase from the Store.

- *In-app purchases*: Another great monetization strategy is to offer in-app purchasing. Lure the user to buy something of value because he or she is already enjoying your Windows 8 app. This model has tremendous potential for games on Windows 8. You could offer new levels, new characters, and so forth, to further monetize on a game that the user has already purchased. Normal apps could benefit from in-app purchases by exposing precious features or user customizations. The virtual marketplace of app accessories is yours to envision.

- *Advertising*: Another monetization option is to feature ads in your Windows 8 apps. Although you may feel guilty to use precious real estate, or reluctant to bother the user, you will be amazed by how little actual users mind a small banner in one corner of a Windows 8 app screen. So, use advertising to your advantage. You could offer your app for free, but be ad-supported throughout. Or, another option may be to use ads in the trial version but remove them once the user buys the app. While you are free to use any ad network, Microsoft offers a robust one that comes with an easy-to-use SDK. For more details on the Microsoft ad network, please visit `http://adsinapps.microsoft.com`.

For more strategies on choosing your business model, or details on specific implementations, please refer to MSDN documentation at http://msdn.microsoft.com/en-us/library/windows/apps/jj193599.aspx. The point is to not be shy about making some money from your Windows 8 app. If you do your job as a developer and wow the user, you more than deserve it!

Summary

This is it, my friend. It has been a long journey for you and for me. Windows 8 presents a huge developer opportunity for you to make a name for yourself. So read well, buckle down, depend on coffee or pop if you have to, and code your dream Windows 8 app. Do not underestimate the last steps discussed in this chapter. Deploy your Windows 8 app correctly through the Windows Store or through LOB enterprise app distribution. Devote some due diligence in testing and validating your app, and you should fly through app certifications and soon have your app in the hands of users. And do not forget your monetization options—it is not OK to leave money on the table.

Thank you immensely for your time and investment in reading through this book. I hope you had as much fun reading it as I had writing it. Best of luck in all of your Windows 8 endeavors!

Index

A

B

C

D

■ E

■ F

■ G

■ H

I, J, K

L

M

N

O

P, Q

R

S

T

U

V

W

X, Y

Z